Bartholomew City Guides

Chester

Bartholomew City Guides

Chester

BRIAN HARRIS

Photographs by A.F. Kersting, F.R.P.S.

John Bartholomew & Son Limited
Edinburgh and London

British Library Cataloguing in Publication Data

Harris, Brian
Chester. – (Bartholomew city guides).
1. Chester, Eng. – Description – Guide-books
I. Title
914.27′14 DA690.C5

ISBN 0–7028–8070–1
ISBN 0–7028–1049–5 Pbk

First published in Great Britain 1979 by
JOHN BARTHOLOMEW & SON LIMITED
12 Duncan Street, Edinburgh EH9 1TA
and 216 High Street, Bromley BR1 1PW

ISBN 0 7028 8070 1 (cased)
ISBN 0 7028 1049 5 (paperback)

Book and jacket design: Frances Dobson
9/11pt Linotron Baskerville
Printed in Great Britain: T. & A. Constable Ltd, Edinburgh

To the Staff of the Chester City Record
Office in grateful appreciation of their
constant help and encouragement

Contents

Chester and Surrounding Area

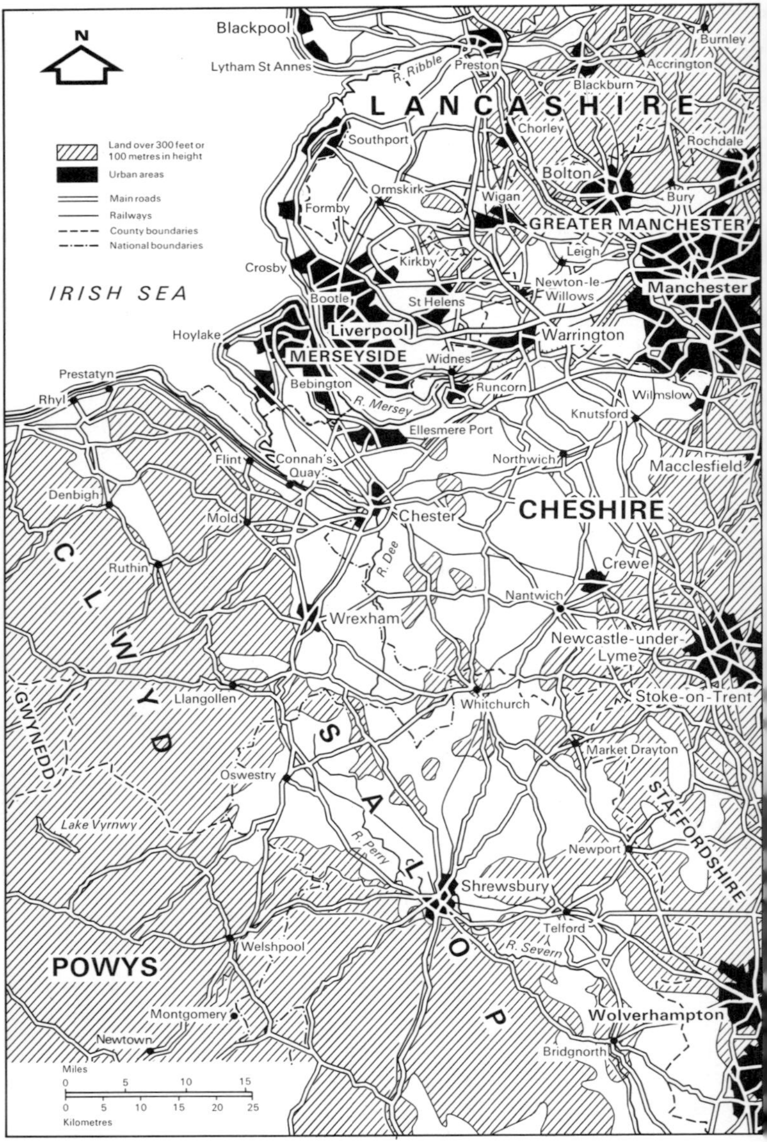

Preface

In 1978 Chester attracted half a million tourists. Many of them bought the *Official Guide*, which outlines the city's attractions and contains much practical information. The volume on Cheshire in the *Buildings of England* series, by Pevsner and Hubbard, is an essential guide to the city's architecture. For many years, however, there has been no detailed guidebook to the city and its main buildings and institutions; in fact the mid-19th-century *Stranger's Handbook to Chester* has never been supplanted. I hope that this book will do something to fill the gap. Its main aim is to tell briefly the story of Chester's history over the past 19 centuries, and to introduce the main physical and institutional features of the city by means of nine perambulations. Since 1974 the term 'City of Chester' has been ambiguous. This book deals with the city as it was before local government reorganization, rather than with the enlarged city that includes the former Chester and Tarvin Rural Districts.

I should like to acknowledge the assistance I have received from many sources in writing this book. Without the help of Miss Annette Kennett, City Archivist, and her staff at the Chester City Record Office, the research for the book could not have been completed. The Clerk and Chief Executive of Chester City Council, Mr D.M. Kermode, and the Chairman of the Amenities Committee, Councillor J. Ross, have expressed their interest on many occasions. I am indebted to Mr J.T. Driver, of Chester College, who first stimulated my enthusiasm for Chester's history when I began to teach at the College in 1969. Mr T.J. Strickland, Field Officer of the Grosvenor Museum, has answered many tiresome questions about the archaeology of Chester.

Mr Christopher Wheeler, of John Bartholomew & Son, has edited the text of the book with skill and tact. The photographs that illustrate it have been taken by Mr A.F. Kersting, F.R.P.S., who has had to cope with such difficulties as the constant congestion of Chester streets and the so-called summer of 1978.

I am conscious that Cestrians and others will notice omissions from this book, and possibly inaccuracies of fact or interpretation. Some of the omissions may be deliberate; all the inaccuracies are accidental, but I shall be pleased to be informed of either, or both.

Brian E. Harris
Chester
September 1978

Editorial Note

References in the text to the book's black-and-white photographs, which form a section between pages 124 and 125, are given as numbers within square brackets.

Chester: the Setting

The Romans named Chester Deva, after the river that flowed past it. The name is said to mean 'goddess' or 'holy one'. About six miles N of Aldford the Dee makes a decisive turn towards the W and then the WNW, and makes for the Irish Sea. It passes between two low hills now occupied respectively by the city of Chester and its suburb Handbridge. In Roman times two opposing gullies led down from the hills to the river, and made the lowest point at which it could conveniently be bridged. The hills were formed of Bunter sandstone of the Triassic period, which could easily be quarried for building.

The site chosen by the Romans for their fortress, which became the nucleus of the medieval and modern city of Chester, enjoyed natural advantages. The hill on which the city stands slopes down quite steeply to W and S. To the W, particularly, it gives a commanding view across the former estuary and the lowlands of eastern Clwyd to the hills – Carboniferous Limestone and Millstone Grit – of the Clwydian range, which attain their highest point in Moel Famau (1,820 ft) W of Mold. The slope to the E is gentler, but the site commanded the low-lying valley of the River Gowy. The view, now obscured by modern buildings, extended as far as the Mid-Cheshire Ridge, which crosses Cheshire from Bickerton Hill (694 ft) in the S to Helsby Hill (462 ft) in the N.

Roman and later settlers found abundant natural resources within easy reach of Chester. Though easily quarried, the Bunter sandstones show poor durability; the harder Triassic sandstones of the Keuper series, however, were available a few miles to the E. For buildings of a less permanent, or less expensive, nature there was abundant timber. Lead was mined in the Clwyds from Roman times onwards. From at least as early as the Tudor period the coalfield of N and E Clwyd has been exploited. As a water supply the Dee was supplemented by abundant springs in the local sandstone, particularly at Boughton and Christleton to the E. The river was harnessed, from the Middle Ages onwards, as a power supply for watermills and, in the present century, for a hydro-electric power station.

Chester was important as a centre of communications. At least until the 15th century the estuary of the tidal Dee up to Chester was deep enough to accommodate the largest ships in use. Chester became an international port. The Dee above Chester was also commercially navigable. Timber was floated down the river on rafts from Bangor-is-y-coed at the end of the 18th century. With the silting of the river at the end of the Middle Ages and the development of bigger ships Chester was forced to fight a long battle to preserve its status as a port: new harbours were established lower down the estuary; in the early 18th century the Dee below Chester was canalized. In the Middle Ages and the Tudor period much of Chester's seaborne trade was with the Continent, but its later associations were particularly with Ireland. By the beginning of the 19th century, however, Chester was eclipsed by Liverpool, and the improvement of road communications to Holyhead robbed it of the Irish trade. Chester was connected to the English canal system, which developed at the end of the 18th century, but its maritime trade could not be revived.

Until 1833, when the Grosvenor Bridge was completed to ease the journey into Wales, the Old Dee Bridge at Chester was the lowest across the river. There was no bridge below Chester until one was opened at Queensferry in 1897, though it had always been possible to cross the river, at some risk, by way of the estuary sands and treacherous fords. In 1693 one Richard Dyason, travelling with coal from Flintshire, was drowned at Blacon Ford. By 1740, after the lower reaches of the river had been canalized, there were two ferries in operation below Chester.

Neither fords nor ferries did much to diminish the traffic

across the Dee at Chester. From Roman times onwards it was a centre of road communication. In the 18th century the turnpike trusts began to rationalize the road network; later both local and national government action improved the roads still further. Chester became an important coaching town. In 1831 eight coaches left it each day for the Liverpool ferries, five for London, four each for Manchester and Shrewsbury, two each for Welshpool and Holyhead, and one for Wrexham. Nine years later the first railways reached the city, and by the end of the 1840s it was a major railway junction with a monumental station proudly presented to the admiration of tourists.

In the present century Chester has become notorious as a traffic bottleneck. Between the World Wars, and after 1945, efforts were made to ease the traffic congestion, so that through traffic can now by-pass Chester on all sides. Nevertheless the main approach roads – the Tarvin, Hoole, Liverpool, and Parkgate Roads and the Grosvenor Bridge – remain congested for much of each working day, in spite of the construction of the by-passes and the inner ring road.

This congestion reflects Chester's present social and economic standing. It is an administrative centre both for the enlarged City of Chester, which includes the former Chester and Tarvin Rural Districts, and for Cheshire. It houses many local service industries. Retail trading is extremely important; Chester serves not only its own suburbs but also large parts of southern Merseyside, western Cheshire, and Clwyd. It is also one of the country's main tourist centres. All these factors have combined to create a major traffic problem in Chester. Few people now live in the city centre. As a result there is an influx of commuters every morning and a corresponding exodus in the early evening, mostly in private cars.

Chester is usually presented as a northern town; geographers tend to associate it with Merseyside. The Redcliffe-Maud Report of 1969 proposed the dismemberment of Cheshire; the city would have become part of Greater Merseyside if the proposal had taken effect. It is true that the capitals of the north-west, Liverpool and Manchester, can each be reached in an hour or less from Chester. Nevertheless the city misses the 'feel' of a northern town. It is not heavily industrialized. The 'true' North is dominated by the Pennines; to catch a first glimpse of the Pennines from Chester one has to travel some 10 miles to the E and climb the Mid-Cheshire Ridge.

The Welsh hills rather than the Pennines dominate Chester. Historically its links are with Wales rather than with northern England. In Roman and early medieval times it stood as a defence against invasion from North Wales and as a base from which the Welsh could be attacked. After the English conquest of North Wales strong economic and administrative ties developed between Chester and the neighbouring Welsh counties. The titles of Prince of Wales and Earl of Chester have been associated since 1301. From the early 14th to the early 16th centuries Flintshire was partly administered from Chester Castle. From the early 16th century to 1830 the Chester Court of Great Session was part of a judicial circuit that included Denbighshire, Flintshire, and Montgomeryshire. Lead and coal came to Chester from Wales. Welsh traders came to the Chester markets. Even today there are Welsh chapels in Chester and it is not uncommon to hear Welsh spoken in the streets. The border with Wales approaches within a mile or two of the city centre.

Set beside this, Chester's 'northern-ness' seems difficult to substantiate, though there have been historic ties with Lancashire. The diocese of Chester created in 1541 included Lancashire and parts of Cumbria as well as Cheshire. The Stanley family of Knowsley in Lancashire, later Earls of Derby, were important in Cheshire government from the mid 15th to the late 17th centuries. The development of road and rail links between Chester and Liverpool and Manchester has tended to strengthen Chester's economic ties with the north-west. When all that is said, however, Chester remains primarily a city on the NE border of Wales and has much in common with other towns of the Marches: Shrewsbury, Ludlow, Hereford.

In climate Chester is generally free from extremes either of rainfall or temperature. It is sheltered from the W and

SW by the Welsh hills, and from the E and NE by the Pennines; the only directions from which there is little protection are the N and NW. Severe frosts and snowfalls are rare. In summer the heat in the city centre can become oppressive, though there may be a breeze on the river.

Roman and Anglo-Saxon Chester

In 1979, the year of this book's publication, Chester will be officially celebrating the 1,900th anniversary of its founding by the Romans. Few historians or archaeologists, however, would be prepared to advance A.D. 79 as the date of the foundation of the Roman fortress of Deva. Recent excavations at the Abbey Green site not far from the Northgate (Walk 3) have confirmed what has been suspected for many years, that there was a fortress on the site in the 50s. It was founded at the time of the Romans' campaign against the Ordovices of North Wales.*

Some 20 years later a more permanent fortress was erected to act as a buffer between the Ordovices and other tribes of North Wales, and the still unsubdued Brigantes of the north of England. The date of this second fort, whose buildings, like those of the earlier one, were of timber, is not clear; building may have begun during the governorship of Frontinus (74–8) or at the very beginning of that of Agricola (78–84). Pigs of lead with inscriptions datable to 74 have been found outside the walls, and these discoveries have led Mr D.F. Petch to suggest that building began in 74 and took about five years to complete. Other writers have suggested starting dates between 76 and 78.

At the end of the last century a section of lead water pipe bearing an inscription attributable to the early part of 79 was found in the city centre. The discovery has produced varying interpretations; it is debatable whether a piped water supply would have been installed early or late in the construction of the second fortress. The water pipe is important as the first

* See J. C. McPeake, 'The First Century A.D.', in T. J. Strickland and P. J. Davey (eds.), *New Evidence for Roman Chester* (1978), pp. 9–16.

dated 'structural' object to be found within the Roman walls.

The walls and buildings of the Roman fort were reconstructed in stone late in the 1st or early in the 2nd century. By that time the Second Legion, whose base had probably been at Chester, was replaced there by the Twentieth, named *Valeria Victrix* as a result of its successes in battle. At the beginning of the 3rd century there was yet another phase of rebuilding. A century later (*c.*300), however, many of the military buildings were apparently demolished. There is evidence of renewed military occupation in the mid 4th century, though timber buildings were then used once again.

It must be stressed that this story is both simplified and tentative. Archaeological excavations continue in Chester under the direction of the Excavations Section of the Grosvenor Museum. Some are long-term projects; others are rescue archaeology undertaken in what little time is allowed between the demolition of buildings and a site's re-development. The evidence for the history of the Roman fortress is derived from many different sources, and its interpretation is a matter for the various skills of the archaeologists and their colleagues. A few finds, like the pigs of lead and the water pipe, are closely datable. Others, such as coins, may be dated by reign and type. Pottery, ornaments, and articles of apparel can also be dated typologically. Finally, the sequence of occupation revealed in one site may be compared with that known from another excavation. Through these researches the story of the Roman occupation of Chester is gradually emerging, though the interpretation of individual pieces of evidence remains controversial.

For the tourist who wishes to know how far excavations have progressed, a visit to the Grosvenor Museum (Walk 5) is essential. Reports of archaeological work in Chester are published by the Museum, and others appear in the *Journal of the Chester Archaeological Society* and in the *Cheshire Archaeological Bulletin.*

The Roman fortress was designed in accordance with a standard plan common, though with variatons in detail, to many such frontier posts throughout the Roman empire.

The walls enclosed a rectangular space, which was marked into divisions by the E–W *via principalis*, now represented by Eastgate Street and Watergate Street from the Cross to the Guildhall, and the N–S *via decumana* (the N part of Northgate Street) and *via praetoria* (Bridge Street). The *via principalis* and the *via praetoria* formed a T-junction, on the N side of which, roughly between St Peter's church and the Town Hall, was the headquarters complex represented by the *principia* and the *praetorium*. The Eastgate and the Northgate stand on the sites of the *porta principalis sinistra* and the *porta decumana*; the medieval extensions of the walls to W and S have resulted in the loss of the W and S walls of the Roman fortress: the Roman W gate (*porta principalis dextra*) stood in Watergate Street, between Trinity Street and the inner ring road, and the S gate (*porta praetoria*) at the junction of Bridge Street and Whitefriars. Comparison of the plan of Chester with other excavated Roman forts has enabled the probable sites of most of the internal buildings to be plotted, and in many cases excavation has confirmed their existence, so that, for example, the sites of the legionary baths and a number of the barrack blocks and granaries are known.

Many traces of Roman occupation have also been found outside the fortress walls. There was a burial ground on the site now occupied by the out-patients' department of the Royal Infirmary (Walk 4). Part of the wall of the Roman quay has been identified by the Roodee (Walk 5). The most dramatic site visible today is the half-excavated amphitheatre [1] E of the Newgate (Walk 7). Foregate Street appears to have been the nucleus of an extra-mural civilian settlement.

Since there has been continuous occupation of the fortress site at least since the late Anglo-Saxon period, it is not surprising that comparatively little evidence of the Roman period remains open to view. Roman masonry may be seen in parts of the walls, e.g. at the Northgate (Walk 3). The SE and NW corner turrets have been discovered: the base of the former can be seen near the Newgate (Walk 6), and the site of the latter has been marked by stone setts in the pavement by St Martin's Gate (Walk 3). In Hamilton Place, S of the

Forum precinct (Walk 1), the *sacellum* of the *principia* (labelled Roman Strong Room) has been preserved for inspection behind glass. Columns from the legionary baths and a reconstructed underfloor heating unit or hypocaust are preserved in the 'Roman Garden' [2] E of the Newgate (Walk 7), and there is part of another hypocaust *in situ* and readily available to inspection at No. 12 Northgate Street (Miss Selfridge) (Walk 1). Much of the material found in Chester, either by chance or throgh systematic excavation, has been deposited in the Grosvenor Museum. Of particular importance is the collection of inscribed and sculptured stones, many of which were found during repairs to the walls in the late 19th century. They include tombstones dedicated to the memory of legionary soldiers and their wives. The Museum's Newstead Gallery contains much information about the rôle and organization of the Roman fortress.

Chester's history after the Roman occupation ended is as obscure as that which preceded it. The town emerges from this obscurity late in the Anglo-Saxon period. Archaeologists, historians, and place-name scholars have investigated the early medieval development of Chester, but few positive conclusions have emerged from their debates. A crucial question is whether the fortress was, either in whole or in part, continuously occupied after the withdrawal of the Roman army, whenever that took place. It has been suggested that this part of Cheshire formed part of a Celtic kingdom of Powis. At some time between 613 and 616 King Ethelfrith of Northumbria defeated a Welsh force at Chester. According to a tradition still widely accepted, St John's church (Walk 8) was founded by King Aethelred of Mercia in 689. If the story is true, Chester had by that time become part of the Midland kingdom of Mercia, and the Welsh had been driven, or had retreated, to the W, a situation confirmed in the 8th century by the construction of Wat's and Offa's Dykes. The Welsh and the Anglo-Saxons of Chester may have lived within the Roman walls, but their buildings would have been of timber and obscured by later rebuilding. Alternatively, their settlement may have taken place outside the walls. There is no evidence to indicate how far the Celtic inhabitants of Chester, in whose ancestry there may well have been the blood of Roman soldiers, intermarried with the English conquerors.

Chester begins to emerge from obscurity at the end of the 9th century. Another tradition tells that in 874 the relics of the Mercian St Werburgh were brought from Hanbury, in Staffordshire, to Chester to keep them safe from the attacks of the Danes. According to the Anglo-Saxon Chronicle a Danish army occupied Chester briefly in the mid 890s; it seems likely that at about the same time the Wirral peninsula was subject to intensive settlement by Norsemen from Ireland. This immigration may have been permitted by Aethelflaed, Lady of the Mercians, daughter of King Alfred the Great and sister of King Edward the Elder of Wessex. She is said to have restored Chester's fortifications in 907, and has been credited with the foundation of St Peter's church and the extension of the Roman walls. At about this time Cheshire appears to have been 'shired': the county as an administrative unit was created as part of a systematic programme developed by the expanding kingdom of Wessex. In 973 Chester was the scene of the submission of various Celtic rulers to King Edgar. According to one account, eight sub-kings rowed Edgar on the Dee in token of their submission to him. Some 15 years before this Edgar, still at that time King of Mercia rather than King of England, had endowed the religious community of St Werburgh in Chester with lands.

Scattered references to Chester in narrative sources are supplemented, from the early 10th century onwards, by numismatic evidence. From the reign of King Athelstan (924–39), and perhaps from that of his father Edward the Elder (900–24), until the mid 12th century there is a continuous history of the minting of silver pennies at Chester by moneyers whose names have been preserved on the coins. The name that the town bore at that time was Legaceaster, a translation into Old English of the Celtic name Caerlleon ('the city of the legion'). The first element, the Lega- denoting 'legion', was only dropped in the 11th century. The names of the moneyers at Chester in the 10th and 11th centuries show Anglo-Saxon, Norse, and Irish influences, indicating the presence of a cosmopolitan community in the town. The existence of a strong Scandinavian element in that community is further witnessed by the dedication of a church to St Olave (i.e. Olaf, King of Norway), by the survival of the Scandinavian name Ulfaldi in Wolfeld gate, the early name of the Newgate, and perhaps by the unique feature of the principal streets of Chester, the Rows (see below, pp. 19–21).

The existence of a mint at Chester indicates that there was a thriving trading community there. The Domesday Survey (1086) was compiled after the Norman Conquest, but its description of the legal and social customs of Chester, which is very full, refers to the late Anglo-Saxon town. In the time of Edward the Confessor (1042–66) there were said to be some 500 houses in Chester. There were then seven moneyers working in the city. There was a court, known as the Hundred. The Reeve, or chief official in Chester, had the power to call on the inhabitants of the county to come to repair the city wall and the bridge over the Dee. A long list of forfeitures is given for various crimes, including bloodshed, robbery, unlawful sexual intercourse on the part of a girl or a widow, and the seizure of land. Certain trading regulations are also specified, including penalties for giving false measure and brewing bad beer.

From the Norman Conquest to the End of the Middle Ages

Tradition asserts that after his defeat at the battle of Hastings in 1066 King Harold came to Chester and ended his life as a hermit. A similar story was produced about the German emperor Henry V (1106–25), whose supposed nickname *Godescallus* provided the origin of the name Godstall Lane (Walk 1); but in fact Henry IV (1056–1106) rather than Henry V bore that nickname, and both Henries are known *not* to have died at Chester. There is no known foundation for the legend concerning Harold.

It is impossible to imagine the immediate effect of the English defeat on a community so remote from the battlefield as Chester. Within three years the men of Chester and Shrewsbury were in revolt against the Normans. In the winter of 1069–70 William the Conqueror led his army across the Pennines into Cheshire, laying waste the lands through which he passed; he captured Chester, and began the construction of a castle. At about the same time he created the Earldom of Chester, at first in favour of a Fleming, Gherbod, and later, after Gherbod's return overseas, for the Norman Hugh Lupus (d. 1101). Hugh's successors retained the Earldom until the death of Earl John 'the Scot' without children in 1237.

From the 1070s onwards, then, Chester was not only an important town in its own right but the administrative centre of an earldom whose possessions included estates in many other English counties and, at first, in North Wales. The tradition later grew up that the Earldom of Chester was almost an independent buffer state on the borders of England and Wales. In the 12th and 13th centuries there certainly seems to have been a distinction in contemporaries' minds between Cheshire, England, and Wales. Earl Ranulph II (d. 1153) was a key figure in the civil wars of the reign of Stephen. Earl Ranulph III (d. 1232) was a figure of international importance. His support was probably crucial in enabling John to attain the Crown on the death of Richard I, and he was powerful enough in 1216 to be offered, though he declined it, the regency over the young Henry III.

After the death of Earl John in 1237, the Earldom of Chester was annexed to the Crown by Henry III; it was given by him to his son the Lord Edward, and when Edward in his turn became King it reverted to the Crown once more. In 1301 Edward created his eldest son, Edward of Caernarfon, Prince of Wales and Earl of Chester, and since that time it has been the normal, though not invariable, practice for the Sovereign's eldest son to receive those titles.

Throughout the medieval period Cheshire was administered as an independent unit. By the end of the 13th century it was known as a county palatine, and its characteristic institutions, which can be seen in embryo under the Norman earls, were allowed to develop. The leading officials of the palatinate were the Justice and the Chamberlain. The Justice, as his name implies, was the chief judicial officer and presided over the county court, which could try any civil or criminal action. The Chamberlain presided over the Chester Exchequer, the county's financial department, and also controlled the secretariat of the palatinate. Commentators in the 16th century and later believed that Cheshire had its own parliament; certainly in the 15th century there is evidence that an assembly from the county was summoned to meet the representatives of Earl or King whenever it was proposed to levy the *mize*, the traditional county tax. Until Tudor times both the county and city were unrepresented in the national parliament.

Chester Castle was the headquarters of the administration of the county palatine. Visits to it by Earls or Kings, however, were comparatively rare, and were often occasioned by the military situation in North Wales. From the late 11th century the area of North Wales under Norman domination tended to contract, either because of the strategic difficulties of holding down the country or because the Earls of Chester were too deeply involved in national and international politics to spend much time in Chester or across the border. It was left, in fact, to the Plantagenet kings to deal effectively with the Welsh. King John led an expedition into Wales from Chester in 1211. Henry III led three expeditions there, in 1241, 1245, and 1257. In 1256 his son, the Lord Edward, used Chester as a base for a tour of his Welsh possessions, but nothing permanent was achieved. Edward I again used Chester as his base for attacks on North Wales in 1277 and 1282; the latter campaign achieved the permanent subjugation of the area, in spite of several subsequent revolts. Shortly after acquiring the titles Prince of Wales and Earl of Chester, Edward of Caernarfon visited Chester to receive the homage of his barons. Thereafter, recorded visits by Earls or Kings were infrequent. In 1309 Edward II came on a brief visit; in 1353 Edward, the Black Prince, son of Edward III, came in order to quell disorders in the county; in 1399 Richard II was brought to Chester from Flint by Henry Bolingbroke, and taken away by him to his eventual deposition. Movements of Kings and their sons during the 15th century are difficult to chronicle precisely; historians have tended to exaggerate the number of royal visits to Chester by assuming, wrongly, that various charters to the city made out in the name of the reigning monarch were actually ordered by him in person at Chester. The formula 'Witness myself at Chester' appears on all letters that went out under the palatine seal, whether the King or Earl was actually there or not. Assertions that Richard II was in Chester in September 1394, and that Richard III was there in April 1484, conflict with those Kings' known movements.

How far the political events that affected the palatinate involved the ordinary citizens of Chester is not clear. From the end of the 13th century, as will be seen, the city progressively became independent of control by the palatine officials. Nevertheless, the operation of the palatine administration from Chester Castle must have had some effects. For example, eight or nine sessions of the county court, each normally lasting two days, were held annually, which necessitated the presence in Chester not only of lawyers but also of gentry drawn from the whole of Cheshire, who came as parties to actions or as jurymen. Relations between England and Wales also had immediate effects on this border town. In 1402 the Mayor and Sheriffs were ordered to array the most substantial citizens for the city's defence. In the following year Welsh men and women were to be expelled from the city between sunset and sunrise; even in the daytime they were not to walk about with any weapon except a knife for cutting their food, or to frequent taverns, or meet within the city walls in groups of three or more.

In times of peace, Chester's trade developed, particularly with Ireland and with the wine-exporting ports of France and Spain. The growth of trade and the development of municipal government coincided: Kings and Earls, by a succession of writs, charters, and letters patent, granted the citizens both trading privileges and an increasing degree of self-government, the latter culminating in the 'Great Charter' issued by Henry VII in 1506. The earliest document preserved in the Chester City Record Office is a letter, undated but assigned to the period between October 1175 and May 1176, in which Henry II required his bailiffs of Dublin to allow the burgesses of Chester the same trading rights there as they had enjoyed in the time of his grandfather, Henry I. Those rights were confirmed by Henry's son John both before and after his accession as King. Earl Ranulph III (d. 1232) granted the citizens power to establish a guild merchant, or trading corporation, and he and his successor Earl John the Scot (d. 1237) confirmed their various liberties and customs.

From the early 12th century there is evidence of the existence of Sheriffs of Chester, distinct from those of Cheshire. The known succession of Mayors of Chester begins in 1238. By the end of the 13th century two law courts had come into existence in the city: the Pentice, controlled by the Sheriffs; and the Portmote, presided over by the Mayor. In 1300 Edward I confirmed the existing liberties of the city, and added to them in three significant ways: the citizens were allowed to retain their liberties and customs in return for a fixed annual payment of £100 to the Chester Exchequer; they were empowered to choose their own coroners rather than being subject to those of the county; they were allowed to try pleas of the Crown, in other words all criminal cases arising within the city's boundaries, fines arising from such trials to be paid to the city instead of to the Crown. These grants, taken together, did much to free Chester from the control of county officials. In 1354 Edward the Black Prince (d. 1376) issued a charter to the citizens, partly of interest in defining for the first time in an official record the city's boundaries, but more significantly making the Mayor escheator within the city and granting admiralty powers over the River Dee. The escheator was the official responsible for administering the lands of royal tenants in chief who had died, until the delivery of the lands to the tenants' heirs. Since the county escheator had hitherto been responsible for executing this office in Chester, the grant of 1354 represented a further extension of the city's independence. In 1506 Henry VII made the city a county in its own right, fully exempt from control by county officials. Chester was by no means the first town in England to gain this privilege: Bristol, York, Newcastle-upon-Tyne, Norwich, Lincoln, Hull, Southampton, Nottingham, Coventry, Canterbury, and Gloucester were already counties corporate. Furthermore, it is quite possible that the 'Great Charter' was in many ways merely confirming practices that had, in effect, been in use for some time. Nevertheless, the government of Chester was now for the first time formulated fairly clearly, and the condition of the charter (strictly not a charter but letters patent) in the Chester City Record Office bears witness to the fact that it was constantly referred to whenever disputes over the form of that government took place. The powers, functions, and method of election of the Mayor, Sheriffs, Recorder, and other officials were defined, and a court of quarter sessions was established for the city, more than 30 years before one was set up for Cheshire.

In the 'Great Charter', the fee-farm, the regular annual payment made by the citizens to the Chester Exchequer, was fixed at £20, only one-fifth of the sum that the citizens had paid in 1300. Throughout the 15th century there were complaints about the poverty of the city, caused by the silting of the Dee and the decline of trade in times of trouble. In 1445 it was said that the silting had been progressing for 50 years, and that now no merchant vessel could approach within 12 miles of Chester. As a result of the complaints the fee-farm was gradually reduced.

The decline of trade, while perhaps not so serious as claimed by the citizens, may have owed something to the civil strife of the 15th century, and to the restrictive practices of the city's tradesmen. By the end of the 15th century the guild merchant, established three centuries earlier, had become indistinguishable from the Corporation, and its place in regulating trade was taken by the craft guilds or companies, which numbered 25 by the 16th century. They insisted that only freemen of a particular company should be allowed to carry on that company's trade. Admission to the freedom was, in general, restricted to those born the sons of freemen, and to those who had served a period of apprenticeship. The guilds' influence on the social life of Chester was not, however, confined to such negative practices. From the late 15th century, if not earlier, they were involved in producing a cycle of miracle plays or religious pageants, which by the early 16th century were performed on the Monday, Tuesday, and Wednesday of Whit week, at various stations in the city. Each company was responsible for producing one play in the cycle, and for providing a movable stage for it. Thus the Drapers and Hosiers staged the Creation of the World, and the Ironmongers and Ropers performed the Crucifixion of Christ. The texts of the plays are extant, and excite lively interest among literary and linguistic historians. From time to time they have been revived. After the late 15th century the companies also produced the Midsummer Show, a procession of religious tableaux, giants, and curious beasts.

Religious activities played a great part in the life of a medieval community, a point illustrated by the number and variety of religious institutions in Chester. For a brief space, between 1075 and 1102, Chester became a bishop's seat; the headquarters of the see of Lichfield was transferred to

Chester in 1075, but removed to Coventry in 1102. The cathedral was not the present one, but St John's church. Even after 1102 bishops of Coventry and Lichfield were still occasionally styled bishops of Chester. There were nine parish churches within the city: Holy Trinity, St Bridget, St John, St Martin, St Mary-on-the-Hill, St Michael, St Olave, St Oswald, and St Peter. St Werburgh's abbey was a pre-Conquest collegiate foundation, but in 1092 Earl Hugh I re-founded and re-endowed it as a Benedictine house. It occupied the NE quarter of the city within the walls, but its influence was due to more than size alone. It had its own trading privileges, including an annual fair, and its own court. Its powers within the city led to frequent disputes with the Corporation, from the 13th century to the end of the Middle Ages. Another religious foundation in Chester was the Benedictine nunnery of St Mary, founded in the early 12th century; in the 13th century houses of Franciscan (Grey), Dominican (Black), and Carmelite (White) friars were established. Earl Ranulph III founded two hospitals outside the walls, St John the Baptist without the Northgate, and St Giles, Boughton.

The chief survivals of medieval Chester are the walls, the street pattern, and the Rows, though there are also parts remaining of several other medieval buildings. Sections of the N and E walls rest on Roman foundations. At some time in the Middle Ages, either in the 10th century or perhaps three centuries later, the walls were extended to W and S to approximately their present line. The medieval gates have been demolished (though the Shipgate has been re-erected in Grosvenor Park – see Walk 8). Most of the defensive towers have also gone, though the sites are still marked, e.g. of Thimbleby's Tower on the E wall (Walk 6). At the NW corner of the wall, Bonewaldesthorne's Tower and the Water Tower (Walk 4) retain their medieval appearance [3], though it is difficult now to appreciate that when the Water Tower was built the Dee ran at its feet.

Towards the end of the 12th century the monk Lucian described the two principal axial streets of Chester, which met at the Cross. We now know that they represent the *via principalis*, the *via praetoria*, and the *via decumana* of the Roman fortress, though by Lucian's time it is evident that the gap between the last two, filled in Roman times by the headquarters building, had been bridged by the S end of Northgate Street. A survey of the streets of Chester made in the time of Edward III (1327–77) was copied into the Assembly Book of the Corporation in the mid 1570s. Expanded and corrected by reference to other records – e.g. those produced by the city courts, and title deeds – the survey enables a reconstruction of Chester in the 14th century to be made: it shows a street pattern recognizably similar to today's. Some of the names have changed: for example, today's Frodsham Street (Walk 3) was Cow Lane, King Street (Walk 3) was Barn Lane, and Weaver Street (Walk 4) was Alvin's or Bereward's Lane. But the only significant alterations to the medieval pattern, apart from the widening of many of the roads, have been the insertion of the diagonal line (NE to SW) of Grosvenor Street (Walk 5) in the 1830s, the extension of Nicholas Street and St Martin's Fields N, as part of the inner ring road scheme, to pierce the walls at St Martin's Gate (Walk 3), and the replacement of the N end of Newgate Street by the Grosvenor-Laing shopping precinct (Walk 1).

Except in one respect Chester is not unique among English towns in its survivals from the Middle Ages; the exception is the Rows. To a Cestrian, or to a visitor once he has seen them, there is no need to describe the Rows; for someone who has not seen them, a verbal description can only partly convey their atmosphere. In Bridge Street and in parts of Eastgate, Northgate, and Watergate Streets the shops are on two levels. Those that are known as 'street level' are really a few feet below the pavement, and have to be reached by steps down. Above these half-basements run a balcony and colonnade, some 7 ft or more above pavement level, and reached by stairs placed at intervals. Behind the balcony is a space of a few feet, sometimes used to display the wares of the shops, beyond which is a pavement of stone or wood, and beyond that again are the shop-fronts at Row level. The upper storeys of the buildings protrude above the walkway and display-space, and are supported by the colonnades, so that they are flush with the 'street'-level shopfronts. The effect is that the Rows provide a covered shopping arcade, open to the street along one side. They were often dismal and dilapidated thoroughfares in the early 19th century. Of the Rows that now exist, Eastgate Street Row S (Walk 1) and Bridge Street Row E (Walk 5) have been fully modernized, as lofty arcades with modern shopfronts [20]. That is true to almost the same extent of Watergate Street Row S (Walk 4); but the Rows on the N side of Watergate Street and Eastgate Street [19], and the E side of Northgate Street, preserve more of their earlier character. Shoemakers' Row, on the W side of Northgate Street (Walk 1), was a true Row up to the end of the 19th century, and is still shown as one on some street maps of Chester, but it was replaced then by a ground-floor colonnade. Similar colonnades, some of which probably date only from the 18th century, are to be found in parts of Northgate Street (Walk 3) and Foregate Street (Walk 8). They are sometimes called *piazzas*, and, unlike the Rows, are found in other towns. The Rows were formerly more extensive than now.

Court records and title deeds prove the Rows to have existed from the late 13th century at least. There is, however, no satisfactory account of their origin. In 1957 P.H. Lawson and J.T. Smith each read papers to the Chester Archaeological Society in which mutually irreconcilable opinions about the beginnings of the Rows were advanced. Smith drew attention to a reference in a near-contemporary chronicle to a disastrous fire that was said to have devastated almost the whole of Chester in 1278, and claimed that the Rows represented a systematic attempt at town-planning after the catastrophe. Lawson put the case for more gradual growth, based on the known practice of erecting stalls in front of the lower floor of shops and workshops, while steps from the stalls gave access to the domestic quarters above. As time went on the stalls, it was claimed, became permanent structures, and the houses and shops on the upper level were connected by elevated footpaths; Lawson believed the process to have started long before the fire of 1278, and to have continued until the 18th century. In 1968 Mr J.McN. Dodgson, in yet another paper read to the Chester Archaeological Society, put forward another possible origin: he pointed out that an early alternative name for the Rows was 'lofts', and suggested a Scandinavian origin, based on the known Scandinavian presence in Chester in the 10th and 11th centuries. The Rows would represent adjacent 'loft-houses' in which the ground or sub-ground level was used for storage, and perhaps as workshops, while the upper floors were used for domestic and business purposes; access to the upper floors would be by an external staircase, and neighbouring buildings might for mutual convenience have their upper floors linked by elevated footways.

A feature of the streets where there are Rows is that several of the shops at 'street' level incorporate medieval stone cellars or crypts. Many of the crypts have been destroyed or drastically altered, but three excellent examples have survived, and should be seen: No. 28 Eastgate Street, Browns' shop (Walk 1), No. 11 Watergate Street, Quellyn Roberts's (Walk 4), and No. 12 Bridge Street, Bookland (Walk 5). All can readily be inspected by individuals or small groups without prior arrangement during hours when the shops are open, but for large parties it would be courteous to make an appointment. All three crypts have been dated to the late 13th century or possibly later.

In domestic architecture the only significant survival of the Middle Ages in Chester is the former Blue Bell Inn [16] in Northgate Street (Walk 3), though medieval timber and structural work have been claimed for many other buildings. Of the castle founded by William the Conqueror the only obvious medieval survival is the so-called Agricola Tower (Walk 6). The medieval churches have suffered considerably, partly because they were built of the local sandstone, which weathers badly. St John's church preserves Norman and Early English work. The Cathedral has specimens of the Norman, Early English, Decorated, and Perpendicular styles, though it is often difficult to distinguish what has been restored from what has been, in effect, rebuilt as the

19th-century architects would have liked to see it (Walk 2). Holy Trinity [9] and St Michael's [10] (Walks 4 and 5), now no longer used as churches, were almost completely rebuilt in the 19th century. St Mary-on-the-Hill (Walk 6), also redundant as a church, and St Peter's (Walk 1) contain more genuine, mostly Perpendicular, work.

The Abbey Gateway [15] (Walk 2), though with an upper floor rebuilt in the late 18th or early 19th century, is a fine piece of 14th-century work. The Old Dee Bridge [35] (Walk 6) was widened in 1826, and the defensive gateways at each end of it have disappeared, but in appearance it remains a medieval bridge. Nothing is left of its famous neighbour at the Chester end, the Dee Mills. The people of Chester and its neighbourhood were obliged to have their corn ground there, and the millers became notorious for their extortion. Such customary payments as those made at the mills were as much an incident of medieval life as today's rates and taxes. The city took tolls on all goods imported and exported through the port. The keepers of the city gates also levied tolls on goods passing through.

The Sixteenth, Seventeenth, and Eighteenth Centuries

The 'Great Charter' that Henry VII gave to the city of Chester in 1506 established a form of government that, in essentials, remained effective until the Municipal Corporations Act, 1835. Nevertheless, in the 16th and 17th centuries there were disputes over the Charter's interpretation, and battles with the courts of the county palatine of Chester, which claimed jurisdiction over the city, and with the Crown. The latter struggle culminated in the dissolution of the Corporation by the government of Charles II in 1684. The city's liberties were not fully restored until 1688, just before the overthrow of James II.

A further stage in Chester's political development was marked in the 1540s by the grant of representation in Parliament. In the later 16th and for most of the 17th century it became the almost invariable practice for the city to return the Recorder as one of its two M.P.s. The dawn of a new age was marked by the election of Sir Thomas Grosvenor of Eaton Hall (d. 1700) as member for Chester in 1679. Two years earlier he had married Mary Davies, heiress to the manor of Ebury to the W of London; the union added vastly to the family's wealth. From the late 17th century the Grosvenors were intimately involved in the political and social life of Chester. Between 1715 and 1874 the Grosvenor family always provided at least one of the city's M.P.s, and often both. Sometimes this success was only achieved by the use of the well-known electoral methods of the time; in 1784 the Grosvenors arranged for potential supporters to be 'treated' at 90 taverns in the city, and their bill for drink amounted to £15,000.

The most dramatic episode in Chester's history during this

period was the siege that it endured during the Civil War. As elsewhere, the choice of sides between Charles I and Parliament depended as much on local as on national issues. Support for Charles was only assured when the Gamull family and their friends managed to gain the ascendancy in the city assembly in the 1630s. Charles visited Chester twice. The first occasion was in September 1642, just after the Civil War had begun. The second was three years later, when Chester was beleaguered by a Parliamentary force. While Charles was in the city, part of his army was defeated near by at Rowton Moor; he is said to have witnessed the defeat from the Phoenix Tower [4] (Walk 3). The siege of Chester had begun in 1644, and lasted until the city's surrender in February 1646. Its most devastating effects were in the suburbs, particularly to the E, but it was afterwards said that no house between the Eastgate and the middle of Watergate Street had escaped damage. In 1645 the city's silver plate was melted down to provide coins. The entry of the Parliamentarian force in 1646 resulted in the dismantling of the High Cross (Walk 1).

In 1745 it was feared that the walls, which had withstood Sir William Brereton's attacks a century earlier, might have to resist the Jacobite force. Bonnie Prince Charlie's army, however, came no nearer than Warrington.

Besides Charles I, the only other reigning monarchs to visit Chester between 1509 and 1800 were James I in 1617 and James II in 1687. One who hoped to become a king, James, Duke of Monmouth, Charles II's illegitimate son, visited the city in 1682; after the visit his supporters rioted in the streets.

Throughout the period Chester remained an important port, though the silting of the Dee continued, and 'havens' at Neston and Parkgate were established to enable vessels to load and discharge their cargoes lower down the Dee. In the 1730s a 'cut' was made between Chester and Connah's Quay to ease the navigation of the river, but its main effect was to allow large parts of the estuary to be drained for agricultural use. Chester's connexion with Ireland in this period was more important than its trade with the Continent. At the time of the Elizabethan wars in Ireland Chester was a major port for the embarkation of troops. Until the development of Holyhead it was frequently used by passengers *en route* for Ireland. Jonathan Swift (1667–1745) is said to have stayed at the Yacht in Watergate Street, and the composer Handel (1685–1759) at the Golden Falcon Inn near the Northgate in 1741, before undertaking the voyage. Both inns have been demolished.

By the end of the 18th century Chester was developing as a canal port [38], with the opening of waterways to Nantwich, Whitby Locks (now Ellesmere Port), and Llangollen (Walk 4). At the same time road communications were being improved by turnpike trusts, and by 1800 Chester was an important coaching centre. The chief coaching inns, again no longer in existence, were the Feathers in Bridge Street and the White Lion in Northgate Street. The production of guidebooks at this time testifies to an embryonic tourist trade in Chester.

Henry VIII dissolved all the religious houses in the Kingdom. The three medieval friaries and St Mary's nunnery became little more than memories preserved in street names. St Werburgh's abbey, dissolved in 1540, became in the following year the Cathedral of Christ and the Blessed Virgin Mary. The diocese of Chester created by Henry VIII included Cheshire and Lancashire and extended into Cumberland, Westmorland, and the W and N ridings of Yorkshire. Its creation was significant in two ways: it linked the county for the first time to NW England rather than to Wales and the marches; and, although the early bishops of Chester were not necessarily or even normally resident in the city, Chester became the headquarters of diocesan administration – a new dimension was added to the city as an administrative centre. The government of the Cathedral itself was in the hands of the Dean and Chapter; this body inherited most of the abbey lands, and thus became one of the most important landowners in the city. Disputes sometimes arose between the Dean and Chapter and the civic authorities. In Abbey Square (Walk 2) non-freemen were able to practise trades, to the annoyance of the city guilds and the Corporation. In 1607 a serious dispute arose over the Mayor's claim to enter the Cathedral with the city sword carried before him with its point upwards.

Like the Cathedral, Chester Castle lay outside the city's jurisdiction. In Henry VIII's reign the quasi-independence of the county palatine was reduced, so that in many respects Cheshire approximated to a normal English county. Nevertheless, the Castle remained important as a military base, as a prison, and as the venue of the surviving palatine institutions, the Exchequer and the court of Great Sessions. Quarter sessions for Cheshire also met there, generally once a year at least, after their establishment in the 1530s. Thus the city remained important as a centre of legal as well as ecclesiastical administration. Visits of bishops and judges were attended with elaborate ceremonial, and the gentry of the county arrived in the city in large numbers. In August 1687 a rare visit by Bishop Cartwright coincided with those of James II and the Quaker William Penn. The opening of the twice-yearly Great Sessions or assizes was normally marked by a sermon preached at the Cathedral. The social gathering was sometimes more important than the process of law; in 1748 the leading gentry of the county appeared, as usual, to form the Grand Jury, but according to the foreman there was no business to deal with 'save eat, drink, smoke, and be jolly'.

The city's relations with the Castle, like those with the Cathedral, were subject to periodic strains. In the 1570s the Corporation lost a battle against the vice-chamberlain of Chester over its claim to exemption from the Chester Exchequer's jurisdiction. In 1715 the Mayor and Recorder became involved in a bitter dispute with Colonel Fane, commander of the garrison at the Castle, who had refused the Mayor's summons to attend him at the Pentice, had placed the Recorder under house arrest, and had tried to make the city accommodate 500 Jacobite prisoners.

A particularly irksome burden was the traditional liability of the city Sheriffs to execute criminals who had been condemned in the palatine court. For most of the period the place of execution was Boughton, to the E of the city (p. 174);

prisoners were handed over to the city Sheriffs at Gloverstone (Walk 6). Some of those executed were religious martyrs; they included the Protestant George Marsh in 1555 and the Roman Catholic St John Plessington in 1679. When the palatinate courts were abolished in 1830 the city Sheriffs claimed, at first unsuccessfully, that they were no longer bound to carry out executions for the assize court; they were not finally relieved of the task until 1867.

There are abundant survivals of the 16th, 17th, and 18th centuries in Chester. The city has long been noted for its specimens of timber-framed, or 'black-and-white' architecture, though it is sometimes difficult for the stranger to distinguish between original examples and those rebuilt or newly erected in the 19th and early 20th centuries. In Lower Bridge Street (Walk 6) the Tudor House claims to be one of Chester's oldest houses, and other examples in the same area are the Falcon, the Bear and Billet [17], and Gamul House. Like Gamul House, the Dutch Houses in Bridge Street (Walk 5) were restored by the City Council to mark European Architectural Heritage Year (1975). In Watergate Street (Walk 4), the Leche House, Bishop Lloyd's House [18], and Stanley Palace are all, at least in large part, genuine timber-framed buildings of the 16th or 17th century; on the other hand, God's Providence House, though prominently dated 1652, is a 19th-century rebuild. There are also unexpected 17th-century interiors, such as the 'Jacobean Room' in Mappin and Webb's shop in Eastgate Street Row N (Walk 1) and the interior of the Pied Bull in Northgate Street (Walk 3). The Cathedral (Walk 2) and its precincts contain work of the early 17th century associated with Bishop Bridgeman, particularly the Consistory Court, the furnishings of St Anselm's chapel, and the two stone houses on the N side of the Abbey Square.

Much rebuilding took place in the city in the 18th century, as prosperity grew. The abundance of visitors, on business, for pleasure, or *en route* to or from Ireland, meant that bigger and better hotels were demanded. Two of the finest Georgian examples were the Royal, now the Grosvenor (Walk 1), and the Blossoms (Walk 3); both have been replaced by 19th-century black-and-white buildings. The exterior of the Pied Bull, however, remains as an example of a coaching inn remodelled in the 18th century, though a great deal of its interior is earlier. Much solid Georgian work in the main streets was swept away in the black-and-white revival of the late 19th century. Nevertheless, many good individual houses remain, such as the Grosvenor Club, Vicar's Lane (Walk 8), and Folliott House, Northgate Street (Walk 3), with minor examples in Castle Street (Walk 6), King Street (Walk 3), and Whitefriars (Walk 5). There are 18th-century terraces in Abbey Street and Abbey Square [22] (Walk 2), Abbey Green (Walk 3), King's Buildings (Walk 3), Stanley Place (Walk 4), and Nicholas Street (Walk 4). There are houses of the late 18th and early 19th centuries at Boughton (p. 173).

At the end of the 18th century the crumbling but picturesque medieval structure of Chester Castle was almost entirely replaced by a monumental Classical complex [23] including barracks, county offices, courts, and a model gaol (Walk 6). The architect was Thomas Harrison, of whose work there are many other examples in Chester. Other buildings of the 18th century that have survived include the Bluecoat School [21] of 1717 (Walk 3) and parts of the Chester Infirmary (Walk 4). Some important buildings have entirely disappeared. The Exchange of 1698 (Walk 1) was so severely damaged by fire in 1862 that it had to be demolished. Matthew Henry's Chapel of 1700 in Trinity Street (Walk 4), the Octagon Chapel, Foregate Street (Walk 9), and the early-18th-century Friends' Meeting House in Frodsham Street (Walk 3) have gone, and the Congregational chapel in Queen Street, built in 1772 (Walk 9), has been demolished very recently.

Except during the short-lived Jacobite scare of 1745, it was felt in the 18th century that the city walls had outlived their purpose as defensive works. Early in the century work began on converting them into a promenade. Much of the paving and repair that this involved was undertaken in the reign of Queen Anne (Walk 4). Later in the century the Eastgate (Walk 1), the Watergate (Walk 4), and the Bridgegate (Walk

6) were demolished and replaced by ornamental gateways [5], which became an integral part of the promenade. Similarly, defensive towers such as the Saddlers' (Walk 3) and Pemberton's Parlour (Walk 4) were either demolished or improved for the convenience of walkers. The rebuilding between 1808 and 1811 of the Northgate [26], which had housed the city gaol (Walk 3), completed the process.

Another area devoted to recreation was the Roodee (Walk 5). Horse-racing in Chester is usually claimed to date from 1540, when the city assembly replaced the traditional Shrove Tuesday football match by foot and horse races and shooting contests. By the early 17th century the Corporation was supporting the annual St George's Day horse-races on the Roodee, both by providing money for the cups that were presented as prizes, and by laying down regulations for the conduct of the races. By the late 18th century the spring races continued for five days each year.

The Nineteenth Century

In 1801 the population of Chester was just over 15,000. A hundred years later it amounted to more than 38,000. Large though that increase may seem, it was much smaller than the average rise in population in England and Wales between 1801 and 1901, and tiny compared with that in some of the industrial towns of the North and Midlands. Chester is not, in fact, usually thought of as an industrial town, though at the end of the 18th century a lead works (Walk 9) was established beside the Nantwich canal, and an engineering works in Charles Street (Walk 9) a few years later. During the 1840s Chester was linked to the expanding national railway network. The General Station of 1847–8 (Walk 9) is a monument to the enterprise of the railway age [37]; the Northgate terminus, which never rivalled the General Station either in business or in magnificence, has been demolished. In the wake of industries and the railway came new suburbs for workers, including Newtown (p. 165), the area SW of the General Station (Walk 9), and much of Hoole (p. 176). In those parts much typical housing of the period between the early 1870s and the First World War may still be seen; the red-brick terraces there and in the Garden Lane–Sealand Road area (p. 176) could belong to the inner suburbs of any large town of the late 19th century, and make an interesting comparison with the more individualistic rebuilding that was going on at the same time in the city centre. One might not tend to associate Chester with the type of slums prevalent in towns of the Industrial Revolution; yet in 1905 there were said to be 122 courts in the city, containing 747 houses and a population of some 2,500 who were living in insanitary conditions.

As in other towns the upper ranks of society tended to move out from the city centre into the suburbs. An early area to become fashionable was Boughton (p. 171); villas for the wealthy were also built at Flookersbrook on the road to Warrington (p. 176), eventually to be isolated among the late-19th-century terraces. The Old Dee Bridge was widened in 1826, and the Grosvenor Bridge [24] was opened in 1832; though traffic on both bridges was subject to tolls until 1885, wealthier citizens could afford to move to the new mid-19th-century estates at Queen's Park (Walk 7) and Curzon Park (Walk 6); at the end of the century more villa residences appeared along Hough Green on the road to Saltney and North Wales.

Chester Corporation, like most others in England, was reformed by the Municipal Corporations Act, 1835, and made subject to the wishes of the ratepayers. Already in the previous century improvement acts of 1762 and 1803 had granted special powers to the city with regard to maintaining its poor in a workhouse, and to lighting, watching, and cleansing the streets. Further acts of 1845 and 1884 added to powers that were, at the same time, also being strengthened by national legislation. By the Local Government Act of 1888 Chester was made a county borough; thus the independence from county control that it had enjoyed since 1506 was confirmed. The symbol of civic pride was the Gothic Town Hall [39] (Walk 1), opened by the Prince of Wales in 1869.

Throughout the 19th century the Grosvenor family remained influential in the political and social life of Chester. For the first three-quarters of the century they continued to represent the city in Parliament. The new bridge over the Dee was called the Grosvenor Bridge, and the road leading to it, Grosvenor Street. In 1883 the Grosvenor Club (now the Midland Bank) was erected opposite the Grosvenor Hotel, formerly the Royal, in Eastgate Street. In 1867 the second Marquess of Westminster presented the Grosvenor Park to the city; 25 years later the first Duke of Westminster gave Edgar's Field in Handbridge. The first Duke also founded the church of St Mary in Handbridge and gave £4,000 to the building fund of the Grosvenor Museum. His work for

Chester was commemorated by the restoration, after his death, of the S transept of the Cathedral, where there is a splendid effigy of him. The magnificent Gothic mansion of Eaton Hall (p. 182), seat of the Grosvenors, was a major tourist attraction in the neighbourhood of Chester, and the visitors' entrance fees were devoted to charitable purposes.

Most of the significant buildings of the 19th century will be described below, in the walks, but some tendencies may be mentioned here by way of introduction. In ecclesiastical building the 19th century witnessed, throughout the country, both the building of new churches and chapels and the drastic restoration of those that already existed. The Cathedral (Walk 2) presents a fascinating, though sometimes confusing, story of a succession of 19th-century restorers, most notably Hussey, George Gilbert Scott, and Blomfield. Trinity church, Watergate Street [9], now used as the Guildhall (Walk 4), and St Michael's, Bridge Street [10], now the Chester Heritage Centre (Walk 5), were virtually rebuilt by James Harrison. St John, St Mary-on-the-Hill, and St Peter, though not altered so completely, nonetheless felt the hands of the 19th-century restorers to some extent. New churches or chapels of ease for the Church of England built during the century included Christ Church, Newtown, St Bartholomew, Sibell Street (Walk 9), St Paul's, Boughton (p. 173), and the parish church of Hoole (p. 177). Churches of other denominations were built in the central area, for example the Roman Catholic churches of St Francis (Walk 5) and St Werburgh [13] (Walk 8), and the Presbyterian, Wesleyan Methodist, and Baptist churches all within a short distance of each other in City Road and Grosvenor Park Road (Walks 8 and 9).

With religion went education. As a county borough Chester did not become involved in building elementary or secondary schools until early in the present century; unlike some towns of equivalent size, it had no school board in the late 19th century, for it could claim that charitable and religious bodies were providing sufficient school places. The King's School (Walk 2) was a foundation of Henry VIII's reign, and the Bluecoat School (Walk 3) dated from the early

18th century. Most of the parish churches in Chester, and some of the non-Anglican churches, had elementary schools attached to them during the 19th century. In 1839 a college for the training of teachers, under the control of the Church of England, was opened at the junction of Parkgate and Cheyney Roads (p. 175), a short distance N of the city. In the Mechanics' Institution founded in 1835, and the classes in science and the arts established in the 1880s, Chester possessed what might in other towns have become a university college, but, though one can assume that the money for such a venture would have been available, the step was never taken.

In the 19th century there were two major changes in the old street pattern of Chester. In the early 1830s Grosvenor Street (Walk 5) was laid out between Bridge Street and the Grosvenor Bridge; it cut diagonally across the established N–S and E–W pattern of the streets. Some 30 years later City Road (Walk 9) was built as a highway from the General Station to Foregate Street and the city centre; it was an alternative to the narrow and congested route via Brook Street (Walk 9) and Frodsham Street (Walk 3). Before the end of the century both City Road and Grosvenor Street lay on the route of the horse-drawn trams that plied between the General Station and Saltney.

Early in the century there was an attempt to improve the 'image' of many of the old lanes of Chester by re-naming them as streets. Joseph Hemingway, in his *History of Chester* (1831), ridiculed the changes: 'they converted all our little close passages, alleys, and entries into more *dignified* appellations. . . . A *street* is now amongst the lowest order of description; whilst we abound in *places* connected with some exalted name, *walks, squares, terraces,* etc. etc. . . . I much question whether the change will supply any additional notion of grandeur to the natives'.

One wonders what Hemingway would have thought about the rebuilding of much of the city centre that took place in the second half of the 19th century. The principal streets must have presented, early in the 19th century, a mixture of crumbling half-timber structures and examples of Georgian elegance. In the first decades of the century, the Classical revival [23–6], of which Thomas Harrison was the greatest local exponent, was in full swing, not only in structures like the Castle (Walk 6), the Northgate (Walk 3), and the City Club (Walk 1), but in commercial buildings such as the earliest part of Browns' shop (Walk 1) and the Old Bank on the corner of Foregate and St John Streets (Walk 3). The Classical style was not dead even in the 1860s, but found expression in the bank on the corner of Eastgate and St Werburgh Streets (Walk 1) and the Presbyterian church [11] in City Road (Walk 9).

In almost any English town one would be prepared to encounter much 19th-century Gothic architecture. The Town Hall [39], opened in 1869, is the most obvious example in Chester; new or rebuilt churches, and the majority of the 19th-century chapels, were also normally given Gothic treatment of one kind or another. In commercial buildings there is a small-scale example of Gothic in the Old Custom House in Watergate Street (Walk 4), and a much larger one in Browns' Crypt Buildings in Eastgate Street [30] (Walk 1). James Harrison was probably the most consistent exponent of mid-19th-century Gothic in Chester.

In 1849 the Architectural, Archaeological, and Historic Society of Chester, Cheshire, and North Wales was founded. Its first object was 'the improvement of Architectural Taste, Science, and Construction'. In 1857 its *Journal* directed its fire against the 'miserable brick, and incongruous piles of heavy Athenian architecture' that had characterized building in Chester during the past 100 years. What had characterized the earlier city were the 'rich and lively façades, the curiously carved fantastical gables, which distinguished the brief but gay rule of the Stuarts'. Existing work of that type must be preserved; furthermore, new buildings should be 'erected after the same distinguishing type'. Thus the demand for a black-and-white revival found expression. Even before 1857 T.M. Penson had introduced 19th-century black-and-white to Eastgate Street [29] (Walk 1). John Douglas and T.M. Lockwood were the two chief exponents of the half-timbered style in Chester in the late

19th and early 20th centuries; as a result of their work Eastgate Street, St Werburgh Street, and the S end of Northgate Street (Walk 1) were largely rebuilt in this style, which penetrated into most of the other main streets of Chester. Douglas and Lockwood were by no means totally committed to half-timbering; Lockwood's Grosvenor Museum [33] (Walk 5) and his building at the corner of Bridge and Watergate Streets (Walk 1) show his interest in Renaissance detail, while Douglas worked happily in brick and stone, as in the Midland Bank, Eastgate Street [32] (Walk 1), the former county police headquarters at the Bars (Walk 9), and his terrace of houses in Grosvenor Park Road (Walk 8). Yet, particularly where the interests of the Grosvenors were directly involved as landowners or as influential patrons, half-timbering tended to prevail. Early in the present century St Michael's Arcade, Bridge Street (Walk 5), was built, its entrance flanked by a Baroque structure; on the insistence of the second Duke of Westminster, the building at the entrance was immediately replaced by a structure in black-and-white. The half-timber revival continued into the 20th century, and resulted, for example, in the rebuilt Royal Oak in Foregate Street (Walk 8) and the District (now Williams and Glyn's) Bank on the W corner of Foregate and Frodsham Streets (Walk 3) in 1920 and 1921.

Throughout the 19th century tourism was important to Chester. Even earlier, some guidebooks had been produced, such as the *Chester Guide and Directory* of 1781, published by P. Broster and dedicated to the city's M.P.s. New and pirated editions of this and other guides followed in large numbers in the early 19th century. The best-known of the early guidebooks is the *Stranger's Handbook to Chester*, by Thomas Hughes, first published in 1856. The *Handbook* went through many editions both during and after Hughes's lifetime; one of the most interesting is that of 1899, written after much of the rebuilding had been accomplished. In the 19th century tourists were no longer visiting Chester as a stage on their route to Ireland; some, like George Borrow (Walk 3), now saw it as the gateway to Wales, but more were visiting it in its own right. Hotels were modernized: the

Georgian Royal (Walk 1) was transformed into the black-and-white Grosvenor, and a similar transformation affected the Blossoms (Walk 3); new hotels, such as the Queen, the Albion, and the Westminster (Walk 9), were built near the General Station, itself an object presented to the tourist for his admiration. An increasing number of visitors came from abroad. A bilingual guidebook, in French and English, was produced by Thomas Pullan in 1851. By the end of the century the presence of many American visitors was noted.

Chester had to contend not only with the interested tourist prepared to spend a week in the city, but with the tourist in a hurry who wanted to 'do' the sights in an hour or two. The latter was recommended, in the *Stranger's Handbook* of 1899, to take a tramcar from the General Station to the Grosvenor Bridge, alight there, and take the next tram back. 'A hasty glimpse of the Rows and the quaint houses and streets can be so obtained which is certainly better than passing through Chester without seeing anything'.

The Twentieth Century

Chester has never developed into a major industrial town, though modern industries have grown up near by. The approaches to the city from the E, the SE, and the S are still largely through unspoiled countryside. On all other sides, however, Chester is surrounded by industry: to the NE the oil refineries of Stanlow; to the N Ellesmere Port, with its Vauxhall motor-car works; to the NW, along the E side of the Wirral peninsula, chemical and other industries from Eastham to Birkenhead; the United Kingdom Atomic Energy Authority complex at Capenhurst; to the W Shotton steel works, and, nearer at hand, Hawker Siddeley Aviation at Broughton. In view of the proximity of industry, it is not surprising that Chester is now sometimes linked in geographers' minds with the Merseyside area. Certainly strong economic ties have developed, through the growth of commuting between Chester and the surrounding areas, and through the use of Chester for shopping and for recreation. Yet the city has managed to stand apart.

Transport problems have influenced Chester's development in the 20th century as in previous centuries. Its importance as a seaport was replaced, at the end of the last century, by its importance as a major road junction and gateway to North Wales, and to a lesser extent as a canal port. In the mid 19th century it became a significant railway town. In the present century it has succumbed in various ways to the influence of the internal combustion engine. The canal, on which trade was fairly brisk at the turn of the century, declined as a commercial route, though cargo vessels were still occasionally to be seen on it in the 1960s. After the Second World War it was the turn of the railways to go into decline: by 1970 the General Station was the only one left in Chester, both Northgate and Liverpool Road Stations having been closed. The vast increase in motor traffic in the 1930s and after the Second World War made Chester notorious as a bottleneck. Traffic from the E and NE heading for North Wales met at Foregate Street and had to traverse the Cross, Bridge Street, and Grosvenor Street to reach the Grosvenor Bridge. By 1945 a project for an inner ring road was being discussed. In an altered form, it came to fruition in the late 1960s and early 1970s. Pepper Street (Walk 6) was widened. A dual carriageway was built from the Castle, through the N wall at St Martin's Gate (Walk 3) to a new roundabout N of the Northgate, then SE to another at Gorse Stacks, site of the 19th-century cattle market (Walk 3), and yet another at the Bars (Walk 8). The needs of the motor car have therefore added a new aspect to Chester's townscape.

Chester's status as a local administrative centre has grown in the present century. Although the diocese of Chester was diminished in size in the 19th century, the city remains important as the diocesan headquarters. From 1907 to 1972 it was also the headquarters of Western Command. Among other organizations to own large administrative centres in Chester and its suburbs are Manweb (the Merseyside and North Wales Electricity Board) and Crosville Motor Services Ltd; the latter started as a very small-scale motor-manufacturing company, branched out *c.*1910 into local motor-bus operation, and developed into a vast network of bus transport operating routes in Cheshire, S Lancashire, and North Wales.

Local government is a major employer in Chester. The increasing complexity of the functions of county councils in the half-century after their formation in 1888 meant that Chester Castle became totally inadequate as an administrative headquarters. Just before the Second World War work began on a new County Hall (Walk 6), adjacent to the Castle. County Hall was opened in 1957, but within a few years it too had become insufficient to house the rapidly increasing number of county officials, and further accommodation had to be obtained in the city – Commerce House in Hunter

Street, for example (Walk 3). In 1967 a large new headquarters building for the county police was completed (Walk 5). At the same time the City Council was also growing, both in functions and in numbers of staff, so that the Town Hall, like the Castle for the county, became inadequate. Temporary accommodation was obtained, and new offices were opened in the Forum (Walk 1), on the site of the old market hall.

As a result of the Local Government Act, 1972, the administrative character of the City of Chester changed dramatically. Chester became a district of the 'new Cheshire'; the district included not only the former county borough of Chester, but also the rural districts of Chester and Tarvin. The reorganization came into effect in 1974, and within two months Chester district secured new letters patent from the Crown, granting it the status first of a borough and then of a city. The offices of Mayor and Sheriff were thus able to continue. Reorganization also made necessary an application for a new grant of arms, since those granted in 1580 were automatically invalidated on reorganization. The new arms, based on the earlier coat but with differences meant to symbolize the association with Chester of the former rural districts, were granted by letters patent in 1977.

In the present century Chester has gained a reputation as a local shopping centre of distinction. Browns of Chester (Walk 1), founded in the late 18th century, earned the nickname of 'the Harrods of the North'. At the turn of the century the antique shops of Chester were well known. From the 1920s onwards multiple stores moved into the city, in some instances replacing old-established small concerns, so that Eastgate and Foregate Streets especially contained exactly the same types of shops as could be seen in other towns of the same standing. Sometimes the new arrivals imposed their standard shopfront styles on the townscape: Burtons and Marks & Spencer in Foregate Street (Walks 3 and 8), for instance. In other cases the new developments took more account of the character of Chester; the building designed for C. & A. in Foregate Street (Walk 8) is a good example. Because of the use made of Chester by residents in the surrounding area, and also perhaps because of its tourist trade, the amount of shopping space in the city grew out of all proportion to its size. When most of the available space was occupied, new room for development had to be found. An answer was discovered in the idea of the shopping precinct: the Grosvenor-Laing precinct to the S of Eastgate Street (Walk 1) was followed by the creation of two lesser ones, the Forum leading off Northgate Street (Walk 1), and Mercia Square, between Frodsham Street and the city wall (Walks 2 and 3). Most of those who now come to shop in Chester arrive by private car, and their demands have led to further invasions of the townscape. There are multi-storey car parks on both sides of Pepper Street (Walk 6); a large underground car park has been provided between the Town Hall and the inner ring road, beneath the new market (Walk 1); long- and short-stay car parks have been provided on open sites throughout the city. Conversely, attempts have been made to remove the private car from the centre of Chester by enforcing partial pedestrianization, so that Eastgate Street, Bridge Street, the S end of Northgate Street, and the E end of Watergate Street are, in theory, restricted to vehicles requiring access to buildings and to public transport.

The period since 1900 has seen in Chester, as in many other towns, a programme of slum clearance that has incidentally led to the virtual depopulation of the central area. Between the World Wars, estates of private housing developed in the suburbs, and the City Council has also provided municipal housing, with its inevitable accompaniment during the 1960s of high-rise flats, at Newtown NE of the city centre and at Blacon to the W. Chester is now almost completely surrounded by suburban housing development to a depth of two to three miles from the Cross. The approach to Chester along most of the main roads leading to it is now no different from the approach to most other English towns, by way of inter-war and post-war housing estates in the outer suburbs and late-19th-century terraces nearer the inner city. Chester's individuality is to a large extent confined within the city walls.

Nevertheless, consciousness of that individuality has never been lost. Whatever one thinks of the buildings of the black-and-white revival, which began in the 1850s and continued well on into this century, one has to admit that they were thought to be in character. Of course, important buildings have been destroyed to make way for 'improvements'. Cestrians often lament the destruction of the market hall that stood to the S of the Town Hall, and its replacement by the new market hall and the Forum precinct. The construction of the inner ring road also involved the demolition of buildings of character. However, a positive interest is now taken in conservation. In 1968, following the Civic Amenities Act of 1967, the Ministry of Housing and Local Government in conjunction with the City and County Councils commissioned *Chester: A Study in Conservation*, by Donald W. Insall and Associates. The Insall Report investigated Chester's past and present character, and brought to light the problems involved in conserving the city's historic heritage. The city centre was made a Conservation Area, and development was more strictly controlled. In 1973 the Committee of Monuments and Sites of the Council of Europe chose Chester as a site for a pilot project for European Architectural Heritage Year (1975). Permanent results have been the restoration of the Dutch Houses, Bridge Street (Walk 5), and of Gamul House, Lower Bridge Street (Walk 6), and the opening of the Chester Heritage Centre at the former church of St Michael (Walk 5). At the end of 1975 the Cross was restored to its position at the road junction S of St Peter's church [8] (Walk 1).

Conservation has not, of course, been uniformly successful. Chester is burdened with its share of glass and concrete office towers, such as Commerce House (Walk 3), Goldsmith House (Walk 1), and Hamilton House (Walk 1), to set against such achievements as the imaginative in-filling of a notorious gap in the buildings on the S side of Watergate Street (Walk 4). While King Street (Walk 3) is being restored with taste, Queen Street (Walk 9) has been sadly neglected, and plans for the large-scale redevelopment of its neighbourhood are not reassuring.

Tourism has remained important to Chester throughout the 20th century. It has received official encouragement in several ways. A well-produced *Official Guide* has been published by the City Council in almost every year since the 1920s: the edition of 1978 was the 42nd. There is a Tourist Information Centre at the Town Hall, which organizes regular and free guided tours of the city centre by qualified guides, who are required to take an examination in the history and features of Chester. A free monthly periodical, *What's On in Chester,* is also published. Since its foundation in 1948 the Chester City Record Office has done much to cater for the casual visitor to Chester as well as for the amateur or professional historian, by providing exhibitions and publications. The same is also true of the Grosvenor Museum. Chester is recognized as one of Britain's leading provincial tourist attractions, rivalling such places as Stratford on Avon and York. It is estimated that half a million tourists visited Chester in 1978.

Chester's reputation is, on the whole, well deserved. The Rows are unique. The circuit of the walls, though not quite as complete or historic as is sometimes claimed, is something that few other towns can offer. The enthusiast for Roman remains is well served, both by surviving evidence of the Roman period *in situ* and by the collections housed in the Grosvenor Museum. There are specimens of every period of architecture from Norman to contemporary. Recreational facilities, too, are good. The Dee above Chester provides excellent boating. Among parks and open spaces may be mentioned Grosvenor Park (Walk 8), the Groves (Walk 7), and the Water Tower Gardens (Walk 4) in the inner city. At Upton, some two miles NE of Chester, is an extensive zoo (p. 177). The Northgate Arena (Walk 3), opened in 1977, provides facilities for swimming and indoor sports. There are golf courses at Curzon Park, Eccleston, Upton, and Vicar's Cross. In Sealand Road are the ground of the Chester Football Club (the 'Seals') and a greyhound racing stadium; the Chester Rugby Union Football Club is at Vicar's Cross.

The only serious defect of Chester as a tourist centre is one common to many town centres as a phenomenon of this century: the problem of evening depopulation. Between 5 and 6 p.m. there is a scramble to leave Chester; the inner ring road and the approach roads are jammed with private cars. By 6.30 the city centre is virtually dead, since very few people now live within the walls. Evening parking restrictions have been blamed for the lack of people in Chester in the evenings, but it is questionable whether many of those who have fought to leave the city at the end of the working day would return even if parking was easier. There are many public houses, wine bars, and restaurants open in the evenings in the city centre, but only one theatre (the Gateway) and one cinema (the Odeon) within the walls. There is no concert hall in Chester; concerts are occasionally given in the Cathedral or the Town Hall. The institution of a Chester Festival fortnight and a Music Festival lasting a week represents an attempt to enliven the city during the evenings as well as in the daytime, but such events serve to highlight the lack of such activities during the remainder of the year.

As a centre for touring a wider area Chester has much to recommend it.* Liverpool and Manchester are easily accessible by road and rail; Liverpool may be reached in well under an hour, Manchester in an hour or a little more. The M56 and the M6 have made it possible to reach the Lake District for a day trip from Chester, although summer weekends should be avoided; the Peak District of Derbyshire is another possible day excursion. The whole of North Wales is also within reach, though the roads to the North Wales coast are again best avoided during summer weekends. Nearer at hand, there is much in Cheshire that is worth exploring. The tourist who is prepared to travel, say, up to 60 miles away from Chester for a day will have within reach a choice of attractions as good as any in the country. Depending on the individual's interests, the city of Chester and its immediate surroundings contain enough to justify a stay of anything from a couple of days to a week or more; as a base for exploring Cheshire, Merseyside and S Lancashire, and North Wales it would justify a stay of another week at least.

* See pp. 178–83 for a short account of suggested excursions from Chester.

Key Map to Walks

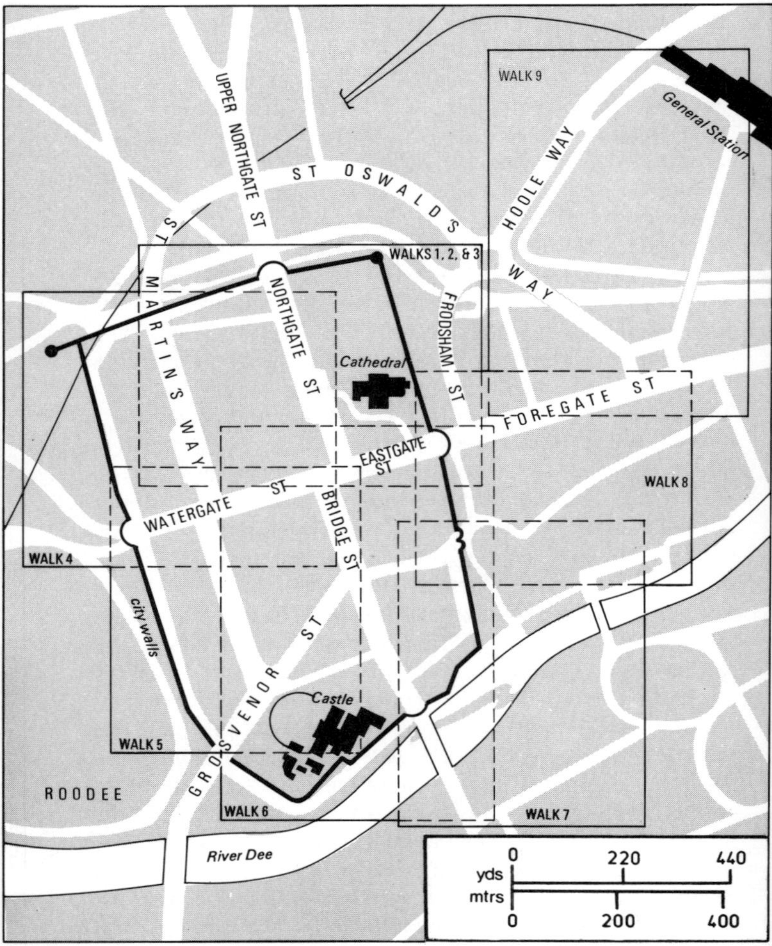

The Walks Preliminary Note

The nine walks described below, if followed systematically, will give the reader the 'feel' of Chester in all the varied aspects of its history. They have not all been chosen for their picturesqueness; the reader will be led through a certain amount of dereliction and neglect, and Walk 9 in particular is intended to present a very different picture of Chester from that which the tourist normally sees.

The centre of Chester is quite small, and several of the walks are short. The average Cestrian going about his business would perform Walk 1, for example, in five minutes. It is assumed, however, that the reader will want to study in detail what is worth studying. A street containing Rows ought to be walked four times, twice at street level and twice at Row level, if its character is to be absorbed. It is also assumed that the more important buildings seen on each walk will be visited. Because the centre of Chester is so small, no attempt has been made to ensure that each walk is circular; the reader can exercise ingenuity by finding a route to St Martin's Gate, for example, to start Walk 4, without covering ground already walked. The street pattern is so simple that it is very difficult to become lost.

Those already acquainted with Chester will immediately discover the surprising omission of a walk round the walls. In fact, such a circuit is made by parts of Walks 1–8, so that the reader who feels that such a perambulation is essential can use the guide selectively. Each walk has been designed to show individual aspects of Chester's heritage, and it was felt that the walls could better be walked in stages. In this as in other respects it is expected that the reader will use his judgement; one who dislikes having routes mapped out for him may nonetheless, by using the index and the sketch-maps, discover quite easily what is said about the various places of interest in Chester. For the visitor with only a short time to spend in the city, Walk 1, a visit to the Cathedral, and Walk 7 ought to provide a sufficient introduction to the atmosphere of Chester to encourage a longer return visit.

Routes of Walks One, Two, and Three

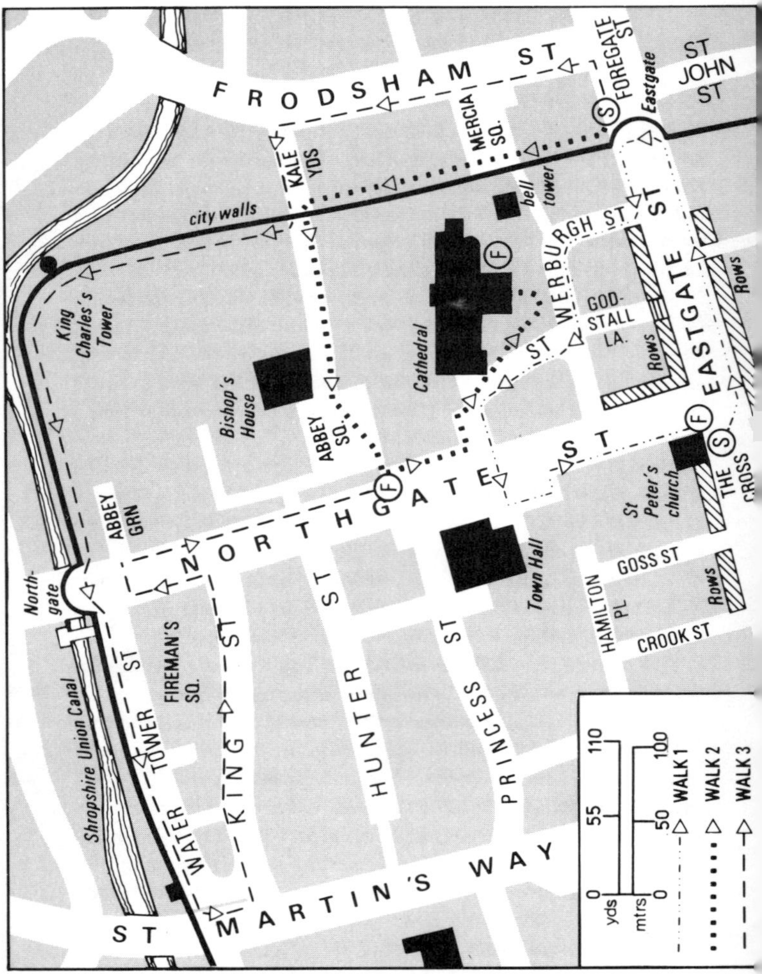

On all the perambulation maps the symbol Ⓢ indicates the start of a walk, Ⓕ the finish.

Walk One

This walk, though very short in distance, introduces much of Chester's character, and is worth the expenditure of a couple of hours at least. It takes in two major buildings, St Peter's church and the Town Hall. Each is worth a visit; both, however, present problems of access. St Peter's is no longer a parish church in its own right, but part of the parish of Chester; it is normally kept locked except during services. Access can usually be arranged by contacting the Rector of Chester Team Parish (telephone 26357; address, The Rectory, Vicar's Lane). For security reasons, casual entry is also discouraged at the Town Hall. The staff of the Chester City Record Office (telephone 40144, extension 2108) will, however, offer advice on obtaining access.

The Cross

Bridge Street, Eastgate Street, Northgate Street, and Watergate Street meet at the Cross, by St Peter's church [8]. During the Middle Ages the High Cross stood at the junction; it was a two-tier six-sided structure on a column, with niches in which stood carved religious figures. It is said to have been demolished when Chester surrendered to the Parliamentarian army in 1646. Early in the 19th century some fragments of it were discovered beneath the steps leading up to St Peter's. After being in private hands for a time, the fragments were re-erected near the Newgate in 1949, but late in 1975 they were restored to their old position in commemoration of European Architectural Heritage Year. The badly weathered sandstone fragment that surmounts the modern pillar seems to date from the 14th century.

A road intersection has existed here since Roman times. Watergate Street and Eastgate Street follow the line of the Roman *via principalis*; Bridge Street follows that of the *via praetoria*. St Peter's church stands on the S part of the site of the *principia*, or headquarters building. The S end of Northgate Street, however, is post-Roman in origin.

During the Middle Ages the Cross became the civic centre of Chester. Along the S wall of St Peter's church the Pentice (i.e. pent-house) was built, a timber erection of two floors with shops at ground level and civic offices above. The Pentice Court, presided over by the city Sheriffs, took its name from the building. (The Pentice Court is still held, but is now a ceremony at which new freemen of the city are sworn in before the Mayor and the officers of the guilds.) In Tudor and Stuart times distinguished visitors were entertained at the Pentice by the Corporation; James I was feasted there in 1617, and Charles I in 1642. The building of the Exchange in Northgate Street at the end of the 17th century provided a new administrative headquarters for the Corporation, though the Pentice remained in place for another century. At its W end, over the steps and porch leading into St Peter's, stood the rector's house.

In the 17th and 18th centuries the open space to the S of the Cross was used for bull-baiting. Near by stood the stocks, pillory, and whipping post. The annual fairs in Chester were announced by the display of a wooden glove outside the Pentice; after the building was removed, the glove was hung at fair times on a pole fixed at the SE corner of St Peter's, until the 1830s. It eventually found its way to a museum in Liverpool. From the 1580s the Cross was the terminus of the Conduit, a piped water-supply from springs at Boughton. The water was conveyed to a cistern raised above street level, with shops or stalls underneath it. On festive occasions the Conduit was filled with wine instead of water; that happened when a new charter from the King arrived at Chester in 1685, and in 1761 when King George III and Queen Charlotte were crowned.

In 1803 the Pentice was removed, in order to improve

access to Northgate Street; the Cross became a notorious traffic bottleneck, however, until the experiment in partial pedestrianization introduced in the early 1970s, since which time buses alone have been allowed to travel from Eastgate Street into Bridge Street, and from Bridge Street into Northgate Street. Today the Cross is an obvious meeting place; there are seats provided S of St Peter's church.

The predominant atmosphere of the surroundings of the Cross is 19th century. The S side of St Peter's [8], and the low spire that surmounts its tower, date from a thorough restoration of the church in 1886–7. Until the late 18th century there was a much higher spire. The restoration changed the tracery of the upper windows from Decorated to Perpendicular, and added the square-headed windows at ground-floor level. The buildings at the other corners by the Cross are all of about the same date. That on the SE corner, between Eastgate and Bridge Streets, is by T.M. Lockwood, designed in the half-timbered style of which much more will be seen on this walk. Together with its ornate neighbour to the E, also by Lockwood and of the same date (1888), it is probably the most frequently photographed building in Chester; it has featured on the covers of guidebooks, on numberless picture postcards, and on one of the postage stamps issued in 1975 to commemorate European Architectural Heritage Year. On the opposite corner of Bridge Street is another Lockwood building, four years later in date, with the half-timbering varied by brickwork, and Renaissance detail in the decoration. Close by, on the N side of Eastgate Street, the department store of Owen Owen is yet another Lockwood building, of 1900, again half-timbered with octagonal copper-roofed turrets at each end. When its site was being prepared, a lead water-pipe from the Roman fortress was discovered there. It bore an inscription datable to A.D. 79. For its significance see pp. 6–7.

St Peter's church

Like most Chester churches, St Peter's was altered considerably in the 19th century, particularly during the restoration of 1886–7. Internally, the basic structure is of the 14th or 15th century. The plan is unusual. There is no nave or chancel; three arcades divide the church into four aisles, so that in plan it is almost square. It has been suggested that in the Middle Ages there were chapels at the E ends of all four aisles.

From the Middle Ages there have survived some carved stone corbels, a monumental brass said to be that of a 15th-century lawyer, and, on the SE pier of the tower, part of a fresco discovered during restoration work in the mid 19th century. There are many mural monuments and brass inscriptions of the 17th, 18th, and 19th centuries. Most of the furnishings are Victorian or Edwardian; the stained-glass E windows are of 1862, one commemorating Prince Albert. There are N and S galleries, much altered in the last century; until 1886 there was also a W gallery.

Tradition asserts that St Peter's was founded on its present site in 907 by Aethelflaed, daughter of King Alfred. It receives a passing mention in the Domesday Survey (1086). Since Tudor times it has been closely associated with the city guilds. A service to celebrate the supposed millenary was held in June 1907, and two years later the local antiquarian Frank Simpson published a history of the church.

To the N of the church, reached by passages from Watergate and Northgate Streets, is St Peter's Churchyard. It was used for burials until the opening of the Chester cemetery S of the river in the mid 19th century, but is now a quiet paved area surrounded by buildings of the 18th and early 19th centuries, including the Commercial Hotel.

Eastgate Street

Eastgate Street represents the E section of the Roman *via principalis,* leading to the *porta principalis sinistra* of which the Eastgate is the successor. Beyond it the Roman road led through a civilian settlement E of the fort and on towards York, following roughly the line of the present A51 and A54. It was the main state entrance to Chester from the English side. In September 1642, for example, Charles I entered the city by the Eastgate and was received by the Mayor and Recorder at the Honey Steps, a site now occupied by Browns' shop. Between the 13th and 15th centuries Eastgate Street was also known as the Cornmarket. In the late 18th century markets for poultry, butter, and cheese were still held there.

By the early 19th century the street presented a mixture of genuine, but dilapidated, half-timber structures and newer Georgian brick buildings. There is an important 13th-century crypt, readily accessible during the shop's opening hours, beneath No. 28 on the S side (Crypt Buildings).* The Boot Inn, Eastgate Row N, is said to date from 1643 but has been extensively restored; on the opposite side, No. 32 Eastgate Row S (Mappin and Webb) has Jacobean woodwork in an upper room above the Row, again open to view during shopping hours.

There are Rows on both sides of the W part of Eastgate Street. They differ widely in character. Eastgate Row S [20] is a modern shopping arcade, high, wide, and light. That on the N [19] preserves more of the earlier flavour of the Rows, which in the 18th and 19th centuries were not particularly salubrious places: it begins as an unprepossessing alley between high buildings, very wet after heavy rain, reached by steps a few yards up Northgate Street; emerging from behind Owen Owen's department store, it continues beneath 18th- and 19th-century buildings to end in another flight of steps at the W side of the National Westminster Bank. Known in Tudor and early Stuart times as the Dark Lofts or Dark Row, it remains unfrequented even when Eastgate Street itself is at its busiest.

Browns of Chester, now part of the Debenham Group, originated in a millinery and haberdashery shop kept by Susannah Brown in the late 18th century. The firm made its first impact on the Chester townscape with No. 38, on the site of the Honey Steps, *c.*1828. Severely Classical, it gained the unqualified admiration of Joseph Hemingway, who thought that it could compare with London's Regent Street shops.

* In December 1978 the crypt was converted into a restaurant.

Thirty years later Browns created another sensation with the Crypt Buildings [30], designed by T.M. Penson in an Early English style to harmonize with the 13th-century crypt beneath. The firm continued to expand; just before the First World War they took over the shop immediately to the E of the Classical building, and thus added a half-timber building to their collection.

Next door to Browns on the E were Bollands, in their own way just as famous. Bollands were one of the leading confectioners in the city, famous as suppliers of a wedding cake to Queen Victoria. One of their 'creations' was a cake designed as a model of the Town Hall, to celebrate that building's opening in 1869.

In the mid 19th century a veritable battle of architectural styles was being fought in Eastgate Street. Shortly before he designed Crypt Buildings in Gothic for Browns, T.M. Penson erected the two shops (now occupied by Browns and Boots) [29] immediately to the E of Browns' 1828 Classical building. They are among the earliest examples of the black-and-white revival, on a smaller scale and much quieter in design than later efforts by Douglas and Lockwood. In 1859–60 George Williams erected the buildings now housing the National Westminster Bank, on the N side of Eastgate Street at the W corner of St Werburgh Street, in a determinedly Classical style (stone, composite columns, and a pediment). In the 1890s G.A. Audsley, bringing up to date the *Stranger's Handbook to Chester*, criticized the building as 'a style of architecture distinctly out of place in such a street'. Within a couple of years of its erection T.A. Richardson had built No. 25 near by, at the entrance to Godstall Lane, for Duttons the grocers; the style was equally determined black-and-white, and hailed by the Chester Archaeological Society as 'one of the boldest and most picturesque [buildings] thus far erected in Chester since the modern revival of the Elizabethan style of architecture'.

T.M. Penson also designed – though he did not live to see its completion – the Grosvenor Hotel. Once again the style chosen was black-and-white, with the upper storeys carried over the street on a colonnade. The hotel was built between

1863 and 1866 for the Marquess of Westminster. It replaced a Georgian building, the Royal Hotel, which had been described in 1856 by Thomas Hughes as '*par excellence* the first and most fashionable of all our Chester Hotels'. Its successor has endeavoured to maintain the Royal's reputation as the leading hotel in the city; it contains some 100 bedrooms, and a ballroom now often used for such activities as antique fairs.

Grosvenor influence is also apparent on the N side of Eastgate Street, opposite the Grosvenor Hotel. The Midland Bank [32], a red-brick building with stone dressings, prominently displays on its upper storey an early version of the Grosvenor arms (*azure a garb or* – a gold wheatsheaf on a blue field). It was designed by John Douglas in 1883 in his Flemish–Gothic style, rather reminiscent of the contemporary work of George and Peto in London, and its upper floor housed the Grosvenor Club. (The Club was founded in 1866, and was housed until 1883 in the Grosvenor Hotel; in 1957 it was transferred from the Bank building to the former St John's Rectory in Vicar's Lane, Walk 8. At the turn of the century it had about 250 members, mostly said to be from Cheshire, Flintshire, and Denbighshire.) The coats of arms above the ground floor windows are those of the 12 counties of Wales (i.e. the counties in existence prior to local government reorganization in 1974); the ground floor was occupied originally by the North and South Wales Bank. A plaque on the building commemorates the fact that it is owned by the trustees of Owen Jones's Charity. Owen Jones, a butcher who died in 1659, directed in his will that the income from his estates in North Wales should be given to each of the city companies in turn, for the benefit of their poor members. The discovery of lead on the lands in the early 18th century considerably enhanced the value of the charity, which invested its income in property and company shares; in 1772, for example, the Weavers' Company decided to invest £2,000 of their income from the charity in the Chester canal.

The narrow entry between the Midland Bank and the Eastgate led to the King's Arms Kitchen, a public house, now closed, with an interesting history. Unsubstantiated legend asserts that after the defeat of the Royalist army at Rowton Moor in 1645, Charles I hid there. In the 18th and 19th centuries it housed the Honourable Incorporation of the King's Arms Kitchen, a drinking and gambling club organized as a burlesque of the City Corporation, with its own mayor, recorder, sheriffs, town clerk, and regalia. Until the closure of the public house in 1978 the room where the Incorporation met was still used; it preserved the members' seats, with places reserved for the officials, and panelling on which was painted the succession of officials' names.

The Eastgate, surmounted by its clock [5], must rival the Lockwood building at the Cross for the distinction of being the most frequently photographed structure in Chester. The medieval Eastgate, said to incorporate arches from the Roman gateway, was taken down in 1766. Illustrations drawn at about that time, though not mutually consistent, agree that it was a pointed archway between two octagonal towers, the whole structure surmounted by a battlement. Some of its lower courses were investigated by archaeologists during excavations in connexion with repairs to a sewer in 1972 (see *Journal of the Chester Archaeological Society*, vol. 59, 1976, pp. 37–49). Like most of the city gates the Eastgate was held not by the Corporation but by individuals from the Earl of Chester: among others, the Earls of Oxford and the Crewe family, who employed gate-keepers and exacted tolls on all goods passing through. An inscription records that the gate was rebuilt in 1768–9 at the expense of Richard, Lord Grosvenor. The clock above it was erected in 1899 by Colonel Edward Evans-Lloyd to commemorate the Diamond Jubilee of Queen Victoria (1897); the iron turret on which it stands was designed by Douglas, and the clock itself by J.B. Joyce of Whitchurch. Until 1974 it was wound by hand once a week.

The Grosvenor-Laing Shopping Precinct

Though not directly included in this walk, the Grosvenor-Laing precinct is worth more than a passing mention.

Immediately to the W of the Grosvenor Hotel, Newgate Street formerly led S from Eastgate Street to the Newgate. It was known, from the 12th to the 18th century, as Fleshmongers' Lane. Since 1965 it has been replaced by Newgate Row, which is the N entrance of a covered shopping precinct that occupies much of the space between Eastgate Street and Pepper Street. The centre of the precinct is St Michael's Square, a covered-in open space used for displays, with seats and a restaurant. A multi-storey car park is incorporated; there is pedestrian access to the walls and St John Street, to Pepper Street, and to the early-20th-century St Michael's Row and Bridge Street (Walk 5). As one might expect from so modern a development, the shops are mostly branches of national or regional multiples. Use of the precinct is very heavy during shopping hours; at other times it is virtually deserted.

St Werburgh Street

This street leads, after several turns, to the Market Square and the Town Hall. Its N side is dominated by the S face of the Cathedral, to be described later (Walk 2). From Eastgate Street, St Werburgh Street first leads N. Until almost the end of the 19th century it was a narrow lane. The range of timber-framed buildings on its E side was designed as a unified scheme by John Douglas, arising from co-operation between the architect, the Corporation, the Duke of Westminster, and others. The range presents a wealth of ornamental detail, with oriel windows, carved figures, and 'barley-sugar' chimneys. At its S end, on the side of Barclays Bank, there is a plaque erected in 1923 to commemorate Douglas's work.

St Werburgh Street now leads W and N towards the Market Square. On the S side, St Werburgh Mount [31] and its neighbours are another example of Douglas black-and-white, but 20 years earlier than that described above. It is more like the half-timbering of Penson, but rather 'cottagey' in style, with the timbers supplemented by herringbone brickwork, and ornamental plasterwork on the upper floors.

An alley leading S from St Werburgh Street to Eastgate Street is Godstall Lane. Most of this lane is now taken up by the grocery, health-food, and wine shops of George Dutton and Son. Formerly Duttons' premises extended to Eastgate Street itself; the shop was then known as the Sigarro Stores. The title came from the first letters of *Signum Arae Romanae* (the Sign of the Roman Altar), and commemorated the discovery, in 1861, during excavations in connexion with the building of the shop, of a Roman altar some 13 ft below ground level. It is now in the Grosvenor Museum.

Another alley, leading W from St Werburgh Street to Northgate Street, is Music-Hall Passage. The building immediately to its N has had a chequered history. From the Passage it will readily be seen to incorporate medieval masonry. It is said to have been built early in the 14th century as the chapel of St Nicholas. Late in the 15th century it became the common hall used by the Corporation. In 1773 it became the New Theatre, and four years later the proprietor obtained a patent that licensed it as the Theatre Royal. Among those who performed there were Mrs Siddons (*Venice Preserved*, in 1786), and Edmund Kean (*King Richard III*, in 1815). In the second quarter of the 19th century it declined in prosperity; when its lease from the Dean and Chapter of the Cathedral expired in 1853, the building was said to be in a state of 'disorganization and decay and dirt'. It was converted into a concert hall by the architect James Harrison, and opened under the name of the Music Hall in 1855. (The Tudor windows at its E end, as seen from St Werburgh Street, are Harrison's: compare his Savings Bank in Grosvenor Street, Walk 5.) In 1867 Charles Dickens gave readings from his novels there. In the present century the Music Hall has seen service as a cinema and as a supermarket. In 1978, after being unoccupied for several years, it opened as a men's outfitters' shop. An account of it as a theatre is given by H. Hughes in *Chronicle of Chester* (1975), chapter 12.

The Town Hall

St Werburgh Street curves round the S side of the Cathedral to reach the Market Square, sometimes known as Town Hall Square, which is not really a square at all but a widening of Northgate Street.

At the end of the 17th century the Exchange was built in the square, a little to the N and E of the present Town Hall. Pictures of the Exchange show that it probably had much in common, architecturally, with the Bluecoat School [21] erected further N in Northgate Street 20 years later (Walk 3); it was built of brick, with stone quoins, and originally its upper floors were carried over colonnades at ground-floor level. By the mid 18th century the structure had become unsafe, and part of the ground floor was filled in and used as shops. The Exchange was used by the Corporation for its meetings, and its courts were held there. There was an assembly room for social events, though by the mid 19th century its place had been usurped by the assembly room at the Royal Hotel (now the Grosvenor) in Eastgate Street. High up on the S front was a niche containing a statue of Queen Anne, which was subjected to acts of vandalism during election riots in 1784 and 1812.

On 30 December 1862 the Exchange was severely damaged by fire; so severely that there was no question of repair, and the Corporation had to demolish it. The statue of Queen Anne eventually found its way to the Water Tower gardens (Walk 4), but disappeared from there a few years ago. A competition was held for designs for a new town hall. Of the 30 designs submitted, that by W.H. Lynn of Belfast (1829–1915)* was declared the winner. Lynn had recently designed a parliament house and government offices at Sydney, New South Wales. There were many delays and difficulties, as was usual in the construction of public buildings of this type. The foundation stone was only laid in October 1865, nearly three years after the fire at the Exchange. A nine-month strike by the stonemasons delayed

* For further information on this architect see C.E.B. Brett, *Buildings of Belfast, 1700–1914* (1967).

completion still further: not until 15 October 1869 did the Prince of Wales, the future Edward VII, formally open the building.

The Town Hall [39] is built of sandstone, generally buff-coloured but picked out in red, in a Gothic style of the 13th century. It has a central tower 160 ft high, a steeply pitched tiled roof, and corner turrets. There is a double arch at the entrance, which is at first-floor level and reached by way of stairs and a balcony. The entrance hall is impressive, as is the main staircase leading to the Council Chamber and other rooms on the second floor. At the W end of the entrance hall is a circular window filled with stained glass; the windows lighting the staircase depict the early Earls of Chester. Relations between the city and the earldom are the constant theme of the sculptures that appear above the entrances to most of the main rooms. They are inventive rather than authentic: for example, the one showing Earl Ranulph III granting a charter to the city in 1181, which appears over the entrance to the Council Chamber, is misinformed in two ways: none of the charters granted by Ranulph to the city can be dated positively to 1181; Ranulph, who in 1181 was about 12 years old, is shown as a mature warrior.

The ground floor was designed as the city police station. It remained in use by the police until the opening of the new County Police Headquarters near the Castle in 1967 (Walk 5). It is now occupied by a magistrates' court, the Chester Tourist Information Centre, and the Chester City Record Office. The two main rooms on the first floor are the Assembly Room and the city's former quarter sessions court, now used by the Chester magistrates. The Assembly Room, which contains a stage, is used for exhibitions, concerts, and other occasional functions. The second floor contains committee rooms, the Mayor's Parlour, and the Council Chamber. The latter was badly damaged by fire in 1897, and restored by T.M. Lockwood. Most of its furniture, however, is of 1869 and, as one might expect from the Town Hall itself, Gothic. The panelling of the Council Chamber is good, and includes carved representations of the city arms. The modern (1977) grant of arms is also displayed there.

The Town Hall houses the city insignia and records and some of the city's collection of plate, the remainder of which is in the Grosvenor Museum. During the siege of Chester in the Civil War the city's plate was melted down for coining, and as a result nothing of earlier date has survived. Most of the late-17th- and early-18th-century plate consists of tankards presented by members of the Corporation when they were elected. One of the remaining duties of the Sheriff of the city is to undertake an annual inspection of the plate. The insignia include 19th- and early-20th-century chains and pendant jewels for the Mayor, the Sheriff, and the Mayoress. The most important items are the city sword, which is said to be of 15th-century manufacture, and is housed in a 17th-century scabbard; the mace, presented to the city in 1668 by Charles, Earl of Derby, who was then Mayor of Chester; and a silver oar 14 in. long, made in 1719, which symbolizes the Mayor's authority as Admiral of the Dee. The sword – which according to the charter of 1506 may be carried upright except in the presence of the Sovereign – and the mace are borne before the Mayor on all ceremonial occasions. The oar is similarly carried whenever the Mayor carries out any duties in connexion with the river.

The Chester City Record Office was established in 1948. The first City Archivist, Margaret J. Groombridge, compiled a well-illustrated *Guide to the Charters, Plate, and Insignia of the City of Chester*; it is still very useful even though recent scholarship has superseded parts of it. The core of the city records is its collection of charters and letters patent by which the Earls of Chester and the Kings of England announced the concession of various liberties to the citizens. These records tell the story of the city's growing independence from the county of Chester, culminating in the charter of 1506 by which Henry VII made Chester a county in its own right. The collection begins with a letter, believed to date from 1175 or 1176, from Henry II to his bailiffs of Dublin instructing them to allow the burgesses of Chester to enjoy their accustomed trading rights there; it ends at present with the two letters patent of 1974 by which Queen

Elizabeth II conferred on Chester district, which was created by the Local Government Act of 1972, the status first of a borough and subsequently of a city, and another patent of 1977 by which the city's new arms were confirmed.

The wealth of material in the Record Office cannot be described adequately in a couple of paragraphs. The city records, apart from the charters, begin in the 13th century and continue to the present time. They deal with the activities of the Corporation and its committees, the work of the various departments, and the proceedings of the city courts. In addition, there is material from the rural districts of Chester and Tarvin, which were absorbed into the new district of Chester in 1974. The Record Office also houses records and manuscripts deposited by private individuals and by corporate bodies; one of the most important deposits is the manuscript collection of the Chester Archaeological Society, whose library is also housed in the Office.

The Forum

Immediately to the S of the Town Hall, and forming a complete contrast in its architecture of concrete, brick, and glass, is the Forum. Its site was occupied in 1863 by a new public market with an ornate Baroque façade. In spite of the feelings of enthusiasts for Victorian public architecture the market was demolished in 1967.

The Forum is part of a comprehensive redevelopment of the area between Northgate Street and the inner ring road. The creation of a new civic centre in the area had been proposed at the end of the Second World War, though luckily the proposals, for a group of neo-Georgian blocks to replace most of the Victorian buildings in the area, came to nothing. The lowest stage of the new complex is a large underground car park extending from the rear of the Town Hall to the inner ring road. At its W end, entered from Trinity Street, is a short-stay shoppers' car park at ground level. The Forum itself is a shopping precinct entered from Northgate Street; above the shops are council offices. To the

NW is the new market hall, opened in 1967, which can also be entered from Princess Street. To the W of the Forum is the Gateway Theatre, which opened in 1968. The name was suggested by an entrant in a competition run by the *Cheshire Observer*, and is said to relate to the theatre's position midway between the Watergate and the Northgate. The theatre and the Forum were designed by Michael Lyell Associates, also responsible for another shopping precinct in Chester, Mercia Square (Walk 2).

To the S of the Forum is Hamilton Place, entered from Northgate Street by a narrow arch that retains a fragment of the Victorian Baroque of the market hall. Behind glass in the S wall of the Forum a small part of the excavated Roman headquarters building is preserved, labelled 'Roman Strong Room'. Hamilton Place itself is dominated by the Forum to its N, and, to the S, by Goldsmith House in Goss Street and Hamilton House. Goldsmith House, built in 1975, contains the Register Office for the Chester and Ellesmere Port districts: part of its site was occupied until 1962 by the Chester assay office, where gold and silver was tested. The closure of that office was followed a few years later by the demolition of the 'listed' Georgian building that housed it. Hamilton House, a six-storey office block built in 1966, houses the Inland Revenue.

Northgate Street (south end)

The S end of Northgate Street has undergone considerable changes since the middle of the 19th century. On the W side the Dublin Packet is the sole survivor (unless the Commercial Hotel in St Peter's Churchyard is counted) of the four inns or taverns that Thomas Hughes noted in 1864; the others were the Legs of Man, the Cross Keys, and the Woolpack. Until the end of the 19th century there was a genuine Row on this side, but it was demolished in the 1890s and a black-and-white 'piazza' substituted. Some of the buildings in this range, which is called Shoemakers' Row, are attributed to John Douglas. At the N end, on first-floor level, is a small carved statue of Edward VII. At the S end, the last building before St Peter's church is the City Club [25], a Classical building designed by Thomas Harrison in 1808 as the Commercial News Room. This was not strictly a subscription newsroom, but was managed by a committee representing the 'proprietors', who numbered 100. London and provincial newspapers and magazines were taken, and the Mayor, the city and county M.P.s, and the leading military officers in the district were automatically entitled to use the facilities. The building also housed, in the early and mid 19th century, the privately-run City Library.

On the E side of Northgate Street an undistinguished block of modern shops replaces the black-and-white Clemence's Restaurant demolished in the early 1960s. Beyond the electricity and gas showrooms, a genuine Row appears on this side. Like the Row on the N side of Eastgate Street, it preserves some of the former character of the Rows; it was apparently so unevenly paved at one time that it was known as Broken-Shin Row. Beneath, one of the shops at street level (Miss Selfridge) preserves, at the rear, a Roman hypocaust. Opposite, No. 23 (Nola Gowns) has in its basement the bases of columns of the Roman *principia.*

Walk Two

The Eastgate, which has been described in Walk 1, is the starting point of this walk. A complete circuit of the exterior of the Cathedral is followed by a description of its interior. The route taken around the exterior is 'widdershins', that is in an anti-clockwise direction as seen from above; anyone who feels that it must result in raising the Devil should follow it in the opposite direction. For the non-superstitious, the advised route is felt to be both logical and satisfying.

The Cathedral

In the late 9th century the relics of St Werburgh, who died *c.*700 and was the daughter of King Wulfhere of Mercia, were brought to Chester from Hanbury, near Burton-on-Trent. A church dedicated to St Werburgh and served by a college of canons was founded in the early 10th century, possibly by Aethelflaed, 'Lady of the Mercians'. In 1086 it held land in Chester and in 21 townships in Cheshire. Six years later Hugh I, Earl of Chester, summoned Anselm, Abbot of Bec and later to be Archbishop of Canterbury, to reorganize the minster as a Benedictine monastery. Hugh himself took a monk's vows there three days before his death in 1101. He and his successors endowed the abbey with lands and other gifts in Chester, Cheshire, and elsewhere. The abbey precinct with its extensive lands and privileges was sometimes seen as a threat to the Corporation of Chester, just as the Cathedral was in the 17th century.

The Benedictine abbey was dissolved in 1540. In the following year it was re-established as a cathedral dedicated to Christ and the Blessed Virgin Mary. It became the administrative headquarters of a diocese that extended N and E into Cumbria and Yorkshire. The Cathedral's establishment consisted of a dean and a chapter of six canons, with six minor canons, six lay clerks, eight choristers, and six bedesmen or almsmen. Its history up to the early 19th century is given in detail by R.V.H. Burne, canon of the Cathedral and archdeacon of Chester, in *Chester Cathedral* (1958), while that of the abbey is told by the same author in *The Monks of Chester* (1962).

Part of the monastic church was used as the parish church of St Oswald. At first it occupied the S aisle of the nave. From the 14th to the early 16th century the chapel of St Nicholas, which later became the Theatre Royal and the Music Hall (Walk 1), was used; but from the early 16th century until 1881 the S transept of the Cathedral was St Oswald's parish church.

The Cathedral today is interesting rather than impressive. It possesses few architectural features of national or international significance; indeed, general works on the cathedrals of the United Kingdom usually find little to say about it. Most of the medieval furnishings apart from the choir stalls have disappeared. The fabric was constructed of the local sandstone, which weathers very badly. As a result, although there is genuine Norman, Early English, Decorated, and Perpendicular work to be found, the dominant impression is created by the work of the Victorian and early-20th-century restorers. In size the Cathedral is undistinguished: its length is 371 ft, its breadth 206 ft, and the height of its central tower is 127 ft. The tower, with its four battlemented turrets, is a dominant feature of the Chester skyline; but the Town Hall tower is 33 ft taller.

From the Eastgate to Abbey Street

The Eastgate should be approached by the rather dingy steps on the S side of Eastgate Street to the E of the Grosvenor Hotel. The view from the top of the gate to the E is not particularly impressive. Foregate Street, which led E through the Roman and medieval suburb of the city, is now lined with multiple stores and ends in a large traffic roundabout at the Bars (Walk 8). To the W, the townscape is much better. The architectural jumble of Eastgate Street, with its interesting mixture of Georgian, Classical, Gothic, and black-and-white styles, leads W to the Cross, beyond which Watergate Street dips down towards the Roodee. In clear weather the view is closed by a glimpse of the Clwydian hills, reminding one that Chester is a border town.

From the Eastgate to the Northgate and beyond, the walls are on Roman foundations. To the N of the Eastgate they are shut in, on the W by the Midland Bank and the unimaginative flank of Woolworths, and on the E by Burtons' shop of 1928. Soon, however, the view opens out. To the E is Mercia Square, more striking in its concept as a two-level shopping precinct than in its use of materials. On the upper level, approached from the walls, is an open space with seats, a restaurant, and two wine bars. Steps lead down to a shopping arcade and Frodsham Street (Walk 3). The square takes its name from the Midland Anglo-Saxon kingdom of Mercia, from which St Werburgh came.

To the W of the wall, opposite Mercia Square, rises the detached bell-tower of the Cathedral, perhaps more like a plump missile on its launching pad than a recognizable piece of ecclesiastical architecture. Completed in 1974, it is 86 ft high and of concrete with brick infilling; above the stone ground floor are three tiers covered with Bethesda slates. Its construction was made necessary by the decay of the bell frame in the central tower of the Cathedral, which put the whole tower at risk. The design of the new tower, by George Pace, consulting architect to the Cathedral, is said to have been dictated by the stresses set up by the ringing of a peal of bells. The tower and its bells are described by A. Whiting in *The Bells of Chester Cathedral* (1974).

From the walls N of the bell tower, the S transept, the crossing tower, the choir, and the Lady Chapel of the Cathedral are seen. A comparison of this view with prints of the early and mid 19th century reveals the extent of the work of the Victorian restorers. The S end of the S transept, with its two small turrets, belongs to an even earlier restoration undertaken by Thomas Harrison between 1819 and 1820. Much of what can be seen from this point dates from the most drastic of the restorations, undertaken by Sir George Gilbert Scott between 1868 and 1876. The crossing tower, up to the height of its louvered windows, is of late-15th-century construction. Its battlements and four turrets, however, are Scott's. Scott would have liked to surmount the tower with a tall spire; opinions differ as to whether that would have been an improvement. The S transept is of about the same length as the choir; its clerestory windows are Perpendicular, and those of its E aisle Decorated. The S choir aisle ends in an unusual polygonal apse with a steeply pitched roof. Originally the aisle had extended further to the E, but Scott claimed that he had found evidence of the existence of the apse. The choir itself ends in two turrets each crowned with tall pinnacles. They are Scott's; but the E window of the choir dates from an earlier restoration carried out in the 1840s, by R.C. Hussey. Early-19th-century pictures of the Lady Chapel show it with Perpendicular windows and a low-pitched roof. In 1859 its E window was replaced with five lancets, and a decade later those on the S side were given lancets, and the roof was given its steep pitch.

As one moves further N along the wall, the monastic parts of the Cathedral come into view, together with its attenuated N transept. Immediately to the N is the chapter house, again with lancet windows. Further to the N is the large E window of the refectory. Its tracery was designed in 1913 by Sir Giles Gilbert Scott.

A slope leads down from the W side of the walls to Abbey Street. A careful search of the coping of the wall near the top of this slope will reveal, among other graffiti, a carved anchor and '692 ft' in the stonework. This is said to have been carved by G. Haswell and J.B. Musgrave in 1858. It is the distance from the mark to King Charles's tower; it commemorates the length of the steamship *Great Eastern*.

Abbey Street, Abbey Square, and the Abbey Gateway

Abbey Street is a cobbled thoroughfare leading W into Abbey Square. The houses on the N side are of the late 18th century (see a rainwater head dated 1764, and two fire insurance plaques), and include the Deanery. Those on the S side were built in the 1820s. Just before reaching Abbey Square, one passes the Bishop's house on the right. It is a large house of the late 18th century, in a walled garden, and was built as the Deanery on the site of a former chapel dedicated to St Thomas.

Cobbled roadways, now unfortunately used as a car park, surround a green space in Abbey Square [22]. The pillar in the middle of the lawn is said to have come from the Exchange (Walk 1). On the E side of the square are two stone-built houses erected by Bishop John Bridgeman in 1626 on the site of the abbey kitchen. On the N and W sides are Georgian terraces, their doorways showing interesting variations on Classical themes.

The exit from Abbey Square is by way of the Abbey Gateway [15], which leads into the Market Square. The gateway is 14th-century, though its upper storey, with Gothic windows, is late-18th or early-19th. The vaulted roof of the gateway has carved bosses, though they can only be seen at some risk as the gate is used by vehicles entering and leaving the car park.

The King's School and the west and south of the Cathedral

Barclays Bank, to the S of the gateway, is a Gothic building of sandstone. It was designed as the King's School by Sir Arthur W. Blomfield, another of the Cathedral's restorers, in 1876. The school was founded by Henry VIII in 1541. From the early 17th century until 1876 it was housed in the Cathedral refectory. The original foundation of the school provided for a master and an usher who were to teach Latin to 24 'poor and friendless boys . . . of good capacity (so far as is possible) and capable of learning'. Fee-paying pupils were taken as well as the foundation scholars. The school was reorganized in 1873, and Blomfield's building, designed to accommodate about 200 boys, cost £20,000. By 1939 there were 280 pupils. In 1960 new buildings were opened in Wrexham Road, S of Chester. A pupil of the school who attained local fame in the 19th century was Thomas Hughes (1826–90), a founder of the Chester Architectural, Archaeological, and Historic Society in 1849 and the author of *The Stranger's Handbook to Chester.* First published in 1856, this guidebook to the city ran into many editions, and still contains much information not readily obtainable elsewhere. Hughes's comments on contemporary Chester are often illuminating. He also edited the *Cheshire Sheaf*, a series of notes and queries on local history that appeared weekly in one of the local newspapers. It began in 1878, and, though there have been several gaps in its production, is still appearing; it is now published monthly in the magazine *Deesider.*

St Werburgh Street, traversed in the opposite direction in Walk 1, leads to the imposing W front of the Cathedral [7], which is basically of the early 16th century, though much restored by Scott. A careful inspection of the great W window will reveal that it is asymmetrical. To its S is the base of an intended SW tower, begun in the early 16th century. To the N is a Norman NW tower, but it is hidden by Barclays Bank. Before 1876 the site of the bank, formerly the King's School, was occupied by the Bishop's Palace, which communicated directly with the Cathedral by way of the NW tower.

The circuit of the exterior of the Cathedral is completed by way of a war-memorial garden. The cross in the middle of the garden was designed in 1922 by F.H. Crossley.

The SW porch is sometimes used as the tourist entrance to the Cathedral. Like the uncompleted SW tower, which it adjoins, it is of the early 16th century. The clerestory windows of the nave are late-15th-century. Below, the tracery of the N aisle windows is Decorated; it is mostly the work of R.C. Hussey, restorer of the Cathedral in the 1840s. Beyond the S transept the S front, facing St Werburgh Street, is reached. It was restored by Thomas Harrison *c.*1820, but its S window tracery is of 1887, and is by Sir A.W. Blomfield. Before the Cathedral is entered, it is worthwhile to walk to the E of the S transept to see the Victorian corbels, dating from Scott's restoration: there are easily recognizable figures of two Prime Ministers, Gladstone, with quill pen, and Disraeli, with a sword; a knight to the right of Gladstone bears a shield with the arms of the Duke of Westminster.

The Cathedral Interior

There are three entrances to the Cathedral in common use. The obvious one for anyone taking this walk is by the S door of the S transept. The Cathedral can also be entered from the SW porch or from Abbey Square by way of the cloisters. Space does not permit a detailed topographical guide to the interior. Instead, the reader is invited to take a position towards the E end of the nave, reached equally easily from any of the three entrances. From that point the main features of the interior can be surveyed, and detailed exploration of the individual parts may be undertaken in any order.

The Nave

The nave is six bays long. Its S side was built in the mid 14th century; the N side was built *c.*1490. The five westernmost bays only illustrate the difference of more than a century in their dates by small architectural details, in the bases and capitals of the columns. The easternmost bays on each side are different again; when the Cathedral was the abbey church the choir probably extended as far W as this point. The vaulting of the nave roof is of timber; it is part of Scott's restoration. The W window, depicting the Blessed Virgin Mary and northern saints including St Werburgh and St Oswald, and also Aethelflaed, Lady of the Mercians, is by W.T. Carter Shapland, and dates from 1961. Towards the W end of the nave, on the S side near the steps leading up to the

W door, there are many mural monuments of the 17th, 18th, and 19th centuries. The black marble font is late-17th-century.

The base of the unfinished SW tower contains the Consistory Court, over which the chancellor of the diocese presides. The furnishings, and the screen dividing the Court from the nave, are of the time of Bishop John Bridgeman (1619–52). The chancellor's seat is canopied, and over it appear the arms of the bishop, together with those reputedly of Earl Hugh I of Chester (d. 1101), who refounded the abbey; of the diocese of Chester; and of Chancellor Edmund Mainwaring.

The W end of the N aisle is in fact the base of the Cathedral's NW tower, which is obviously Norman. Since 1885 it has been used as the baptistry. Until the removal of the former Bishop's Palace to make room for the new King's School building in the 1870s, the tower was walled off from the church and divided into two floors. The font was presented to the Cathedral by Earl Egerton of Tatton (d. 1909) in 1885. Until recently it was thought to be Italian work of the 6th or 7th century, but is a 19th-century imitation.

The N wall of the N aisle is decorated with mosaics designed in the 1880s by J.R. Clayton. They depict scenes in the lives of Abraham, Moses, David, and Elijah.

The stalls at the E end of the nave were designed by George Pace (noticed earlier as the designer of the bell tower); they date from 1966.

The South Transept

The most remarkable feature of the S transept is its size. It is five bays long, similar in length to the choir. It has E and W aisles; the four S bays of the E aisle are occupied by chapels dedicated respectively (from N to S) to St Mary Magdalene, St Oswald, St George, and St Nicholas. Those of St Oswald, St George, and St Nicholas have stained glass windows by C.E. Kempe (1837–1907), who also designed the reredos in St Oswald's chapel. St George's chapel is associated with the

Cheshire Regiment, whose colours are displayed on the E wall.

The transept was built in the 14th century, though its clerestories are Perpendicular in style. Until 1880 it was used as the parish church of St Oswald; from 1828 it was separated from the main body of the Cathedral by a screen. The S end was restored by Thomas Harrison, *c.*1820, and Sir A.W. Blomfield restored the E aisle of the transept and designed the tracery of the S window, which was filled with glass by Heaton, Butler, and Bayne representing the triumph of faith. Between 1900 and 1902 the remainder of the transept was restored by C.J. Blomfield (d. 1932) in memory of Hugh Lupus Grosvenor, first Duke of Westminster (1825–99). Blomfield also designed the Duke's monument, which stands in the transept; the recumbent effigy is by F.W. Pomeroy (1857–1924).

There are many other monuments of interest in the transept. One, of particular interest to Americans, commemorates Frederick Philips of New York (d. 1785), who opposed the American War of Independence and came to England after it. The battle ensigns worn by H.M.S. *Chester* at the battle of Jutland (31 May 1916) are displayed, together with the ship's roll of honour, which includes the name of Jack Cornwell, V.C.

The North Transept

This presents a complete contrast to the S transept. It is of two bays only; to its N the monastic buildings prevented further expansion. Some of the earliest visible work of the Cathedral is in the NE bay, where a late-11th-century arch is surmounted by a triforium. To its E is a former chapel. The transept roof is of timber, and is early-16th-century, bearing the arms of Henry VIII and Cardinal Wolsey. The most striking monument in the transept is that to John Pearson, Bishop of Chester (1673–86). It dates not from the 17th century but from 1863. It was designed by Sir A.W. Blomfield. Bishop Pearson was the author of an *Exposition of the Creed*, and the base of the monument shows the heads of the 12 Apostles, with the words of the Creed below. A mural monument to Samuel Peploe (d. 1781), chancellor of the diocese of Chester, is by Joseph Nollekens.

The Crossing and the Choir

The crossing between N and S transepts is now uncluttered. Until Sir George Gilbert Scott's restoration, the choir stalls had extended further to the W, into or beyond the crossing. Scott removed the stone screen or *pulpitum* that had divided the choir from the nave. He designed the present timber screen to replace it, and also the organ loft and organ case that divides the crossing from the N transept. The rood above the choir screen was designed by his son, Sir Giles Gilbert Scott, and executed by Ferdinand Stuflesser (1883–1958) of Ortisei in the Tyrol, in 1913.

The choir stalls are probably the most famous single feature of Chester Cathedral. They are of late-14th-century date, and were restored in the 1870s. Above the stalls are richly carved canopies. The ends of the stalls are also carved (see, for example, the tree of Jesse, the pilgrim, and the pelican in her piety), and beneath the seats the misericords present as fine a selection of the art of the late-14th-century woodcarver as any in the country. The catalogue of the carvings, by B.T.N. Bennett, obtainable at the Cathedral bookshop, lists 48 misericords, 96 corbels, and 36 bench ends. Some of the carvings were replaced during the Victorian restoration, either because they were badly decayed or, in some cases, because they offended the restorer's sensibilities.

The choir itself was built in the early 14th century. At its E end is the high altar, with a mosaic reredos of 1876. Above it is the E window, whose tracery dates from Hussey's restoration in the 1840s and whose glass is of 1884. There are aisles both to N and S of the choir. In the Norman abbey church they ended in semi-circular apses, the positions of which have been marked in black marble paving. Each aisle has at its W end wrought iron gates made in Spain in the mid 16th century and presented to the Cathedral in 1876.

Plan of Chester Cathedral

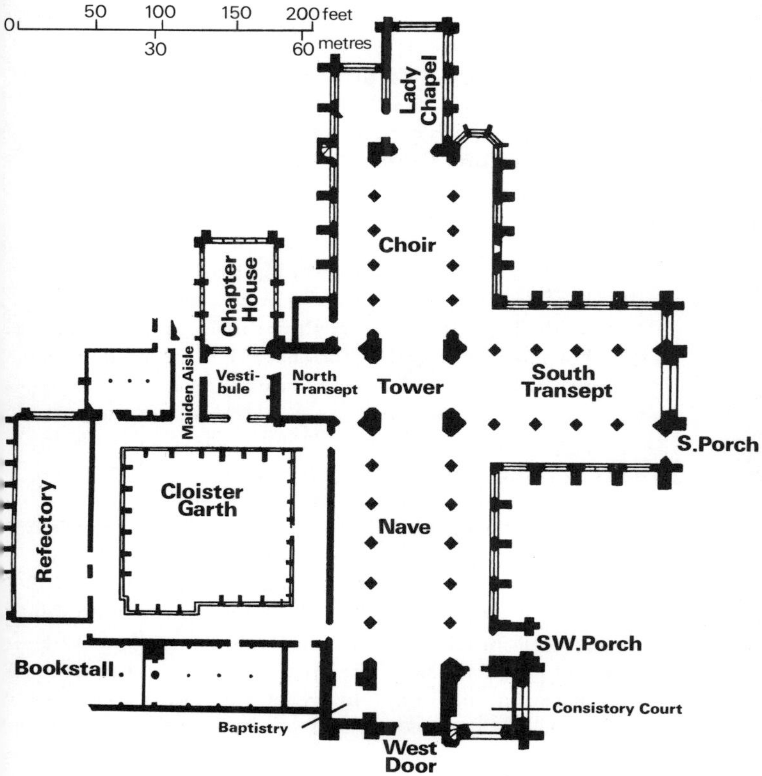

The S choir aisle is now the chapel of St Erasmus, and is set aside for those who seek a place for private prayer. Until Scott's restoration the aisle extended further to the E: Scott, claiming that he had found architectural evidence to support him, built a shorter aisle ending in a polygonal apse. At its E end, to the N of its altar, is a monument to Thomas Brassey (d. 1870), railway builder.

The N choir aisle extends further to the E than that on the S side. It terminates in a late-Perpendicular chapel dedicated to St Werburgh, which contains, S of its altar, a recumbent effigy of Bishop John Graham (1848–65).

The Lady Chapel

The Lady Chapel, at the E end of the Cathedral, is said to be of the third quarter of the 13th century. Pictures of the exterior in the early 19th century show that its windows were by then Perpendicular; inside, the chapel had retained more of its original features when Scott addressed himself to its restoration. The E window is of 1859 (the stonework designed by Scott, the glass by William Wailes), a decade in advance of Scott's main restoration work. The 13th-century vaulting contains three large bosses, depicting the Trinity, the Virgin and Child, and the murder of St Thomas Becket at Canterbury in 1170. At the W end of the Lady Chapel is the early-14th-century shrine of St Werburgh, which until 1876 was used as the base of the Bishop's throne. It was restored by Sir A.W. Blomfield after the discovery of some missing fragments in the Baptistry. The shrine is made of sandstone, and much of it, including many of the figures said to represent Anglo-Saxon kings and saints, is badly decayed.

The Monastic Buildings

To the N of the nave, and reached by a door from the N aisle, are the cloisters around which most of the monastic buildings were grouped. The S wall of the cloister walk contains Norman work. The cloisters themselves were rebuilt in the early 16th century, but after four centuries they were badly decayed: much of the Perpendicular tracery had disappeared from the windows overlooking the cloister garden. Shortly before the First World War Sir Giles Gilbert Scott undertook a thorough restoration of the cloister walk. In the 1920s the windows were filled with stained glass, mostly by F.C. Eden and A. Nicholson, depicting (in the order E, N, W, S) the saints whose festivals were celebrated in the Anglican calendar. The S and part of the W cloister are wider than the remainder. The recesses formed between the columns supporting the roof and the windows overlooking the cloister garden were used as carrels, or booths in which the monks sat to copy manuscripts. The N cloister contains a long stone shelf in its N wall; this was the *lavatorium* where the monks washed before meals, and probably had a stone or lead trough to contain the water.

Abutting the N transept of the Cathedral, and entered either from the transept or from the E cloister, is the 13th-century chapter house, where the monastic community, and later the dean and chapter of the Cathedral, met to discuss matters of common business. The chapter house is entered by way of a vestibule, also of the 13th century, and unusual because the columns that support the roof run directly into the vaulting without capitals. The chapter house itself contains a portion of the Cathedral library, with some of its more valuable items on display. At the E end is a cupboard with 13th-century ironwork. The five lancet windows at the same end are filled with glass of 1872 by Heaton, Butler, and Bayne: a memorial to Dean Anson (1839–67), who was responsible for Hussey's restorations in the 1840s, it depicts the history of the Cathedral; Earl Hugh I, for example, is shown endowing the new foundation in 1092, and Henry VIII's commissioners are shown dissolving the abbey in 1540. Most of the Norman Earls of Chester were buried in the chapter house.

To the N of the chapter house is a slype, or passageway, once apparently known as the 'Maiden Aisle'. It led to the monastic buildings, such as the infirmary, which lay to the E, and beyond them to the Kaleyards Gate (Walk 3). To the N again is the 13th-century parlour, not open to visitors; at its entrance may be seen the day stair, which in monastic times led to the dormitories above.

North of the N cloister is the refectory or frater, where the monks met for meals. It was rebuilt at the end of the 13th century, and one of its most interesting features is the stone pulpit in its SE corner, approached by a flight of steps. During the monks' mealtimes one of their number read aloud from this pulpit. The tracery of the E window was designed by Sir Giles Gilbert Scott in 1913; the glass, showing St Werburgh and her relations, is of 1920 and is by James Powell and Sons. The timber roof was designed by F.H. Crossley (d. 1955). Crossley, who also designed the war memorial outside the SW porch of the Cathedral, was a well-known writer on architectural history; he contributed many articles on church-building in the Chester area to the Chester Archaeological Society's *Journal*, and added some valuable appendices to a standard work on the county's ecclesiastical architecture, *Old Cheshire Churches* by Raymond Richards (1947).

The refectory has been equipped with a modern kitchen, and light refreshments are sold there.

To its W, part of the Norman undercroft, most of which is not accessible, was opened in 1977 as the Cathedral bookshop. Among the books on sale there, A. Whiting, *The Bells of Chester Cathedral* (1974) has already been mentioned in connexion with the bell tower. B.T.N. Bennett, *The Choir Stalls of Chester Cathedral* (1965) is a complete descriptive catalogue of the carvings and their history. Dean G.W.O. Addleshaw's *The Pictorial History of Chester Cathedral* (1969) is an excellent chronologically written introduction to the subject, and his *Chester Cathedral: The Stained Glass Windows, Mosaics, Monuments and some of its other Treasures* (1965) gives a far more comprehensive account than could be attempted here.

The cloister garden was laid out in the 1920s in the time of Dean Frank Bennett (1920–37). The author of a detailed guidebook to the Cathedral (1925), which is still very useful, Bennett was also responsible for encouraging the use of the former monastic parts of the Cathedral, such as the parlour and the refectory, for meetings, so that they were once more involved in the life of the institution. The fountain in the middle of the garden occupies the site of the abbey's reservoir, which was fed by a piped water supply from Christleton, to the E of the city. Dean J.S. Howson (1867–85), who is buried in the cloister garden, was responsible for supervising the major restoration undertaken by Scott between 1868 and 1876, and the further work done by Sir A.W. Blomfield in the early 1880s. He planned the stained-glass windows in the N and S windows of the Lady Chapel as an illustration of the Acts of the Apostles.

To the S of the undercroft, forming an extension of the S cloister, is the passage to the abbot's lodging, over which is the chapel of St Anselm. The chapel is approached by way of the roof of the undercroft. It adjoined the Bishop's Palace, the site of which is now occupied by Barclays Bank, and was used by the bishops of the 17th century as a domestic chapel. Originally of the 12th century, the chapel was altered by Bishop John Bridgeman (1619–52), who provided its chancel with a Gothic ceiling, carved wooden screen, and altar rails. The chapel is normally kept locked, and enquiries about access should be directed to the verger on duty. Adjacent to the chapel is the main part of the Cathedral library, which contains a valuable collection of theological and historical works; the library is available for use by students: access may be obtained by application to the Cathedral officials.

Walk Three

Foregate Street

Foregate Street is the street 'before' or 'outside' the Eastgate. It leads E from the Eastgate to the Bars. Most of it will be described in Walk 8, but its W end is visually a part of the Eastgate townscape. The earliest surviving building here is the Old Bank, now Lloyds, at the W corner of Foregate and St John Streets. It is stone-built, of Classical design, and of the early 19th century. Like the earliest part of Browns' department store in Eastgate Street, and the City Club in Northgate Street (Walk 1), it belongs to the series of improvements undertaken by Thomas Harrison and his contemporaries. Lewis Wyatt is said to have been the architect.

The Old Bank is flanked, to the W and, across St John Street, to the E by Lockwood exercises in black-and-white. Old Bank Buildings [34], to the W, was built in 1895. Its upper floors are carried out over the pavement, continuing the 'piazza' effect of the Grosvenor Hotel and its neighbour, on the W side of the Eastgate. The Blossoms Hotel was described in 1856 as 'a house of the highest standing and respectability'. At that time it was a Georgian brick building; it was rebuilt, with its upper storeys half-timbered, in 1896. To its E is the former entrance, stone-built in a Baroque style in 1911.

The N side of Foregate Street was rebuilt rather later. Two forlorn alleys now leading nowhere, between the shops on this side, were, to the W, Old Post Office Yard, where Chester's post office stood until 1842, and, to the E, Bank Place, described by Hemingway in 1831 as 'a row of small neat cottages'. The former District Bank, now Williams and Glyn's, on the W corner of Frodsham Street is a late exercise (1921) in black-and-white. Just to its W stood the Hop Pole Hotel, another Georgian brick building. Apart from the modernized Georgian Macfisheries, and the standard Burton shopfront of 1928 next to the Eastgate, black-and-white prevails on this side of the street. On the opposite corner of Frodsham Street, the site of H. Samuel's shop was occupied until the 1950s by another public house, Ye Olde Bear's Paw.

Frodsham Street

Frodsham Street is different in scale from Eastgate and Foregate Streets. Its former rustic name, Cow Lane, belies its importance as one of the main roads into Chester. Before the construction of the inner ring road it bore most of the traffic to and from Warrington and the North, by way of Hoole Road and Brook Street. Until City Road (Walk 9) was built, it was also the means of reaching the city centre from the General Station. Hemingway described Frodsham Street as 'narrow, filthy, and inconvenient'. Much of it was rebuilt in the 19th century and afterwards, but it has failed to achieve a better press. The Insall Report of 1969 described it as 'a largely undistinguished and disjointed street scene'. It is now a one-way street, in which much of the traffic heads for a short-stay shoppers' car park. Moreover, one of its important historic buildings has disappeared since 1969: on the S corner of Frodsham Street and Union Walk, in a potentially attractive garden, stood the early-18th-century Friends' Meeting House, pulled down in the early 1970s and replaced by a new meeting room, which occupies the first floor of a colonnaded building [14] on the site of the garden. Quakers are recorded in Chester from the mid 17th century, when several of them were punished for various offences by confinement in the Northgate.

There are no major buildings in Frodsham Street, but one or two features of interest. On the E side, the Chester Hearing Aid Centre occupies a pleasant red-brick Tudor-style building of 1892. An alley near by led in the 19th century to the Commercial Hall, built in 1815 and approached by pedestrians from Foregate Street. Like the Union Hall built six years earlier on the other side of Foregate Street (Walk 8), the Commercial Hall was a market hall intended to be used by tradespeople attending the July and October fairs in Chester. It was a two-storeyed structure built around a quadrangle. Also on the E side of Frodsham Street are two public houses in contrasting styles, the rather rustic City Arms of 1892 on the N corner of Union Walk, and, further N, the Georgian Oddfellows' Arms of 1771.

On the W side of Frodsham Street, a short way to the N of Foregate Street, is the ground floor of the Mercia Square shopping precinct (Walk 2). To the N, the shoppers' car park has retained the trees that were there before it was opened. The Witches' Kitchen occupies a late-19th-century black-and-white building. Further along, at the corner of Kaleyards, Duttons' art shop is also late-19th-century black-and-white, almost on the scale of the Eastgate Street buildings. On the upper storey appear the arms of the Joiners', Turners', and Carvers' Company.

The Kaleyards were the kitchen garden of St Werburgh's abbey. A footpath leads beside the art shop, between an unexpected playground for children and the forecourt of North Western Farmers, to the Kaleyards Gate. Tradition asserts that this breach in the city wall was permitted by Edward I, *c.*1275, so that the monks could reach their vegetable garden without having to make the longer journey by St Werburgh Street, Eastgate Street, and Frodsham Street. The gate is still under the control of the Dean and Chapter, and is locked at nine each evening.

The Wall from Kaleyards Gate to the Northgate

Kaleyards Gate leads into Abbey Street (Walk 2), but slightly to the N a flight of steps leads up to the city wall. At about this spot stood the Saddlers' Tower, one of the defensive towers placed at intervals around the wall. It was used as a meeting place for the Saddlers' Company. In 1779 it was demolished. On 25 July 1828 during a heavy rain storm some 15 yards of the wall in this area fell down into a ropewalk below and to the E. It was probably as a consequence of the repairs that followed this damage that the last remaining traces of the tower were obliterated.

The walk from here to the NE angle of the wall comes as a refreshing change after Foregate and Frodsham Streets, as there is plenty of greenery in sight, with a cricket pitch to the left and trees to the right. At the corner stands one of the surviving towers [4]. It is said to have been known at an early date as Newton's Tower, but by the 17th century was called the Phoenix Tower, or the Golden Phoenix – the emblem of the Painters' and Stationers' Company, which used the tower as a meeting place. Above the door at wall level is a carving of a phoenix, with the date 1613.

The Phoenix Tower is also known as King Charles's Tower. On 24 September 1645 Charles I stood there while his army was sustaining a heavy defeat by the Parliamentarians at Rowton Heath, a few miles to the SE. It would have been impossible for Charles to see events at Rowton from the tower, but he may have seen fugitives from the battle being pursued through the eastern suburbs. He is said to have moved to the Cathedral tower for a better view; while there, he was narrowly missed by a bullet fired from St John's church. King Charles's Tower has been fitted up as a small museum, with dioramas representing various scenes of the Civil War, and, on the upper floor, a model of the battlefield.

The wall now turns W towards the Northgate. Writers of the 19th century spoke highly of the views over the N and NE suburbs from the walls: today the view to the NE is obscured by high-rise flats in Newtown. Below and to the N of the walls is the Shropshire Union Canal (Walk 4). Trees on its N bank mask the large car park at Gorse Stacks, and, further W, the Delamere Street bus station. Beyond there is a glimpse of the Northgate Arena [40], a large leisure centre opened in April 1977. It includes two swimming pools – one for leisure, the other for training – a sports hall, and refreshment facilities. It occupies the site of one of Chester's railway stations,

Northgate, which was the terminus of the Cheshire Lines Railway route from Manchester via Northwich.

The section of the N wall from the Phoenix Tower to St Martin's Gate was repaired in the 1880s and 1890s. During the repair work, some of the most spectacular discoveries relating to Roman Chester were made. About 150 Roman tombstones, most of them inscribed to the memory of soldiers of the Second or Twentieth Legions, had been incorporated into the masonry during the rebuilding of the wall in the 3rd century; the stones are now housed in the Grosvenor Museum (Walk 5). A descriptive catalogue by R.P. Wright was published by the Chester Archaeological Society in 1955.

To the S of the wall, a terrace of Georgian brick houses at right-angles to it is Abbey Green. A former entrance to the Green from the wall has been bricked up. Nearer at hand may be seen work undertaken by the Excavations Section of the Grosvenor Museum. This archaeological site, just within the wall, has yielded valuable information about the history of Chester in Roman times and afterwards.

Between the Abbey Green excavation and the Northgate there are a shop and a house opening on to the wall. In the early 1830s the shop was occupied by George Batenham (d. 1833), whose engravings of the principal streets of Chester are one of the best records of the appearance of the city in the early 19th century.

The Northgate

The Eastgate (Walk 1) was erected at the expense of Richard Grosvenor (d. 1802), who was created first Baron Grosvenor of Eaton in 1761 and Earl Grosvenor and Viscount Belgrave in 1784. His son Robert, the second Earl, was elected Mayor of Chester in 1807. In the following year the new Mayor commissioned Thomas Harrison to rebuild the Northgate: it was completed in 1810, when the Earl's cousin, General Thomas Grosvenor, was Mayor. The gate [26] is built of grey stone, its central arch flanked by two narrower pedestrian arches of the same height supported by Doric half-columns. The solid parapets contain inscriptions commemorating the rebuilding. The effect is more austere than that of the 18th-century gates, the Eastgate (Walk 1), the Watergate (Walk 4), and the Bridgegate (Walk 6). Its sombreness owes something to the colour of the stone, compared with the warmer sandstone of the other gates. The others are also relieved by rustication and by either pierced parapets or, in the case of the Eastgate, iron railings and the Douglas clock tower.

The sombreness of the Northgate is in keeping with its earlier history. Until 1807 the gatehouse was used as the city gaol; it was described by Hemingway as 'an inconvenient and unseemly pile of buildings'. Both gate and gaol were under the control of the city Sheriffs. Parts of the gaol were excavated from the rock below the wall. Descriptions of it in the 17th century refer to a 'dark stinking place called *dead men's room*' where prisoners who had been condemned to death were confined, and another cell called Little Ease, which was about 4 ft 6 in. high and 17 in. at its greatest in width and depth; it was said that the height could be lessened, as a form of torture, by fixing wooden boards across the cell. Shortly before the gaol was demolished, the gaoler reported that he found an iron glove useful for restraining refractory prisoners.

To the N of the Northgate, Upper Northgate Street is a confusion of traffic islands and signals, leading to the Northgate roundabout where the Liverpool and Parkgate Roads join the inner ring road. The roundabout, described by the Mayor at its opening in 1967 as 'the crowning glory of the completed part of the inner ring road', was stigmatized in the local press as 'Chester's most notable non-place'. It was provided with a lawn and fountains, but no pedestrian access; pedestrians have to burrow beneath it in subways. For that reason it failed to win a Civic Trust award in 1969. Further E, the Gorse Stacks roundabout has been contrived much more attractively; its subways lead to a pleasant central garden.

Nearer at hand, immediately beyond the canal on the W

side of Northgate Street, is the former Bluecoat School [21]. It is built of brick, with stone dressings and a copper-roofed cupola. It has two projecting wings flanking a central entrance, over which there is a statue of a Bluecoat boy. It was built in 1717 to house the charity school founded by Bishop Nicholas Stratford of Chester (1689–1707) 17 years earlier. The boys at the school were clothed, boarded, and educated at the expense of the charity. In 1790 a junior branch, whose pupils were known as the Green Caps, was established; the Bluecoat scholars were usually chosen from among the Green Caps. In 1831 there were 28 Bluecoat boys and 64 Green Caps. The Bluecoat School closed in 1949.

Immediately to the W of the school, and reached by way of its central entrance, is a group of almshouses rebuilt in 1854 around a central courtyard. They represent the hospital of St John the Baptist, founded according to tradition by Earl Ranulph III of Chester (1181–1232), for 13 'poor and feeble men' of the city. A chapel attached to the hospital, known as St John without the Northgate or Little St John, occupied the S wing of the Bluecoat building. The building as a whole is now used as the Chester Youth Centre.

A few yards to the W of the road bridge over the canal a narrow and dangerous-looking stone footbridge links the wall and the Bluecoat building. Known as the Bridge of Sighs, this structure, which originally had iron railings, was built in 1793 as a means of secure communication between the gaol and Little St John's chapel; it is particularly associated in popular tradition with visits by condemned felons to receive their last rites.

Northgate to St Martin's Gate

To the S of the wall and parallel with it is Water Tower Street. On its S side is Centurion House [16], part of which was opened in 1977 as the local branch of H.M. Customs and Excise. Centurion House partly occupies the site of the Northgate Brewery, which closed in 1969 and was demolished two years later. Archaeological excavation of the site revealed evidence of the Roman rampart buildings, *intervallum* road, and barracks. Cellars of the 14th and 15th centuries were also discovered, and the foundations of late-18th- and early-19th-century houses that had occupied part of the brewery site.

Another defensive tower on the N side of the wall, just E of the inner ring road and St Martin's Gate, is Morgan's Mount. It is said to derive its name from Captain William Morgan or his son Edward; one of them is supposed to have commanded a Royalist gun battery mounted on the tower. Guidebooks written in the 19th century praised its upper level as a viewpoint, but better views may now be obtained from St Martin's Gate.

This gate is the most recent to have been made in the city wall. Beneath it runs the dual-carriageway inner ring road, from the Grosvenor Street roundabout in the S to the Northgate roundabout in the NE. This section of the road, and the gate, were opened in 1966 by the Minister of Transport, Mrs Barbara Castle. As will be seen (Walk 4), the construction of the inner ring road caused extensive changes in Chester's townscape in the interest of motor traffic. Whatever one may think of these changes in principle, one cannot fail to be impressed by the viaduct that carries the road N and E of St Martin's Gate, as a piece of civil engineering. The gate itself, designed by A.H.F. Jiggens, the City Engineer, and Grenfell Baines of the Building Design Partnership, has been praised for its elegance and combination of simplicity and lightness.

From the top of the gate there is a wide view to the W, with the Clwydian Hills forming a panoramic background. Nearer at hand, the seven-storeyed concrete office block of Manweb (Merseyside and North Wales Electricity Board) can be seen in Sealand Road, with the floodlights of the Chester football ground to its right. Beyond are the high-rise blocks of the city's Blacon estate. Where the Welsh hills slope down to the Dee estuary, the cooling-towers of Shotton can be seen.

King Street

The descent from the wall should be made to the E of St Martin's Gate. At this point the Roman and medieval walls of Chester diverged. The Roman wall turned S here, a few yards E of the inner ring road. Stone setts in the pavement to the SE of the gate, and a commemorative plaque, mark where the Roman NW angle tower was discovered during excavations for the new road.

A few yards further S, King Street leads back W towards Northgate Street. King Street was known in the 13th century as Barn Lane (it led to a barn owned by St Werburgh's abbey in 'the Crofts' to the W). Before 1966 its W end was not a T-junction but a right-angled turn into St Martin's Fields (anciently Crofts Lane). At the corner stands a terrace of Georgian houses, built in 1776, known as King's Buildings. Unfortunately, structural damage caused by settlement has made it necessary for the houses at the E end of the terrace to be shored up by ugly timber buttresses.

King Street is one of the most pleasing side-streets of Chester. It rises in gentle curves towards Northgate Street. Most of its houses, of the 18th and 19th centuries, are individually undistinguished, but the effect of the street as a whole is attractive. When the Insall Report was written, in 1968, much of the property was in need of urgent repairs. A comprehensive scheme of restoration and rebuilding is now in progress. There are several minor streets of similar quality in Chester, but the condition of some of them has been allowed to deteriorate beyond hope of renewal.

Northgate Street (north end)

King Street enters Northgate Street between the Red Lion and the Pied Bull. Both have their upper floors built over the pavement to form an arcade. This is a feature common to the main streets of Chester beyond the Rows, and is being preserved wherever possible when rebuilding takes place.

To the N of the Red Lion is the former Blue Bell Inn [16],

now a shop for children's clothes called Snow Whites. It is claimed to be Chester's sole remaining example of medieval domestic architecture; most of it dates from the 15th century. The upper storey, over the pavement, has a braced king-post roof. Another unusual feature is its detached shopfront, between the pavement and the roadway. The building is fortunate to have survived. It closed as an inn in 1930, and demolition was threatened on several occasions. After the Second World War it seemed likely that it would have to give way to the inner ring road, which was originally planned to run inside the north wall.

A much taller black-and-white building N of Snow Whites, built in 1911, was the city fire station. From 1863 Chester had a body of voluntary firemen, the Earl of Chester's Volunteer Fire Brigade. The Corporation provided a paid superintendent and the necessary fire-fighting equipment. In 1914 the brigade came under Council control. Built for three horse-drawn fire appliances, the fire station had become obsolete by the 1960s and a new one, to the E of the Northgate Arena, was opened in 1970. Four years later, as a result of local government reorganization, the fire service became the responsibility of Cheshire County Council.

The façade of the old fire station has been preserved, though the building is now dwarfed by Centurion House. Behind it is Fireman's Square, whose houses, originally built for the firemen, have recently been modernized. Before 1911 the site was occupied by Valentine's Court, one of Chester's slum areas, which contained 14 cottages, wash-houses, a smithy, a stable, and two warehouses.

Opposite the former fire station an entry leads E into Abbey Green. On the return S down Northgate Street to the Town Hall, the only features of interest on the E side of the street are the Little Abbey Gateway (a single sandstone arch), and a development of 1972 immediately to its S (Jobcentre, etc.), which takes up once more the arcade or 'piazza' theme.

On the W side of Northgate Street, immediately to the S of King Street, is the Pied Bull. From the outside it appears to be quite an impressive 18th-century inn; inside, there is much earlier work including a 17th-century staircase. The

Pied Bull is said to have been the 'old-fashioned inn in Northgate Street' where George Borrow stayed with his wife and daughter in 1854. He was more impressed by the 'strapping chambermaid' at the inn than by the quality of the ale and the Cheshire cheese that he was offered.

On the corner of Hunter Street is the Odeon Cinema, opened in 1936 but recently rebuilt internally to house three cinemas and re-named the Odeon Film Centre. A narrow entry to the N leads to a Georgian residence, Folliott House, occupied by the Citizens' Advice Bureau and the Chester City lottery office.

Hunter Street is worth a short detour for anyone interested in the architecture of the late 19th and early 20th centuries. Until the 1890s it was Hunter's Walk, which was bounded on its N by the garden of Folliott House and made a right-angled turn S into Princess Street. The name Hunter's Walk is now preserved merely for the short street connecting Hunter and Princess Streets. Towards the W end of the new street, on the N side, there are two late-19th-century villas. On the S side, from E to W, there is first a terrace of red-brick houses, which look like Douglas's work. To the W stands the former Primitive Methodist chapel of 1898–9, designed by Howdills of Leeds for a congregation that had for the previous 30 years used a small chapel in Commonhall Street. The chapel was closed for worship in 1967.

To the W, beyond Hunter's Walk, is the former Hunter Street School, which originated as a 'Sunday and working' school for girls in 1787. After several changes of location the school became a 'higher grade' girls' school in 1886, taking pupils from the local elementary schools. Successive re-organizations turned it into a 'central' and a secondary modern school before its closure in 1963. The building was then occupied for some time by the Chester Register Office, now in Goldsmith House (Walk 1). Further W again is the Freemasons' Hall, Classical, of brick with stone facings, built in 1909.

Hunter Street is dominated by two modern office blocks. At its W end, facing the inner ring road, is St Martin's House, a clinic centre and headquarters of the Chester Health

District, built jointly by the City and County Councils and opened in 1967. On the N side of Hunter Street, facing Hunter's Walk, is Commerce House – a private office development of the mid 1960s – criticized by the Insall Report as an excessively dominant feature of Chester's skyline. At the time when the Report was compiled Commerce House was vacant. Soon afterwards, however, it was taken over by the County Council as an alternative to a major extension of County Hall (Walk 6). It now houses the County Planning and Social Services Departments.

The block between Hunter and Princess Streets on the W side of Northgate Street contains public houses at each end, the Shropshire Arms and the Coach and Horses. A third, the Elephant and Castle, formerly occupied the building immediately N of the Coach and Horses. To the N again is an imposing Edwardian frontage displaying the legend 'Westminster Coach and Motor Car Works'. A century ago the site was occupied by a coach-building firm. It subsequently became a motor-car showroom and part of it was occupied as offices by the City Council. In the early 1970s it was taken over by the Chester Arts and Recreation Trust. The Insall Report suggested it as a site for a conference centre. Plans are now (1978) going ahead for its development as a central library by the County Council; the Northgate Street façade, however, is to be retained.

Until the early 19th century Princess Street (also known as Prince's Street) was Parson's Lane, where the vicar of St Oswald's church had a house. In the late 19th century it was occupied by terraced houses; by the 1930s the whole area behind the Town Hall and the old market hall, as far as Trinity Street (Walk 4), had become a notorious slum area. When the Princess Street Clearance Area was designated in 1934, there were 224 inhabited houses there, of which 37 were said to be overcrowded; 214 of them were without baths, and 167 had no proper food store. More than half were said to be verminous, damp, and defective in brickwork. The street now shows no trace of that part of its history. Its S side as far as Trinity Street is occupied by the new market and car park. On the N side, beyond Hunter's

Walk, a temporary structure houses the Excavations Section of the Grosvenor Museum, where current archaeological work in Chester is supervised. To its W, the City Mission occupies a small Gothic building bearing the date 1845. From 1868 this housed the Bishop Graham Memorial School, a ragged school founded to commemorate John Graham, Bishop of Chester (1848–65). Ragged schools were intended to provide free education for poor or neglected children. This was one of three schools provided by the Chester Ragged School Society, founded in 1851.

Walk Four

The Shropshire Union Canal

This walk begins at the W side of St Martin's Gate. Immediately to the NW of the Gate a footpath leads down to the Northgate locks [38] of the Shropshire Union Canal. It is worth a brief detour, and for the transport history enthusiast there are interesting towpath walks to the E, where the canal runs below the N wall as far as King Charles's Tower (Walk 3), and to the W as far as the junction with the Dee at Tower Wharf.

The Northgate locks are a 'staircase' of three locks with a total fall of 33 ft. They were excavated from the sandstone rock. A free-standing plaque at the bottom of the footpath commemorates the inauguration of the canal in 1772. Seven years later it was opened as far as Nantwich. In 1776 its western end was extended to communicate with the Dee to the W of Tower Wharf. The Wirral branch of the Ellesmere Canal, opened in 1796, enabled boats to reach the Mersey at what became known as Ellesmere Port; a regular passenger service to Liverpool from Chester began to operate soon afterwards. A decade later the southern branch of the Ellesmere Canal was completed from Hurleston Junction to Ellesmere and, via the Pontcysyllte aqueduct, to Llangollen.

In the 1830s Chester was linked to the national canal network. A branch of the Chester Canal led to the Trent and Mersey Canal at Middlewich. An extension of the Chester Canal from Nantwich to Autherley Junction, near Wolverhampton, established a connexion with the Staffordshire and Worcestershire Canal. The Chester and Ellesmere Canal Companies had been amalgamated in 1813; in 1846

Route of Walk Four

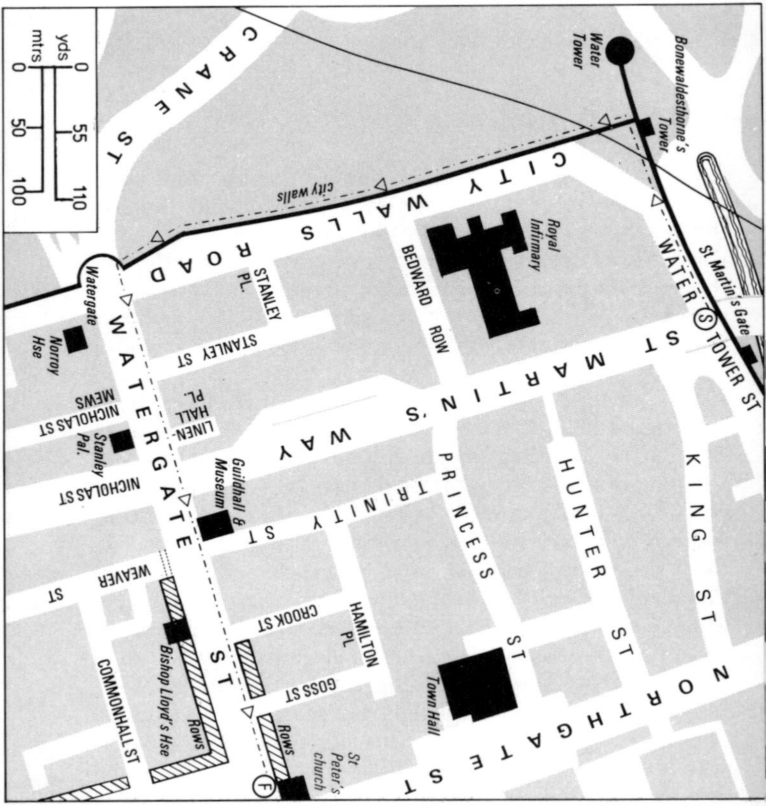

they were merged into the Shropshire Union Railways and Canal Company, which in turn was bought by the London and North Western Railway (later the London, Midland, and Scottish) in 1922.

Some history textbooks claim that canals were never able to compete effectively with the railways. In fact Chester became and remained throughout the 19th century a thriving canal port. Most of the vessels using the canals were used as dwellings, and under the Canal Boats Act they had to be registered with a local authority and inspected by the Medical Officer of Health. At the end of 1905 there were 448 boats on the Chester register; they accommodated 893 men, 317 women, 173 children of school age and 120 children under school age. The canal traffic through Chester continued between the wars, with oil products and metal forming the main cargoes, but since the 1960s use of the canal has been almost exclusively confined to pleasure craft.

From St Martin's Gate to the Watergate

To the W of St Martin's Gate the wall is only a few feet above the level of the road inside it. A few yards along the wall is Pemberton's Parlour, the remnant, rebuilt in 1894, of a defensive tower known formerly as Dill's or the Goblin Tower. Much of the N wall suffered badly from Parliamentarian cannon late in 1645. An inscription on the tower records that in the reign of Queen Anne 2,000 yards of the wall were 'new flagged or paved, and the whole improved, regulated, and adorned'. The Corporation officials responsible for keeping the wall in repair were the murengers, two of whom were elected annually; the inscription records their names and those of the Mayors from 1702 to 1708. The tower was originally a round one, but the S side was demolished and the N side converted into an alcove with seats. Another Mayor, John Pemberton, is said to have given his name to the Parlour; he owned a ropewalk beneath the wall and supervised his men from this tower.

In 1914 a hoard of Saxon silver pennies was found to the E

of Pemberton's Parlour. They were of the late 10th century; a few of them had been minted at Chester.

Between Pemberton's Parlour and the NW corner of the wall, the view to the N offers an interesting microcosm of transport history. The Shropshire Union Canal passes under a railway bridge and then makes a right-angled turn to the N, broadening into the Tower Wharf basin. To the W a branch leads down through three locks to the Dee. The railway, after crossing the canal, passes under the wall. Its four tracks bear the traffic between Chester General Station (Walk 9) and North Wales; S of the Dee a branch leads to Wrexham, Shrewsbury, and Wolverhampton. To the NE can be seen the viaduct carrying the inner ring road from St Martin's Gate to the Northgate roundabout.

To the W of the railway a flight of steps leads N from the wall to Tower Road. In the mid 19th century the Chester baths and wash-houses were established at this point N of the wall. They were opened in 1849 under private management, but taken over by the Corporation soon afterwards. The swimming and shower baths, typically of their time, were run according to a class system: subscribers of one guinea a year were allowed to use them at the most favoured time, between 10 a.m. and noon; the general public was admitted only between sunrise and 9 a.m., or between 4 p.m. and sunset. The baths were still located here in the late 1870s, but by 1892 they had been replaced by a floating bath on the Dee (Walk 7).

The tower at the NW corner of the wall is Bonewaldesthorne's Tower. A spur wall to the W, about 100 ft in length and 11 ft wide, connects it to a round tower, the New or Water Tower [3]. The contract for the building of this tower has survived. It is said to date from the sixteenth year of Edward II's reign (i.e. between July 1322 and July 1323). In return for 100 pounds the mason John de Helpeston was to build a round tower where the Dee flowed W of Bonewaldesthorne's Tower, and a wall to connect it with the main city wall. Helpeston was also employed at about this time on work at Flint Castle. His tower consists of two floors, with octagonal rooms inside the round walls. A fighting platform was erected over the E entrance from the spur wall. It is difficult now to appreciate that when the tower was built the river flowed up to it; it is said that mooring rings were attached to the tower.

In the 1830s the Water Tower was taken over as a museum by the Mechanics' Institution, and a camera obscura was erected on the roof of Bonewaldesthorne's Tower. Like King Charles's Tower at the NE corner of the wall, the Water Tower was later fitted up with dioramas and models illustrating the medieval history of the city. At present, however, the tower is closed for restoration work.

A few yards to the E of Bonewaldesthorne's Tower a stairway descends to the S. It leads to the Water Tower Gardens, which contain tennis courts and putting and bowling greens. A path branching off to the N passes through the spur wall; an inscription on the N face of the spur records that it was rebuilt in 1730 during the mayoralty of John Pemberton. The path bears round to the E, so as to come near the stairway, mentioned earlier, leading N from the wall. Near its E end a small model of the Grosvenor Bridge (Walk 5) may be seen against the N face of the wall.

The wall now turns S from Bonewaldesthorne's Tower towards the Watergate. The railway line makes a second breach in the wall, and is seen passing to the E of some gasholders, on a long viaduct, the approach to the Dee railway bridge. A few yards further S, the wall fades into the W pavement of City Walls Road. Below it to the W are the playing fields of the Queen's School.

Nothing has been said so far of what can be seen on the inner, or S and E, sides of the wall. The Roman wall diverged from the present one at the E side of St Martin's Gate and followed a line approximately represented by the E side of the inner ring road (Walk 3). Between it and the Dee there was some settlement in Roman times. South-east of Bonewaldesthorne's Tower, in what was known as the Infirmary Field, 40 Roman graves containing the bodies of men, women, and children were discovered in the second decade of this century. The remains of several buildings of Roman date have been found between the NW part of the wall and

Watergate Street. In the Middle Ages, however, much of the area was unoccupied by buildings. It became known as the Crofts, and probably consisted of small enclosed plots of agricultural land.

The N part of this area is now entirely taken up by the Chester Royal Infirmary. The Infirmary was founded as a charitable institution in 1755, at a time when philanthropists were founding similar establishments in many towns. At first it was situated in part of the Bluecoat building (Walk 3), but in 1761 a purpose-built hospital designed to accommodate 100 patients was erected fronting City Walls Road. It forms the southernmost part of the range that can be seen from the W wall, and bears its date over the porch. The Infirmary was supported by subscriptions and donations, and to be admitted a patient had to obtain a letter of recommendation from a subscriber (by the 'statutes' of 1763 a subscriber of two guineas a year was entitled to recommend one in-patient or two out-patients). The Infirmary was intended to benefit the poor; the admissions register included a note of a patient's home parish, so that application could be made to the parish officials for a contribution towards his subsistence.

Until 1868 the Infirmary turned away cases of infectious disease such as cholera (of which there were epidemics in 1849 and 1867) and typhus, but in that year a fever hospital was opened in its grounds. There were many more improvements and enlargements of the Infirmary in the 19th and early 20th centuries. In 1914 George V bestowed on it the title 'Royal'. In 1963 Princess Marina, Duchess of Kent, opened a new out-patient and accident wing. In effect the Royal Infirmary was now turned back to front, since the main entrance is today from the inner ring road rather than from City Walls Road. The history of the Infirmary is described by Enid M. Mumford in *Chester Royal Infirmary 1756–1956*, a booklet published to commemorate its bicentenary. Many of its records have been deposited in the Chester City Record Office at the Town Hall.

To the S of the Infirmary is the Queen's School. It occupies the site of the city gaol, which was built there in 1807 to replace the Northgate gaol (Walk 3). Hemingway commented that immediately after the building of the new gaol escapes from it were very frequent. He also relates how a prisoner in the mid 1820s, being taken by two constables to the gaol to await his trial, induced them to accompany him first to a public house, and then made his escape by jumping from the city wall. At the W entrance to the gaol the public execution of condemned criminals took place. The gaol was closed in 1872.

The Queen's School was founded in 1878 in a house in Watergate Flags (the N side of Watergate Street). It was intended to provide an academic education for middle-class girls. Queen Victoria allowed the school, which had previously been called the Chester School for Girls, to take the title 'Queen's' in 1882. In the following year the new building to the S of the Infirmary was erected to designs by E.A. Ould. Ould was a pupil of John Douglas, and his design, of patterned brickwork in a 'Tudor-Gothic' style, shows Douglas's influence. To the S and E are 20th-century additions to the school. A history of the Queen's School by a former pupil, Miss Gladys Phillips, was published in 1978.

To the S of the Queen's School there are two elegant terraces of Georgian houses, built in the early 1780s, with a lawn between them. They are called Stanley Place (not to be confused with Stanley *Palace* on the other side of Watergate Street). The house at the W end of the southern terrace has a porch with two side entrances; it was designed to accommodate a sedan chair, so that passengers could enter or leave the house without being exposed to the weather.

The Watergate

The wall walk leaves City Walls Road, sloping up to cross Watergate Street by the Watergate. This gate was constructed in 1788 to replace a medieval archway. Its arch is round, like that of the Eastgate; it is built of sandstone, and rusticated. There is only one arch for pedestrians, on the S side.

As its name implies, the Watergate of the Middle Ages

stood not far from the edge of the Dee. It was the principal entrance for goods, which were unloaded from the wharves. After the canalization of the river in the 1730s new wharves were built to the W, and New Crane Street was constructed to link them to the Watergate. It is now a main route W from the city centre, leading to the modern trading estate at Sealand Road. Until the late 1960s it contained a major bottleneck, in the form of a swing bridge over the spur that connected the Shropshire Union Canal with the Dee.

At an unknown date the control of the Watergate passed into the hands of the Earls of Derby. Thomas, Lord Stanley (d. 1504) was created Earl of Derby by Henry VII soon after the battle of Bosworth. The Stanley family were based on Lathom and Knowsley in Lancashire, but from the mid 15th century they were associated with the administration of the county palatine of Chester. Thomas, the first Earl, had been made Justice of Chester by Edward IV in 1462. He was the chief legal officer of the palatinate, though in practice he normally acted through deputies. His successors as Earls in the 16th and 17th centuries often held the positions of Chamberlain of Chester (the official in charge of the Chester Exchequer, again usually acting through a deputy) and Lord Lieutenant of the county; the latter post empowered them to supervise the organization of the local militia. In Chester affairs the Stanleys were in a position of influence comparable with that of the Grosvenors in the 18th and 19th centuries; this particular quarter of the city is especially associated with them. In 1778 the Corporation bought the custody of the Watergate from Edward, the twelfth Earl, who had succeeded to the title two years earlier.

Watergate Street

It is easy to forget that Chester is sited on a hill. The view up Watergate Street from the gate is, however, a sufficient reminder; the street rises 30 ft from a point just S of the gate to the inner ring road, and another 20 between the inner ring road and the Cross. The slope, and the comparative narrowness of the street, together with the survival of Rows for a considerable part of its length and the generally sympathetic nature of most of the modern developments, give Watergate Street a particular interest.

On the N side, between the Watergate and the inner ring road, there are Georgian houses, some in poor condition. The W end of these terraces is known as Watergate Flags. In 1779, when the site was being prepared, the remains of what is thought to have been the Roman legionary bath house were discovered. They included a hypocaust and two tessellated pavements. An altar discovered on the site was presented to the British Museum in 1836.

Stanley Street leads N into Stanley Place. On its E side are stables used for racehorses during race weeks (Walk 5). In the Middle Ages the site was occupied by a Franciscan friary, which, confusingly, has given its name to Grey Friars, a street to the S of Watergate Street. The friary was established on this site between 1235 and 1245; it was dissolved in August 1538, with the other friaries in Chester. William Wall, its last warden, became Sub-Dean of Chester Cathedral in 1541; he survived all the religious changes of the 1540s, 50s, and 60s, retaining his position until his death in 1574. An inventory of the goods of the friary at the time of its surrender to the commissioner appointed by Henry VIII lists the buildings as the choir, vestry, kitchen, brewhouse, buttery, and bakehouse. No systematic archaeological survey of the site has been possible, since it is built over, but isolated finds of floor tiles and carved pieces of sandstone have been made there. J.H.E. Bennett described the known history of the friary in an article in the *Journal of the Chester Archaeological Society*, new series, vol. 24, part 1 (1921), pp. 5–80.

By the end of the 16th century the site of the friary had passed into the hands of the Stanley family of Alderley in E Cheshire, who were kinsmen of the Earls of Derby. In the mid 1770s a body of merchants purchased a part of it for the purpose of erecting the Linen Hall there. This was a building intended for the use of the importers of Irish linen. It was a quadrangular building containing 60 shops, built in 1778. The erection of Watergate Flags and Stanley Place immediately afterwards must have created the impression of a new inner suburb.

Like the Commercial Hall near Frodsham Street (Walk 3) and the Union Hall to the S of Foregate Street (Walk 8), the Linen Hall was only successful for a short period. Hemingway noted in 1831 that very few of the shops were let at the time of the annual fairs, and that the proprietors wanted to close the hall down. It was afterwards used as a cheese market. The site was sold in 1919 to the Chester Race Company for conversion into stables. The Linen Hall was demolished, but although some traces of the friary walls were found, thorough excavation was not carried out.

On the S side of Watergate Street the westernmost building is an office block constructed early in the 1960s, Norroy House, which houses the Chester branch of the Department of Health and Social Security. It stands in the former garden of the adjacent building to the E, Watergate House, built in 1820 by Thomas Harrison for the Clerk of the Peace to the county, Henry Potts. Its entrance porch is set on the angle between Watergate Street and Nicholas Street Mews. Above the porch is the monogram E R, referring to Edward VII. In 1907 Chester was made the headquarters of Western Command (formerly the NW District), the military area comprising Wales and the border counties, the NW of England, and the Isle of Man. The headquarters was moved to Boughton in 1935 and to Queen's Park in 1938. Watergate House is now the office of the Cheshire Community Council.

To the E, beyond Nicholas Street Mews, is Stanley Palace. This black-and-white building now faces an open area provided with seats; until the 1930s it was shut off from Watergate Street by another building, and could only be reached through a narrow entry. One of the carvings on its face bears the date 1591. It is said to have been built by Peter Warburton of Grafton (d. 1621). Warburton was a lawyer favoured by two 16th-century Chamberlains of Chester, Robert, Earl of Leicester, Queen Elizabeth I's courtier, and Henry, Earl of Derby. He was an active official of the Chester Exchequer, and became Vice-Chamberlain in the 1590s. Leicester strongly recommended his election as one of the city's Members of Parliament in 1584, but although the Mayor and one of the Sheriffs supported Warburton's candidature, the Assembly refused to elect him. Nevertheless he was chosen M.P. in 1586 and 1593. In 1600 he became a Justice of the Common Pleas. On his death in 1621 his property, including the sites of the Grey and Black Friaries, was inherited by his daughter, who had married Sir Thomas Stanley of Alderley, a kinsman of the Earls of Derby. The Stanley Palace descended, with Sir Peter Warburton's other property, in the family of Stanley of Alderley. In 1831, when Hemingway wrote, it was 'a striking illustration of the mutability of all human affairs'; it was no longer a mansion but occupied as cottages. By the middle of the 19th century it was under threat of demolition, and it was suggested that it might be reconstructed in the United States. The Chester Archaeological Society purchased it, and in 1889 sold it to the Earl of Derby on condition that it should be preserved.

In 1928 the then Earl of Derby offered Stanley Palace, otherwise known as Derby House, to Chester Corporation as a gift. (The commemorative plaque for some reason assigns the gift to 1931.) The Council purchased and demolished a house at the corner of Watergate and Nicholas Streets, and carried out a restoration of the Palace involving the extension of the black-and-white front to the N. The new work is quite obvious from the street. The Palace is at present occupied by the Chester branch of the English-Speaking Union.

Watergate Street now crosses the inner ring road. The junction is one of the busiest in Chester, and pedestrians need to take great care when crossing between the W and E parts of Watergate Street: no special provision is made for them. The construction of the ring road in the mid 1960s involved the widening of Linen Hall Street to the N and Nicholas Street to the S. There is nothing attractive about the inner ring road between Watergate Street and King Street (Walk 3); to the W are the stables occupying the site of the Linen Hall, and to the E the shoppers' car park, with Hamilton House (Walk 1) and the Gateway Theatre beyond it, followed by St Martin's House (Walk 3). The widening of

Linen Hall Street and of St Martin's Fields to the N involved the demolition of several houses to the S of King Street.

Nicholas Street, to the S of Watergate Street, has fared slightly, but only slightly, better. On the W side is a terrace of what Hemingway called 'handsome modern brick buildings in the London style, with sunken kitchens, inclosed with a neat iron railing, built in 1781'. These houses were known collectively as Pill-Box Promenade in the 19th century, because many of them were occupied by doctors. They are now mostly used as offices, though one is the Chester Liberal Club. A modern building further S, with a car showroom beneath it, is the Conservative Club. The widening of Nicholas Street has improved the view of the Georgian terrace from the N. On the W side, however, Nicholas Street has less to commend it. To the S the modern rectangular blocks of Stops House and More and Gamon are followed by a derelict site used as a Corporation car park, and unoccupied and decaying buildings at the end of Cuppin Street.

At the NE corner of Nicholas Street there is now a paved area outside the Axe Tavern. Before the inner ring road was built, a post office occupied the site, and to the W of it, on the corner of Nicholas Street, stood the Yacht Inn. Thomas Hughes, in the *Stranger's Handbook* of 1856, described it as 'without exception, the most picturesque and curious of all our Chester inns', and recommended it particularly to visiting Americans in search of the curious. Hughes recounted the story, many times repeated, of Jonathan Swift, author of *Gulliver's Travels,* scratching a sarcastic verse on a window pane when the Cathedral dignitaries refused to accept his hospitality at the Yacht.

A new post office was built on the opposite corner of Watergate Street. In 1969 the building was awarded a commendation from the Civic Trust as 'a very commendable townscape contribution made under unusually difficult conditions'. To its E is the 'new' custom house for the port of Chester, built in 1868. It replaced a small Classical building. In 1869 Thomas Hughes described the new building, with its Gothic windows, as 'a complete wart upon the beautiful Church it adjoins'.

The 'beautiful Church' was Holy and Undivided Trinity [9], on the corner of Watergate and Trinity Streets. The medieval church on this site was altered in the 17th and 18th centuries. In 1811 Thomas Harrison was asked to report on the condition of its spire; as a result of his findings the spire was dismantled. In the early 1860s a restoration was proposed, with James Harrison as the architect; the plans were later amplified so as to involve the virtual rebuilding of the church, with its N aisle becoming a nave and chancel and a new N aisle being constructed. The tower was reinforced so that a new spire could be erected on it. The work was not completed until 1869, after Harrison's death.

Since the early 1960s the building has been used as the Guildhall. The church plate was transferred to Holy Trinity church, Blacon, in the W suburbs of Chester; Blacon cum Crabwall had been a township in the medieval parish of Holy Trinity, which had extended beyond the city boundary. The Guildhall is used for the functions of the 23 guilds that still exist (see pp. 188–9), and is also available for other activities. The S part of the Guildhall has the arms of the guilds displayed along its N wall, and an interesting collection of maps and prints of Chester. The former vestry of the church has been converted into a tiny museum, where some of the records and other relics of the guilds are on display. The exhibits include some of the guilds' charters and account and minute books, as well as indentures recording the conditions under which apprentices were bound to freemen in order to learn their trade. A silver seal presented at Chester in 1499 by Arthur, Prince of Wales and Earl of Chester, son of Henry VII, is also on display.

Between the inner ring road and the Cross, Watergate Street contains examples of the architecture of every period from the 16th century to the present day. There are Rows on the S side from Weaver Street to the Cross, and on the N side to the E of Crook Street. The Row on the N side preserves more of its antique character.

Trinity Street is a narrow entry to the E of the Guildhall. It leads N to Princess Street, between the shoppers' car park and the W end of the Forum development. Until the early

1960s the earliest surviving Nonconformist place of worship in Chester, Matthew Henry's chapel, stood towards its N end, between Trinity and Crook Streets. Matthew Henry (d. 1714) was a Presbyterian minister who founded a congregation in Chester in 1687 after James II had allowed toleration to dissenters. The chapel in Trinity Street was built in 1700. While he was minister, Matthew Henry wrote an *Exposition of the Old and New Testaments.* In the mid 18th century the chapel became Unitarian under John Chidlaw (d. 1800); as a result some of the congregation left, and eventually founded the Congregational chapel in Queen Street (Walk 9). Matthew Henry's chapel remained Unitarian until its closure, to make way for the city's central redevelopment, in the early 1960s. Like Holy Trinity church, it was re-housed on land at Blacon in the western suburbs.

On the N side of Watergate Street, most of the buildings appear to be Georgian or later. The house at the E corner of Trinity Street was built early in the 18th century by Alderman Henry Bennett to replace one that had acquired a certain notoriety: in 1700 equipment for forging coins was discovered there, and the occupier, Joshua Horton, was tried and convicted; but sentence was not immediately carried out and he managed to escape from the Northgate gaol. The city Sheriffs were fined heavily for failing to prevent the escape.

Immediately to the E is a terrace of five large Victorian houses. They were built in 1852, and replaced a timber-framed house that had belonged to the Mainwaring family. George Mainwaring (d. 1695) established the family's connexion with Chester; born in London, he married into a Chester family and became Mayor in 1681–2 and one of the city's M.P.s in 1689.

Further to the E, between Crook and Goss Streets, is a large house known as the Booth Mansion (Nos. 28–34). In external appearance it is of the early 18th century. Inside there is earlier work, and the arches at Row level that support the upper floors are medieval. The house has had a chequered career. In the 18th century it became an Assembly Room. The opening of a new Assembly Room in the Royal (now the Grosvenor) Hotel (Walk 1) at the end of the century diverted the fashionable clientele from the Booth Mansion. In 1892 it became the Chester Liberal Club. Forty years later part of it was in use as a billiard hall. In 1946 it was said to have 'recently been vacated by the military' and to appear 'rather neglected'. It became an adult education centre and, in 1947, the Chester College of Further Education. The Insall Report (1968) criticized the use of the upper floors for college purposes as inappropriate to the architectural style of the building. Shortly afterwards the College of Further Education was moved to Eaton Road, S of the river. In 1976 the *Chester Conservation Review Study* expressed serious concern about the condition of the Booth Mansion. In October 1978 plans for its restoration and conversion into an auction room and 'cultural centre' were announced.

To the E of Goss Street, which is now only accessible to pedestrians, part of Astons' furniture store displays a rebuilding of the early 1970s, which, in spite of its modernism, has not conflicted with the character of the street. The Deva Hotel also underwent major reconstruction, in the late 1960s. Once again a Georgian front conceals timber work of the 16th and 17th centuries.

The S side of Watergate Street to the E of Nicholas Street contains several buildings of exceptional interest. The Custom House Inn, though bearing the date 1637, has been extensively restored in the present century. Weaver Street to its E, now closed to vehicles, was known in the Middle Ages first as Bereward's Lane and later as Alven's (corrupted into St Alban's); from the 16th century it was Weaver Lane, but like many of the Chester lanes it was promoted to the status of a street early in the 19th century.

The building immediately to the E of Weaver Street has been restored very recently. Again, to outward appearance, it is Georgian. It is said to occupy the site of the house of Henry Gee (d. 1545), Mayor of Chester in 1533–4 and 1539–40. He is known to historians of Chester as the Mayor who initiated the first Assembly Book, a record of decisions reached by the Corporation that also contains valuable information on the boundaries and wards of the city in Gee's time. During his second term of office the Assembly made regulations about the restriction of trade to freemen; poor relief; the times at which corn could be sold in the market; compulsory instruction on weekdays and attendance at divine service on Sundays for all children over six years old, and archery practice for boys after church; annual races on foot and on horseback on the Roodee; the prohibition of alehouse keeping by women aged between 14 and 40; and the colour of women's caps and hats. It is not surprising that Gee, as the head of the Assembly, attained a reputation as a reformer.

A little to the E there was for several years a notorious area of dereliction known as The Gap. Between 1968 and 1970 the site was redeveloped as shops and dwellings. Both here and, to a lesser extent, in Refuge House further to the E (which is a development of the early 1960s, rather too tall for the scale of the street), modern materials have been used quite effectively to replace earlier structures without destroying the character of street or Row. The Victorian solution to the need to replace buildings may be seen immediately to the W of Refuge House, in two black-and-white structures of the late 19th century.

A famous disaster occurred in the area of The Gap in November 1772. A barrel of gunpowder exploded in a grocer's warehouse below a room where a puppet show was being given. Twenty-three people were killed, and more than 80 injured.

A little to the E of The Gap is a genuine timber-framed building [18], Bishop Lloyd's House (or 'Palace'). George Lloyd was Bishop of Sodor and Man (1599–1605) and of Chester (1605–15). If the date inscribed on the house, 1615, is the date when it was built, he cannot have used it as his residence for long, since he died in that year. In fact the association with Bishop Lloyd is derived from the arms carved above the Row, depicting the Legs of Man (for the bishopric) and three horses' heads (for Lloyd). To the left appear the arms of James I. The abundance of carving here and below the gable of the house adds greatly to its picturesqueness. Below the gable the carvings appear to show heraldic beasts, including an elephant and castle and a bear. The lower panels, on either side of the two coats of arms, depict scenes from the Bible, including Adam and Eve in Eden and the Crucifixion. Inside, there is 17th-century work in the panelling and ceilings of the rooms above the Row. These rooms are used for the meetings of various local societies; visits may be arranged through the Chester Tourist Information Office at the Town Hall. T.M. Lockwood restored the house in the 1890s and enlarged the windows of the floor above Row level. In 1973 further major structural repairs were found to be necessary; they were undertaken by the Corporation, which owns the house, and completed in 1976.

The Leche House, to the E of Refuge House, is another genuine black-and-white building. It is now occupied by an antique dealer. Somewhat earlier in date than Bishop Lloyd's, it preserves a great hall two floors in height. On the E side of the hall is a large fireplace with the arms of the Leche family over it. The house is believed to have been the residence of Alderman John Leche. He died in 1639, and there is a painted memorial tablet showing his coat of arms in the S choir aisle of the Cathedral.

The next three buildings to the E are all, to outward appearance, Georgian. At 'street' level (in other words, reached by steps *down* from the street) they are occupied by Messrs Quellyn Roberts, wine and spirit merchants. At the E end is one of the best of the preserved medieval crypts of Chester, measuring 44 ft by 22 ft, and divided by three octagonal columns into four bays. The owners describe it as a 'Norman crypt' but it has been dated to the late 13th century. Like the other crypts that now form parts of shops, Browns' (Walk 1) and Bookland's (Walk 5), this one is readily accessible during the shop's opening hours, without formality. The wine and spirit business of Quellyn Roberts was established in 1863. Their crypt is occasionally used for private functions, and wine-tasting evenings are arranged for organized groups.

Immediately to the E is a half-timber building known,

from the inscription above it, as God's Providence House [28]. It was built, according to the inscription, in 1652, and it is usually said that the phrase 'God's Providence is Mine Inheritance' refers to the house's escape from a visitation of the plague. The last major outbreak of plague in Chester was in 1647–8, when more than 2,000 people are said to have died in 10 months. In 1861 the owner of the house, Mr Gregg, proposed to demolish it. Five years earlier Thomas Hughes had described it as a 'quaint old spot' with its low, small rooms. In reporting the imminent demolition to the Chester Archaeological Society in 1861, he expressed the hope that both the timbers and the external character of the house might be preserved in the rebuilding. The architect who supervised the work was another active member of the Society, James Harrison. Some of the original timbers were included in the new building, but the resemblance to the old one is small. The height of the Row was increased to match that of the adjoining buildings. The height of the house above it was also increased, so that the level of the second-floor window above the Row matched that of its neighbours. The windows themselves were enlarged; the plasterwork in between the timbers was enriched by decoration. On the top frame of the first-floor window above Row level was inscribed 'Reconstructed 1862'. The inscription has been painted over, but can just about be read. The house is now a kitchenware shop.

Walk Five

Nuns Road

South of the Watergate (Walk 4) Nuns Road follows the line of the city wall. To the E, as far as Black Friars, there are 18th- and 19th-century houses. The area between the wall and Nicholas Street, and between Watergate Street and Black Friars, was the site of the friary belonging to the Dominicans, or Friars Preachers. They were known as the Black Friars because they wore a black mantle over their white habit. Their house in Chester, established in the mid 1230s, was the first friary in the city. The Dominicans are said to have objected to the establishment of the Grey Friars a few years afterwards on the opposite side of Watergate Street (Walk 4): possibly they felt that a neighbouring institution would compete for alms on what was Chester's main commercial thoroughfare. What is known of the Dominicans' subsequent history has been set out by J.H.E. Bennett in the *Journal of the Chester Archaeological Society*, vol. 39 (1952), pp. 29–58.

Together with the Franciscans and the Carmelites, the Dominicans surrendered their house to Henry VIII's Visitor in August 1538. The site of the friary passed into the hands of the Dutton family. The N side, fronting Watergate Street, was built over in part late in the 16th century; much of the remainder was open ground until the late 18th. The Black Friars' buildings have entirely disappeared. They possessed a church to the E of the friary, dedicated to St Nicholas, which gave Nicholas Street (formerly St Nicholas Lane) its name, but that has also gone without trace. When the large Victorian house at the N corner of Grey Friars and

Route of Walk Five

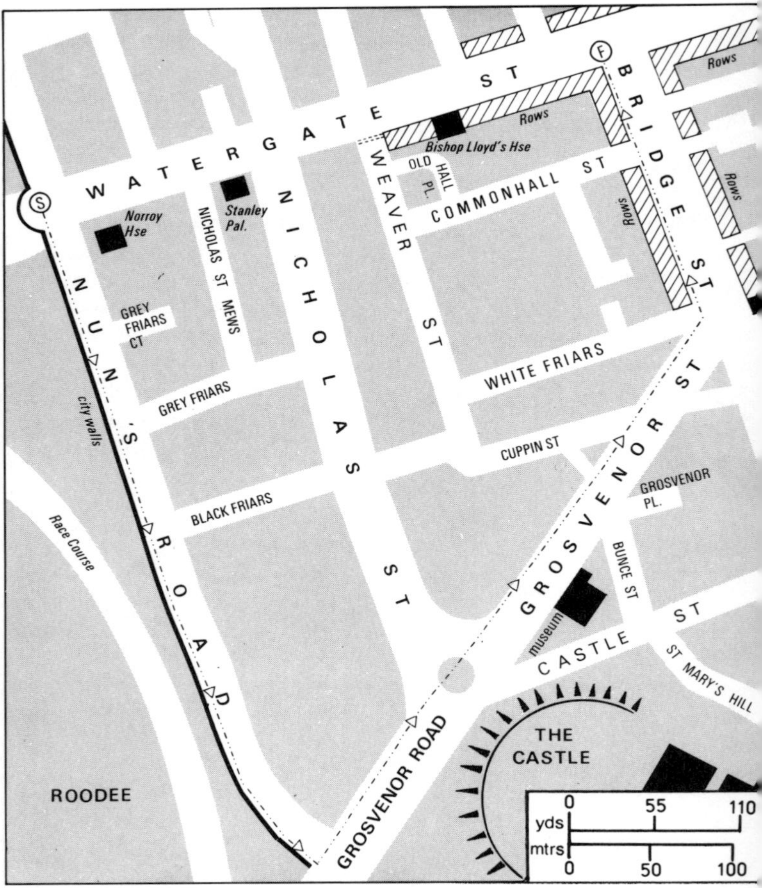

Nuns Road was built in 1895 skeletons were found on the site. In 1977 and 1978 excavations were carried out by the Grosvenor Museum staff to the N, between Grey Friars and Watergate Street, revealing what is thought to be the W end of the friary church.

The names of the two streets leading W from Nuns Road are comparatively modern. Grey Friars was known as Smith's Walk at least until the end of the 18th century. It is thought to mark the site of a road between the E and W entrance gates of the friary. The modern name is misleading, since the Grey Friars had their house on the N side of Watergate Street. The name 'Black Friars' is said to date from 1856. In the 14th century it was known as Arderne Lane, and in the 18th as Walls Lane.

The Roodee

In Roman and medieval times the Dee flowed immediately W of the wall. Traces of the Roman quay have been found in this area. It is possible that the river was split by an island in those times, but that the island was covered by water during the highest tides.

The name 'Roodee' means 'Rood island'. According to legend, a cross or rood stood on the island, carried there by an image of the Virgin from the sands near Hawarden (in Clwyd), where it had been put on trial and subsequently dumped after falling on the lady of the castle while she was praying for rain.

In the 16th century the Roodee was used for pasturing cattle. It was also used as a place for recreation. In November 1539 the Assembly ordered all boys to go to the Roodee or some other convenient place on Sundays to practise archery. In the following January the traditional Shrove Tuesday football match between the Roodee and the Common Hall was discontinued; in its place were established an archery competition and races on foot and on horseback.

The Assembly's order of 1540 is usually taken to mark the beginning of the Roodee's use for horse racing. By the early

17th century the date of the horse race had been established as St George's Day (23 April). The prizes were at first silver bells, which the winners had to return after a year; by the early 17th century a silver bell was to be presented outright to the winner. The Corporation and the guilds supported the races in the 17th and 18th centuries by contributing towards the prizes. The value of the City Plate was increased from £50 to 60 guineas (£63) in 1808, but the Municipal Corporations Act of 1835 prevented the Corporation from continuing to support the races in this way. In 1813 the Palatine Stakes and Dee Stakes were added to the list of races run; the Chester Cup originated in the Chester Tradesmen's Cup first run in 1824. In the late 18th and mid 19th centuries race meetings were held in the autumn as well as in the spring. There are now three meetings a year, held in May, July, and September.

By the late 17th century the Chester races were attracting the leading gentry of the county. Hemingway, in 1831, described the cleaning-up of the city that preceded the meetings: 'painters, whitewashers, and char-women all being placed in requisition'. He pointed out that over the previous 70 years both the prize money and the number of horses entered had increased ten-fold. A grandstand was first built in 1817; it was enlarged several times in the 19th century, and rebuilt in 1901.

The Roodee has also been used for other events requiring a large open space. Thomas Hughes, in the *Stranger's Handbook* of 1856, proudly announced that he had been there on 2 April in that year to witness the presentation of colours to the first regiment of Royal Cheshire Militia.

Across the Roodee the viaduct carrying the railway to its bridge over the Dee is seen, backed by a gasworks. The gasworks was originally built by the Roodee Gas Company in the early 19th century as a rival to the one in Cuppin Street operated by the Chester Gas Light Company. The two concerns were amalgamated in 1856. To the N of the gasworks stood the Chester workhouse, erected in the late 1750s.

Up to that time, each of the parishes in Chester had

been responsible for maintaining its own paupers. In 1757 the nine parishes agreed to unite for the purpose of providing poor relief. Five years later an Act of Parliament was obtained establishing a board of guardians of the poor in the city. The board consisted of the Mayor, the Recorder, and the aldermen, and annually elected representatives from each of the parishes. The existence of this body meant that in 1834 the city was able to stay outside the new system of large poor-law unions established by the Poor Law Amendment Act. Thirty-five years later, however, Chester was brought into the national system, and in 1871 the Chester Poor-Law Union was enlarged by the addition of 43 townships from neighbouring unions. By the end of the 19th century a new workhouse had been built at Hoole; it eventually became the City Hospital.

In 1831 Hemingway wrote enthusiastically of the treatment of the poor in Chester. In the workhouse 'the food of the inmates is good and nutricious; their treatment, gentle and humane, while an appearance of cleanliness and an air of comparative comfort are prominently discoverable'. Within the previous 12 years a new building had been erected as an asylum for pauper lunatics, and another as a school, while a warm bath had been installed in the workhouse itself. In 1829 the guardians had taken over about 40 acres of waste ground at Saltney, and the able-bodied poor were set to work producing crops there.

The railway bridge over the Dee was first used in 1846. In May of the following year it collapsed under a passenger train, but although the coaches fell into the river only four people were killed.

The Nunnery and the County Police Headquarters

The County Police Headquarters stands to the S of Black Friars, in the middle of a landscaped area. In the Middle Ages the Benedictine nunnery of St Mary stood here. It was apparently founded by Earl Ranulph II of Chester (d. 1153). A plan drawn after its dissolution shows a cloister, with a church to the N, a chapel to the S, and a range of domestic buildings to the W. The date of its dissolution is not known; both 1537 and 1540 have been suggested. The last prioress, who was still receiving her pension of £20 a year in 1556, was Elizabeth, daughter of Richard Grosvenor of Eaton.

Part of the site of the nunnery was excavated in 1964. The church was found to have virtually the dimensions described in the 16th-century plan; it was divided into two by a central arcade. Tiles and pottery of the 13th or 14th century were found.

After the dissolution the lands of the nunnery came into the possession of the Brereton family of Handforth. Sir William Brereton (d. 1661) was the Parliamentarian leader in Cheshire during the Civil War. In the 1630s he was at odds with the Corporation of Chester, claiming that the lands of the nunnery, which he had inherited, were exempt from both local and national taxes, as they had been during the Middle Ages. In 1642 he provoked a riot in the city by trying to recruit for the Parliamentarian army; several of his supporters were imprisoned. Within less than a year Brereton led his first armed attack against the eastern defences of the city. The tenacity with which he directed the siege has been seen as his retaliation for earlier injuries. During the siege his house on the nunnery site was destroyed by the citizens.

The site of the nunnery passed through various other hands, but in 1806 was sold to the county authorities. Some walls and arches remained from the nunnery; nothing is visible now, but one of the arches has been re-erected in the Grosvenor Park (Walk 8). In the 1860s a barracks for the local militia was erected on the E part of the site, facing the Castle. It was demolished to make way for the new County Police Headquarters.

The history of the Cheshire police force has been described by a former Chief Constable, R.W. James, in *To the Best of our Skill and Knowledge* (1957). By an Act of Parliament obtained in 1829 the county J.P.s in quarter sessions were enabled to appoint Special High Constables in each hundred in Cheshire, and paid Assistant Petty Constables in groups of villages, but there were only about 80 of the latter in the whole of Cheshire in 1856. The County and Borough Police Act of that year obliged quarter sessions to set up a paid police force for the whole county; the force was to be under Government inspection. The original headquarters of the Cheshire force was at a private house, No. 4 Seller Street (Walk 9). It was moved a few years later to another, larger, house in Egerton Street near by, and subsequently to Foregate Street, where the building erected for it by John Douglas may still be seen (Walk 9). Under the Police Act of 1946 the independent police forces of Congleton, Macclesfield, Hyde, and Stalybridge were amalgamated with the county force.

The city of Chester's police were not incorporated into the county force until 1949. As a county borough, Chester was exempt from amalgamation under the 1946 Act until after a local public inquiry had been held. The city police continued to use the Town Hall (Walk 1) as their offices until the new headquarters building was opened, in 1967. Designed by Edgar Taberner, the County Architect, the new building aroused fierce controversy, particularly over its size in relation to the Castle opposite. In 1969 it won a Civic Trust award. It is a severely rectangular block, eight storeys in height. The end walls are of concrete worked into reliefs.

Grosvenor Bridge

Nuns Road terminates at Grosvenor Road, which leads SSW to the Grosvenor Bridge. By the early 19th century the Old Dee Bridge had become incapable of taking all the traffic from Chester into Wales. It might have been widened or even rebuilt, but there remained the two problems of the steepness of the ascent on the Handbridge side (Walk 7) and the sharp turn of the road to the W at the top of the hill in Handbridge. It was therefore decided that a new bridge should be built to the SW of the Castle, with a connecting road running SW from Bridge Street at its junction with Pepper Street. The designer of the new bridge was at first the county surveyor, Thomas Harrison. He resigned in 1826, pleading age and infirmity, and the work was carried on by his pupil William Cole the younger. The foundation stone was laid by Robert, Earl Grosvenor, on 1 October 1827. Five years later the bridge, though still unfinished, was named by Princess Victoria, daughter of the Duchess of Kent, later to become Queen Victoria. Work only finished in November 1833.

The bridge [24], which consists of a single segmental arch, has a span of 200 ft. The main material used is sandstone from Peckforton in the Mid-Cheshire Ridge. At each end are semi-circular arches of Cheshire sandstone, and the abutments between those arches and the central span have niches below and architraves, friezes, and pediments in the Doric order. It was the largest single stone arch in the world; Harrison's critics confidently, but wrongly, believed that it would collapse. J.W. Clarke has described the building of the bridge in the *Journal of the Chester Archaeological Society*, vol. 45 (1958), pp. 43–56.

Although the bridge was subject to toll until 1 January 1885, its construction opened up the possibility of development on the S side of the Dee. Some of the mid-19th-century villa residences in Curzon Park can be seen from the Roodee. An equally important development was the establishment, in the late 1840s, of a new cemetery S of the river (Walk 7).

Castle Esplanade

Grosvenor Road passes NE between the new Police Headquarters and the propylaeum of the Castle (Walk 6). Between the two buildings, on an island in the middle of the road, is a bronze equestrian statue of Stapleton Cotton, Viscount Combermere (d. 1865), by Baron Marochetti. Lord Combermere was a distinguished soldier who fought in the French Revolutionary and Napoleonic Wars. He was later Governor of Barbados and Commander-in-Chief first of Ireland and then of India. The base of the statue records some of the battles in which be fought. A subscription to erect the statue had been started before his death.

A large roundabout forms the S end of the inner ring road. A short distance along the ring road, on the W side just beyond the police headquarters, is a villa built by Thomas Harrison for himself *c.*1820. After the death of his daughter in 1857 it became the rectory of St Bridget's with St Martin's. It is now used by the County Council as offices.

St Martin's church was another casualty of the inner ring road. It stood on the E side of St Martin's Ash, the southward continuation of Nicholas Street, opposite Black Friars. The medieval parish of St Martin was one of the smallest in Chester. Its church had become ruinous by 1721, and it was then rebuilt. In 1842 the parishes of St Martin and St Bridget were united. By the 1870s the church was in use for Welsh services. The building was bought by the Corporation for demolition in 1964.

The church of St Bridget, with which St Martin's was united in 1842, originally stood on the W side of Bridge Street, opposite St Michael's. In 1828 it was demolished to make way for Grosvenor Street. The site of the new church that replaced it is now marked by the roundabout at the junction of Grosvenor Street and the inner ring road, and by the lawned area immediately to the NE of it. It was an elegant Classical structure designed by William Cole the younger, Harrison's pupil, with Doric pilasters supporting a pediment at the W end and a cupola supported on Ionic columns above. Hemingway thought that it was 'executed in a superior style of elegance'; Thomas Hughes, however, criticized it bitterly: 'The structure presents outwardly none of the characteristics of a Christian Church; and might easily be mistaken for some pagan temple'. In 1891 the church of St Mary-on-the Hill (Walk 6) became the parish church for St Bridget's and St Martin's, and in the following year St Bridget's was demolished. The churchyard, however, remained until the construction of the new roundabout. Most of it was then grassed over, but some gravestones remain in place, and at the S side of the roundabout is an obelisk commemorating Matthew Henry, founder of the Presbyterian chapel in Trinity Street (Walk 4).

On the corner of Grosvenor Street and Castle Street is the

Trustee Savings Bank [27]. The Chester Savings Bank was established in 1817. At first it occupied a room in the Exchange (Walk 1), but in 1839 it took over premises in Goss Street. The site at the corner of Grosvenor Street was purchased from the county authorities in 1847, and a competition was held for designs for a building in the Tudor style to house the Bank. James Harrison won the competition, and the building was opened in 1853. Built of buff-coloured stone, it has Perpendicular windows and a clock tower. The clock, like that on the Eastgate (Walk 1), is by Joyce of Whitchurch. The building was commodious enough to be used for Council meetings in the 1860s after the Exchange was burned.

The Grosvenor Museum

In the early 1880s four local organizations set up a joint committee to consider how a museum could be provided in Chester. The bodies concerned were the Chester Archaeological Society, the Chester Society of Natural Science, the School of Science, and the School of Art. A public meeting was held at the Town Hall to inaugurate a subscription fund. The Duke of Westminster subscribed £4,000, and donated some land that belonged to him on the proposed site. T.M. Lockwood prepared the design for the Museum; the Duke laid the foundation stone in February 1885, and the Museum was opened in August of the following year. The building [33] is in a free Renaissance style, with Dutch gables; the material used is red brick, with stone dressings.

The Museum was an immediate success. Admission charges and other fees enabled its debt to be cleared by 1888, and in 1911 the annual number of visitors was said to be approaching 50,000. Until 1956 it housed the School of Art, which had amalgamated with the School of Science in 1886. It also maintained close links with the two learned societies that had been prominent in its formation.

The Architectural, Archaeological, and Historic Society

of Chester, Cheshire, and North Wales had been founded in 1849. In the 1850s and 60s it formed an important pressure group campaigning for high standards in local architecture. By the 1880s it was becoming prominent in local archaeology; in 1888 it published an account of the Roman remains discovered during repairs to the N wall of the city. In 1871 the Chester Society of Natural Science was established. Its president was Charles Kingsley, then a canon of the Cathedral. In the 1880s and 90s it extended its interests to applied science, literature, and art. Both societies held their meetings in the Museum.

Among the permanent displays at the Museum pride of place must go to the Roman exhibits. The Newstead Gallery is named after a former curator, Robert Newstead (d. 1947), the leading archaeologist in Chester between the wars. It contains models and dioramas illustrating the history of Roman Chester; one of its most popular exhibits is a life-size model of a legionary soldier. The Inscribed Stones Gallery houses material found during the repairs to the N wall, including altars and tombstones. Other galleries illustrate the history of furniture and costume, and the natural history of the Chester area. On the second floor there is an art gallery.

The collections are augmented through purchase and through gifts. In 1952, for example, Dr Willoughby Gardner offered to sell to the Chester Archaeological Society, for housing in the Museum, his collection of 652 silver pennies of Anglo-Saxon and post-Conquest date minted at Chester. The purchase price was raised through private and corporate subscriptions. Accumulations of Anglo-Saxon coins had previously been presented in 1925 and 1941. Among other items in which the Museum specializes are topographical paintings and silver with the Chester hallmark.

Special temporary exhibitions are produced each year: the monthly publication *What's On in Chester* gives details of current displays. The Museum employs a field officer to supervise archaeological excavations, and information about work in progress can be obtained there. The results of this work are usually published, and a wide range of local literature on archaeology, history, and natural history is available at the publications counter.

Grosvenor Street

Grosvenor Street was constructed in the late 1820s as an approach road from Bridge Street to the Grosvenor Bridge. It marked the first significant alteration to the Roman and medieval pattern of N–S and E–W streets intersecting at right angles. As has been mentioned earlier, its building involved the demolition of St Bridget's church.

Opposite the Grosvenor Museum is the Roman Catholic church of St Francis. In 1858 a mission of Franciscan friars was established in Cuppin Street. Four years later the foundation stone of a new church was laid, but various difficulties prevented the completion of St Francis's church until 1875. The architect was J. O'Byrne. The church is stone-built, its design involving a free use of 13th-century motifs. The building immediately to the NE of the church is the Franciscan friary.

Cuppin Street leads W from Grosvenor Street towards the inner ring road. Immediately W of its junction with Grosvenor Street is one of the few surviving 'courts' of Chester, Union Place. Further W in Cuppin Street was the site of the original gasworks established in 1817. By Hemingway's time all parts of Chester were gas-lit, but he pointed out that 'complaints . . . are occasionally made by the citizens of the offensive stench produced by the escaping of the gas, and sometimes for the dimness of the light'. The Cuppin Street works was replaced by the new one W of the Roodee before the First World War.

The name of Cuppin 'Street' was changed from 'Lane' in the early 19th century; it has been traced back to the 13th century, and is said to be derived from the name *Copin.* On the opposite side of Grosvenor Street is another former lane with a long recorded history, Bunce Street (from the Bunte or Bunce family), which has been traced back to the early 14th century.

On either side of Grosvenor Street there are 19th-century terraces of brown patterned brickwork. They were put up after Hemingway's time, for he complained about 'this skeleton of a street', the buildings of which had not, apparently, been systematically planned. On the S side of the street, at the corner of Bunce Street, the Saddle is a half-timbered pub of the late 19th century, asymmetrical with its ground floor of brick. At the corner of Grosvenor and Lower Bridge Streets is a red-brick building, possibly by Lockwood, now belonging to the W.R.V.S. It is dated 1898, and was built to house the Chester Benevolent Institution. This was an organization formed in 1798 to assist 'poor married lying-in women at their own houses'. A staff of midwives delivered the babies without charge, and linen, sheets, sugar, tea, and soap were provided. The Institution was financed by private subscriptions and donations, and subscribers were allowed to recommend patients in proportion to their subscriptions. In 1830 it was responsible for nearly 300 deliveries, and its staff included a matron, five surgeons, and four midwives. After the First World War the building became a district nurses' home run by the Chester Maternity Hospital and District Nursing Association.

The junction between Grosvenor Street, Bridge Street, Lower Bridge Street, and Pepper Street was widened in the 1960s. In the second half of the 19th century a well-known landmark at the intersection was The Fountain, an ornate water trough for horses, surmounted by a large gas lamp.

White Friars

The S wall of the Roman fortress of Chester ran immediately to the S of White Friars. Nothing of the wall can now be seen; nevertheless a brief detour along White Friars is worthwhile. Like King Street (Walk 3) it is an attractive lesser thoroughfare, though on weekdays there is obstructive parking along it. Most of the houses in White Friars are of the 18th century, and several have dated rainwater heads. No. 1, on the S side, is one of the least known genuine timber-framed houses of Chester; it is dated 1658 and has carved timbers and decorative plasterwork.

White Friars Cottage, on the W corner of White Friars and Bollands Court, is also timber-framed, but of the late 19th century. When the foundations were being prepared in 1884, Roman remains were found, and 3 ft above their level a floor believed to have belonged to the Carmelite friary that stood here in the Middle Ages. A commemorative plaque records the discoveries.

The order of Carmelite friars was established slightly later in the 13th century than the Dominican and Franciscan orders. The Carmelites were known as 'White' because they wore a white mantle over a brown habit. Their house in Chester was founded in the late 1280s. Its history has been narrated by J.H.E. Bennett in the *Journal of the Chester Archaeological Society*, new series, vol. 31, part 1 (1935), pp. 5–54. Together with the houses of Black and Grey friars, it was surrendered to the Visitor appointed by Henry VIII in August 1538. In the early 1590s its site, which lay between Bridge Street, White Friars, Commonhall Street, and Weaver Street, was acquired by Thomas Egerton, the Attorney-General, who soon afterwards became Chamberlain of Chester and, in 1603, Lord Chancellor, and received the titles of Lord Ellesmere and Viscount Brackley. Egerton dismantled the spire of the friary church, which had been a prominent local landmark, and built a mansion on the site of the friary. His descendants, who became Earls and later Dukes of Bridgwater, retained the property until the end of the 18th century, though they did not live there but leased it out to various tenants.

Chester Heritage Centre

On the corner of Bridge Street and Pepper Street stands the former St Michael's church [10]. St Michael's was one of the nine medieval parish churches of Chester. In 1841 St Olave's parish was added to St Michael's, and at the end of the decade the church was almost entirely rebuilt, in the Perpendicular style, by James Harrison. The W tower extends beyond the body of the church, and the Row passes through it.

In 1971 the Chester parishes were reorganized, and St Michael's was closed for worship in 1973. As part of its contribution to European Architectural Heritage Year, the City Council reopened it in 1975 as the Chester Heritage Centre. The building combines exhibition space with a small theatre where an audio-visual presentation of Chester's architectural history is given. As an introduction to the heritage of the city it is well worth the moderate admission charge. Temporary exhibitions are also staged at the Centre, usually in connexion with current conservation projects.

Bridge Street

Hemingway described Bridge Street in 1831 as 'generally wide and commodious'. Both before and after the building of the Grosvenor Bridge it was the principal exit from the city to Wales. It was the *via praetoria* of the Roman fortress, leading up from a gate in the S wall at roughly the level of St Michael's church to the headquarters complex N of the Cross. On its E side, St Michael's Row marks the position of a large Roman building, which has been variously described as the club for legionary officers or the legionary baths. Excavations there have revealed column bases, hypocausts, and mosaic floors.

There are Rows on both sides of Bridge Street. That on the E side is high, wide, and light, and is used as a modern shopping arcade. It is continuous from the Heritage Centre to the Cross. Bridge Street Row W begins suddenly as an entrance to the first floor of Owen Owen's department store. It is not continuous, for although a modern footbridge carries it over Pierpoint Lane one has to descend from it in order to cross Commonhall Street. It contains few shop entrances, and is much less used than the Row opposite. At one time it was apparently known as Scotch Row, because tradesmen from Scotland frequented it at the times of the annual fairs.

In Hemingway's time the shops at street level on the E side of Bridge Street were mainly occupied by butchers; he described those at street level on the W side as 'of a more respectable character'. On market days the middle of the road was blocked by coal-merchants' carts. In the early 19th century the Feathers Inn stood on the E side of the street, a little to the S of the present St Michael's Row. It was, when Hemingway wrote, the principal coaching inn of Chester. Out of 26 coaches that left Chester daily all but six went from the Feathers. The remainder used the White Lion in Northgate Street.

Hemingway wrote that Bridge Street displayed 'every gradation of architecture, from the rude clumsy wooden hut, to the open airy commodious hotel'. There remains a variety of architectural styles in spite of Victorian and later efforts to enforce the domination of black-and-white.

No. 12 Bridge Street, on the W side, now occupied by Bookland, includes an excellent medieval crypt, 42 ft long by 15 ft wide. It is thought to date from *c.*1270, and, used as part of the bookshop, is accessible during opening hours. At its W end there are three lancet windows, of which the two at the sides are believed to be original. In the S wall of the crypt there is a 13th-century stone staircase. The building above is timber-framed and of the mid 17th century. It was the residence of the Cowper family. Alderman Thomas Cowper (d. 1671) was Mayor of Chester between 1641 and 1642 and a Royalist. When Charles I visited Chester in September 1642 Cowper arranged for a gift of £200 to be presented to him, and £100 to his son Prince Charles, to be made out of an assessment on the inhabitants. His great-grandson William Cowper (d. 1767) was Mayor in 1754–5, and is well known as the compiler of *Collectanea Devana*, a collection in manuscript of material on the history of Chester.

Lower down Bridge Street on the W side, Owen Owen's department store incorporates some medieval remains including the 'three old arches' at Row level, which give their

1 The Roman amphitheatre: view NW across the excavated N part towards St John Street

2 Reconstructed columns in the 'Roman Garden' by the Newgate

3 The 14th-century Water Tower, connected by a spur wall to the NW corner of the city wall

4 The Phoenix Tower, or King Charles's Tower, at the NE corner of the city wall

5 The Eastgate, rebuilt in 1768–9. The clock above was erected to commemorate Queen Victoria's Diamond Jubilee (1897)

6 The Newgate, built in 1938

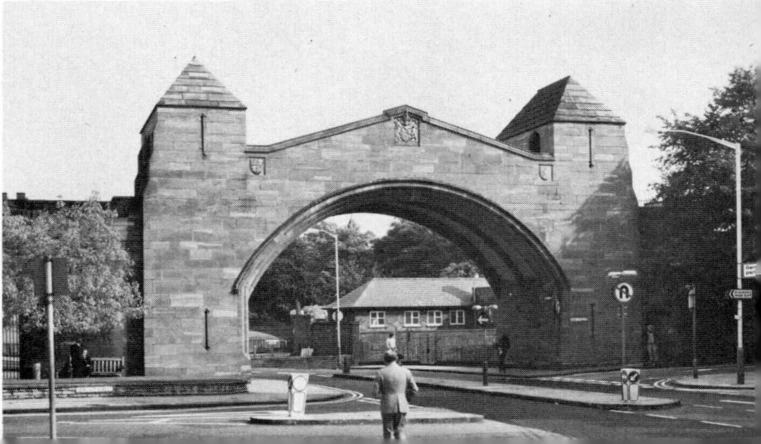

7 The W front of the Cathedral. To the right is the unfinished SW tower; to the left is the King's School building designed by Blomfield

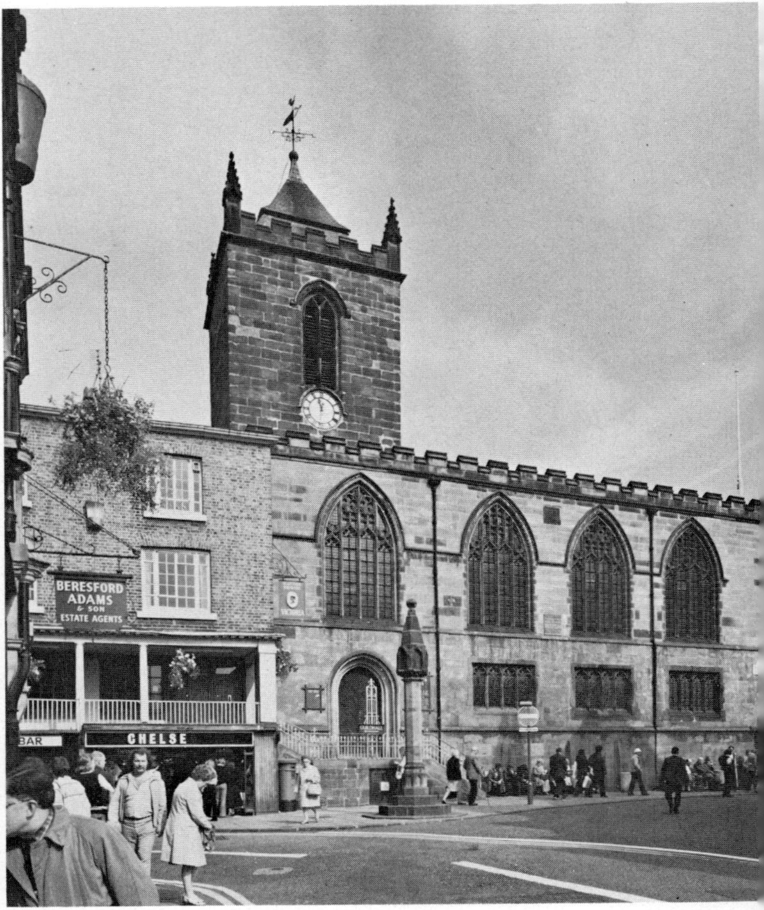

8 St Peter's church. The High Cross was restored to its position S of the church porch in 1975

9 Holy Trinity church, now used as the Guildhall

10 St Michael's church, now used as the Chester Heritage Centre

11 The Welsh Calvinistic Methodist church of 1864 in City Road: a Classical front

12 Nonconformist Gothic: the Wesleyan Methodist church of 1873, also in City Road

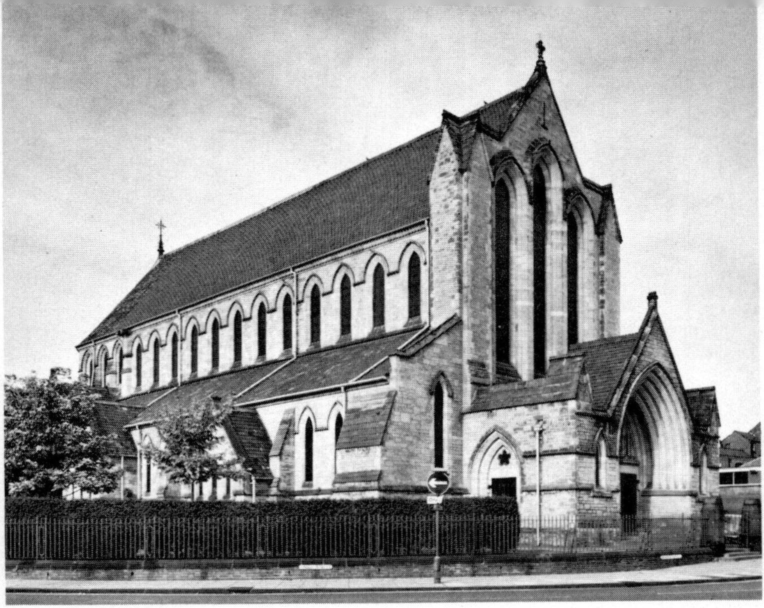

13 St Werburgh's Roman Catholic church, Grosvenor Park Road, opened in 1876

14 The new Friends' Meeting House, Frodsham Street

15 The 14th-century Abbey Gateway. Its upper storey is 18th or early 19th century

16 The Blue Bell Inn (Snow Whites), Northgate Street, said to be of the 15th century. To the right are the former Fire Station of 1911 and the recent Centurion House

17 The Bear and Billet Inn (dated 1664), Lower Bridge Street

18 Bishop Lloyd's House (dated 1615), Watergate Street

19 Eastgate Row N: a Row little changed since the early 19th century

20 Eastgate Row S: a modern shopping arcade

21 The early-18th-century Bluecoat School, Northgate Street

22 Eighteenth-century houses at the NW corner of Abbey Square

Thomas Harrison (also overleaf)

23 Chester Castle: the portico (*c.* 1797)

24 The Grosvenor Bridge (completed 1833)

25 The City Club (1808), Northgate Street

26 The Northgate (1808–10)

27 The Savings Bank (1853), Grosvenor Street

28 God's Providence House, rebuilt in 1862

29 Eastgate Street S: early examples of the black-and-white revival. The right-hand shop was occupied in the 19th century by Bollands, wedding cake manufacturers to Queen Victoria

30 Browns' Crypt Buildings (1858), Eastgate Street S. To the left is Browns' Classical shopfront of *c.* 1828

31 St Werburgh Mount, built in the 1870s. Beyond is part of Douglas's range on the E side of St Werburgh Street, built 20 years later

32 Detail of the Grosvenor Club (1884, enlarged 1908), Eastgate Street N. The Jubilee clock turret is also by Douglas

33 The Grosvenor Museum (1886), Grosvenor Street

34 Detail of Old Bank Buildings (1895), Foregate Street

35 The Old Dee Bridge

36 View E from City Road canal bridge towards the former steam mill (on the right)

37 Chester General Station (1847–8)

38 The inner ring road viaduct over the Shropshire Union Canal at the Northgate Locks

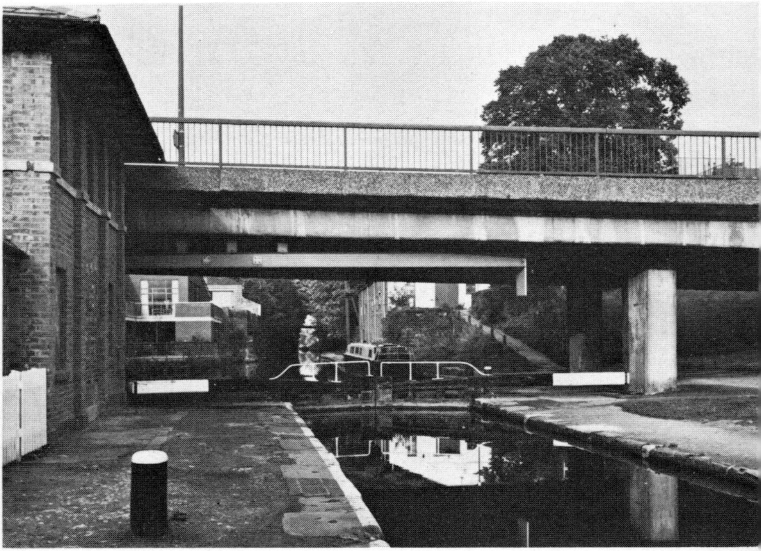

39 Chester Town Hall (1865–9): the expression of civic pride in Gothic

40 The Northgate Arena: (1977): Chester's swimming and sports centre

name to part of the store. The 'Dutch Houses' (Nos. 22–6), further N, are timber-framed and of the mid 17th century, but with the timbers covered by plaster. They were extensively restored by the Council as a project for European Architectural Heritage Year. During restoration, earlier remains were discovered inside the building. Another 17th-century survival in Bridge Street is No. 43 on the E side (Row No. 49). It is said to have been given to St Michael's church for use as a rectory. It too was restored between 1974 and 1975.

As might be expected, Bridge Street has its share of modern timber-framing. Immediately to the N of the Dutch Houses No. 20 Bridge Street (the Plane Tree Restaurant) was designed by T.M. Lockwood in the early 1870s. It is very tall, and out of proportion to the buildings to N and S of it, but much less ornate than Lockwood's later designs, such as the buildings at the Cross (Walk 1) and Old Bank Buildings in Foregate Street (Walk 3). By contrast, No. 55 (street) on the E side of Bridge Street shows Victorian half-timbering at its most elaborate. The shop at Row level was occupied by Sherratts, dealers in works of art: their name can still be seen over the shop, together with a carved figure of Charles I, and representations of various Biblical scenes. The 1899 edition of the *Stranger's Handbook* described this building as 'perhaps rather over-loaded with ornament' but thought that it would 'doubtless be much admired by the visitor who may not have very critical eyes, or be possessed of any decided architectural bias'.

To the N there is a massive timber-framed range of gabled buildings flanking the entrance to St Michael's Row. The latter was designed as a shopping arcade, and was built on Grosvenor property in 1910. The architect was W.T. Lockwood. His first attempt at a building on this site aroused much local criticism because of its Baroque style and facing of white tiles. The second Duke of Westminster accepted the criticism and ordered the replacement of the tiled front with timber-framing. Traces of the original tiling can still be seen at street level, and Lockwood's treatment of the arcade behind it was allowed to survive. It is high, wide, and well lit by large skylights, and the modern Grosvenor-Laing shopping precinct with which it connects (Walk 1) seems tunnel-like by comparison.

Bridge Street houses the offices of the *Cheshire Observer* and the *Chester Chronicle.* The earliest weekly newspaper in Chester was the *Chester Weekly Journal,* first printed in 1721. In 1732 *Adams' Weekly Courant,* later renamed the *Chester Courant,* was started. Its rival, the *Chester Chronicle,* began publication in May 1775; to mark its bicentenary a detailed account of its history, *Chronicle of Chester* by H. Hughes, was published. Until the mid 19th century attempts to start a third weekly newspaper in Chester met with little success. In 1854, however, the *Cheshire Observer* was launched. In 1891 it took over the *Courant.* Joseph Hemingway, whose *History of Chester* published in 1831 contains so much that is still useful, was successively editor of the *Courant* from 1817 to 1824 and of the *Chronicle* from 1824 to 1830.

Since 1804 the shop at No. 11 Bridge Street Row, on the E side not far from the Cross, has been occupied by Lowe and Sons, jewellers. This firm celebrated its bicentenary in 1970. The Lowes were goldsmiths, and several of the family held the position of Assay Master at Chester. (The city had an Assay Office from 1701. Silver hallmarked in Chester bore the coat of arms of the city; from 1779 this was not the official coat of arms but the unofficial one – an erect sword between three wheatsheaves – which had been in use before the official grant of arms in 1580.) George Lowe was Assay Master in 1840. His son Thomas succeeded him, holding the office for 24 years, and Thomas's nephew James Foulkes Lowe occupied it for 45 years. Lowes have produced much silver for use on ceremonial and other occasions, including the annual Chester Cup presented at the races and wedding presents from the county of Cheshire to Princess Elizabeth (now Her Majesty The Queen) and Princess Margaret. Their wares no longer bear the Chester hallmark, for the Assay Office (in Goss Street, Walk 1) closed in August 1962.

Commonhall Street

Hemingway described two exits from the W side of Bridge Street. One was 'a small filthy opening, denominated with great propriety *Dirty*-lane'. It is now known by its earlier name of Pierpoint Lane, apparently taken from the Pierpoint family who had some connexions with the city and county in the 13th century. The other outlet from Bridge Street is Commonhall Street. In the 13th century it was known as Norman's Lane, again after a family of that name. In the following century it became Moot Hall Lane, and, by the late 15th century, Commonhall Lane. Between it and Pierpoint Lane was the Common Hall, often named in court records as the Common Hall of Pleas. The hall seems to have been abandoned by the Corporation in the early 16th century in favour of the former St Nicholas's chapel (Walk 1) between St Werburgh and Northgate Streets.

The former Common Hall subsequently became the chapel of the hospital and chantry of St Ursula the Virgin, the history of which has been described by J.H.E. Bennett in *Journal of the Chester Archaeological Society*, new series, vol. 32, part 2 (1938), pp. 98–129. In 1508 Roger Smith, a former Sheriff of Chester, left his house in Commonhall Lane for the use of aldermen or common councilmen of the city who might fall upon hard times, or for others who might be chosen by 'the Mayor and his brethren'. Two years later, royal letters patent established the 'Fraternity or Guild of St Ursula' as a religious community to which wealthy citizens might retire. The community was probably dissolved along with all such chantries and guilds in the reign of Edward VI, but the benefaction survived as almshouses until the mid 19th century.

Route of Walk Six

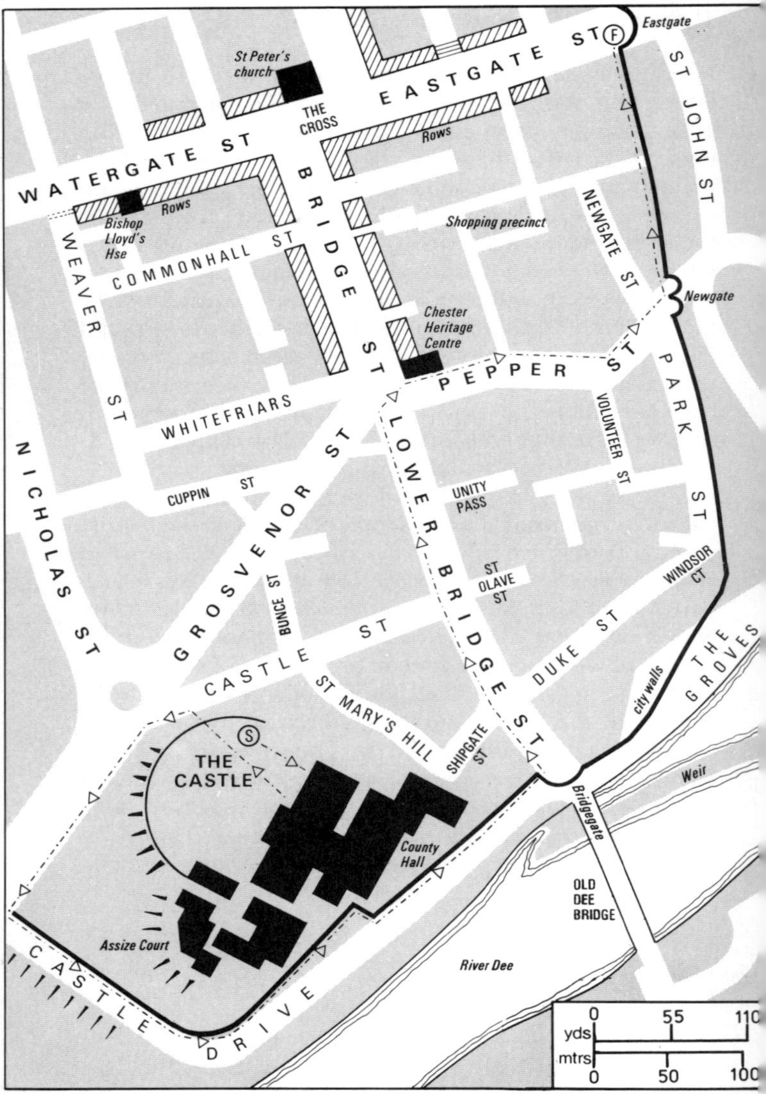

Walk Six

Chester Castle

William the Conqueror is said to have founded Chester Castle during his campaign in the area in 1069–70. It is situated within the extended circuit of the city wall, and as the wall's enlargement has usually been attributed to Aethelflaed, Lady of the Mercians, in the early 10th century, it has been assumed that there was an Anglo-Saxon fortification on the site of the present castle. This, however, has yet to be proved.

From the late 11th century the Castle was of both strategic and administrative importance. Chester was the base from which North Wales was attacked and eventually conquered in the 12th and 13th centuries. The Castle was the administrative headquarters of the county palatine of Chester. The two most important institutions of the palatinate, the Exchequer and the county court, were based there. The Castle also served as a garrison and as a prison. Richard II is said to have been lodged there after his surrender in 1399 to Henry Bolingbroke, who was shortly to supplant him as King. In 1651 James, Earl of Derby, was held there after his trial by court martial for his support of Charles II, until he was taken to Bolton for execution.

The palatine courts were held in the Castle until their abolition in 1830, and afterwards the Cheshire Assizes, now replaced by the Crown Court, were held there. Moreover, after the establishment of quarter sessions in Cheshire in the 1530s at least one session of the court a year was held at the Castle. It was the only gaol in the county until a second was built at Knutsford early in the 19th century. By long-established tradition criminals sentenced to death in the palatine court were handed over to the jurisdiction of the city sheriffs at Gloverstone, a kind of no-man's-land to the N of the Castle.

Although it was geographically within the city wall of Chester, the Castle remained outside the jurisdiction of the city until the reorganization of local government in 1974: Henry VII's charter to Chester in 1506 expressly excluded the Castle from the city's authority.

No satisfactory historical description of the medieval castle has yet been written. Drawings and plans made in the 17th and 18th centuries show an impressive structure consisting of an upper and a lower ward. The principal entrance to the lower ward was by a gateway facing N; it was reached by a drawbridge across a moat. Along the E side of the lower ward were the chief administrative buildings, the Shire Hall and the Exchequer, the latter also known as the 'Parliament' because it was believed that the Cheshire 'Parliament' had met there in the Middle Ages. Another moat divided the lower from the upper ward. A bridge across it led to a gateway facing NE. Along the E wall of the upper ward were the Castle's domestic quarters.

Very little of the medieval castle remains visible today. From the city wall to the SW parts of the medieval wall of the upper ward, extensively restored and altered, can be seen. One medieval tower survives, to the SW of the main block of the modern castle. Containing two chambers, it is known as Agricola's Tower, and stood in the NE corner of the upper ward. The lower chamber was rebuilt after a fire in the early 14th century; the upper is a chapel of the late 12th or early 13th century, named St Mary de Castro. The tower, now preserved by the Department of the Environment as an Ancient Monument, was re-faced by Thomas Harrison in the early 19th century.

By the end of the 18th century much of the medieval castle was ruinous. John Howard, the prison reformer, compared its gaol to what he had heard of the Black Hole of Calcutta. The court-rooms and administrative offices were also inadequate for the needs of the time. An Act of Parliament was obtained for rebuilding the lower ward, and after a competition Thomas Harrison was commissioned as architect. The rebuilding was begun in 1788 but not completed until 1822. The upper ward was levelled and rebuilt later in the 19th century.

The entrance to the Castle is by way of a *propylaeum*, a massive gateway in the Doric order flanked by two smaller pedimented lodges. This was the last part of Harrison's work to be completed. It leads into a large parade ground (now used as a car park except when needed for ceremonial occasions), which is on the site of the former lower ward but much bigger. Beyond is a central block facing NW with two wings at right angles to it. In the middle of the central block is a portico [23] with massive Doric columns of Manley stone supporting a pediment. The wings have half-columns in the Ionic order. They are connected to the central block by short colonnades.

The central block contains the main court-room, a semi-circular chamber with a domed roof and Ionic columns. To the SE, across two courtyards behind the central block, lay the new gaol. Its plan was half an octagon. The gaoler's house was built on the same level as the entrance and court-room. To its SE the ground falls steeply, and the windows of the house overlooked the courtyards in which the prisoners were housed and exercised; this accorded with the 'panoptic' principle giving the prison governor full supervision of his charges. The gaol was taken over by the government in 1877 and closed seven years later. Eventually the cell blocks were demolished, and the site was used as a parade ground and afterwards grassed over, until just before the Second World War the erection of County Hall began. The central block of the Castle had long been used for administrative offices by the County Council, and the rear of County Hall was built on to the former gaoler's house.

The two wings at right angles to the central block of the Castle were designed as a barracks and as an armoury, though the northern wing held the Exchequer court until its abolition in 1830. At about the same time the southern wing was converted into officers' quarters. The northern wing now houses a small museum devoted to military history, and particularly to that of the Cheshire Regiment.

Chester Castle contains the County Record Office. The records of the palatinate of Chester were taken to the Public Record Office in London in the 1850s. Those of the Cheshire quarter sessions, however, remained. A record office was established between the Wars, but no full-time archivist was appointed until 1949. Since then the records of the diocese of Chester that relate to Cheshire, including wills and inventories and transcripts of parish registers, have also been deposited at the Castle. The collection has been augmented by numerous private deposits of deeds, and by the records of subordinate local authorities. For the student of the history of the city of Chester, the main importance of the County Record Office lies in its holding of wills and parish registers, and its microfilm copies of the census returns of the mid 19th century up to 1871, the last census to have been opened to public inspection.

St Mary-on-the-Hill

From the Castle parade-ground the tower of St Mary's church can be seen above the castle buildings to the NE. A good view of the church is obtained by leaving the parade ground by the colonnade at its NE corner: a footpath leads into Castle Street, and to the right the church is seen.

St Mary-on-the-Hill was one of the nine medieval parish churches of Chester. The appearance of the church, which is built of red sandstone, is Perpendicular. It was extensively restored by James Harrison in the early 1860s. In the late 19th century a complex series of adjustments in parishes in Chester took place: a new church was built for the parish of St Mary, across the river in Handbridge (Walk 7), and St Mary-on-the-Hill became the parish church for the combined parishes of St Bridget and St Martin (Walk 5). The creation of the united parish of Chester in 1972 made St Mary's church redundant. It was closed for worship, and has been taken over by the County Council as an educational resources centre. This has meant that public access is now restricted. The building contains some interesting features. The nave roof, which is of timber, is said to have come from Basingwerk Abbey in Flintshire in the mid 16th century, but the story rests on no good authority. There are recumbent effigies of Thomas Gamull, who died in 1613, and his wife, and of Philip Oldfield, who died in the same year.

The history of the church and parish was described in 1898 in *The History of the Church and Parish of St Mary-on-the-Hill, Chester,* by J.P. Earwaker, edited by R.H. Morris.

To the N and E of the church St Mary's Hill is an attractive cobbled street running steeply downhill towards Shipgate Street. At the top is St Mary's School, which was opened in 1846. Lower down is the early-19th-century Tudor-style rectory.

The City Wall south of the Castle

The Castle should be left by way of the parade ground and the *propylaeum.* In the parade ground there is a statue of Queen Victoria by F. W. Pomeroy, who was also responsible for the effigy of the first Duke of Westminster in Chester Cathedral (Walk 2). It was unveiled in 1903. Two-thirds of the cost of its erection were borne by the county, and the remainder by the city of Chester.

The approach road to the Grosvenor Bridge (Walk 5) leads SW from the Castle entrance, and the wall walk is soon reached leading off to the left. It maintains a high level and runs S of the Castle, with a view to the N of the wall of the upper ward and to the S of the Little Roodee, which is an open space used as a car park and also occasionally as the site of a fun fair.

The wall's course is SE, then ENE for a short stretch and NE. Between it and the river is Castle Drive, a road made early in the present century. In the early 19th century a road called Skinner's Lane ran between the wall and the river. It housed the workshops of animal skinners, and an acid factory. In the early 1830s the county authorities acquired this industrial area and extended the city wall to enclose it. The wall now makes a right-angled turn to the SE and drops to the level of Castle Drive.

To the left is the large neo-Georgian block of County Hall. Until the 1930s the administrative offices of the County Council were scattered through Chester and elsewhere in the county. The building of a new administrative headquarters, designed by the County Architect, E. Mainwaring Parkes, was started just before the Second World War, but County Hall was only opened in 1957. During the 1960s and early 1970s the number of County Council staff increased rapidly, and County Hall was found not to be big enough. As a result other offices in Chester have since been taken over, such as Commerce House in Hunter Street (Walk 3).

Bridgegate

The wall walk rises above road level once more just to the NE of County Hall. it crosses Lower Bridge Street by the Bridgegate. A few yards to the SW stood another gate, the Shipgate, which was demolished when the wall was altered in 1831. The archway of the Shipgate was eventually re-erected in the Grosvenor Park (Walk 8).

The Bridgegate in the Middle Ages was of great military importance, as it guarded the approach to Chester from across the Dee by way of the Old Dee Bridge. The custody of the gate, like that of the Eastgate (Walk 1) and the Watergate (Walk 4), passed into private hands in the Middle Ages; it carried with it the right to take toll on goods passing through. Because of a division among co-heiresses, the custody of the Bridgegate was shared between two families, the Norrises, who sold their portion to the Corporation in 1624, and the Troutbecks, whose descendant, the Earl of Shrewsbury, sold his part in 1666. The old gateway was flanked by two towers. In 1600 John Tyrer, a lay clerk in the Cathedral, was licensed by the Assembly to build a tower above the gate. Water was raised from the Dee into the tower, and supplied through pipes to properties in the city. Tyrer later extended his operation with another water tower at Boughton, which supplied water to the conduit near the Cross (Walk 1).

The medieval Bridgegate was demolished in 1781, and the present sandstone archway with two pedestrian arches and an ornamental balustrade above was built in the following year. The expense was defrayed by the Corporation.

To the S of Castle Drive a low stone structure may be seen jutting out into the river. This was a hydro-electric power station erected by the Corporation and opened in 1913; it was designed to supplement the generators at the Corporation's power station in New Crane Street, which had been opened at the end of the 19th century.

The hydro-electric works stand on the site of the Dee Mills. It is usually suggested that Earl Hugh I of Chester (d. 1101) first constructed a causeway or weir across the Dee at Chester for the purpose of providing power for a water mill. The mill belonged not to the city but to the Earldom, and since all citizens were compelled to have their corn ground there, it was a rich source of profit. The Earls of Chester were able to let the mill out to individuals for a high annual payment; the lessees kept the fees for grinding, and earned a reputation for the harshness of their exactions. During the Middle Ages the mill was several times repaired and enlarged, so that it is usually known as the Dee Mills. In the early 17th century there were 11 water-wheels at work there, six for grinding corn, three for fulling cloth, and two for raising water from the river to the water tower on the Bridgegate. In the early 1550s the corn mills were granted by the Crown to Sir Richard Cotton. Afterwards they were leased to the Gamull family, but in the late 18th century the Wrenches purchased them outright and continued to operate them until the end of the following century. In 1831 they were said to contain 22 pairs of millstones.

The Dee Mills were several times badly damaged by fire. The Corporation acquired them in 1895, and another fire broke out soon afterwards. Although they were put back into operation, they did not prove successful and were demolished in 1910.

The Old Dee Bridge

A wooden bridge existed across the Dee at this point at least in the early 13th century. During that and the following century it was destroyed by flood waters on several occasions. Among the royal grants preserved in the Chester City Record Office is one from Richard II dated 25 July 1387, in which he allowed the city to use certain taxes and tolls for the rebuilding of the bridge. The present stone bridge [35] is late-14th-century in style. It consists of seven arches, which are irregular in both size and shape. The S end of the bridge was again rebuilt at the end of the 15th century. At that end there was another gate, which, like the old Bridgegate, was demolished in the 1780s.

The Old Dee Bridge was widened on the W side in 1826 by the construction of a footway. Animals and vehicles making the crossing had to pay toll until 1 January 1885. The bridge is too narrow for vehicles to pass on it, and traffic is controlled by traffic lights at each end.

Lower Bridge Street

One of the most interesting parts of Hemingway's *History of Chester* is his perambulation of the City. Surprisingly, he devoted little space to Lower Bridge Street, which contains many buildings of character and historical interest. Unfortunately the street also contains areas of dilapidation and neglect, in spite of efforts by the Conservation Section of Chester's Technical Services Department.

At one time there were Rows in Lower Bridge Street. Part of the Row on the E side can be seen at No. 11, a building of the mid 18th century. Elsewhere traces of Rows have been discovered behind the façades of buildings. Some of the shops at 'street' level are reached by steps down from the pavement, as in the streets where there are 'proper' Rows. Several of the houses have their main entrances at first-floor level, another characteristic of properties in former Rows. These details add character to a street that has the natural advantage of a fairly steep rise up from the Bridgegate.

On the E side of the street there is one of the medieval parish churches of Chester, St Olave's. St Olave was Olaf, King of Norway (d. 1030), and this early dedication to him has been taken as an indication of Scandinavian influence in this part of Chester. The church was in existence by 1119. Both church and parish were very poor in the Middle Ages and afterwards, and in 1841 the parish was united with St Michael's.

Until the early 19th century this part of Chester must have seemed exceedingly well provided with places of worship: St Mary-on-the-Hill is not far away, up the short but steep St Mary's Hill; St Michael's and St Bridget's stood on opposite corners of Bridge Street; at the top of the street was the Cross and St Peter's.

St Olave's is a small sandstone church with a bell cote at its W end. It was restored by James Harrison in the late 1850s. To the E, in St Olave Street, the First Church of Christ Scientist occupies the former elementary school for the parish of St Michael with St Olave. A ragged school was established there in 1852 by the Chester Ragged School Society, which also founded the Bishop Graham Memorial School in Princess Street (Walk 3). The elementary school that replaced it in the late 1870s closed down in 1941, because the residential population of the area had declined.

There are several houses of the 17th century in Lower Bridge Street. On the E side the Tudor House, a little way above St Olave's, has on occasion been claimed as the oldest house in Chester. Below the gable is an inscription, now partly obscured but said at one time to bear the date 1503. In fact it is more likely to be 1603, and there are other houses in Chester that incorporate earlier work, for example the former Blue Bell Inn in Northgate Street (Walk 3). At first-floor level there was a Row, which is said to have been enclosed in the early 18th century. The house has been extensively restored.

On the W side of the street, the first 17th-century building from the S end is the Bear and Billet [17], which bears the date 1664. It was owned by the Earls of Shrewsbury until

1867; they had held half the custody of the Bridgegate in the mid 17th century. In the gable of this timber-framed building there are doors through which grain was hoisted for storage in the attic. The bear and billet (or staff) is heraldically associated not with the Shrewsbury family but with the Earls of Warwick. As a name for this inn, however, it probably goes back no further than the 19th century.

Just above the Bear and Billet, on the S corner of Shipgate Street, is the King Edgar Tavern, or Ye Olde Edgar. It is another timber-framed building, restored towards the end of the last century. The name commemorates the episode of 973 when King Edgar visited Chester and was rowed on the Dee by tributary rulers of the Celtic kingdoms in token of their submission to him.

Between Shipgate Street and Castle Street there is a terrace of houses whose entrances are approached from a footpath above street level. At the N end is what appears to be a building of the 18th or early 19th century, with oval windows to the upper storey and a pedimented porch. It is Gamul House, which together with the Dutch Houses in Bridge Street (Walk 5), is a major example of restoration work carried out by the City Council as part of the European Architectural Heritage Year programme. Its brick façade conceals timber framing and the remains of a Row. There is a 17th-century plaster ceiling inside, and a carved sandstone fireplace. It is thought likely that the house was built over the courtyard of an earlier structure that lay slightly to the W. Gamul House is associated with the Gamul family, often spelt Gamull, which was very influential in early-17th-century Chester. There is a monument to Thomas Gamull, Recorder of Chester (d. 1613), in the church of St Mary-on-the-Hill. His son Francis was Mayor of Chester in 1634–5 and one of the leading Royalists in the city when the Civil War began. He is said to have entertained Charles I in Gamul House during the King's visit to Chester in September 1645. In 1978 Gamul House was opened as a Greek restaurant and *taverna*.

Further N again, on the N corner of Castle Street, is the Old King's Head. The name 'Old' distinguishes this timber-framed building from the Victorian 'King's Head' on the N corner of Bridge Street and Grosvenor Street. In the 17th century the Old King's Head was a private residence. It was rebuilt, or enlarged, by Randle Holme (d. 1655), who was Mayor of Chester in 1633–4. There were four generations of Randle Holmes working in Chester in the 17th and early 18th centuries. Randle I, who rebuilt or enlarged this building, was an armorial painter and the local deputy of the Heralds' College, an important position in the 17th century. The right to bear arms was an indication of social status, and after an armigerous person's death arms-painters were in demand; they painted representations of the bearings for use in the funeral procession, and wooden memorial tablets to be hung in churches. Randle I, Randle II (d. 1659), Randle III (d. 1700), and Randle IV (d. 1707) all pursued this trade. They were leading members of the Company of Painters, Glaziers, Embroiderers, and Stationers. All four served as churchwardens of St Mary-on-the-Hill. They were devoted antiquaries who collected and copied deeds and other evidences of local topography and genealogy. Their collections now form Nos. 1920–2177 of the Harleian Manuscripts in the British Library. Randle Holme III published, in 1688, an heraldic encyclopaedia entitled *The Academy of Armoury*. He is also said to have built for himself a timber-framed house further N in Lower Bridge Street, which was later converted into the Lamb Inn. Early-19th-century pictures of it show a crazily picturesque structure. It fell down in 1821.

At the corner of Lower Bridge Street and Grosvenor Street is yet another 17th-century timber-framed building, the Falcon. It was built as a town house for the Grosvenor family. Richard Grosvenor petitioned the Assembly for permission to enlarge it in October 1643. It afterwards became an inn. In the 1880s it was restored by John Douglas for the Duke of Westminster, and was reopened as a cocoa house. By 1976 it was in need of major structural repairs, and temporary shoring was erected. Extensive repair and restoration work is planned for it.

Georgian architecture is well represented in Lower Bridge

Street. The S end of the W side of the street is named Bridge Place, and consists of a terrace of 18th-century houses. Other examples of medium-sized Georgian town houses may be seen elsewhere in the street and in Castle Street, which leads W towards the N entrance of the Castle. To the N of Castle Street, above an unhappy vista of dereliction and demolition, stands the Oddfellows' Hall, or Bridge House. This is a large house of six bays with much Classical ornamentation. It was built early in the 18th century for John Williams, Attorney-General of Denbighshire and Montgomeryshire in 1702 and of Cheshire and Flintshire as well in 1727. On the opposite side of the street, just below the Tudor House, is another early-18th-century building, with its entrance porch, in the Tuscan Doric order, approached by steps. It was built in 1715 as Park House; it subsequently became the Albion Hotel, and is mentioned by Hemingway as 'elegantly fitted up' and containing an assembly room. To the rear were gardens and a bowling green. It later became the Talbot Hotel. In 1978 its upper floors were opened as an antiques hypermarket. The ground floor is partly occupied as a wine bar.

Pepper Street

There is a marked change in character as one turns E from Lower Bridge Street at the traffic lights by St Michael's church (now the Chester Heritage Centre – Walk 5) into Pepper Street. This road was widened in the 1960s as part of the inner ring road scheme. To the E of the Heritage Centre, most of the N side as far as Newgate Street is occupied by the S face of the Grosvenor-Laing shopping precinct (Walk 1). The S side begins with Windsor House, an office block built on the site of a public house, the Red Lion, which was said to date from 1642. There follows an extensive motor-car showroom, the interior of which incorporates four fluted pillars that fronted the Methodist New Connexion chapel built in 1835. Volunteer Street, leading off Pepper Street to the S, contains terraced housing of the late 19th century. At its S end is the Territorial Drill Hall established in 1869 as a base for the local volunteers. The Hall has Gothic features and a turret at the NE corner. In 1978 it was planned to transfer the Chester Arts and Recreation Trust there from the building between Hunter and Princess Streets (Walk 3), which is to be converted into a new central library.

Beyond Volunteer Street the S side of Pepper Street contains a multi-storey car park. On a tower above this building is the figure of a lion, which formerly surmounted the brewery that stood on this site from the 1840s. When the brewery was demolished in the late 1960s the lion was given to the Chester Civic Trust; it was placed on the car park tower in 1971.

The truncated Newgate Street leads N from Pepper Street into the shopping precinct's car park. It formerly connected with Eastgate Street. On its W side is St Andrew's Presbyterian Church of England, now St Andrew's United Reformed Church, a Gothic building erected in 1860 and substantially reconstructed in 1884. On the opposite side are some minor 18th-century houses and the 19th-century Plumbers' Arms.

Pepper Street ends at the Newgate [6]. This wide stone archway flanked by towers was built in 1938, to designs by Sir Walter and Michael Tapper. At that time Pepper Street and its continuation to the E, Little St John Street, were diverted from the former Newgate or Wolf Gate, which can be seen immediately to the N. In the Middle Ages this was a small postern in the wall, but it was rebuilt in 1608, and again in the late 1760s. The battlements above were added in 1890. In 1925 it was feared that the Council's plan to improve communication between Pepper Street and Little St John Street would involve the destruction of the Newgate, but the new archway was sited a few yards to the S.

The wall can only be ascended on the S side of the Newgate by way of steps in Park Street. Immediately to the N of the earlier gateway the wall makes a short bend to the NW. Outside it can be seen the foundation of the SE angle-tower of the Roman fortress. From this point to the Eastgate and beyond (Walk 3) the wall is once more on Roman foundations. A few yards further N is the base of a defensive tower, known as Thimbleby's Tower. It was restored in 1879. The lower parts of the vaulting of the tower room can be seen. The upper room or rooms were demolished during the siege of Chester in the Civil War.

From this point to the Eastgate is the least attractive part of the city wall. On the left is the multi-storey car park belonging to the Grosvenor-Laing shopping precinct, followed by the undistinguished flank of the Grosvenor Hotel. To the E are the backs of the buildings in St John Street (Walk 8).

Walk Seven

The Roman Garden and Amphitheatre

Immediately to the SE of the Newgate (Walk 6) is the 'Roman Garden', an area between the city wall and Souter's Lane in which various architectural remains found during the excavation of Roman sites in Chester have been placed. They include a reconstructed underfloor heating chamber or hypocaust. Between 1949, when this area was laid out, and 1975 the High Cross (Walk 1) also stood here, before its removal to its old position S of St Peter's church.

On the far side of Souter's Lane is the most dramatic survival of Roman Chester, the amphitheatre [1]. A Roman legionary fortress would normally have an amphitheatre outside its walls, as would a large civilian settlement. These arenas were used not only for the sort of gladiatorial combats commemorated in epic films, but for military training exercises. It was natural, then, for the existence of an amphitheatre at Chester to be suspected. It was only proved in 1929. The Chester Archaeological Society sponsored an appeal for money to purchase the buildings that occupied the N half, accidentally revealed during building operations. Archaeological excavation started in 1960 and the N half of the amphitheatre was opened to the public in August 1972. This stone-built structure appears to have replaced an earlier timber one. The oval arena of the amphitheatre measured 190 by 162 ft, and it is thought that there was accommodation for more than 7,000 spectators. There is a full description of the amphitheatre displayed on the site, but the leaflet said there to be available is unfortunately out of print. The excavation is, however, described in

Route of Walk Seven

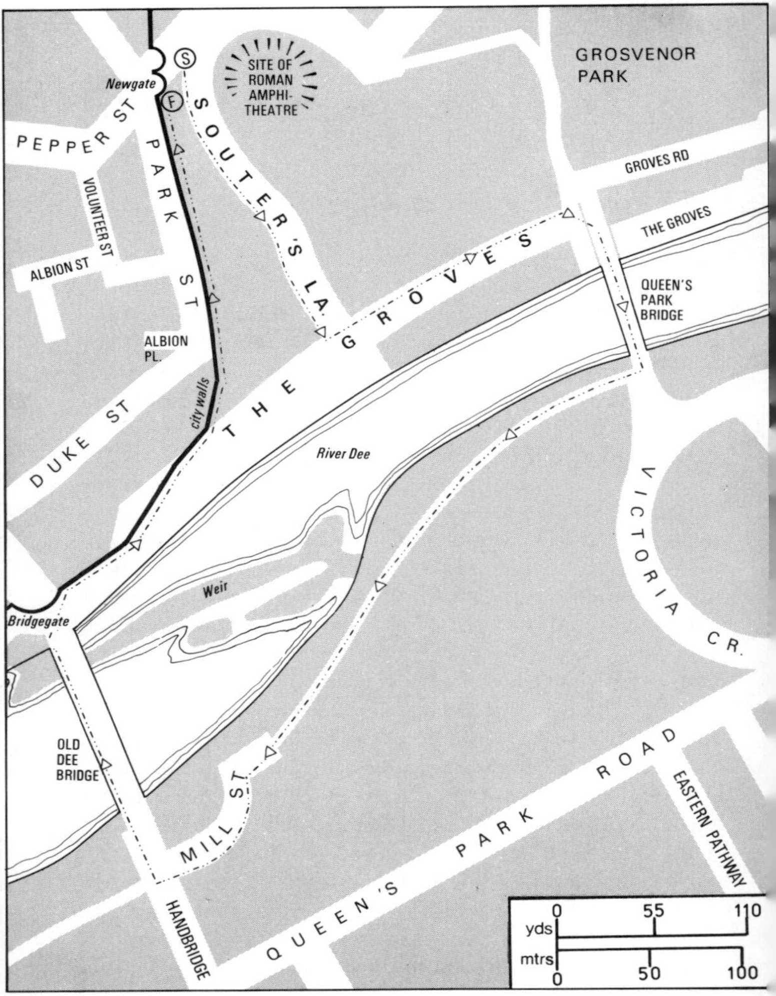
GROSVENOR PARK
SITE OF ROMAN AMPHI-THEATRE
Newgate
PEPPER ST
VOLUNTEER ST
PARK ST
SOUTER'S LA.
GROVES RD
THE GROVES
ALBION ST
QUEEN'S PARK BRIDGE
ALBION PL.
city walls
DUKE ST
River Dee
VICTORIA CR.
Weir
Bridgegate
OLD DEE BRIDGE
MILL ST
QUEEN'S PARK ROAD
EASTERN PATHWAY
HANDBRIDGE
yds
0
55
110
mtrs
0
50
100

detail by F.H. Thompson in *Archaeologia*, vol. 105 (1975); off-prints of that paper are obtainable from the Grosvenor Museum.

Souter's Lane and the Groves

Souter's Lane drops steeply to the riverside. In the Middle Ages it was *Souterlode*, the river-passage of the shoemakers. To the E is the former Ursuline convent of Dee House, now owned by the Post Office, which overlies the S half of the Roman amphitheatre. The nucleus of the convent was a small Georgian house, which was opened in 1854 as a boarding school. In 1925 it was taken over from the order formerly in charge of it, the Faithful Companions of Jesus, by the Ursulines of Crewe. By that time considerable extensions had been made to the original building; a Gothic wing, for example, can be seen immediately to the E of the original Georgian house. The convent became a direct-grant girls' school, but in 1972 it was decided to phase it out.

Below Dee House is the Chester Y.M.C.A. hostel. Its core is a red-brick Georgian house dating from the mid 18th century. From the 1870s until 1921 it was the palace of the Bishop of Chester; formerly the Bishop's Palace had adjoined the Cathedral, occupying the site later developed as the King's School and now used by Barclays Bank. From the 1920s the Bishop's house has been the former Deanery at the NE corner of Abbey Square (Walk 2).

Souter's Lane ends at the Groves, Chester's riverside promenade. This embankment above the Dee is one of Chester's leading tourist attractions. The W end of it, towards the Old Dee Bridge, was laid out at the expense of Alderman Charles Brown (d. 1900), one of 'the' Browns of Chester (Walk 1), in the early 1880s. There are refreshment kiosks, an attractive late-19th-century bandstand, and landing stages from which pleasure boats leave for cruises up the Dee. Rowing boats and small motor boats can also be hired. Regattas and canoeing events are regularly held during the summer and autumn.

In the 19th century a floating swimming bath was set up by the Corporation at the Groves, replacing the public baths established earlier in the century at the NW corner of the city wall (Walk 4). In January 1898 it was carried away by a flood, and came to rest on the top of the weir. It was replaced in position but does not seem to have survived long after the opening of the new public baths in 1901 (Walk 8).

Queen's Park

Upstream from Souter's Lane the suspension bridge that leads to the suburb of Queen's Park on the other side of the river is seen. Just before the suspension bridge is reached, a building is half visible behind trees and bushes to the N of the Groves. A better view of it is obtained by ascending a short way up the path leading from the bridge end: the building can then be seen across a bowling green. It is the 'Anchorite's Cell', a medieval hermitage restored during the 19th century; it is a sandstone building of two floors, with a window at the E end of reticulated tracery. The building as a whole is suffering from neglect. Tradition asserts that King Harold II, after the battle of Hastings in 1066, came to Chester and ended his days in this cell as a hermit.

The suspension bridge was first erected in 1852 to link Chester directly with Queen's Park. It was rebuilt in 1923; the date is prominently marked at each end of the bridge, where there are also the real or supposed coats of arms of the Norman Earls of Chester.

Queen's Park was a villa estate laid out in the mid 19th century by Enoch Gerrard; James Harrison designed some of the houses. In 1856 Thomas Hughes warmly praised this new development: 'The salubrity of the air, and the high commanding situation of Queen's Park, together with its beautiful river scenery, and its close proximity to the city, combine to render it peculiarly suitable for villa residences'. The same could have been said of Curzon Park, which lay W of the S end of the Grosvenor Bridge (Walk 5). The mid-19th-century villas are still there, but there has been

much in-filling of the spaces between them by modern houses and there are also some unsightly army huts. To the W, along Queen's Park Road, is the Neo-Georgian building erected as the headquarters of Western Command in 1937. Further W again are the two parts of the Queen's Park High School, which was formed in 1971 by amalgamation of the former City Grammar School for Boys and the City High School for Girls. The former had its origin in day technical classes held at the Grosvenor Museum in the 1890s. The City High School for Girls was founded in 1905 and had as its first site the stands on the Roodee.

Handbridge may be reached by way of Queen's Park Road, but the more pleasant route is by way of the riverside promenade. It leads to a modern block of flats near the site of the former snuff mills in Handbridge. A water wheel has been preserved on the river side of the footpath, and between the river bank and the weir supposedly made by Earl Hugh I of Chester (Walk 6) can be seen the salmon leap.

Handbridge

The suburb of Handbridge was dismissed by most writers of the 19th century as unworthy of the tourist's attention. 'It consists', wrote Hemingway, 'of narrow steep streets, built on a red rock, and almost exclusively inhabited by the lower orders'. Thomas Hughes is even less flattering: 'We might, if we chose, wander forth into Handbridge, were there anything in that suburb deserving our special notice'.

At that time Handbridge was an industrial suburb. The watermill was run by the firm of Nicholls, tobacco and snuff manufacturers. The area between the mill and the Old Dee Bridge was occupied by skinners or tanners. There were also rope makers. Further to the W much of the land was taken up by horticulture, with extensive nurseries belonging to the firm of Jarvis and Son. The housing in Handbridge seems to have been like that associated with most industrial settlements of the 19th century; the workers' houses were crowded into courts between Mill Street, the W side of

Handbridge, and the sandstone cliff to the N. In the early 1920s this was declared an unhealthy area, and the Council obtained the City of Chester (Handbridge Improvement Scheme) Order, 1925, which enabled them to purchase the properties for demolition. The result may be seen in the half-timbered shops erected in the late 1920s that now line the E side of Handbridge between Mill Street and Queen's Park Road. On the opposite side of Handbridge there remain houses of the 18th and 19th centuries.

The return to Chester can now he made by way of the Old Dee Bridge, but a detour of half an hour to investigate the W parts of Handbridge is worth making. The main road bends sharply to the W, and Eaton Road leads off to the left in the direction of Eccleston and Eaton Hall. At the junction is the Chester Boys' Club, formerly the Handbridge Institute, a red-brick building of 1895 with Renaissance detail, believed to be by Lockwood. Handbridge now becomes Overleigh Road, and to the S is the church of St Mary without the Walls. It was completed in 1887, the architect being F.B. Wade (1851–1919). The first Duke of Westminster paid for this building, which was to serve as a parish church for the truncated parish of St Mary-on-the-Hill (Walk 6). Wade used a free form of 13th-century Gothic. The church has a reredos of 1888 by Frederic Shields.

Overleigh Road continues between, to the N, late-19th-century terraces, and, to the S, very recent Neo-Georgian town houses. Further to the W is the Chester Cemetery, which extends on both sides of Overleigh Road. The N side, towards the river, is the more picturesque. It was designed by T.M. Penson in the late 1840s, and is most attractively landscaped. Among the trees and winding footpaths is a fascinating variety of Victorian monuments. Thomas Hughes aptly commented in 1856: 'Nature and Art have alike combined to produce here a retreat worthy of the dead, and yet full of beauty and allurement for the living', though the lake, which was an added ornament to the cemetery in his day, has now disappeared.

The return to Handbridge and the Old Dee Bridge can be made by way of a riverside footpath. To the W there are good views of the Grosvenor Bridge (Walk 5). The river bank at the end of Greenway Street is particularly associated with the Dee salmon fishermen. Between there and the Old Dee Bridge the path passes through a recreation ground, Edgar's Field, named after the king who in the 10th century was rowed by his tributary kings on the Dee. It was presented to the city by the first Duke of Westminster in 1892. The sandstone rock, first used by the Romans as a source of building stone, outcrops here at several points. Behind an iron grating is a Roman carving of Minerva, but it is so badly worn that it has to be viewed with the eye of faith.

Old Dee Bridge to Newgate

Something has been said of the history of the Old Dee Bridge and the Dee Mills in Walk 6. The footpath across the bridge is on its E side and gives an excellent view of the causeway or weir said to have been first constructed in the late 11th century. The weir was tidied by the Corporation early in the present century, and Cestrians bemoaned the resulting loss of picturesqueness. It is covered by the highest tides.

At the N end of the Old Dee Bridge the city wall rises above the Groves, to the E of the Bridgegate. There are good views upstream towards the suspension bridge and the suburb of Boughton, and across the river towards Handbridge. On the inner side of the wall there are Georgian and later houses. A plaque erroneously commemorates the construction in 1700 of the 'Recorder's Steps', which lead down to the Groves: they are said to have been built for Roger Comberbach (d. 1719), successively Clerk of the Pentice and Recorder of Chester, but in fact were built after his death, between 1720 and 1722.

Further along the wall there is a succession of short flights of stairs, known as the 'Wishing Steps' and said to have been constructed in 1785 during improvements to the walls. The name is derived from a local tradition that someone who makes a wish at the bottom and then runs up, down, and up again without drawing breath will have his desire granted.

To the W of the wall late-19th-century terraces surround the Drill Hall at the S end of Volunteer Street (Walk 6). The road just inside the wall on this side is Park Street. Between Albion Street and the Pepper Street multi-storey car park there is a short terrace of six timber-framed houses with their ground floors of sandstone. They are the survivors of a range known as the Nine Houses, built *c.*1650. By the late 1950s they had become so dilapidated as to be unsuitable as dwellings, and by 1962 all the occupants had been moved elsewhere. Further deterioration of the properties was rapid while endeavours were made to find the means of restoring them. By 1966 demolition of the houses appeared inevitable, but the Historic Buildings Council gave the City Council a grant towards their restoration, and they were extensively restored and modernized in 1968 and 1969.

At the N end of this terrace is a black-and-white house of 1881, which provides an interesting juxtaposition of 17th-century timber-framing and its revival two centuries later. The modern building is in an entirely different scale. It is a dental surgery, and coincidentally bears the inscription 'The fear of the Lord is the fountain of life'. This is said to have been an inscription on a coin found on the site.

☆

The reader who has followed these walks in order has now completed the circuit of the walls. This walk has been mostly outside the line of the medieval walls. The remaining two itineraries lie entirely outside their circuit and take in the inner suburbs to the E of the city, on both sides of Foregate Street.

Walk Eight

St John Street

St John Street is a short thoroughfare that runs parallel to the SE section of the city wall (Walk 6) between Foregate Street and the Newgate. It is now a one-way street for vehicles. Short though it is, it contains several major public and other buildings. On the E side, the Blossoms Hotel (Walk 3), whose main entrance is now in St John Street, is succeeded by the Victorian or early-20th-century black-and-white Marlborough Arms. There is a minor 18th- or early-19th-century house, then the side entrance to Marks & Spencer, and the Welsh Presbyterian church of 1866, designed by W. and G. Audsley of Liverpool and built of grey stone in an Early English style with a large rose window facing the street. It is one of the two remaining churches in Chester where services are held in Welsh; the other is the Penri Memorial Chapel, a Baptist church in Gorse Stacks. Before the Second World War there were several others, including St Martin's (Walk 5), and chapels in Albion Street and in Queen Street (Walk 9). Further S, at the end of St John Street, is the telephone exchange, a Neo-Georgian building of 1940.

On the W side of the street the Old Bank (Walk 3) is succeeded by Chester's main post office, a high building in Tudor style. At the beginning of the 19th century the post office was in Old Post Office Yard, on the N side of Foregate Street near the Eastgate (Walk 3); in 1842 a new one was built, apparently at the postmaster's own expense, on the E side of St John Street on land now occupied by the Blossoms Hotel. The present building dates from 1876 and is on the

Route of Walk Eight

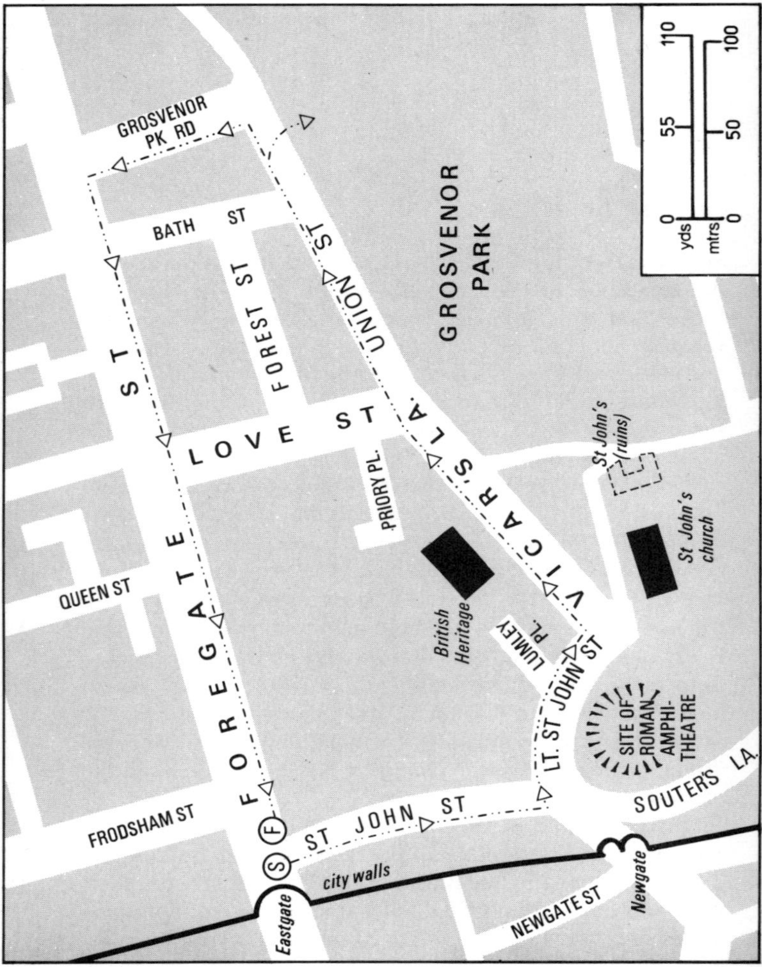
GROSVENOR PK RD
BATH ST
FOREST ST
UNION ST
GROSVENOR PARK
LOVE ST
FOREGATE ST
QUEEN ST
PRIORY PL.
VICAR'S LA.
St John's (ruins)
St John's church
British Heritage
LUMLEY PL.
ST JOHN ST
LT. ST JOHN ST
SITE OF ROMAN AMPHI-THEATRE
SOUTER'S LA.
FRODSHAM ST
ST JOHN ST
city walls
Eastgate
Newgate
NEWGATE ST
S
F
yds 0 55 110
mtrs 0 50 100

site of a garden that formerly lay to the S of the Old Bank.

To the S of the Post Office the Central Library, opened as a Free Library in 1874, makes an architectural contrast with the Post Office; it is of brick with stone dressings, and the style is Classical. The former entrance doorway has a broken segmental pediment incorporating the city arms, and Ionic pilasters. To the S is a much lower and plainer 20th-century addition; it was opened in 1931. In the early 19th century there were several subscription libraries in Chester: a Mechanics' Institute was opened in St John Street in 1835, but like many such organizations elsewhere it met with only limited success. In 1856 Thomas Hughes in the *Stranger's Handbook* bemoaned the fact that 'so few mechanics, comparatively, avail themselves of this, their own Institution'. Shortly after this it seems to have collapsed. The Free Library succeeded, and was managed by a committee consisting of city councillors and co-opted members. A century later local government reorganization removed it to county control. The library contains a lending department, a children's department, and a reference section. It is too small for the numbers requiring its services, and the reference library in particular is overcrowded and under-equipped. Plans have been announced for a new library complex to be built in Northgate Street between Princess and Hunter Streets (Walk 3).

The library's neighbour on the S side is an imposing town house of the mid 18th century, of brick but with stone dressings in the Corinthian order. It is used as insurance offices, and was extensively restored in the early 1970s.

Towards the end of St John Street, on the W side, is a large Methodist church. A plaque on the wall of the building immediately S commemorates the first occasion when John Wesley preached in Chester, in 1752. The Wesleyans erected the Octagon Chapel at the E end of Foregate Street in 1765. It was demolished to make way for the new City Road (Walk 9) in the 1860s, but half a century earlier the Wesleyans had left it in favour of their new church in St John Street, built in 1811, possibly to the designs of Thomas Harrison. Part of the interior survives from that time, but the exterior was rebuilt in 1906 in dark-red brick, with stone ornament; there is a very large E window facing the street, with a kind of debased Perpendicular tracery.

Little St John Street

Little St John Street curves round to the N of the N half of the amphitheatre (Walk 7). To the E of the telephone exchange, Lumley Place is a picturesque terrace of seven cottages built in brown patterned brick, probably by John Douglas. Lumley Place, the N side of Little St John Street to its S, the N side of Vicar's Lane, and Priory Place leading off Love Street are all part of the Grosvenor Estates.

South-east of Lumley Place is the former Grosvenor St John's School, founded by Robert, Earl Grosvenor, and Countess Grosvenor in 1810 for the free education of poor children. After three years in temporary accommodation the school moved to premises in Little St John Street in 1813. When Hemingway described it in 1831 some 500 children were being taught there, with their materials supplied free; on each New Year's Day

> an excellent dinner of roast beef and plum-pudding is provided at his lordship's cost, who, with other branches of his family, usually attend; when his lordship delivers an appropriate address to the scholars, distributing an immense quantity of books to those children who have been returned by the master as deserving of distinction for their progress in learning or good behaviour.

'His lordship' was, in the year when Hemingway's *History of Chester* was published, created first Marquess of Westminster; he died in 1845.

The school building of 1813 was demolished 70 years later when a new and improved school was opened. This was designed for the first Duke of Westminster, the founder's grandson, by E.R. Robson (1835–1917), architect to the London School Board. After the Second World War

Grosvenor St John's School became a junior and infant school, then a junior school alone, and finally an annexe to the neighbouring Love Street girls' school. It closed in 1967. In 1974 the building was reopened as the British Heritage Exhibition, not to be confused with the Chester Heritage Centre (Walk 5). The British Heritage Exhibition, a privately owned institution, incorporates an audio-visual presentation of Chester's history, displays of maps and prints, and a reconstruction of the Rows as they appeared in the mid 19th century. Associated with the Exhibition is an organization that promotes guided tours of Chester and the surrounding area.

St John's church

The entrance to St John's church faces the British Heritage Exhibition. Like St Peter's at the Cross (Walk 1), this church will often be found locked when no one is available to supervise visitors. Enquiries about access should be made to the Rector of Chester Team Parish, at the Rectory in Vicar's Lane (telephone Chester 26357).

In 1892 the Reverend Samuel Cooper Scott, who had become vicar 15 years earlier, published his *Lectures on the History of S. John Baptist Church and Parish.* He accepted the traditional claim that St John's was founded before the Norman Conquest, either by King Aethelred of Mercia in 689 or by Aethelred, *ealdorman* of Mercia, and his wife Aethelflaed, Alfred the Great's daughter, in the early 10th century. It is known that Peter, Bishop of Lichfield (1072–85), transferred his see to Chester in 1075 and that his successor, Robert de Limesey (1086–1117), removed it to Coventry in 1102. During the intervening 27 years St John's church was the cathedral of the diocese, and it is said to have retained the status of a cathedral even after the removal of the see to Coventry. The church was collegiate, and at the time of its dissolution in 1547 or 1548 was served by a dean, seven canons, and four minor canons. After the dissolution it became a parish church.

Part of the church fell out of use after it had lost its collegiate status, and the E end of the chancel, the Lady Chapel, and the choir chapels built in the 14th century now only survive as ruins outside the church. The N and S transepts have been truncated, so that all that remains as a place of worship is most of the nave with N and S aisles, the crossing, and the westermost part of the chancel or choir.

The exterior of the church looks Victorian. This appearance is partly the result of a restoration by R.C. Hussey undertaken between 1860 and 1866. The E window, Norman in style but un-Norman in size, was designed by T.M. Penson in 1863. The NE clock tower of 1887 and the NW porch of 1882, however, owe their origin to a dramatic event that occurred on the evening of 14 April 1881 and the following morning, Good Friday, when the W tower of the church collapsed. Scott described the event graphically:

> I was aroused by a rumbling noise, which was succeeded by a terribly and indescribably long drawn-out crash, or rather rattle, as though a troop of horse artillery was galloping over an iron road; this was mingled with a clash of bells, and when it had increased to a horrible and almost unbearable degree, it suddenly ceased, and was succeeded by perfect stillness.

In its ruin the tower demolished the Early English porch. The porch was rebuilt, as a reproduction of the old one, by John Douglas, but it proved impossible to raise the money required to rebuild the tower.

In his *Lectures* Scott described how, on his first visit to St John's in 1868, he was disappointed by its exterior but impressed by the grandeur within. The nave of the church, and the crossing, are Norman work of the early 12th century undertaken at about the time when the see was removed to Coventry. Above is a triforium in Transitional style, which has been dated to the end of the same century; the clerestory is in the Early English style of the 13th century. The Norman work at St John's is more impressive, because it has been preserved better, than that in the Cathedral (Walk 2).

A medieval wall painting said to represent St John the Baptist has survived on a pier at the NE corner of the nave. Three 14th-century effigies are also preserved. A painted wooden board known as the Mace Board commemorates those Mayors of Chester from 1529 to 1794 who lived within St John's parish. There are also painted heraldic memorials executed by members of the Holme family (Walk 6), a good Classical monument to Diana Warburton (d. 1693), and stained glass in the E window, by Clayton and Bell, commemorating the marriage of Edward, Prince of Wales, later King Edward VII, in 1863. The reredos was designed by John Douglas in 1877 and commemorates Scott's predecessor as vicar.

Vicar's Lane and Union Street

To the NE of St John's church a red-brick town house of the mid 18th century, now occupied by the Grosvenor Club, was until 1957 the vicarage of St John's. For some reason it was often referred to as the rectory. The Grosvenor Club moved there from the building NW of the Eastgate that Douglas had designed for it (Walk 1). The vicarage was re-sited in a house of 1892 at the corner of Vicar's Lane and Love Street. This house is now the rectory of Chester Team Parish.

A small red-brick pedimented building next door to the Grosvenor Club is St John's parish room. It was built in 1888. To the E and set back from the street is the former Blue Girls' School, founded in 1720 for the instruction of poor girls. In the early 19th century instruction was said to be in 'religious and moral duties, and . . . every part of household business; such as washing, cleaning, plain cooking, sewing, knitting, etc.' Girls were expected to enter domestic service when they left the school. In the early 19th century the school was housed in St Martin's in the Fields, now part of the inner ring road. The school house was demolished in 1865 to enable extensions to be made to the Infirmary (Walk 4) and in 1872 the new building was erected in Vicar's Lane. The school was closed in 1940.

Vicar's Lane becomes Union Street E of the junction with Love Street. To the S is a convent founded on this site in 1913 for the Little Sisters of the Assumption, who had established themselves in Chester as nurses two years earlier. It is now the house of the Sisters of Charity.

On the N side of Union Street, at its junction with Bath Street, are the City Baths opened in 1901. They were public baths open all the year round, unlike the floating bath of the 1890s (Walk 7), which was only in use during the summer months. Social segregation was practised here as it was in the mid-19th-century baths at the NW corner of the walls (Walk 4). There were two swimming baths, named 'Atlantic' and 'Pacific', with admission charges of sixpence and twopence respectively. The bath building was designed by Douglas and Minshull with an upper storey in black-and-white.

Grosvenor Park

John Douglas's work also appears in the entrance lodge to the Grosvenor Park. It is a black-and-white building dating from the late 1860s. It bears carvings representing the Norman Earls of Chester – a common theme in Chester; they appear in stained glass in the Town Hall (Walk 1) and their arms are shown at each end of the Queen's Park Suspension Bridge (Walk 7).

In 1867 Richard Grosvenor, second Marquess of Westminster, presented the Corporation with about 20 acres of land, which became in due course the Grosvenor Park. The park's designer was Edward Kemp, who was a pupil of Sir Joseph Paxton, architect of the Crystal Palace, and had supervised the execution of Paxton's work at Birkenhead Park in the 1840s. The statue of the second Marquess, by Thomas Thornycroft, was erected in 1869; it was believed to have been carved from a single piece of marble, but in the winter of 1869–70 a part of one shoulder that had been let in to the block became loose. Thornycroft is famous as the sculptor of Queen Boudicca's statue near Westminster Bridge in London.

The park contains an ornamental pond, a children's playground, and a scented garden for blind people to enjoy. The Shipgate, which formerly stood W of the Bridgegate (Walk 6), has been re-erected in the park, together with a surviving arch from St Mary's nunnery near the Castle (Walk 5).

Grosvenor Park Road

On the W side of Grosvenor Park Road is the Roman Catholic church of St Werburgh [13]. It was built between 1873 and 1875 and opened in 1876. The architect was Edmund Kirby of Liverpool, who designed many Catholic and other churches in the North-West in the late 19th century; St Werburgh's was designed early in his career. As originally planned, the church, which is in an Early English style, would have had a spire 200 ft high, but because of a shortage of funds this was never built and, indeed, the E end of the church could not be completed until 1914.

The E side of Grosvenor Park Road is all Douglas. It contains a Baptist church in Early English style, built in red brick, and a terrace of large red-brick houses with Tudor-Gothic detailing. The whole group dates from the late 1870s and is comparable with that architect's Grosvenor Club building in Eastgate Street (Walk 1).

Foregate Street

Foregate Street is, as explained above (Walk 3), the street 'before', that is to the E of, the Eastgate. It follows the line of the main Roman road out of Chester to the N of Britain. Excavations undertaken when buildings have been demolished in Foregate Street have revealed evidence of a *vicus* or civil settlement that existed outside the Eastgate in Roman times.

Foregate Street is not Chester's most attractive approach. At its E end it has since the late 1960s become a complex system of traffic gyration, so that vehicles approaching Chester from the E only reach Foregate Street by way of Grosvenor Park Road, Union Street, and Love Street. At the W end, towards St John Street and Frodsham Street, it becomes very busy, for Chester's chain stores have tended to congregate in that area: C. & A., Tesco, Marks & Spencer, British Home Stores, and Littlewoods are all at that end of Foregate Street.

To the S, there are two side streets worth brief investigation. Bath Street, which leads to the old City Baths, has another terrace in which Douglas took a hand; the houses are on a much smaller scale, with Gothic decorations and stone fronted, and are about 25 years later than those in Grosvenor Park Road. Love Street, and Priory Place, which leads off to the W of it, have Grosvenor Estate terraced cottages of 1898–9. On the E side, S of the Co-operative department store, is all that is left of the late-18th-century Forest House, which originally had a large oval courtyard to the N facing Foregate Street. In the early 19th century Forest House was the residence of Colonel Roger Barnston (d. 1837), who became Colonel of the Chester local militia in 1803. The Barnston family came from Churton, S of Chester.

South of Forest House is the former Love Street Council School opened in 1909 to replace a Wesleyan school in St John Street. From 1944 to 1967 it was a secondary modern school, for children of both sexes until 1953 and afterwards for girls alone. In 1967 it was taken over by St Werburgh's Roman Catholic junior school, which had originally been housed in Queen Street.

In the 18th and early 19th centuries Love Street was well known as the home of Chester's clay-pipe manufacture: in 1840 five of the seven clay-pipe makers named in a local directory had premises there. The making of tobacco pipes, a craft said to have been introduced to Chester by Dutch settlers, produced one of the city's chief exports in the 18th century; but Hemingway noted in 1831 that the manufacture was by then only for the home market.

Hemingway described the houses that then lined the W

side of Love Street as 'a range of miserable cottages, few of which are one remove for convenience or appearance, above an Irish cabin'. There is little sign today, either in Love Street or in Foregate Street, that until late in the 19th century this area was one of the most crowded in Chester, with residential courtyards and passages leading off Foregate Street on both sides. In 1879 Bateman's Court, Edwards's Court, Hamilton Court, Crown Court, Crossgun Court, and Parry's Entry between them contained 102 houses. These slum areas have disappeared in the course of several generations of modernization of the street, which is now commercial rather than residential.

A few buildings of interest have survived. No. 70 on the S side bears the date 1571, though supporting evidence for that dating is not known and the building itself appears to be of the mid 17th century. It is timber-framed, with its upper storey overhanging the pavement and supported on timber columns. On the opposite side, Nos. 75 and 77 are also timber-framed and of roughly the same date. There are three heavily restored black-and-white inns, the Old Nag's Head and the Old Queen's Head on the N side and the Royal Oak on the S. At the E corner of Foregate Street and Queen Street is a Georgian brick building with an arcade at ground-floor level. Opposite is the C. & A. department store, opened in 1972. Its construction involved the demolition of the Classic Cinema and the Swan Hotel. Although designed (by the Building Design Partnership) in a modern idiom the structure does not harm the character of the street as a whole, and in 1973 it was awarded a Civic Trust commendation as one of the best contributions of 1972 to civic design. Between Nos. 30 and 32 on the S side a passage leads to the surviving S and E sides of the Union Hall of 1809. Like the now vanished Commercial Hall on the N side of Foregate Street (Walk 3), it was a block of shops arranged on two floors around a central courtyard; it was built to accommodate tradesmen visiting the annual fairs in July and October. In the early 19th century it was the first home of the Grosvenor St John's School, which later established itself in Vicar's Lane.

Walk Nine

Queen Street

Queen Street could have been one of Chester's most attractive minor thoroughfares, like King Street (Walk 3) or White Friars (Walk 5). It contained several listed buildings, including Georgian terraced houses and the late-18th-century Congregational church. Unfortunately many of these buildings were allowed to deteriorate beyond hope of practical restoration. At the time of writing (September 1978) most of those on the W side, including the church, have been demolished to make way for a new commercial complex to be sited between Canal Side and Foregate Street.

On the E side of Queen Street most of the buildings are still standing. They include some Georgian houses at the N end, near the Shropshire Union Canal, and the former Welsh Methodist chapel of 1884. Built of red brick in a Norman style, this chapel was closed early in the 1970s.

The Congregational church, which formerly stood on the W side of Queen Street N of the junction with Union Walk, was demolished in 1978. The congregation it housed broke away in the 18th century from Matthew Henry's chapel in Trinity Street (Walk 4) and established itself as a separate church in 1772. The first pastor, William Armitage, preached a sermon on 5 November 1772, which, he claimed afterwards, attracted several people who might otherwise have attended the ill-fated puppet show held in Watergate Street on that evening (Walk 4), the scene of a major disaster occasioned by the explosion of a barrel of gunpowder. Those who attended Mr Armitage's sermon instead of the puppet show understandably regarded their escape as providential.

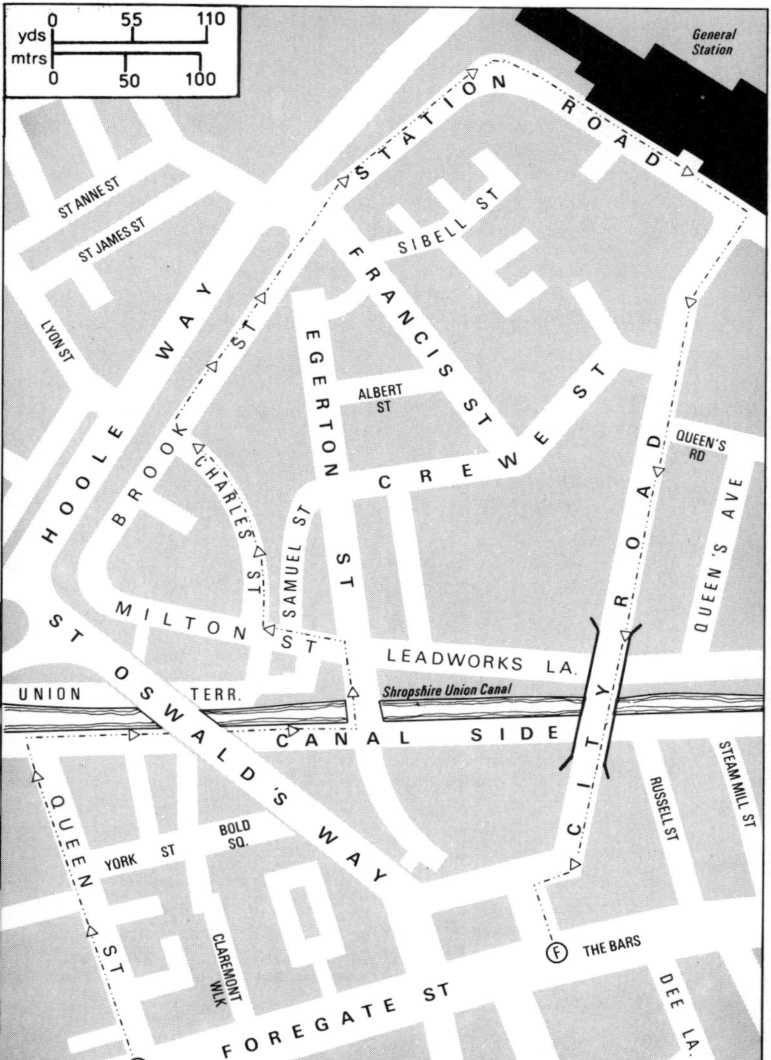
0
55
110
yds
mtrs
0
50
100
General Station
STATION ROAD
ST ANNE ST
ST JAMES ST
SIBELL ST
FRANCIS ST
LYON ST
HOOLE WAY
BROOK ST
EGERTON ST
ALBERT ST
CREWE ST
QUEEN'S RD
CHARLES ST
SAMUEL ST
CITY ROAD
QUEEN'S AVE
MILTON ST
ST OSWALD'S WAY
LEADWORKS LA.
UNION TERR.
Shropshire Union Canal
CANAL SIDE
STEAM MILL ST
RUSSELL ST
QUEEN ST
YORK ST
BOLD SQ.
CLAREMONT WLK
THE BARS
DEE LA.
FOREGATE ST
S
F

The chapel itself appears to have been built between 1776 and 1777 and enlarged in the early 19th century. It was a brick building with a stone façade in Greek Revival style. In 1966 a new church was opened for its congregation at Vicar's Cross to the E of the city, and the Queen Street building became a furniture warehouse.

The area N of Union Walk and W of Queen Street was known formerly as the Jousting Croft; according to tradition the medieval pursuit of tilting was practised there.

Canal Side to Brook Street

The remainder of this walk concentrates particularly on a theme in Chester's history unnoticed by most tourists: its development as an industrial and a railway town in the 19th century. The origin of the Shropshire Union Canal has been described in connexion with the Northgate locks (Walk 4). In the Canal Side district Chester's townscape is that of an industrialized area. To the S of the canal, E of Queen Street, is the former flour mill of Messrs Griffiths, an early-19th-century structure badly damaged by fire in October 1975 and now in ruinous condition. The canal towpath passes under the viaduct that carries the NE section of the inner ring road, opened in 1971. To its E across the canal is another former flour mill built in the mid 19th century. It was closed down *c.*1970 and reopened in 1974 as a furniture warehouse.

Further E again, the canal is crossed by a road bridge, with Seller Street to the S and Egerton Street to the N. These streets were laid out early in the 19th century; Seller Street was built by and named after Alderman Seller, who owned a brewery in Foregate Street. The canal bridge was built at the expense of Thomas Lunt, who owned an iron foundry N of the canal. At the S end of Seller Street Lunt laid out Bold Square, named after the family who formerly owned a mansion there, as a residential area for 'the man of slender independence'. Hemingway, praising Lunt's schemes, thought that the improvements when completed would make the area 'one of the most interesting parts of this city'.

North of the canal bridge, Milton Street and Charles Street lead to Brook Street. Between Charles Street and Egerton Street is the factory of the Hydraulic Engineering Company, one of Chester's leading industrial concerns. Here we seem far away from the Chester of Rows, walls, and timber-framed buildings. This factory started in 1805 as the Flookersbrook Foundry of William Cole, Thomas Whittle, and John Johnson. The title 'Hydraulic Engineering Company' dates from 1874; from that time the factory produced hydraulic lifts, cranes, and similar machinery, specializing in hydraulic-powered hoists used for coaling steamships.

Until the construction of City Road, Brook Street was the approach road to Chester from the General Station. It also carried all the traffic from Hoole and areas to the NE of Chester, which approached the city by way of Cow Lane Bridge and Frodsham Street (Walk 3). In 1859 Thomas Hughes, in the edition of the *Stranger's Handbook* published that year, described the route from the station to the city centre as 'in many parts inconveniently narrow, abounding in sharp curves and unsightly projections, and certainly in nowise equal to the continually increasing traffic'. Brook Street is now a one-way street used as a secondary shopping area; to the N a dual carriageway carries the traffic to and from Hoole and the NE.

Brook Street ends, to the E, in a complex road junction. To the N, on the far side of the dual carriageway, is the mid-19th-century suburb of Newtown. This was an area of working-class housing designed to meet the needs of workers on the railway and in associated trades. Its eastern boundary is marked by Black Diamond Street, which, as its name implies, was given over to coal merchants. Christ Church in Newtown was established in 1838 and rebuilt by Douglas during the last quarter of the 19th century. Much of the S part of Newtown has been demolished and three high-rise blocks of flats now dominate it.

South-east of the Brook Street–Egerton Street intersection is another, but slightly later, area of artisans' houses. These too were provided with an Anglican place of worship,

St Bartholomew's in Sibell Street, built in 1877 as a chapel of ease to St John's church (Walk 8), in whose parish the area lay. Again, much of the original housing has been replaced by flats.

Chester General Station

East of the intersection Brook Street continues as Station Road, which curves to the right and passes in front of the General Station, with the postal sorting office on the opposite side.

The first railways came to Chester in 1840. In September of that year a line was opened from Chester to Birkenhead, and in the following month the one from Chester to Crewe. In 1846 Chester was connected with Ruabon. By 1848 the Chester and Holyhead Railway had reached Bangor, and in 1849 a branch S to Mold was opened. Another line, opened in the following year, headed NE from Chester to Warrington. The line from Tattenhall Junction S to Whitchurch was opened in 1872. The early lines were built by individual companies, but many takeovers and mergers took place in the mid 19th century; by the end of the century all these lines, which connected at the General Station, were under the control of the London and North Western and Great Western Railway Companies.

From 1840 to 1848 a temporary station was used to the N of the present General Station. The latter was built between 1847 and 1848. Its architects were C.H. Wild and Francis Thompson; the contractor was Thomas Brassey, who is commemorated in St Erasmus' chapel in the Cathedral (Walk 2). The station has always been regarded as a significant contribution to the city's architecture. Its façade [37] is of brick, with stone dressings; the detailing is Classical, in an Italianate style. Its great size was dictated by its need to accommodate not only a large number of trains but also the administrative offices of the railway companies using it.

Thomas Hughes, in the *Stranger's Handbook,* quotes

impressive statistics about the station and its facilities in the mid 19th century. In the refreshment rooms 'the utmost wish of your soul will be incontinently gratified', he promised. There were then 'upwards of ninety-eight' arrivals and departures of passenger trains each day. By the late 1920s that number had doubled, and the station, with 20 platforms in active use, was at its zenith. Even after the post-war cutbacks in railway services Chester station has remained very busy. In the summer of 1978 more than 100 passenger trains departed from it on an ordinary weekday, in spite of the fact that several of the services established in the 19th century no longer run. The lines to Mold, and from Tattenhall Junction to Whitchurch, have been abandoned. The last through train from Birkenhead to Paddington ran in 1967; the service to Birkenhead now terminates at Rock Ferry, where passengers change to the Merseyrail underground line. On the other hand, the closure of Chester Northgate Station at the end of the 1960s resulted in the diversion of trains from Manchester (Oxford Road) to the General Station. This line, opened to passengers in 1875, had been operated by the Cheshire Lines Committee. The Great Central Line from Chester to Hawarden Bridge, opened in 1890 and served by Northgate and Liverpool Road Stations, has now lost its passenger traffic altogether.

City Road

City Road was laid out early in the 1860s as a better approach to Chester than the old route by Brook Street and Frodsham Street. As indicated above, Hughes lamented the inadequacy of the old approach to Chester in 1859. Ten years later he was able to write in another edition of the *Stranger's Handbook*: 'It is not too much to say of City Road and the Station adjoining that few cities or towns now equal Chester, either in respect of railway accommodation or in the convenience of access to it'.

City Road is straight and wide, and leads to Foregate Street at the Bars, though the junction is now part of a complex gyratory traffic system (Walk 8). From 1879 to 1930 it formed the first stage of Chester's main tramway route. A service of horse-drawn trams began in Chester in 1879. The route went down City Road and along Foregate Street and Eastgate Street to the Cross. The trams then headed S down Bridge Street, turned into Grosvenor Street, passed the Castle, and travelled over the Grosvenor Bridge. South of the river they headed W for Saltney. In the *Stranger's Handbook* of 1899 the visitor to Chester with little time to spend was advised to take a tram to the Grosvenor Bridge and return by the same route, since this would introduce him to something of the character of the city.

At the turn of the century the tramway, run hitherto by a private company, was taken over by the Corporation, and the system was electrified on the overhead-wire system. Extensions to the original route were made along Boughton and for a short distance E along Tarvin and Christleton Roads. Plans for further extensions were never taken up, and Chester abandoned its electric trams in favour of motor buses in 1930. The trams have left their legacy in Tramway Street and Car Street S of the General Station, which now lead into the Corporation's bus depot, formerly the tram shed. In those streets short sections of tram track can still be seen. Chester City continues to operate its own bus services, though many of its suburbs are served not by Corporation but by Crosville routes.

At the N end of City Road there are two hotels facing each other across it, the Queen and the Albion. The Queen dates from 1860, though it was badly damaged by fire in 1861 and had to be rebuilt. The Albion, formerly the Queen Commercial Hotel, was opened by the company that owned the Queen in 1867. There are several other hotels at the end of City Road nearest the station.

There are two Nonconformist places of worship in City Road. On the E side is the Gothic Wesleyan Methodist Central Hall of 1873 [12], described in the 1899 *Stranger's Handbook* as 'a building of some pretensions'. It contrasts with the former Welsh Calvinistic Methodist chapel of 1864 [11] further along City Road on its W side, which is stuccoed and Classical with Ionic columns and a pediment. To G.A. Audsley, author of the 1899 edition of the *Stranger's Handbook*, 'Architecturally considered, the building lays no claim to the visitor's attention': Audsley disliked Classical architecture in Chester, and was equally critical of the bank at the W corner of Eastgate and St Werburgh Streets (Walk 1), which was built at about the same time as this church. The church became Presbyterian in the 20th century.

The chapel of 1864 was built as nearly as possible on the site of the Octagon Chapel, which had been demolished to make way for City Road. The Octagon Chapel had been built for the Wesleyan Methodists in 1766 and had served as their church in Chester until they moved to St John Street in 1811 (Walk 8).

Between the Methodist Central Hall and the Presbyterian chapel City Road crosses the Shropshire Union Canal by a bridge built in 1866. The view to the E along the canal [36] shows more of Chester's early-19th-century industrial development. On the S side a large building named 'Milns Seeds' incorporates the steam-powered flour mill that gave its name to Steam Mill Street; parts of the building are obviously of the early 19th century. The mill was owned by the Frost family, who became prominent in Chester's local government. Sir Thomas and Robert Frost were each three times Mayor of Chester; Meadows Frost was Mayor twice; James Garrett Frost was Mayor at the time of Edward VII's coronation in 1902.

Further to the E, on the N side of the canal, is the Chester leadworks, whose tall chimney and shot tower are prominent features of Chester's skyline. It was established by Walker, Parker and Company at the beginning of the last century to produce red and white lead as well as lead shot. The circular tower is designed so that molten lead can be dropped inside it: during the fall it solidifies as round shot. Very few shot towers have survived (probably the most famous, though no longer in use, is the one on the S bank of the Thames in London, which featured in the Festival of Britain exhibition in 1951).

South of the canal bridge is the former Royalty Theatre,

not to be confused with the Theatre Royal (Walk 1). It was built in 1882. When it was described by Audsley in 1899 as 'entirely devoid of external effect' it was the only theatre in Chester. Among music-hall stars of the early 20th century who performed there were Albert Chevalier, G.H. Elliott, Sir Harry Lauder, and Marie Lloyd. By 1966, when its licence was surrendered, it was variously used for pantomime, opera, wrestling, and bingo. In 1978 it was opened as a skateboard rink.

City Road ends at the Bars, so named because in the Middle Ages an outer gate in the city's defences stood there. The junction of City Road and Foregate Street is now part of a complex traffic system. On the SE corner of City Road is a stone-built former bank building by Lockwood. Opposite is a red-brick building with a stepped gable in Flemish or Dutch Renaissance style. It was designed by John Douglas in 1884 as the Cheshire police headquarters; a black-and-white extension to its W has been demolished.

Chester Suburbs

Until the 19th century most of Chester lay within the medieval walls. The only significant suburban developments were in Handbridge across the Old Dee Bridge (Walk 7); for a short distance N of the Northgate (Walk 3) along the Liverpool and Parkgate Roads; and to the E, along Foregate Street (Walk 8) and beyond into Boughton. The 19th century witnessed the development of new suburbs, some of which have been treated in these perambulations as 'inner city' areas. South of the river Queen's Park (Walk 7) and Curzon Park were developed as fashionable estates of villa residences in the middle of the century, while the principal roads into Chester became lined with prosperous gentlemen's residences towards the end of the century. The latter can be seen along the Liverpool Road, and in Hough Green, the road from Chester to Saltney and North Wales, as well as in Hoole (see below). At the same time, i.e. from *c.*1850, industrial development and especially the coming of the railways (Walk 9) resulted in the growth of working-class suburban areas, such as Newtown and parts of Hoole and the Parkgate Road–Garden Lane area. This expansion was into former agricultural land; there are no significant medieval or Tudor or Stuart remains in Chester's suburbs.

Boughton

The name 'Boughton' is rather confusing to a non-Cestrian, because it has different meanings in different contexts. It describes the main road E from the city, to the E of the Bars (Walk 9). It also describes the suburb at the E end of that

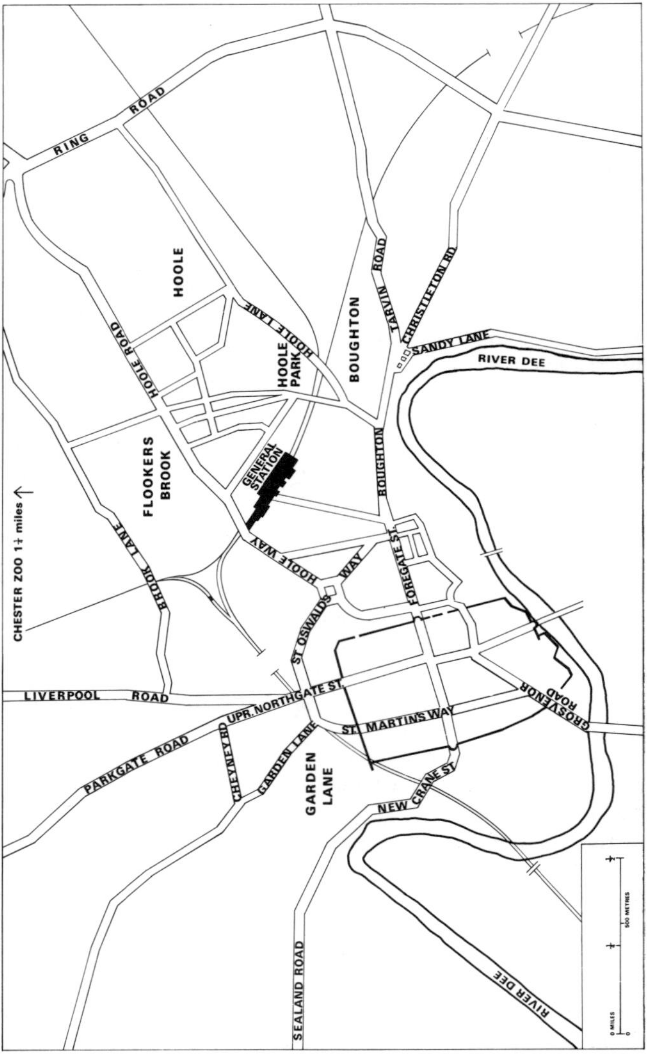
RING ROAD
HOOLE
HOOLE ROAD
HOOLE LANE
HOOLE PARK
BOUGHTON
TARVIN ROAD
CHRISTLETON RD
SANDY LANE
RIVER DEE
GENERAL STATION
FLOOKERS BROOK
BOUGHTON
CHESTER ZOO 1½ miles
BROOK LANE
HOOLE WAY
FOREGATE ST.
ST. OSWALDS WAY
LIVERPOOL ROAD
UPR. NORTHGATE ST.
ST. MARTINS WAY
GROSVENOR ROAD
PARKGATE ROAD
CHEYNEY RD
GARDEN LANE
GARDEN LANE
NEW CRANE ST
SEALAND ROAD
RIVER DEE

road, where the Tarvin and Christleton Roads diverge. Finally, it is an element in 'Great Boughton', a village that lay slightly further E between the Tarvin and Christleton Roads.

The road named Boughton is not the most pleasant of Chester's approach roads. To the N, between it and the canal, there has been much demolition of mid-19th-century terraced housing. The N side of the road, for some distance E of the Bars, is lined by small shops. To the S there has also been more recent demolition, this time to allow the road to be widened. Boughton was formerly just wide enough for three traffic lanes, but it proved totally inadequate to cope with commuter traffic at rush hours, and widening is currently (1978) in progress.

Hoole Lane branches off to the NE to cross the Shropshire Union Canal. West of its junction with Boughton there were formerly two schools, St Paul's elementary, later junior and infant, and Boughton Industrial School. Both have now been demolished. The Industrial School was opened as a ragged school in 1852.* At that time some of the meanest of Chester's slums were in the Boughton area. Some years later it became an industrial school, to which magistrates could commit juveniles who had been convicted of minor offences, and later a reformatory. It closed in 1929.

Further E in Boughton there is some late-Georgian and Regency housing bearing witness to its popularity as a genteel suburb at the beginning of the 19th century. It was valued for its views over the Dee. In 1830 an Anglican church was built on the S side of the road, as a chapel of ease to St John's parish church. It was Classical in style, and Thomas Hughes wrote disparagingly of it in 1856: 'What is this white conventicle-looking edifice . . .? Surely it is the refuge of some Mormon congregation – the temple, perchance, of some pagan fanaticism? Nay verily, good sirs, – assuage your indignation, for here is a Church of your own communion. . . . One less becoming the outward character of a Church it is impossible to conceive'.

The chapel of ease was made into a distinct parish church

* Like the Bishop Graham Memorial School (Walk 3) and St Olave's Ragged School (Walk 6), it was controlled by the Chester Ragged School Society.

in 1846. Thirty years later it was rebuilt by John Douglas in Early English red brick, and in 1900 the timber framed S aisle and W porch were added. The spire carries a clock by Joyce of Whitchurch. Inside, the church embodies Victorian and *Art Nouveau* furnishings and decor; the guidebook obtainable there describes it justly as 'the finest Victorian Church in Chester'. To the E is the Campbell Memorial Hall, by Lockwood, built in the 1890s as a recreational centre for the parish in memory of the Reverend Edward Augustus Pitcairn Campbell (d. 1892) by his widow.

To the W of St Paul's church a small public garden overlooking the river marks the site of Gallows Hill. Until the beginning of the 19th century, when the Northgate gaol (Walk 3) and later the city gaol near the Infirmary (Walk 4) were used, this was the place of public execution of condemned criminals. It was the scene of two martyrdoms: of an Anglican priest, George Marsh, in 1555, during the persecution of Protestants in the reign of Queen Mary – a commemorative obelisk records the event; of the Roman Catholic priest John Plessington, later canonized, in 1679. The last three executions there took place on 9 May 1801; one of the three prisoners condemned for burglary attempted to escape but was drowned in the Dee; the other two were kept waiting until his body was recovered, when it was hung in chains with them. This story is recounted by Hemingway in his list of executions from the 16th century to 1829.

Further E, to the N of Boughton, are the reservoirs and water tower of the Chester Waterworks Company. From Roman times onwards, wells and springs at Boughton and Christleton were used to supplement the supply of water available from the Dee. The Conduit at the Cross (Walk 1) was the terminus of a water main from Boughton laid in the 16th century. In the following century new waterworks were constructed at the Bridgegate (Walk 6), but by the early 19th century all existing supplies had become inadequate and a Waterworks Company was set up in 1829. When Hemingway wrote, it cost 30 shillings a year for a supply of water.

South of the junction between Tarvin and Christleton Roads is a small burial ground. It marks the site of St Giles' hospital, founded as a refuge for lepers under the control of St Werburgh's abbey by Earl Ranulph III of Chester (1181–1232). The hospital itself with its chapel is said to have been destroyed during the siege of Chester in 1645. The burial ground was used for victims of the plagues of the 16th and 17th centuries. Because of the presence of the hospital, Boughton was known formerly as Spital Boughton to distinguish it from Great Boughton to the E.

A walk of about half a mile along Sandy Lane, to the S of Christleton Road, takes one downhill to the bank of the Dee. From there, good views extend towards the early-19th-century houses of Boughton and St Paul's church.

Parkgate Road and Garden Lane

Parkgate Road and Liverpool Road diverge N of the Northgate roundabout. On the W side of Parkgate Road is the church of St Thomas of Canterbury. This is an Anglican church in Early English style designed by Sir George Gilbert Scott and erected in the late 1860s; it was originally designed to have a tower, but that was never built. Confusingly, the church became a parish church in 1881, for the parish of St Oswald, whose church had formerly been the S transept of the Cathedral (Walk 2). The vicarage, immediately S of the church, is by Douglas.

To the N, on the corner of Cheyney Road and Parkgate Road, is Chester College. This was established in 1839 as a Church of England training college for schoolteachers. The administrative building fronting Cheyney Road is in a Tudor style, though with a modern entrance porch, and was completed in 1842; it was opened by W.E. Gladstone. In 1847 its chapel, in the Decorated style, was opened; the furnishings were made by students at the college. In its early days the college incorporated two schools: one was a boys' elementary school, which later became a central and a secondary modern school for boys and closed in 1963; the other was a commercial and agricultural school, which took in boarders. Numerous extensions were made to the original college buildings, including laboratories, gymnasia, and a swimming pool, besides several halls of residence in a mixture of architectural styles and media. The college is dominated by the glass and concrete Price Tower completed in 1971 and named after the Reverend A.J. Price, principal from 1953 to 1965. Since the mid 1970s Chester College has been reorganized to offer degree courses as well as teacher-training courses. Its history is described in J.L. Bradbury, *Chester College and the Training of Teachers* (1975).

Cheyney Road leads W to cross the Shropshire Union Canal's northern branch from Chester to Ellesmere Port. To the S is Garden Lane, an area of late-19th-century red-brick terraced houses. Like Newtown (Walk 9) this is a reminder of Chester's growth in the late 19th century; Garden Lane is typical of the inner suburbs of most English towns.

Hoole and Flookersbrook

Hoole Road crosses the railway by a large bridge N of the Station (Walk 9). The bridge is inconveniently narrow, for it carries all the traffic between Chester and the N, leading ultimately to the M56, Warrington, and Manchester. To the N of the bridge is a magnificent example of the effect of railways on urban geography. By the end of the 19th century Chester was hemmed in to the N by two vast but unconnected triangular railway junctions. One, which is still in continuous use, divides the line from Chester to Rock Ferry and that from Chester to Wrexham and North Wales. The other and later junction fed the now demolished Northgate Station; one branch led E towards Manchester, the other W towards Hawarden. Only the N arm of this triangle has survived, parallel with Brook Lane; it is used only by freight trains. A third station was sited W of Liverpool Road near the junction with Brook Lane.

Immediately E of the railway line, but now mostly culverted, is Flookers Brook, a stream that gave its name to a 19th-century suburb. This suburb lay outside the city boundary. It is now more generally known as Hoole, since in the 1860s it was governed by Hoole Local Board, which in 1894 became Hoole Urban District; it was only absorbed into Chester City in the mid 1950s. For the student of suburban domestic architecture it presents curious contrasts in styles. All Saints' church in Hoole Road was built in 1867 and became a parish church five years later. In Hamilton Street near by, and in Ashby Place to the N of Hoole Road, there are houses built for prosperous citizens in the early 19th century. Along Hoole Road itself and for a short distance along some of the side streets there are later 19th-century villa residences, also marking considerable prosperity. To the N in the Ermine Street area, however, and particularly to the S of Hoole Road, are artisans' dwellings of the later 19th century. The growth of Hoole's population at that time was almost entirely the result of the railways, for whose workers these houses were built. Hoole developed its own suburban shopping centre in the Faulkner Street–Charles Street–Westminster Road area. Before the Second World War the Urban District Council had laid out Alexandra Park, to the E of the parish church. Beyond the park, and N of Hoole Road, further housing developments took place in the inter-war period, and have continued since 1945.

Chester Zoo

Chester Zoo is on the E edge of the suburb of Upton. It was founded in the early 1930s after Mr G.S. Mottershead (1894–1978) had purchased the site, Oakfield. The zoo, controlled by the North of England Zoological Society, extends over 700 acres. Many of the animals are housed in large paddocks rather than in cages, and the zoo is excellently landscaped with ornamental gardens and waterways. In 1977 Chester Zoo established a record when Jubilee, the first baby elephant to have been bred in the United Kingdom, was born.

There is a Crosville bus service to the zoo from Northgate Street.

Excursions

The following notes are intended for visitors to Chester who wish to travel outside the city but within a radius of about 30 miles. Chester is a good centre for excursions even further afield. The cities of Liverpool and Manchester are within easy reach both by car and by rail. The whole of Derbyshire and much of S Lancashire and SW Yorkshire are accessible to the motorist who does not object to a round trip of 120–50 miles. Roads in Wales are in general less good than those in England, and suffer much from weekend congestion; nevertheless the whole coast of North Wales and most of Snowdonia are within reach of Chester. The M6 has made it possible to reach Blackpool or even the Lake District and to return the same day. To give even a selective list of possible excursions within that range, however, would demand much more space than is available here.

Areas of interest will be described in a clockwise direction, beginning with the Wirral peninsula.

North-West

There are two main roads up the Wirral peninsula from Chester; they begin as the Parkgate and Liverpool Roads, which diverge N of the Northgate roundabout. The Parkgate Road (A540) is rural until Heswall is reached, about 12 miles NW of Chester. A diversion should be made through Neston to Parkgate, the last of Chester's outer havens and the point of embarkation for Ireland in the 18th century. Parkgate became an estuary resort, and it preserves a waterfront promenade, though the Dee has receded from it. The Wirral Country Park is a system of public footpaths using abandoned railway track. Beyond Heswall there are picturesque views from the A540 around Thurstaston, and the road then drops down to West Kirby. West Kirby is partly a seaside resort, and partly a commuter town for Birkenhead and Liverpool. There are fine views across the estuary of the Dee to the hills of Clwyd, and at low tide it is possible to walk across the sands to Hilbre Island. Hoylake is another resort; it faces the Irish Sea. To the E are Bidston Hill, a well-known viewpoint, and New Brighton on the Mersey estuary.

The Liverpool Road becomes the A41 N of Upton. A diversion can be made N from it to Ellesmere Port, where there is interesting canal architecture at the N end of the Shropshire Union Canal and a new waterway museum. The A41 passes Hooton and Eastham; Eastham was the terminus of a ferry service from Liverpool. North of Bebington is Port Sunlight, the model village created by Lever Brothers for their employees at the end of the 19th century. At Port Sunlight the Lady Lever Art Gallery contains important collections of 19th-century paintings and furniture. A detour from the main road at Rock Ferry brings one to an interesting 19th-century villa estate with a riverside promenade from which there are good views over Liverpool. The A41 passes through Tranmere, and the shipbuilding yards of Cammell Laird are seen on the right. A road tunnel leads to Liverpool. Birkenhead preserves the remains of a medieval priory and some interesting examples of 19th-century town planning: e.g. Hamilton Square and Birkenhead Park (the park was laid out by Joseph Paxton in the mid 1840s).

North-East

The A56, which leads to the M56 and thus connects Chester with the national motorway network, tends to be congested as far as Dunham-on-the-Hill. Plemstall church to the S of the road contains interesting furnishings. Helsby Hill, and

Overton Hill above Frodsham, are good viewpoints from which Liverpool, the Mersey estuary, and the industrial areas of S Lancashire can be seen. Beyond Frodsham a road leads N to Runcorn, a riverside resort on the Mersey in the early 19th century that expanded into a port and industrial town and is now the nucleus of a New Town. Its features of interest include Norton Priory, the site of which has been revealed by archaeological excavations; the ruined castle of Halton, with some old houses near by; Shopping City and the housing estates of the New Town; and the Runcorn–Widnes road bridge opened in 1961 with, to its W, the railway bridge built a century earlier.

East

The A51, the Tarvin Road, leads E from Chester for five miles, after which it branches SE towards Nantwich. The eastward road continues as the A54. At Kelsall it passes through the Mid-Cheshire Ridge. To the N is Delamere Forest, a well-known tourist attraction with nature trails and picnic places provided. South of the A54 is an outlying part of the forest, and there are good views from the hills above Willington. On summer Sundays the gardens at Tirley Garth S of Kelsall are worth visiting for their display of rhododendrons and azaleas. The A556, which branches N from the A54, leads to the industrial town of Northwich; this is the centre of the Cheshire salt and chemical industry. At Anderton N of Northwich there is a lift to transfer canal boats from the Weaver Navigation to the Trent and Mersey Canal. North-east of Northwich is Knutsford, with its literary associations (Mrs Gaskell) and the unusual later 19th-century architecture of R.H. Watt. Near Knutsford is the imposing late-18th- and early-19th-century Tatton Hall in a vast park.

The A54 continues E through the salt and chemical towns of Winsford and Middlewich, and eventually leads to the medieval borough of Congleton, which, like Macclesfield nine miles to the NE, achieved prominence in the late 18th century as a centre for silk manufacture. Above Congleton and Macclesfield is the Pennine fringe of Cheshire, with hills of Millstone Grit.

South-East

The A51 passes through Tarvin and Tarporley, both of which have medieval churches, on its way to Nantwich. To the S of Tarporley, reached by minor roads, is the early-13th-century Beeston Castle. For the walker the Sandstone Trail has been dedicated as a waymarked path leading from Delamere Forest along the Mid-Cheshire Ridge as far as Bickerton in the S of the county; Beeston Castle is a good central point from which the Trail may be explored. Near by is the medieval church of Bunbury. Nantwich, like Northwich and Middlewich, was a salt-producing town in the Middle Ages. It is now a market town, with an impressive medieval church and several good timber-framed houses.

South

The Christleton Road, the A41, passes W of the Mid-Cheshire Ridge. A short detour SW of it leads to Malpas, where there are 18th-century buildings and one of the best medieval churches of Cheshire.

The B5130 leads S from Spital Boughton to Aldford and Farndon, two villages from which the Dee above Chester can be explored. South of Farndon minor roads lead across the Welsh border to Bangor-is-y-coed and Overton; SW of Overton is the 14th-century Chirk Castle.

Many of the villages S of Chester display Grosvenor influence, with model farmhouses, schools, and other buildings designed for the Eaton estate by Douglas or Lockwood. The finest examples are to be found at Eccleston, reached by a minor road from Handbridge. The mid-

Victorian Eaton Hall S of Eccleston was demolished in the 1960s except for its chapel, clock tower, and stables. The gardens are sometimes open to the public in summer.

South-West

The Wrexham Road (A483) S of the Grosvenor Bridge enters Wales at Rossett. Gresford and Wrexham have interesting churches, though their surroundings are industrialized. South of Wrexham is the late-17th- and early-18th-century Erddig Hall, a National Trust property. Beyond Ruabon a road branches W from the A483 to Llangollen in the Dee valley. About two miles W of Ruabon is the dramatic Pontcysylltau aqueduct of the Shropshire Union Canal. The Vale of Llangollen offers fine scenery and many survivals of industrial history.

West

Chester's main exit to North Wales is the A55 through Saltney, though a less congested route to the coast is by way of the Sealand Road (A548) N of the Dee, and the Queensferry road bridge. Hawarden preserves the remains of a medieval castle but is better known as the home of William Ewart Gladstone (1809–98), four times Prime Minister: 19th-century tourists were advised to make a pilgrimage to Hawarden Castle in the hope of seeing the great man, perhaps engaged in felling trees in the park.

The A494 leads through Mold to cross the Clwydian range. From Loggerheads the ascent can be made of Moel Famau (1,820 ft), a well-known viewpoint with the remains of Thomas Harrison's Jubilee Tower of 1810. The A541 passes through the range further N on its way to the medieval town of Denbigh. Further N again, the A55 is the main route from Chester to the North Wales coast, which it reaches at Abergele. At Holywell St Winifred's Well can be visited. The A548 is the coast road proper. At Flint it passes near the late-13th-century castle that commands the lower estuary of the Dee, and near Greenfield are the ruins of Basingwerk Abbey. Prestatyn and Rhyl are seaside resorts; beyond are Abergele, Colwyn Bay, and Llandudno, The roads to the North Wales coast, and those that lead via Denbigh or Ruthin to the A5 and Snowdonia, tend to be very congested during summer weekends.

☆

As a guidebook to the architecture of Cheshire N. Pevsner and E. Hubbard, *The Buildings of England: Cheshire* (1971) is essential. R. Richards, *Old Cheshire Churches* (1947; revised and enlarged edition 1973) is a valuable guide to ecclesiastical architecture. Elisabeth Beazley and P. Howell, *The Companion Guide to North Wales* (1975) is as indispensable for Clwyd as Pevsner and Hubbard are for Cheshire.

Appendix I: Chester Corporation

The Unreformed Corporation

No full-scale study has yet been made of the history of the Corporation of Chester in the Middle Ages, from the first recorded mention of Sheriffs and Mayors (see p. 15) up to the 'Great Charter' of 1506, which regulated it and probably added something to its powers. The process by which the guild merchant became the Corporation is still obscure. The system of local government in Chester from 1506 to 1835 underwent various changes, but, stated as simply as possible, the Corporation and its officers were as follows:

Common Councilmen: these numbered 40. In theory they were elected by the citizens, but in practice they decided who should fill any vacancies that arose.

Aldermen: there were 24. Again, in practice, they themselves filled casual vacancies as they arose.

The Mayor: originally elected on the Friday after the feast of St Denis (9 October) but later, in the 18th-century, on the Friday after 20 October. He was to be an alderman. Chosen in practice by the Corporation itself, in theory by election by the citizens. The Mayor presided over the court of Quarter Sessions established in 1506 and over the Portmote and Crownmote Courts, which were much earlier in origin. The Portmote was particularly concerned with civil actions dealing with land; the Crownmote was a criminal court established after Edward I's charter of 1300. The Mayor had admiralty powers over the Dee by virtue of the Black Prince's charter of 1354; he was also clerk of the market, and escheator. The latter office gave him power to take into custody the lands of dead tenants in chief of the Earl of Chester within the city, and to hold inquisitions into their value and the nearest heir.

The Recorder: in theory elected annually; in practice an alderman who was also a trained lawyer who held office until resignation or dismissal. In the 16th and 17th centuries the Recorder often represented the city as one of its M.P.s.

Justices of the Peace: these consisted of the Mayor and Recorder and all former Mayors. The Mayor and former Mayors also formed a kind of 'inner cabinet' known as 'the Mayor and his Brethren', which decided matters of policy.

Sheriffs: there were two, chosen annually, one by the Mayor and the other by the citizens, i.e. in practice by the Assembly. They presided over the *Pentice Court*, which dealt mainly with cases of debt.

Treasurers: two were elected each year. They also acted as *coroners* in the city, holding inquests in cases of unexplained death.

Leavelookers: these two officials had the duty of collecting certain customs payments and annual fines paid by those who were not freemen who traded in the city.

Murengers: two officials who were responsible for the repair of the city walls and for collecting *murage*, a tax imposed for that purpose. Sometimes '*Muragers*'.

Town Clerk: the chief legal official of the Corporation.

Minor Officials included a swordbearer, a mace-bearer, four serjeants at mace, four ministers of the Pentice Court, a yeoman of the Pentice, and a crier.

The Assembly is the name given to a meeting of the Mayor, aldermen, and common councilmen. Its decisions from 1539 are recorded in the *Assembly Books*.

Theoretically the city was divided into 12 wards for the purposes of local government elections. In practice, as has been shown, the Corporation, like so many others in England, became self-perpetuating.

Voters, members of the Assembly, and the major officials

had to be *freemen.* The freedom of the city could be obtained in several ways: by birth as the son of a freeman; by apprenticeship to a freeman; by purchase; and by special order of the Assembly. Traditionally the Mayor on his election had the power to create one freeman. The names and trades of new freemen were enrolled solemnly before the Mayor. The city of Chester has preserved its freemen; new ones are enrolled now in a ceremony, usually held annually, known as the Pentice Court in the Council Chamber of the Town Hall.

The Reformed Corporation

As a result of the *Municipal Corporations Act,* 1835, Chester, like most other ancient boroughs, found its electoral system radically reformed. The ratepayers were now to elect the councillors. The city was divided into five wards, each returning six councillors. The councillors, 30 in number, were to elect 10 aldermen. The councillors and aldermen together elected the Mayor. There was only one Sheriff, also elected annually. The Recorder and Treasurer were now paid officials, not members of the Council.

When the Corporation of 1835 came to an end in 1974, the number of six-councillor wards had been increased to seven. By that time much of the Council's work was delegated to standing committees of aldermen and councillors, and to special committees set up as required. In 1901 there were 16 standing committees, apart from the general purposes committee which consisted of the whole Council. During the 19th century there was also a vast increase in the number of paid officials employed by the Council as the scope of local government activities grew ever wider.

Since 1974

Under local government reorganization Chester City became a part of Chester District, which included the former

Chester and Tarvin Rural Districts. Aldermen were abolished. Chester applied successfully for the status of a borough, and then for that of a city; as a result the 'new' city of Chester, which includes places as far distant as Puddington to the NW and Malpas to the S, still has a Mayor and a Sheriff. The independence from county control that Chester had enjoyed as a county in itself since 1506 and as a county borough since 1888 was lost; Chester became one of eight districts of the new county of Cheshire.

Appendix II: The City Guilds

In the Middle Ages and afterwards there were many craft guilds established in Chester to regulate trade in their own particular fields. Freemen of the city were, and are, expected to belong to one of the guilds. In the list of the guilds that follows some unlikely juxtapositions of trades will be seen. These arose because many of the smaller guilds found that they could only survive financially by amalgamating with others. One of their heaviest burdens was the production of the Mystery Plays.

The history and records of the city guilds are described briefly by Miss Margaret J. Groombridge, first City Archivist in Chester, in the *Journal of the Chester Archaeological Society*, vol. 39 (1952), pp. 93–108.

The guilds still in existence are:

Tanners
Merchant Drapers and Hosiers
Brewers
Barbers, Surgeons, Wax and Tallow Chandlers
Cappers, Pinners, Wire Drawers, and Linen Drapers
Bricklayers
Carpenters, Slaters, and Sawyers
Joiners, Carvers, and Turners
Painters, Glaziers, Embroiderers, and Stationers
Goldsmiths
Smiths, Cutlers, Cardmakers, and Plumbers
Butchers
Wet and Dry Glovers
Cordwainers
Bakers
Fletchers, Bowyers, Coopers, and Stringers

Grocers, Ironmongers, Mercers, and Apothecaries
Innholders, Cooks, and Victuallers
Skinners and Feltmakers
Saddlers and Curriers
Merchant Tailors
Clothworkers and Masons
Weavers

Others, such as the Fishmongers and Dyers and the Drawers of Dee, have become extinct.

The guilds' records are housed in various places. Many remain in the hands of the guilds' stewards. Some have been deposited in the Chester City Record Office in the Town Hall (Walk 1). Others are on display in the Guildhall Museum (Walk 4), and the genuine or supposed arms of the guilds are also displayed in the Guildhall. Historical and current information about the guilds and freemen is given in their magazine, the *Deva Pentice.*

Appendix III: Some Chester Architects

Douglas, John (1829–1911)

A pupil of E.G. Paley of Lancaster (1823–95). Practised in Chester. Worked in partnership from 1885 (Douglas and Fordham; Douglas and Minshull). Undoubtedly the most prolific of the Chester architects, and also responsible for much building in Cheshire and North Wales. Designed Gothic churches and chapels, in brick (St Paul's, Boughton, with much timber work; Baptist chapel, Grosvenor Park Road) as well as in stone. A leading figure in the black-and-white revival of the later 19th century, early works include the Grosvenor Park lodge and the S side of St Werburgh Street [31] (facing the S transept of the Cathedral). Developed the style to its most elaborate, in the late 1890s, on the E side of St Werburgh Street and in parts of Shoemakers' Row, Northgate Street. Also used brick with stone dressings, mixing Gothic and Renaissance detail, e.g. in a terrace on the E side of Grosvenor Park Road, the former county police headquarters, Foregate Street (1884), and the Grosvenor Club, now the Midland Bank, Eastgate Street [32]. On the E side of Bath Street is a stone gothic-Renaissance terrace of the first years of the 20th century.

Douglas was employed by the Grosvenors for much work around the Eaton estate; he also built them model farms, e.g. at Aldford and Bruera.

The works of Douglas are far too numerous to list here; but see N. Pevsner and E. Hubbard, *The Buildings of England: Cheshire,* and E. Beazley and P. Howell, *The Companion Guide to North Wales,* for two comprehensive accounts.

Harrison, James (1814–66)

Unrelated to Thomas Harrison. A native of Chester. A founder member, and Honorary Architectural Secretary, of the Chester Architectural, Archaeological, and Historic Society.

In 1847 he won a competition for a design for a Savings Bank in Tudor style (the Trustee Savings Bank [27], Grosvenor Street, opened in 1853). In the mid 1850s he rebuilt the Theatre Royal (formerly St Nicholas's chapel), between Northgate Street and St Werburgh Street, as the Chester Music Hall; it was opened in 1855. He reconstructed God's Providence House in Watergate Street [28] in 1862. He is best known, however, for building or rebuilding Gothic churches: he designed the new St Michael's (1849–50), now the Chester Heritage Centre, and the new Holy Trinity, Watergate Street, now the Guildhall, which had not been completed at his death. In 1861 he restored the church of St Mary-on-the-Hill. Designed other churches in Cheshire: Capenhurst (1856–9), Dunham-on-the-Hill (1860–1), much of Handley (1853–5), and Upton by Chester (1852–4). In the early 1850s laid out Queen's Park S of the Dee as a villa estate.

See *The Modest Genius*, a catalogue of an exhibition vol. 28, part 1 (1928), pp. 132–6 (article by F. Simpson).

Harrison, Thomas (1744–1829)

Born at Richmond, Yorkshire; studied architecture in Italy. Lived in Lancaster in the 1780s, and in Chester from 1793. Appointed County Surveyor and Bridgemaster by Cheshire quarter sessions, 1815.

Between 1785 and 1822 worked on Chester Castle [23]; most of the medieval castle was demolished to make way for a new shire hall, barracks, and county gaol. Other work in Chester includes the Commercial News Room [25] (now the City Club), Northgate Street (1808), the Northgate [26] (1808–10), and three houses, Dee Hills, St Martin's Lodge, and Watergate House. In 1827 work began on his Grosvenor Bridge [24], not completed until after his death. He restored the S transept of the Cathedral (1818–20).

Harrison's work elsewhere includes Woodbank House, Stockport; the Shire Hall, Lancaster Castle; the Lyceum, Liverpool; and the Portico Library, Manchester. He designed a Jubilee Tower for Moel Famau in the Clwydian hills to commemorate the golden jubilee of George III in 1810; the tower, built in 1812, collapsed in 1862.

See *The Modest Genius*, a catalogue of an exhibition illustrating Harrison's life and work (Grosvenor Museum, 1977). He was a leading exponent of the Greek Revival of the late 18th and early 19th centuries, though occasionally (not in Chester) he built in the Gothic style.

Lockwood, Thomas Meakin (1830–1900)

A pupil of T.M. Penson. Like Penson and John Douglas he was a leader of the black-and-white revival; most notable examples in Chester are the buildings on the corners of Bridge Street at the Cross (1888), Old Bank Buildings [34] (1895), the Blossoms Hotel (1896), and Owen Owen's, Eastgate Street (1900). A much earlier and more restrained example is No. 20 Bridge Street (early 1870s). He restored Bishop Lloyd's House, Watergate Street. Lockwood used Renaissance ornament, e.g. in the building on the corner of Bridge and Watergate Streets, and sometimes designed in that style (Grosvenor Museum [33], 1885–6). The centre-lights of his windows often have semi-circular heads (perhaps influenced by Norman Shaw).

Lockwood rebuilt the Council Chamber in the Town Hall after a fire, in 1896–7.

His sons P.H. and W.T. Lockwood worked with him in the 1890s. W.T. Lockwood was responsible for St Michael's Buildings, Bridge Street (1910 – rebuilt in black-and-white after the Duke of Westminster objected to Lockwood's first version in Baroque white Doulton ware) and the City High School, Queen's Park Road.

Penson, Thomas Mainwaring (1818–64)

Son of the architect Thomas Penson of Wrexham (1791–1859). County Surveyor of Flintshire. Practised in Chester. Chiefly known for the part he played in the early black-and-white revival in Chester, shown in Nos. 34–6 Eastgate Street [29] (1856) and the Grosvenor Hotel (completed after his death by the partnership of his elder brother R.K. Penson and A. Ritchie). Also worked in Romanesque and Gothic: in early 1860s designed the Norman E window of St John's church, and built a Norman chapel in the cemetery S of the Grosvenor Bridge, which he laid out in the late 1840s; built Browns' Crypt Buildings, Eastgate Street [30] (1858), in Early English style to harmonize with the 13th-century crypt. Used the Renaissance style for the Queen Hotel, near the General Station (1860–1, rebuilt in same style in 1862 after extensive fire damage).

Glossary of Architectural Terms

Abacus Slab-like, upper part of a capital.

Abutment Mass of masonry resisting a structural thrust.

Acanthus Stylized lobed leaf form much used in classical decoration, especially on Corinthian and Composite capitals.

Aedicule Classical surround to a window or door; from *aedicula*, a small temple.

Ambulatory A processional way behind a main altar.

Apse Semicircular or polygonal end to a building or room.

Arabesque Delicate surface ornament of fronds, flowers, vases, etc.

Arcade Free standing line of piers and arches.

Arch Structural device for spanning openings, usually to a curved outline, consisting of wedge-shaped elements called *voussoirs*. Many forms indicative of period. (See fig. 1.)

Architrave Lowest member of the classical entablature. The moulded frame to an opening.

Ashlar Evenly worked masonry with squared edges and thin joints.

Atrium The internal courtyard of a Roman House. A forecourt.

Attic The space within a roof. Part of a classical design above the main cornice.

Aumbry Cupboard to house sacred vessels.

Bailey The open court or courts of a castle (inner and outer bailey).

Ball Flower Early-14th-century ornament of a ball set inside a three-lobed globe.

Baluster Small pillar of moulded and swelling outline to support a parapet.

Barbican Defensive outwork to a gate consisting of parallel walls linked by an outer arch.

Bargeboards Boards, often decorative, set against gable ends to protect structural elements behind.

Baroque Style originating in Rome in the 17th century; a reaction against classicism; though the vocabulary remained the same its use was much freer and more emotional.

Basilica An aisled hall, essentially Roman or Early Christian.

Bastion Projecting defensive tower on the line of a wall.

Battlement (*crenellation*) Indented parapet, originally defensive but frequently purely decorative. The low parts are *embrasures*, the high parts are *merlons*.

Bay A compartment, usually repeated, defined by principal structural elements.
Beakhead Formalized bird's head with prominent beak. Norman.
Berm Level ground between defensive wall and ditch.
Billet Norman ornament of small cylindrical elements.
Black-and-White See *Timber Framing.*
Blind Arcade Small-scale arcade used decoratively on a wall face.
Block Capital Norman capital; cubical, the underside rounded and tapered to column shape.
Bond The arrangement of brickwork in a wall.
Stretchers are bricks laid with long side showing.
Headers are bricks laid with short end showing.
Stretcher Bond is laid with all stretchers.
English Bond is laid with alternate courses of stretchers and headers.
Flemish Bond is laid with stretchers and headers alternating in a course.
Boss Carved, projecting block at the intersections of vaulting ribs, etc.
Bow Window Curved projecting window. Late Georgian, Regency, and, alas, modern.
Box Pew High panelled church pew with a door.
Bressumer Horizontal beam to support a projecting upper storey.
Broach Spire Octagonal spire drawn out of lower pyramidal form.
Buttress Projecting masonry or brickwork support to a wall. Angle buttresses meet at the corner. Clasping buttresses enclose the corner like a turret. Diagonal buttresses are set at an angle to the corner. Flying buttresses are half arches set against buttresses especially to support high stone vaults.

Cable Mould Cord-like Norman ornament.
Campanile Detached bell tower.
Canopy Projecting feature protecting an opening, statue, etc., often richly ornamented.
Capital The upper termination of a column or pier.
Cartouche Acanthus, cherubs, flowers, etc., composed to frame an inscription or coat of arms.
Caryatid Female figure supporting an entablature.
Chamfer The most basic of mouldings where the angle between two planes at right angles is cut away at 45°.
Chancel The eastern arm of a church.
Chantry Chapel endowed for saying Mass for the soul of the founder etc.
Chevet Fully developed apsidal end to a church with ambulatory and radiating chapels.
Chevron Norman zigzag ornament, capable of great variety.
Choir The place where service was sung, loosely applied as the eastern arm of the church, cf. chancel.

Clerestory The upper stage of a building pierced by windows.
Coadestone Late-18th-century, early-19th-century artificial stone of great durability.
Coffering Repeated square or polygonal panels sunk in the face of a ceiling or vault.
Colonnade Range of columns supporting an entablature.
Console Classical bracket of complex outline like a drawn-out volute.
Corbel Projecting block supporting a structural or decorative feature.
Corbel Table Range of corbels along the upper part of a wall.
Cornice The uppermost, projecting section of a classical entablature. Any projecting crowning feature running horizontally.
Cove Prominent concave surface between wall and ceiling.
Crocket Regularly spaced leaf-shaped knobs. Gothic, on gables, pinnacles, etc.
Crypt Underground or semi-underground stage of a church – usually below the eastern arm – or of a secular building.
Cupola Domed turret, popular on stable blocks.
Cusp The pointed element formed between the foils of a foiled opening.

Dado Panelling along the lower part of a wall.
Dagger Symmetrical, cusped tracery element pointed at both ends.
Decorated English architecture of the last quarter of the 13th century and first half of the 14th century.
Diapering Repeated surface patterning of square or lozenge shapes, foliated.
Dogtooth Universal Early English ornament of pyramidal star shapes.
Dormer Window within a roof slope with its own roof above.
Dutch Gable A gable of curved outline crowned by a pediment, loosely used of all curving gables.

Early English English architecture of the first three-quarters of the 13th century.
Embrasure Small defensive window, widely splayed inside. The openings in battlements.
Encaustic Tiles Glazed earthenware tiles, patterned.
Engaged Column Half or more of a column attached to a wall face.
Entablature Horizontal structural element in classical architecture, spanning between columns. Comprises architrave, frieze, and cornice.

Feretory Chapel behind the high altar to house the chief relics.
Finial Foliated top ornament of a canopy or pinnacle.
Flamboyant Late French Gothic with flamelike and waving forms.
Fleche Tall spirelet of light construction set on a roof ridge.

Flushwork East Anglian decoration of stone tracery and panels inset with cut flint.
Fluting The vertical channels on a classical column, usually 24 in number.
Foil Lobe of a cusped form; hence *Trefoil, Quatrefoil*, etc.
Foliated Leafed.
Fresco Painting on wet plaster.
Frieze Central section of a classical entablature, between architrave and cornice.

Gable The flat end of a pitched roof.
Galilee Western chapel or porch.
Gardérobe A medieval lavatory.
Gargoyle Horizontal waterspout often carved with great fancy.
Gazebo Look-out tower or summerhouse.
Geometrical English architecture of late 13th, early 14th centuries with tracery formed of circles and other simple geometrical forms.
Gibbs Surround Early-18th-century door and window treatment where orthodox classical elements are alternated with large stone blocks.
Grisaille Painting in shades of grey.
Groin The intersection of two vaulting surfaces, without ribs.
Grotesque Fanciful ornament.

Hagioscope Squint, an internal window allowing a view from one part of a building to another.
Half-timbering See *Timber Framing.*
Herringbone Anglian and Early Norman masonry; small stones set on a slope reversing direction with each course.
Hood Mould or *Label* Weathering moulding over a window.
Hypocaust Hollow floor on short pillars for hot-air central heating.

Impost Horizontal band or moulding on which an arch rests.

Jetty The overhang of the upper floors of a timber-framed house.

Keep or *Donjon* The most strongly fortified tower of a castle, usually with extensive living accommodation.
Keystone The apex of an arch.

Lacing Course Horizontal band bonding together the face and core of a wall, may be large stones or bricks.
Lancet Narrow, sharply pointed openings characteristic of Early English style.
Lantern Open, traceried tower or turret.
Light The individual glazed areas of a window.
Linenfold Tudor panelling carved with a representation of linen in vertical folds.
Lintel Horizontal member spanning an opening.
Loggia Covered colonnade or arcade open on one or more sides.

Long and Short Work Anglian system of quoining with stone posts alternating with flat slates.
Louvre Roof opening to let out smoke from a central hearth. Infilling of belfry windows with inclined slabs for sound transmission.
Lozenge Diamond shape.
Lychgate Roofed churchyard gate for the reception of a coffin.

Machicolation Military. Deeply projecting parapet on brackets. Designed for dropping missiles on attackers below.
Mannerism · Highly intellectual style in 16th-century Italy involving subtle reinterpretation of classical themes, often with very disturbing results.
Mansard Roof Roof with a double slope, admitting an extra storey.
Mathematical Tiles Interlocking tiles applied to timber framing to give an appearance of brickwork.
Mezzanine An intermediate storey.
Misericord Tip-up seat with carved bracket beneath to provide support during long services. Also called a *miserere.*
Modillion Bracket repeated beneath the main projecting element of an Ionic or Corinthian cornice.
Mouldings Narrow flat or curved bands designed to catch the light. The Gothic and classical styles each had its characteristic repertoire of profiles, the classical ones being minutely governed by rules of proportion. (See fig. 2.)
Motte and Bailey Earliest form of Norman Castle with a mount and bailey, both moated and defended by timber pallisades.
Mouchette Cusped tracery element with asymmetrical curving outline.
Mullion Vertical member between window lights.

Nailhead Late-12th-century, early-13th-century ornament of small pyramids.
Newel The main structural vertical of a staircase.
Newel Stair A spiral staircase round a central newel, usually stone.
Nodding Ogee Ogee arch projecting in three dimensions.
Norman English Romanesque style, mid 11th, late 12th century.

Order Concentric layers of an arch, especially Norman.
Orders Backbone of classical architecture, originating in Greece, adapted by the Romans and revived during the Renaissance. Five principal orders: *Tuscan, Doric, Ionic, Corinthian, Composite* (see fig. 3). Capable of infinite variation. The subject is vast.
Oriel Window Window projecting from an upper storey.

Palladian Architecture following the rules, though seldom the inspiration of Andrea Palladio.
Palladian Window Popular 18th-century motif of a three-light

window with a tall arched central light between lower rectangular lights.

Parapet Low wall surrounding a roof.

Pargeting External ornamental plasterwork.

Patera Small circular classical ornament.

Pedestal Block supporting classical statue or column.

Pediment Low gable end to a classical temple with horizontal and raking cornices. Essential to the vocabulary of 18th-century windows and doors. Segmental pediments were common, and they sometimes took on fanciful shapes. *Broken pediments* have a gap in the horizontal cornice. *Open pediments* have a gap between the two raking cornices.

Pendant Boss or vaulting form elongated downwards.

Pendentive The device for converting a square or polygonal plan shape to a circular one to take a dome: consisting of sections of a hemisphere struck from the largest diameter.

Perpendicular English Gothic from the mid 14th to early 16th century, characterized by vertical lines. A wholly English creation in startling contrast to French Flamboyant.

Piano Nobile The principal, usually first floor of a classical house.

Pier The support for an arcade.

Pilaster Shallow sections of classical columns applied to wall face, or broad, flat, Norman buttresses.

Pinnacle Upper termination of Gothic buttresses, parapets, and towers, of tapering crocketed outline. May be structural in providing additional weight to resist a thrust, or purely decorative.

Piscina Stone basin for washing Sacred vessels.

Podium The stepped base of a classical building.

Poppyhead Foliated finial to bench ends.

Portico Classical feature based on a temple front.

Postern Small gateway.

Presbytery The part of a church where the altar is placed.

Pulpitum Stone screen separating choir from nave.

Quoins Dressed angle stones of a building.

Rendering The plastering of an external wall.

Reredos Screen with canopies, images etc. behind an altar.

Respond Half column or other termination of an arcade against a wall.

Rococo Late, lighter phase of Baroque; mid 18th century.

Romanesque Norman style of the late 11th, early 12th century, characterized by round-headed arches.

Rood Cross or crucifix generally placed at the entrance to the chancel above a screen with gallery approached by staircases, known respectively as rood screen, rood loft, and rood stairs.

Roofs Common rafters were the basis of all traditional roof construction. Single-framed roofs had only these transverse elements, often with collars, ties and struts, but not tied together longitudinally. Double-framed roofs introduce trusses at intervals supporting purlins, which in turn support the common rafters, allowing more economical construction and greater spans. (See fig. 4.)

Rose Window A traceried circular window.

Rotunda A circular building usually domed.

Rustication Rock-faced stonework used particularly on quoins and on the lower storeys of classical buildings.

Saddleback Short gabled roof over a church tower.

Sanctuary Area round an altar.

Sash Window Georgian and after. Window designed in two planes, which slide in front of one another, either vertically or horizontally.

Scagliola Imitation marble.

Scalloped Capital Block capital with conical elements on the under surface.

Screen Timber or stone partition used in both domestic and ecclesiastical work.

Screens Passage Passage between kitchen and hall in medieval planning.

Sedilia Seats for priests on south of chancel.

Soffit Underside of an arch or horizontal member.

Solar Medieval living room, almost always upstairs.

Sounding Board Flat canopy over a pulpit.

Spandrel The flat area between two arches.

Spire Pyramidal or conical tower termination. The junction with tower capable of endless variety. (See *Broach Spire.*)

Springing The level at which the curve of an arch starts.

Stanchion Upright steel member.

Stiff Leaf Lobed conventional foliage of Early English capitals.

Storey Posts The main posts in a timber-framed wall.

Stoup Stone bowl for holy water near church door.

Strapwork Elizabethan and Jacobean ornament of flat interlacing bands.

Stretcher See *Bond.*

String Course Projecting horizontal moulding or band on the surface of a wall.

Stucco Plaster.

Studs Subsidiary verticals in a timber-framed wall.

Swag Carved decoration based on suspended cloth.

Terracotta Unglazed, burnt clay used for decorative elements.

Tessellated Pavements Flooring made of tesserae, small pieces of marble, stone, brick, or glass set in cement to form patterns, figures, etc.; Roman.

Three-decker Pulpit Pulpit, reading desk, and clerk's desk on descending levels.

Timber Framing Also known as *half-timbering* and *black-and-white.* Structural system of wooden beams, posts, struts, etc., often involving one or more overhanging storeys. The spaces between the frame are filled with lath and plaster or brickwork.

Tomb Chest Medieval box-shaped tomb, often with supporting effigies and richly decorated.

Tracery The stone framework of a Gothic window, developed from the coupling of lancets and the piercing of the space between their heads to windows of great size and elaboration designed to show off the products of the stained-glass artist. Plate tracery, the earliest form, is cut out of flat slabs. Bar tracery is formed of moulded or chamfered sections common both to straight mullions and curved tracery elements. Tracery designs were also much used as a wall decoration. (See fig. 5.)

Transept The cross arm of a church.

Transom A horizontal member in window tracery.

Tribune Large gallery at triforium (q.v.) level.

Triforium Central horizontal subdivision in Romanesque or Early Gothic church above the arcade and below the clerestory.

Tympanum Panel, carved or traceried, between the springing line and an arch.

Undercroft Underground or semi-underground room below more important building.

Vault Stone vaulting was one of the great ambitions of the medieval architect.

Barrel Vault. Early Romanesque, continuous semicircular section on side walls.

Groin or *Cross Vault.* Intersecting barrel vaults concentrating thrust.

Rib Vault. With introduction of pointed arch. The ribs built first as permanent shuttering then the *webs* or spaces between filled in.

Quadripartite Vault. Each bay divided into four quarter vaults.

Sexpartite Vault. Double bays transversely divided so that each has six parts.

Tierceron Vault. Additional ribs from springing to ridge, from early 13th century.

Lierne Vault. Has more ribs joining the tiercerons etc. to form star patterns etc., from end of 13th century.

Fan Vault. Ribs fanning out from springing, all the same length and curvature. Ribs and panels no longer formed of separate stones, from mid 14th century.

Vaulting Shaft Wall shaft to support a vault.

Venetian Window Wide-arched opening between two lower rectangular ones. Popular 18th-century motif from Palladio.

Volute Spiral scroll of Ionic capital (also used in Corinthian and Composite).

Waggon Roof Roof with closely set curved braces.
Wainscot Panelled wall linings and partitions.
Waterleaf Capital Late-12th-century flat leaves turned in at the top corners.
Wealden House Timber-framed hall between two jettied wings, the eaves running across at the outer line leaving deep cove over recessed centre.
Weatherboarding Overlapping horizontal boards to weatherproof exterior.

The publishers are grateful to John Hutchinson for compiling this glossary and drawing the accompanying figures.

ARCHES

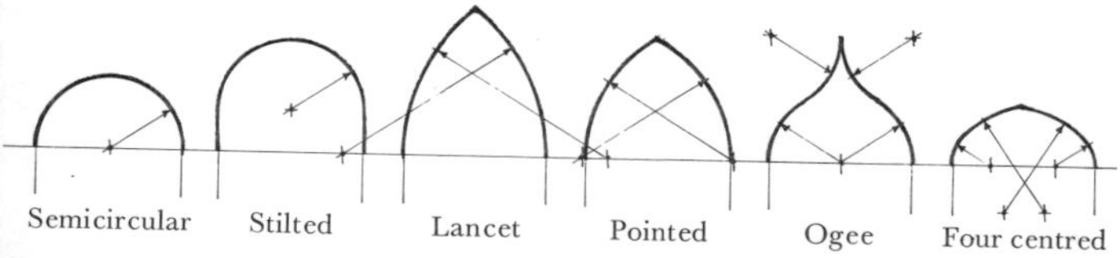

Fig. 1

MOULDINGS

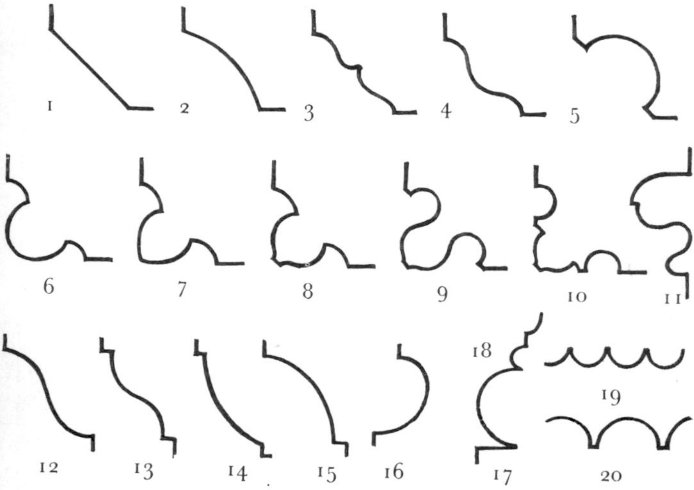

1 Chamfer
2 Hollow chamfer
3 Double ogee
4 Wave mould
5 Hollow
6 Roll
7 Keeled roll
8 Filletted roll
9 Filletted roll between hollows
10 Triple Filletted Roll
11 Scroll Mould
12 Cyma
13 Cyma reversa
14 Ovolo
15 Cavetto
16 Scotia
17 Torus
18 Astragal
19 Reeding
20 Fluting

Fig. 2

Roman orders based on the designs of James Gibbs

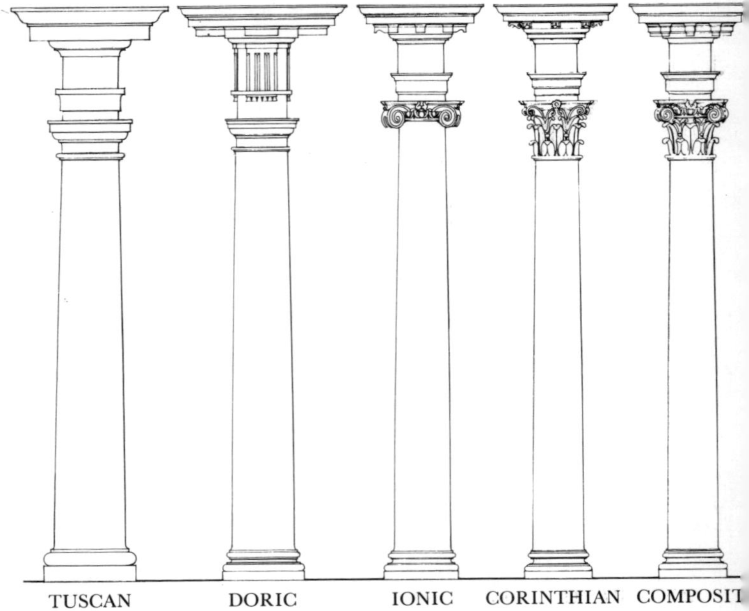

Fig. 3

ROOFS

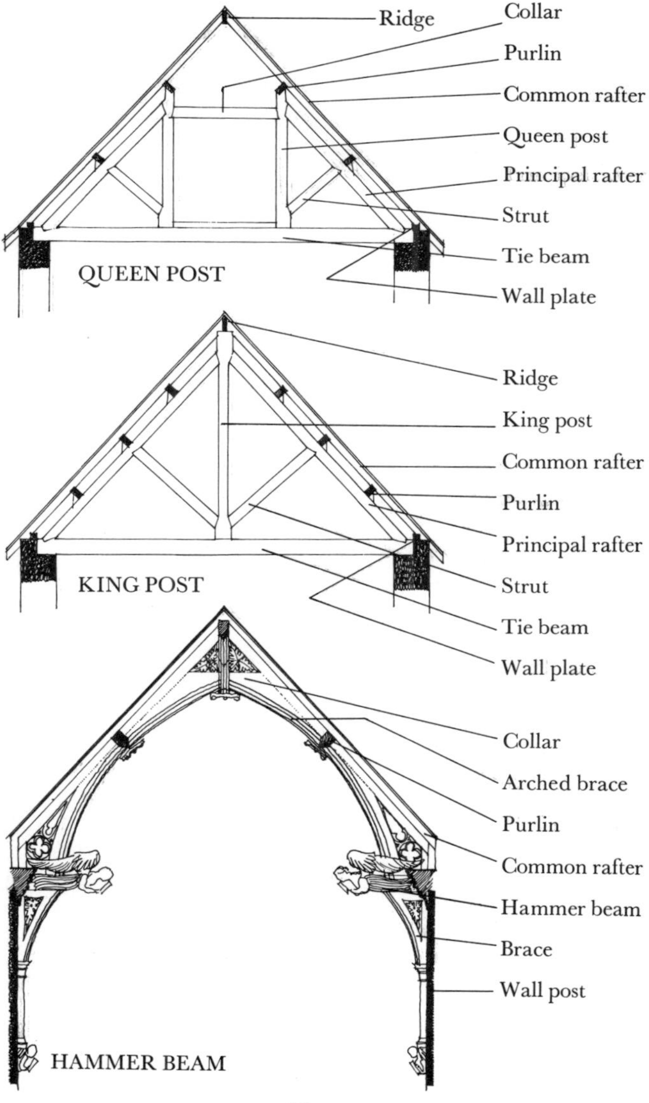
Ridge
Collar
Purlin
Common rafter
Queen post
Principal rafter
Strut
Tie beam
Wall plate
QUEEN POST
Ridge
King post
Common rafter
Purlin
Principal rafter
Strut
Tie beam
Wall plate
KING POST
Collar
Arched brace
Purlin
Common rafter
Hammer beam
Brace
Wall post
HAMMER BEAM

Fig. 4

TRACERY

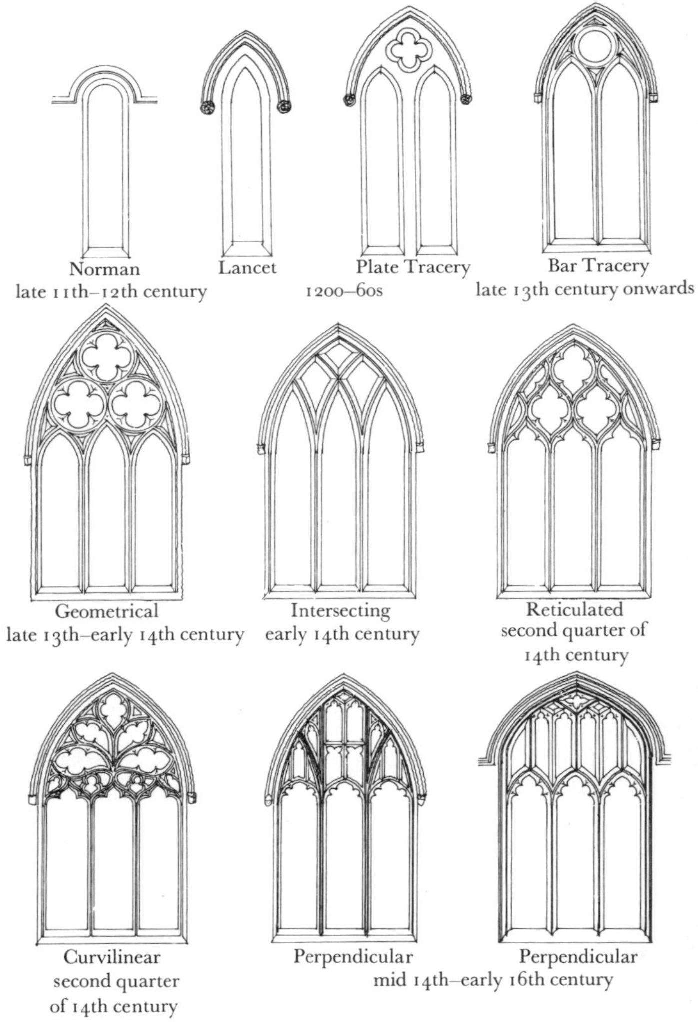
Norman
late 11th–12th century
Lancet
Plate Tracery
1200–60s
Bar Tracery
late 13th century onwards
Geometrical
late 13th–early 14th century
Intersecting
early 14th century
Reticulated
second quarter of
14th century
Curvilinear
second quarter
of 14th century
Perpendicular
Perpendicular
mid 14th–early 16th century

Fig. 5

Further Reading

It is hoped that this guide will answer most straightforward questions about the growth and main features of Chester. Nevertheless, its treatment of many subjects is necessarily limited. The reader may well wish to enquire further, and he can be helped in two ways. First, since it is impossible in a book of this size to give the source of every statement made in the text, a fully annotated copy is being prepared that will be placed in the Chester City Record Office, so that anyone wishing to verify a fact that is not simply a matter of general knowledge may be able to trace its source. Secondly, the following note has been compiled as a guide to books and articles that are fairly easily available. Again, because of limitations of space it must necessarily be rather an individual and selective one.

For the visitor who wishes to spend some of his time in Chester on further investigation, the obvious sources of information are the Public Library and the Chester City Record Office. The Chester Library, in St John Street (Walk 8), is open until 7 p.m. on Mondays, Tuesdays, Thursdays, and Fridays, until 5.30 on Wednesdays and only until 1 p.m. on Saturdays. The Reference Library contains a good collection of works on the history of Chester, most of which, however, are not on open access. It also possesses an important collection of local newspapers, either in the original or on microfilm, and a very good collection of photographic records of Chester.

The Chester City Record Office is housed in the Town Hall (Walk 1). It is open from 9 a.m. to 1 p.m. and 2 p.m. to 5 p.m. on Mondays to Fridays; in the summer of 1978 an experimental scheme of Monday evening opening from

5 p.m. to 9 p.m., by appointment, was inaugurated. The Office houses the records of the city of Chester, which begin with the charter issued by Henry II in 1175 or 1176. Since local government reorganization it has also taken over some of the records of the former rural districts that were merged with the city. In addition, it has custody of various private collections of documents, including that of the Chester Archaeological Society. The Record Office library contains most of the works that have been published on the history of Chester, as well as various unpublished theses and dissertations; it has also a collection of works of reference indispensable to the local historian, such as directories and both official and unofficial guidebooks. Many of the gaps in the Office's own library of works on Chester are filled by volumes in the Chester Archaeological Society's library, which is also housed there. That library contains many rare and early works on Chester, but also includes most of the current periodical publications of archaeological and historical societies in the region. The City Record Office often provides exhibitions of some of the material in its possession; the catalogues of the exhibitions, such as *Chester and the Monarchy* and *Chester and Wales*, both produced in 1977, provide useful introductions to their subjects. Sadly, there is as yet no published guide to the city records, but the Record Office has produced a series of excellent publications: the early but still interesting *Guide to the Charters, Plate, and Insignia of the City of Chester*; *Chester Mystery Plays*; *Chester 1066–1971*, which records descriptions of Chester by various visitors over the centuries; and *Chester Schools*, which gives a list of the records of each school within the city and a brief history of the schools.

Three important series of records concerning the city that are not housed in the City Record Office are the archives of the Diocese and the Cathedral, parish registers, and census returns. The Cheshire Record Office in Chester Castle houses the first two, except for some of the Cathedral's administrative records, which remain in the Cathedral muniment room; it also has microfilm copies of the census returns for 1841, 1851, 1861, and 1871 (the latter being the last available for public inspection until 1981). Like the City Record Office, the Castle also contains private collections, some of which contain material relating to Chester; it has an extensive library, but covers Cheshire as a whole and has only a limited collection of books in Chester. Its opening hours are from 9 a.m. to 5 p.m. on Tuesdays to Fridays; on Monday evenings it remains open until 9 p.m., and it is also open on Saturday mornings.

The Chester Architectural, Archaeological, and Historic Society (now normally known simply as the Chester Archaeological Society) was founded in 1849. One of its objects was the promotion of what it considered to be good architectural standards, but it was also equally interested in furthering archaeological and historical research in Chester and its surrounding area. Between October and April it organizes monthly lectures, usually at the Grosvenor Museum; its *Journal* has gained an international reputation for its scholarly articles on the archaeology and history of the area. There is a branch of the Historical Association in Chester, but it has not primarily concerned itself with local history. Other societies with interests in the history of Chester are the Historic Society of Lancashire and Cheshire (which meets at Liverpool), the Lancashire and Cheshire Antiquarian Society (which meets at Manchester), the Chetham Society, and the Record Society of Lancashire and Cheshire; the two last-named are purely publishing societies.

Odd though it may seem, there is no published history of Chester that is comprehensive or scholarly enough to be satisfactory. The standard work on the history of Cheshire is George Ormerod's *History of the County Palatine and City of Chester*, originally published in the early 19th century but replaced, after Ormerod's death, by a much enlarged edition by Thomas Helsby (1882). Unfortunately, both Ormerod and Helsby decided that nothing of importance happened in Chester after 1745, although they record changes to ecclesiastical buildings, including Scott's restoration of the Cathedral. In 1831 Joseph Hemingway published a *History of Chester* in two volumes. It was partly based on earlier work, such as that of J. Poole (1791), but in many respects it has never been replaced. Thus it contains good accounts of the political history of Chester in the 18th and early 19th centuries; for the latter period it becomes a contemporary source, and Hemingway's descriptions of the walls, the streets, and such buildings as the Castle and the newly built lunatic asylum at Upton are still valuable. Later authors who attempted to cover the whole history of Chester include G.L. Fenwick (*A History of the Ancient City of Chester*, 1896) and J. Williams (*The Story of Chester*, 1907). Williams's book is quite useful for events of the late 19th and early 20th centuries. A recent publication in paperback, Marion Seal's *Chester of Yester-Year* (2nd edn, 1977), contains chronological notes of events in Chester from the Anglo-Saxon period to 1899. There is a great deal of information stored in the volumes of the *Chester Sheaf*. They contain material of the 'notes and queries' type relating to Chester, Cheshire, and North Wales; the *Sheaf* appeared in various local newspapers from 1878, and was bound together in annual volumes: it now appears as a feature in the monthly periodical *Deesider*. There is an incomplete index to the Chester material there in the City Record Office.

Individual periods of Chester's history have been extensively covered, but there are surprising gaps.

Roman and Anglo-Saxon

There are two excellent short introductions to Roman Chester: F.H. Thompson's *Deva: Roman Chester* (1959), and D.F. Petch's *Deva Victrix* (1971). Reports of archaeological excavations have appeared in the Chester Archaeological Society's *Journal* throughout its history, and more have been published by the Grosvenor Museum.* The only modern work on the Anglo-Saxon period is J.D. Bu'Lock, *Pre-Conquest Cheshire* (1972), one of a series of works published by the Cheshire Community Council on the history of the county.

* The most recent archaeological conclusions on Roman Chester are summarized in T.J. Strickland and P.J. Davey (eds.), *New Evidence on Roman Chester* (1978).

1066–1500

The standard work on medieval Chester is R.H. Morris, *Chester during the Plantagenet and Tudor Reigns* (1894). It is often a difficult book to follow, but has the advantage that Morris used original sources whenever he could, though he sometimes misunderstood them. Other works have drawn largely upon Morris, such as those in the Community Council's series: B.M.C. Husain, *Cheshire under the Norman Earls* (1973); H.J. Hewitt, *Cheshire under the Three Edwards* (1967); and J.T. Driver, *Cheshire in the Later Middle Ages* (1971). All deal with the county as a whole, but have much to say about Chester as the largest and best recorded town in Cheshire and the seat of palatine administration. R.V.H. Burne's *The Monks of Chester* (1962) is a competent account of the history of St Werburgh's abbey. J.McN. Dodgson, 'Place-Names and Street-Names at Chester', *Journal of the Chester Archaeological Society*, vol. 55 (1968), pp. 29–61, is an invaluable article.

The Sixteenth, Seventeenth, and Eighteenth Centuries

For the Tudor period Morris, *Chester during the Plantagenet and Tudor Reigns*, is essential; Morris used the city's archives as a rich quarry for his work, and particularly the first Assembly Book, large extracts from which are printed in the volume. After Morris's death his book *The Siege of Chester* (1924) was completed and edited by P.H. Lawson, and published both as volume 25, new series, of the Chester Archaeological Society's *Journal* and separately. There are two Community Council books covering the 16th and part of the 17th century, Joan Beck's *Tudor Cheshire* (1969), and R.N. Dore's *The Civil Wars in Cheshire* (1966).

For the 18th century there is very little available, apart from the relevant information in Hemingway's *History of Chester*, though some interesting background detail is provided by *Browns of Chester*, a history of Browns' shop published by Mass-Observation *c.*1946, and by H. Hughes, *Chronicle of Chester* (1975), which is a history of the *Chester Chronicle.*

The Nineteenth and Twentieth Centuries

Despite, or perhaps because of, the abundance of material available for studying the history of Chester since 1800, there is no satisfactory book covering the period. Thomas Hughes, *The Stranger's Handbook to Chester* (1856; available as a reprint in facsimile), is a valuable description of the city as it appeared in the mid 19th century, and subsequent editions can be used to chronicle many of the changes that took place later in the century. D.W. Insall and Associates, *Chester: A Study in Conservation* (1968), is of great value in describing the recent growth and geographical, economic, and social standing of Chester. *Browns of Chester* and *Chronicle of Chester* again provide interesting information; G. Huxley, *Victorian Duke* (1967), is a biography of Hugh Lupus, first Duke of Westminster, head of the all-important Grosvenor family.

On the history of buildings in Chester the relevant part of N. Pevsner and E. Hubbard, *The Buildings of England: Cheshire* (1971), is essential, though there are some omissions (e.g. no mention of the Royal Infirmary), and much has happened architecturally in Chester since 1971. Chester's walls are described by Frank Simpson in *The Walls of Chester* (1910); but Simpson, a prolific writer who helped to popularize local history in Chester, did not always get his facts right, and what he says needs to be checked wherever possible against his sources. A short and very popular account of the walls is given by Marion Seal, *A Walk Round the Walls of Chester* (1968). The history of the Cathedral has, as one might expect, been written from several viewpoints. R.V.H. Burne, *Chester Cathedral* (1958), is an account of the Cathedral as a building and as an institution from the foundation to 1837. Dean Frank Bennett produced a detailed topographical guide (*Chester Cathedral,* 1925), but the earlier account by C. Hiatt (*Chester Cathedral and See*, 1897) is still valuable as a subjective judgement on the Victorian restorations. A short and popular work, but one of great worth, is G.W.O. Addleshaw, *The Pictorial History of Chester Cathedral* (1969); Dean Addleshaw also wrote *Chester Cathedral: The Stained Glass Windows, Mosaics, Monuments, and some of its other Treasures* (1965 and later editions), an essential guide to the Cathedral's furnishings. There are full-length histories of three of the other parish churches of Chester: S. Cooper Scott, *History of S. John the Baptist Church and Parish* (1892); J.P. Earwaker, *History of the Church and Parish of St Mary-on-the-Hill, Chester* (1898); and F. Simpson, *History of the Church of St Peter* (1909). The Town Hall is briefly described in *Chester Town Hall and its Treasures* by H.T. Dutton (1928). The schools of Chester and their records are described by Annette M. Kennett, *Chester Schools* (1973). Needless to say, there are many articles scattered through the *Cheshire Sheaf* and the *Journal of the Chester Archaeological Society* on individual buildings.

Various short and well-illustrated guides to Chester are available. No visitor should omit to purchase a copy of the *Official Guide*, which has always given excellent value for money: moderately priced, it is well illustrated and carries up-to-date details of all educational and recreational facilities, including opening hours and telephone numbers, and also guidance on accommodation in Chester. An unusual pictorial souvenir, and an excellent source of information on Chester at the turn of the century, is J. Tomlinson, *Victorian and Edwardian Chester* (1976), a collection of photographs with commentary.

Index

Note: This index refers only to places in Chester, institutions, artists, and architects. Numbers in italic type refer to the plates between pages 124 and 125.

ELECTROACOUSTIC MUSIC

Recent Titles in
Contributions to the Study of Music and Dance

Perspectives on the Grateful Dead: Critical Writings
Robert G. Weiner, editor

The Cultivation of Body and Mind in Nineteenth-Century American Delsartism
Nancy Lee Chalfa Ruyter

Domenico Cimarosa: His Life and His Operas
Nick Rossi and Talmage Fauntleroy

The Writings and Letters of Konrad Wolff
Ruth Gillen, editor

Nomai Dance Drama: A Surviving Spirit of Medieval Japan
Susan M. Asai

The Wind and Wind-Chorus Music of Anton Bruckner
Keith William Kinder

Modern Myths and Wagnerian Deconstructions: Hermeneutic Approaches to Wagner's Music-Dramas
Mary A. Cicora

Virtue or Virtuosity? Explorations in the Ethics of Musical Performance
Jane O'Dea

Beethoven in Person: His Deafness, Illnesses, and Death
Peter J. Davies

The Character of a Genius: Beethoven in Perspective
Peter J. Davies

Sing Sorrow: Classics, History, and Heroines in Opera
Marianne McDonald

Feminist Aesthetics in Music
Sally Macarthur

ELECTROACOUSTIC MUSIC

Analytical Perspectives

Edited by
Thomas Licata

Foreword by Jean-Claude Risset

Contributions to the Study of Music and Dance, Number 63

GREENWOOD PRESS
Westport, Connecticut • London

Library of Congress Cataloging-in-Publication Data

Electroacoustic music : analytical perspectives / edited by Thomas Licata, foreword by Jean-Claude Risset.

p. cm.—(Contributions to the study of music and dance, ISSN 0193–9041 ; no. 63)

ISBN 0–313–31420–9 (alk. paper)

1. Electronic music—History and criticism. 2. Musical analysis. I. Licata, Thomas, 1961– II. Series.

ML1380.E36 2002

786.7—dc21 2001054717

British Library Cataloguing in Publication Data is available.

Library of Congress Catalog Card Number: 2001054717
ISBN: 0–313–31420–9
ISSN: 0193–9041

First published in 2002

Greenwood Press, 88 Post Road West, Westport, CT 06881
An imprint of Greenwood Publishing Group, Inc.
www.greenwood.com

Printed in the United States of America

The paper used in this book complies with the Permanent Paper Standard issued by the National Information Standards Organization (Z39.48–1984).

10 9 8 7 6 5 4 3 2

Copyright Acknowledgments

The author and publisher gratefully acknowledge permission for use of the following:

James Dashow, "Looking into Sequence Symbols," *Perspectives of New Music* 25, nos. 1 & 2 (Winter/Summer 1987): 108–135, and Pascal Decroupet and Elena Ungeheuer, "Through the Sensory Looking-Glass: The Aesthetic and Serial Foundations of *Gesang der Jünglinge*," *Perspectives of New Music* 36, no. 1 (Winter 1998): 97–142. Used by permission of authors and *Perspectives of New Music*.

Karlheinz Stockhausen, *Texte zur Musik 3* (1971): 79–84. (This book and all Stockhausen scores, CDs and books about Stockhausen may be ordered directly from the Stockhausen-Verlag, 51515 Kurten, Germany).

Emilio Vedova, *Intolleranza '60, n. 2 (a Luigi Nono)*, 1960.

Risset's manuscript of his PLF4 Fortran Program in Chapter 7 is used by permission of Jean-Claude Risset.

for my parents

Margot and Vincent

Contents

Illustrations

Foreword

Jean-Claude Risset

This book on the analysis of electroacoustic music is a timely and significant one. Electroacoustic music blossomed in the second half of the twentieth century. Not only did it expand instrumental music to a wider range of sound material, but it also opened a new sonic art form—another branch of music, as different from instrumental music as cinema is from theater.

This new music has been little discussed in writing, in part because much of electroacoustic music does away with the score, a document that had heretofore seemed essential. The lack of an objective representation makes it difficult to study these works. This has resulted in few textbooks about electroacoustic music and even fewer analyses of electroacoustic works. The present book purports to fill this gap and to shed light on some important works of this medium.

I wish to provide some historical background concerning electroacoustic music. Around 1875, two inventions brought a considerable change to our relationship with sound: the gramophone and the telephone. The gramophone, invented by Thomas Edison, engraved sound, which allowed its replication in the absence of the vibrating object that had produced it. From this point on, one could no longer say "verba volent, scripta manent" (words fly away, writings remain with us): recording provides a durable trace of the sound, enabling one to scrutinize it as an object and to modify it in novel ways—for instance, to play it in reverse. The telephone, invented by Alexander Graham Bell, transformed sound into electrical vibrations that could be transported on wires and converted back into sound. The composer Hugues Dufourt has termed this an "electric revolution": the elaboration of sound can benefit from the resources of electric technology.

Initially, these new possibilities were used to transport and reproduce sound and music rather than to produce new sounds and new music. However, at the turn of the century, Thaddeus Cahill built the "dynamophone"—an electrical machine that produced musical sounds with electric dynamos (it was also called the "telharmonium"). Being in the form of electricity, the musical signal could be carried on telephone lines and sent remotely, a concept later evoked by

Stockhausen in his piece *Telemusik* (a work analyzed in this book). The success of Cahill's machine, however great, was short-lived, yet it excited the imagination of Varèse, who insisted all his life that science and technology were to provide new resources for music.

In the first half of the twentieth century, some "electronic instruments" appeared, for instance, the Theremin and the Martenot. These were mostly used to mimic existing acoustic instruments such as the violin. However, during the 1930s there were a few attempts to experiment with recording and electricity in music by such composers as Milhaud, Hindemith, Toch, Varèse, and McLaren. Stokowski called for the realization of scores "directly in tone, not on paper." John Cage's *Imaginary Landscape No. 1* (1939), in all likelihood, is the first musical work that exists not as a score but as a sound recording.

These concepts became especially practical after 1948. In this year, Pierre Schaeffer invented *musique concrète*—recording sounds and then modifying and assembling them to realize the musical work as a concrete recording rather than an abstract score. In 1950, Schaeffer and Pierre Henry composed *Symphonie pour un homme seul*—a single man monitoring the recording at the console. Schaeffer and Henry, as well as Luc Ferrari, François Bayle, and Beatriz Ferreyra, composed "by ear," experimenting and critically listening to sounds and their combinations.

In contradiction, the early practitioners of "electronic music," following Herbert Eimert, Karlheinz Stockhausen, and Gottfried Michael Koenig in Cologne around 1950, were concerned with creating precise, sonic realizations of complex scores, formally elaborated in advance, in the spirit of the serial methods of composition. They insisted on using only electronically produced sounds, whose physical parameters could be precisely controlled. Milton Babbitt had similar preoccupations when he realized such works as his *Ensembles for Synthesizer* on the RCA machine, a precursor of the synthesizers that later became popular.

One of the first major works that combined both electronic and "concrete" sounds was Stockhausen's *Gesang der Jünglinge*. Analyzed in this book by Pascal Decroupet and Elena Ungeheuer, this work was very successful and highly influential. Luigi Nono, also represented in this book, likewise adopted this syncretic approach, as well as associated electronic sounds with instruments (as did Luciano Berio, Mario Davidovsky, Milton Babbitt, and number of others).

In 1957, Max Mathews implemented the first digital computer synthesis of sound at Bell Laboratories. The computer in itself is a neutral medium, since it permits the implementation of a great variety of processes with unprecedented precision and reproducibility. Indeed, nearly all electroacoustic music is now produced digitally.

I had myself begun composing with instruments, and I hadn't been attracted to either *musique concrète* or "electronic music." It seemed to me that *musique concrète* afforded a great variety of sonic material but that the ways to process or assemble the sounds were rudimentary with respect to their richness, which made it hard to avoid an aesthetics of "collage." "Electronic music" offered a more ductile material. The sounds could be better controlled in their parameters, but I found them dull, lacking life, richness, and identity. I was intrigued when I learned of the new digital possibilities—perhaps they could reconcile richness and control. In the 1960s, I had the good fortune to collaborate with Max Mathews (and, indirectly, John Chowning) in developing the musical possibilities of sound synthesis. Indeed, the sonic resources of the computer had to be conquered, and this exploration provided valuable insight to the perception of musical sounds—one had to find ways to produce interesting sounds, so the development of specific knowledge and expertise was needed. Fortunately, the computer permits the implementation of a large variety of processes as well as the storing of thorough and accurate records of them, making it easy to communicate sonic descriptions, recipes, and sound catalogs.

The categories of "electronic music" and *musique concrète* still exist in the digital domain within two branches: the *synthesis* and *processing* of sound. However, the gap between synthesis and processing can be bridged through such methods as analysis-synthesis. There are still aesthetic arguments between the defenders of "live electronic music" and those who realize "music for tape." A few composers (among them Pierre Boulez) have viewed electroacoustic music as a prolongation of instrumental music, offering a mere extension of the available sound material. According to this conception, electroacoustic music should be performed live in an instrumental fashion. Others insist that music should not remain confined in an instrumental context. Beyond composing solely with ready-made sounds, electroacoustic composition can offer the possibility to compose the sounds themselves. The craft of composition must therefore be liberated from the real-time constraints of performance, resulting in a recording that constitutes the musical work itself—a "cinema for the ear," according to François Bayle. The expression "music for tape" has become somewhat archaic, since sounds today are recorded in digital form (DAT, other format audiotape, compact discs, or any other form of digital memory) rather than on analog tape. In France and Quebec, one often uses the more accurate expression *musique sur support*—"music for the recording medium"—but "music for tape" is still popular and well understood.

Most compositions for tape do not come with a score. The lack of a written document creates great difficulties for the musicologist who insists on carrying out rigorous, "objective" work. One might object that sound recording is an objective trace of the work—in the case of "music for tape," it could almost be said to coincide with the work itself—but it is certainly not a convenient document to consider, no more than Jorge Luis Borges' fictitious maps that coincide with the territories that they represent. Because of this problem, music for tape has been somewhat disregarded by musicology.

In an article for the *Contemporary Music Review*, Marco Stroppa enumerated the difficulties that he confronted in analyzing my piece *Songes*. The lack of a representation analogous to the conventional score prompted Stroppa to renounce the performance of his analysis. Because he found them too gross and approximate, he dismissed "listening scores": descriptive sketches realized, generally a posteriori, enabling one to follow the piece. As for the technical and operational data, which can give valuable information about works realized with computers, he generally considers them as disheartening and even incomprehensible for nonspecialists, especially since they refer to specific hardware and software that are ephemeral due to the rapid evolution of technology.

These difficulties are real. However, if the software used is structured in a way that provides exploitable archives, the coded traces left by the use of the computer can yield considerable amounts of valuable information for analysis. This is the case for C-synthesis programs such as Csound and Music V. I used the latter in my piece *Songes* (however, Stroppa did not have access to my computer "scores"). Therefore, it proves helpful if the composer makes his or her archives available with proper explanations. To take full advantage of these somewhat cryptic traces, those who undertake the analysis must be enlightened specialists, often composers themselves. This is the case for a number of the analyses presented in this book. For instance, the chapter by Konrad Boehmer describes the precise procedures that Koenig used and explicated in composing his piece *Essay*. In two other chapters, the methods used in computer compositions are discussed and elucidated by the composers themselves: Otto Laske and James Dashow. The chapters on Iannis Xenakis' *Diamorphoses* by Thomas DeLio, Luigi Nono's *Omaggio a Emilio Vedova* by Thomas Licata, and Joji Yuasa's *A Study in White* by Kristian Twombly resort to technical tools that can be great assets for musical analysis, such as sonograms and amplitude graphs, which provide some kind of portrayal or cartography of electroacoustic music.

Apart from the case of early electronic music pieces constructed in a very precise and formal fashion, only a few examples can be cited of earlier analyses of electroacoustic music. Around 1970, François Delalande of GRM-Paris wrote a significant article on the analysis of electroacoustic music, and Enrico Chiarucci produced perceptual ("phenomenological") analyses of works by Stockhausen and Penderecki. As DeLio, Licata, and Twombly do in the present volume, Robert Cogan's *New Images of Musical Sound* used sonograms to portray and analyze several musical works of various times, including electronic and digital works. Insightful analyses have been published by Stanley Haynes, Denis Smalley, Simon Emmerson, Hans Ulrich Humpert, Wolfgang Thies, and Michel Chion. Denis Lorrain's analysis of my piece *Inharmonique* was also a reconstitution, since he provided Music V scores that permitted the replication of certain sections through computer synthesis. This approach was also followed in the computer music synthesis manuals by Charles Dodge and Thomas Jerse and by Richard Boulanger. In a volume edited by Wolfgang Gratzer, *Nähe und Distanz*, the composers themselves, as well as other musicologists, provide analyses of instrumental, electroacoustic, and mixed works. The second volume produced by the Academy of Bourges, entitled *Analysis in Electroacoustic Music*, presents both a few general essays insisting on the importance of this issue as well as some analyses of electroacoustic pieces, with most of them documented by their authors.

The present book is an important contribution to the corpus of music analysis, which one can by no means reduce to a blind and automatic dissection according to a priori principles; each work requires its own approach, which may yield surprises. The detailed study of my own piece *Contours*, by composer Agostino Di Scipio, has been fruitful to me, unveiling certain features that I was unaware of. An insightful analysis participates in the life of the work by revealing unsuspected aspects and novel perspectives, enlightening listeners, and inspiring composers—teaching composition consists largely of analyzing musical works. In the case of electroacoustic music, a proper analysis clearly explicates the technical processes involved and their musical necessity and significance. Thus, the chapters that follow will be helpful to the understanding of electroacoustic music and its raison d'être.

REFERENCES

Analysis in Electroacoustic Music (1996). (All essays are published in English and in French). Proceedings of Session II, Académie de Bourges. Bourges: Editions Mnémosyne.

Boulanger, R., ed. (2000). *The Csound Book: Perspectives in Software Synthesis, Sound Design, Signal Processing, and Programming*. Cambridge: MIT Press.

Chiarucci, H. (1973). "Essai d'analyse structurale d'oeuvres musicales." *Musique en jeu* 12: 11–43.

Chion, M. (1983). *Guide des objets sonores: Pierre Schaeffer et la recherche musicale*. Paris: INA et Buchet/Chastel.

Cogan, R. (1984). *New Images of Musical Sound*. Cambridge: Harvard University Press.

Delalande, F. (1972). "L'analyse des musiques électroacoustiques." *Musique en jeu* 8: 50–56.

Die Reihe (1955). "Electronic Music." Vol. 1. Vienna: Universal Editions.

Dodge, C., and Jerse, T. (1985, 1998). *Computer Music: Synthesis, Composition and Performance*. New York: Schirmer Books.

Emmerson, S., ed. (1986). *The Language of Electroacoustic Music*. London: McMillan, 61–93.

Emmerson, S. (1998). "Acoustic/Electroacoustics: the Relationship with Instruments." *Journal of New Music Research* 27, nos. 1–2: 146–164.

Gratzer, W., ed. (1996). *Nähe und Distanz: nachgedachte Musik der Gegenwart*. Hofheim: Wolke Verlag.

Haynes, S. (1982). "The Computer as a Sound Processor: a Tutorial." *Computer Music Journal* 6 (1): 7–17.

Humpert, H. U. (1987). *Elektronische Musik: Geschichte, Techik, Kompostionen*. Mainz: Schott.

Lorrain, D. (1980). "Analyse de la bande d'Inharmonique de Jean-Claude Risset." Paris: Rapport IRCAM 26.

Mathews, M. (1969). *The Technology of Computer Music*. Cambridge: MIT Press.

Mion, P., Thomas, J.C., Nattiez, J.J. (1982). *Pour en finir avec le pouvoir d'Orphée, de Bernard Parmegiani*. Paris: INA et Buchet/Chastel.

Risset, J. C. (2001). "Problèmes posés par l'analyse d'oeuvres musicales dont la réalisation fait appel à l'informatique." In *Analyse et creation musicale*, Paris: L'Harmattan, 131–160.

Schaeffer, P. (1966). *Traité des objets musicaux*. Paris: Editions du Seuil.
Smalley, D. (1986). "Spectro-morphology and Structuring Processes." In *The Language of Electroacoustic Music*, edited by S. Emmerson, London: McMillan, 61–93.
Thies, W. (1987). In Batel, G., Kleinen, G., and Salbert, D. *Computermusik*. Laaber-Verlag.

Acknowledgments

First and foremost, I would like to thank each of the authors for contributing their valuable time and work in helping to create this collection of essays. I would also like to thank my editors at Greenwood Press, Pamela St. Clair, Eric Levy, and Nina Duprey for their invaluable assistance during the preparation of the manuscript. I would like to express my sincere appreciation to my friends and colleagues for their insightful comments and suggestions about various parts of the manuscript: Paul Berg, Konrad Boehmer, Linda Dusman, Alan Fabian, Wes Fuller, Patricia Julien, Orlando Legname, Liviu Marinescu, Scott McCoy, Diane Paige, Jerry Tabor, and Kees Tazelaar. I would like to especially thank Thomas DeLio, whose own music and teaching have played a decidedly influential role in bringing this project, among many others, to light. A special and heartfelt thanks goes to Jasenka Rakas, whose boundless enthusiasm and uncompromising honesty have inspired me to reach for more than I thought was possible. And to my parents and sisters Susan and Gabriele, for without their support and encouragement this book would never have come about.

Introduction

Thomas Licata

Electronic and computer technologies have equipped composers with the means to conceive, realize, and convey their musical ideas in ways never before possible. Indeed, since the inception of the electronic age, the music world has witnessed a veritable flood of extraordinarily diverse creative efforts, at times resulting in music of uncommon richness and diversity. Composers from around the globe have come to recognize the enormous creative potential of these resources, which, even today, continue to stimulate new modes of musical thought.

Over the course of the past fifty years, much has transpired within the realm of electroacoustic music. As the technology has grown increasingly more sophisticated and accessible, composers have embraced an ever-growing multiplicity of compositional approaches. Moreover, a considerable amount has been written about electroacoustic music, with much of it directed toward areas such as sound generation and transformation practices, new technological developments and applications, aesthetics, among others. Of course, these areas of inquiry are extremely important and, for the composer of electroacoustic music, even essential. However, only modest attention has been directed toward the actual analysis of electroacoustic works themselves.

Admittedly, the analysis of electroacoustic music presents unique challenges. In general, no score exists for such compositions. Moreover, as many electroacoustic works employ a full gamut of sound materials, from a pure sine tone to a virtual kaleidoscope of noise, music theory has not yet fully developed the means to confront such a wealth of sound materials. Despite such challenges, music theorists (in collaboration with those in computer science, psychology, acoustics, among other fields) must develop ways to effectively study this music. Invariably, new tools and methods will be created that will enhance our abilities to consider electroacoustic music. However, we must always be mindful of the fact that the importance of any new analytical tool or method lies in what it tells us about a musical work that we could not have gleaned in any other way.

The chapters in this book present detailed analyses of important electroacoustic works while also demonstrating some recent approaches to the analysis of this music. Drawn from music composed for "tape" alone by distinguished American, Asian, and European composers, the compositions under consideration span the mid-1950s to the late 1980s. The authors of these chapters are all distinguished composers and/or theorists who have actively worked in the field of electroacoustic music. The wide-ranging methodologies used throughout the book offer a variety of perspectives on the analysis of electroacoustic music. Whether through some form of existing documentation (composer's sketches and annotations, process scores, graphic notational scores, computer programs, among others) and/or some application of computer technologies (sonograms, amplitude graphs), each author endeavors to elucidate the overall sonic design of the work under investigation.

The works examined in the first three chapters, all written between the mid- and late 1950s, reflect the two prevailing aesthetics of electronic composition during its early years: *musique concrète* (based in Paris and drawn upon recorded sound materials) and "electronic music" (based in Cologne and drawn from synthesized sound materials). In Chapter 1, Pascal Decroupet and Elena Ungeheuer present a collaborative analysis of one of the seminal works of this period, indeed of Western music history, Karlheinz Stockhausen's *Gesang der Jünglinge* (1955/1956). This was one of the first works to integrate prerecorded sound materials (a boy's voice) and synthesized sound materials. Largely based on the examination of the composer's sketches, the authors undertake a comprehensive analysis of this work's rich amalgam of vocal and electronic sound materials as well as the serial and various extended serial procedures used throughout the piece. In Chapter 2, Thomas DeLio presents an analysis of Iannis Xenakis' first electroacoustic work, *Diamorphoses* (1957). Through the use of numerous and revealing sonograms of this work's recorded source materials (bells, airplane noises, and explosions), DeLio offers penetrating insight into the overall development and ultimate synthesis of these contrasting sounds, thereby revealing the work's dynamic formal design as it emerges from its sonic materials. In Chapter 3, Konrad Boehmer investigates Gottfried Micheal Koenig's *Essay* (1957/1958). Through the examination of this work's realization score, Boehmer devotes particular attention to the various processes needed to realize the piece. What is especially interesting about this analysis is that it is not so much an analysis of the product of the compositional process (the musical work itself) as an examination of the actual technical and compositional procedures that ultimately give rise to the musical work. Thus, the author affords the reader an intriguing look at this pioneering composer's thinking vis-à-vis the creative process.

The works examined in the next two chapters, both written in the 1960s, exemplify a compositional approach that further integrates the different aesthetics of *musique concrète* and "electronic music," not only through a deepening convergence of sound source materials but through compositional methodology as well. In Chapter 4, through the use of sonograms and amplitude graphs, the editor presents an analysis of Luigi Nono's first electroacoustic work, *Omaggio a Emilio Vedova* (1960). The images of these sonograms differ dramatically from those found in the analysis of *Diamorphoses*, most notably by the fact that the sound material of *Diamorphoses* was drawn from prerecorded, real-world sounds, while those of *Omaggio a Emilio Vedova* are entirely of electronic origin (the only electronic piece that Nono created in this way). In Chapter 5, Jerome Kohl investigates Stockhausen's work *Telemusik* (1966). Kohl approaches his analysis through an examination of this work's study/realization score. After providing a broad overview of Stockhausen's evolving thoughts on the subject of serialism, Kohl details the composition's overall moment-form as it relates to both its serial and nonserial moments as well as its electronic and nonelectronic moments.

With advancements in digital technology during the 1970s and early 1980s came the arrival of progressively more powerful and accessible digital computer systems, dramatically transforming the musical landscape of sound production and composition. Jean-Claude Risset, a pioneering composer and researcher, has commented on the considerable importance of computer applications in electro-acoustic music: "The computer can serve as a refined tool to probe into the deep microstructure of sound. It can help to set up situations whereby the composer can interact in various ways with his sound material, develop formal, graphic, gestural or sonic representations, and experience the control of sound and music both sensually and intellectually" (Risset 1996, 176).

The works examined throughout the last four chapters, all written in the 1980s, are by composers who, in a variety of ways, have used the computer in realizing their musical soundscapes. In Chapter 6, Otto Laske presents a procedural analysis of his piece *Terpsichore* (1980). While discussing his use of "outside-time" structures both compositionally and analytically, Laske considers the compositional processes and overall sonic design of this work as well as the integration of the computer programs and systems used in its construction. He concludes with a discussion of another piece written some twenty years later, *Trilogy* (1999–2001), a work that employs similar compositional methods but was created with altogether different technologies. In Chapter 7, Agostino Di Scipio examines Jean-Claude Risset's *Contours* (1982). Through detailed examination of the Music V instrument and score designs created by Risset for this work, as well as of his sketches and annotations (generously provided by the composer), Di Scipio surveys the resultant sound structures of the various synthesis techniques employed as well as their integration to the work's overall form. In Chapter 8, James Dashow provides an analysis of his own composition *Sequence Symbols* (1984). After furnishing an overview to the basic concepts of his generating-dyad compositional technique, Dashow illustrates the instrument designs of his computer orchestra and details the implementation of these instruments throughout the composition. In the last chapter, Kristian Twombly investigates *The Sea Darkens*, the first movement of Joji Yuasa's text piece, *A Study in White* (1987). Using sonograms of electronic and vocal sounds, Twombly examines the evolution of this work's many local and large-scale oppositional relationships. It is especially interesting to consider this analysis alongside those of Xenakis' *Diamorphoses* and Nono's *Omaggio a Emilio Vedova*, for all three employ the same technology for the computer-aided analysis of sound, sonograms.

This book represents not only a collection of analyses of electroacoustic works but also a collection of diverse and wide-ranging perspectives on the nature of analysis itself. Of course, the diversity of analytic approaches encountered throughout these chapters reflects the diversity of compositional approaches undertaken by this extraordinary group of composers. One hopes that these chapters will act as a point of departure for further investigations, and not only into music composed for tape alone but also into the myriad of other means and forms of creating music with modern-day technologies. As the field of electroacoustic music continues to grow, music theorists will be continually challenged. New, as yet unimagined analytical approaches will be envisioned, bringing us ever closer to a greater understanding of the medium known as electroacoustic music; a medium that continues to inspire, for the composer and listener alike, new modes of inquiry, reflection, and discovery.

REFERENCE

Risset, J. C. (1996). "Composing Sounds, Bridging Gaps: The Musical Role of the Computer in My Music." In *Musik und Technik: Funf Kongressbeitrage und vier Seminarberichte*, edited by Helga de la Motte and Rudolf Frisius. Mainz, Germany: Schott, 152–181.

1

Through the Sensory Looking-Glass: The Aesthetic and Serial Foundations of *Gesang der Jünglinge*

Pascal Decroupet and Elena Ungeheuer

Gesang der Jünglinge is an emblematic composition, both for its composer and for electronic music. In spite of certain bitter opposition due to the use of a child's voice, at the time of its premiere this work gave the feeling that the phase of etudes was over; we are faced here with an opus, in the most emphatic sense of the term. In the context of European work of the 1950s, it played the role of a real turning point in musical thought, on the one hand, precipitating certain beginnings of a broadening and reassessment of serial thought as it had been formulated in the first half of the decade and on the other hand, making this same thought permeable to some new influences or interpretations. Its antecedents date back to some instrumental works conceived only in anticipation of new technical means; later on, certain strategies implemented here would lead to *Kontakte* and the concept of "Momentform."

In the autumn of 1951, Pierre Schaeffer opened the doors of his studio for *musique concrète* to a younger generation of composers, in order to carry out a consciousness-raising training course. The works most resolutely turned toward the serial universe were the two *Etudes concrètes* produced by Boulez, at the end of 1951 and at the beginning of 1952, respectively. Their bases are significantly different from those of the *Konkrete Etüde* that Stockhausen undertook in December 1952. Boulez abides by the natural facts of the materials used (duration and dynamic curve, both functions of resonance) and applies to them a quantified system of the serial type, whereas Stockhausen, as early as the first phase of work, is seeking to constitute a malleable material that can, without restrictions, undergo a whole series of transformations—and this independently of its starting nature. This is the real beginning of work on pure sound, this amorphous "atom" of timbre, which it would be possible to order according to the same principles of global serial organization. The sense of projection is all-important: it is really a question of carrying the general, aesthetic, and technical principles right into the sound. In his first theoretical writing, "Situation des Handwerks" (1952), which remained unpublished at the time, Stockhausen summarized his then-current concerns in the formulation: "There is the consequence that for a work *X* alone, tones exist which bear the ordering character *X* and only as such and alone in this work have their meaning."[1] The first legitimate realization in this direction, although still posing some problems,[2] is *Studie I*, which Stockhausen realized in the electronic music studio of the Westdeutscher Rundfunk in Cologne from July to November 1953. In *Studie II*, an expression of a new fundamental questioning, the fusion of the partials is improved, certainly, but the sonorities are also noisier than the crystalline constellations of *Studie I*. These studies made it clear that too simple an acoustic premise had been used: the conception of new timbres as stable entities. However, with the conclusion of *Studie II*, Stockhausen writes that "the majority of the sound phenomena that we know are 'nonstationary'"[3] and that such things as the attack, the decay, and the minimal duration necessary to identify a sound intervene in the perception of timbres of phenomena. He infers nothing less than a new definition of the series, as a "series of 'general factors of modification' . . . applicable, according to its internal functional definitions, each time to another sound aspect or several sound aspects at the same time."[4] From repeated hearing of *Studie II*, Stockhausen extracts new criteria of composition, which he calls "statistical" and which he presents to the public through his analysis of *Jeux* by Debussy.[5] He focuses his attention on the overall directional tendencies of movement: the change from one state to another, with or without returning motion, as opposed to a fixed state. These motions can be descending or ascending in relation to some scale or other (on the level of pitches: from low to high; in dynamics: from weak to strong; in tempo: from slow to rapid; etc.). There results a system comprising, if one sets aside the forms created by the superposition of several curves, five situations:

For his new electronic music project, Stockhausen derived the shapes of articulation for sound complexes in time from the articulation of a sound, in phases of attack, sustain, and decay. In a work from that time, Fritz Winckel describes these different stages in the following way: the attack is "the setting into acoustic oscillation" of the phenomenon; in the sustain phase, "the various partials react to each other and modify qualities of the sound at every moment"; finally, during the decay, "the timbre is destroyed gradually and is reduced to some elements which fade away."[6] Whereas the middle part requires more specific means of description and characterization, the extreme parts can in all cases be subjected to the same restricted whole of directionalities to produce a limited number of temporal forms: setting into oscillation and decay from high to low (1), from low to high (2), or these two forms combined (3) or setting into oscillation from low to high and decay from high to low (4).

In choosing musical materials, the first stage concerns the acoustic matter to be integrated within a network of relations that gives them direction. Reversing the attitude that had prevailed in his studies, from now on Stockhausen sets out from the acoustical characteristics of the fundamental material itself, which he projects onto the form.

The sine tone and white noise are diametrically opposed in their spectral constitution; the sine tone provides a single precise pitch; white noise, provides a statistical mixture of all the sounds contained in a given frequency band. However, on the level of their duration these two materials function in an identical way, since neither the one nor the other is subjected to a specific dynamic curve. The impulse is, in terms of its spectrum, between the sine tone and white noise but has, like percussive sounds, a natural decay. One can thus arrange these materials in a triangle, the third point being located between the first two and at the same time on another level. As for the human voice, it is placed in the third dimension, as the fourth corner of a tetrahedron, because it includes specific cases of all the acoustic characteristics mentioned earlier: vowels are like harmonic unfoldings, setting out from sine tones; the fricatives and sibilants are like filtered noises; and the plosives are like impulses with variable intensity and attack.

From each of these materials, Stockhausen derives a certain number of criteria, which are then generalized to the other levels of composition: to the other sound dimensions or to the parameters of formal articulation. For vowels, by transference from the realm of pitch to that of durations (rhythm, pitch, and timbre merely constituting the qualitative realms that perception distinguishes within a physical continuum), Stockhausen passes from "spectra to rhythmic formants," as he calls them in his account relating to the techniques of composition implemented in *Gruppen*.[7] Noise, considered quite generally as chaotic matter, introduces the elements of statistics, of approximation, and of global qualification (as opposed to control down to the smallest detail). As for the impulse, in the systematic relation between sound and silence of the particular orderings, it prefigures in particular the alternation of families of different textures.

Whereas in "Aktuelles," a reflective article presenting the project as it existed in the spring of 1955,[8] the number 6 is said to be at the base of all the serial determinations, Stockhausen deviates as far back as the first realization sketches, dating from June 1955. The basic series of the work has seven elements and is deployed according to the principle of a function of functions developed by Boulez, meaning the transposition of the series onto its own elements.[9] The basic series and its transpositions constitute the top lines of serial squares of 7 × 7 elements, the vertical derivation of which is made by the unfolding of cycles of selection with increasing intervals (recall the principle of variable width for sonorities of *Studie II*): in the first square this interval is nonexistent, and so the series is repeated on each line; in the second square, the interval is 1, and the basic series is presented vertically in various rotations; in the third square, the interval is 2; that is, the new order of succession applied to each element of the transposition makes a value selection on 2 in the original; and so on.

Read horizontally, according to which direction each sound dimension is varied, this systematic transformation of the vertical forms leads to a constant redistribution of the elements of the series, modifying as much as possible the intervals from one serial form to another. The nonrepetition of contour of the serial forms is the aesthetic principle of "'statistical' permutation,"[10] which justifies the distribution of the organizing numbers in *Gesang der Jünglinge*. Example 1.1, a combination from various sketches, contains the complete serial grid, and the grid of the durations of reference, as well as the scale of variation for each dimension. There are four temporal parameters in the work:

1. the *value*: the fundamental duration, which regulates the intervals of entry between successive complexes;
2. the *duration*: the actual duration of each complex obtained by a positive or negative transformation of the value; depending on the duration/value ratio, the complexes will be partially superimposed or will be separated by a silence;
3. the *group of formants*: the number of "octaves of durations" within which the durations will be taken for carrying out the various harmonic subdivisions of the duration, the octave grouping being limited to five octaves; and
4. the *evolutionary form in time*, where the concepts of attack and decay of the sound, developed earlier, take place.

The temporal reference grid has seven octaves with seven equidistant subdivisions and extends from 4 to 512 centimeters, which—for a tape playing speed of 76.2 cm/sec—corresponds to a scale extending from a twentieth of a second to nearly seven seconds.

To realize the first six complexes, constituting a first element of the work, Stockhausen genuinely carves the blocks of rhythmic spectra according to the characteristic forms obtained by application of the serial system.

a. On the level of the *value/duration ratios*, we have:

I	420	:	490	+ 1/6
II	282.6	:	518.1	+ 5/6
III	256	:	213.4	- 1/6
IV	156	:	260	+ 4/6
V	172.3	:	258.4	+ 3/6
VI	116	:	116	unmodified

b. The *groups of formants*, where the limits for the various octaves of duration are 4/8/16/32/64/128/256/512 cm (durations exceeding this plan not being counted), giving the following vertical articulation:

I	group 3: 490/245-163.5/122.5-98-81.66-70; ratios: 1:2:4
II	group 7 = 2: 518.1/259.05/172.7-129.5; ratios: (1):1:2

Example 1.1
Serial Data for the Beginning of Part *F* (Combined from Sketches I/1–5 and 57)

value	3716524	7453261	1564372	6342157	5231746	2675413	4127635
duration	3716524	1327456	5427163	4617235	7154263	6741532	2753146
formants	3716524	6741325	4736521	1425763	2476135	7453126	5364721
time	3716524	5136742	7612435	2173546	1623457	4512367	6412357
pitch	3716524	2675134	6253714	7256314	4315672	5136274	1275463
dynamic	3716524	4512673	2341657	5734621	6547321	1327645	7536214
timbre	3716524	3264517	3175246	3561472	3762514	3264751	3641572

VALUE							
	4						
	8	7.25	6.6	5.95	5.4	4.9	4.4
	16	14.5	13.1	11.9	10.8	9.7	8.8
	32	29	26.3	23.8	21.5	19.5	17.7
	64	58	52.5	47.6	43.1	39	35.3
	128	116	105	95.1	86.2	78	70.7
	256	231.9	210	190.2	172.3	156	141.3
	512	463.7	420	380.4	344.6	312.1	282.6

DURATION (1) –1/6 (2) 0 (3) +1/6 (4) +2/6 (5) +3/6 (6) +4/6 (7) +5/6

GROUP OF FORMANTS

number (1) 1 (2) 2 (3) 3 (4) 4 (5) 5 (6) 1 (7) 2

from among the following possibilities:

1	12	123	1234
2	13	124	1235
3	14	125	1245
4	15	134	1345
5	23	135	2345
	24	145	
	25	234	
	34	235	
	35	245	
	45	345	

EVOLUTIONARY FORMS

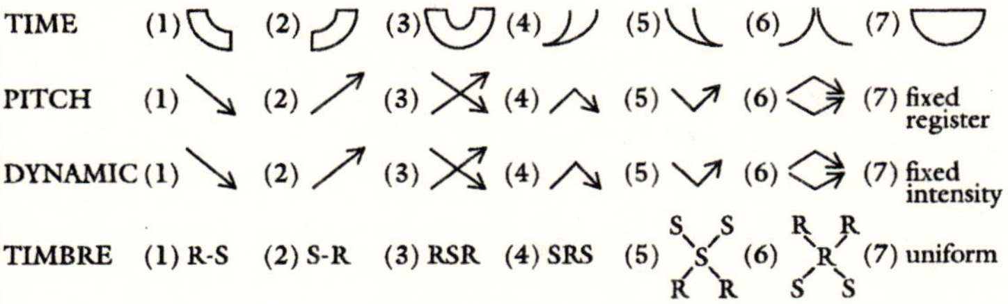

III group 1; selection: octave 2 [213.4]/106.7-71.1; ratios: [1]:2

IV group 6 = 1; selection: octave 1—the only component sound in the entire duration of the complex

V group 5: 129.2/86.1/51.7-36.9/28.7-23.5-19.8-17.2/15.2-13.6-12.3-11.23-10.34-9.57-8.9-8.33; ratios: 1:1:2:4:8[11]

VI group 2; selection: octaves 1 and 3 116/29-23.2-19.33-16.57; ratios: 1:4

(We note that what Stockhausen calls "rhythmic formant" here is a relatively faithful adaptation of the formant notion from acoustics, consisting of more or less dense frequency *regions*, which give each sound its specificity. In the instrumental works composed on the same bases, the final part of *Zeitmaße* and *Gruppen*—as well as in the theory related to it, formulated in the article "wie die Zeit vergeht"[12]—"formant" is made the equivalent of "rhythm harmonic," meaning therefore an integral periodic subdivision of the fundamental duration. The vertical proportional grouping in bands with a width of one octave each, characteristic of the first complexes composed for *Gesang der Jünglinge*, is therefore later replaced by an individual serial treatment of each rhythm harmonic.)

c. By the application of *evolutionary forms of in time*, we obtain Example 1.2. Spectra I and II should make comprehensible the difference between two spectra with settings into vibration from high to low and symmetrical decay, the first hollow, the second solid. However, because of its group of formants, spectrum II does not have enough elements to render this difference perceptible. The evolutionary forms of movement of spectra III, V, and VI are simple, either a setting into vibration from high to low (III and V) or a decay from low to high (VI). The appearance at the end of spectrum V expresses the difference between the "pointed" spectra and those that are denser at the end (III and VI). With only one component, complex IV obviously cannot describe any evolution.

d. For the *pitches*, as formulated in "Aktuelles," Stockhausen works with various scales, at this stage of the project still all dodecaphonic. Their subdivision can be harmonic, subharmonic, or chromatic (equal-tempered) or even result from the mixture of several of these scales. The scale worked out for the realization of the first complexes combines harmonic (*h*) and subharmonic (*sh*) degrees; it is cited here according to the first state of the sketch; by the time of realization, these figures had been rounded: 100, 104.35 (*sh*), 108.33 (*h*), 116.66 (*h*), 127.05 (*sh*), 133.33 (*sh*), 141.66 (*h*), 150 (*sh*), 158.33 (*h*), 171.4 (*sh*), 183.33 (*h*), 191.66 (*h*), 200.

The series used for the distribution of pitches contains, in fan shape, all the intervals: 12-1-11-2-10-3-9-4-8-5-7-6. For the later orders of succession, it is divided into three segments of five (a), one (b), and six (c) elements, respectively, then permuted. With each new line, the preceding result is presented in the form *c* retrograde, *a* retrograde, *b*, which amounts to isolating the seventh element of each form and then placing it at the end of the retrograde of the preceding form. After twelve permutations, we have returned to the starting point.

Example 1.2
Sketch Transcription, Beginning of Part *F*

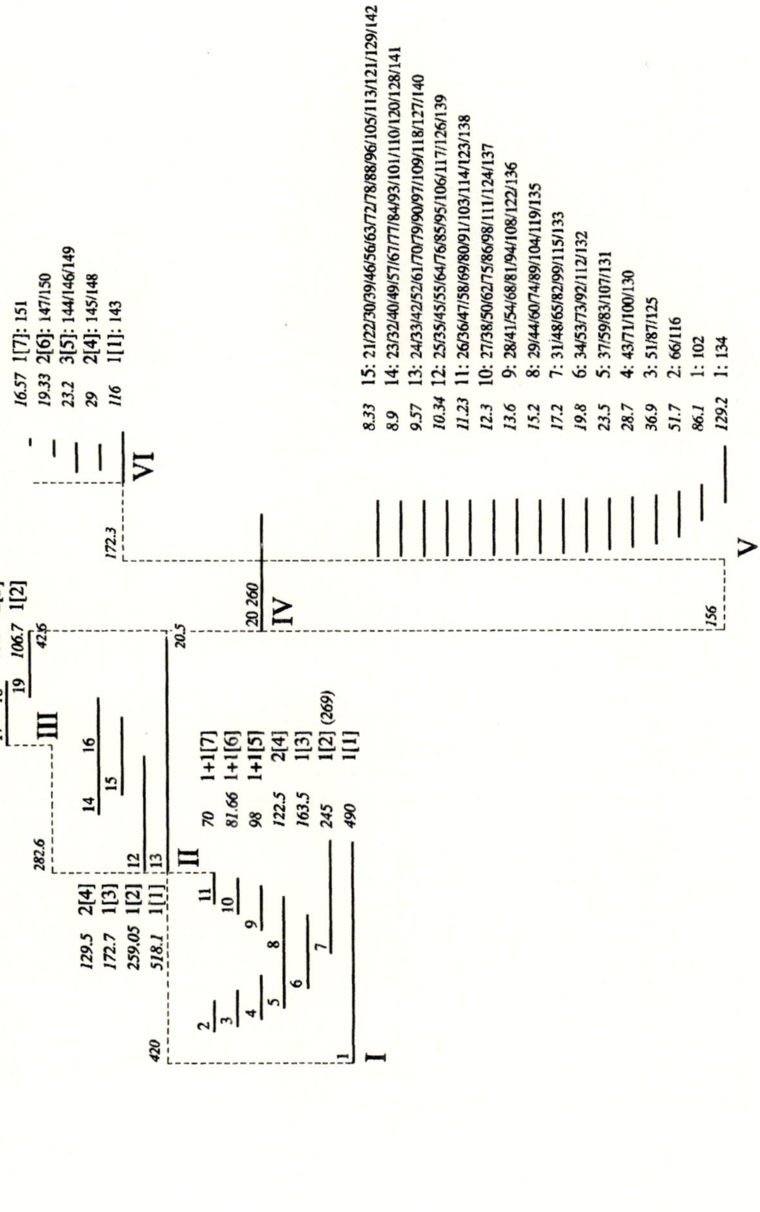

The range uses the seven available octaves (numbered from low to high—the first two sounds presenting these limits precisely), and the orientation of the figures follows the envisaged global determinations. Here, by way of example, is the movement of pitches in complexes I and VI:

Complex I: crossing of (*a*) a downward segment and (*b*) an ascending segment possessing a small final relapse

a:	*octave*	*sound*	*b:*	*octave*	*sound*
1:	7	12	2:	1	1
3:	6	11	4:	2	2
6:	5	3	5:	4	10
7:	4	9	7:	4	9
8:	4	4	9:	6	8
10:	3	5	11:	5	1

Complex VI: ascending movement in two stages (double wave)

	octave	*sound*
143:	3	5
144:	3	8
145:	4	4
146:	4	9
147:	5	10
148:	5	2
149:	4	11
150:	6	1
151:	6	12

The evolutionary form of movement of the pitches for complex V is limited to the middle octaves for the beginning and the end and spreads out to the full range at its center.[13] Now, this motion corresponds to the serial determination planned for complex IV, whereas complex V should have described a simple departure-and-return: descending-ascending. However, since complex IV, with its single component, cannot describe an evolutionary form, Stockhausen transfers its determination (the most complex among the forms selected) to the complex that has the greatest number of particles (V). Thus, he will not be missing an extreme in his grid, which he considers important to present in the most exhaustive possible way from the very beginning. Moreover, this modification breaks up the parallelism between the forms of movement of the pitches and of the intensities.

e. On the level of *dynamics*, spectra 1 to 6 fluctuate within an ambitus of two octaves, whereas spectra 7 to 15 move about over a range of three octaves of intensities. One can observe more or less marked local symmetries, which are produced during the systematic symmetries in the organization of the pitches.

f. As for the *evolutionary forms of timbre*, the elements contained in the fundamental sketch indicate a statistically prevalent state in the mixture at any given moment, the

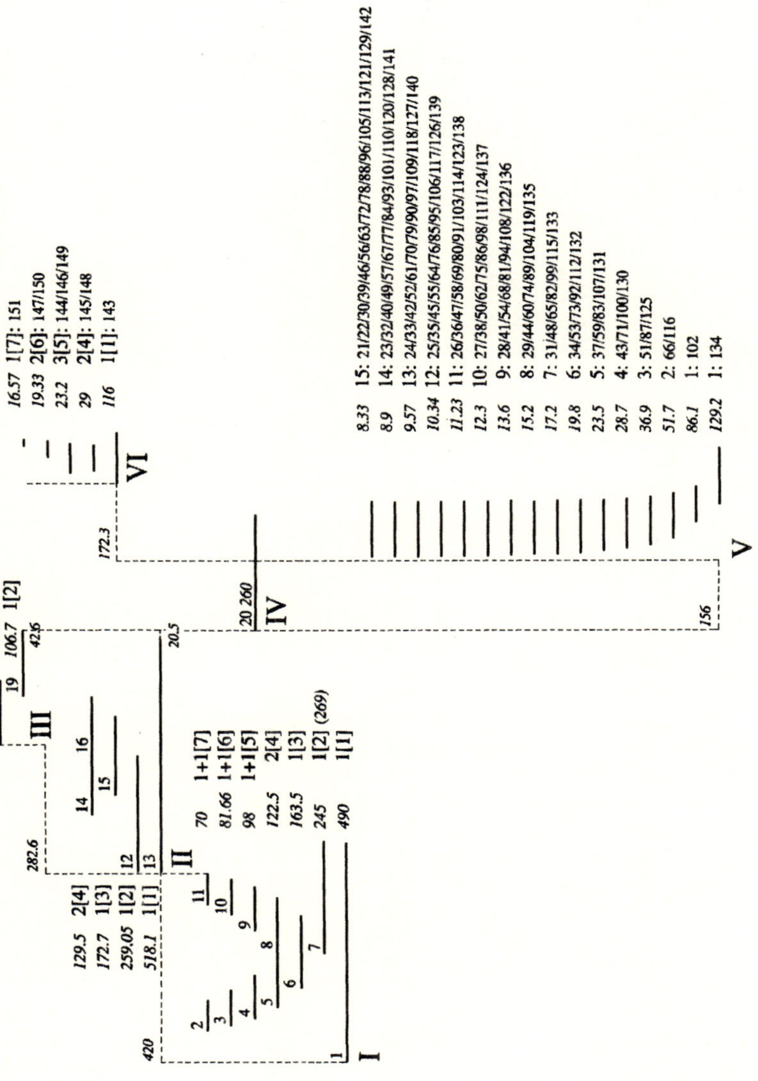

letters *R* and *S* being the abbreviations for *Rauschen* (noise) and *Sinus* (sine tone) and appearing there only as an indication. For the first six complexes, the distributions of the materials evolve as follows (with *N* = noise; *I* = impulse; *V* = vocal; *S* = sine tone)[14]:

1. *I I* *N V N* *N N*	2. *I I* *V* *N N*	3. *N S V* *I*
4. *V*	5. *S S* *I N I* *V V*	6. *V S I* *N*

For reasons similar to those raised earlier, which had led to changing the form of pitch movement, complexes II and IV exchanged their determinations for timbres. The observation raises an additional discrepancy, namely, that the form with the noisy element in the center is applied to complex V, not IV. It is not enough, however, to see simply an extra permutation there, because the interferences between the determinations, which have been isolated up to now, can have consequences in regard to which the composer must take a stand. In order not to distort the sung elements (the permutations of the letters to constitute syllables free from any semantic value were sung as such and do not result from a sound-editing operation), they can be placed only at the respective ends of complex V, which restricts their pitches to the two middle octaves, a tessitura where it is precisely the vocal element that prevails. Stockhausen realizes concretely, within only one sound complex, the fundamental thought that underlies the whole of this composition, namely, the transition from simple phenomena (sine tones and voice) via impulses to noise—here with a return to the starting situation.

On the level of the text, as this section was intended to be the introduction of the composition, Stockhausen used only the very first line of the Song of the Youths in the Burning Fiery Furnace, the apocrypha of the third chapter of the Book of Daniel, a generic phrase of praise of divine works that will be enumerated subsequently in the canticle.[15] In a second section, also based on temporal spectra but reducing the utilized material to some sine tones and a few syllables, the second element of the initial clause is subjected to permutations controlled by a construction on the level of the vocal timbres (the position of the vowels *a* and *i* in the phrase). From the initial clause, which is completely intelligible, one evolves toward another significant phrase while passing through entirely artificial intermediate stages. The complete vocal material of the work is presented in the Appendix, where, for this passage, one may refer to part *F*, sections D4 and H8.

On 6 August 1955, Stockhausen wrote to Pousseur, having finished twenty-five seconds of his new electronic work. The following day, he left Cologne for Paspels in Switzerland, where he withdrew until the beginning of October in order to start the composition of *Gruppen* and *Zeitmaße*. He also gave thought to how *Gesang der Jünglinge* should be continued. For the reformulated project, he sketched a new beginning consisting of four moments, which are written down in a large dramatic curve (parts *A* to *D*). The materials that he plans to realize pursue the route begun at the beginning of the summer, even while introducing new criteria. This differentiation of the criteria is pursued still in part *E*, the whole generating the logic that may be seen here (see Example 1.3).

The spectra of rhythmic formants, which is the starting point of the composer's thinking, are subjected to a serial generalization by the application of a double variation: in the horizontal direction and the vertical direction.

The horizontal organization of the layers can be periodic, as in the harmonic rhythm spectra, or, on the other hand statistical, as in the choral and impulse swarms produced in the autumn. By "statistical," one understands here that the composer has only an overall, qualitative control over the result, but not a quantitative one on the detailed level. Stockhausen goes so far as to integrate this approximation into the realization regulations themselves. Thus, for the choral swarms, he submitted to the young singer approximate graphs of pitch movement in a given time, where only the number of syllables per layer and the number of layers per complex were determined.[16] However, at the time of the realization it appeared that the young singer could not execute the graphic models with a precision to the nearest centimeter in regard to the overall duration of each layer, and Stockhausen decided to prefer approximate, but lively, results to a meticulous editing job that would break the phrasing. For this reason one hears in the work some complexes whose beginnings and/or ends give the impression of a setting into vibration or of a progressive decay, which extends certain of Stockhausen's initial ideas and are thus integrated perfectly into the system. As for the impulse swarms, they result from the superposition either of various realizations of the same overall process with a statistical description (the results having movement of definite pitches in parts *A*, *B*, and *D*) or of different processes carried out within the same temporal limit (nondirectional results in *C*). The parameters of variation, dependent on the machine used (Abstimmbarer Anzeigeverstärker of the firm UBM), are pitch, regulated through a filter device, the speed of impulse, and approximate duration of the impulses, regulated via the level of resonance.[17]

Between these two extremes of periodic articulation and statistical articulation extends the field in which the horizontal dimension is governed by the serial organization: the elements that make up a layer are, in general, whole-number multiples of a unit value in permuted order, the level of periodicity being a function of the vertical.

- The global form of part *C* (*C* form) is made up of four layers of 7, 14, 21, and 28 elements, with the layers in a ratio of 1:2:3:4.
- For the global form of part *E* (*E* form), Stockhausen carried out a regular selection of formants: 1, 3, 5, 7, 9, 11 (spectrum with odd formants).
- For the eleven stratified complexes of deep impulse groups in part *E* (*E* deep impulses), each layer is a mechanical transposition of a loop of impulses at irregular intervals; the lengths of the layers that make up a group are all multiples in irregular progression of a unit value (in Example 1.3, all the durations, expressed in centimeters of tape, are multiples of 90). Each layer, realized in its prescribed duration and

provided with a direction for the frequencies (in the example, ascending), is then broken up into proportional sections for permutation. The temporal shape of the spectra depends on a preestablished catalog of forms of synchronization, consisting in synchronization of the layers at the beginning and/or end of the complex, or following a central axis.

- For the vocal polyphonies inserted in the electronic texture of *E* (*E* vocal polyphony), the serial determinations deliver up a grid of variable durations and an index of polyphonic density for each duration, specifying the number of vocal parts that simultaneously articulate a syllable. Moreover, the distribution over the polyphonic voices takes into account the number of resultant syllables per voice; for each vocal insert, there is a different extract from the scale of integers (4 to 6; 4 to 8; 6 to 9 + 5 to 8; 7 and 8), reflecting the idea of the acoustic formant characterizing the sonorities.
- The groups of deep sounds presented melodically in part *C* are joined together polyphonically in *E* (*E* groups of deep sounds) according to an index of density and a form of synchronization describing the profile of the movement of density (in Example 1.3, a maximum density at the beginning; the figures indicate the duration of each layer in centimeters and the number of deep sounds by layer).

The implications of the changes of perspective are felt especially on the level of the working out of timbres, the other dimensions being less immediately dependent on the means of production specific to the period. Independent of obvious implications that will be noted, the aesthetic and technical bases are largely maintained, even if the visionary Utopia gives way to a certain pragmatism, which leads the composer to imagine translating processes of a kind even more proximate to the statistical principle, of permutation from the most elementary level of numerical determinations up to the practical realization of the sound complexes.

Part *A* (0:00–1:01) opens with an impulse swarm, which, as it breaks up, gives way to isolated impulses, which are controlled on the level of their frequency.[18] Over a background of supporting sounds consisting of combinations of variable timbres, there follows an alternation of isolated words (with a grouping into 2–3–1–4 syllables) and of choral swarms (whose vertical density varies according to serial forms: 6–4–3–7–5–1–2/4–6–3–7–5–2–1/etc.—see the Appendix), until some isolated impulses are accelerated until they become transformed into a new impulse swarm, at the same time a complement to, and a counterpart of, the first. With the exception of the final gesture, the simple phenomena are concentrated in loudspeaker I, whereas the mass phenomena sound, in turn, in one or several other loudspeakers. For the evolutionary forms of pitches, only the elementary forms and their simplest combinations (successive directions of movement without intertwinement) were retained. As for the spacing of events, it is subject to a distribution in zones with a duration from 1 to 7 seconds, partially following the basic series. Significantly, parts *A* and *B* each starts with a transposition of the original form, whereas the other serial forms utilized have statistical permutations of the elements.

A: 7453261/1653472
B: 6342157/6271435/2765134/1534627

Example 1.3
Table of Materials

acoustical references	SOUND sine-tone vowels						NOISE consonants / filtered noise	NOISE white noise
layers' intern. articulation	PERIODIC	SERIAL ORGANIZATION					STATISTIC	
vertical organization	spectra	spectra / formants subdivision of a unit		multiplication of a smallest unit	density		density	
complex forms	F (D4/H8)	C form	E form	E low filtered impulses	E vocal polyphony	E groups of deep sounds	A/B/D choral swarms	A/B/D and C impulse swarms
	harmonic time-spectra with timbre changes	proportional number of events 1:2:3:4	odd-numbered spectra regular selection	proportional lengths of layers (irregular progression) + permutations	density repartition on a grid of points of entrance	layers regulated through forms of synchronization	approximatively realized durations and pitches	approximative behavior following specific evolutionary forms
examples	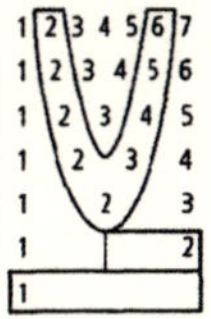 Sm 1	28 movements of impulses 21 syllables (3 groups) 14 groups of deep sounds 7 impulse swarms	11 low filtered impulses 9 groups of deep sounds 7 groups of high filtered impulses 5 filtered noises 3 reverberated deep sounds 1 low noise 1 2 3 4 inserts	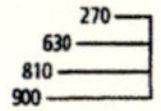 with ascending pitch-direction  permuted to  I 3/1	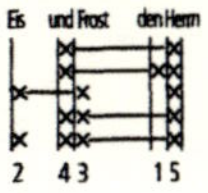 density beginning of insert 2	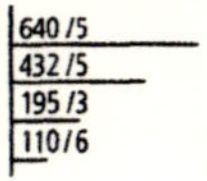 B3	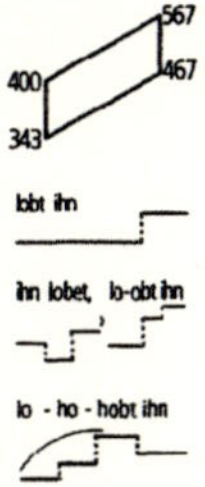 Cs 3	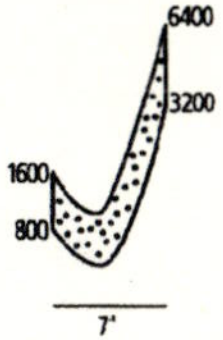 Is 1 beginning of part A
spatial distribution	spectra / speaker			layer / speaker	layer / speaker	layer / speaker	spectra / speaker	spectra / speaker

In addition, the actual durations in centimeters are drawn from the grid of tempered durations; it follows that the indications in seconds are approximate and can even vary in number of seconds for one and the same reference. Thus, for the theoretical value of one second (i.e., 76.2 cm), Stockhausen uses various durations: 86.1, 78, and 70.7 cm.

Whereas in *A* there is an overall opposition of simple and complex phenomena in the two "rich" timbres—voices and impulses—parts *B* and *C* divide them up between them. In *B* (1:02–2:42), Stockhausen makes use exclusively of choral and impulse swarms. The double temporal determination consisting of interval of entry and actual duration of the events opens up silences here and there between the choral swarms, which, usually, are partially superimposed. These zones of silence are filled by impulse swarms. The new choral swarms in *B*1 no longer exhibit characteristic pitch profiles but are restricted to a fixed frequency band; in *B*2 and *B*3, the previously introduced stable and mobile forms interact, either successively or simultaneously. The three sections of part *B* are distinguished, moreover, on the level of their spatial effect: in *B*1, the dynamics are constant by event; in *B*2, the variations of amplitude give way to a sensation of variable depth; in *B*3, the choral swarms move irregularly around the audience, anticipating the rotation of the long impulse swarm, which is at the same time the result of the thickening and compressing of the events in *B*2 and *B*3 and the beginning of part *C*. A similar phenomenon governs the utilization of the canticle's text. *B*1 continues the statement of verses 1 to 3 begun in *A*, whereas in *B*2 and *B*3 the principle of permutation becomes more widespread, directed at first in the choral swarms drawn only from verse 2 (*B*2) and then upon all of creation, which praises the Lord (*B*3—where the generic expression "ihr Werke alle des Herrn" no longer occurs).

The arrangement of the impulse swarms on the grid of intervals of evolutionary forms shows how Stockhausen adapted his ideas concerning forms of movement to this new context (Example 1.4). An exception occurs in the second impulse swarm in *A* (which is necessary to mark the symmetrical articulation of this part on the level of the form of the timbres: a very large form, of impulse-noise-impulse, on which is superimposed the double layer of vocal elements), and the durations of the swarms in seconds are varied according to a series of seven elements, whereas the forms of pitch movement describe the different possible forms, with a double interpretation of the "fixed register," that is, of the model of variation number 7. Over the whole of parts *A* and *B*, the evolutionary form for the timbres of these complexes is impulses / impulses intercut with complexes of sine tones / impulses—that is, a symmetrical form once again. In spite of its simplification, the parameter of timbre retains all its revelatory power: among the complexes with two timbres, only the two materializations of the model of variation 7 make exception regarding the principle of an impulse swarm broken off by an artificial resonance.

Part *C* (2:43–5:12—graphic transcription in Example 1.5)[19]—exhibits the full extent of the world of impulse variation. In order to distinguish the three types of sections that alternate irregularly, two statistical variants of impulses (IN1 and IN2) appear alongside regular melodic successions (IK). IK stands for

Example 1.4
Impulse Swarms in *A* and *B* (with durations)

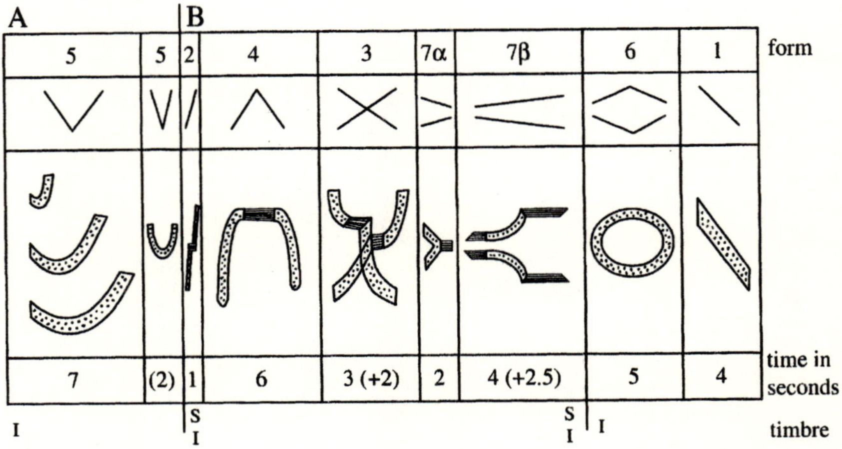

Impulse künstlich (i.e., isolated impulses stuck onto leader tape according to a serial grid of spacings); IN stands for *Impulse natürlich* (i.e., successions of impulses delivered directly by the generator). Despite the fact that these abbreviations date back to a first intention for realization, and Stockhausen changed the mode of production of the IKs (generating them directly with the machine, as well), the different sections reflect well the initially selected characterizations, which can therefore always serve the needs of analysis as well as those of hearing. An additional mode of orientation between these two large families is the movement of the sounds in space, because the periodic and statistical phenomena rotate in opposite directions. The beginning of each section is announced by a short, but dense, impulse swarm, to which choral swarms are assimilated three times. The voice intervenes, always with distinct syllables, in the sections with only isolated impulses, thereby showing analogous melodic-treatment criteria for the two phenomena of different material origin.

On the level of serial organization, several factors interact, to begin with, the number of events per timbre. The principle of the harmonic formant is transferred into the realm of form (with the number 7 as basic unit)—see Example 1.3. These numerical data were slightly altered: for instance, there are twenty-two vocal entities, some of which do not consist of isolated syllables but of groups of syllables of variable density (4, 3, 2); and the reckoning of impulse swarms includes neither the big initial swarm nor the last at the beginning of the background layer of part *D*, both with the profile of frequencies polished over the course of time.

The durations of the sections and the spacing of the vocal sounds or of groups of deep sounds draw their values from the tempered grid of seven elements by the application of a cycle of selection with interval 5.[20] Such a mode

Example 1.5
Part *C*, Score

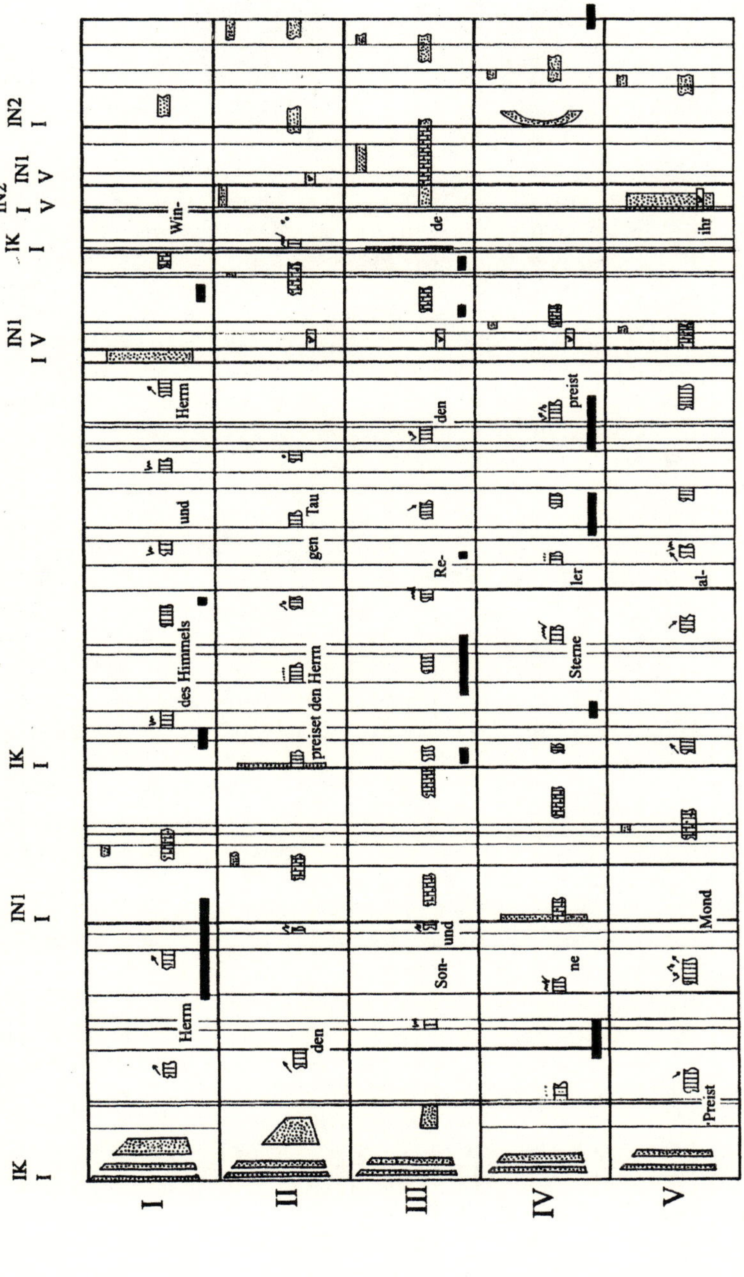

of selection of value within the grid reproduces in a completely different context the principle of derivation by a variable cycle from the initial serial table. What is remarkable for this cycle of interval 5 is that the values selected are in ratios surprisingly close to those of one of the Fibonacci series, the sum of two consecutive elements always approximating the following element closely enough.

The durations for the fragments making up the impulse swarm that opens part *C* are taken from the tempered grid but, this time, according to a cycle of interval 3: 5.4, 7.25, 9.7, and so on, up to 190.2.

The sections, in addition, will be subdivided in order to control the organization of the background elements: bands of filtered noise and groups of impulses, distinct or statistical. To this end, Stockhausen extends the principle adopted for parts *A* and *B*, that is, the durations of reference expressed in seconds. As such, they apply to the sections with distinct impulses; for the sections with statistical impulses, they alternate with values taken from an original scale of "dotted" values: 110 (78 + 32), 258 (172 + 86), 326 (210 + 116), 439 (283 + 156), 570 (380 + 190), 696 (464 + 232), 795 (512 + 283) cm.[21]

A setup governed by the number 7, which is the foundation of the first serial data of *Gesang der Jünglinge*, is effective on several levels in the working out of figures with distinct impulses. The various parameters are the evolutionary form of pitches, the ambitus (the base of which, theoretically, is the subdivision of the octave into seven equidistant steps), the number of impulses per second that the machine delivers (even-numbered settings only), and intensity. On the level of ambitus, the transfer into the pitch realm of the principle previously tied to the organization of durations demonstrates in a way such that it actually could not make more plain the equality between the dimensions in the serial universe, an equality that is the very basis of the concept of "parameter," which is used by Stockhausen precisely from the moment where the determinations exceed the framework of the acoustic dimensions of the sound phenomena.[22] Example 1.6 shows these data as they appear in the work, taking into account the various modifications that occurred while working them out, up to the final realization; it contains, moreover, the indications of grouping of the twenty-eight figures in fourteen sequences (one of density 2, two of density 4, three of density 3, and eight of density 1—another allusion to Fibonacci: 1-2-3-[5]-8).[23]

In part *D* (5:13–6:20), tracks III to V from the middle section of part *B* are heard in reverse. Onto this mixture of choral swarms (immediately identifiable as being of vocal origin, though the text is not comprehensible) and impulse swarms are grafted vocal chords of variable density in a homorhythmic setting. The spacing of the vocal chords, whose density varies syllable by syllable according to the serial forms 2-6-5-3-7-4-1/5-3-6-4-2-1-7, is calculated on the basis of a cycle of interval 5, transposed in respect to the grid of reference according to the length of the segment, taken again from part *B*. The end of *D* marks a reduction of the voice to its simplest means, isolated syllables more declaimed than sung, accompanied by very fine impulse sizzlings in the high register to begin with and then alone.

Part *E* is built from a scale of electronic timbres developed from those of part *C*. On the level of form, electronic and polyphonic-choral sections alternate

Example 1.6
Figures of Distinct Impulses in *C*

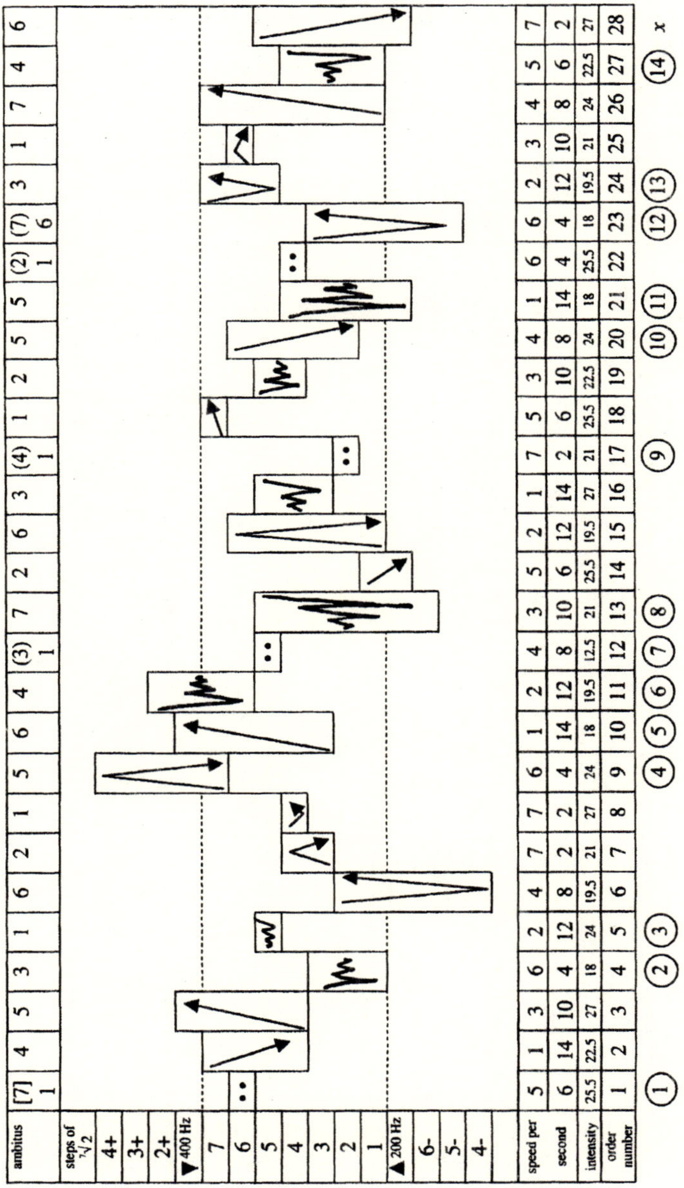

antiphonally, interrupting the continuous course of the electronic part, which is organized over the whole of *E*'s duration according to a spectrum with odd formants—see Examples 1.3 and 1.7. Each layer is divided into groups of variable density, multiples of a different basic unit. In addition, the two most complex layers—the groups of impulses and of deep sounds—vary with each of their appearances in density and on the level of their form of synchronization.

The collection of groups of deep impulses is based on a single tape loop 540 cm in length, on which the impulses are spaced according to a serial distribution (128-60.4-36.5-13.3-22-77-10.3-100-17.1-47-28.4 cm, i.e., a permuted order in the scale according to the series 11-8-6-2-4-9-1-10-3-7-5). The proportions that regulate this smallest-scale spacing also serve to determine spacings of the various groups. The values of durations are chosen again by means of a cycle of selection, this time with interval 4. But instead of resorting to the grid of the durations used up to now, Stockhausen turns to a scale of eleven degrees per octave, which was used in *C* to determine the pitches of the vocal interventions. This loop of impulses is then transposed (brought to a duration of 900 cm in the example in Example 1.3) and provided with a pitch direction, then divided into proportional parts in permutation, and finally synchronized at the rate of one layer per loudspeaker. The relationships between the lengths of the various layers are also proportional, but the progressions are not regular, as is also the case for the spectrum of odd formants organizing the distribution of timbres.

Example 1.7
Formal Sketch of Part *E* with Indications of the Overall Durations and of the Subdivisions for Each Layer

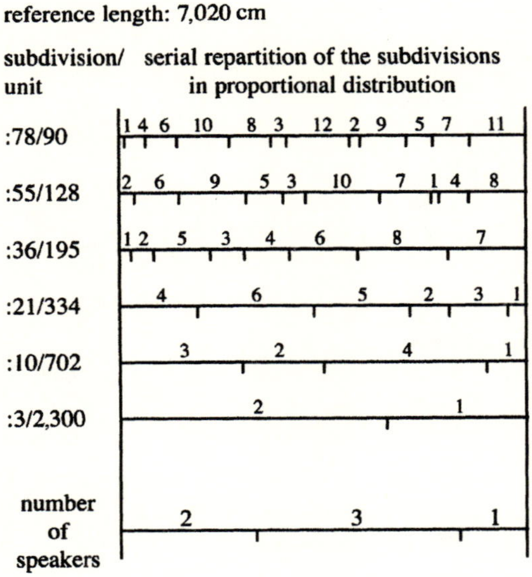

The groups of deep sounds are constructed on the basis of groups introduced in *C*, with the possibility of being transposed before being integrated in the new entity. The fifth presents a special feature because it is, according to Stockhausen's expression, "rhythmicized"; that is, the parts of sound and silence alternate, for a total duration of 540 cm for the sounding parts and 740 cm for silences. The length of the loop of deep impulses is 540 cm, and the isolated durations in the mixing of deep sounds vary according to the subdivisions of this loop. The scale with the overall value of 740 cm is taken from the same scale of eleven degrees per octave and according to the same interval of selection. These two numbers also govern the vocal polyphonies, which last 990, 740, 1,280, and 540 cm, respectively (1,280 = 540 + 740; the 990 cm are divided according to the same durations as the eleventh group of impulses, which is of the same length and which had been produced by transposition of the initial loop in the ratio 50:27.3).

The filtered impulses in the high register attest to a strict organization on the level of the group (2-1-3-4/1-4-2-3)—there are eight groups in all, because part *E* starts with high impulses, a timbre common to parts *D* and *E* that serves them as a pivot. Durations and transpositions of the filtered fragments change independently; for the first, Stockhausen returns to the grid of seven equidistant degrees from which he takes, in a cycle of interval 4, a total number of seven values: 11.9-17.7-26.3-39-58-86-128, which appears in the order *x*-3/7/1-6-5/2-4-6-7/5/4-1-3-2/6-5/4-7-3, reproducing first the basic series and a transposition in rotation: 3-7-1-6-5-2-4 and 2-6-7-5-4-1-3 starting from the 6.[24]

The vocal polyphonies inserted into this electronic texture have a different number of voices each (3-5-4-2), clearly perceptible because each voice sounds from a different loudspeaker (for the insert with maximum density, Stockhausen has, in addition, superimposed two voices per loudspeaker). The serial organization extends to the number of attacks per layer and their variable vertical density (see Example 1.3)[25]; the durations for the syllables were selected from the scale of eleven degrees per octave by means of a cycle of interval 4. Precision in the realization of the durations is made possible by the fact that the young singer stresses the consonant aspect of the words here: Eis, und, Herrn, preist, Frost. The spectral nature of consonants, in fact, allows an a posteriori assembly more easily than for vowels, which are more sensitive to dephasing. As these polyphonies were to be assembled sound by sound, the intonation could be refined and very precisely controlled. The scale comprises sixty equidistant degrees per octave and is, in each insert (*i*), traversed according to a different cycle of selection (*cs*)[26]: *i*1-*cs*2; *i*2-*cs*4; *i*3-*cs*3; i4-*cs*1. These frequencies are gathered into sets of five pitches and then permuted according to a series of five elements (2-1-4-5-3) deployed accordingly (Example 1.8).

On the level of number manipulation, Stockhausen returns here, as in the groups of deep sounds of part *C*, to the technique advocated in *Studie I*, that is, to a series deployed in a function of functions whose elements are joined together in aggregates of variable density by an index of grouping. This may be surprising in a work in which, until then, the composer has constantly carried out statistical permutations according to ever-new principles, some of which

Example 1.8
Frequencies of the Syllables of the Second Vocal Polyphony (cf. Example 1.3)

scale (subdivision of 60 steps per octave) and selection following a cycle of 4

634.5	und	a1	503.6	Frost	b1	399.7	Herrn	c1
627.2			497.9			395.11		
620			492.1			390		
612.9			486.5			386		
605.9	und	a2	480.9	Frost	b2	381	Herrn	c2
598.9			475.4			377.3		
592			469.9			372.9		
585.2			464.5			368.6		
578.5	und	a3	459.2	und	b3	364.4	Herrn	c3
571.9			453.9			360.2		
565.3			448.7			356		
558.8			443.5			352		
552.4	Eis	a4	438.4	den	b4	347.9	Herrn	c4
546			433.4			343.96		
539.7			428.4			340		
533.6			423.5			336.1		
527.5	Eis	a5	418.6	Frost	b5	332.2	Herrn	c5
521.4			413.8					
515.4			409.04					
509.5			404.35					

series for ordering		21453
		15342
		43125
	a	54231
	b	32514
	c	15342
		54231
		32514
		43125
		21453
density series for syllables		Eis (2) und (4) Frost (3) den (1) Herrn (5)
order of syllables		Eis (a5 + a4)
		und (a2 + a3 + a1 + b3)
		Frost (b2 + b5 + b1)
		den (b4)
		Herrn (c1 + c5 + c3 + c4 + c2)

are systematic whereas others are irreducible to a unique process. Does this diversity of strategies necessarily suffice to explode the unifying serial idea? No, because Stockhausen's concern is detached from the processes themselves in order to focus even more on their results, independently of the path that led there. In the vocal polyphonies, the quantity of data to be managed is relatively important, and a systematic procedure facilitates their organization. In addition, the variable grouping, the durations partly independent of the simultaneously attacked syllables, the spatial distribution of the voices of the polyphony, and the different scales for each insert so effectively thwart the emergence of isomorphisms that the chosen tool is only seemingly in contradiction with the subjacent thought. The actualization within the piece, which is dependent on intermediate manipulations that really do modify the appearance, prevails over the elementary preparations, chosen for their simplicity and their speed of execution.

The temporal plan, which is the basis of the final part, *F*, and which Stockhausen had worked out at the time to produce the first complexes with mixed timbres, follows a long departure-and-return curve between long and short values of duration traversing seven octaves of durations.[27] However, the new overall proportions required a longer duration for this sixth part, for which reason Stockhausen grafts onto the returning movement toward longer values two "rhythmic inserts," which occupy only the four highest octaves of the scale of durations. The internal organization of these inserts combines determinations of duration in seconds (from 1 to 6) and of directional tendencies, simple in the first insert, compound in the second. The simple directional tendencies are:

1. values statistically all rapid (higher octave)
2. values statistically all slow (lower octave)
3. accelerando
4. rallentando
5. accelerando-rallentando
6. rallentando-accelerando

The compound variants combine one of the static possibilities (1 or 2) with one of the emphatic movements (3 to 6).

Serially, the order of succession of the durations of sections in the inserts is regulated by the transpositions of a serial form of six elements (4-1-2-6-3-5) obtained by filtering starting from the last transposition of the basic series of seven elements 4-1-2-(7)-6-3-5, by analogy with the limited ambitus of durations available in these inserts.

4 1 2 6 3 5	
1 4 5 3 6 2	first insert
2 5 6 4 1 3	
6 3 4 2 5 1 + 2	second insert

At the beginning of part *F*, Stockhausen places those first few seconds that had been realized in the summer of 1955. The distinction between value and duration of an event that had prevailed there will be maintained only up to the thirtieth value, the later ones taking concrete form in terms of complexes each having but a single sonority. From here on, the sounds follow one another continuously, sometimes interrupted by silences that constitute an additional means of articulation. The possible superpositions between loudspeakers result from a new criterion, namely, a regulation of polyphonic principles by section (in the spirit of the synchronization forms in *Studie II*), the extremes of the scale being strict alternation between the loudspeakers ("Wechsel") and the superposition of a new element onto a resonance in one or more other loudspeakers ("Polyphonie"), the intermediate cases resulting from combinatorial operations on these two strategies ("Kombiniert").

The articulation of the formal plan for this final part (see Example 1.9) fulfills a principle of polyphony as well, because it superposes two partially independent temporal structures. They have in common their overall durations, each divided according to a different principle (a procedure similar to the independent movements of tempo in *Zeitmaße*). The framework is provided by a series expressed in seconds (54-36-45-27-9-18), in which the internal articulation is made up, in the first structure, of multiples of the unit of 3" (initially according to the same series 6-4-5-3-1-2 and then according to permutations that allow the lower level to adopt the proportions from the higher-level framework) and, in the second structure, according to a division of the overall duration into four proportional sections. Each global duration is brought out, on the one hand, by a particular polyphonic type and, on the other, by a prevalent loudspeaker in the spatial setup. The first structure combines the determinations relating to grouping (the maximum number of sonorities that can constitute a figure), to the ambitus of the scales (number of octaves), and to their subdivision (all in equidistant steps); the second ties together the number of loudspeakers (and their selection), the combination of timbres in terms of homogeneity or heterogeneity, and the selections from the scale of timbres, adding up to twelve different categories (i.e., their grouping form).

For the first set of structures, the direct relation between the ambitus of the scales and the durations of the sequences must be emphasized: this close correspondence between the horizontal and the vertical is the very basis of the temporal organization of *Gruppen*, where the maximum number of rhythm harmonics per group corresponds to its number of fundamental durations. In addition, the subdivisions of the scales used per polyphonic type attest to a taxonomy of distribution that anticipates *Kontakte* on several levels: for "Polyphonie," the scale progresses by steps of 1 (7-8-9-10-11-12); for "Kombiniert," by steps of 2 (7-9-11-13-15-17); for "Wechsel," by steps of 3 (7-10-13-16-19-22). The distribution of pitches does not ensure, however, throughout part *F*, any real function of formal articulation: it is rather used to describe the different scales of variable rates for filling-in by a statistical scanning.

The articulation of the form depends, on the contrary, upon decisions relating to timbre, namely, the type of combination within the figures formed by

Example 1.9
General Plan for Part *F*

1st rhythmic insert (from the 18-sec. field of section 36 to the 6-sec. field of section 45); 2nd rhythmic insert (from the 12-sec. field of section 27 to the end of section 9)

section duration in sec.	**54**	**36**	**45**	**27**	**9**	**18**
field duration in sec.	*18* / *12* / *15* / *9*	*3* / *6* / *18* / *9*	*3* / *15* / *12* / *6* / *(9)8*	*15* / *12*	*3* / *6*	*18*
polyphonic type	Wechsel	Polyphonie	Kombiniert	Polyphonie		Kombin.
group (number of sounds per unit)	1 / 2 / 4 / 6	5 / 3 / 5 / 4	6 / 3 / 1 / 2 / 3	2 / 5	4 / 1	(6) 5/1 (synchr. 2/4)
number of octaves	6 / 4 / 5 / 3	1 / 2 / 6 / 3	1 / 5 / 4 / 2 / 3	5 / 4	1 / 2	6
scales (subdivision per octave)	7 / 13 / 10 / 16	12 / 11 / 7 / 10	17 / 9 / 11 / 15 / 13	8 / 9	22 / 19	7
prevalent speaker	1	4	2	5	3	1
duration for speaker changing in sec.	21.6 / 10.8 / 5.4 / 16.2	3.6 / 14.4 / 10.8 / 7.2	18 / 13.5 / 4.5 / 9	2.7 / 8.1 / 5.4 / 10.8	0.9 / 2.7 / 1.8 / 3.6	5.4 / 3.6 / 1.8 / 7.2
number of speakers	5 / 3 / 2 / 4	3 / 4 / 2 / 5	2 / 3 / 5 / 4	4 / 5 / 5 / 3	3 / 2	—5—
selection of speakers	1 2 3 4 5 / 145 / 13 / 1 2 3 5	42 1 / 4 3 2 1 / 4 1 / 43 215	25 / 235 / 23 45 1 / 23 41	54 32 / 543 21 / id. / 531	32 / 33 15 2 / 3 4	1 2 3 4 5
grouping form	I V / III / I / II	IV / III (I) / II / II (III)	IV / III / IV (II) / I	IV— / I / II	III I / II	III
timbre field	D 4 / H8 / R6 / N10	V2 / M11 / F6 / B2	J10 / P8 / X1 / T4	W1 C3 / G7 / K11	S5 / E5 / O9	—L12—
0 dB						

grouping and the portion of the timbral scale exploited in each section. Spatial projection, in addition to its dramaturgical function, also serves the clarification of this double articulation of timbres.

First of all, the four fundamental materials were increased to a catalog of twelve categories[28]:

1. sine-tone complexes
2. impulse complexes
3. vocal sounds or syllables
4. white noise filtered to about 2% width (in Hz)
5. single impulses with definite pitch
6. synthetic vowel sounds (spectra rich in overtones with varying formant combinations)
7. white noises filtered to a width of 1 to 6 octaves
8. impulses in swarms of statistically defined density, filtered to a width of 1 to 6 octaves
9. single impulses synchronized in chords
10. chords of narrowly filtered noises
11. sine-tone chords
12. vocal chords

The extremes are the elements with the simplest spectra (sine-tone complexes) and those with the most complex spectra (sung chords). The gradation is, according to Stockhausen, the most continuous possible. Having established this hierarchy, Stockhausen works twenty-three combinatorial possibilities out of it, designated successively from A1 to L12, then from M11 to W1: the index represents the number of timbral categories contained in a field, it being understood that from A to L, a new category is always added to the scale in order of increasing complexity, and from M to W the categories are subtracted one by one until finally only the vocal chords are retained.[29] To obtain these fields' order of succession, Stockhausen deploys their representatives vertically in six columns, the first three in correct order, the last three with an interchange of the second and fourth elements or, put another way, in rotated retrograde:

A	E	I	M	Q	U
B	F	J	P	T	(X)
C	G	K	O	S	W
D	H	L	N	R	V

In the composition the fields will appear, interrupted by two long silences, in the order:

D H R N V M F B // J P X // T W C G K S O E L

that is, a free arrangement by line; the exchange of the fields M and L results from a later operation; the fields not used were not related to the draft of the formal plan.

For the combination of timbres, Stockhausen distinguishes the bodies and the endings of the figures, ringing the changes independently between a homogeneous situation and heterogeneous successions of timbres. The four possibilities are:[30]

	body	*endings*
I	heterogeneous	homogeneous
II	homogeneous	heterogeneous
III	heterogeneous	heterogeneous
IV	homogeneous	homogeneous

In order that this timbral structure may be really effective as a guide to perception, Stockhausen increases its obviousness by interrupting the course of sonorities on various occasions, entrusting to the silences thus created some revealing functions of various orders. The first silence separates the first thirty values, which are obtained by modification of the fundamental duration, from the remainder of the curve of values, where sonorities follow one another without automatically generated superpositions or interruption. As the overall determinations for part *F* were distributed over the large form according to durational proportions in centimeters of tape, not according to key points of group articulations, the overlapping or transitional groups between harmonic fields and polyphonic types are the rule, not exceptions. The field of timbres that follows this first interruption, N10, includes at its beginning and end the last group of R6 and the first of V2 (the latter does not yet adopt the new scale of timbres but does already have the new form of internal timbral articulation, IV: =,=). N10 is articulated by silences according to a grouping series for the figures (1-5-3-7-6-4-2), which implies, with the first interruption, a total of eight silences, the first seven of which follow the original series 3-7-1-6-5-2-4, in duration classes selected from the grid of reference durations (values: 52.5-70.7-32-39-86.1-58-47.6; elements 1, 5, and 7 are multiplied by 2, the third by 4); the eighth silence again takes a duration of class 7, that is, the beginning of a serial form on the second term of the series—a logical procedure according to the principle of the function of functions. The following silence lasts nearly eight seconds and includes four nonstructural chords of impulses grouped in 1+1+2 attacks: it separates off the large sections of "Polyphonie" from the following ones, which are in "Kombiniert" mode. Fields J10-P8-X1 form the central section of this part. In J10, the silences are colored by choruses in the background (choral swarms of voices from *A* and *B* repeated in a loop), and they separate some groups of figures with an identical final timbre, changing group by group. In P8 and X1, the silences are really empty and isolate the rhythmic insert's various temporal zones, measured in seconds and each provided with an internal movement of different durations (2-5-6-4-1-3 seconds). X1 is followed by a second long silence, filled in gradually in the fifth loudspeaker by the syllable "ihn," reverberated for a long time and played backward. The last two silences, at the beginnings of O9 and L12 respectively, isolate the short section in "Wechsel" mode before the final section in "Kombiniert" mode, which returns, after the second rhythmic insert, to the long values of the beginning of part *F*. The closing gesture of the work appears as if cut off from the rest of the final structure because of the elimination of a long vocal chord on "Herrn," which was to have joined parts *F* and *G* and which, structurally, belongs already entirely to the unfinished part *G*.

The two elements put forward by Stockhausen in the general introductory texts to *Gesang der Jünglinge* are the composition of timbres and spatial articulation. The desire to have at his disposal electronic sounds of a complexity comparable to vocal sounds had spurred him toward the composition of sound complexes integrating particles of various material origins. The difficulty and the slowness of realization of such complexes, however, led the composer to imagine, for the interaction of timbres, different transpositions to formal levels by a variety of grades. The majority of the events, taken separately, have a homogeneous timbre, and only their combination in the form gives rise to significant distributions. In the most general way, the principles of interaction are summarized by polyphony (parallel control, largely independent of the various layers of events) and by alternation (interruption of one type in favor of another). A typical instance of polyphony clarified by spatial disposition occurs at the beginning of the work, with all the behavioral types of electronic sounds in one and the same loudspeaker; alternation is presented for the first time in part *B* with the impulse swarms, which fill in the empty spaces of the vocal structure. In part *C*, these two principles are combined in different respects:

- the continuous weft of groups of deep sounds, which constitutes a polyphonic element independent of articulation into sections;
- within the sections with distinct impulses, the unfolding without any reciprocal interference of impulses and syllables;
- the alternation of groups of distinct and statistical impulses and, on a lower level, of presence and absence of the weft of noise and impulses in the sections with distinct impulses, of presence and absence of groups of filtered impulses in the high register in the sections with statistical impulses.

In part *E*, the relation of alternation between vocal elements and electronic material is the opposite of the situation in *B*, because it is the vocal inserts that come to interrupt the electronic weft. What's more, in *E* the most clear-cut juxtaposition coexists with polyphony of the greatest number of independent layers.

The degrees of intelligibility of the text to which Stockhausen drew attention for the beginning of the work[31] are precisely a function of the degree of structural transparency, of the relative potential for analysis that the listener is offered. From this point of view, the electronic and vocal parts of *E* have a common denominator: each layer being heard in one loudspeaker, the distinction of the components of the polyphony is, if not easy, at least possible. On the other hand, the choral and impulse swarms packed together into compact blocks assigned to only one point in the hall (parts *A* and *B*, especially) make impossible any attempt to distinguish the components. In the sections of part *F* where the bodies as well as the ends of the figures are different, Stockhausen exploits two different strategies. In M11 (see Example 1.10), where the grouping makes it possible to put together units of a certain length, he takes advantage of the speed of succession of the events delivered by the first rhythmic insert to produce, thanks to a certain fusion of the components, the illusion of timbral transformations within the same complex (a perspective that prolongs the complexes that were the first ones realized and came to be integrated into this final part). In P8, where the grouping of density 1 would normally bring about a complete and utter explosion, the spatialization that intervenes to clarify the composition of the timbres by allotting to certain loudspeakers all the variants of one category of timbre and by concentrating the irregular changes in only one loudspeaker.[32]

In the more analytical commentary that Stockhausen has devoted to *Gesang der Jünglinge*, "Musik und Sprache III," there occurs a particularly cryptic sentence relating to the fields of timbres in part *F*, whose solution could well contain the cornerstone of the entire edifice: "*x* receives a structure with a particular definition, resulting from the general layout of the work."[33] However, field X1 comprises exclusively chords of isolated impulses, a timbre that had just already been added at the end of field *B*2 in the form of three interventions at the beginning of the first long silence in this part. *B*2 contains, according to

Example 1.10a
Key to Examples 1.10b and 1.10c

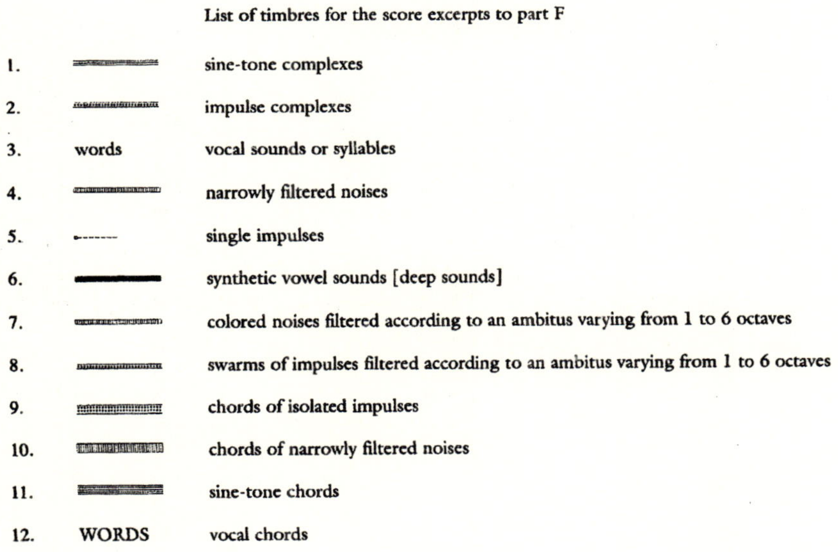
List of timbres for the score excerpts to part F
1. sine-tone complexes
2. impulse complexes
3. words vocal sounds or syllables
4. narrowly filtered noises
5. single impulses
6. synthetic vowel sounds [deep sounds]
7. colored noises filtered according to an ambitus varying from 1 to 6 octaves
8. swarms of impulses filtered according to an ambitus varying from 1 to 6 octaves
9. chords of isolated impulses
10. chords of narrowly filtered noises
11. sine-tone chords
12. WORDS vocal chords

Note: To differentiate class 2 from 8, and 4 from 7, refer to the vertical placement (at the top of the fields and in their center, respectively); the chords are drawn twice as large. The durations of the words/WORDS are indicated by empty boxes (words above, WORDS generally below). R signifies that a sound is reverberated.

Example 1.10b
Extracts from the Study Score: Passage from R6 to N10 (one system)

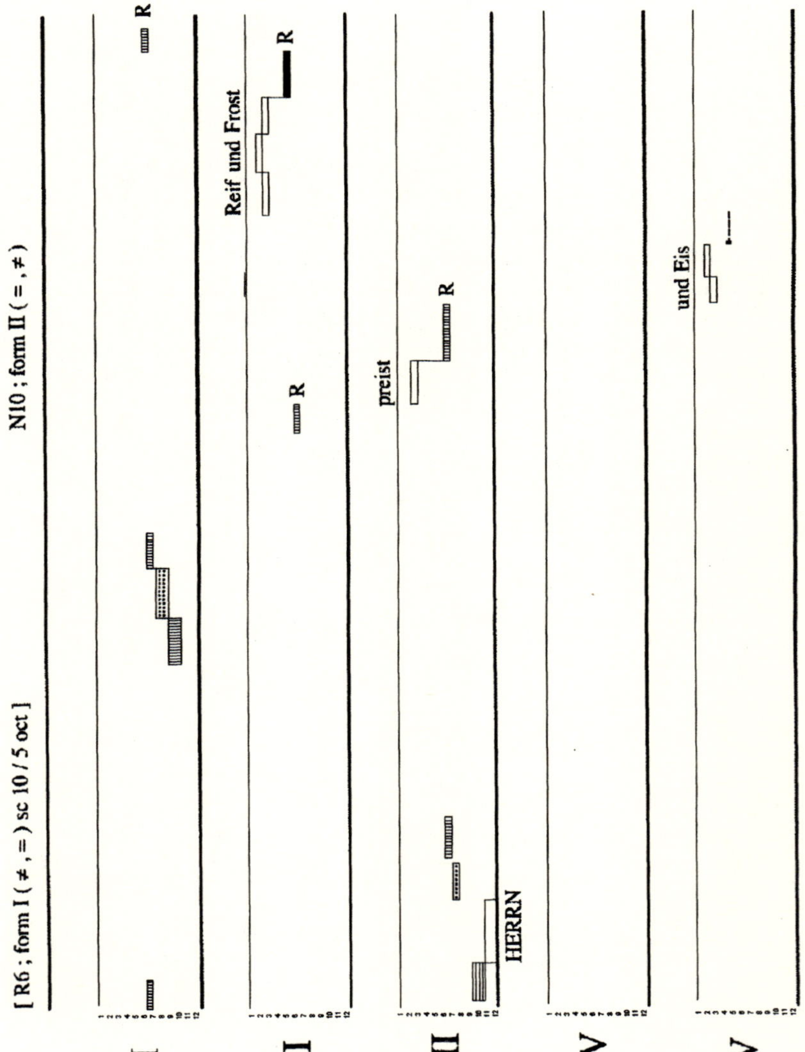

Example 1.10c
Extract from the Study Score: Passage from V2 and the Beginning of M11 (two systems)

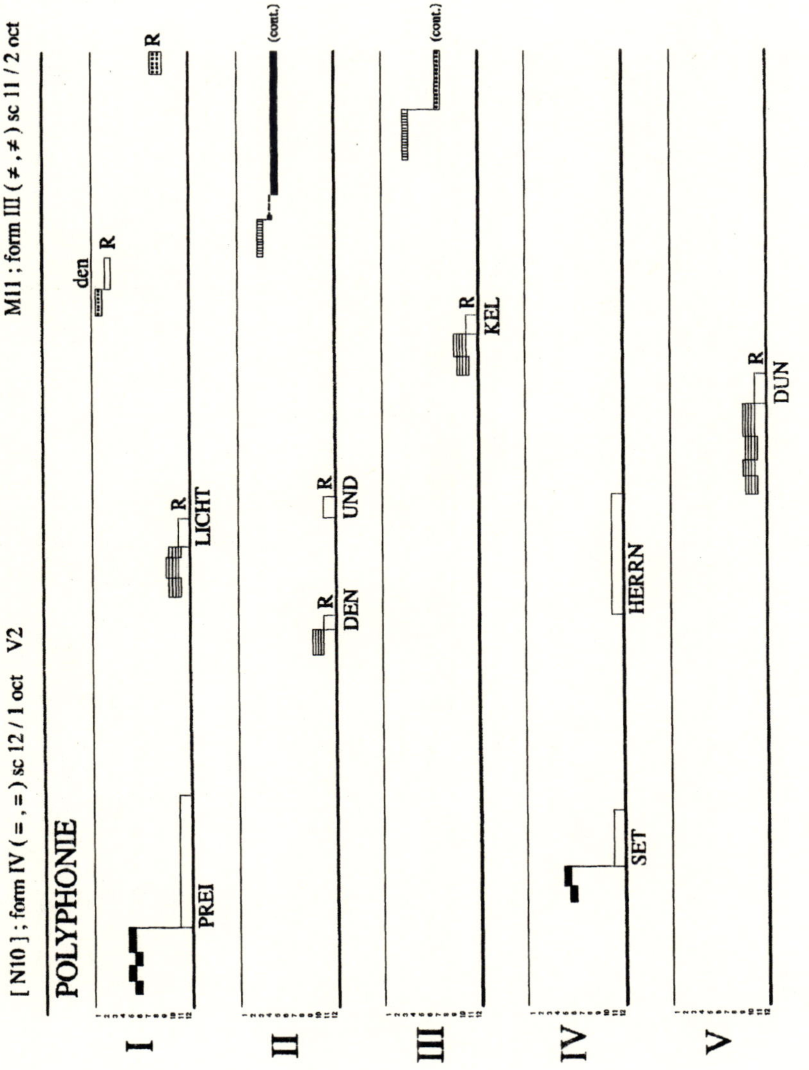

(Example 1.10c continued)

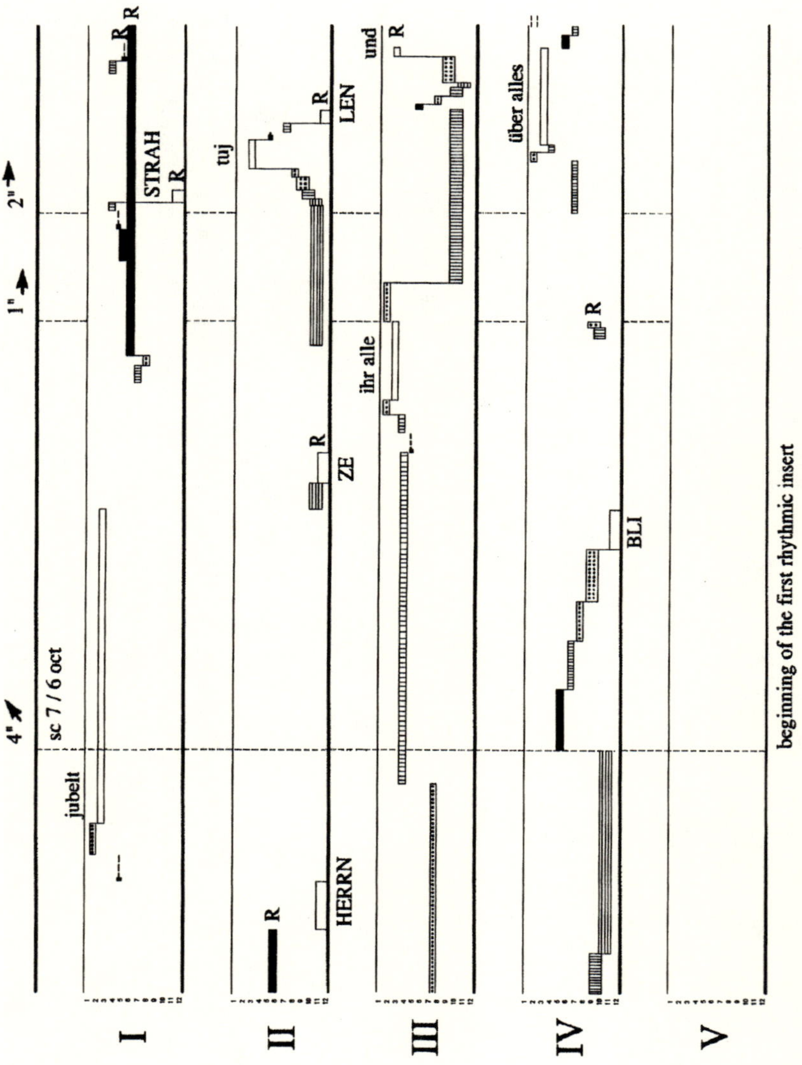

the schema, nothing but complexes of sine tones and complexes of impulses. However, the only complex of sine tones that Stockhausen retains for this passage is complex V from the beginning of *F*, that is, a mosaic of timbres in which one of the verbal permutations carried out upon the word "jubelt"—the syllable "tuj"—is particularly prominent. Its percussive character to some extent predestined this complex to be associated with the impulse structures. The impulses have played a signposting role throughout the composition, and it is the same here: framing function in *A*; filling in of silences in *B* (and *D*); articulation into sections and individualization of basic texture in *C*; main framework in *E* (the proportions of which govern the other phenomena); emphasized ending of each of the large sections in *F*. In the closing gesture, finally, again a complex of impulses predominates. In the network of serial relations the impulses, which are located metaphorically between the sine tone and noise, assume a function of vital mediation that makes them also equivalent to being agents of the key points of the form.

APPENDIX

verse	basic text
1a	Preiset (Jubelt) den(m) Herrn, ihr Werke alle des Herrn
1b	lobt ihn und über alles erhebt ihn in Ewigkeit.
2a	Preiset den Herrn, ihr Engel des Herrn
2b	preiset den Herrn, ihr Himmel droben.
3a	Preiset den Herrn, ihr Wasser alle, die über den Himmel sind
3b	preiset den Herrn, ihr Scharen alle des Herrn.
4a	Preiset den Herrn, Sonne und Mond
4b	preiset den Herrn, des Himmels Sterne.
5a	Preiset den Herrn, aller Regen und Tau
5b	preiset den Herrn, alle Winde.
6a	Preiset den Herrn, Feuer und Sommersglut
6b	preiset den Herrn, Kälte und starrer Winter.
7a	Preiset den Herrn, Tau und des Regens Fall
7b	preiset den Herrn, Eis und Frost.
8a	Preiset den Herrn, Reif und Schnee
8b	preiset den Herrn, Nächte und Tage.
9a	Preiset den Herrn, Licht und Dunkel
9b	preiset den Herrn, Blitze und Wolken.

Explanation of symbols

Vocal categories

sy	syllable or monosyllable
vc	(text in capitals) vocal chord, variable in density according to the superscript
cs	choral swarm, variable in density according to the superscript (the alternative versions "Herr(e)n" and "lob(e)t" are not being constantly repeated)
vp	vocal polyphony, variable in density
sm	temporal harmonic spectrum of mixed timbres, numbered
sm'	modified spectrum
sy/sm	syllable in a spectrum of mixed timbres (the underlined syllables are made conspicuous)

unities

[ ] staggered: superimposition of successive entries

[ ] enclosed in brackets: superimposition of simultaneous entries

nomenclature of sections (with the exception of the subdivisions of *B*, the abbreviations are Stockhausen's)

in *C*: IK: section with distinguishable impulses
IN: section with impulses in a statistical accumulation

In *F*: the letters refer to the nomenclature of timbral groupings ("Musik und Sprache III," 64–65; Engl. ed. 60); the numbers indicate density

Everything in italics in the following is editorial.

timing	*section*	*text*	*vocal category*
0:00	*A*	jubelt	sy
		[jubelt dem Herrn]	cs^6
		[preiset den Herrn ihr Werke alle des Herrn]	cs^4
		[lobt ihn]	cs^3
		lobet ihn	sy
		[lobt ihn und über alles erhebt ihn]	cs^7
		IHN	vc^7
		IN EWIGKEIT	vc^2
1:02	*B* 1	[jubelt dem Herrn ihr Engel des Herrn]	cs^5
		[preiset den Herren]	cs^1
		[jubelt den Herrn ihr Himmel droben]	cs^2
		[ihr Wasser alle]	cs^4
		[preiset/jubelt den(m) Herrn]	cs^6
		[die über den Himmeln sind]	cs^3
		[alle]	cs^7
		[jubelt]	cs^5
		[ihr Scharen alle des Herrn]	cs^2
		[jubelt dem Herrn ihr Scharen alle des Herrn preist ihn alle ihr Scharen]	cs^1
	2	*permutation of the cs of A and B1*	
1:43		[ihr Wasser alle]	cs^4
		[lobt ihn]	cs^3
		[jubelt dem Herrn]	cs^6
		[die über den Himmeln sind]	cs^3
		[preiset den Herrn]	cs^1
		[preiset/jubelt den(m) Herrn]	cs^6
		[ihr Scharen alle des Herrn]	cs^2
		[preiset den Herrn ihr Werke alle des Herrn]	cs^4
		[jubelt]	cs^5
		[jubelt dem Herrn ihr Himmel droben]	cs^2

	3	*in superposition: one cs per loudspeaker*	
2:24		[lobt ihn und über alles erhebt ihn]	cs^7
		[jubelt dem Herrn ihr Engel des Herrn]	cs^5
		[jubelt dem Herrn ihr Scharen alle des Herrn preist ihn alle ihr Scharen]	cs^1
		partial cs	
		[die über den Himmeln sind]	cs^3
		[jubelt dem Herrn]	cs^6
		in spatial rotation	
		[preiset den Herrn]	cs^1
		[ihr Scharen alle des Herrn]	cs^2
		lobet ihn	sy
		[ihr Wasser alle]	cs^4
		[alle] *in four loudspeakers*	cs^7
		ihn	sy
	C	*each section begins with a swarm of impulses or with cs assimilated to these swarms*	
2:43	IK	preist den Herrn Son ne und Mond	sy
3:17	IN1		
3:36	IK	preiset den Herrn	sy
		des Himmels	sy
		Sterne	sy
		al ler Re gen und Tau	sy
		den Herrn preist	sy
4:29		*impulse swarm alone*	
4:31	IN1	[preiset/jubelt den(m) Herrn] *in 3 loudspeakers*	cs^6
4:43	IK	ihr Win de	sy
4:49	IN2	[ihr Wasser alle]	cs^4
4:52	IN1	[lobt ihn]	cs^3
4:59	IN2		
5:13	*D* α	*over a background of B2 (tracks 3 to 5) played backwards*	
		DEN HERRN PREISET	vc
		FEUER UND SOMMERSGLUT	vc
		PREISET DEN HERRN	vc
5:56	β	Kälte und starrer Winter	sy
	E	*vocal parts inserted*	
6:21			
6:51	1	[preist den Herrn Tau und des Regens Fall]	vp^3
7:02			
7:17	2	[preis(e)t den Herrn Frost und Eis]	vp^5
7:26			
7:51	3	[preis(e)t den Herr(e)n Reif und Schnee]	vp^4
8:07			
8:14	4	[preiset den Herrn Nächte und Tage]	vp^2
8:21			

8:39	*F* D4	ju	sy/sm1
		belt	sy/sm2
		dem	sy/sm3
		Herrn	sy/sm4
		dem Her ju bel tuj ult ren Herrn belt tuj	sy/sm5
		leb ju dem jeb leb ju be dem Herrn tuj lt	
		bel dem ju dem ihr Herrn Herrn belt	
		Wer ke al le des Herrn	sy/sm6
9:00	H8	al i (h)ir des le Her Wer ren ke	sy/sm9
		des Wer al ihr Herrn le ke	sy/sm10
		Wer a des ihr (h)al Her ke ren le	sy/sm12
		al	sy/sm13
		le des Her ren Wer ke	sy/sm14
		ihr	sy/sm15
9:12	R6	HERRN	vc
9:20	N10	preist und Eis Eis Reif und Frost	sy
		ZE Re STRA gens	sy+vc
9:42	V2	PREISET DEN HERRN LICHT UND DUNKEL	vc
9:49	L12	den HERRN jubelt	sy+vc
9:53	———	*beginning of the first rhythmic insert* ———	
		BLI ZE ihr alle STRA tuj LEN über alles und WOL KEN	sy+vc
10:03	F6	droben [sm15'] ihr Scharen alle	sy+sy/sm
		[sm10'] jubelt [sm14']	sy+sy/sm
		dem Herren jubelt ihr	sy
10:14	B2	[sm5' *nine times*]	sy/sm
	I10	*cs in the background sonority*	
10:26		Schnee [sm15']	sy+sy/sm
		[ihr Wasser alle]	cs^4
		[lobt ihn und über alles erhebt ihn]	cs^7
		Frost	sy
		[alle]	cs^7
		[lobt ihn]	cs^3
		und	sy
		[die über den Himmeln sind]	cs^3
		[jubelt dem Herrn]	cs^6
		Eis Glut jubelt Scharen ihr Werke des Herrn	sy
		jubelt	sy
		[jubelt dem Herrn ihr Engel des Herrn]	cs^5
		alle und	sy
		[preiset/jubelt den(m) Herrn]	cs

		[jubelt dem Herrn ihr Himmel droben]	cs
		über alles	sy
11:06	P8	BLI ZE DUN KEL	vc
		STRA LEN	vc
11:23	X1		
11:30	———	*end of the first rhythmic insert* ———	
		Schnee ihn (*retrograde*)	
11:46	T4	FEU ER	vc
11:53	W1	WOL KEN NÄCH TE TA GE [sm9', sm1']	vc+sy/sm
11:57	C3	Reif [sm6', sm 12']	sy+sy/sm
12:05	G7		
12:07	———	*beginning of the second rhythmic insert* ———	
		Schnee Bli ze Bli Reif Bli ze ze preiset	sy
		den Herren	sy
		ihr Scharen die über	sy
		Himmels und sind	sy
		[sm5'] alle [sm5']	sy+sy/sm
12:10	K11	jubelt dem Herrn	sy
		[sm5'] ihr Engel	sy+sy/sm
		[sm5'] preiset den Herren [sm5' *two times*]	sy+sy/sm
12:22	S5	LICHT	vc
12:25	O9	SOMMERSGLUT	vc
12:27	M11	lobet [sm5', sm8'] preist	sy+sy/sm
		glut Stra len Licht Wol	sy
		ken LICHT Bli ze ju-bel und über alles	sy+av
		erhebt ihn	
12:34	———	*end of the second rhythmic insert* ———	
		Coda TAU [sm5']	vc+sy/sm
		[sm13'] *in the final chord*	sy/sm
12:54			

NOTES

The present study is based on an investigation of the composer's sketches, such as were made accessible in a limited edition published in 1983, and carried out within the framework of a grant from the Paul Sacher Foundation in Basle, which we wish to thank for its hospitality and generosity.

1. Karlheinz Stockhausen, "Situation des Handwerks," *Texte* 1 (Cologne: Verlag DuMont Schauberg, 1963), 23.
2. See the articles on this subject by Pierre Boulez and Henri Pousseur in *Die Reihe 1: elektronische Musik* (1955; English edition 1958), as well as their correspondence from the spring of 1954 (deposited in the Paul Sacher Foundation, Basle).
3. Karlheinz Stockhausen, "Situation du métier de compositeur," *Domaine musical* 1 (1954): 140; Karlheinz Stockhausen, "Situation des Metiers," *Texte 1*, 56.
4. Stockhausen, "Situation du métier," 141; Stockhausen, "Situation des Metiers," 56.
5. The original text, intended for a "Musikalisches Nachtprogramm des Nordwestdeutschen Rundfunks" of 23 December 1954, significantly has as its title: "Von Anton Webern zu Claude Debussy—Formprobleme der elektronischen Musik."
6. Fritz Winckel, *Klangwelt unter der Lupe* (Berlin and Wundsiedel: Max Hesses Verlag, 1952), 8; French trans. as *Vues nouvelles sur le monde des sons* (Paris: Dunod, 1960), 2.
7. Karlheinz Stockhausen, "wie die Zeit vergeht," *Texte 1*, 108–109 [English ed. of *Die Reihe* 3: 17].
8. Karlheinz Stockhausen, "Aktuelles," *Texte* 2 (Cologne: Verlag DuMont Schauberg, 1964), 51–57 [English trans., as "Actualia," *Die Reihe* 1: 45–51].
9. Pierre Boulez, "Eventuellement . . . ," *Relevés d'apprenti* (Paris: Seuil, 1966), 153–155; *The Boulez-Cage Correspondence*, edited by Jean-Jacques Nattiez (Cambridge [England]: Cambridge University Press, 1993), 98–103.
10. Stockhausen. "Aktuelles," 54 [English ed., 48].
11. This constitutes a deviation compared to the system (1:2:4:8:16), as is still reflected in the first sketch relating to the temporal organization of the six complexes, where it appears, however, that Stockhausen also means to realize only one layer out of every two—that is, half of the layers contained in each octave of duration. The reasons for this modification must be sought in the means of production. In fact, the synchronization was done starting from monophonic tapes onto a four-track, multichannel machine; by a return mixing operation from the multitrack to the monophonic apparatus, the total number of voices could be brought to sixteen—exactly the number of layers in complex V as it was realized. Along with the very laborious realization of the sixteen additional layers, the theoretical proportions would have always implied new copying operations, which would have meant a notable increase in background noise each time as well.
12. Stockhausen, "wie die Zeit vergeht," 108–109, and 122–123 [English ed. of *Die Reihe* 3: 17 and 27–28]. For an explication of applications in *Zeitmaße* and *Gruppen*, cf. Pascal Decroupet, "Gravitationsfeld *Gruppen*. Zur Verschränkung der Werke *Gesang der Jünglinge*, *Gruppen* und *Zeitmaße* und deren Auswirkung auf Stockhausens Musikdenken in der zweiten Hälfte der fünfziger Jahre," *Musiktheorie* 12, no. 1 (1997): 37–51.
13. A transcription of the corresponding sketch may be found in Elena Ungeheuer, "Statistical Gestalts—Perceptible Features in Serial Music," *Music, Gestalt, and Computing* (*Lecture Notes in Artificial Intelligence* 1317), edited by Marc Leman (Berlin: Springer, 1997), 107.
14. A version of the present Example 1.2 with the timbres included may be found in

Elena Ungeheuer, "From the Elements to the Continuum: Timbre Composition in Early Electronic Music," *Contemporary Music Review* 10, no. 2 (1994): 27.
15. The vocal material has been augmented by the word "Strahlen"; the cries of "jubelt" and "preis(e)t," which are synonymous, are freely interchanged.
16. Cf. Karlheinz Stockhausen, "Musik und Sprache III," *Texte* 2, 68 [English trans. as "Music and Speech," *Die Reihe* 6: 63]; the durations depicted and notated are the durations actually realized; originally, all of the layers were to have had a duration of 210 cm, which is about three seconds.
17. The process of realization is described by Stockhausen in "Wille zur Form und Wille zum Abenteuer [Gespräch mit Rudolf Frisius]," *Texte* 6 (Cologne: DuMont Buchverlag, 1989), 338; cf. also the sketch transcriptions in Richard Toop, "Stockhausen's Electronic Works: Sketches and Work-Sheets from 1952–1967," *Interface* 10 (1981): 180–182.
18. A transcription of the first two pages of Stockhausen's second realization score was published by Richard Toop in "Stockhausen's Electronic Works," 178–79; this same transcription is reproduced in Robin Maconie, *The Works of Karlheinz Stockhausen*, 2d ed. (Oxford: Clarendon Press, 1990), 60–61.
19. This reduction shows the five loudspeakers vertically and the temporal sequence of events horizontally. The overall duration is 3:13. The logic of spatial linkup confirms that the five loudspeakers were located according to the same plan, around the audience, and that speculations concerning a loudspeaker placed above the audience are purely a matter of myth.
20. The durations of the sections according to the scale 128–210–344–565–928–1, 520–2, 496–4,096 cm; the final section, with a length of 1,066 cm, is at the same time the beginning of part *D* and no longer fits into this scale. The spacing for the vocal sounds follows the scale 43.1–70.7–116–190.2–312–512–840 cm (applied three times). The two collections of groups of deep sounds draw the values for their spacing from the scale 26.3–43.1–70.7–116–190.2–312.1–512 cm, values that are multiplied by 4.5 to yield a total corresponding approximately to the collective duration of this part.
21. The values in parentheses come from the 7 × 7 square of basic durations. The first terms constitute a scale progressing by whole seconds; the second ones, by half seconds. As before, these values are approximate, because Stockhausen caused to intervene as a supplementary criterion the presence of all the classes of durations, that is, of all the columns of the table (except that in the scale of half seconds a doubling of column 2 occurs, compensating for the absence of column 3). The scale of dotted values results from their combination. The alternation between the scales follows those of the base elements and of the figures (or high noises): in the sections with distinct impulses, the alternation operates between the scales of seconds (presence of a noisy background) and of half seconds (absence of a noisy background); in the sections with statistical impulses, the areas coming from the scale of dotted values are marked by bands of high noises, and they alternate with areas in which the durations are extracted from the scale of half seconds.
22. Karlheinz Stockhausen, "Musik im Raum," *Texte* 1, 161 [English trans. as "Music in Space," *Die Reihe* 5: 73].
23. Figure 28 (marked with an *x* in Example 1.6) consists of two isolated impulses in a descending melodic direction, right after the words "ihr Winde," since there is no noiseband in the background, this figure does not integrate the grouping strategy.
24. The initial *x* is equivalent to 195 cm, the unit of subdivision for this layer.
25. The continuation of this vocal polyphony is contained in "Musik und Sprache III," 67 [English ed. of *die Reihe* 6: 62].

26. The sketches of the unrealized part *G* show that Stockhausen had derived the pitches for the vocal as well as the electronic elements from this same scale, read in a cycle of interval 5.
27. A transcription of this sketch has been published in Ungeheuer, "Statistical Gestalts," 111.
28. "Musik und Sprache III," 64 [English ed. 59–60].
29. Stockhausen. "Musik und Sprache III," 64–65 [English ed. 60].
30. See also ibid., 65 [English ed. 61].
31. Ibid., 61–62 [English ed. 58–59].
32. The extract relating to a study score was published in Pascal Decroupet, "Timbre Diversification in Serial Tape Music and Its Consequence on Form," *Contemporary Music Review* 10, no. 2 (1994): 19.
33. "Musik und Sprache III," 65 [English ed. 60].

2

Diamorphoses by Iannis Xenakis

Thomas DeLio

The second half of the twentieth century certainly will be remembered as one of the richest periods in the history of Western music. Indeterminacy, serialism, the dissemination of a variety of world musics, and, of course, the advent of electronic music all had a significant impact on Western musical practice in this era. Significantly, the first decade of this half century witnessed not only the beginnings of the electronic era but also an extraordinary outpouring of some of its most vibrant creative offerings: John Cage's *Williams Mix* (1952), Toshiro Mayazumi's *XYZ* (1953), Pierre Henry's magnificent and austere *Voile d'Orphée* (1953), Gottfried Michael Koenig's *Klangfiguren* (1954), Karlheinz Stockhausen's *Gesang der Jünglinge* (1956), Edgard Varèse's justly celebrated *Poème Electronique* (1957–1958), Luciano Berio's *Thema-Omaggio a Joyce* (1958), and many more, in Europe, Asia, and the United States. Subsequent years may have witnessed an explosion in technological advancements (hyper-instruments, interactive CD-ROMs, etc.) but surely never again such an exceptional burst of creativity. Iannis Xenakis, one of the great figures of twentieth-century music, was, of course, also one of the pioneers of electronic composition. Since the 1950s, he has produced a succession of works that are among the most original and rigorous ever created in this medium.

Diamorphoses

dia-	prefix [fr. Gk, dia: through, apart]: through, across
-morphoses	*comb form*, plural of *–morphosis* [fr. Gk mōrphōsis: process of forming]: development or change of form of a (specified) thing or in a (specified) manner

Diamorphoses, Xenakis' first electronic work, was written in 1957 and premiered in October 1958 at the Journèes Internationales de Musique Experimentale in Brussels together with works by Pierre Schaeffer and Luc Ferrari.[1] It was composed at the studio of the Group de Recherche de Musique Concrète in Paris, founded and directed by Schaeffer in 1951. This studio was one of the first and most important centers for the creation of electroacoustic music in the world, where composers as diverse as Xenakis, Schaeffer, Boulez, Henry, Messiaen, and Stockhausen worked. *Diamorphoses* exemplifies the approach to electronic composition known as *musique concrète*, which characterized all the work done at this studio. Speaking of this work, Xenakis has said that he wanted "to mix timbres in order to arrive at a body of sound like white noise; to study the evolution of timbres, dynamics and register; to make unisons with attacks only with or without transposition; to make chromosomes of attacks."[2] In describing more general aspects of Xenakis' early electronic works, Joel Chadabe has written:

> In his early tape pieces . . . [Xenakis] used recorded acoustic sounds modified by tape manipulations—changing speed, playing backward, splicing—and mixing, but without electronic processing such as filtering and modulation. His compositions, however, were not juxtaposed "objects," as in normal musique concrète, so much as they were complex sound masses that transformed in time as the result of shifting distributions and densities of small, component sounds.[3]

Chadabe adds: "In composing *Diamorphoses* (1957), Xenakis used the sounds of jet engines, car crashes, earthquake shocks, textures of sliding pitches, and other noiselike sounds, and sometimes contrasted them with thin, high bell sounds."[4]

Little has been said about the structure of this work, and, unfortunately, what has been said offers little insight into its unique sonic design. Indeed, many observations have been downright misleading and belie the richness of both form and sound that constitutes its unique sonic and expressive design. Nouritza Matossian, in her book *Xenakis*, states that, in this piece, "a strongly shaped rich section at the beginning and the end frame a much sparser, short middle section."[5] Makis Solomis, in his notes for the CD "Xenakis: Electronic Music," observes that the work is "far from the genre of an 'étude,' due perhaps to its ternary form."[6] James Brody in his notes to an earlier recording, "Iannis Xenakis: Electro-Acoustic Music," says that the piece "is in four parts, the outer ones being of high density, the inner ones sparse."[7] Contradicting Xenakis own observations about the work, all of these commentators see the design of *Diamorphoses* as static and discontinuous, a design in which the beginning and ending are somehow similar. Moreover, all of these critics seem to dissect the piece into several distinct sections and fail to understand the continuous, evolutionary nature of its form. Indeed, the work is not at all sectional (either in three or four parts), but, in rather Carter-like fashion, evolves from the simultaneous unfolding of two overlapping layers of sound, which separate, merge, intercut, and disrupt one another over the course of the piece. The interactions of these layers and their ultimate synthesis constitute the form of the work.

In general, Xenakis' music is far too continuous in its evolution to be considered in terms of distinct and separable parts. In this respect, *Diamorphoses* is no exception. Even taking into account its sudden shifts and numerous disruptions, it unfolds as a dynamic process from beginning to end. However, in order to facilitate discussion of the piece, the use of some term to delineate its various sonic events was felt to be necessary. I have chosen to use the term "stage," as in the various stages in an evolutionary process, or process of transformation. The reader must always bear in mind that the beginnings and endings of these stages often overlap or merge into one another, so their value is primarily in facilitating our discussion of the work rather than in isolating distinct points of demarcation. This emphasis on terminology may seem fussy to some, but the way that we speak of things has a direct bearing on how we experience them and ultimately how we understand them. It seems to me that the term "stage" has fewer connotations of closure than terms such as "section" or "part," and this piece exhibits only one real moment of closure, its conclusion.

In dealing with any electronic work, we must consider the question of how to go about analyzing its sonic events. Typically, there is no score, and each work uses sounds that may be wholly unfamiliar, at least in the world of traditional instrumental/vocal music—a rather narrowly defined sonic environment. With an instrumental work, we study the score, knowing that its notations represent sound. However, in order to deal with an electronic work such as *Diamorphoses* we must develop some way to represent its sonic elements that reveals the nature of those elements, as well as their combinations and transformations, in some useful way. This seems to me to require a new approach to analysis itself (one that, I feel, probably would be of value in the study of *all* music as it necessarily would be based on the acoustical substance of the music rather than any linguistic framework—such as tonality or serialism—imposed upon that substance). Following in the footsteps of a few pathbreaking studies of electronic music by recent scholars, most notably, Robert Cogan, I have chosen to examine *Diamorphoses* with the help of a series of sonograms of a monophonic reduction of the composition.[8] *Diamorphoses* was originally composed for four channels of sound. It was reduced to two channels by the composer for distribution on record (and later compact disc).[9] Both channels on this stereo version are identical, so nothing has been lost in the further reduction to one channel. The sonograms used in this chapter were created with the aid of the Sound Technology Inc. SpectraPLUS FFT Spectral Analysis System.[10] The vertical axis of each of these graphs represents frequency in hertz (Hz), while the horizontal axis represents time. The relative darkness of the various images in the picture reflects their relative amplitude levels (a lighter image reflects a soft sound; a darker image, a louder sound). On these sonograms, frequency is plotted logarithmically along the vertical axis.

The sonogram of the entire composition clearly shows three stages of evolution (Example 2.1). I indicate the approximate start and end points of each stage:

Stage 1 (0:00–2:47): the introduction of two contrasting frequency regions and two contrasting types of sound distinguished primarily by their different sonic envelopes.

Stage 2 (2:47–4:11): the complete separation of these two regions and their respective sound types.

Stage 3 (4:11–6:50): the transformation, juxtaposition, and opposition of these two regions and sound types and their eventual synthesis.

The first thing that we might note about these three stages is how closely their start and end points coincide with both the Golden Section and the Inverse Golden Section of the composition. The work is 6:50 long. The Inverse Golden Section (.382) falls at precisely 2:37; stage 2 begins at about 2:47. The Golden Section (.618) falls at precisely 4:13; stage 3 begins at about 4:11. Again, these points do not so much signify boundaries, as areas where change is most noticeable. One suspects that these proportions served as guides in helping Xenakis design the general shape of the piece. Of course, as is well known, Xenakis was for many years an associate of the architect Le Corbusier. Thus, his use of the Golden Section in this manner is not at all surprising. Le Corbusier championed the use of the Golden Section in all forms of design, as documented in his path-breaking book, in two volumes, *Modulor.*[11] Indeed, in the second volume he even comments on Xenakis' use of the Golden Section and offers examples drawn from the composer's earliest instrumental music, written at about the same time as *Diamorphoses*.

As already stated, the work consists of multiple and contrasting layers of sound that evolve simultaneously and in opposition to one another. To see these layers in their clearest, most distinct manifestations, we need only look at the opening moments of stage 2 (Example 2.2). At approximately 8,137 Hz we find a string of identical bell sounds (short attack, quick decay); below these, at about 500 Hz, short bursts of sound (explosions, plane engines) consisting of wider frequency bands with less focused attack characteristics; in between, a yawning gap of about four octaves! (There is also a third, subsidiary layer of sound at about 16,175 Hz derived from upper partials of the bell, which I will discuss later.) Over the course of stage 1 Xenakis builds to this separation. Later, in stage 3, he juxtaposes and finally synthesizes these two frequency regions. Their dialogue constitutes the form of the piece.

STAGE 1

Stage 1 (0:00–2:47) traces the unfolding of the two principal layers of sound that constitute the primary materials of the piece (Example 2.3). Starting in a very low frequency region (below 100 Hz), Xenakis constructs a sound mass derived from the noise of jet plane engines and earthquake explosions that slowly and steadily rises to about 8,137 Hz. This ascent peaks at about 2:22. At this same moment, the aforementioned 8,137 Hz bell sound enters. This bell contrasts dramatically with the engine sounds. It has a sharp attack and a very short decay, while the jet engines and even the explosions have less defined attacks and much greater sustain and decay periods. From this moment on, the bell remains at 8,137 Hz and becomes more prominent. Meanwhile, the engine sounds begin to recede and become quite sparse. By 2:47, the engine/earthquake sounds have dropped back to their starting point and so appear to have completely separated from the bell.

Preceding the first appearance of the 8,137 Hz bell at 2:22, we hear an intermittent succession of pure sonorities resembling sine tones, which begin at about 2,500 Hz at 0:30 and gradually rise all the way up to about 16,000 Hz at 1:18. These brief interjections introduce the upper frequency regions that will figure prominently in stage 2. The sonorities themselves appear to be derived from the aforementioned bell, which is transposed and played backward, occasionally with its attack cut off. Finally, at the peak of this ascent, at 1:18, the bell, for the first time, is played forward with the attack clearly in evidence. At this moment, we begin to recognize it as a bell-like sound. However, Xenakis still distorts the bell somewhat by stretching its decay into a glissando. It does not appear unaltered until 2:22. So, the first complete appearance of this source bell sound is ushered in by a series of transpositions, distortions, and reversals of itself, which rise to the highest frequency regions of the piece (and indeed of human hearing—16,000 Hz) and then finally settle down at 8,137 Hz. Stage 1, then, consists of two layers of sound that simultaneously ascend to the 8,137 Hz region. When they reach this peak, they separate; the bell remains there, while the engine sounds reverse direction and drop back down to their starting point.

STAGE 2

At 2:47 the two layers of sound have completely separated, and they remain so throughout the second stage (Example 2.4). At 8,137 Hz we find a string of identical bells; below these, at about 500 Hz and lower, short bursts of sound (crashes and explosions); in between, a gap of about four octaves. In comparison to stage 1, the second stage is quite static spatially but quite active rhythmically. As stage 2 unfolds, the bell repeats faster and faster and, consequently, the 8,137 Hz region becomes steadily more dense.

The bell contains a strong formant region at about 16,175 Hz, about one octave above 8,137 Hz. As mentioned earlier, this higher region was introduced briefly in stage 1 at 1:18. Here it seems to strengthen the bell sonority and, coupled with the steadily increasing density in the 8,137 Hz region, pulls our attention away from the more static and sparse lower register toward the upper one (see Example 2.2). This constitutes a shift in emphasis from that heard in stage 1.

STAGE 3

The steadily increasing density in the 8,137 Hz region in stage 2 propels the music forward into stage 3: 4:11–6:50 (Example 2.5). Significantly, this third

Example 2.1
Sonogram of *Diamorphoses* (total duration 6:50)

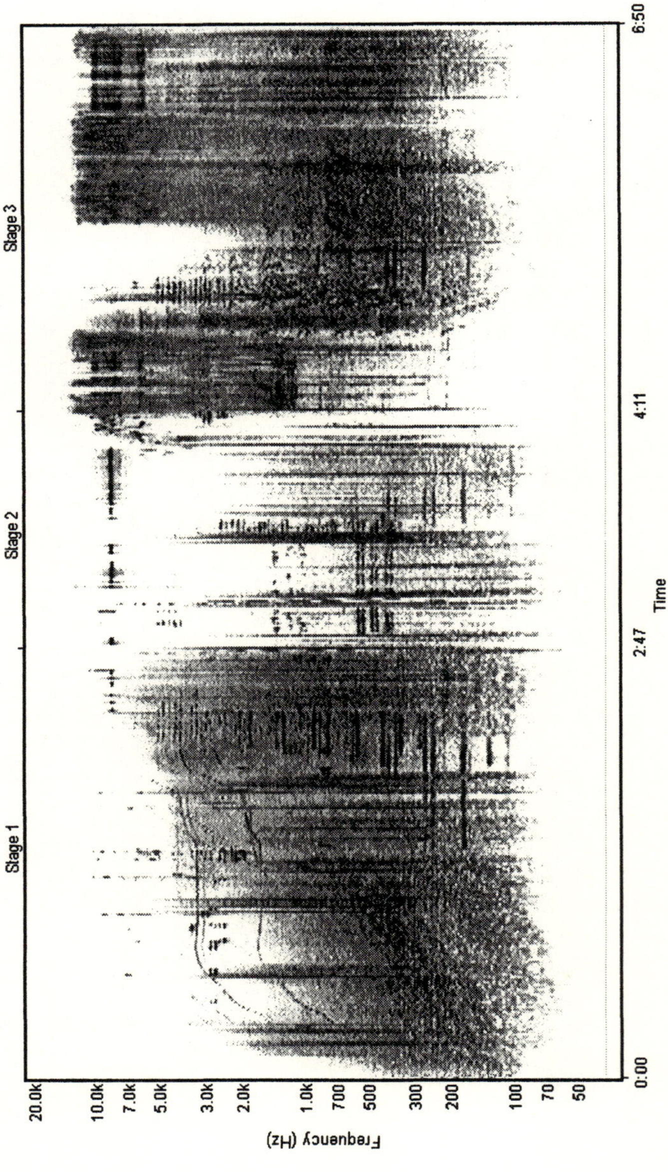

Example 2.2
Sonogram of Eleven Seconds of Stage 2 (3:10–3:21)

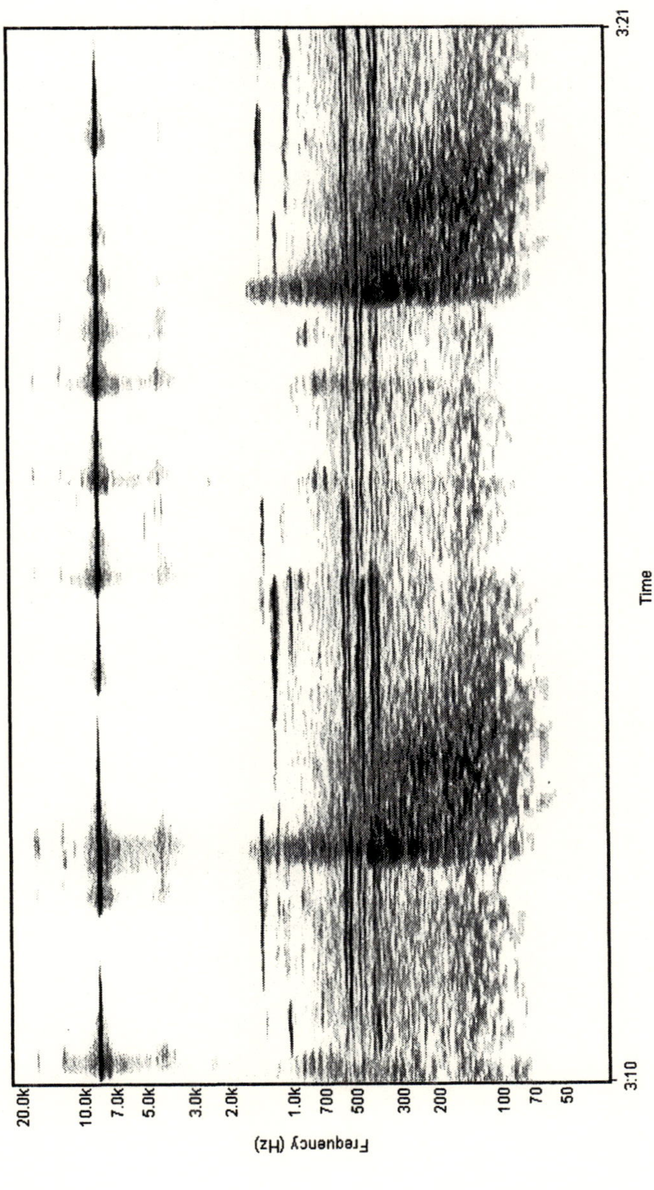

Example 2.3
Sonogram of Stage 1 (0:00–2:47; total duration 2:47)

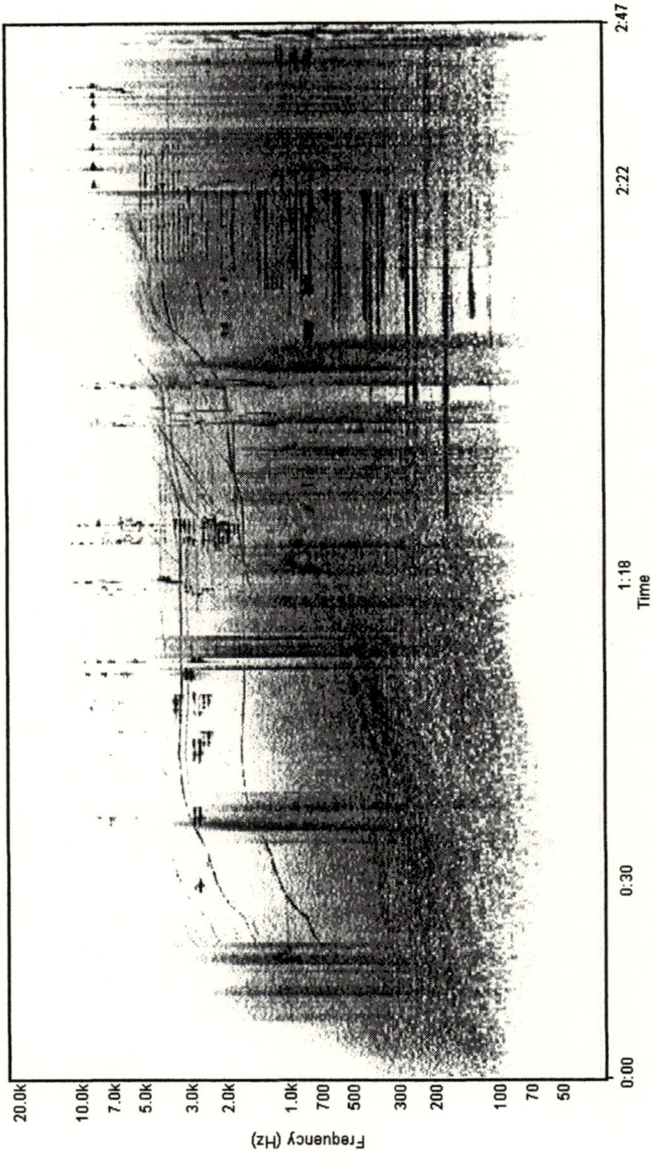

Example 2.4
Sonogram of Stage 2 (2:47–4:11; total duration 1:24)

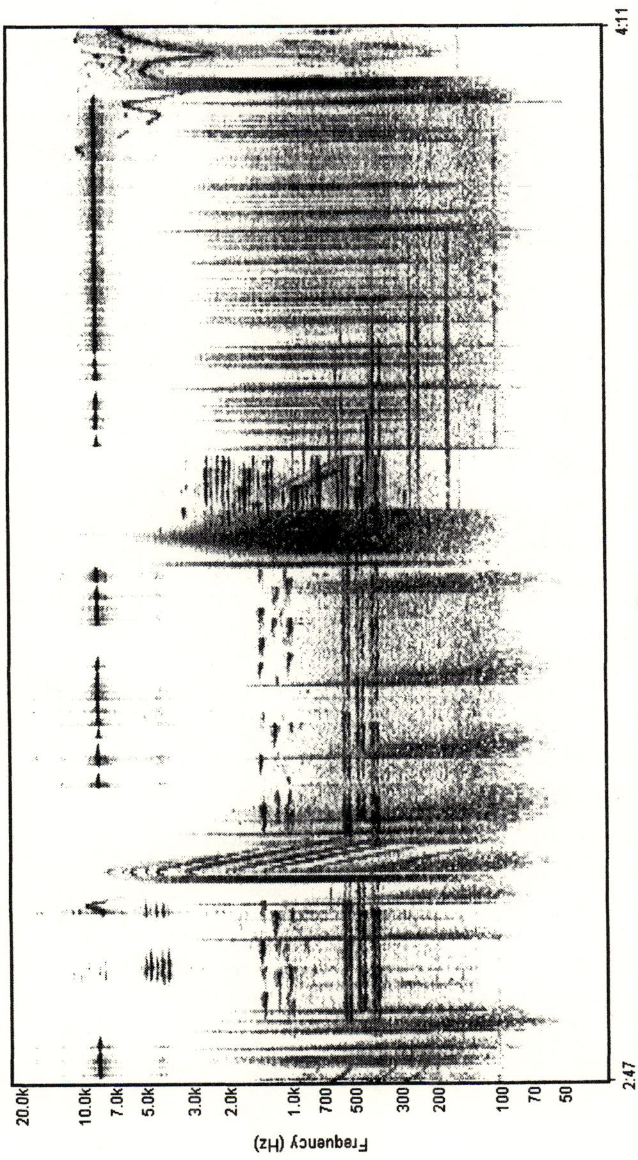

and final stage is the least continuous of the three, consisting of dramatic and sudden juxtapositions of contrasting materials. Stage 3 itself can be divided into three general areas of activity: 4:11–4:49, 4:49–5:32, and 5:32–6:50. At the start of stage 3 the 8,137 Hz region explodes into a dense band of glissandi clearly reminiscent of the bell (and also reminiscent of the ascending sequence of glissandi heard at the opening of the piece). This wide band of sound fills a frequency region spreading out from about 1,000 Hz to 13,000 Hz, enveloping the narrowly focused 8,137 Hz bell region that had evolved through stages one and two. At the same time, the region below 1,000 Hz is almost empty. Only an occasional eruption intrudes to remind us of the activity that once filled this space. This situation represents the inverse of what happened in stage 1 where the lowest region was quite dense but the upper region rather sparse. It constitutes the *first sonic inversion* of the piece.

Later, at about 4:49, the upper region drops off (both in terms of register and density) in several descending waves of sound, and emphasis returns to the lower region below 1,000 Hz. As the lower region fills, the upper region empties. This constitutes the *second sonic inversion* of the piece.

In the final minute and a quarter of *Diamorphoses* (5:32–6:50) Xenakis brings the two regions back together again (Example 2.6). In contrast to stage 2, however, each frequency region is now articulated with densely packed bands of sound approaching white noise. This synthesis itself occurs in two stages: 5:32–6:15 and 6:15–6:50. In the second of these stages, the upper band narrows into a dense core of sound between 5,500 Hz and 10,000 Hz. This contraction tends to separate the regions somewhat, while still maintaining a connection between them. Significantly, the distinguishing characteristics of attack and decay that helped differentiate the sound types associated with each frequency region in stage 2, all but disappear in stage 3. We hear nothing that clearly resembles a bell or an engine, just a general wash of sound partitioned into two registers.

THE ENTIRE COMPOSITION

As stated earlier, the form of the piece can be described as a three-stage progression. In the first stage, Xenakis introduces two contrasting frequency regions and two contrasting sound types. In the second stage, these two regions and sound types are completely separated. In the third and final stage, they are pitted against one another through a pair of sonic inversions. In the first of these inversions, the upper region is emphasized, and the lower one drops out. In the second, the lower region is emphasized, and the upper one drops out. The alternating presence and absence of these regions in stage 3 constitutes the central dramatic dialogue of the piece. The composition concludes with a brief synthesis in which the two frequency regions are fused into what appears to be one sound comprising two bands of noise. Thus, *Diamorphoses* ends with a real fusion of its two primary frequency regions into one complex sonority.

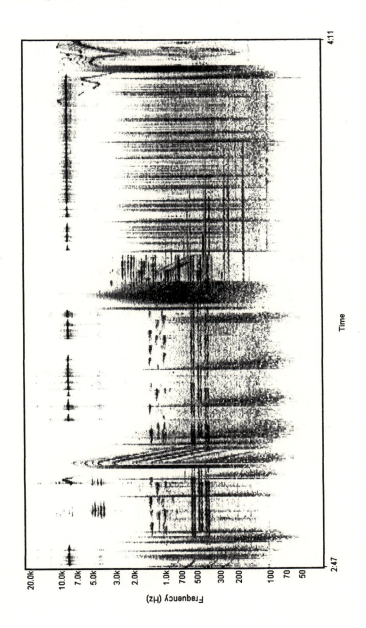

A FEW DETAILS

The richness of this piece lies not only in its remarkable macrostructure but also in some of its details and the relationship of these to its larger formal design. Returning to the opening minutes of the piece, we notice that the slow, steady ascent in the lower region (jets engines etc.) is quite continuous until about 2:22, when the bell first appears peak at 8,137 Hz. As mentioned earlier, at that point the jet sounds recede to the lowest frequency regions of the piece. However, they recede less continuously, in successive waves of sound, each wave dropping farther and farther down (Example 2.7). These waves gradually become quite sparse and finally segue into the intermittent explosions, which continue through the second stage and on into the opening of the third and final stage. A subsequent and similar descent back to the lower register occurs between 5:00 and 5:30, also in successive waves of sound, quite reminiscent of those heard between 2:22 and 2:47.

One significant *inversion* of these falling waves occurs at 4:06 where we find a deliberate ascent—the first one since the opening (Example 2.8). This is beautifully exploited for full dramatic effect. It rather suddenly interrupts the bells, which at this point have grown quite dense. The music seems to drop out momentarily and then rush on to the explosion of sound that ushers in stage 3. This constitutes yet another clear sonic inversion in the piece, though on a more local level than those discussed previously.

CONCLUSIONS

With few exceptions, music theorists have avoided electronic music. Only those with a truly comprehensive understanding of both acoustics as well as musical design could ever really attempt to analyze it. In discussing Varèse, Risset, and Babbitt, Robert Cogan has illuminated electronic works that had previously eluded explication.[12] Richard Toop and Seppo Heikenheimo, in their studies of the electronic works of Karlheinz Stockhausen, have also provided numerous insights.[13] Of course, theory follows practice, usually by many generations, for theory can evolve only from a clear examination of all the particulars of many specific cases. Certainly, the most analyzed literature of Western music—that of the so-called common practice—came to be understood theoretically to any degree only through the work of Schenker and his successors in the early years of the twentieth century, when, for all intents and purposes, the common practice had ended. Yet, even this body of music remains relatively unexplored on many levels (e.g., rhythm, space, tone color). We know that the first chord of the *Eroica* symphony is a tonic triad, but why does Beethoven space it, orchestrate it, articulate it as he does, and why does he repeat it? A theory of such music cannot ignore so many factors that shape what we experience when we hear a piece. Similarly, the music of Schoenberg, Stravinsky, Varèse, and their colleagues in the first half of the twentieth century remains virtually unexplained, for, in their music, pitch, tone color, time, and

Example 2.5
Sonogram of Stage 3 (4:11–6:50; total duration 2:39)

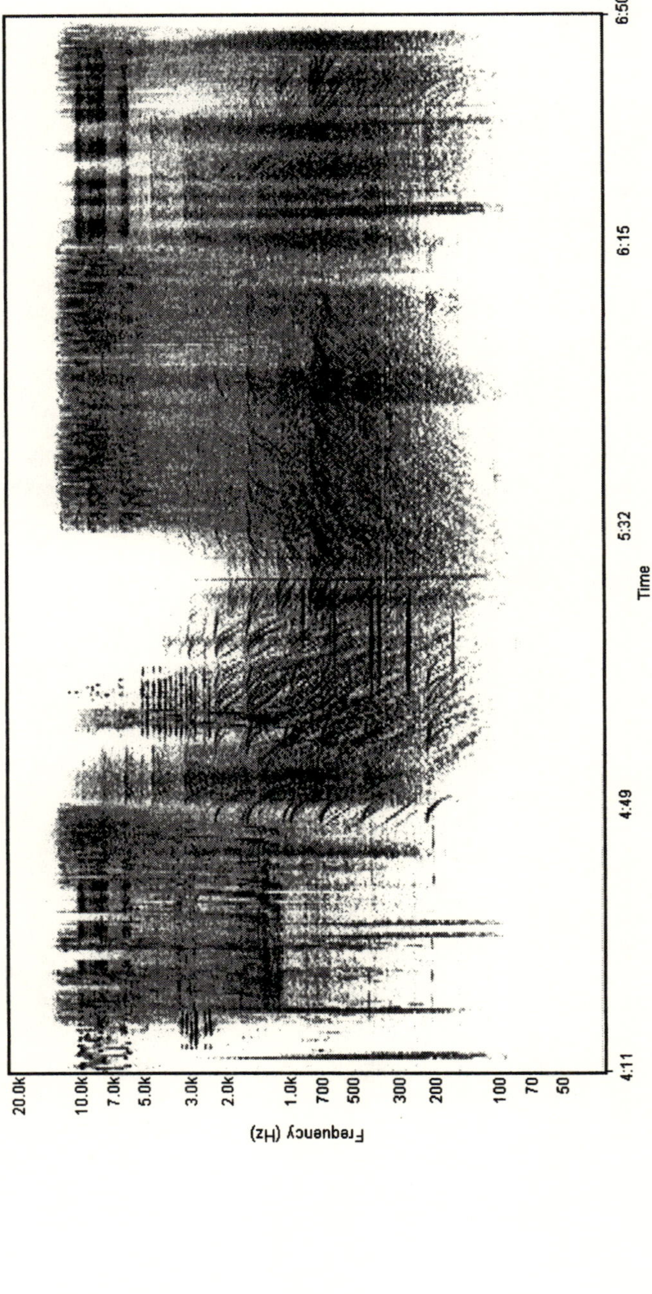

Example 2.6
Sonogram of Conclusion of Stage 3 (5:32–6:50; total duration 1:18)

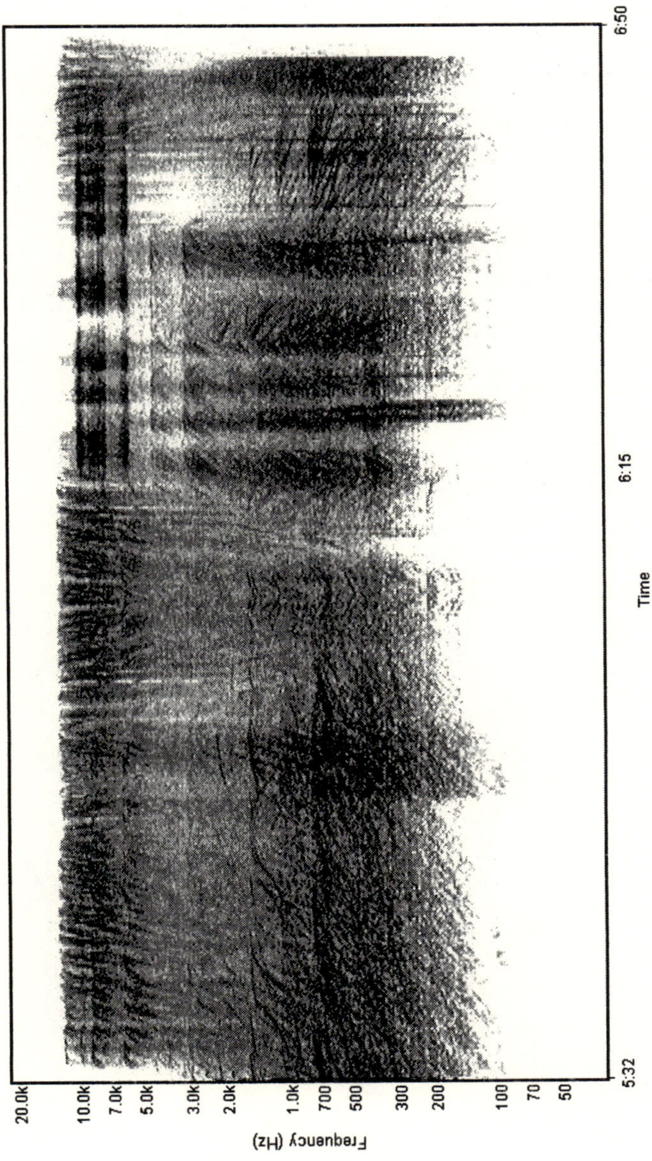

Example 2.7
Conclusion of Stage 1 (2:22–2:47; total duration 0:25)

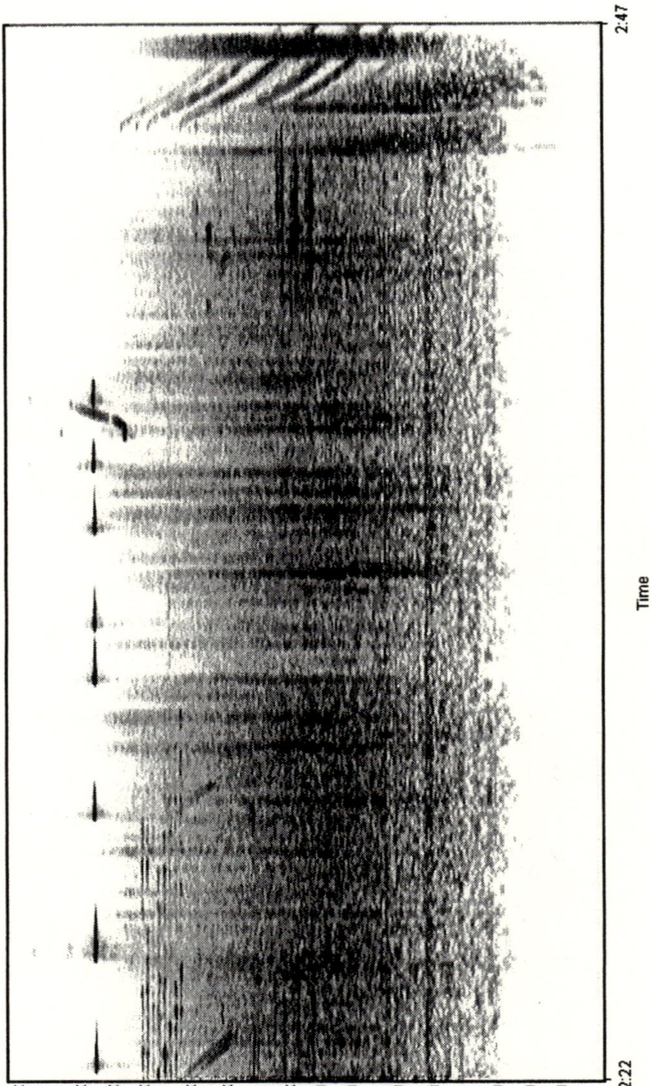

Example 2.8
Conclusion of Stage 2 and Beginning of Stage 3 (4:06–4:50; total duration 0:44)

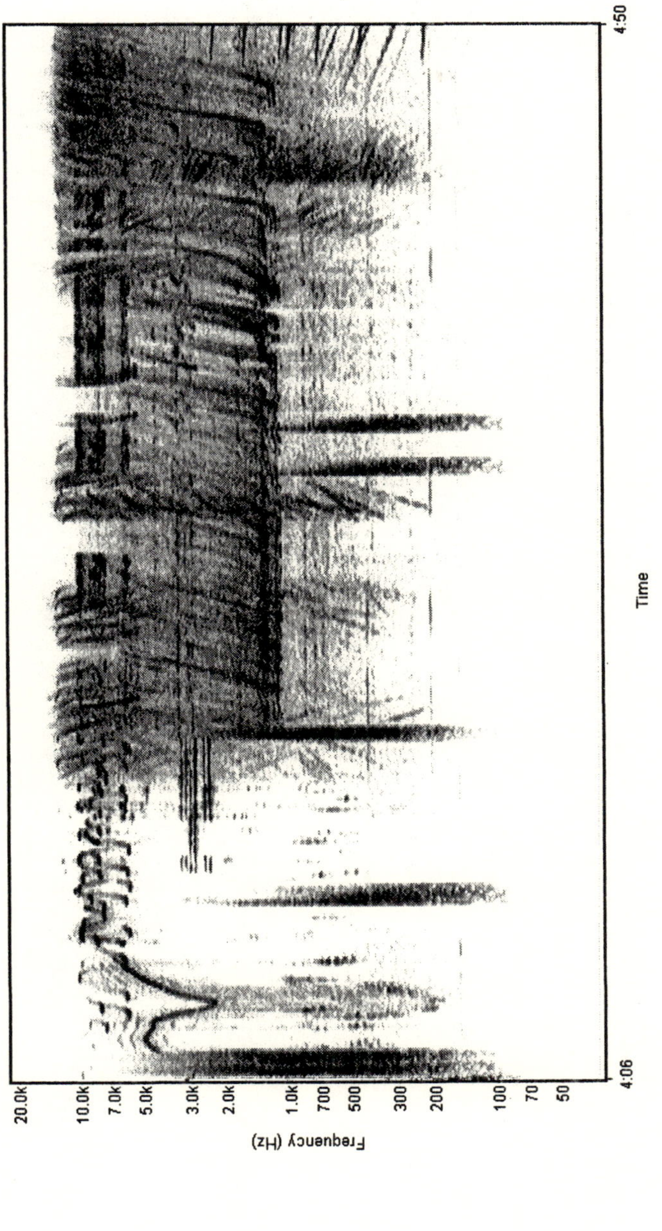

space work as more or less equal partners in shaping our sonic experience. The search for a theory of this music has hardly begun. *Comprehensive* analysis of specific works from this period has rarely been undertaken. Indeed, at this point, any attempt to formulate a general theory of this music would be sadly premature.

In electronic music, frequency, time, tone color, and space become inextricably fused. Such music challenges us to discover new ways to think about composition and forces us to examine each piece from a new theoretical perspective. We can look at each particular case only as thoroughly as possible and hope that, in time, the accumulated wisdom gleaned from many such examinations will offer a glimpse at a possible theoretical basis for this music. The analysis of an electronic work is a bracing musical experience. Practice has already leaped so far ahead of theory (and only fifty years since the inception of the electronic era!) that one can only wonder at the prospects for theorists who attempt such an examination. Certainly, this brief study of Xenakis' *Diamorphoses* has only scratched the surface of the work. We must continue to dig as archaeologists, slowly unearthing new data, formulating tentative theories for future generations to revisit.

NOTES

1. Iannis Xenakis, *Diamorphoses*, in "Xenakis: Electronic Music" (Albany, NY: EMF CD 003, undated).
2. Iannis Xenakis, as quoted by Nouritza Matossian in *Xenakis* (London: Kahn and Averill, 1986), 125; found originally in a notebook in Xenakis' hand in the Xenakis Archives.
3. Joel Chadabe, *Electronic Sound: The Past and Promise of Electronic Music* (Saddle River, NJ: Prentice-Hall, 1997), 34.
4. Ibid., 34–35.
5. Matossian, *Xenakis*, 125.
6. Makis Solomis, program notes for the CD "Xenakis: Electronic Music."
7. James Mansback Brody, program notes for the LP "Iannis Xenakis: Electro-Acoustic Music" (New York: Nonesuch Records, H-71246, undated).
8. Robert Cogan, *New Images of Musical Sound* (Cambridge: Harvard University Press, 1984); Robert Cogan, *Music Seen, Music Heard* (Cambridge: Publication Contact International, 1998).
9. Xenakis, "Xenakis: Electronic Music."
10. SpectraPLUS FFT Spectral Analysis System (Campbell, CA: Sound Technology, 1998).
11. Le Corbusier, *Modulor I, II* (London: Faber and Faber, 1954).
12. See Robert Cogan's analyses of Varèse's *Poème Électronique* in "Varèse: An Oppositional Sonic Poetics," *Sonus* 11, no. 2 (1991): 26–35; Jean-Claude Risset, *Little Boy*, in Robert Cogan, *New Images of Musical Sound* (Cambridge: Harvard University Press, 1984); Milton Babbitt, *Ensembles for Synthesizer*, in Thomas DeLio, *Contiguous Lines; Issues and Ideas in the Music of the '60's and '70's* (Lanham, MD: University Press of America, 1985).

13. See Richard Toop's analyses of Stockhausen's electronic music in "Stockhausen's Electronic Works: Sketches and Work-Sheets from 1952–1967," *Interface* 10, no. 3–4 (1981): 149–198. Also, see Seppo Heikenheimo's study of Stockhausen's electronic music in *The Electronic Music of Karlheinz Stockhausen* (Helsinki: Acta Musicologica Fennica No. 6, 1972).

3

Koenig—Sound Composition—*Essay*

Konrad Boehmer

To those composers who stood beside the cradle of "electronic music" at the beginning of the 1950s, *synthetic sound composition* was a central concern. Although the instruments of production that the composers at that time had at their disposal were extremely primitive (none of the equipment had been designed specifically for compositional purposes), the music of the Cologne studio, in particular, makes a considerably more lasting impression than a large majority of compositions that have been produced in later years. It seems to me that this was precisely due to the primitive and bulky nature of the production tools, which challenged these composers to extremes. Within the field of "electronic music," the subsequent mediation between various production techniques and the serial way of thinking led to results that would have otherwise been impossible to obtain through a mechanical serialization of orchestral instruments.

In Pierre Schaeffer's *Studio d'Essai*, in which *musique concrète* made use of recorded sounds that were subsequently "de-naturalized," the production instruments, in contrast to those in the Cologne studio, were much more refined. (This was not, however, entirely due to the genius of Pierre Schaeffer.) Nevertheless, the musical results were considerably more primitive than in the Cologne studio. Through the process of an increasing "occupation" of compositional intentions and methods through the automation of machines, the Paris studio had initiated a process that proved disastrous for much of the electroacoustic music that followed. The facilitation of work that became possible by the automatic functions of machines corresponded to timbral, rhythmic, and formal textures that were of a naive simplicity and whose repetitive character reflected the very essence of the machine: mechanical repetition. In 1958, ten years after the founding of the Paris studio, Schaeffer drew radically different theoretical conclusions from the methods developed up to that time, laying the foundations of what later became known as *acousmatic* modes of production. After this turning point, *musique concrète* grew closer to the aesthetic presuppositions of the Cologne school. Moreover, in 1958 Pierre Schaeffer proposed to abolish the term *musique concrète*, unfortunately without success. Still today, when referring to the early stages of *musique concrète* (as well as to the composer Pierre Henry) the impudence of various disc jockeys—who in a musical sense, are as illiterate as they are pretentious—reveals a kind of triumphant helplessness.

The pretension to "compose even the sound itself" (Stockhausen 1963, 42) encountered numerous theoretical and aesthetic obstacles. It is understood that it would be irrational to synthetically produce currently nonexisting sounds that would strike up as if they had originated from a Stradivarius or a jet fighter. The idea of a quasi-infinite quantity of currently unheard of sounds also proved to be quite naive. It began from the tacit assumption that these sounds would already have a *virtual* existence that needed only to be unveiled by the composer. Yet, reality is different: without some form of existence there can be no structure and no possibility of determination. It is not surprising that this idea settled mainly in the minds of journalists and hardly in those of serious composers. At least in Cologne, this idea was quickly swept away in favor of the more concrete intention of reconciling the structure of the sound with that of the form with the aid of serial techniques. However, even this notion contains a fair amount of utopian naïveté. Despite all Cagean animisms, the "new sound" is *not* an *ontological* quality, as every sound is a derivation of material causes. As long as these causes are bound to movement and atmosphere, the number of causes is not infinite, although the derivations may manifest numerous subtle variations so that their quantity can be considered unrestricted—at least in relation to the capacities of the human brain. This "infinity" is of a very restricted aesthetic relevance: no sea wave surging toward the shore will ever sound exactly like any other sea wave before or after it, and thus, its countless variants have only an extremely restricted aesthetic and thus compositional significance. (This is one of the main problems of most compositions that make use of sounds "captured" by composers themselves. They may have very specific associations or remembrances concerning the respective sound that they confuse with musical relevance, believing that they are "specific." The listener hears only the sound, which, in general, is exposed solely within the framework of a composition and is not integrated within its formal structure.) Electroacoustic compositions that are chiefly based on these (subjective) factors may, at best, be useful for psycho-acoustic listening tests. Their aesthetic value is rather dubious. "Natural" variants are the result of stochastic or other aleatoric processes for which their mutual relation can be defined only as a relation with their common source. The fact that one tree rustles this way and another slightly differently may be fascinating for friends of nature and disciples of Thoreau's *Walden*; however, the difference makes no musical sense at all. Musical variants differ from all extra-artistic-acoustic variants by their mutual *intentional* relations. These do not have a *material* cause but a *spiritual* one. Their (possible) quantity shows no direct relation to their structural meaning. For example, at every concert performance of Beethoven's *Great Fugue* (which has an amazing richness of musical variants) the work will sound slightly different from how it sounded at all its previous performances. Yet, the aesthetic essence of the composition is untouched by these differences. Moreover, one can find much more acoustic variants in the works of John Cage than in Stockhausen's music. Nonetheless, Stockhausen's music is much richer in an aesthetic sense than is that of Cage. Even the "new" sounds that result from the process of industrialization in the nineteenth century cannot escape—as far as one wants to apply them in an electroacoustic composition—from the dialectics of varied differentiation and aesthetic relevance. Composers who would like to make use of the "new" sounds for the mere reason that they seem *to them* to be interesting or "original" dodge the central problem of composition, which is the problem of an *intratextual* mediation—the prerequisite of any structural organization on an aesthetic level.

Sound composition cannot rely on a kind of *mimesis* of mechanically produced or "natural" sounds, nor can it start from the fiction of "yet unheard" *virtual* sounds. The essence of Western art music of the past 1,000 years has rested on the fact that it has generated *artifacts* that differ in a substantial way from "nature," from the earliest Saint-Martial motets to the era of electroacoustic music. The crux of the matter could be formulated as follows: the trombones in Berlioz's *Requiem* were not shocking because their effect had not been exploited before (in fact, other French composers had used them before Berlioz); they were radically new because of their textual function. Sine waves existed long before Stockhausen; factory noise, long before Nono. What made their integration into a musical context so "new" was their *structural function*. In this respect, we could call to mind Varèse's significant idea in which he conceives of sound not so much as a "real" phenotype but as a *process*. It is precisely this idea that can be considered as the core element of electroacoustic composition—not to embed sound into formal processes but to let it unfold over the course of time, in accordance with its elemental characteristics. In this instance the boundaries between what Stockhausen calls "macro-" and "micro-" time begin to merge, opening entirely new dimensions for the compositional imagination; at least the boundaries between "texture" and "sound-shape" will be merged, for the "new" sound is, above all, "art(ificial) sound." It owes its existence to musical-structural conceptions. Outside of this, it is, at the very most, of anecdotal value.

From the moment of his first collaboration with the "Studio of Electronic Music" of the Cologne Radio WDR (1954) Gottfried Michael Koenig was acutely aware that electronic music must, in *all* its aspects, be a *noninstrumental* music—a music that transcends the traditional dichotomy of composition and sonorous realization. This has had radical consequences for the methodology of composition (and notation!), only because the composer largely becomes his or her own performer but also because the history of music has not brought forth any techniques to notate sound *as such*. In traditional music, a performer translates various symbols that suggest specific (vocal or instrumental) *actions*, whereas the composer of electroacoustic music is confronted with a completely different set of actions. In the electronic studio, every action can be rejected long before the composition is performed in public. Within the framework of a traditional concert, this opportunity would lead to numerous protests. For electroacoustic music, however, it provides an essential function: the singular intent of the composition requires a "safety mechanism" from the composer (or the sound-engineer) that should allow only results that are optimal to human standards. During the "classical" period of the Cologne studio I have observed Koenig, Stockhausen, and other composers repeating simple actions and working long hours until the results, in an optimal way, corresponded to their musical imagination (e.g., applying a specific dynamic curve to a short sound). Eventually, nerves were "laid bare," and French cigarettes (deep black tobacco) were consumed in such sufficient quantities that it would be enough to poison every U.S. citizen in a single day. Those were healthy, fantastic times.

The score of Koenig's composition *Essay* (1957), on whose methodology of sound-texture composition I will comment shortly, was conceived from the start in relation to the new situation of studio-production. It contains, down to the smallest detail, technical instructions (in text and figures) for its *production*. One cannot "read" the score for the purpose of "following" the work while listening (e.g., such as with the funny graphical score of Ligeti's *Artikulation* or the score designed by Bussotti, with erotically graphic talent, of Pousseur's *Elektra*). The score's comprehensive introduction explains the compositional presuppositions of the work in order that those who intend to realize it understand precisely *what* they are doing and *why*. In the introduction of the score, we find a passage that refers to the "elementary timbres." This may be of interest for our further investigations, above all, if we want to trace the relationship between the "elementary timbres" and the ultimate sound composition. Let's unveil the secret, for it is so simple: "The following are used for elementary timbres: sinus tones, filtered noise, filtered impulses" (Koenig 1960, 7). Is that all? No, not yet, for the different sound-sources *as such* are quite bare and for this reason rather uninteresting. The next step is of far more interest: "[e]mployment of these elements as: individual timbres, combined timbres, transference of timbres" (7). This passage needs historical comment. Koenig not only assisted Stockhausen with the realization of his piece *Gesang der Jünglinge* (and later with *Kontakte*) but also—and at crucial points of its production—had significant influence on the methods of production of these works. For example, at the beginning of *Gesang der Jünglinge* we hear marvelous sound-clouds comprising sinus tones, impulses, and noise-particles that merge with transformed fragments of a young boy's voice (just as if it were the question to transport Bach's choral *Vom Himmel hoch, da komm' ich her* into an age of flights to outer space). This passage is significant, for the elementary, rude sounds obtainable from the primitive studio apparatus were melded into a texture that, at its very heart, flourishes as richly as perhaps the overture to Mendelssohn's *Midsummernights-Dream*. How did this soaring Stockhausen overture originate? Simply, Koenig was convinced that it would not be at all sensible to record thousands of centimeter-long particles of sinus tones and to then measure, cut, and finally glue them together. For this reason, he proposed a quasi-aleatoric production process in which he began with tapes of short magnetic and white-taped sections and then recorded a sinus-glissando that would be automatically divided into distinct, small particles. If several such tapes are synchronized (with different "rhythms" and glissandi), one hears a "cloud" of tiny sound-particles with an all-embracing global direction. Although the composer might not have absolute control over every detail, he or she can control the audible result. Consequently, in *Essay*, Koenig wanted to understand the entire process more accurately.

In *Essay* Koenig placed the three elementary categories of sound into three groups (S = sinus tones, N = noise, I = impulses).

1. individual (only S, N, or I is used)
2. vertical combinations (synchronizations): S+N, S+I, N+I, S+N+I
3. horizontal combinations (following the time-arrow): S→N, N→S, S→N→I, I→N→S...

In total, these three forms result in nineteen possible combinations of elementary categories. Because of these combinations, especially at the "microrange," Koenig creates various types of sound in which the temporal *process* extends from absolute homogeneity to absolute heterogeneity, leading ultimately to the formation of compositional categories. The different steps of this process can be determined by serial methods, which I comment upon shortly. Having obtained nineteen different categories (three single, four vertical, and twelve horizontal combinations), what can now be done with them? We could permute ("serialize") them to infinity for the sole purpose of picking raisins from that immense permutational cake. This, regrettably, is the practice of inferior serial composers who neglect the simple fact that their *selection* never coincides with their compositional methodology. Only the most dim-witted seagull confuses a grain of sand on the beach—one of trillions—with a savory shrimp. During this time Koenig was already a rather systematic hawk who, *before* flying downward, took aim of his prey in a very precise manner. Even if the story becomes somewhat technical, we should try to descend a little further into the methodical details of *Essay*.

The "serial" methodology of the Cologne school never conceived of a "series" as an agglomerate, a simple addition of concrete "values" (pitch, duration, etc.—as Boulez had done during a certain period). The composers of the Cologne school conceived of a "series" as a "modulor" (termed by the architect Le Corbusier), as a *configuration of (possible) proportions,* which was applicable, in like manner, to all primary (sound) and secondary (texture, form) parameters. In this respect, *Essay* was developed simultaneously from two extremes: form *and* material. The "form" is not simply "capped" atop the "head" of the material; rather, the dialectical interference of both extremes (as well as their intermediate steps) can be considered as the essence of serial composition. If one cannot say more about the "form" of *Essay* other than that it has eight parts of different length, such an observation (from a serial perspective) would mean nothing more than that *a form as such* has no substantiality at all, but that it is *defined* by those *elements* by which it is *constituted.*

Let us return to the question of how Koenig continues to proceed with his "elementary timbres." These timbres are placed into various "groups" (whose elements are composed to the smallest detail), which Koenig labels as "material"; already this material contains very specific characteristics. This "material" is not *nature*, nor is it *convention,* for in itself, it is already the result of compositional and formal decisions.

To each of the eight parts of the form (A–H) is attached "material," with each part divided into a different number of sections of different total lengths (length is calculated in centimeters (cm) and is based on a tape-speed of 38.1 cm/sec). No single "part" of the total "form" contains only one or two sections, as this would lead to rather weak polyphonic textures. As a result, the series (as it pertains to the number of total sections in each part) begins with the value 3 and ends with 10. The total length of each part is based on a divisional ratio of 3/2, with all parts ordered along a prescribed "sequence" (Example 3.1).

The total lengths of the different "materials" already provide some indication as to (1) the density of "events" within the different parts of the form (thereby beginning to form their first concrete definition) and (2) the density of the "elementary timbres" within the sections of "material." As the procedures from any one part to the next are the same, I focus on the disposition of the material-sections in part A, thereby illustrating the various steps that are to be repeated in

Example 3.1
Parts of *Essay* (sequence: 5 4 1 7 6 2 8 3; ratio: 3/2)

Part	Number of sections	Total length (in centimeters)	Total duration (in seconds)
A	7	384.7	10.10
B	6	256.5	6.73
C	3	76.0	2.00
D	9	865.7	22.72
E	8	577.1	15.15
F	4	114.0	3.00
G	10	1,298.5	34.08
H	5	171.0	4.49

Example 3.2
Part A (sequence: 1 2 5 4 3 7 6; ratio: 3/2)

Section	Tape length
1	12.0 (cm)
2	17.9
3	60.5
4	40.4
5	26.9
6	136.2
7	90.8

Example 3.3
Section 1, Part A (sequence: 5 4 1 7 6 2 8 3; ratio: 12/11)

Subsection	Tape length	Frequency
1	1.5 (cm)	456 + 703 (Hz)
2	1.4	441 + 644
3	1.1	400 + 591
4	1.8	486 + 542
5	1.7	471 + 519
6	1.2	413 + 566
7	2.0	502 + 617
8	1.3	427 + 673

Example 3.4
Section 2, Part A (sequence: 4 3 8 6 5 1 7 2; ratio: 11/10)

Subsection	Tape length	Frequency
1	2.1 (cm)	476 (Hz)
2	1.9	508
3	3.0	542
4	2.5	578
5	2.3	617
6	1.6	658
7	2.7	703
8	1.7	750

each of the remaining parts. Part A (total tape length: 384.7 cm) is divided into seven sections with the total length of each section based, once again, on a divisional ratio of 3/2 (Example 3.2).

Each section is further divided into eight subsections that are "filled in" with concrete "elementary timbres," as well as with their specific definitions (frequency). The division into subsections of the first section (total length: 12.0 cm) of part A is based on a divisional ratio of 12/11, with each subsection assigned two frequencies to each timbre (Example 3.3).

The subsections in section 2 (total length: 17.9 cm) are based on a divisional ratio of 11/10, with each subsection "filled in" this time with only one frequency (Example 3.4). Similarly, all subsections in the remaining five sections of part A have different divisional ratios, with either one or two frequencies assigned to each timbre.

The shorter the time-value (tape length), the less they are determined by serial methods (in which case they are defined by dividend ratios of the total duration). While the sequence of subsections is serially determined, how are the sequences themselves determined? For this Koenig developed a double parameter that determines (1) the frequencies and (2) the ambit (range) in which frequency movements will develop. Throughout the piece, the directions of movement are derived from two basic categories:

1. directionally undefined (a highly permutable sequence)
2. directionally defined (unpermutable), upward or downward

As was the case with the short time segments, the structural divisions of the frequencies are once more determined by a geometric series. For the range of frequencies, Koenig designed eight basic schemes (Example 3.5) that, if desired, can be modified to a high degree without affecting their global tendency. These forms of movement, which can vary between one and eight octaves, are projected onto various sound spaces that are different in each of the work's eight parts (Example 3.6).

These directions of movement are also applied to materials with an indefinite direction. Within the overall frequency range of each part (which is further divided into eight separate ranges) "layers" are formed in which the dispositions of frequencies follow principles of aleatoric permutation. For example, frequency development in part A is static (between ca. 400–800 Hz). The directions of movement, again determined from the scheme of eight directions, develop "freely" within the various pitch ranges of each section. This scheme provides an effective summary of the global frequency movements throughout the entire composition and, consequently, of the evolving contraction and expansion of its sound space. Here again, an aspect of the quality of the form was defined by criteria that initially concerned the material.

Example 3.5
Directions of Movement Used in *Essay*

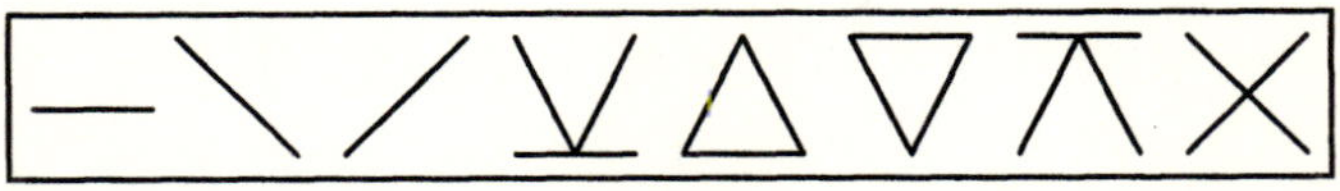

Example 3.6
Frequency Ranges of *Essay* (sequence: 1 7 6 2 8 3 5 4)

Part	# of octaves	Octave range
A	1	400-800 (Hz)
B	7	50-6,400
C	6	200-12,800
D	2	400-1,600
E	8	50-12,800
F	3	200-1,600
G	5	100-3,200
H	4	200-3,200

How does Koenig carry on further with these "elementary timbres," which, as sinus tones, impulses, or noise, have so incredibly little substance? The disposition of these timbres (their distribution within the shortest temporal units of each subsection) is once more based on global definitions of movement. Throughout the piece, these timbres can be distributed in the following ways:

1. Static (only one category): for example,

   N N N N N N N N

2. Transitional: for example, from N to I

   N N N N N N N N
   I N N N N N N N
   I I N N N N N N *etc., until*:
   I I I I I I I N
   I I I I I I I I

   (these transitional sequences can also be affected with all three "elementary timbres").

3. Combinations (relatively undirected): for example, for two or three of the "elementary timbres." Part A makes use of this category of distribution. In each of its sections, the distribution is as follows:

		subsections							
	1.	S	S	S	S	S	N	S	S
	2.	S	S	N	N	S	S	S	N
	3.	N	N	S	S	N	N	N	N
sections	4.	S	N	N	N	N	N	N	I
	5.	N	N	N	N	I	I	N	N
	6.	N	I	I	I	N	N	I	I
	7.	I	I	N	I	I	I	I	I

As these "elementary timbres" are distributed within the shortest units of time (e.g., 1.1 cm lasts approximately 0.029 sec.), we do not, in general, hear "timbre-melodies" but compact *timbral movements*, which extend from having rather "homogeneous" to "heterogeneous" characteristics. A sequence that consists exclusively of *S* sounds homogeneous and quite smooth; a sequence consisting exclusively of *N* sounds homogeneous and rough; and a sequence consisting of *S* + *I* + *N* sounds heterogeneous and quite rough. A sequence that moves from *S* to *N* sounds relatively homogeneous, at first smooth and then increasingly rough. Koenig is not in the least interested in the (three) categorical timbres that were available to him at the Cologne studio (which at that time was still rather undeveloped). Instead, he focused his efforts entirely on their subtle and consistent *combinations* that might render entirely new global timbral impressions—timbres that are neither of "instruments" nor of "machines." The conjunction of acoustic qualities and the organization of musical time lead to such a result.

Up to this point, the "musical material" has been defined in relation to its relevant parameters. It is indeed remarkable that the application of these compositional techniques owes nothing to the "mechanical" serial techniques as the young Boulez had used them, when he simply summed up values until he became completely muddled in the process (e.g., in his *Structures I*). For Koenig, every type of serial determination is derived from superior criteria of musical perception. This simple truth of the Cologne school conception of serialism has been neglected by those who could see nothing beyond its methods other than a "discharge" from compositional efforts or imagined a "series" as a kind of insurance policy for modernism. Later polemics of this kind from "serial fetishists" against the aesthetic baseness of serialism sound as dilettante as the "serial sins" from their youth. They seem to me to be along the same lines as the polemics of the conservative parson Artusi against Monteverdi.

What other procedures does Koenig employ to treat his minutely composed "material" (For, as it stands, it is still quite bare)? Koenig next combines the different sections of material into more complex configurations, as well as increases the total length of sections. In addition, he takes the following steps, which (1) lead the "material" to musical textures and (2) lend specific qualities to the sequences of "material" *within the textures*. These qualities are developed from the technical possibilities of the Cologne studio at that time. Let us take a closer look at them, concentrating once again on form/part A. The sections of "material" in part A undergo the following transformations:

1. ring-modulation
2. transposition (this alters each section's total duration. For example, when transposed twice its speed, the pitch will be one octave higher, while the durations will be half that of the original sound). The total length of each section of part A before and after transposition is shown in Example 3.7.
3. filtering
4. reverberation
5. intensity curves (applied only to sections at this stage of elaboration)
6. other transformations

The score indicates precisely in what manner the transformations of the original sections must be operated upon. (Some "parts" make intentional use of distortions, sending the "material" through an overdriven amplifier to make the alteration more clearly audible.) All these measures of sound alteration can be applied successively. For example, after a sequence is first ring-modulated and then reverberated, the inversion of these operations leads to different results. All these activities are still related to the separated sequences of "material." Only after

Example 3.7
Tape Length before and after Transposition in Part A

Section	Total length *before* transposition	Total length *after* transposition
1	12.0 (cm)	96.2 (cm)
2	17.9	384.7
3	60.5	3,078.0
4	40.4	192.4
5	26.9	48.1
6	136.2	1,539.0
7	90.8	769.5

being transformed with the various methods mentioned earlier have these sequences been modified and then assembled into larger forms. This occurs in two ways:

1. Entry delays definitions for the different sections. This is based on a series of time-intervals whose structure is once again based on a geometric series. The entry delays for part A are shown in Example 3.8 (the entry of the first section is evidently 0, with the last entry of the sequence being the start time for the first section of the next part, part B).

2. Combination of resultant polyphonic layers. For part A the layers produced are:

Layer I: transformation results of A1 and A2, as well as A4, A5 and A6 (ring-modulation, transposition, filtering)
Layer II: transformation results of A3 (ring-modulation, transposition, constant reverberation)
Layer III: transformation results of A7 (ring-modulation, transposition, filtering, increasing reverberation)

As far as the transpositions are continually developed (as transposition-glissandi), single sections of "material" often "float" between "micro-" time, a continuous perception (where the details as such do not enter the conscience), and "macro-" time, a discontinuous perception (where the singular "atoms" of sound become perceptible). This is what I have described as the "hovering passage from textures to timbres." If these transitions are based, for example, entirely on sinus tones (and are of different frequencies), the result forms a "melodic" perception. Within a "polyphonic" interaction of different sections, several forms of perception are activated simultaneously, leading to a colorful kaleidoscope. These many variants are characteristic of *Essay*. It is precisely these "transitions in time" that are typical of the specific "electronic" character of the composition, and *in no way* could this have been realized by instrumental means. The result is an extremely vivid composition! Although realized with the aid of extremely simple tools, *Essay* sounds fresher and more immediate after

Example 3.8
Entry Delays for Part A (sequence: 1 2 5 4 3 7 6; ratio: 3/2)

Section	Total length
1	116.4 (cm)
2	174.5
3	589.1
4	392.7
5	261.8
6	1,325.4
7	883.6

forty years than many later works that borrowed their material from pre-established programs or from computers. In many of these cases the impression of apparently "complex" sounds seemed to be decisive to such an extent that the composer completely overlooked addressing their formal integration, leaving the form as a simple summing up of its parts, comparable to that of a baroque suite. The total duration of *Essay* is exactly eight minutes, and this is only one reason that the polyphonic or polymorphic ramifications of its textures escape the dangers of repetition and redundancy.

Koenig invested a considerable amount of time and work into this piece. This was due not only to the use of rather primitive technology but, above all, to the aesthetic presuppositions of the composition itself. A work's presuppositions do not wholly depend on the demands of *sound composition* but also on the considerably more essential presupposition that "sound" is *not* a preestablished category at the composer's disposal that he needs only to place into formal patterns. The question—whether the composer has in advance "heard" the object of his calculations and definitions—could be answered with the objection that the composer of a "traditional" work does not hear his or her "form" before realizing it. From Machaut, to Beethoven, to Schoenberg, "form" has always been *forma formans,* exactly as the great Arabic philosopher Averroës, who understood "form" as the "possibility of matter," defined it some 900 years ago. Since the time of Wagner and Debussy, European music began to detach itself from "categorical" conceptions of sound, integrating timbre as something "moved" and "moving" within the formal process. Only with the advent of "electronic" music did it become possible to mediate, in a dialectical way, between form (as the dynamic aspect) and timbre (as the direct appearance) and to proceed in such a way that it becomes impossible to separate both dimensions in a scholastic-academic way. This step manifests itself in Koenig's *Essay* in a much more radical way than in other compositions of that period. *Essay* is a composition that set the standards for a new type of "thinking in music." Consequently, it provided in a very decisive manner the first steps toward a *terza prattica* of European art music. The existence of "standards of a new type of thinking *in* music" does not at all suggest that these standards can be imitated.

Any academician is a sworn enemy of the arts. In new music, it is a deadly poison, leading only to the most dreadful kinds of "arts-and-crafts." In short, sound, as a new compositional paradigm, is *not an object* that one can first listen to and to which, furthermore, then dispose of. It is, on the contrary, exactly that which rises *above* the purely physical sounding matter that in itself is already form.

The "Score and Instructions for Realization" of *Essay* was originally published by Vienna Universal Edition. As it was not fit for reading while listening and thus does not offer a graphic representation of the music, it was difficult to sell to amateurs interested in modern music. It was also not possible to commercialize it as "rental material," for the work (on tape) is already its own performance. For this reason the publisher—whose politeness toward composers had been experienced long before Koenig (e.g., by Kurt Weill)—simply sent back the remaining exemplars to the composer without even discussing the dissolution of the contract. When the publisher "PFAU-Verlag" began working on the edition (in German) of Koenig's collected theoretical writings,[1] they then decided to publish the score of *Essay*. With the availability of a CD recording of this work,[2] *Essay* can now be studied in both its forms by those who not only want more information about this important document of early electronic/serial music but also want to have aesthetic pleasure with it. It is worthwhile.

NOTES

1. PFAU Verlag, Postfach 102314, D 66023 SAARBRÜCKEN, tel: 0049-681-41.63.394, fax: 0049-681-41.63.395. Currently, four volumes have been published: G. M. Koenig, Ästhetische Praxis, Texte zur Musick, Band I-IV.
2. G. M. Koenig: Klangfiguren II, Essay, Terminus I | II, Output and Funktionen (2 CDs), BVHAAST CD 9001/2 (Serie: Acousmatrix 1/2). United States—Distribution: North Country Distributors, The Cadence Building, Redwood, NY 13679, tel: (315) 287-2852, fax: (315) 287-2860, E-mail: northcountry@cadencebuilding.com.

REFERENCES

Koenig, G. M. (1960). *Essay, Score and Instructions for Realization*. Vienna, Austria: Universal Edition, PFAU Verlag.

Stockhausen, K. (1963). "Die Entstehung der elektronischen Musik." In *Texte zur elektronischen Musik*, Cologne, Germany.

4

Luigi Nono's *Omaggio a Emilio Vedova*

Thomas Licata

In 1960, Luigi Nono initiated a lifelong exploration of electronic media with the creation of his first composition for tape, *Omaggio a Emilio Vedova*. Nono's initial experimentation with the use of electronic sound came about through a variety of musical, extramusical, and, to a large degree, ideological concerns and influences. Dissatisfied with the postwar music establishment and the traditional "concert-hall" performance environment, electroacoustic music supplied Nono with not only a means of exploring new modes of artistic expression but also a medium in which he could present his music in rather unconventional venues for an audience other than that of the typical urban concertgoer. For instance, *La fabbrica illuminata* for soprano and tape (1964), a work commenting on the exploitation of the industrial worker, was not only generated in part from factory noises and the spoken words of factory workers but created to be presented in the very environment that provided much of its source materials: factories.

While Nono was striving to break new ground in the musical arts, he found in Emilio Vedova (b. Venice, 1919) an artist, collaborator, and friend with similar creative and ideological views working in the visual arts. Their first collaboration, the opera *Intolleranza 60'*, was marked by important artistic developments in the work of both artists. In designing the opera's striking sets and costumes, Vedova felt that he had made significant strides forward in his experiments in creating original structures, which he later labeled *plurimi*: artworks comprising various assemblages of interlaced panels. In his *Sketchbooks of Preparatory Drawings to the Plurimi, 1961–1965*, Vedova refers to the importance of these opera sets: "In *Intolleranza '60* . . . this plurimo of mine found its first free-natural-existence, finding itself in the dynamic-light, a constant in my work" (Eccher 1996, 41). In addition to the opera's many musical innovations and stylistic developments, Nono for the first time integrated electronic sound with live performers—a practice that he was to employ in many of his subsequent compositions. Following *Intolleranza 60'*, these two artists were to collaborate on a number of other projects over the course of the next three decades. With his painting *Intolleranza '60, n. 2 (a Luigi Nono)*, created during the same year as both *Omaggio a Emilio Vedova* and the opera *Intolleranza '60*, Vedova conveys his mutual admiration for Nono (Example 4.1).

xample 4.1
***ntolleranza '60, n.2 (a Luigi Nono)*, Vedova, 1960 (145 x 145 cm)**

Omaggio a Emilio Vedova was composed at the RAI (Radio Audizioni Italiane) studios in Milan. Established in 1955 by Luciano Berio and Bruno Maderna, it was considered one of the best-equipped electronic facilities in Europe during the late 1950s and early 1960s. Moreover, it was through the work of many of the composers who worked in the RAI studios, in large part, that the distinctions between the compositional aesthetics of *musique concrète* (based in Paris and drawn upon recorded sound materials) and "electronic music" (based in Cologne and drawn from synthesized sound materials) were further eroded, if not thoroughly discarded. Premiered in Rome in 1961, *Omaggio a Emilio Vedova* is not only Nono's first electroacoustic work but also his only tape piece composed entirely of electronic sounds. Though created in this way, this work (and, above all, Nono's artistic stance regarding music making in general) is far removed from the compositional methods of the Cologne school, for its design—as in much of his musical output—is primarily concerned with the musical and sonic properties of texture, sonority, and timbre. While working in the RAI studios throughout much of the 1960s and 1970s, and initiated with the creation of *Omaggio a Emilio Vedova*, Luigi Nono created some of the most innovative, provocative, and indeed socially minded electro-acoustic music of the postwar era.

METHODS OF ANALYSIS

As is typical of most works for tape alone, there is no score for *Omaggio a Emilio Vedova*. In studying this work sonograms and amplitude graphs were used as a means to graphically represent its rich and diverse sonic environment. Spectrographic study of sound had its beginnings with Helmholtz in the 1860s. More recently, it has been applied to the analysis of both electroacoustic music and instrumental music, most notably in the work of Robert Cogan (1984a, 1998, 1999). Sonograms provide a means of delineating the structural outline of a work's sonic design through the graphic representation of frequency on the vertical axis and time on the horizontal axis. Furthermore, as music encompasses not only movement in time and space but also the projection of tone color, sonograms also provide views of a work's timbral properties. The intensity (amplitude) of any given sound is represented by various shades of gray (lighter shades represent softer sounds, while darker shades signify louder sounds). Amplitude graphs, the second means of graphic representation used in this analysis, depict amplitude levels on the vertical axis and time on the horizontal axis, providing yet another perspective of a work's structural design. These tools provide the analyst with considerable means to examine both the macrostructure and microstructure of a composition's sonic landscape. In his book *New Images of Musical Sound*, Cogan comments on the broad implications of using new analytical technologies in studying musical sound: "[T]hrough a new synthesis of scientific and musical analysis, can we begin to probe the sonic enigma. Photographs of spectral formation of musical works provide a bridge that makes a new understanding of sound and music, sound *in* music, possible" (Cogan 1984a, 12).

OVERVIEW OF FORM

Example 4.2 presents a sonogram and an amplitude graph of *Omaggio a Emilio Vedova* in its entirety.[1] (In this and all such examples that follow, sonograms are always placed above amplitude graphs.) These images show the division of the piece into three large sections of successively shorter duration, each with its own unique sonic design. In general, section 1, while displaying a wide frequency range throughout (ca. 50–18,000 Hz), is the only section characterized by a gradual movement from a relatively diffuse to a more compact spectral distribution, which runs in parallel with a movement from low to high amplitude levels. At 1:54, significant reductions in both spectra and amplitude levels signal the start of section 2. Section 2, while carrying over the wide frequency range of section 1, returns to diffuse spectra and low amplitude levels. Beginning at 2:31, while spectra and amplitude remain at relatively low to moderate levels, there is a distinct and significant compression of the overall frequency range (ca. 100–7,000 Hz)—the narrowest frequency range in the piece. The immediate shift to the widest frequency range in the piece, in combination with the most compact spectrum and highest amplitude levels in the piece beginning at 3:32, marks the rather abrupt and dramatic start of section 3. These high levels of activity remain relatively constant throughout most of this third section. In general, *Omaggio a Emilio Vedova* may be characterized as comprising a gradual movement from a high degree of contrast and opposition in section 1, leading toward, and set against, far greater degrees of compression and uniformity in both sections 2 and 3.

SECTIONS

Section 1

Section 1 (Example 4.3), the longest section of the piece, is divided into three subsections of relatively equal durations (0:43, 0:37, 0:34). As mentioned, on the macro level, section 1 (operating within the framework of a wide frequency range) gradually moves from a diffuse to a more compact spectrum and from low to high levels of amplitude. On the micro level, each of its three subsections exhibits similar behavior. In addition, subsections 1b and 1c (after returning to low levels of spectra and amplitude) subsequently move to a more compact spectrum and to even higher amplitude levels than subsections 1a and 1b, respectively—in effect not only mirroring the sonic design of the preceding subsections but eclipsing their parametric levels as well.

What further delineates these three subsections, as well as contributes to their overall evolution throughout section 1, are the various gestural configurations contained in each subsection. Generally, these gestures are comprised and differentiated by two contrasting sound types: short, percussive-like sounds with hard attacks, and long, sustained sounds, of varying length, and, if at all, generally with soft attacks. Intersecting, alternating, and opposing one another in a variety of ways, these sound types play important roles not only in section 1 but also, as will be shown, throughout the entire piece. In the examples of sonograms that follow, short sounds (designated with arrows in Example 4.4) are identified with sharp, densely packed vertical peaks with a fast decay, while sustained sounds (designated with brackets in Example 4.4) are characterized by horizontal bands of varying length, distributed throughout various regions across the overall frequency range.

Throughout section 1 there is a motion from a rather rich interplay between sound types toward a more distinct separation of the two, gradually leading further to a more pronounced separation from one gesture to the next. Subsection

Example 4.2
Sonogram (Top) and Amplitude Graph (Bottom) of Entire Piece

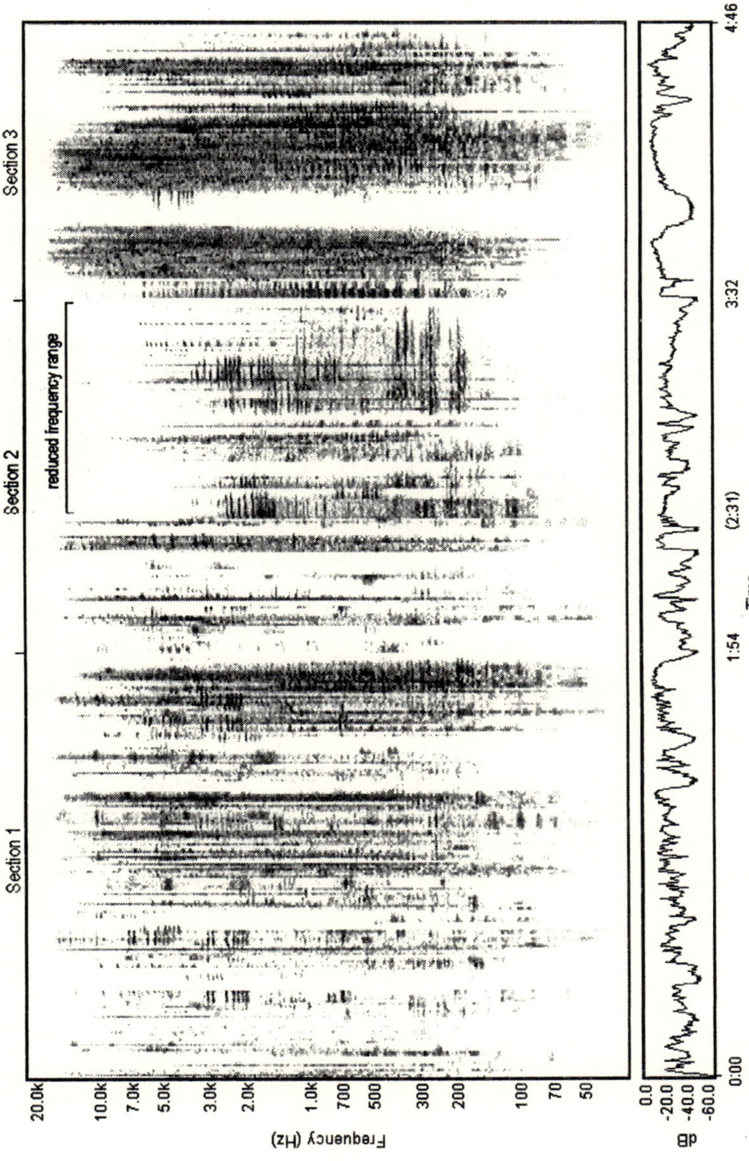

Example 4.3
Section 1 (0:00–1:54, total duration: 1:54)

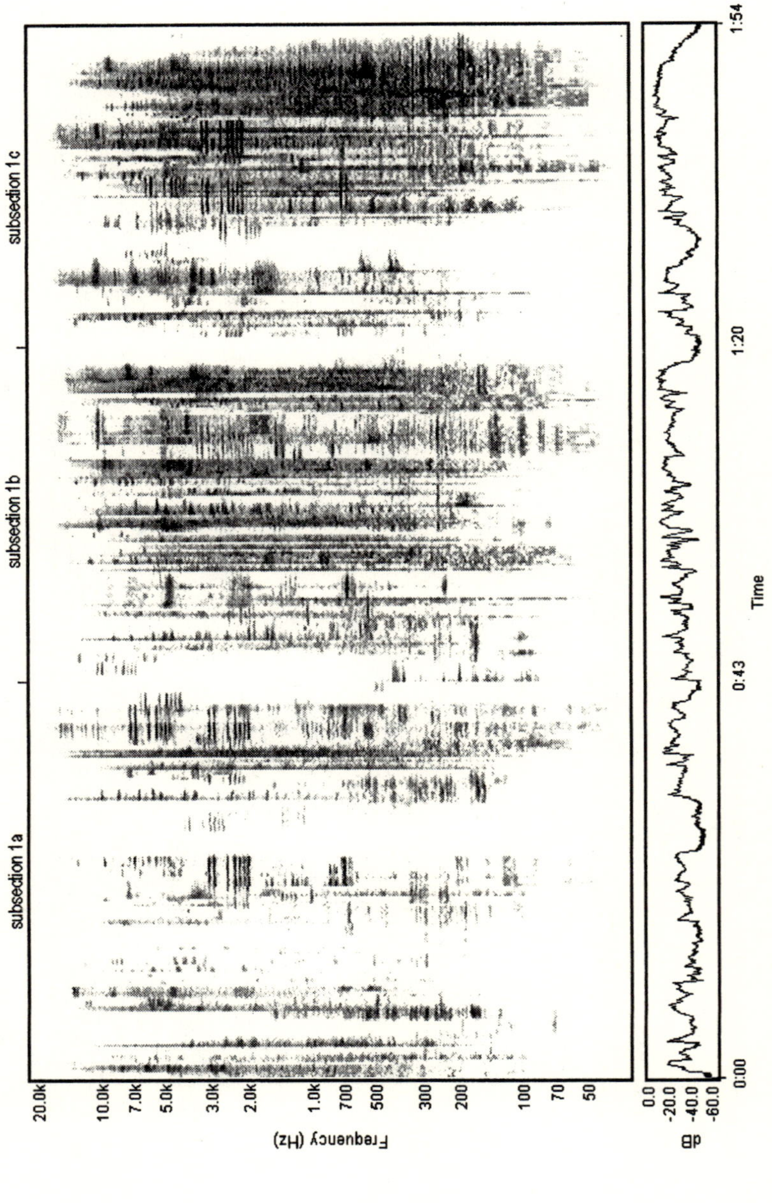

Example 4.4
Subsection 1a (0:00–0:43), General Mixing of Sound Types within Gestures (arrows = short sounds, brackets = sustained sounds)

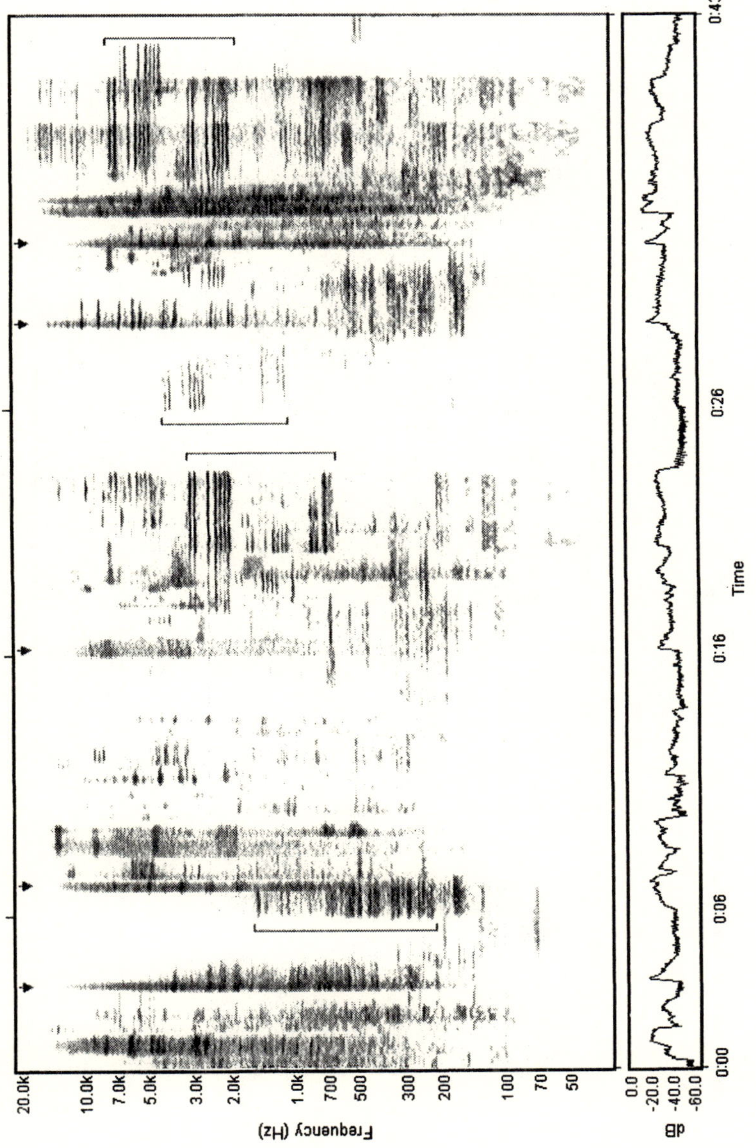

Example 4.5
Subsection 1b (0:43–1:20), Growing Separation of Sound Types between Gestures

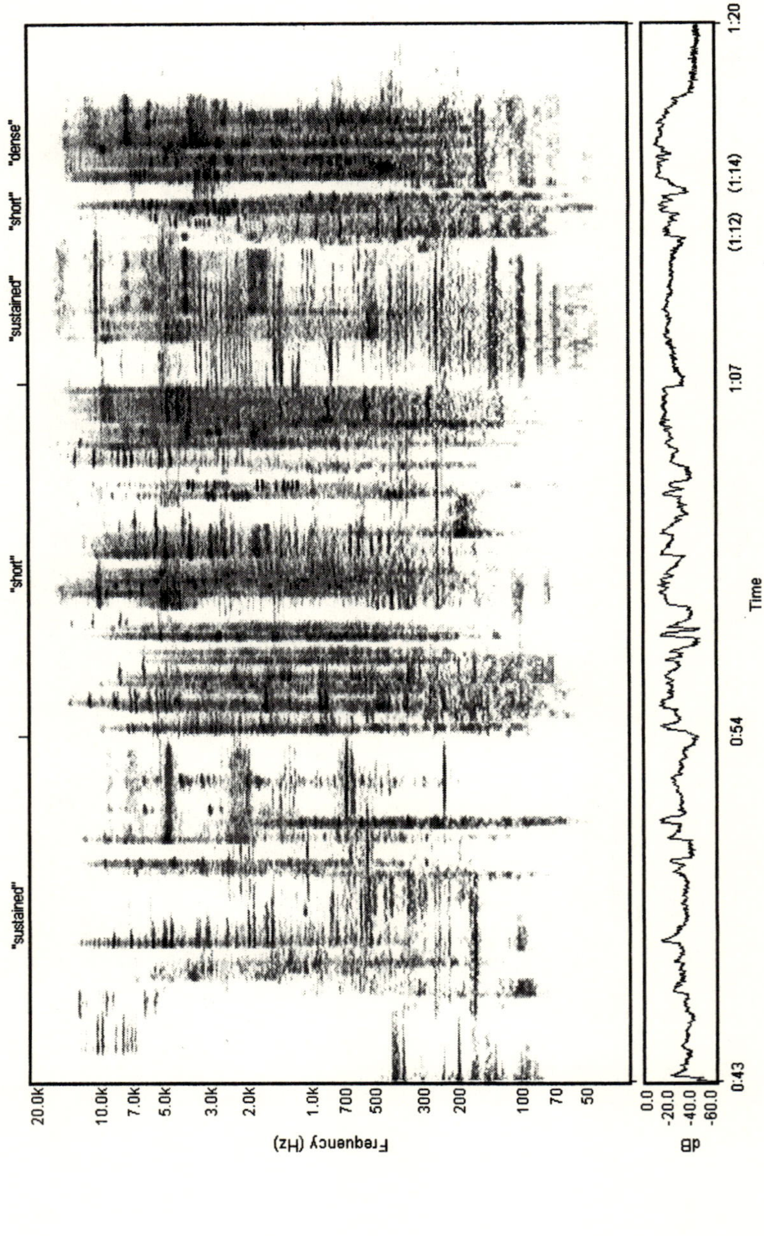

Example 4.6
Subsection 1c (1:20–1:54), Greatest Separation of Sound Types between Gestures

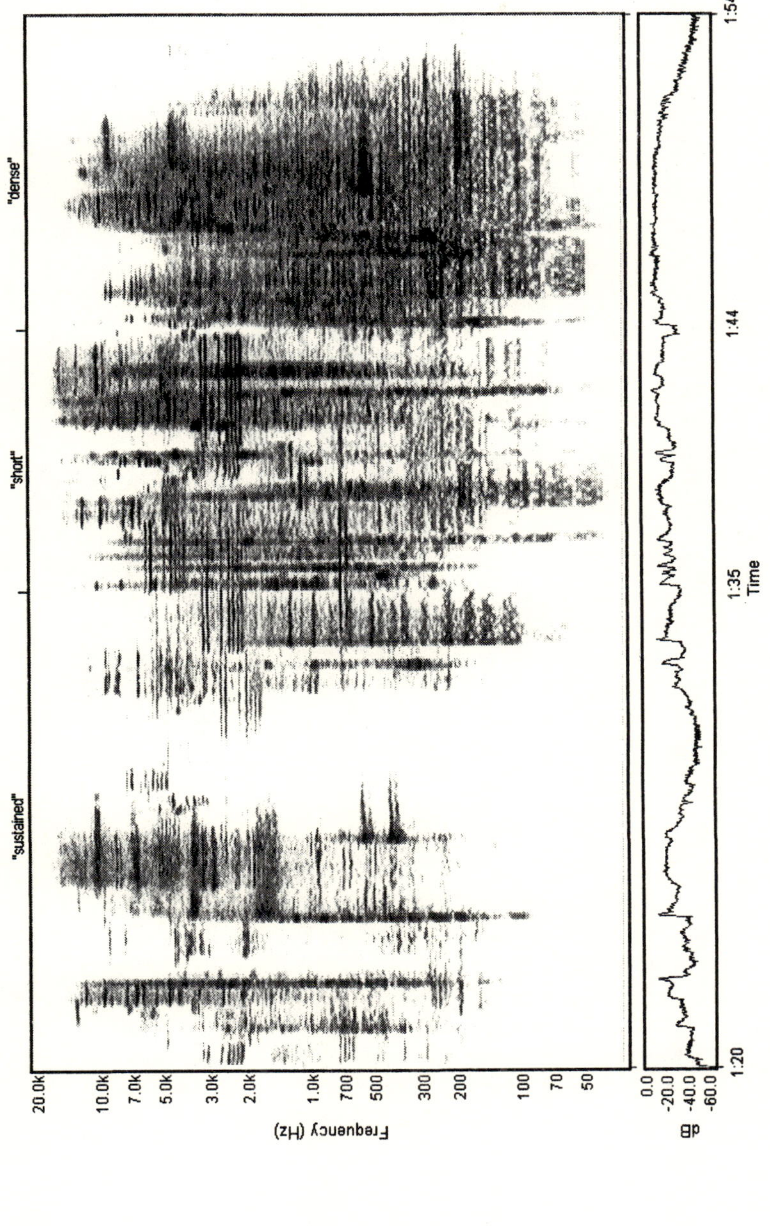

Example 4.7
Movement from One State of Activity to Another throughout Section 1

	subsection 1a	subsection 1b	subsection 1c
Spectrum	diffuse	→ →	compact
Amplitude	low	→ →	high
Sound types	mixture of sustained/short	→ →	separation of sustained/short

1a (Example 4.4), comprising of four gestures, each separated by a pause, consists of short and sustained sound types that alternate and interact with one another throughout. Subsection 1b (Example 4.5), containing three gestures, though no pauses separate these gestures, is marked more by a general shifting of sound types from one gesture to the next. This is particularly the case with the third gesture of subsection 1b, which begins with sustained sounds (1:07), immediately moves to short sounds (1:12), and, at 1:14, shifts to a rather dense sonic event. This progression, while clearly separating short and sustained sound types within this last gesture, foreshadows the same separation that occurs between the three gestures in subsection 1c overall. The three gestures of subsection 1c (Example 4.6), again none of which are separated by pauses, are more clearly differentiated than those of the previous two subsections. This is particularly significant, for not only has the separation of sound types grown to their most distinct, but also at this point, as mentioned, spectra and amplitude have reached their highest levels thus far in the piece.

As summarized in Example 4.7, section 1 comprises a rather diverse collection of parametrical progressions that gradually move from one state of activity to another.

Section 2

Section 2 (Example 4.8) is divided into two subsections, the second being of considerably longer duration than the first (0:37, 1:01). Subsection 2a, while carrying over the wide frequency range of section 1 (ca. 50–18,000 Hz), is characterized by extremely diffuse spectra and low amplitude levels. The material at 2:22, still stretched across a wide frequency range, is far denser compared to the material before it. This "column" of sound, which is similar to the frequency range of the material before it, as well as to the spectral distribution of the material that follows, provides a link between the sonic materials of subsections 2a and 2b. Subsection 2b is clearly set apart from 2a (and indeed from the rest of the piece) through the widespread compression of the overall frequency range beginning at 2:31. In 2b, spectra, which are comparatively more compact than

2a, and amplitude levels, while somewhat higher than 2a, still consistently remain at generally low to moderate levels.

Subsection 2a comprises primarily sustained sound types. However, at its center (2:09) a sharp and comparatively much louder short attack initiates a drop in both spectra and amplitude in the material that follows. By contrast, there had been a modest increase in these levels before this point. With this in mind, subsection 2a can be viewed as comprising two gestures, separated by a short attack, that move in similar ways but in opposite directions. Subsection 2b also comprises predominantly sustained sounds—and of a markedly far greater length than those in 2a, as well as at any other point in the piece (clearly distinguishable by the long horizontal stretches of soundbands). Subsection 2b likewise comprises two gestures, which, preceded and followed by a brief pause, are once again separated by a short, loud attack (2:57). This second gesture, however, contains considerably more shorter sounds than the first, and this serves an important function: by expanding to higher frequencies, they help prepare for the return of the high frequency levels of section 3. Consequently, notwithstanding the compression of its overall frequency range and the considerable lengthening of its total duration, subsection 2b can be viewed as a structural imitation of the sonic design exhibited in subsection 2a.

Section 3

Section 3 (Example 4.9) has two subsections, the first being nearly twice as long as the second (0:48, 0:26; the inverse of the durational relationship found between the two subsections of section 2). Subsection 3a is dominated by two massive columns of sound (beginning at 3:37), resulting from a unique combination of the highest parametric levels found in the entire piece: the widest frequency range, the greatest concentration of short sounds, the highest amplitude levels, and the most compact spectrum. These columns are separated by significant reductions in amplitude as well as the nearly total absence of spectra (about 3:55). Subsection 3b, with an apparent structural inversion of the material exhibited in 3a, consists, at its center (4:32), of a single column of sound comprising a wide frequency range and high levels of spectra and amplitude, which is surrounded by two areas of significantly lower levels.

Similar to the structural mirroring and incremental expansion of parametric levels from one subsection to the next found in section 1, as well as to the structural imitation between the two subsections of section 2, there is also, significantly, a similar interrelationship between the two subsections of section 3. However, in Section 3 it is achieved through the process of structural inversion.

THE OVERALL FORM

As summarized in Example 4.10, the three sections of *Omaggio a Emilio Vedova* each exhibits its own distinguishing set of characteristics. These features not only help to shape the work's form within and between sections but also help

Example 4.8
Section 2 (1:54–3:32, total duration: 1:38)

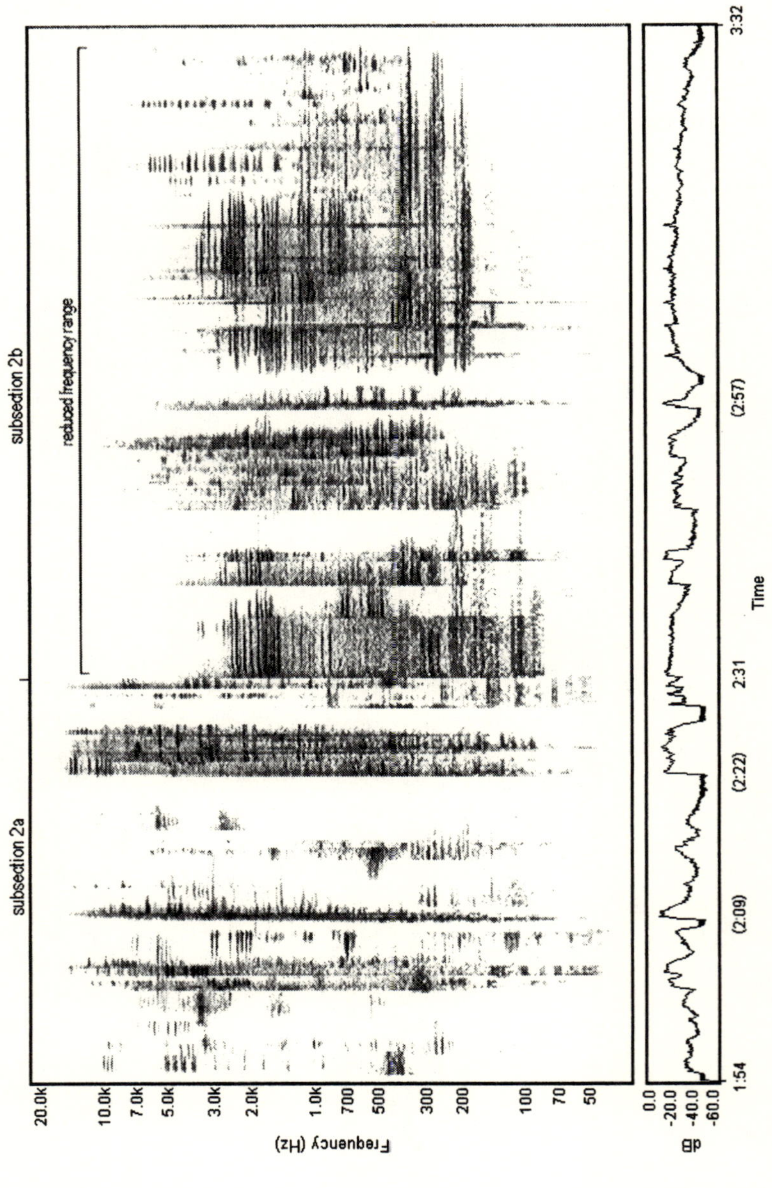

Example 4.9
Section 3 (3:32–4:46, total duration: 1:14)

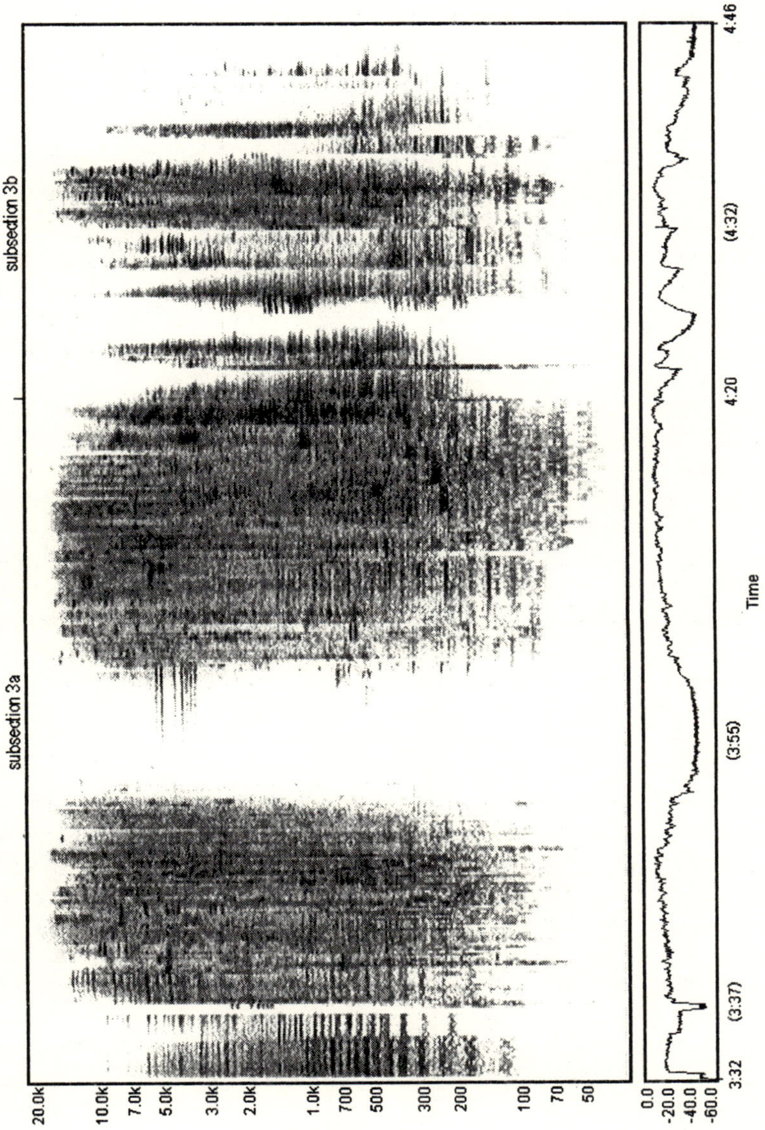

Example 4.10
General Characteristics of the Three Sections of *Omaggio a Emilio Vedova*

	Section 1	Section 2	Section 3
Spectrum	diffuse → compact	diffuse	compact
Amplitude	low → high	low	high
Sound types	mixture of → separation of sustained/short	sustained	short

contribute to the overall evolution of the piece. Of the three sections, section 1 stands alone as the only one that moves, in a variety of ways, from one state of activity to another. This clearly sets it apart from the material in sections 2 and 3, which, by contrast, generally remain stationary. While sections 2 and 3 are set apart from section 1, these two sections bear additional oppositional relationships other than those listed in Example 4.10. Section 2 contains the narrowest frequency range in the piece, while section 3 contains the widest. Furthermore, while each section has two subsections, the overall durational relationship between the subsections of section 2 is *short/long* (0:37, 1:01), while in section 3 it is *long/short* (0:48, 0:26). By constrast, in section 1, the only section with three subsections, the durational relationship of its subsections is relatively uniform throughout (0:43, 0:37, and 0:34). Significantly, the distinctions between sections 2 and 3 as well as their further separation from section 1 help contribute to the ultimate unfolding of the work's form.

While there are many oppositional characteristics between these three sections, there are also some rather important and distinctive similarities. For instance, section 1 exhibits a number of characteristics that are found in sections 2 and 3. However, these unfold in a different way. Section 1 begins with *diffuse* spectra and *low* amplitude levels and gradually moves to, and concludes with, *compact* spectra and *high* amplitude levels. This same progression is formed when the material of section 2, comprising *diffuse* spectra and *low* amplitude levels, is joined with that of section 3, which consists of *compact* spectra and *high* amplitude levels. However, instead of the gradual movement from one state of activity to another as displayed in section 1, there is an immediate and dramatic shift from one state (*diffuse/low*) to the next (*compact/high*) at the very point where section 2 ends and section 3 begins (3:32). What's more, this moment is further emphasized through the shift from the narrowest frequency range in the piece exploding outward to the widest frequency range in the piece. Consequently, when placing section 1 alongside the pairing of sections 2 and 3 (both seen as a single and distinctly separate structural unit), *Omaggio a Emilio Vedova* can be viewed as divided into not three but two overall parts (Example 4.11)—extrapolating and further expanding upon the properties of structural imitation, which is so prevalently found throughout the piece.

Example 4.11
Overall Two Part Division of *Omaggio a Emilio Vedova*

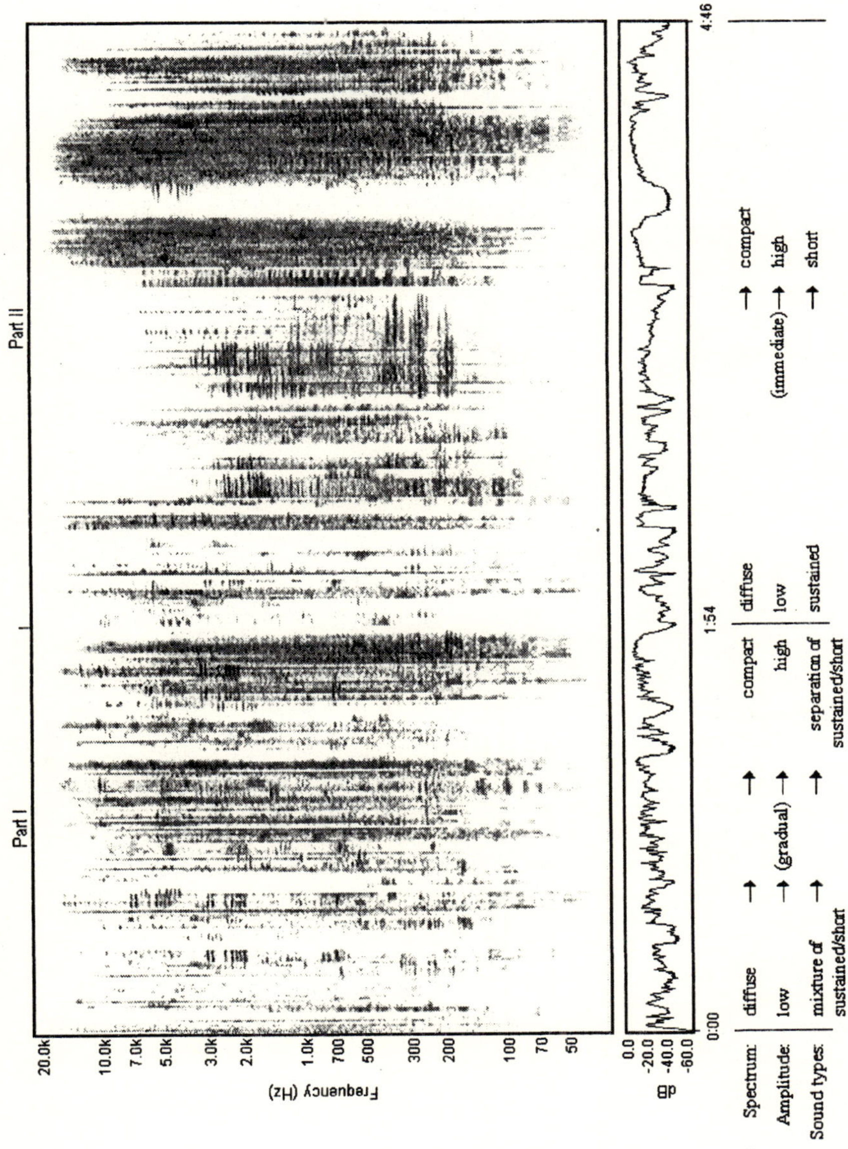

It is noteworthy to recall that throughout section 1 there was a movement from a general mixing of sound types toward a more pronounced separation between the two. At its greatest point, subsection 1c (see Example 4.6), the separation is at its clearest and most immediate. Occurring near the end of section 1, this moment points to the broader and more complete separation of sound types present in section 2 (which is dominated by *sustained* sound types) and section 3 (dominated by *short* sound types). The separation of sound types at the end of section 1 is additionally significant because it also forecasts the separation of various other parametric levels found between sections 2 and 3: spectra (*diffuse/compact*), amplitude (*low/high*), and overall frequency range (*narrow/wide*).

At the heart of *Omaggio a Emilo Vedova* there appear to be two similar, although opposing, schemes at work (parallel to the two contrasting sound types operating throughout the piece). Through the various forms of structural imitation within and between subsections, the piece always seems to be looking in on itself, while, at the same time, through the foreshadowing of the ultimate division of the entire piece into two parts, these internal structures seem to project themselves outward as well. Ultimately, this results in a rich and intricately composed work comprising various, multilayered unfoldings of a rather wide array of mirrored structures and complementary pairs.

NOTE

1. The original version of *Omaggio a Emilio Vedova* is for four channels. However, for the commercial recording this was mixed down to two (Wergo 6229-2). All sonograms and amplitude graphs, which were created using Sound Technology's SpectraPLUS Spectral Analysis System, are the result of a monophonic mix of the two-channel version.

REFERENCES

Appleton, J., and Perera, R. (1975). *The Development and Practice of Electronic Music.* Englewood Cliffs, NJ: Prentice-Hall.

Chadabe, J. (1997). *Electric Sound: The Past and Promise of Electronic Music.* Upper Saddle River, NJ: Prentice-Hall.

Code, D. L. (1990). "Observations in the Art of Speech: Paul Lansky's *Six Fantasies.*" *Perspectives of New Music* 28, no. 1:144–170.

Cogan, R. (1984a). *New Images of Musical Sound.* Cambridge: Harvard University Press.

Cogan, R. (1984b). "Penetrating Ensembles: Some Sounds from Milton Babbitt's *Ensembles for Synthesizer.*" In *Contiguous Lines: Issues and Ideas in the Music of the 60s and 70s*, edited by T. DeLio, Lanham, MD: University of America, 57–79.

Cogan, R. (1991). "Varèse: An Oppositional Sonic Poetics." *Sonus*, 11, no.2: 26–35.

Cogan, R. (1998). *Music Seen, Music Heard: A Picture Book of Musical Design.* Cambridge, MA: Publication Contact International.

Cogan, R. (1999). *The Sounds of Song: A Picture Book of Music for Voice.* Cambridge, MA: Publication Contact International.

Davismoon, S., ed. (1999). *Luigi Nono: The Suspended Song* and *Luigi Nono: Fragments and Silence.* In *Contemporary Music Review*, 18, parts 1 and 2.

Eccher, D. (1996). *Emilio Vedova.* Torino: Hopefulmonster.

Gianelli, I. (1998). *Emilio Vedova*. Milan: Charta.
Manning, P. (1994). *Electronic and Computer Music*. Oxford: Clarendon Press.
Riede, B. (1986). *Luigi Nono's Kompositionen mit Tonband: Ästhetik des musikalischen Materials, Werkanalysen, Werkverzeichnis*. Munich-Salzburg: Emil Katzbichler.
Spangemacher, F. (1983). *Luigi Nono, Die elektronische Musik: historischer Kontext, Entwicklung, Kompositionstechnik*. Regensburg: Gustav Bosse.

5

Serial Composition, Serial Form, and Process in Karlheinz Stockhausen's *Telemusik*

Jerome Kohl

In the mid-1970s, Stockhausen reacted to a question about the concept of "post-serialism" as follows:

> When writers about music speak today of a "post-serial" phase, they simply mean that music of recent years sounds different from that of the fifties, and since they have no concept of music of the fifties other than that it was "serial music," then today's music must be "post-serial." Isn't that dreadfully trite? Anyone who understands the spirit of the serial manner of composition knows that this spirit has brought something into consciousness that can never be undone: to arrive at an equality of all the elements in a composition and yet heed the law of natural difference. A misunderstanding has arisen which must be quickly cleared up: composition with series of proportions has been applied for many years now not only to individual notes, to their individual properties, but also to groups and collectives. Furthermore, composing in the sense of a qualitative serial technique is changing more and more into the serial ordering of perceptual qualities, and not just quantities. Because of this, many people today do not recognize, in works that sound completely organic and "free," even "chaotic" in places, that this all originates right within a very comprehensive conception of musical forms of organization. (Thomas 1975; Stockhausen, *Texte* 4, 550)

Serialism in Stockhausen's frame of thinking is more broadly applied than most people imagine. Karl H. Wörner, who was the first to publish a book devoted to Stockhausen's work, described two levels of serial thinking, "special and general serial formation" (Wörner 1973, 85–90), the former referring to specific local manifestations and the latter to "ways of interpreting more comprehensively all the individual parameters with the help of adequate flexibility in the serial process of composition" (87–88), a concept that "respects a law that applies not in the realm of music alone" (90).

Stockhausen expanded on this generalized conception of serialism in a conversation with the American poet Jonathan Cott (1973, 100–101):

Serialism means nothing but the following: rather than having everything based on periodic values in any parameter, what we do is use a set, a limited number of different values—let's say 1, 2, 3, 4, 5, 6. And a series which is based on a scale of different values is simply the permutation of these individual steps in a given scale. We have two conditions to follow. In order to have a serial sequence of individual values—whether it's pitch, timbre, duration, the size of objects, the color of eyes, whatever—we need at the base to have a scale with equal steps. If we leave out certain steps of a scale we get a modal construction, as in old folk music. Chromatic music is the most neutral kind because it doesn't seem to belong to any particular style, it incorporates all the other scales within itself—you use all the steps with equal importance. In serial composition, we use all the notes within a given scale of equidistant steps. It could be 5, 13, 15, or 32 to an octave—32 is an important scale. But we have to use them, statistically speaking, with an equal number of appearances so that there's no predominance, no one tone becomes more important than the other. And we don't leave out notes. I make a series, a particular order of these scalar steps, and use this as a constructive basic principle for certain sections of a composition.

As I've said, you can apply this to anything—Le Corbusier's modular system, with its red and blue scale of proportions, for example . . . He stated that you could use all the measures of this scale, permutate them, and make series—then create, for example, a facade of a building with the permutations of these basic measures.

Wörner presents the generalized concept of "serial thought," in its broadest manifestation, seemingly in Stockhausen's own words:

Serial thought—the term is deliberately chosen, rather than "serial technique"—sets out to mediate between any given extremes. What is new about it is that this mediation between two extremes is to be established through at least two intermediate stages. Without first putting this idea in musical terms let us take the extremes of black and white. Here serial thought would be nothing more than setting up between black and white, according to the complexity of the proposed form, a scale having a sufficiently large number of degrees of grey, so that black appears not simply as an antithesis in direct contrast to white, but also as a degree of white itself, by virtue of the different values of grey in between. Now the transition from the one extreme to the other may be made either continuously or discontinuously: in the first case as a *glissando* from black to white—a transformation completely free of hiatuses—and in the second case as a scale of equidistant degrees (a scale in equal intervals, such as might correspond to the chromatic scale on the piano). If, given a specific number of equidistant degrees in such a scale, we now permutate the succession of degrees in the series so as to bring them into a new order, no longer having a regular sequence of intervals, then we no longer have a scale but a "row," or "series." Hence the musical definition of "series" (not to be confused with the term's mathematical definition). (Wörner 1973, 82–83)

Between 1960 and 1964, Stockhausen developed this continuum conception, extending it even to the relationships between different types of musical form. Helmut Kirchmeyer (1963, 6) offers the most sophisticated representation of these formal ideas in what he calls a *Neunerschema* (nine-schema), dated 1961, and so possibly derived by Kirchmeyer himself from Stockhausen's article of that year, "Erfindung und Entdeckung" (*Texte* 1, 222–258):

	Periodicity	⟷	*Aperiodicity*
Elements:	Collective ["mass"]	Group	Point
Connection:	Determinate	Variable	Polyvalent
Form:	Developmental ("dramatic")	Serial ("suite") ["epic"]	Moment ["lyric"]

The bracketed items do not appear in Kirchmeyer's table. The terms in parentheses are taken from the list in "Erfindung und Entdeckung" (*Texte* 1, 250–251), where the first row is presented in reverse order to Kirchmeyer's (though without the periodicity/aperiodicity rubric); the terms added in square brackets are from Stockhausen 1964; and it should be noted that the German word rendered here (following Stockhausen's own practice in his English-language lectures) as "polyvalent" is not the term *mehrwertig* from chemistry, but rather *vieldeutig*, which normally means "ambiguous."

It should be understood that these nine elements are not necessarily mutually exclusive categories but may be combined in various ways. The "elements," in particular, "can be combined with each other and with all the others. (For example: pointillistic moment formation, determined; statistical sequence formation, polyvalent; groups in developmental formation, variable.) Or, within one work *simultaneous* combinations can take place" (*Texte* 1, 251).

In order to explore these notions of serial composition, it is useful to examine a composition in some detail. Stockhausen's fifth electronic composition (leaving out of account the student work *Konkrete Etüde*, from 1951), *Telemusik*, has been selected for this purpose.

Telemusik, according to a note in the score,[1] "was realized between January 23 and March 2, 1966 in the Studio for Electronic Music of the Japanese broadcasting system Nippon Hoso Kyokai (NHK), in collaboration with the director of the studio, Wataru Uenami and the studio technicians Hiroshi Shiotani, Shigeru Satô and Akira Honma." The first of two works commissioned by NHK,[2] it is dedicated to the Japanese people. The first public performance took place at the NHK studios in Tokyo on 25 April 1966, in a program that also featured the first and second performances (in versions for trombone and for flute) of *Solo*.

In an interview first published in *Christ und Welt* (CuW), 7 June 1968,[3] Stockhausen explained at some length the circumstances surrounding the origin of *Telemusik* and also some of his philosophical, aesthetic, and technical ideas. Because this is not available elsewhere in English and contains several ideas of importance for our investigation, I quote here an extensive excerpt from it:

<u>CuW</u>: How did your composition *Telemusik* come about?

<u>Stockhausen</u>: *Telemusik* was realized in 1966 during a quarter-year in the Studio for Electronic Music of the Japanese broadcasting system, Nippon Hoso Kyokai (NHK). During my first eight or nine days in Tokyo I couldn't sleep. I didn't mind, since sound-visions, ideas, and movements ceaselessly passed through my head while I lay

awake. Then a vision returned ever more frequently: a vision of sounds, new technical processes, formal relationships, images of notation, and human relationships. Beyond this I wanted to come nearer to a long-established and recurring dream: to take a step further in the direction of writing not my music, but a music of the whole earth, of all countries and races.

CuW: The idea of an all-encompassing musical language isn't new, even if an electronic realization offers new possibilities of blending the day before yesterday and tomorrow, the here and the there in the manner of, as you said earlier, "a free encounter in the mental realm." In general, modern music of our century speaks a language which is understood all over the world, a language in which national elements play practically no role any longer—which is understandable after the nineteenth-century period of nationalist styles. So, is there now a "world music" instead of "individual" music, or is this idea too journalistic?

Stockhausen: No, the idea is correct. In America I have recently often heard the formulation "universal music" as a comment. However, "Telemusik" also means something more, that some things which are very widely separated will be composed near to each other. Things which are quite "tele," therefore far away—also in history, chronologically—distantly separated, I have *composed* [i.e., in the etymological sense: French *com* "together" + *poser*, "to place, put down"]. So there are in this work "electronic" passages, which are therefore of today, together with tape recordings of music of the southern Sahara, for example, or of the Shipibos from the River Amazon, of a Spanish village festival, Hungarian and Balinese music, recordings of temple ceremonies in Japan—such as the Omizutori ceremony at Nara, in which I participated for three days and nights, or of the Kohyasan temple, or music of the Buddhist priests of the Jakushiji temple—music of the inhabitants of the mountain highlands of Vietnam, etc.

CuW: So you chose folk and ritual music as a component of a composition of world music?

Stockhausen: You do not hear this "found" music in its original form. I have attempted instead to bring these apparently so heterogeneous phenomena together into close relationships—to be precise, through various processes of modulation. The old concept of "modulating," of changing to another tonality, is here applied to styles. I modulate from one musical event to another; or else I modulate one event with another, as I have learned through recent experiences.

CuW: Can you give an example of this new kind of modulation?

Stockhausen: Yes. I modulate the rhythm of one event with the amplitude curve of another. Or I modulate electronic chords, which I produced myself, with the amplitude curve of a priest's chant, and then I modulate this with the monodic chant (that is, the pitch line) of a Shipibo song, and so forth. In this way I have in *Telemusik* united other people's music with my own for the first time. Up to that point I had not accepted into my compositions any previously existing, pre-formed music. But I wanted to get out of this system of exclusivity. And so, as I increasingly integrated what occurs in life (not just artificially constructed instruments) into sounds, so I also am attempting to bring every sort of music—whether it is now three thousand years old or originated yesterday or today—into a new relationship, since temporal intervals are of course artificial and everything exists simultaneously in our consciousness.

CuW: Is this related to collage procedures?

Stockhausen: No. Collage-work was the problem of the first half of the century—juxtaposing things, like the people in New York still live today, initially without any relationship; but they soon collide. The next stage is simply to strive for a real integration—something like a universal music . . .

I won't deny that essentially new experiences, which continue to be true, were made from time to time in the great works of the first half of the century. Only perspectives diminish. Firstly with distance, and secondly, we always see what is nearest to us as inordinately large. In this respect the transformation of consciousness which has taken place in recent years seems enormous to me. This transformation is decisively linked with people growing out of the national sphere of music and the purely personal sphere, beyond individualistic music. The composer no longer strives for "his own" music or a personal style. We are becoming increasingly aware of the fact that the entire earth is a single village. People are coming very close together. And as a result, levels of consciousness which were simply asleep rise up in individuals—me, for example. You sense that there are ever more supra-personal things. I know that I am a member of a whole.

CuW: And also of yesterday, of tradition?

Stockhausen: I no longer understand tradition in the sense of having occurred "previously," but rather tradition is everything that comes to me, that has already been formed. It is now my task to consider everything on a higher level, not as something which just falls apart into many details, but rather also has things in common which concern the whole of humanity. We don't just use the term "humanity" as a vehicle. Rather, it really describes our experience today. And then it finds immediate expression in music. One feels that music is increasingly attempting to open up. The desire for integration is an expression of this consciousness. Something else is involved too: We are being greatly changed by the experiences of space research. We observe that our monistic concept that the earth should of course be the center of consciousness, is being relativized. And many people are already thinking—and it shouldn't be assumed that they are wrong—about other beings in the cosmos at a different level of development. Entirely apart from what effective experiences look like: this relativity is sticking in our consciousness.

CuW: And that is immediately reflected in art?

Stockhausen: It is expressed artistically in that people are less interested in writing their own music, which is less important, but rather a music aimed at creating a very open musical world where diverse pluralistic manifestations can find their place in an integrated world. Composing a polyphony of styles is now becoming highly interesting. People used to think of a polyphony of *voices*—or even of harmonic planes. That was a technology of symbolism. However I now see "polyphony" as a qualitatively more determinable conception—as a polyphony of styles, times, and regions.

CuW: Then even such wildly divergent forms as folklore on the one hand and electronic music on the other can really attain a new unity?

Stockhausen: Yes, if one manages it—there is the immensely exciting task of constantly composing bridges between new and preformed structures, still emphasizing the one by way of the other . . .

CuW: Isn't there the danger of a violation of those cultures which are spatially and sometimes also temporally distant from us, when we today include them in our trains of thought?

Stockhausen: No, no. You must just avoid trying to level things down. I am not striving for a "synthesis" in which everything becomes absorbed in a colossal mish-mash. On the contrary: the characteristic structure must even be supported in a chosen context. I don't want to destroy anything, but rather to preserve the independence of the individual phenomena in the sense of the above-mentioned polyphony. Individual aspects of a structure are brought into relationship with other details. Existing music is not to be obliterated, but rather is ambiguously [*mehrdeutig*] effective. In *Telemusik* you will hear that the quantitatively dominant sound-world is the electronic one, which I myself have made. A new experience occurs: something that is already shaped and is very old, has an unusual hardness and strength—like the old Californian redwoods which are as much as 5,000 years old and are indestructible. That's how music is too: it is necessary to invent very strong new music and give it more time and space, in order to be able to relate it to ancient preformed phenomena, if a balance is to be found between the new and the naturally evolved, or let us say, between what is unknown to us (that is, what we make today ad hoc) and what is more or less familiar. I see the task as: bringing different strata of consciousness into balance. That is our new task.

The fascination with metamorphosis in the idea of "modulating" from one event to another; the Augustinian concept of the presence of past and future in the present consciousness (a fundamental principle of moment form, here extended to spatial as well as temporal dispersion); and relating all the elements of a continuum in a polyvalent (here the word is *mehrdeutig*, rather than *vieldeutig*, however) manner are by the mid-1960s all long-established factors in Stockhausen's thinking (Kohl 1981, Chapter 1). The chief innovation here is the sudden enthusiasm for "found" material. "*Telemusik* in fact marks a paradigm shift in the history of electronic music" (Fritsch 1999, 179).

Stockhausen expanded on this aspect eight years later, in an interview with Ekbert Faas (1977, 198–199):

At some point I was quite shocked to find that I had suddenly changed my whole way of thinking and my approach to composition. Before my first arrival in Japan in 1966 these had been absolutely abstract. Then suddenly I was ready to integrate Japanese music into compositions of my own and to transform them. I mean music I found on the spot, like recorded music. *Before that I had staunchly refused to let any melody or otherwise preformed piece of music enter my compositions.*

(The English here is Stockhausen's, as the whole interview was conducted in that language, but the emphases are mine.) While *Telemusik* is certainly the first of Stockhausen's works to extensively and openly employ "found" material, it is not, strictly speaking, true that Stockhausen had previously "accepted into my compositions no music that already existed." His first use of musical "found objects" had already occurred, albeit very briefly and heavily disguised, when he quoted the "Marseillaise" in the 1964 orchestral-electronic work *Mixtur* (Kohl 1981, 70, 92–94, 100–102). Shortly afterward, the orchestral composition *Stop* (1964–1965) contains what seems to be a quotation from nineteenth-century tonal music at rehearsal number 41, though the source of this tune has not been identified—it could be Stockhausen's own invention. Furthermore, *Mikrophonie II*, completed in 1965, also quotes from Stockhausen's own earlier compositions, though this is a somewhat different matter. Perhaps the answer lies in the clause "At some point I was quite shocked," which implies that the conscious realization of this sudden willingness to use "found" material may have occurred in 1966 in Japan, even if some earlier manifestations exist in the scores mentioned.

In any case, in the earlier works this kind of found object occurs as exceptional, "inserted" material, while in *Telemusik* only seven of the thirty-two moments are entirely restricted to electronic sounds (all are in the first half: nos. 1, 2, 4, 6, 8, 10, and 16); the rest use the "found" materials as essential matter. This "polyphony of styles," as Stockhausen calls it, subsequently becomes a very important aspect of his music, from the vast electronic composition *Hymnen* (1966–1967) through the so-called process-plan compositions, *Prozession* (1967), *Kurzwellen* (1968),[4] *Spiral* (1968), *Pole* (1969–1970), and *Expo* (1969–1970), down to the "sound scenes" of the *Licht* operas *Montag* (1984–1988), *Dienstag* (act 1, "Jahreslauf," 1977), and *Freitag* (1991–1994), and the electronic music for *Mittwoch aus Licht* (1995–1996).

It may also be that Stockhausen wished (unconsciously?) to attribute to Japan a change in his outlook that he considered to be of the utmost importance. His infatuation with that country, which began with that first visit in 1966, is evident from the continuation of the previous quotation:

> It all started in Japan. I bought myself Japanese clothes—old clothes—and dressed up in a kimono etc. And I went and participated in their ceremonies. And I got so absorbed in them—even more than the Japanese themselves—that I said to myself: This is impossible, I don't at all feel like a stranger. Instead, I feel like someone who is coming home. I was so much in love with Japan, and love, as I have said many times, is recognition; It's not seeing something new, it's recognition. You recognize something that you are, that you have been. (Faas 1977, 199)

This is quite understandable considering the close relationship that his Catholic mystical outlook of the early 1950s has with Oriental (including Japanese) attitudes, particularly with respect to ritual and music (Kohl 1981, 31–39), and how relatively little this has to do with the modern, secular West.[5]

Stockhausen's horror of "synthesis" and the destruction of cultural referentials, expressed in the *Christ und Welt* interview, is reflected in later expressions of satisfaction, upon revisiting Japan, in finding that (apparently) due to his having used Japanese elements in *Telemusik*, young Japanese composers who had formerly been interested only in imitating European "avant-garde" music were turning to traditional instruments and music from their own cultural past.[6]

Insofar as the "modulations" described by Stockhausen are concerned, while it is essential to the technique of *Telemusik* that the material be transfigured in various ways (principally by ring-modulation, filtering, transposition by varying tape speed, playing the tape in reverse, splicing, varying playback-levels, and amplitude modulation), the only specific example that he gives ("I modulate electronic chords . . . with the amplitude curve of a priest's song, and then this with the monodic song . . . of a Shipibo song") seems to be purely hypothetical. Neither of the priest-songs used (which occur only in moments 22, 30, and 31) occurs in the same moment as the Shipibo music (only found in 13, 14 and, 20), and the latter is never connected in a circuit to anything other than steady sine-tones (through a double ring-modulation circuit—called the "Gagaku circuit" in the score, because it is first used, in the third moment, to modulate a recording of Gagaku music). Similarly, the even more complicated example given by Wörner (1973, 143) seems to be a fiction. The other, more general example given by Stockhausen ("I modulate the rhythm of one event with the amplitude-curve of another") could very well reflect some transformation process in the score, though it is not clear just what he means by modulating rhythm with an amplitude-curve. It should not be supposed that this operation would be carried out "automatically" with some sort of electronic apparatus (e.g., an amplitude modulator certainly could not do this); but there are numerous instances where the speed of a variable-speed tape recorder is regulated manually (by changing the frequency of the driving-generator), according to curves drawn in the score, and it is quite possible that some of these curves represent the "amplitude-curve" of some other event.

These processes, controlled by hand and eye, are therefore what Stockhausen calls "variable" devices (cf. the *Neuenerschema*, earlier) similar to those used in *Gesang der Jünglinge* (1955–1956) and described by the composer as follows:

> Let me describe how we've gone about making a sound texture [i.e., as opposed to a gestalt—see Kohl 1981, 157] of twenty seconds' duration [in *Gesang der Jünglinge*]. I sat in the studio with two collaborators. Two of us were handling knobs: with one hand, one of us controlled the levels and, with the other hand, the speed of pulses from a pulse generator which were fed into an electric filter; a second musician had a knob for the levels and another for the frequency of the filter; and the third one would manipulate a potentiometer to draw the envelope—the shape of the whole event—and also record it. I drew curves—for example: up down, up-down up-down, up-down, up, which had to be followed with the movement of a knob (let's say for loudness) for the twenty-second duration. And during these twenty seconds, another musician had to move the knob for the frequency of the pulses from four to sixteen pulses per second in an irregular curve that I'd drawn on the paper. And the third musician had to move the knob for the frequency of the filter following a third curve. So, everyone had a paper on which different curves were drawn. We said, "Three, two, one, zero," started a stopwatch . . . we'd all do our curves, individually produce one sound layer which was the product of our movements; and this resulted in an aleatoric layer of individual pulses which, in general, speeded up statistically. But you could never at a certain moment say, "*This* pulse will now come with *that* pitch." This was impossible to predetermine. Then we'd make a second, third, fourth, fifth layer—the number of layers was also determined—and I'd synchronize them all together and obtain a new sound. (Cott 1973, 71–72)[7]

Recently, in a response to a paper by Winrich Hopp, Stockhausen expanded on this description, clarifying the way in which realization in classical electronic studio technique resembles performance, with a variable result from one attempt to the next (Hopp 1999, 176):

> It is not exactly as if each [musician] were in a separate room all by himself. The second in the chain can only determine pitches if the first produces impulses, and the third can

only produce or modify volumes if impulses with pitches are available. If nothing sounds and he drew the controller up, he does not hear anything: *mezzoforte* produces zero . . .

In other words: this interaction between the three is important, and one notices this above all when by accident a beautiful result came and I decided: don't mess with it, it will not likely get better, because all actions cooperated accidentally in such a way that the result is interesting, i.e. a good musical relationship of pitches to durations to dynamics. We then left the result as it was, but that is very rare.

Mostly two, three, four repetitions had to be realized, apart from errors in following the curves. You adjust to the musicality of your partners, and this results in a real interaction. This was more emphatically the case in the detail, in relation to a sound complex, than in the later works, where whole gestalts were played, one imitated or transformed gestalts (either transposed upward, or accelerated downward, and so on). Do not underestimate this.

One very great difference exists between the processes of *Gesang der Jünglinge* and those of *Telemusik*: the former took most of a year to realize (early 1955 to early 1956), while the latter took less than six weeks. This is because *Telemusik* was designed to be realized in (more or less) "real time"—that is, the various processes do not involve the painstaking construction of rhythmic structures, which are then speeded up thousands of times to produce pitches, as was the case in *Kontakte* (1958–1960) and *Gesang der Jünglinge*. The choice of preformed material (and for the electronic sounds, pitches generated by beat-frequency, sine-wave, triangular-wave, and function generators) enabled *Telemusik* to be realized in such a fashion. But the time imperative of Stockhausen's short stay in Japan had a further determining influence on the structure of *Telemusik*: while the various partial structures in each moment could be tried out over and over until the desired result was achieved, the schedule of producing about one moment per working day precluded any extensive editing after the fact. So *Telemusik* was produced straight through on the master tape, from beginning to end just as it plays (one exception: moment 26 was produced before 24 and 25), which means that, unlike earlier moment-form pieces, there is a decided tendency to develop a forward momentum through the piece since (among other things) the employment of inserts from later moments into earlier ones is all but impossible.

This tendency toward a directed process for the whole form is intensified by the particular character of the first and last moments. The quiet, high-pitched blocks of sine-tones in the opening moment create the same sense of "measuring" found in the introductions of *Gruppen* (1955–1957), *Mantra* (1970), and *Luzifers Tanz* (1983, the third scene of *Samstag aus Licht*), the simple presentation of the opening pitch series in *Zeitmaße* and *Kontra-Punkte*, and the time-marking first thirteen measures of *Kreuzspiel*. The sudden sweep of activity in the concluding moment, coming after the sustained sounds of the longest moment in *Telemusik*, and then the hovering in the second part followed at the very end by the emphatic, loud stroke of the temple instruments in all five channels are an unequivocal closing gesture. This is, of course, contrary to Stockhausen's view of moment-form having no "beginning" and no "end," the music simply "starting" and "stopping" (cf. "Momentform: Neue Zusammenhänge zwischen Aufführungsdauer, Werkdauer und Moment" [*Texte* 1, 207]). This and the emphasis in the discussion on "process" should not lead to the false conclusion that *Telemusik* is not essentially a moment-form work, however. The processes that operate within the moments are, for the most part, self-contained, although a few continue straight through two or more moments, linking them into moment-groups; but the independent function of each moment is still quite strong. By contrast, the "process-plan" works (several of which were already composed or sketched by the time of *Telemusik*) act with some defined process upon a musical entity, or "event," to produce the succeeding event, which is then, in turn, modified by another process to produce the next, and so on, thus resulting in a continuity of process, contrasted with the essentially discontinuous nature of moment form.[8] Nevertheless, the influence of the evolving conception of "process" composition may be seen in *Telemusik*, which brings it very close to *Mikrophonie I*, a work in which the contents of successive moments are defined largely in terms of processes relating to the preceding moment's content.

It is not my purpose to examine in detail all the various processes used in *Telemusik*, nor shall I deal with the structures of individual moments to any great extent. The overall plan of the work is of prime interest, for two reasons. First, it is quite strikingly different from the plans of the earlier moment-form works. Second, there is a similarity to the construction of the later cycle of intuitive music compositions, *Aus den sieben Tagen* (for a detailed analysis of this cycle, see Kohl [1981, Chapter 5]).

THE FORM PLAN

Stockhausen has not published a form plan or, indeed, any sketches for *Telemusik* from which we may perhaps infer that he considers the realization score to be a sufficiently detailed document.[9] Stockhausen has referred specifically to such a plan for *Telemusik*, however: "You were speaking about the possibility of anticipating in a dream a complete new work: you hear and see it. This has happened in *Telemusik* for the general form plan and now in *Trans*" (Cott 1973, 54). Just what this dreamed form plan included and whether it was ever written down I do not know. But from the score it seems clear that the principal forming element is duration.

Telemusik consists of thirty-two moments[10] of various durations, each beginning with the stroke of a Japanese temple instrument.[11] The durations in seconds of these moments are derived from the six members of the Fibonacci series from 13 to 144.[12] Each step occurs a different number of times, the number being inversely dependent on the length of the step and drawn from the first six Fibonacci numbers, thus: 144 × 1, 89 × 2, 55 × 3, 34 × 5, 21 × 8, and 13 × 13. This seems to be according to the principle that "you must give more time and space to a weak sound, otherwise the strong one just buries it. And I don't mean strong only in terms of dynamics" (Stockhausen, in Cott 1973, 192). If this were carried out exactly as I have just described it, the total durations of all the occur-

Example 5.1
***Telemusik*: Table of Durations**

identifying instrument	*durations (in seconds)*	*number of instances*	*totals*
4 large bells	144	1	144
Keisu	91 89	1 1	180
Rin	57 56 55	1 1 1	168
Mokugyo	37 36 35 34	1 1 1 2	176
Bokusho	23 22 21	2 3 3	175
Taku	14 13	8 5	177

rences of each scale step would be 144, 178, 165, 170, 168, and 169 seconds, respectively, thus bringing them all into roughly the same degree of (temporal) prominence. However, the lengths are varied slightly according to a regular scheme whereby the single 144 value is left alone, the next smaller step has one of its two values increased (in this one case increased by two, to 91), the next step has three values of 55, 56, and 57 (the Fibonacci value, plus the same value increased by one, and then by one again), the next step has four, and then the fifth and sixth values reverse the trend, having three and two values each. The relative prominence of the scale steps is not significantly altered by this operation, though the complexity of the scale is. The resulting data are tabulated in Example 5.1, where it may also be seen that the *number of instances* of each subscale step (the third column of the table) is determined by dividing the field of each scale step into Fibonacci proportions.

Whether this really makes any difference to the final audible result seems doubtful, but it is characteristic of Stockhausen's view of the universe:

> Periodicity is one aspect, of the very large and the very small. And it should always be shown as being just one aspect of the universe . . . And going down to the atoms and even the particles of the atoms, there is always periodicity. Nevertheless, periodicity is, as I say, like the abstract year, but what changes within the year? Sometimes the snow comes earlier, or later.
>
> Actually, within this periodicity, no day is the same. We shouldn't forget this, that's all. There has been a lot of music where this periodicity becomes so absolute and dominating that there's little left for what is happening within the periods. (Cott 1973, 27)

The temple instruments were selected according to their natural resonance (decay-time) to mark the beginnings of the various duration scale-steps. The Taku, a high-pitched wood block, the sound of which has the fastest decay (almost instantaneous), is thus assigned to the shortest duration value of the form scheme. The Bokusho, a larger temple block with a somewhat longer duration, is assigned to the next longer step. The deep-pitched Mokugyo is assigned to the next longer value, the higher-pitched Rin (a cup-bell), with the next longer reverberation, is assigned to the next value, and then the Keisu and the group of four large bells are assigned to the longest two. Jonathan Harvey, in his attempt to explain some facets of this structure, erroneously ties the *pitch* of these instruments to the duration of their corresponding sections and suggests that the temple instrument came first and that the duration was derived from it (Harvey 1975, 100–101). Clearly, neither was the case: according to the score's preface, the Rin is much higher in pitch (a quarter tone above $B\flat_4$, with a strike-tone a minor thirteenth higher) than the Mokugyo (at $E\flat_3$, in the bass clef).

The various durations are distributed in the score as is shown in Example 5.2. Although Harvey describes this construction as "fairly symmetrical," it quite obviously is nothing of the sort. However, four of the six structural layers (called "formant rhythms" by Harvey, after Stockhausen's terminology in ". . . How Time Passes . . ." [Stockhausen 1959]) are internally symmetrical, though their centers (marked by the + signs in Example 5.2) do not coincide, which at once shows the lack of symmetry in the composite structure, even without considering the other two "formants."

These formant rhythms are, in the arguments presented in ". . . How Time Passes . . ." (Stockhausen 1959; *Texte* 1, 99–139), a way of unifying the conception of form with those of pitch and timbre. Thus, the large-scale form plan of *Telemusik* is the analog of a single note, with the fundamental represented by the large temple-bell layer. The second harmonic is absent (or perhaps subsumed by the fourth), while the third, fourth, and fifth are represented by the Keisu, Rin, and Mokugyo layers, respectively (we shall temporarily set aside the remaining two layers). Each of these layers consists of regularly spaced "pulses," with the distance between pulses measured in number of moments, rather than in seconds (though the actual time distances are extremely close to exact values anyway, thanks to the displacement of the 144-second moment to near the end and the insert of moment "7 Forts."). But there is a regular *phase shift* pattern. The Keisu layer, with a pulse every eleventh moment, is centered on the form plan. The Rin layer's center is shifted one position to the left, the Mokugyo layer is two to the right of this, and the Bokusho layer is three to the left of the Mokugyo's. The Rin layer would seem, by the "formant rhythm" analogy alone, to require another "pulse" at moment 32, but the Fibonacci proportioning allows only three instances at this level. The Bokusho level does not have regularly spaced pulses but rather represents a complex wave-form of symmetrical construction, with intervals between pulses ranging from three to five. The Taku moments then simply fill in the remaining positions, after the "fundamental" pulse has been

Example 5.2
Formal Layout of *Telemusik*

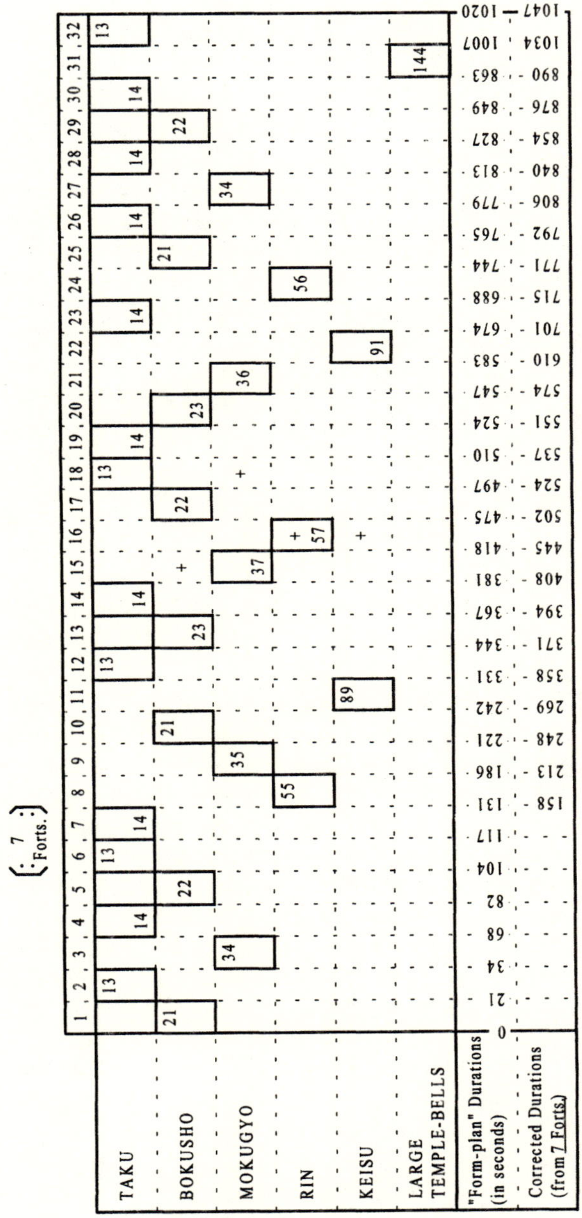

positioned at moment 31 (where the great length of the moment enhances the "cadential" quality of the succeeding short, final one).

Within each of these "formant" layers there is also a consistent pattern formed out of the subscales. The first appearance at each level is in all cases the principal (Fibonacci) value. Toward the center, the greatest deviation is reached, after which there is a general tendency back toward the principal value for the last appearance (the temple-bell and Rin layers, with only one and two appearances, respectively, are, of course, excepted). The symmetrical nature of this process is most fully developed in the Bokusho layer (which is symmetrical without being periodic in terms of its "vibration" structure), where the three subscale degrees (21, 22, and 23) occur in the order 1 2 1 3 2 3 1 2. Considered rotationally (i.e., as one "cycle" of a continuing vibration), this has centers of symmetry at the first and fifth elements. The Mokugyo layer, with only one occurrence of each of the subvalues other than the prime one (see Example 5.1), is only approximately symmetrical: 1 2 4 3 1, and the Rin layer has its three elements arranged 1 3 2. The Taku layer seems concerned more with keeping up a regular alternation of values (13 and 14) in the first portion (through moment 19) than with arranging these symmetrically, though the last 13-duration is saved for the end.

The aperiodic internal construction of the Taku and Bokusho layers has its counterpart in Stockhausen's use of the function generator in moments 6–7, 8, and 18. This instrument, built by NHK engineers for the studio, is pictured in the front of the score. It has the unusual feature of allowing the construction of any envelope that can be represented by partial amplitudes, up to about fifty consecutive equal parts (the photograph shows only the lower part of the instrument, where forty-one sliders are visible—each is presumably a potentiometer—but in the eighteenth moment Stockhausen calls for a period with fifty positions). Stockhausen uses this generator to construct wave-forms with irregular sequences of pulses ("square" waves) for each period. These periods are repeated at relatively slow frequencies, from 300 Hz down to 1/4.5 Hz in moments 6–7, 6 Hz in moment 8, and 2.5 Hz in moment 18 (possibly this reflects the limits of the instrument). In moments 8 and 18 these pulses are used to amplitude-modulate sine waves, and the product is then used to modulate other events.

In the score, there is an inserted moment immediately following moment 7, labeled "7 Forts." (7 cont.). This begins with a stroke on a temple-bell (called "Kane" in the score and described in the preface), which has no place in the schema of form-marking instruments. In fact, this inserted moment is a repetition of the pulse-structure mentioned earlier, a long compound of descending glissandos that continues from the beginning of moment 6 to the end of moment 7 in tracks I–IV, except for an insert from moment 5 that replaces this glissando on track II of moment 6 (track V contains the main differentiating material for moments 6 and 7, together with the two Taku strokes, and is not used in "7-Forts."). This structure is ring-modulated in "7-Forts." with a 12,000 Hz sine wave and copied onto tracks II and V, with a "notch" at the original division point between moments 6 and 7 (at 13 seconds into the structure) where the modulating sine wave dips quickly down to 2,000 Hz and then back up. Very much more softly (for the most part about 25 dB below the level of tracks II and V), an unmodulated recording of a Buddhist chant is recorded on track III (a sustained C♯$_3$, with a brief dip to B$_2$ at the 13-second mark). This entire inserted moment recalls those of *Momente* that are played twice in succession, but in different versions. However, the purpose there is to exhibit the polyvalence of the internal structures and to emphasize the inserts, which are omitted in one of the two statements. Here the purpose seems to be to correct the positioning of the formant rhythms of the Keisu and Rin layers, which, with respect to time measured in seconds, are closer to their symmetrically proper positions with the addition of this 27-second event (the 144-second moment 31 caused a displacement toward the beginning—see Example 5.2).

The original form plan may well have included additional structures, but until and unless sketches are made available, it will be difficult to determine what these might involve. The duration structure obviously does not exhibit any serial elements in the form plan, though serial structures within individual moments are not difficult to find.

EXAMPLES OF LOCAL SERIAL CONSTRUCTION

Together with what Stockhausen terms "individual" (i.e., not divisible into structural subparts) moments, there are in *Telemusik* many structures that may clearly be analyzed and heard in terms of the relationships of distinct subordinate parts,[13] and the relationships are in most cases easily seen to be serial ones. For example, there is a structure that occurs during the first part of the longest moment, no. 31 (see page 42 of the score). During the first eighty-nine seconds of this moment, comprising the first of two main temporal subdivisions, four simultaneous structures occur on tracks I, II, IV, and V. It is the structure on track IV that I wish to examine in detail.

This structure begins with the simultaneous stroke on four large temple-bells, which marks the longest moment duration (Example 5.3 shows the durations). Each of these bells continues with further strokes, forming four independent layers within the structure. The first bell, Kohyasan (Kongobu-ji), from the large pagoda at Daitoh, is struck a total of five times at intervals of 17 seconds (16.5 seconds between the third and fourth and between the fourth and fifth strokes). This seems to complete its pattern, as there would have been time for yet one more stroke before the end of the partial moment (the fifth stroke is 22 seconds before the end of the part—by which I mean the structure under examination). The other bells toll in progressively longer intervals-of-entry. The second bell, Kohyasan, Fukushima Masanori, is struck also five times, at time intervals of around 18 seconds (18.5, 16.5, 18, and 20 seconds), the last stroke falling 16 seconds before the end of the part. Hohko-ji, at Kyoto, the third bell, also has five strokes, at intervals averaging a little more than 20 seconds (21.5, 20.5, 20, and 19.5 seconds), with the last stroke continuing until it is cut off by the end of the part. The fourth bell, Myoshin-ji, also at Kyoto, is heard only four times,

Example 5.3
***Telemusik*, Moment 31, Page 1, Track IV: Durations of the Four Large Temple Bells**

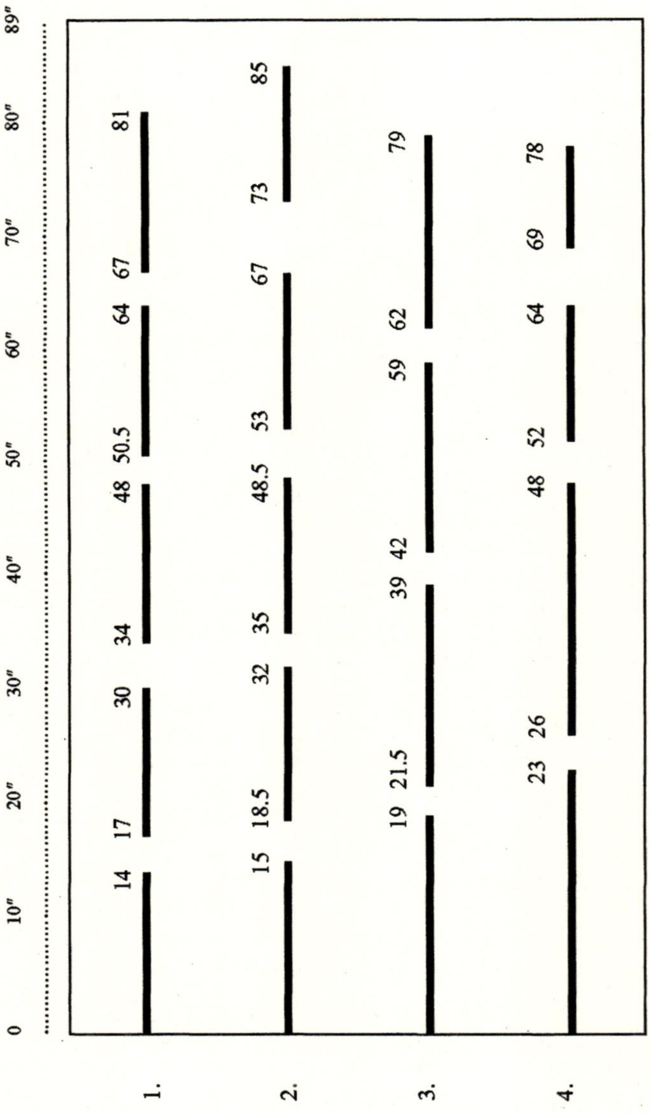

modulating sine wave dips quickly down to 2,000 Hz and then back up. Very much more softly (for the most part about 25 dB below the level of tracks II and V), an unmodulated recording of a Buddhist chant is recorded on track III (a sustained C♯$_3$, with a brief dip to B_2 at the 13-second mark). This entire inserted moment recalls those of *Momente* that are played twice in succession, but in different versions. However, the purpose there is to exhibit the polyvalence of the internal structures and to emphasize the inserts, which are omitted in one of the two statements. Here the purpose seems to be to correct the positioning of the formant rhythms of the Keisu and Rin layers, which, with respect to time measured in seconds, are closer to their symmetrically proper positions with the addition of this 27-second event (the 144-second moment 31 caused a displacement toward the beginning—see Example 5.2).

The original form plan may well have included additional structures, but until and unless sketches are made available, it will be difficult to determine what these might involve. The duration structure obviously does not exhibit any serial elements in the form plan, though serial structures within individual moments are not difficult to find.

EXAMPLES OF LOCAL SERIAL CONSTRUCTION

Together with what Stockhausen terms "individual" (i.e., not divisible into structural subparts) moments, there are in *Telemusik* many structures that may clearly be analyzed and heard in terms of the relationships of distinct subordinate parts,[13] and the relationships are in most cases easily seen to be serial ones. For example, there is a structure that occurs during the first part of the longest moment, no. 31 (see page 42 of the score). During the first eighty-nine seconds of this moment, comprising the first of two main temporal subdivisions, four simultaneous structures occur on tracks I, II, IV, and V. It is the structure on track IV that I wish to examine in detail.

This structure begins with the simultaneous stroke on four large temple-bells, which marks the longest moment duration (Example 5.3 shows the durations). Each of these bells continues with further strokes, forming four independent layers within the structure. The first bell, Kohyasan (Kongobu-ji), from the large pagoda at Daitoh, is struck a total of five times at intervals of 17 seconds (16.5 seconds between the third and fourth and between the fourth and fifth strokes). This seems to complete its pattern, as there would have been time for yet one more stroke before the end of the partial moment (the fifth stroke is 22 seconds before the end of the part—by which I mean the structure under examination). The other bells toll in progressively longer intervals-of-entry. The second bell, Kohyasan, Fukushima Masanori, is struck also five times, at time intervals of around 18 seconds (18.5, 16.5, 18, and 20 seconds), the last stroke falling 16 seconds before the end of the part. Hohko-ji, at Kyoto, the third bell, also has five strokes, at intervals averaging a little more than 20 seconds (21.5, 20.5, 20, and 19.5 seconds), with the last stroke continuing until it is cut off by the end of the part. The fourth bell, Myoshin-ji, also at Kyoto, is heard only four times,

Example 5.3
***Telemusik*, Moment 31, Page 1, Track IV: Durations of the Four Large Temple Bells**

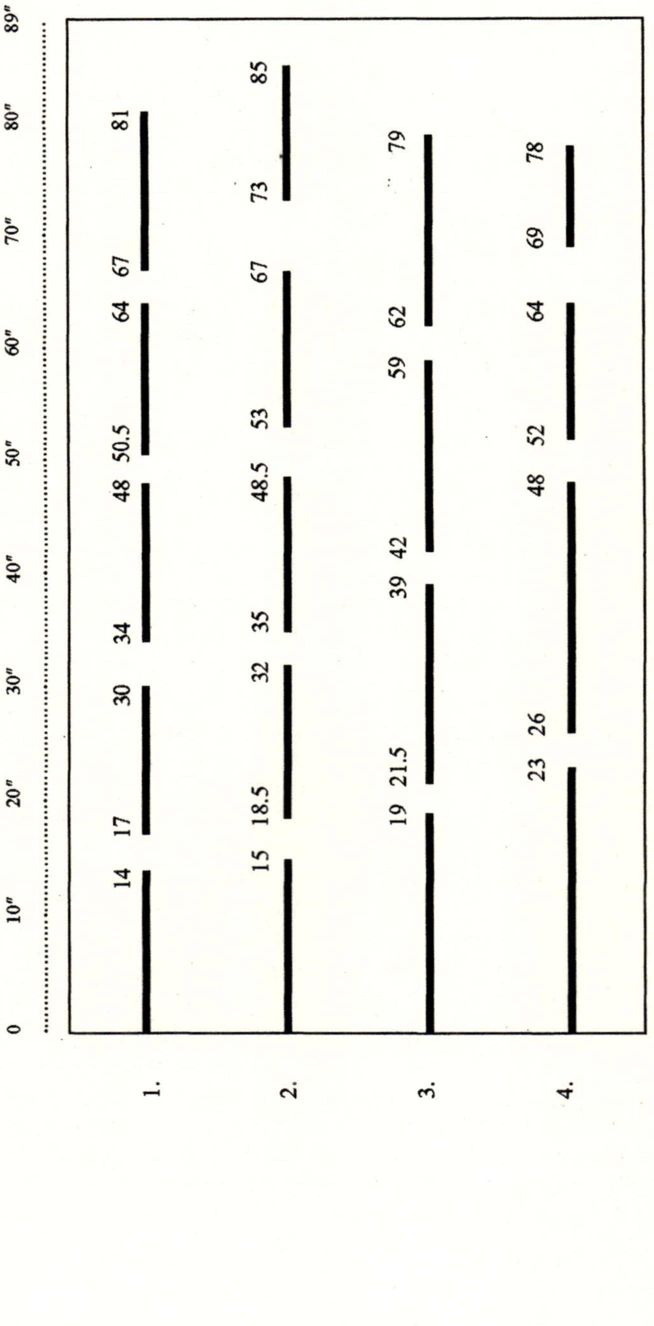

presumably because its time interval of 26 seconds would put the fifth stroke beyond the end of the 89-second part. The fourth stroke is actually moved up a bit in time, so that the intervals of entry become 26, 26, and 17, the last stroke occurring 20 seconds before the end of the part (this adjustment in the last stroke causes the sound to end precisely where it otherwise would have begun). If we read the third bell's average as 21 (the others similarly average a little less than the norms given), the differences between the time intervals (17, 18, 21, 26) are Fibonacci numbers: 1, 3, and 5. The duration of each bell-stroke is less than the interval-of-entry, resulting in a detached (staccato) articulation between successive strokes. In general, the percentage of the interval-of-entry represented by the duration decreases in each line (slight inflections within this tendency occur in the first and second bells), thus making the articulations progressively more staccato. Unless this directed tendency is to be interpreted as a scale of distinct values, which does not seem likely, the rhythmic structure cannot be said to exhibit serial patterns.

However, the successive strokes of each bell are subjected to differing degrees of timbral transformation through the "Gagaku circuit," a double ring-modulation circuit that first modulates the recorded sound with a sine wave (in this case always 12,000 Hz), yielding summation and difference tones, which are then fed into a second ring-modulator. At the other input of this second modulator (the *B* input of the score), various frequencies are used. These frequencies are shown in Example 5.4. Rows 1 through 4 show the frequencies at the point of attack of each bell. However, each bell has also its own particular "mode of attack" in this second modulating frequency. The first bell has a constant frequency; the second bell has a series of glissandos down 50 Hz from the basic frequency and back up to it (the third stroke ends with the lower frequency, by way of exception); the third bell has smaller glissandos, 6 Hz above *and* below the basic frequency, in differentiated rhythmic patterns: rit., accel.-rit., rit.-accel., accel., rit.; and the fourth bell has the most complex pattern, a series of five steps for each attack, which are subordinate to the main modulating-frequency for that attack. These five-step series are shown in Example 5.4 by the diagonal series extending below series 4 and labeled with the letters *A* through *D*.

It will be seen that the frequency-successions of (1), (2), (3), (4A), (4B), (4C), and (4D) are all drawn from scales of equidistant 100-Hz increments, each therefore representing a bandwidth of 400 Hz. The four bands of 4A through 4D themselves comprised a band 1,400 Hz wide, with steps between equivalent points of successive bands (top-to-top, let us say) of 300, 700, and 400 Hz, from lowest to highest. The "lopped off" fifth bell-stroke in this layer, therefore, may be inferred to have been in the "missing" central band (which would make a scale of equal, or nearly equal, degrees), probably covering 11,800–12,200 Hz. This completes a five-set for this layer, and the resultant series for all of the five-sets in Example 5.4, expressed in terms of scale-degree numbers (zero through four), is shown in Example 5.5. While it would be sufficient merely to have shown this set structure to establish the presence of serial composition

Example 5.4
Moment 31, Track IV, Ring-modulator B-input Frequencies

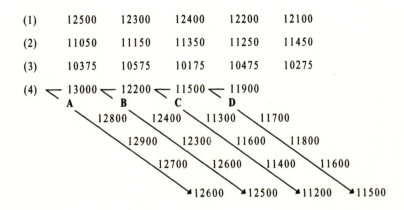

(1)	12500	12300	12400	12200	12100
(2)	11050	11150	11350	11250	11450
(3)	10375	10575	10175	10475	10275

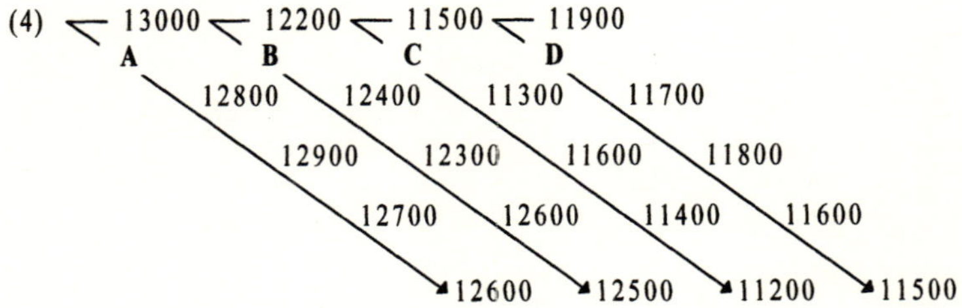

techniques—since Stockhausen's practice, dating back to *Kreuzspiel* in 1951, admits permutation in general, not restricting relationships to the "classical" retrograde, inversion, and rotation—in fact, most of the series in Example 5.5 are of a single type, that represented by the first line, and so arbitrarily designated T_0. In this example, the relationships are also shown.[14]

Foreseeing the inevitable objection that this has nothing to do with what the listener hears, I must point out that (1) the structure–form relationship does not require that the structure be audible as such; (2) the resultant colorations, in which the original sound, together with the outputs of both ring-modulators are recorded, are all quite easily differentiated by ear (by *my* ear, at least, listening to the recording)[15]; and (3) the products of the ring-modulation are really very easy to foresee and were certainly so foreseen by the composer who could construct the ring-modulation schemes of *Mixtur* (Kohl 1981, Chapter 2).

These timbral transformations will, because of the uniform 100 Hz interval between scale-steps in each set, necessarily result in the addition of two pitches from the A-modulator (the sum and the difference tones—of course, the overtones are also modulated and produce weaker sums and differences) and the two difference-tones between these pitches and the sine wave in the B-modulator (the summation tones are filtered out by a 5,500 Hz low-pass filter in the "Gagaku circuit" but are all above 22,000 Hz in any case and therefore inaudible to most people), these differences themselves forming scales of 100-Hz steps. Furthermore, because of the particular selection of modulating frequencies relative to each bell-note, the bands within which the difference-tones of the B-modulator vary are distinct for each bell, though there is a small amount of overlap between those of the first two bells. The considerable overlap between the bandwidth of the B-modulator outputs of the fourth and second bells is rendered distinct through the particular forms of modulation variation (the "attack characteristics"

Example 5.5
Serial Structure of Moment 31, Track IV

	Series of Modulating Pitches					*Relationships*
(1)	4	2	3	1	0	T_0
(2)	0	1	3	2	4	RT_0 (or r_1T_2I)
(3)	2	4	0	3	1	r_2RT_0, last two exchanged
(4)	4	3	0	1	(2)	r_2RT_1 (or r_4T_3I)
(4A)	4	2	3	1	0	T_0
(4B)	0	2	1	4	3	T_1I, last two exchanged
(4C)	3	1	4	2	0	(permutated)
(4D)	4	2	3	1	0	T_0

mentioned earlier), the specific pitch differences resulting from the bells' fundamentals being a minor seventh apart.

The dynamic levels of the successive attacks in the composite structure are varied ad lib, but from a particular scale of values and with the stipulation that the first (simultaneous) attack be the loudest. The score specifies "0 dB at the beginning, then maxima mostly -14, -12, -16 dB (one time -10 dB)." This is, therefore, a statistical variation among set scale-steps, which, if they were used in the order given (0, -14, -12, -16, and -10 dB) would give scale order numbers 4, 1, 2, 0, 3, which is r_4R of the series shown at 4B in Example 5.5.

Similar structures may be found elsewhere in *Telemusik*, for example, in tracks II and III of moment 29, where the initial Bokusho stroke is repeated into the structure, together with strokes from the Mokugyo, Rin, and Keisu, in a layered structure much like the one that we have just examined. But here each sound is *transposed* with each stroke by means of a variable-speed tape recorder, each according to the same scale of transpositions (one slight variation: the Bokusho's lowest transposition is 41:31 on the control-generator's frequency scale, while all the others are 41:32), but in different orders (see Example 5.6). All of these are rotations of the first series or of its retrograde (untransposed and therefore without having to rely on the admittedly doubtful use of mod 5 to demonstrate relationships), but with exchange of the last two resulting members in the row and the omission of scale-degree 3 from the last.

A simpler example may be found in track II of moment 14, where transposition is similarly applied to the initial Taku stroke to achieve a scale of nine transposed forms, which then are ordered 5, 1, 0, 2, 6, 3, 4, 7, 8. This series is not, as the other two structures' series were, retrograde or retrograde-inversion symmetrical, but nonetheless it fulfills Stockhausen's definition of serial composition. That this series is not the same as either of the other two or even easily related to them, since its scale consists of nine elements as opposed to the others' five each, may by almost any definition disqualify this work as "total" or

Example 5.6
Serial Structure of Moment 29, Tracks II and III

2	4	1	0	3
3	0	-1	4	2
1	0	3	4	2
4	1	0	2	

"integral" serial in construction. As shown in Kohl (1981, Chapters 1 and 2), this does not in any way represent a change from Stockhausen's earlier practice, and it would seem that the freedom to choose scales of such diversity for the same composition (though even these may be supraordered by a uniform scale) is a contributing factor to the richness of texture that characterizes his works.

OTHER ASPECTS OF THE FORM

The three examples that we have just considered all use the temple instruments internally, within the structure of the moments. This is by no means typical of *Telemusik*, but it does occur from time to time, in degrees varying from a simple immediate echo of the initial stroke, as in moment 10 (Bokusho), through such internal form-marking as is found in moment 11 (Keisu), to the full-fledged structural use that we have seen in moments 14, 29, and 31 and even beyond, into dense, statistical echoes, as in moment 19 (Taku). The distribution of these internal usages of the temple instruments is fairly even throughout the composition and in no way suggests a through-line of *development* (Harvey 1975, 101).

Nevertheless, certain features do tend to make *Telemusik* less discontinuous than one might expect from a moment-form work. Chief among these is the connection of two or more consecutive moments in one or more tracks by the uninterrupted continuation of a single process, such as we have already seen in the case of moments 6 and 7. (Such more or less casual fusion of neighboring formal units occurs in Stockhausen's music as early as *Klavierstück I* [1952], where the composer describes them as "Hauptgruppen.")[16] Also, a recognizable process from one moment may be immediately repeated as an insert in the following moment, as we have seen in track II of moments 5 and 6. Such connections provide considerable continuity in the cases of the following groups of moments: 1-2-3 (the continuities here are analyzed in detail by Fritsch [1999, 177–178]), 5-6-7-7 Forts., 10-11, 12-13-14, 17-18-19-20-21-22-23, 24-25-26, and 27-28-29-30-31—in short, through almost the entire composition. It should be pointed out, however, that in most of these moment-groups there is not a single, long process binding them all but rather a series of shorter, overlapping multimoment processes, and in some cases the processes themselves undergo a distinct change in some aspect of their character at the point of transition to a new moment, while the basic material continues. An example of the latter occurs in track I during the moments 27 through 30, where a scrambled track of alternating segments of two different pieces of Vietnamese music provides the basic material, and the processing is essentially the same for all four moments, but the rhythm of the output amplitude-envelope is very different in each (the same is true of track IV in these moments, which is reprocessed from track 1, except that in the last two moments a single, diminuendo process occurs).

There are further, more subjectively based connections of similar type. Robin Maconie (1976, 211–212) points out one, the link between 15, 16, and 17, where a structure in the first sends a succession of glissandos up into the highest range of hearing, followed in the middle moment by a sustained sound in this same area (with some dips to lower pitches) and then by a reverse of the glissandos in the third. In this case, however, the sounds in the middle moment, while audibly similar to the end of the preceding and the beginning of the following moments, are produced by quite different means and have a distinctly different (audible) bandwidth and internal movement. This is because the sounds in moment 16 are entirely "electronic" (i.e., they are produced by sine-wave generators), while the other moments use a mixture of layers of electronic and processed "natural" sounds. The relatively simple, calm internal movement of the electronically produced sounds has a quite different texture from the restless activity within the processed "natural" sounds.

This grouping of moments by single processes and inserts does not appear to follow any particular scheme. Indeed, the moments that I grouped together earlier are not all bound together by anything like the same degree of similarity and use a wide variety of different techniques. This rather seems to have come about from more or less intuitive conceptions, perhaps in part by the working schedule, in which sometimes two or three moments would be produced in a single day, and it might have been convenient to execute a single, continuous process in one track for the duration of that day's assigned task.

More distant connections also occur, in the sense of both temporal separation and degree of recognizability. As an example of the former, moment 16 takes up again the sine-wave chords that were produced for moment 13, tracks II and III, and subjects them to further manipulations. As an example of the latter, moment 32 uses the same excerpt of Balinese music as moment 7 but treats it in such a radically different way as to render the connection all but unrecognizable.

The distinctly different qualities of the purely electronic sounds and the "natural" materials produce in the first half of the work a sense of directed line also (though this may not have been the composer's intent). The first two moments use exclusively electronic sounds, the first quite static and the second rather more active. The third moment introduces the first "natural" sounds (in track V only),[17] after which the moments alternate electronic and mixed electronic/natural materials up to moment 10, with ever-increasing prominence given to the natural materials in the odd-numbered moments. After this point, only the sixteenth moment is entirely given over to electronically produced sounds, though these continue to be used in mixture with the processed natural materials to the end of the composition. This process of gradual oscillation away from the steady, simple sounds of the electronically generated textures may not be reducible to measurable quantities, but it certainly provides a tendency as far as the middle of the piece, though that it is quite different from a *developmental* tendency, which implies manipulation of material that is recognizably "the same."

The five channels of sound used in *Telemusik* superficially recall the five channels of *Gesang der Jünglinge* but actually stem from the equipment available in the NHK studio. Stockhausen says in a note in the preface to the score that the *six*-channel tape recorder used is "so far only to be found in Japan, and for that reason the original can only be performed there."[18] The sixth track was used in the production process, as may be seen by a glance at almost any moment, but apparently the flexibility allowed by leaving one track out as a "production tool" was great enough to command a five-channel result. Unlike the cases of *Kontakte* and *Sirius* (1975–1977), the separate channels here are used only to keep simultaneous structures distinct from each other. There is no attempt to compose "spatial" structures, with the sounds moving from channel to channel. This is doubtless because, unlike the situation at the Westdeutscher Rundfunk (WDR) studios, where *Kontakte* and *Sirius* were produced, there was no "rotation table" available at NHK.[19] We may infer from the instructions in the preface to the score regarding performance of the mixed-down, two-channel "stereo" version that the intention of the original was that the five channels be placed more or less in a circle around the audience. In *Gesang der Jünglinge*, the situation may have been slightly different. In the composer's words, the five loudspeaker groups are "to be distributed in space around the listeners. The side from which the sounds and sound-groups are emitted, from how many loudspeakers at once, whether moving clockwise or anticlockwise, sometimes static and sometimes mobile—all this becomes decisive in the work" (*Texte* 2: 49, trans. Richard Toop). While this suggests the rotational and "flood sound" movements of *Kontakte*, it does not necessarily confine them to one plane, as in that work; nor does the experience of hearing *Gesang* in the four-channel version (with speakers in the four corners of the surrounding space) convey very much of this sort of spatialization. Pascal Decroupet and Elena Ungeheuer (1998, 141, n. 19) conclude from a study of the sketches: "The logic of spatial link-up confirms that the five loudspeakers were located according to the same plan, around the audience [i.e., in a circle], and that speculations concerning a loudspeaker placed above the audience are purely a matter of myth." The "myth," however, comes with an extremely good pedigree. In an interview conducted in October 1980 (Tannenbaum [1985] 1987, 24), the composer himself asks, "And do you know that the original conception also included a fifth track with a boy's voice sounding from above in the first bars? No technician has ever wanted or known how to arrange a loudspeaker on a ceiling." His continuation gives an indication of the principal reason behind the spatialization in *Gesang*: "[This] forced me to superimpose the final track, the fifth, on the fourth. But once the voice which sings 'Jubelt' ('Rejoice') was incorporated with the rest, it didn't achieve the necessary prominence." The instructions for *Telemusik* read:

From this original the composer made several 2-channel stereo copies in the same studio, with the following spatial distribution of the 5 channels (Panorama-console):

III
IV II
channels: I V

In this distribution small dynamic alterations were adjusted by ear in order to clarify the directions and to produce a balance in the multi-leveled structures . . .

In public performances of the stereo tape it is recommended that each of the two outputs of the 2-track tape recorder be connected to two separate regulators (or to 2 preamplifier-balance controls), and these controls be connected to 4 loudspeakers (in the corners of the hall on stands about 2.5 meters high), in order that the dynamics may be adjusted to the acoustical characteristics of the hall: channel I left-rear and left-front, channel II right-front and right-rear, controlled from the center of the hall. With a good balance, one can achieve a projection of the sound that comes very near to the 5-channel original.

But whether this means that the channels were not intended to be arranged in numerical order from left-rear around to the front and then to the right-rear is hard to say. In any case, there are to be found in the score none of the "moving sound" techniques of *Kontakte* nor any evidence of structures calculated according to the principles outlined in Stockhausen's article "Music in Space."[20] The spatial conception of this work seems, therefore, to be closer to the concept of *Gruppen* and *Gesang der Jünglinge* than to those of *Kontakte*, *Sirius*, or *Oktophonie* (from *Dienstag aus Licht*).

While the distinction between groups of moments and divisions within moments themselves is maintained with a fair amount of precision through the degree of unity that was from the outset the leading characteristic of the independent moment, and the use of spatially separated, simultaneous events (or structures) gives a degree of the polyvalent connections associated with such earlier moment-form works as *Momente*, *Mixtur*, and *Mikrophonie I*, there nevertheless exists in *Telemusik* an overall tendency toward a unidirectional time-flow, whether dictated by personal preference, subconscious factors, or the pressures of a tight production schedule. While *Telemusik* must still be described basically as a moment form with determinate connections, made up primarily of group and statistical (gestalt and textural) elements, the ideas of process formation with which the composer had already been occupied for several years are clearly at work not only within individual moments but also in the shaping of the whole work.

NOTES

1. *Nr. 20 Telemusik* (Vienna: Universal Edition, 1969) (UE 14807).
2. The other was *Solo*, which dated back to a sketch of 1964 (*Texte* 3, 86), and so received the earlier work-number, 19, even though it was not completed until April 1966.
3. Reprinted in *Texte* 3, 79–84. The first paragraph is very similar to the program note in *Texte* 3, 75–77.
4. For a discussion of process plans in general and *Kurzwellen* in particular, see Kohl (1981, Chapter 4) and Hopp (1998). Hopp offers particularly valuable analyses of the manipulation of "found" material in several individual performances of *Kurzwellen* and, beyond this, gives an account of Stockhausen's construction of the tape-collage of Beethoven's music used in the version of *Kurzwellen* variously known as *Stockhoven-Beethausen*, *Kurzwellen mit Beethoven*, and *Opus 1970* (pp. 263–415).
5. Later works also pay homage to Japan in very explicit terms: *Japan* from *Für kommende Zeiten* (6 July 1970), *Inori* (1973–1974, whose title is Japanese for "Adorations"), and *Der Jahreslauf* (The Course of the Years, 1977, from *Dienstag aus Licht*), composed originally for Gagaku orchestra and dancers (see *Texte* 4, 346–357). Some scenic elements in *Licht* are also based on the composer's experiences in Japan: the Third Station of *Michaels Reise um die Erde* (Michael's Journey round the Earth, act 2 of *Donnerstag aus Licht*) is set in Japan, and the "colouring of the soundscape" is determined by Geisha bell, Keisu, and other instruments simulating characteristic Japanese sounds (harmonium=Shô, harp=Koto, bongo=Kakko); the "Mädchenprozession" in act 2 of *Montag aus Licht* depicts a nocturnal ritual procession witnessed near Kyoto (*Texte* 6, 279); and the noise of wooden shoes worn by the monks' choir in *Luzifers Abschied* (Lucifer's Farewell, scene 4 of *Samstag aus Licht*) is taken directly from the Omizutori (water-consecration) ceremony at the Todai-ji temple in Nara (*Texte* 4, 446). Of course there are also smaller references in other works, notably the Nô-percussionist's signaling cries near the end of *Mantra* (1970) and the further use of Japanese percussion in *Licht*: *Donnerstag*, act 3, scene 1 "Festival"; *Samstag*, scene 1, *Luzifers Traum* (Lucifer's Dream), and scene 3, *Luzifers Tanz* (Lucifer's Dance). Stockhausen has also spoken of less direct influences, such as that of Nô theater on *Kathinkas Gesang als Luzifers Requiem* (scene 2 of *Samstag*) (*Texte* 6, 275–276). The employment of the Japanese national anthem starting about ten minutes into the third region of *Hymnen*, on the other hand, is scarcely remarkable in the context of dozens of other national anthems.
6. *Texte* 4, 457, and 475, in two articles dating from 1976 and 1973, respectively.
7. It will be observed that while the individual events are "statistical" within composed guidelines, the connections between the layers (and even between the guidelines of different parameters within layers) are "variable" (see Kirchmeyer's *Neuenerschema*, earlier).
8. Some process compositions, such as *Kurzwellen* (Kohl 1981, Chapter 4; Hopp 1998), are structurally divided into segments with the continuity broken (more or less) at the boundaries. In this way, it would be possible to compose a moment form of processes, but the reverse would require a unidirectional flow of (inherently directionless) moments!
9. Moment 8 from Stockhausen's original manuscript score is reproduced in *Texte* 3, 78 (the published score was redrawn by Péter Eötvös). This shows that a few details that might have been of use to the analyst (grids with more precise time, frequency, and loudness values for the curves) were omitted in the final score.
10. They are called simply "structures" in the score, but in *Texte* 3, 77, the previously mentioned manuscript page is described as showing "the composition of the five tape tracks of the *8th Moment*."

11. This sort of form-marking cycle of percussion (usually with the various instruments finally coming together in a unison stroke to signal the end) is found in various Oriental musics, but Stockhausen no doubt borrowed it from the Buddhist temple ceremonies to which the instruments pertain. (Some ethnomusicologists extend to this generalized type of percussion function the term "colotomic"—presumably derived from the Greek: κόλλα "glue" + τομή "cut, sector," hence, "glue between the sectors"—which is more strictly applied to the pattern-within-pattern rhythms found in Indonesian gamelan music.) Moment 26 lacks any indication of such an instrument in the score, but this is apparently an oversight: the expected Taku is heard in the recording. The thirty-first moment begins not with a single instrument but with "four large temple bells" (the four deepest of the five mentioned in the score's preface).

12. The Fibonacci series is the succession of numbers in which each value is the sum of the preceding two: 1, 1, 2, 3, 5, 8, 13, 21, 34, . . . For a discussion of the aesthetic values believed to be inherent in the Fibonacci series, its relation to the Golden Section, and some of its special properties, see Chapters 4, 10, 11, and 12 in Huntley (1970). A more comprehensive treatment of the mathematical properties of the series may be found in Vorob'ev (1961). For specifically musical applications, see Kramer (1973). The utility of the series for the composition of durations lies in the approximately (and increasingly) constant value of the proportions between successive members. Binet's formula (Vorob'ev 1961, 20)

$$u_n = \frac{\left(\frac{1+\sqrt{5}}{2}\right)^n - \left(\frac{1-\sqrt{5}}{2}\right)^n}{\sqrt{5}}$$

yields values that, when rounded to the nearest whole number, are the *n*th term of the series. From this it may be seen that, as n increases, the proportion of n to $n + 1$ approaches a limit, which happens to be the so-called Golden Section. Therefore, this series provides a scale "whose stepwise distances are felt to be equally large." (Compare the logarithmic tempo scale proposed in ". . . How Time Passes . . . ," *Texte* 1, 9–139.) So far as I am aware, Stockhausen first employed the Fibonacci series in a thoroughgoing way in *Zyklus* (1959), though Pascal Decroupet and Elena Ungeheuer (1998, 115–116) believe they have found traces of it in *Gesang der Jünglinge*. In a conversation with the author in Florence on 2 June 1984, Stockhausen asserted that he first learned of the properties of the Fibonacci series in school during World War II, and may have used these proportions in *Gruppen* (1955–1957).

13. "[We] shouldn't fall into the trap of composing only statistical structures while not considering the relativity of these structures—which implies the importance, in one and the same composition, of composing a whole scale between the individual—the indivisible—and the dividual—the divisible—which means between gestalt and texture. There are such marvelous examples in Paul Klee's *The Thinking Eye* in which you see a fish as a gestalt; but looking at its gills, you find a statistical, aleatoric texture" (Cott 1973, 72–73). See also Kohl (1981, 156–158).

14. I have excluded the equivalents of the cycle-of-fifths and cycle-of-fourths transformations, which in a mod-5 system would be M2 and M3, on two grounds: Stockhausen has never shown an awareness of this kind of transformation, and admitting these to the "canonic operations" of a system of five-membered sets reduces the number of set-types in that system to only two.

15. Stockhausen Complete Edition, CD 9 (Kürten: Stockhausen-Verlag); previously released on LP by Deutsche Grammophon Gesellschaft (DGG) as 137 012 (side 1).
16. Stockhausen, "Gruppenkomposition: *Klavierstück I* (Anleitung zum Hören)," in *Texte* 1, 69. The term is provisionally translated as "group aggregation" in the draft of the English edition of *Texte* 1 (Kürten: Stockhausen-Verlag, forthcoming).
17. The Gagaku music, heavily modified by the double ring-modulation circuit, and the entirely "natural" recording of the Mokugyo, which originally consisted of forty-eight accelerating strokes (a diminuendo is effected artificially). Maconie (1976, 207) refers to "the characteristic accelerating beat-pattern of the Mokugyo injecting from time to time an element of dynamic relief." While one might ask, "Relief from what?" it is also pertinent to note that moment 3 is the *only* place in *Telemusik* where the Mokugyo is heard to accelerate. Presumably, Maconie means that in the Buddhist temple ceremonies it is characteristic of the Mokugyo to do this.
18. The original master tape became inaccessible soon after the 1966 premiere in Japan, when the NHK's custom-built, six-channel tape machine fell out of use. Beginning in 1988, thanks to efforts made by sound technician Shigeru Satô (one of Stockhausen's original collaborators in 1966), the old machine was made functional again, but it was not until 1996 that a satisfactory transfer to standard eight-channel tape was accomplished, enabling public performances of the original five-channel version for the first time in thirty years. The correspondence documenting this recovery is planned for publication in volume 11 of Stockhausen's *Texte*.
19. See Kirchmeyer (1963, 34–36) for a description of this "rotation-table" and an *ersatz* picture (according to the caption, "Die Aufnahme ist allerdings gestellt. Der abgebildete runde Tisch ist nicht drehbar, sondern diente als Photoersatz für das Original, das nicht zur Verfügung stand. Die elektrische Apparat hingegen ist echt" [The photo is posed, however. The round table depicted is not rotatable, but served as a photo-substitute for the original, which was not available. The electrical equipment, on the other hand, is genuine]). (This photograph and several similar ones with the same manifestly unrotatable table, posed at the same time—1962 or 1963—have appeared elsewhere, usually misrepresented as dating from the time of composition. See, for example, Kurtz [1992, 102] photograph captioned "Stockhausen experimenting with new 'spatial projection' for Kontakte in the WDR electronic studio, 1959.") See also Stockhausen, "Die Zukunft der elektroakustischen Apparaturen in der Musik," *Musik und Bildung* 6, no. 7/8 (1974): 412–417, reprinted in *Texte* 4, 425–436.
20. *Die Reihe* 5 (1959; English ed. 1961), 67–82. German text reprinted in *Texte* 1, 152–175.

REFERENCES

Cott, J. (1973). *Stockhausen: Conversations with the Composer*. New York: Simon and Schuster.

Decroupet, P., and Ungeheuer, E. (1998). "Through the Sensory Looking-Glass: The Aesthetic and Serial Foundations of *Gesang der Jünglinge*." *Perspectives of New Music* 36, no. 1 (Winter): 97–142.

Faas, E. (1977). "Interview with Karlheinz Stockhausen Held August 11, 1976." *Interface* 6: 187–204. Reprinted in *Die Feedback Papers* no. 16 (August 1978): 23–24.

Fritsch, J. (1999). "*Telemusik*: Fragment des Verstehens." In *Internationales Stockhausen-Symposion 1998, Musikwissenschaftliches Institut der Universität zu Köln, 11. bis*

14. November 1998: Tagungsbericht, edited by Imke Misch and Christoph von Blumröder, in association with Johannes Fritsch, Dieter Gutknecht, Dietrich Kämper, and Rüdiger Schumacher. Signale aus Köln 4. Saarbrücken: Pfau-Verlag, 177–185.

Harvey, J. (1975). *The Music of Stockhausen: An Introduction*. London: Faber and Faber.

Hopp, W. (1998). *Kurzwellen von Karlheinz Stockhausen: Konzeption und musikalische Poiesis*. Kölner Schriften zur Neuen Musik 6, edited by Johannes Fritsch and Dietrich Kämper. Mainz: Schott Musik International.

Hopp, W. (1999). "Interaktion und akustisches Photo: Überlegungen zur live-elektronischen Musik Karlheinz Stockhausens." In *Internationales Stockhausen-Symposion 1998, Musikwissenschaftliches Institut der Universität zu Köln, 11. bis 14. November 1998: Tagungsbericht*, edited by Imke Misch and Christoph von Blumröder, in association with Johannes Fritsch, Dieter Gutknecht, Dietrich Kämper, and Rüdiger Schumacher. Signale aus Köln 4. Saarbrücken: Pfau-Verlag, 155–177.

Huntley, H. E. (1970). *The Divine Proportion: A Study in Mathematical Beauty*. New York: Dover Publications.

Kirchmeyer, H. (1963). "Zur Entstehungs- und Problemgeschichte der 'Kontakte' von Karlheinz Stockhausen." In booklet for the original "Luxusalbum" edition of the LP of Stockhausen's *Kontakte für elektronische Klänge, Klavier und Schlagzeug*. David Tudor, piano; Christoph Caskel, percussion. Studio-Reihe neuer Musik, edited by Dr. Werner Goldschmidt. Großkönigsdorf bei Köln: Wergo Schallplattenverlag, WER 60009. Later reprints of this article (on the more modest sleeve for the reissued Wergo LP and in *Neuland: Ansätze zur Musik der Gegenwart: Jahrbuch* 3 (1982/83), edited by Herbert Henck, 152–176 [Bergisch-Gladbach: Neuland Musikverlag Herbert Henck, 1983]) omit most of the illustrations.

Kohl, J. (1981). "Serial and Non-serial Techniques in the Music of Karlheinz Stockhausen from 1962–1968." Ph.D. diss., University of Washington, Seattle.

Kramer, J. (1973). "The Fibonacci Series in Twentieth-Century Music." *Journal of Music Theory* 17, no. 1 (Spring 1973): 110–148.

Kramer, J. (1988). *The Time of Music: New Meanings, New Temporalities, New Listening Strategies*. New York: Schirmer Books.

Kurtz, M. (1992). *Stockhausen: A Biography*. Trans. R. Toop. London: Faber and Faber.

Maconie, R. (1976). *The Works of Karlheinz Stockhausen*. Foreword by Karlheinz Stockhausen. London: Oxford University Press (2d ed. Oxford: Clarendon Press, 1990).

Stockhausen, K. (1959). ". . . How Time Passes . . ." Trans. C. Cardew. *Die Reihe* 3 [English ed.]: 10–40.

Stockhausen, K. (1964). [Untitled lecture]. Adolf and Felicia Leon Lecture Series. University of Pennsylvania, 15 April. A recording of this lecture was broadcast on the radio in three parts in programs 5, 6, and 7 of the series *Stockhausen in Retrospect*, WUHY-FM, Philadelphia, 1965.

Stockhausen, K. *Texte zur Musik*, vols. 1–3, edited by Dieter Schnebel. Cologne: Verlag M. DuMont Schauberg 1963, 1964, 1971; vols. 4–6, edited by Christoph von Blumröder. Cologne: DuMont Buchverlag, 1978, 1989; vols. 7–10, edited by Christoph von Blumröder. Kürten: Stockhausen-Verlag, 1998. English editions of vols. 1–3 (translated by Jerome Kohl, Richard Toop, Tim Nevill, et al.; edited by Jerome Kohl) are currently in preparation, and translations of all subsequent volumes are planned (Kürten: Stockhausen-Verlag, forthcoming).

Tannenbaum, M. (1987). *Conversations with Stockhausen*. Trans. David Butchart. Oxford: Clarendon Press.

Thomas, E. (1975). "Zur Situation." In *Darmstädter Beiträge zur Neuen Musik* 14. Mainz: B. Schott's Söhne, 8–23. Thomas printed responses to a questionnaire from four composers, Christian Wolff, Mauricio Kagel, Iannis Xenakis, and Stockhausen. The questions with just Stockhausen's responses are reprinted as "Interview II: Zur Situation (Darmstädter Ferienkurse '74)" in his *Texte zur Musik* 4, edited by Christoph von Blumröder (Cologne: DuMont Buchverlag, 1978), 550–555.

Vorob'ev, N. N. (1961). *Fibonacci Numbers.* Trans. Halina Moss. Popular Lectures in Mathematics Series, vol. 2. London: Pergamon Press.

Wörner, K. H. (1973). *Stockhausen: Life and Work.* 2d ed. Trans. Bill Hopkins. Berkeley and Los Angeles: University of California Press.

6

Subscore Manipulation as a Tool for Compositional and Sonic Design

Otto Laske

INTRODUCTION

This chapter elucidates issues regarding the production and analysis of electroacoustic music from a compositional perspective.[1] I review the *musicological* notion of score and define the *compositional* notion of score in contrast to it. On this theoretical basis, I discuss the manipulation of subscores as a tool for the sonic design of compositions for loudspeakers. To exemplify my ideas, I analyze the structure of the process that yielded my composition *Terpsichore* (1980) for dancers and tape. I also review the design of *Trilogy* for loudspeakers (1999–2001).[2] I conclude with remarks on the utility of the *procedural* approach to music analysis for understanding electroacoustic music.

Computer music composition is conventionally viewed as involving the use of a sound synthesis program taking as input data manually provided by the composer. This *sound synthesis view* of computer music is historically lopsided since computer music started out as the attempt to model compositional procedures of classical instrumental music (Xenakis 1957). The one-sidedness of this view lies in the fact that it fails to acknowledge that the resources of musical software and software engineering potentially extend to the programmed generation and manipulation of the score itself and the viability of composition that is rule- rather than model-based (Laske 1989b).

In terms of music theory, the sound synthesis view of computer music adheres to a notion of score that is more *musicological* than strictly *compositional*. Viewed musicologically, the score documents the end result of a compositional process that itself remains unelucidated. More precisely, a score viewed musicologically documents the product of a compositional process that itself remains unelucidated. In accordance with this musicological view of score, composers almost exclusively use what Xenakis calls *in-time structures* (structures-en-temps; Xenakis 1971), shying away from *outside-time structures* (structures-hors-temps), or dismissing them as "precompositional" idiosyncracies. In-time schemata by definition do not extend beyond the time flow of an individual composition, while outside-time structures define classes of compositions independent of time flow.

When one approaches composition from the design of outside-time structures, the meaning of "score" changes. In strictly compositional terms, a score is a deep-structure (outside-of-time) matrix for generating a *base score.* When sequenced in the medium of time and projected into the sonic domain, variations derived from the base score accumulate to form individual compositions. In short, the individuality of compositions is largely based on the way in which time flow is employed to articulate outside-time structures.

It is tempting to suggest that while generating outside-time material is a matter of musical *competence*, articulating such material in musical time is rather a matter of *creativity*, and the two are to be distinguished for analytical reasons. (In traditional musicology, this distinction is never made.) Only human beings aware of their own personal and cultural history and limited lifetime can use time flow appropriately, while anybody capable of formal logical thought can manipulate outside-time structures. The latter is a capability that most (though not all) individuals reach in late adolescence, while the former is an adult-developmental achievement linked to how meaning is made of life experiences over the course of adulthood (Kegan 1982; Basseches 1984).

Studies in musical creativity, when based on insight into the outside-time structures employed in a composition (competence), may have a better grasp of what creative (i.e., adult-developmental), achievement is manifest in a composition. In terms of cognitive musicological research, giving one and the same outside-time structure to composers at different adult-developmental levels and analyzing the resulting compositions yield differences in these composers' articulation of time flow (based on identical materials) that manifest their creative and adult-developmental *differences*. Employing outside-time structures of music, therefore, not only is of composition-theoretical interest but also permits novel research into the relationship linking creativity and adult-developmental achievement, on one hand, and musical competence and creativity, on the other.

In this chapter, I highlight compositional procedures used in composing *Terpsichore* (1980) for loudspeakers and dancers that are apt to shed light on the potential of using outside-time structures both compositionally and analytically. To demonstrate the transfer of these compositional ideas to a contemporary sound synthesis medium, in addition I comment on *Trilogy* for loudspeakers (1999–2001). I refer to the use of outside-time structures, such as grammatical and aleatoric ones, as *score synthesis* and exemplify a *score synthesis view* of electroacoustic music in contrast to the widely accepted sound synthesis paradigm of that music. I furthermore show that outside- and in-time structures can be linked by the use of compositional macros. Actually, it makes good sense to distinguish three and not just two levels on which computer-based music composition potentially takes place (Example 6.1).

Example 6.1
Three Levels of Computer Music Composition

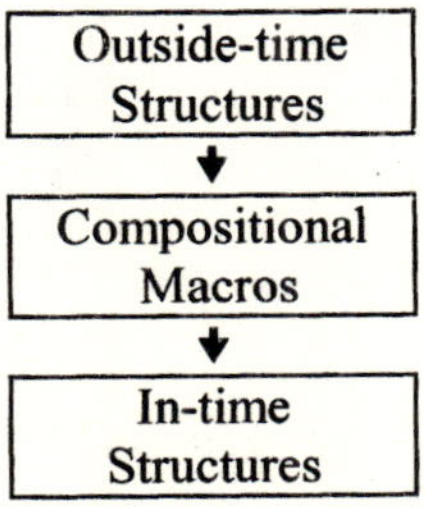

Rather than defining these levels abstractly, I demonstrate how they are used in *Terpsichore*. In *Terpsichore*, I saw it as my task to define a set of abstract relationships between musical parameters and to make parametric change manifest through its projection into a particular temporal sequence. Since no single program afforded me the tools to do so, I chose three different programs to work with: G. M. Koenig's Project 1 (1964–1970), W. Buxton's SCED (1979), and Buxton's OBJED (1976–1980). These programs complement each other: Project 1 delivers a *base score* from which compositional materials are derived, SCED generates syntactic variants of these materials, while OBJED defines sonic variants. These variations together explore the full scope of sonic and semantic implications of the base score.

TERPSICHORE: THE COMPUTER PROGRAMS USED

Koenig's Project 1

Koenig's Project 1 is a computer program for defining a class of compositions. Based on a minimal input given by the composer,[3] the program outputs seven parametric *data streams* for the definition of timbre, time-delay (start times), pitch, register, and intensity.[4] In their intersection, these data streams form musical *events*. The data streams computed by Project 1 articulate decisions about the outside-time structure on which a family of compositions is based, decisions partly made by the composer himself, and partly made by the program. These data streams differ from each other by the degree of variability that they embody, which is measured along a scale from 1 to 7. Variability of degree 1 is the classical serial case of nonrepetition of elements in a repertory. Variability of degree 7 is the case of maximum recurrence of elements in a repertory. Variability and redundancy have different manifestations in each of the different parameters to which they are applied. In the domain of pitch, redundancy can manifest as the repetition of a single tone or group of tones, while in the domain of *start-time*, redundancy appears as a recurrence of one and the same time-delay linking successive events.

The composer using Project 1 is required to make four basic decisions. These decisions concern (1) the contents and size of parameter repertories, (2) the degree of variability in each section (subscore), (3) a "structure formula," or mapping of parametric data streams onto each other (which may differ from composition to composition), and (4) the direction in which materials are projected into the time-domain. The program delivers data for individual sections; it does not prescribe the number of sections or their real-time sequence.

In *Terpsichore*, I chose repertories comprising nine instruments, thirteen time-delays, twelve pitches, four registers, and eight intensities. Since repertory size differs between different parameters, when mapped onto (coupled with) each other, parametric data streams naturally create syntactic counterpoint, in that instrument sequences, taleas, colors, and dynamic lines change at different times, even if following the same degree of variability. In *Terpsichore*, I use the parameter mappings (combinations of different degrees of change) shown in Example 6.2. This set of mappings suggests, but does not determine, decisions about projection into time; it remains valid and effective whether displayed forward, backward, or disjunctively. It is truly an outside-time structure. Read horizontally, the matrix of the mappings displays a tendency of parameter development over time; read vertically, it defines a compositional section or "movement" occurring "before" or "after" another. In semantic terms, each mapping (set of variants of the base score) constitutes a high-level building block of the composition. Example 6.2 shows a sequence of structures that, read from left to right, initially adhere to an utmost degree of recurrence (degree of variability 7). The strength of the recurrence factor is then consistently lessened, until one reaches the classical serial case. The only exception to this tendency is found in the register parameter, which counterbalances the increase of variability.

The Project 1 output for *Terpsichore* consists of 7 x 108 events (=756). Each event comprises from one to six tones. In total, the output consisted of 1,600 single events of approximately 4.5 minutes length (at tempo MM 60). I wanted to compose a piece in three distinctly different movements, as befitted the choreography that I envisioned, and of a length about three times as long (ca. 13.5 to 14 minutes). I thus needed a compositional procedure or set of proce-

Example 6.2
Variability Mappings in *Terpsichore*

	mappings						
	no. 1	no. 2	no. 3	no. 4	no. 5	no. 6	no. 7
instruments	7	6	5	4	3	2	1
time-delay	7	6	5	4	3	2	1
pitch class	7	6	5	4	3	2	1
dynamics	7	6	5	4	3	2	1
register	6	4	5	2	1	3	7

dures that would enable me to elaborate the base scores obtained to the full extent of the in-time output (musicological "score") planned. I found only a single program to be available for this purpose: the program SCED ("score editor") of the Structured Sound Synthesis Project (SSSP), Computer Systems Research Group, University of Toronto (Buxton 1979).

Buxton's SCED

W. Buxton's SCED is not only a score editor but, more importantly, a score manipulator. The program accepts a single subscore of up to (about) 800 events as input and from it derives related scores of at least the same size. The relationship between the input and output score is very flexible, in that the output score may differ from the input score in either one or all parametric domains specified. It is thus possible to compose scores of varying degrees of similarity, extending the classical idea of *Durchkomponieren*. More generally, it is possible to strengthen, weaken, or maintain the outside-time structure characterizing the input score by computing score variants. To my mind, SCED is a superb tool for elaborating scores that embody germinal ideas. Its use is particularly striking when combined with that of a program such as Project 1.

For SCED as a score editor, I refer to the literature (Buxton 1979, 1985). I restrict myself here to documenting its capabilities as a score manipulating tool. SCED enables the composer to formulate "shell commands," or compositional macros, through which outside-time structures serving as input are systematically varied in one or more parametric domain(s).[5] The variants obtained form a derivative material that exhibits outside-time structural features. In the case of *Terpsichore*, I decided to use the seven event lists (mappings of parameter streams) in a strictly forward direction, so as to proceed from utmost recurrence to utmost variability (7 to 1). In order to modulate the continuity of change that the base score embodies, I used event lists no. 1 and 2 (degrees 7 and 6) for movement one, lists no. 3 to 5 (degrees 5 to 3) for movement two, and lists no. 6 and 7 for movement three. In this way, I took advantage of the form-building dimensions of the base score. I also decided to use different compositional macros for each of the movements, thereby basing semantic differences on procedural ones. Partly, these macros were determined by precompositional decisions, and partly they developed during the real-time interaction with SCED. Following, I first define what I mean by a compositional macro and then outline the compositional procedure used in each of the individual movements of the score, by discussing the respective macroexpansion.

A compositional macro ("shell command") in SCED is a sequence of operators each of which applies to a particular parametric dimension and produces a variant of the material to which it is applied. The macro produces a sequence of transformations that apply to entire (sub)scores. Operators are invoked by commands such as "retrograde score *x*," "mix scores *x* and *y*," "time-scale score *x* in duration only," "randomize score *y* in pitch class term," and so forth. Already powerful in themselves, these individual operators take on new significance when linked to form a macro; they represent a compositional procedure whose formulation provides a protocol of compositional decision making, which makes it possible to reconstruct a composition from its base materials. The existence of compositional macros further generalizes the notion of a score: beyond its being a mapping of parametric data streams onto each other, in the sense of Project 1, the score becomes a tool for the derivation of material unified by certain outside-time features. Only in its definitive form is the score also a musicological document.

TERPSICHORE: THE COMPOSITIONAL MACROS USED

Movement 1

In working out movement 1, I went through a first-order and second-order derivation of materials; results of the first-order derivation are not sounded. In the first derivation, the macro embodied two commands: partition (combination of copy/delete) and retrograde; the second derivation was also based on two commands: mix and splice. In both cases, the combined Project 1 material of variability degrees 7 and 6 was subjected to transformation. The first-order derivation of new materials is shown in Example 6.3. The second-order derivation is shown in Example 6.4. The solid lines stand for splicing; the broken lines, for mixing. In short, the material was halved and retrograded, and halves and retrogrades were either spliced or mixed to form new materials.

Example 6.3
First-order Derivation of Movement 1

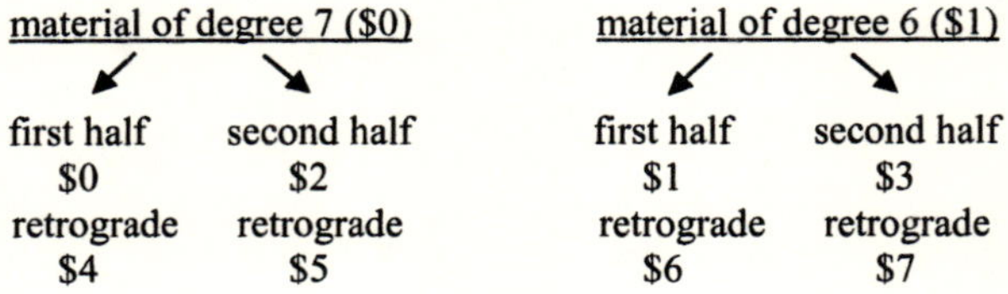

Example 6.4
Second-order Derivation of Movement 1

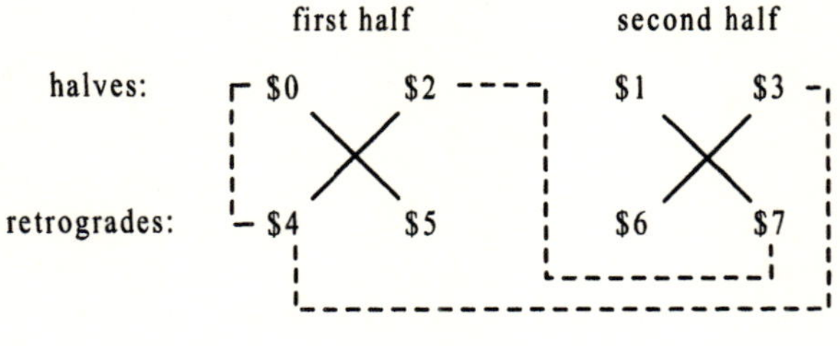

While halving and retrograding are obvious operations, splicing and mixing require some comment. One best thinks of tape procedures. Splicing means linking together. Mixing creates a new sequence of time-delays (starting times), by interlacing two series of events in strict temporal order. The compositional macro used for movement 1 is shown in Example 6.5 (the left side represents input; the right side, following the colon, the output).

Example 6.5
Compositional Macro of Movement 1

```
MACRO ONE
; first-order derivation
half    $0 : $0 $2        ; half is a combined operation of copying and deleting,
half    $1 : $1 $3        ; to effect a partitioning $0 and $1 are redefined.

retro   $0 : $4           ; retrogradation leaves the score unchanged,
retro   $2 : $5           ; it merely reverses the temporal order of events.
retro   $1 : $6
retro   $3 : $7

; second-order derivation
mix     $0 : $4 : $10     ; mixing creates a new time-delay structure by
mix     $0 : $0 : $11     ; inserting time-points of two different scores
mix     $0 : $0 : $12     ; according to their consecutive starting times.

splice  $0 : $5 : $13     ; splicing does not create new structures, it merely
splice  $4 : $2 : $14     ; links them together.
splice  $6 : $3 : $15
splice  $1 : $7 : $16
ENDMACRO
```

In this macro, the commands used in the first-order derivation originated from a decision made prior to the actual work with sounding results; each new material, as it emerged, was listened to in a default-orchestration to decide about its overall semantic ("musical") acceptability. All inputs to the second-order derivation operators are thus determined via listening. The in-time projection of accepted materials in movement 1 is shown in Example 6.6.

Example 6.6
Movement 1 (total duration: 4:45)

	$10	$12 $11 $14	$15 $16
duration	1:55	1:15	1:05
MM	60	57	53

Movement 2

In composing movement 2, I applied two derivations, as in the first movement, but of a totally different kind. Essentially, I used *scorchestration*, retrogradation, and splicing. Scorechestration is what Boulez once called *multiplication*, namely, the erection of a chord (considered the scorchestrating factor) on every single element of the "multiplied" structure. Since I was multiplying up to six-tone events with a chord of three tones, eighteen-tone chords resulted that had to be pruned (reduced in chord size) to be acceptable to the SSSP synthesizer. As materials for chord multiplication, I used the subscores conforming to an overall degree of variability from 5 to 3 (event lists no. 3–5).

Example 6.7 summarizes the derivational history of materials in movement 2. \$0 stands for the material of degree (of variability) 5, \$1 for material of degree 4, \$2 for that of degree 3. The three-note subscores (chords) used for scorchestration are named \$3 and \$4, respectively; \$4 is a transposition upward of \$3 by six semitones.

Example 6.7
Summary of the Derivational History of Materials in Movement 2

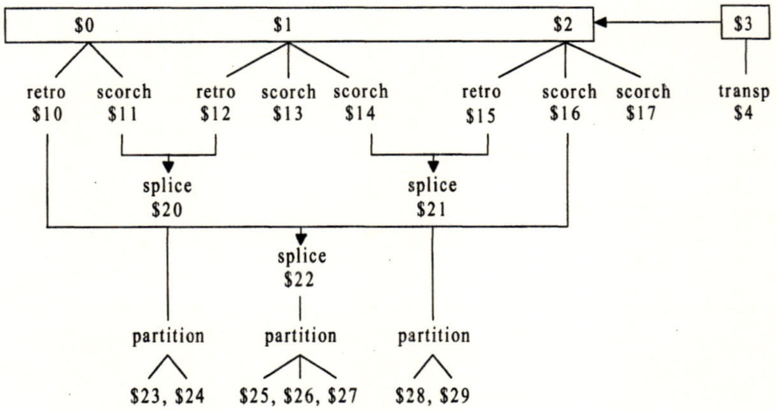

The compositional macro used to compose movement 2 is shown in Example 6.8 (transformation results are stated at the right side of the colon).

Example 6.8
Compositional Macro of Movement 2

MACRO TWO
; first-order derivation
transp $3 $6 : $4 ; *transpose* the multiplier by six semitones
; (upwards).

(Example 6.8 continued)

```
    retro       $0 : $10
    scorch      $0 $3 : 11          ; multiply all events in $0 by $3.
    retro       $1 : $12
    scorch      $1 $3 : $13
    scorch      $1 $4 : $14
    retro       $2 : $15
    scorch      $2 $3 : $16
    scorch      $2 $3 : $17         ; scorchestration yielded a maximal
                                    ; chordsize of 18 tones.
    prune       $11 $8 : $11        ; reduce chordsize in $11 to 8 and
                                    ; delete the old score.
    prune       $13 $8 : $13
    prune       $14 $8 : $14
    prune       $16 $8 : $16
    prune       $17 $8 : $17

; second-order derivation
    splice      $11 $12 : $20
    splice      $14 $15 : $21
    splice      $10 $16 : $22       ; $13 and $17 were not used.
    partition   $20 : $23 : $24     ; partitioning is "unsplicing"; it is a
    partition   $21 : $25 : $26     ; combined operation composed of
                $27                 ; copying and deleting.
    partition   $22 : $28 : $29     ; $20-$22 were partitioned
                                    ; according to semantic criteria (listening).
ENDMACRO
```

The in-time sequence of materials in movement two are shown in Example 6.9.

Example 6.9
Movement 2 (total duration 5:10)

	$23	$25 $26 $24	$28 $29
duration	2:15	1:45	1:10
MM	90	45	45

Movement 3

The end materials presented in movement 3 are derived in five steps, and only the fifth-order derivation materials are sounded. As a new strategic element, I used time-scaling of durations alone (i.e., not of time-delays), to obtain durations half and twice as long as were found in the basic subscores. Additional transformations were inversion and delay (fugal entry). In going through five derivational steps, the force and subtlety of SCED became quite obvious. In Example 6.10, I state a general summary of the derivational history

Example 6.10
Summary of the Derivational History of Materials in Movement 3

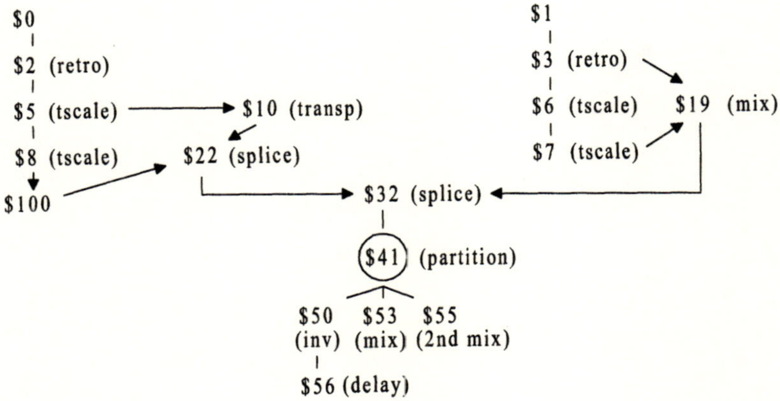

of movement 3, which, however, needs to be decoded in terms of the following macro. $0 stands for material of degree—of variability—2, $1 for material of degree 1 (serial case).

More evidently than the previous two macros, macro 3 documents the real-time compositional interaction of a composer with SCED. Only the time-scaling (i.e., the shortening and lengthening of durations in both subscores [$0, $1]) goes back to a precompositional decision, whereas all other commands express decisions based on auditory findings (semantic criteria). Macro 3 (Example 6.11) is a compositional protocol that I have discussed in much of my compositional-theoretical research.[6]

Example 6.11
Compositional Macro of Movement 3

```
MACRO THREE
; first-order derivation
   retro      $0 : $2
   retro      $1 : $3
   tscale     -s $0 .5 : $4      ; in SED, durations are initially set equal to
   tscale     -s $0 2. : $5      ; time-delays, a state of affairs that can be
   tscale     -s $1 .5 : $6      ; changed by mixing or time-scaling.
   tscale     -s $1 2. : $7      ; "-s" is a flag indicating that only durations
   tscale     -s $2 2. : $8      ; are to be divided or multiplied. The
   tscale     -s $3 2. : $9      ; outside-time structure of time-delays
                                 ; remains unaffected.
; second-order derivation
   transp     $5 6 : $10         ; transposition by tritone upwards mix first
```

(Example 6.11 continued)

```
   transp     $7 6 : $11                ; material with its own retrograde mix.
   mix        $0 $2 : $12               : second material the same way mix a
   mix        $1 $3 : $13               ; time-scales version of $1 ($7) with the
   mix        $7 $2 : $14               ; retrograde of $0 ($2) and repeat for
   mix        $4 $3 : $15               : other materials.
   mix        $4 $0 : $16
   mix        $4 $2 : $17
   mix        $7 $1 : $18
   mix        $7 $3 : $19
   splice     $5 $8 : $100              ; join 2 time-scales versions of $0.
   splice     $7 $9 : $101              ; join 2 time-scales versions of $1.
   splice     $12 $13 : $20             ; join 2 mixings of $0 and $1.
   splice     $14 $15 : $21             ; join 2 mixings of $0 and $1.
   splice     $10 $100 : $22            ; join a time-scales transposed version of $0
   splice     $11 $101 : $23            ; with a time-scaled transposed version of
                                        ; of both; $0 and $2 (=$22), and
                                        ; correspondingly for $1

; third-order derivation
   splice     $20 $14 : $30             ; join different mixings of $0 and $1.
   splice     $15 $18 : $31

; fourth-order derivation
   partition  $32 : $40 $41 $42 $43 ; partition $32 according to semantic criteria.

; fifth-order derivation
   invert     $41 : $50
   sdelay     $50 4 : $51               ; insert an initial silence of 4 seconds.
   splice     $50 $51 : $52             ; fugal entry of $50, $51.
   mix        $52 $51 : $52             ; mix fugal entry with delayed theme.
   retro      $52 : $54                 ; retrograde fugal entry.
   mix        $54 $53 : $55             ; mix retrograde and previous mix.
   prune      $55 8 : $55               ; reduce chordsize to 8 tones.
   $50        settime/4 : $56           ; slow down $50 by a factor of 4.
ENDMACRO
```

In a more compact form:

```
$41  →  $32
$32  →  $19  $22
$19  →  $7  $3      →  $1
$22  →  $10  $100   →  $0  $1
```

In order to trace the rather convoluted history of movement 3 backward to its origins, I rewrite the derivations in the form of a transformational grammar (starting from the end of the fourth derivation (Example 6.12).

Example 6.12
Derivations in the Form of a Transformational Grammar

$41	→	$32	
$32	→	$19 $22	
$19	→	$7 $3	
$22	→	$10 $100	
$7	→	$1	; tscale by 2.
$3	→	$1	; retrograde
$10	→	$5 $6	; tscaling by .5 & 2.
$100	→	$5 $8	; tscaling by 2. of retrograde
$8	→	$2	; tscaling by 2. of retrograde
$2	→	$0	; retrograde
$5	→	$0	; tscaling by 2.

As one can see, the final material ($41) that underwent the last-step derivations embodies elements of both $0 and $1 materials, of degree of variability 1 and 2. As the grammar formalism suggests, certainly a grammar approach supportive of SCED procedures could be developed.

The in-time projection of fifth-derivation materials in movement three is shown in Example 6.13.

Example 6.13
Movement 3 (total duration: 3:50)

	$50 $53	$55	$56
duration	1:00	1:40	1:10
MM	30	30	7.5

OBSERVATIONS ON SONIC DESIGN IN COMPUTER MUSIC

General Notions

The *mapping* of a score onto an orchestra and vice versa are the aesthetic crux of computer music composition; however, score and orchestra may be delimited in software terms. This mapping can be only as good as the two elements being mapped. Complexity for its own sake is not the point. However, a certain complexity of both score and orchestra is indispensable in music that is to satisfy the mind's quest for informational complexity. It is not often considered that a simple score remains a simple score no matter how beautified it may appear through orchestration. Many compositions following the *sound synthesis view* have, to my mind, embarrassingly simple scores. By contrast, the syntactic complexity of a score can, and in most cases does, carry over into sonic complexity.

According to my compositional experience, one of the most effective ways of achieving sonic complexity is not via instrument design or instrument usage but via the design of a complex time organization of musical events. The time organization of a composition can be viewed on two levels: in terms of time-delays on the outside-time level and in terms of durations on the in-time level. (The rendition of time-delay as "starting time" of instruments reduces this two-level hierarchy to a one-level affair.) Composition theoretically, the time at which a sound starts (its onset), and its duration have nothing to do with each other: *they are completely separable aspects of the temporal behavior of sounds.* Time-delays account for the "metric" of compositions, while durations account for degree of connectedness (topology).

In theory, two distinct logical relationships can hold between time-delay and duration: identity and nonidentity. In the latter case, the relation of "smaller than" and of "larger than" exists. It is important to realize that one and the same time-delay structure, whether used forward or backward, can be interpreted by durations in entirely different ways and can thus yield entirely different textures and articulations. One can conceive of a scale or transitions leading form "time-delay smaller than duration" to "time-delays larger than duration." At one end of the scale, sound overlap, thus sound mixture, occurs, while at the other, hocket is created; in the middle of the scale lies the point at which time-delay equals duration (the classical metric case). In short, the relationship between time-delays and duration is a sonological parameter of the first order, thus of great relevance in sonic design. Given the fact that very slow and very high speeds pose no problem in computer music composition, the full range of sonic designs from hocketlike segregation to complex sound mixtures can be explored in this medium.[7]

Observations on *Terpsichore*

In *Terpsichore,* I was especially interested in exploring marginal and extensive sound overlap, thus sound mixture, at high speeds. The degree of sound mixture that results from the time organization of musical events can be measured by considering the relationship between the shortest (or longest) time-delays and durations in a section. The three movements of *Terpsichore* differ considerably in this regard (Example 6.14).

While in the first movement, the average duration is about four times as long as the corresponding time-delay (1:4), the relationship of time-delay to duration is 1:1.12 in the second movement and 1:2 in the third movement. Consequently, extensive sound mixture results in the first movement. This mixture is realized by relatively simple (frequency-modulation) instruments. In the second movement, whose time-delays are more varied than is the case in movement 1, there is a slight overlap of 1:1.12 between time-delays and durations. Complexity is created by the speed of events following each other and their slight overlapping

Example 6.14
Shortest (or Longest) Time-delays and Durations in a Section

	time-delay	duration	relationship
movement 1	25 ms.	100 ms.	(shortest) 1:4
movement 2	42 ms.	37.5 ms.	(shortest) 1:1.12
movement 3	20.5 sec.	51.2 sec.	(longest) 1:2

in time. Finally, in the third movement, durations are never longer than twice their time-delay; but since the time-delays are very diverse (nearly serial), irregularity of overlap is created and becomes obvious on account of slow speed. Tempo affects both time-delay and duration, being their common link. Tempo can be used to highlight or to de-emphasize complex temporal relationships, which, in turn, support or counteract a specific degree of variability of materials.

Since in *Terpsichore* the degree of variability of instruments and time-delays develops according to the same tendency, from homogeneity to diversity, the number of distinctly different instruments increases over the course of the composition, as does the diversity of time-delays. Specifically, the orchestration of *Terpsichore* follows the matrix in Example 6.15.

The orchestra was designed for the purpose of clarifying the syntactic and semantic relationships inherent in the score. Complexity of the score is balanced by (relative) simplicity in the orchestra. This is one of the many different balances between score and orchestra that can be realized in computer music.

Example 6.15
Orchestration of *Terpsichore*

	1.1	1.2	1.3	2.1	2.2	2.3	3
Total number of instruments	9	9	9	9	9	9	9
Distinctly different instruments	6	6	7	8	8	9	9
Shared with previous section	–	7	6	–	5	4	2
Duration	1:55	1:15	1:05	2:15	1:45	1:10	3:50

REFLECTIONS ON *TRILOGY*

In the introduction, I distinguished between the musicological and the compositional notions of *score*. The first describes a musical end product; the second, a deep-structure model of a composition to be produced. Pertinently related to this distinction is that of model- and rule-based composition (Laske 1989b). In model-based composition, a preexisting piece of music or a "style" abstracted from a group of musical pieces is chosen as the model upon which to base new work. Emphasis is on the in-time flow of linear time. By contrast, in rule-based composition, a composition is envisioned abstractly in terms of a set of rules, whether or not these take the form of one or more computer programs.

Rule-based composition can be *interpretive, stipulative,* or *improvisational* (Laske 1989). When dealing with a "black box" score generator such as Project 1 (or Xenakis ST10), which accepts only a limited range of input data, the composer acts as an interpreter of generated parametrical materials. When the composer defines his or her own rules of score generation, as in Koenig's Project 2, stipulative composition occurs. Such composition yields an output that can only be either accepted or rejected, but not interpreted, by the composer. Given an appropriate computer-based task environment, interpretive as well as stipulative compositional task environments additionally allow for improvisational designs. In short, the distinctions made earlier between three different types of rule-based composition are not meant to exclude the use of hybrid procedures. Using a rule-based composition program producing outside-time material (base score), the composer is free to stipulate his or her own rules for employing it and can interact improvisationally, in real time, with sounds derived from it.

A few words about *interpretive* composition using Project 1 are in order. Project 1 is a composer's assistant, not a composing machine. It is a design tool that outputs abstract compositional designs and thus provokes reflection on the composer's process. This feature is a result of the fact that the program outputs uninterpreted parameter values for tone colors (instruments), tone-height, register, and dynamics and lets the composer decide what the values should stand for. Most importantly, the program leaves certain parameters, such as duration, entirely open, thus enabling the composer to make texture and density decisions as required by the emerging context. In its newer version, the program permits the composer to vary harmony (intervallic content) by section. In the domain of sonic design, the composer can experiment in a systematic fashion, simultaneously following the program's rules and his or her own. For instance, the composer may decide to define a series of durations to be used throughout a particular section and may vary register assignments as required by musical logic.

When using Project 1 in combination with a sound synthesis language, such as Kyma, the composer works *top-down,* by selecting instruments that read scores. Kyma instruments are written in the Smalltalk language. Together, they form orchestras. In *Trilogy,* I make use of the *TextFileInterpreter* instrument, attempting to simulate Buxton's SCED. I do so by editing Smalltalk code in order to satisfy compositional requirements emerging in interactive listening.

In what follows, I note some features of *Trilogy*. I refer to Buxton's SCED as the model used in composing this new piece.

Buxton's SCED score editor is one among several editing tools developed for the SSSP synthesizer (Buxton, et al., 1979, 1985). SCED is driven alphanumerically, rather than graphically. SCED pioneers the notion of *scope*, meaning a subset of musical events of an event list. As Buxton et al. say: "Composers should be able to define a group of notes on the basis of their own constraints (a scope as defined above) and operate on such a group" (1979; reprinted 1985, 395). In contrast to SCED, operations such as (1) scoping, (2) halving, (3) mixing, (4) splicing, and (5) pruning are not predefined in Kyma, although a composer with a working knowledge of the Smalltalk programming language can easily implement them. Most generally, scoping requires selecting start-time boundaries so as to define a *group of events* to be manipulated, while the syntactic context of the group delimited remains unchanged. This is a welcome means of transcending the linearity (one-dimensionality) of event lists (Laske 1992, 270–275). *Halving, mixing*, and *splicing* require the automatic handling of start times. Halving entails resetting the beginning of the second part of a score to 0:00 and determining all successive start times accordingly, while splicing and mixing require an automatic recalculation of start times depending on the initial time values that bound the manipulated segments. Finally, *pruning* entails a systematic reduction of chord sizes in order to stay within computational limits or simply to thin out undesired densities. Before discussing some of the simple score manipulation operations used in *Trilogy*, in Example 6.16 I present the matrix on which the design of the composition's tape part is based, documenting abstract *precompositional* design decisions. Their overriding goal is to define a balance of continuity and contrast. The design attempts to balance increasing rates of change in some parameters (degrees of change 7 to 1) with decreasing rates of change and redundancy (not constancy) in others (degrees of change 1 to 7). As a result, each of the ten sections of the score is characterized by a particular *mapping of event list parameters adhering to a particular degree of change* (see Example 6.16). Parametric "counterpoint" gives rise to patterns of increasing and decreasing rates of change that follow auditory and aesthetic criteria of musical meaning-making. Individual sections derive their character from the way in which long-range syntactic tendencies meet, fuse, oppose, and balance each other. For instance, section C3 is unique in its relatively long delay times and slow harmonic change (degree of change 7), contrapuntally opposed by high registral change (degree of change 1), and further marked by slow tempo (tempo range MM 20–60) and a relatively high degree of instrumental and dynamic change (degree of change 3). The repetition rate of the section is 2, as in the rest of movement C, thus higher than in sections A, B, and D. These features are emphasized by the section's total duration (121 seconds).

In more global terms, the score of *Trilogy* is initially characterized by a gradual decrease of instrumental (4→7), harmonic (1→7), and dynamic change (5→7), balanced by an increased rate of change in start times (6→1) and register (7→1). The beginning of section C (C1) marks abrupt changes in tone color (7→1) and dynamics (4→1), compensated for by continuity in start times (2→1), harmony (5→6), and register (4→3). The number of octave registers gradually increases until section B (2→5), then oscillates around degrees 3 and 4, all of them represented by nonsuccessive registers (e.g., 5.0, 7.0, 9.0, 11.0 in C1). Registral range peaks in section D1 (7 registers), then decreases toward the end of the piece (3 registers). Intervallic structure, indicated in semitones, starts quasi- "tonally" (5, 5/3, 7) and then proceeds to more "dissonant" interval combinations, which, however, remain balanced by tonal combinations (i.e., 2, 3/7,

Example 6.16
Matrix of Compositional Parameters, *Trilogy*

Section/Parameters	A1	A2	A3	B	C1	C2	C3	D1	D2	D3
Instrument Change	4	5	6	7	1	2	3	6	5	4
Delay Change	6	5	4	3	2	1	7	4	3	2
Harmonic Change	1	2	3	4	5	6	7	1	2	3
Interval Structure	5,5/ 3,7	5,8/ 3,10	5,10/ 3,11	4,9 6,8	2,3/ 7,7	2,5/ 7,10	2,7/ 7,11	8,10/ 1,7	3,10/ 5,6	7,7/ 1,5
Register Change	7	6	5	4	3	2	1	7	6	5
Register Range	7.0- 8.0	8.0-10.0	6.0- 9.0	7.0 to 11.0	5.0, 7.0, 9.0, 11.00	6.0, 8.0, 10.0	7.0, 8.0, 9.0, 10.0	5.0 to 11.0	6.0 to 10.0	7.0, 8.0, 9.0
No. of Registers	2	3	4	5	4	3	4	7	5	3
Dynamic Change	5	6	7	4	1	2	3	4	1	7
Dynamic Pattern	a	b	c	g	f	e	d	h	i	j
No. of Events	100	100	100	200	150	75	125	100	75	50
Tempi Sequence	a 30-75	d 45-61	a' 75-30	b 30-50	e 60-100	g 45-80	i 20-60	g' 80-45	d' 61-45	b' 50-30
Redundancy	1	1	1	1	2	2	2	1	1	1
Total Duration	84"	53"	75"	182"	69"	53"	121"	43"	61"	45"

7). At the same time, dynamic patterns (comprising different arrangements of eight dynamic levels) are changing continuously, as are tempo sequences (comprising six different tempi), although some of the latter are retrogrades of earlier sequences. By way of these tendencies and countertendencies, an overarching syntactic and sonic framework is created that seeds the creation of musical form and articulates a peculiar kind of *Durchkomponieren.*

Working inside this framework, the composer interprets computed parameter values in concordance with rules partly inherent in the program output, and partly stipulated by himself or herself and thereby creates one among many possible *interpretations* of the outside-of-time structure chosen. The interpretation is arrived at through listening, which informs the parametric changes that the composer makes in order to create a foundation for further compositional work. The interpretation functions as a *default score* for the composition and is sounded in a *default orchestration.* Once the default score is in place, it is then considered as the composition's *base score.* Subsequently, two processes are applied to it: first, *score manipulation* (achieved by writing Smalltalk code in the framework of instrument definitions), and second, *orchestral redefinition* (achieved by redefining instrument parameters in a group of instruments called an "orchestra"). Following, I give an example of simple score manipulation procedures applied to the subscore A3 of the composition.

In Kyma, score manipulation regards changes in the score text read by TextFileInterpreter (TFI) instruments, while orchestra redefinition regards changes in a set of four (or more) TFI instruments ("voices"). In the act of composing, the musician can freely alternate between score and orchestra redefinition. This challenges the musician to bring the *syntactic* representation of the score into balance with its *sonological* representation. Together, these two representations determine (1) the potential meanings of the composition for a musical listener and (2) the way the composition makes sense for the listener. In short, the balance between syntactic and sonological representation defines *semantic* representations.

After producing a score for some number of instruments, using a computer program such as Project 1, the composer obtains an "event list" of chosen length in which each event is of the form shown in Example 6.17. In this list, events

Example 6.17
Kyma Event List

			instr	start	dur	freq	ampl
C (event)	#1	I	2	0.00	0.17	7.07	17000
C	#2	I	2	0.17	0.33	7.00	17100
C	#3	I	2	0.33	0.50	7.01	16900
		I	2	0.41	0.50	7.10	16500

are defined in "music-N" (4BF) fashion, comprising the specification of five parameters: (1) the instrument synthesizing the event, (2) its start time, (3) duration, (4) frequency, and (5) amplitude. In event 1, instrument I2 is activated to sound pitch/octave 7.07 (G below middle C) at amplitude 17,000 (ff) for 0.17 seconds. To audition the score in a *default orchestration*, the composer starts out with a default setup of the TFI orchestra (written in Smalltalk), for example:

```
| paramArray |
MM := 60.
[file atEnd] whileFalse: [
    paramArray := file nextParameters.
    (paramArray at: 1) == #I
        ifTrue: [
            (orchestra at: ((paramArray at: 2) min: orchestra size))
            start: (paramArray at: 3) beats
            duration: (paramArray at: 4) beats
            frequency: (paramArray at: 5) octavePointPitchClass hz
            amp: (paramArray at: 6) / 2000.0]
].
```

The preceding Smalltalk code defines each one of the five event parameters mentioned earlier. In composing, the composer uses *listening* as the major tool for a stepwise approximation of the envisioned "ideal" sonological representation of the adopted base score. In this process, the composer can freely alternate between making changes in how the orchestra interprets the score and the orchestra itself. (Manual changes in the base score are not typically made, except for changes suggested or required by certain orchestral representations of the score.) Example 6.18 is an example of the score manipulation that the listening composer has decided to of the score untouched (paramArray at: 5) but has redefined (1) *start time* (paramArray at: 3), (2) *duration* (paramArray at: 4), and (3) *amplitude* (paramArray at: 6). As a result, the orchestra "reads" (computes) the score differently from how it reads the unedited base score, by taking the changes introduced by the composer into account.

In a first step, taking advantage of the distinction between start time (time delay) and duration, the composer has delayed the attack point of partials under middle C (8.00) that last longer than three seconds, by multiplying start time by 1.25. All other start times remain unchanged. In a second step, the composer has introduced *register contrast*, by lengthening both low (frequency < 7.06) and high (frequency > 9.06) partials to almost double length (1.85) and by shortening partials in the middle frequency range (0.85).

The composer has applied the most complex conditional changes to the amplitude parameter, in the attempt to lessen the density of partials in the octave above middle C (8.00 to 9.00), as well as in the highest frequency region of the score (frequency > 9.06). The low-region partials of the subscore (< 8.00) have been left untouched. Amplitude has been reduced by more than half (* 0.4) for partials in the octave above middle C. The amplitude of the highest partials has been reduced under the condition that their durations are longer than two

Example 6.18
Kyma Score Manipulation

```
| paramArray |

MM := 60.

[file atEnd] whileFalse: [
    paramArray := file nextParameters.
    (paramArray at: 1) == #I
        ifTrue: [ (orchestra at: ((paramArray at: 2) min: orchestra size))

        "(1) stretch tones under middle C if their duration > 3.0 seconds"
        ifTrue: [(paramArray at: 5 < 8.00) & (paramArray at: 4 > 3.0)]
            start: (paramArray at: 3) * 1.25 beats
        ifFalse: [(paramArray at: 5 < 8.00) & (paramArray at: 4 > 3.0)]
            start: (paramArray at: 3) beats

        "(2) lengthen low & very high durations, & shorten all others"
        ifTrue: [(paramArray at: 5 < 7.06) | (paramArray at: 5 > 9.06)]
            duration: (paramArray at: 4) * 1.85 beats
        ifFalse: [(paramArray at: 5 < 7.06) | (paramArray at: 5 > 9.06)]
            duration: (paramArray at: 4) * 0.85 beats
            frequency: (paramArray at: 5) octavePointPitchClass hz

        "(3) leave lows alone; reduce amplitudes above middle C, in the high only
            if > 2.0 in duration & betw. 12 & 18K"
        ifTrue: [((paramArray at: 5 > 8.00) | (paramArray at: 5 < 9.00))
            & ((paramArray at: 5 > 9.06) & (paramArray at: 4 > 2.0)
            & (paramArray at: 6 > 12000) | (paramArray at: 6 < 18000))]
            amp: (paramArray at: 6) * 0.4 / 2000.0
        ifFalse: [((paramArray at: 5 > 8.00) | (paramArray at: 5 < 9.00))
            & ((paramArray at: 5 > 9.06) & (paramArray at: 4 > 2.0)
            & (paramArray at: 6 > 12000) | (paramArray at: 6 < 18000))]
            amp: (paramArray at: 6) / 2000.0]
].
```

seconds, and their amplitudes lie between 12 and 18K (approximately "mf" to "ff"). Overall, the score's *amplitude profile* has been reshaped. The density contour of the score in the lower register has been maintained. By contrast, the density of higher partials has been altered, either depending on their frequency definition alone or conditional upon their duration as well as amplitude profile. The composer has carried out all of these changes by analyzing the content of his listening experience. By formulating hypotheses as to what changes need to be made to remove less than optimal auditory features of the sounding score, the composer has moved the score closer to the "ideal score." At times, the composer has also changed features of the instruments playing the score by adjusting sonic features, for example, modulation indices, pitch bend, wave table, envelope, and start times of individual instruments.

The preceding example demonstrates a particular style, that of *functional orchestration*. Orchestra definition serves *score articulation*, rather than being an aesthetic end in itself. The syntactic and sonological representations of a score are brought into balance to achieve an optimal semantic rendition of the computer-generated base score. The latter thus serves as a *working model* of the definitive piece.

Score editing is not limited to local changes in a *base score* by way of score manipulation, manual or automated. It can also be used to derive entirely new scores experimentally, aided by auditory rehearsal. Presenting a base score in reverse (reversing the order of samples) or in retrograde (retrograding the events of the instrument script) is an example. In this way, entirely new, starkly contrasting *variants of one and the same base-score* can be produced, each of them resulting from a separate editing process. The composer can subsequently mix these variants in any way desired, either with the original subscore or with different subscores used in the composition, by employing one of the many available mixers and combiners in the Kyma instrument repertory. Through these procedures, *subscore manipulation becomes a principle of defining aesthetic form, not just a way of managing syntactic and sonic design.*

CONCLUSIONS

The possibility of composing at the intersection of rule-based processes defined outside oneself, by programs, and one's own rule stipulations is the fruit of more than forty years of musical software engineering. When first emerging in the early 1980s, this possibility seemed to herald a new age of compositional design, of composition theory, and of studies in musical creativity. In addition, awareness of this possibility introduced new ideas of music analysis, especially for electroacoustic music. For the first time in musicological history, there existed a way to link process descriptions of music—descriptions of the structure of compositional processes—to static "analytical" descriptions of musical objects, thus to define models that I have referred to as *process models of music* (Laske 1977, xiii).

When surveying different contemporary approaches to music for their appropriateness to studying electroacoustic music, it makes sense to distinguish four essentially different choices: the (1) semiotic, (2) formal-language, (3) machine, and (4) procedural, approach (Laske 1999). Of these four approaches, three entirely rely on notation, while the fourth one lends itself to analyzing electroacoustic music as a product of compositional processes. In the *semiotic* approach (Nattiez 1975), music is approached as extending between three "poles," the neutral, aisthetic, and poietic. While the *neutral* pole embodies syntax, the *aisthetic* pole represents the auditory and "esthetic" features of a music. In contrast to these, the *poietic* pole regards the making of the music. Despite paying lip service to understanding the poiesis by which music comes into existence, semiotic composition theories have generally imprisoned themselves within an outdated theory of artistic creativity. The resulting theories have not been "scientific" in the sense of hypothetical formulations that can be tested empirically, in real time.

By contrast to semiotic approaches to music analysis, *formal language* approaches to music are literally bound to musical symbol systems without regard to their auditory referents. As a result, such approaches must assert that audition is determined by abstract structures functioning as epistemological enablers of music listening. While this is an interesting hypothesis, as shown by the work of Kassler (1963), Lerdahl and Jackendoff (1983), and a diversity of programmed analyses (e.g., Balaban 1992; Baroni et al. 1984), the hypothesis misses out on capturing the *sonic* dimension, which is paramount in electroacoustic music. Only when expanding this approach to modal (rather than traditional) logic, as Kunst (1976, 1978, 1997) has done, does it become possible to take sonic features of the music into account, without reducing them to a by product of music-syntactic relationships. Similarly, when time-object structures are taken as the unit of analysis, as in Bel (1992), there is a possibility to make sonological statements about music.

While akin to the formal language approach to music analysis, the *machine* (artificial intelligence) approach is not bound to ideas of grammar as much as to the idea of *patterns* in the most general sense (including patterns of neural firing in the human brain). Depending on the underlying conception of what a musical listener is, machine approaches are based on programs searching for patterns of a syntactic, semantic, or sonological nature. For instance, Ebcioglu (1988) searched Bach chorales for syntactic (melic and harmonic) patterns for purposes of harmonization, while Smoliar (1993) went further in the direction of searching for structures embodying mental processes, using "process theory." None of the approaches discussed so far seem to be a propitious choice for analyzing electroacoustic music.

As this chapter demonstrates, a *procedural* approach to music analysis consists of capturing the mental processes giving rise to a music, rather than simply analyzing the end results of such processes, objectified as static objects (Laske 1977, 1984). In the procedural approach, music structures are present as *agents propelling compositional processes forward.* In no way does such an approach imply a reduction of musical structures to mental processes (Laske 1977, xiii–xvi). Rather, what is topical is the relationship between musical structure and the processes that generate them.

The first attempt in the direction of a strictly procedural analysis of music was made by G. M. Koenig when giving a description of his electroacoustic composition *Essay* (1958) in terms of the procedures used to put the work in place. Koenig indicated the order but not the interactive process in which the mental processes underlying the composition had been activated, thus giving a static description of dynamic processes. The major reason for the lack of descriptions of a temporal and interactive nature in *Essay* was a technical one: in 1958, electronic music composition had not yet been transferred from hardware to software synthesis. With the advent of computer programs, the tracking of compositional processes, both of a syntactic and sonological nature, has become a possibility. (This possibility is, by the way, not restricted to music but is to be found in all of the arts that use computers for realizing aesthetic artifacts.)

In light of the ultimate goal of a process model that elucidates the linkage between the musical structures composing a work and the mental processes that produce them, one would hope that procedural analyses of music would further expand in their scope and sophistication. Forty years is a short time for such an ambitious goal to be realized. This holds true especially for research in an intellectual culture bound to a level of mental growth at which a majority of individuals cognitively thrive on static "features" of music and static "traits" of personality (Laske 1999b). Clearly, a fixation on traits and features hinders music theory from achieving a level of sophistication that is commensurable with its dynamic subject matter, *music*.

To conclude, I briefly consider the changes wrought by the Internet as a result of the computer revolution in music and their link with the score editing and manipulation procedures. These changes regard the *transformation of the listener into an arranger*, not only of electroacoustic music. Listeners of the future will have at their disposal digital controls that invite them to "edit" a "base score" represented by the piece of music that they have chosen. As a result, what musicology considers "works" will be transformed into *working models* for listeners' preferential ways of making music.

In the 1940s, Arnold Schoenberg suggested that listeners could be educated by engaging them in compositional "exercises." Practicing elementary composition would enhance their understanding of what the composer had done to produce the piece of music to which they were choosing to listen. Schoenberg thereby suggested a way of making music education more democratic, by letting musical laypersons participate in the craft of composition to the extent of their own abilities. Changes in music technology and distribution during the twentieth century have led to a situation in which Schoenberg's idea seems more prophetic than ever. The Internet is about to redefine not only the methods by which music is distributed in society as an item of consumption ("entertainment") but also the mental set or attitude with which listeners will increasingly approach what society markets as *music*.

I suggest that the so-called revolution caused by the Internet in the musical domain is essentially an extension of the revolution that composers working with computers have brought about during the second half of the twentieth century. Composers' work has focused on refining the digital means of editing and manipulating acoustic material as well as alpha-numerical score texts. It seems obvious that many of the techniques that have been forged, especially in the domain of electroacoustic composition, will be transferred to interactive listening via the Internet. Score editing and score manipulation will become a hallmark of interactive listening.

I conclude from this state of affairs that the musicological notion of *musical score* is increasingly being transformed into that of a *working model for possible musics*. This notion of a musical score is already commonplace among present-day composers working in a computer-assisted manner, especially in electroacoustic music. This turn of events points to a new raison d'être for developing novel notions of music education *based on digital score manipulation*. In addition, the new musical soundscape defined by the Internet sheds new light on composition theory as a theory of the mental processes by which what society regards as *music* is actually produced. In the new musical culture created by the Internet, composition theory is becoming a foundation of interactive listening.

APPENDIX: Subscores from *Terpsichore*

Score Example 1 Section 1.1, in the format of SCED

event number	note	(hz)	sound object	volume	duration	time -delay
1	f3	(174)	obj7	160	1/10	0/1[8]
2	b3	(246)	obj7	200	3/5	0/1
3	a3=	(233)	obj7	200	3/5	0/1
4	d3	(146)	obj7	200	3/5	0/1
5	b3	(246)	obj7	200	3/5	0/1
6	a3=	(233)	obj7	200	3/5	1/10
7	f3	(174)	obj7	160	1/10	1/10
8	f3	(174)	obj4	160	1/10	1/10
9	f3	(174)	obj4	160	1/10	1/10
10	f3	(174)	obj4	160	1/10	1/10
11	f3	(174)	obj4	160	1/10	1/10
12	d3	(146)	obj6	200	3/5	1/10
13	f2	(87)	obj6	160	1/10	0/1
14	f2=	(92)	obj6	160	1/10	0/1
15	a2=	(116)	obj6	180	1/10	0/1
16	d2	(73)	obj6	160	1/10	0/1
17	d2=	(77)	obj6	160	1/10	1/10
18	f2	(87)	obj6	160	1/10	1/10
19	f2	(87)	obj6	160	1/10	1/10
20	f2	(87)	obj6	160	1/10	1/10
21	e2	(82)	obj6	160	1/10	0/1
22	c2	(65)	obj6	160	1/10	1/10
23	f2	(87)	obj6	240	1/10	0/1
24	f2=	(92)	obj6	240	1/10	0/1
25	a2=	(116)	obj6	240	1/20	1/10
26	a3=	(233)	obj6	200	3/5	0/1
27	d3	(146)	obj6	200	3/5	0/1
28	b3	(246)	obj6	200	3/8	0/1
29	f2	(87)	obj6	240	3/8	0/1
30	f2=	(92)	obj6	240	3/8	3/8
31	f3	(174)	obj8	240	3/8	0/1
32	f3=	(184)	obj8	240	3/5	9/40
33	a3=	(233)	obj8	200	3/8	3/20
34	a3=	(233)	obj8	240	3/8	0/1
35	g3=	(207)	obj8	240	3/8	0/1
36	g3=	(207)	obj8	240	3/8	3/8
37	c3	(138)	obj8	200	3/8	3/40
38	d3	(146)	obj8	200	3/5	0/1
39	b3	(246)	obj8	200	3/5	0/1
40	a3=	(233)	obj8	200	3/5	3/10

Length of this segment is 2.833 seconds (real time).[9]

Score Example 2 Section 2.1, in the format of SCED

event number	note	(hz)	sound object	volume	duration	time -delay
1	c5	(522)	obj8	160	4/5	0/1[8]
2	e5	(659)	obj8	160	4/5	0/1
3	b4	(493)	obj3	160	4/5	1/5
4	e3	(164)	obj3	40	5/3	1/20
5	f5=	(739)	obj3	4	3/2	1/3
6	f5=	(739)	obj3	4	3/2	13/60
7	c5=	(553)	obj3	160	4/5	4/5
8	d5	(587)	obj3	160	4/5	0/1
9	f4=	(369)	obj3	160	4/5	0/1
10	g4	(391)	obj3	160	4/5	0/1
11	g6=	(1661)	obj3	160	4/5	3/20
12	c5=	(553)	obj3	4	3/1	7/60
13	e3	(164)	obj7	140	5/3	13/60
14	c5=	(553)	obj7	4	3/1	19/60
15	c7	(2094)	obj7	220	4/5	0/1
16	e7	(2637)	obj7	220	4/5	4/5
17	f7	(2794)	obj8	220	4/3	0/1
18	a6	(1760)	obj7	220	4/3	1/3
19	a3	(219)	obj7	140	5/3	1/1
20	a6=	(1864)	obj7	220	4/3	0/1
21	b6	(1975)	obj7	220	4/3	13/60
22	d5	(586)	obj7	4	3/1	0/1
23	f5=	(739)	obj7	4	3/1	1/3
24	d5	(586)	obj7	4	3/1	0/1
25	f5=	(739)	obj6	4	3/1	7/60
26	f3=	(184)	obj6	140	1/2	1/2
27	f4=	(369)	obj6	140	1/2	1/6
28	e7b	(2490)	obj6	100	4/3	0/1
29	d7b	(2218)	obj6	100	4/3	0/1
30	d7	(2350)	obj2	100	4/3	1/3
31	f4=	(369)	obj6	140	1/2	1/2
32	f4=	(369)	obj6	140	1/2	1/2
33	f4=	(369)	obj6	40	5/6	0/1
34	g4	(391)	obj6	40	5/6	0/1
35	f6=	(1480)	obj2	100	4/3	11/20
36	c5=	(553)	obj2	180	3/1	0/1
37	d5	(586)	obj2	180	3/1	17/60
38	f2=	(92)	obj2	40	5/6	1/20
39	c5=	(553)	obj2	180	3/1	0/1
40	d5	(586)	obj2	180	3/1	9/20

Length of this segment is 6.4 seconds (real time).[10]

Score Example 3 Section 3, in the format of SCED

event number	note	(hz)	sound object	volume	duration	time -delay
1	g4=	(415)	obj6	180	3/4	0/1[9]
2	f5	(698)	obj2	100	4/3	0/1
3	e3	(164)	obj2	120	3/2	0/1
4	f3	(174)	obj8	120	3/2	0/1
5	g3=	(207)	obj5	120	3/4	0/1
6	c4	(261)	obj5	180	3/4	0/1
7	e4	(329)	obj5	180	3/4	1/6
8	f4	(349)	obj5	180	6/5	0/1
9	c4=	(277)	obj1	140	6/5	5/4
10	f4	(349)	obj5	140	1/1	0/1
11	b4	(493)	obj9	120	1/1	1/12
12	d4=	(311)	obj9	120	1/1	0/1
13	f3=	(184)	obj2	100	1/1	0/1
14	g3	(195)	obj7	100	1/1	1/15
15	a3=	(233)	obj6	100	1/1	0/1
16	d4=	(311)	obj6	120	1/1	11/60
17	b4	(493)	obj6	120	1/1	29/60
18	a5	(880)	obj6	140	1/1	0/1
19	a4=	(466)	obj6	200	2/3	4/15
20	a4	(440)	obj6	200	2/3	0/1
21	c3=	(138)	obj4	100	3/4	19/60
22	c3	(130)	obj4	100	3/4	0/1
23	f4	(349)	obj4	140	6/5	1/6
24	c4=	(277)	obj3	140	6/5	0/1
25	f4	(349)	obj4	180	3/4	0/1
26	e4	(329)	obj4	180	3/4	0/1
27	c4	(261)	obj4	180	3/4	1/60
28	g4=	(415)	obj4	180	3/4	1/4
29	c5	(523)	obj7	220	5/4	1/4
30	d3=	(155)	obj5	200	1/4	0/1
31	d3=	(155)	obj8	160	8/5	0/1
32	d3	(146)	obj8	160	8/5	31/60
33	b3	(246)	obj2	160	8/5	0/1
34	d4=	(311)	obj2	120	3/4	0/1
35	d4	(293)	obj2	120	3/4	0/1
36	a4=	(466)	obj9	120	3/4	17/30
37	a4	(440)	obj9	120	3/4	3/40
38	g4	(391)	obj1	240	8/5	0/1
39	f4=	(369)	obj1	240	8/5	0/1
40	d4	(293)	obj1	240	8/5	2/5

Length of this segment is 9.968 seconds (real time).[11]

NOTES

1. This chapter is dedicated to Bill Buxton.
2. The three movements of *Trilogy* are entitled *Echo des Himmels*, *Erwachen* and *Ganymed.*
3. In the 1970 version of Project 1, only the number of events, the tempi, and a set of time delays needed to be specified by the user. The 1979 version of the program, which is connected to VOSIM oscillators and works in an interactive mode, permits further input specifications. (The 1970 version was used for this composition.)
4. The Project 1 score contains two additional data streams (columns), namely, for tempo and for an additional optional parameter called "sequence." The latter can be used to control the succession of tones in a chord (thus replacing register) or the succession of instruments in a class of instruments.
5. In-time structures, such as motivic structures, can also be used, but they do not fully exploit SCED's capability in that they are not valid beyond the scope of an individual composition.
6. See Laske.
7. Both segregation and mixture are, of course, relative concepts, since their experience is dependent on speed. Disjunct hocketlike structures can be heard as "streams," thus as continuous, while overlapping structures, due to high speed, may appear as being almost metric, with time-delay and duration seeming to be nearly identical.
8. The scale for volume in SCED extends from approximately 10 to 240 (fff). Durations are indicated as fractions, such as 1/10. In the time-delay column, the expression "0/1" indicates that the respective tone is part of a chord.
9. The relationship of duration and time-delay stated for this section is an average one; in the ninth line from the bottom on this page one finds duration: time-delay = 3/8:9/40, which constitutes a relationship of Dur = Delay x 12.7.
10. Extreme duration/time-delay relationships occurring in this fragment are Dur = Delay * 33.3 (5/3:1/20), Dur = Delay * 25.6 (3/1:7/60), and Dur = Delay * 16 (5/6:1/20).
11. Extreme duration/time-delay relationships occurring in this fragment are Dur = Delay * 45 (3/4:1/60), Dur = Delay * 15 (1/1:1/15), and Dur = Delay *12 (1/1:1/12).

REFERENCES

Balaban, M. (1992). "Music Structures: Interleaving the Temporal and Hierarchical Aspects in Music." In *Understanding Music with A.I.*, edited by M. Balaban, K. Ebcioglu, and O. Laske. Cambridge: MIT Press, 110–139.

Baroni, M., Brunetti, R., Callegari, L. and Jacoboni, C. (1984). "A Grammar for Melody." In *Music Grammars and Computer Analysis*, edited by M. Baroni and C. Jacoboni. Florence, Italy: Leo S. Olschki, 201–218.

Basseches, M. (1984). *Dialectical Thinking and Adult Development*. Norwood, NJ: Ablex.

Bel, B. (1992). "Symbolic and Sonic Representations of Time-Object Structures." In *Understanding Music with A.I.*, edited by M. Balaban, K. Ebcioglu, and O. Laske. Cambridge: MIT Press, 64–109.

Buxton, W., Sniderman, R., Reeves, W., Patel, S. and Baecher (1985). *The Evolution of the SSSP Score-Editing Tools*. In Roads, C., and Strawn, J., eds. *Foundations of Computer Music*. Cambridge: MIT Press.

Buxton, W. (1980). *Music Software User's Manual*. Toronto, Ontario, Canada: Computer Systems Research Group, University of Toronto.

Buxton, W. (1985). "The Evolution of the SSSP Score-Editing Tools." In *Foundations of Computer Music*, edited by C. Roads and J. Strawn, Cambridge: MIT Press, 1985, 376–402. (reprinted from *Computer Music Journal* 3, no. 4, [1979]:14–25).

Ebcioglu, K. (1988). "An Expert System for Harmonizing Four-part Chorales." *Computer Music Journal* 12, no. 3: 43–51.

Kassler, M. (1963). "Sketch of the Use of Formalized Languages for the Assertion of Music." *Perspectives of New Music* 1, no. 2.

Kegan, R. (1982). *The Evolving Self.* Cambridge: Harvard University Press.

Koenig, G. M. (1970). "Project One." *Electronic Music Reports*, no. 2, Institute of Sonology, Utrecht, The Netherlands.

Koenig, G. M. (1993a). "Aesthetische Integration mit einem Computer komponierter Partituren" [1983]. In *Aesthetische Praxis*, edited by W. Frobenius, S. Fricke, S. Konrad, and R. Pfau, vol. 3. Saarbruecken, Germany: Pfau Verlag, 263–271.

Koenig, G. M. (1993b). "Begegnung mit Komponierprogrammen" [1991]. In *Aesthetische Praxis*, edited by W. Frobenius, S. Fricke, S. Konrad, and R. Pfau, vol. 3. Saarbruecken, Germany: Pfau Verlag, 358–364.

Koenig, G. M. (1993c). "Computerverwendung in Kompositionsprozessen" [1969]. In *Aesthetische Praxis*, edited by W. Frobenius, S. Fricke, S. Konrad, and R. Pfau, vol. 3. Saarbruecken, Germany: Pfau Verlag, 27–38.

Koenig, G. M. (1993d). "Die Entwicklung von Computerprogrammen fuer musikalisch-creative Zwecke" [1970]. In *Aesthetische Praxis*, edited by W. Frobenius, S. Fricke, S. Konrad, and R.Pfau, vol. 3. Saarbruecken, Germany: Pfau Verlag, 57–76.

Koenig, G. M. (1993e). "Erfahrungen mit programmierter Musik" [1975]. In W. Frobenius, S. Fricke, S. Konrad, and R. Pfau, eds., *Aesthetische Praxis* (vol. 3, 169–191). Saarbruecken, Germany: Pfau Verlag.

Koenig, G. M. (1993f). "Programmierte Musik. Eigene Erfahrungen und Arbeiten" [1975]. In *Aesthetische Praxis*, edited by W. Frobenius, S. Fricke, S. Konrad, and R. Pfau, vol. 3. Saarbruecken, Germany: Pfau Verlag, 182–190.

Koenig, G. M. (1993g). "Programmierte Musik" [1985]. In *Aesthetische Praxis*, edited by W. Frobenius, S. Fricke, S. Konrad, and R. Pfau, vol. 3. Saarbruecken, Germany: Pfau Verlag, 272–276.

Koenig, G. M. (1993h). "Project 1: Modell und Wirklichkeit" [1979]. In *Aesthetische Praxis*, edited by W. Frobenius, S. Fricke, S. Konrad, and R. Pfau, vol. 3. Saarbruecken, Germany: Pfau Verlag, 223–230.

Koenig, G. M. (1993i). "Umgang mit Project 1. Erfahrungen mit Computermusik" [1990]. In *Aesthetische Praxis*, edited by W. Frobenius, S. Fricke, S. Konrad, and R. Pfau vol. 3. Saarbruecken, Germany: Pfau Verlag, 332–340.

Koenig, G. M. (1993j). "Zu *Essay*" [1958]. In *Aesthetische Praxis*, edited by W. Frobenius, S. Fricke, S. Konrad, and R. Pfau, vol. 1. Saarbruecken, Germany: Pfau Verlag, 5, 111, 115, 116, 297.

Koenig, G. M. (1999). "Protocol." *Sonological Reports*, no. 4. Institute of Sonology, Utrecht, The Netherlands [1975]. German edition: Protokoll. In *Aesthetische Praxis*, edited by W. Frobenius, S. Fricke, S. Konrad, and R. Pfau, vol. 4. Saarbruecken, Germany: Pfau Verlag, 1–172.

Kunst, J. (1976). "Making Sense in Music I: The Use of Mathematical Logic." *Interface* 5: 3–68.

Kunst, J. (1978). "Making Sense in Music." Ghent, Belgium: *Communication and Cognition.*

Kunst, J. (1997). "Muziek & wetenschap." *Dutch Journal for Musicology*, 6, no. 1: 27–40.

Laske, O. (1977). *Music, Memory, and Thought: Explorations in Cognitive Musicology.* Ann Arbor, MI: UMI Research Press.

Laske, O. (1980a). "Composition as Self-Reference." In *Allos,* edited by K. Gaburo. La Jolla, CA: Lingua Press, 419–431.

Laske, O. (1980b). "Preliminary High-Level Specification of a Computerized Music System." Unpublished manuscript.

Laske, O. (1980c). "Requirements Analysis and Specification for a Computerized Music System." Unpublished manuscript.

Laske, O. (1983). "Composition Theory: A New Discipline for Artificial Intelligence and Computer Music." In *Music and Mind,* vol. 2 (collected papers 1971–1981). San Francisco: International Computer Music Association, 157–196.

Laske, O. (1983). "Models of Musical Planning." Unpublished manuscript, Boston: NEWCOMP.

Laske, O. (1984). "Keith: A Rule System for Making Music-Analytical Discoveries." In *Musical Grammars and Computer Analysis,* edited by M. Baroni and L. Callegari, Florence, Italy: Leo S. Olschki, 165–200.

Laske, O. (1988a). "Composition Theory as a Basis for Second-Generation Computer Music Systems." Unpublished manuscript.

Laske, O. (1988b). "On Cognitive Musicology: Holding, Eliciting, and Modeling Musical Knowledge: Observations about PROJECT ONE." Unpublished manuscript.

Laske, O. (1989a). "Composition Theory in Koenig's PROJECT ONE and PROJECT TWO." In *The Music Machine,* edited by C. Roads. Cambridge: MIT Press, 119–130.

Laske, O. (1989b). "Composition Theory: An Enrichment of Music Theory." *Interface* 18, nos. 1–2: 45–59, (*Kompositionstheorie: Ein neues Konzept musikalischerTheorie*, unpublished manuscript.)

Laske, O. (1989c). "Die Integration neuer Technologien in die Denkweisen der Musiker." Unpublished manuscript.

Laske, O. (1990). "The Computer as the Artist's Alter Ego." *Leonardo* 23, no. 1: 53–66.

Laske, O. (1991a). "Composition musicale et assistance informatique: Un exemple de composition interpretative." In *Actes, seminaire creativite en art,* edited by B. Bel and B. Vecchione. Universite Aix-en-Provence: Centre de Recherche en Sciences de la Musique.

Laske, O. (1991b). "Toward an Epistemology of Composition." *Interface* 20, nos. 3–4: 235–269.

Laske, O. (1992). "The OBSERVER Tradition of Knowledge Acquisition." In *Understanding Music with A.I.*, edited by M. Balaban, K. Ebcioglu, and O. Laske. Cambridge: MIT Press, 259–289.

Laske, O. (1999a). "Furies and Voices: Composition-Theoretical Observations." In *Otto Laske: Navigating New Musical Horizons*, edited by J. Tabor. Westport, CT: Greenwood Press, 151–167.

Laske, O. (1999b). "Music Theory: Three Syllabi." Unpublished manuscript.

Laske, O. (1999c). *Transformative Effects of Coaching on Executives' Professional Agendas*. Ann Arbor, MI: Bell and Howell.

Laske, O. (2000). "Mindware and Software: Can They Meet? Observations on A.I. and the Arts." *Proceedings*, IAKTA/LIST Intern. Workshop on Knowledge Technology in the Arts, Osaka, Japan, 1993, 1–18.

Lerdahl, F. and Jackendoff, R. (1983). *A Generative Theory of Tonal Music*. Cambridge: MIT Press.

Nattiez, J. J. (1975). *Fondements d'une Semiologie de la Musique*. Paris: Union generale d'editions.

Smoliar, S. (1993). “Process Structuring and Music Theory.” In *Machine Models of Music*, edited by S. M. Schwanauer and D. A. Levitt. Cambridge: MIT Press, 189–212.

Wilber, K. (2000). *Integral Psychology*. Boston: Shambhala.

Xenakis, I. (1957). “In Search of a Stochastic Music.” *Gravesaner Blaetter*, no. 11/12.

Xenakis, I. (1971). *Formalized Music*. Bloomington: Indiana University Press.

7

A Story of Emergence and Dissolution: Analytical Sketches of Jean-Claude Risset's *Contours*

Agostino Di Scipio

INTRODUCTION

The late 1970s and early 1980s represent an important period in the history of electroacoustic music. During these years the work of many musicians and researchers underwent the final transition from analog to digital production technologies. Moreover, the artistic relevance of the musical results achieved with these new means was to show that a free and aesthetically fruitful relationship with this new technology could be established. Near the end of this period, Jean-Claude Risset (b. Le Puy, 1938) composed *Contours* (1982), a tape piece created entirely by computer sound synthesis. This piece was realized with a version of Music V running the Telemecanique T1600 processor, an old computer system available at the National Center for Research (CNRS) Laboratory of Mechanics and Acoustics (LMA) in Marseilles from 1974 to 1983.

Although not among Risset's better-known pieces, *Contours* does feature many elements characteristic of other music that he composed during these years, including a particular focus to processes of sonic transformation and development (e.g., *Inharmonique* for soprano and tape, 1977; *Profils* for ensemble and tape, 1981; and *Passage* for flute and tape, 1982). When first listening to *Contours*, it reveals a music of highly expressive and technical concentration, with a deep sense of intimacy, perhaps due to its nature as music for "solo tape"—an intimate monologue, rather than a dialogue, as would be more customary to the "instrument and tape" medium. (*Dialogue* incidentally, is also the title of a Risset work for ensemble and tape from 1975.) The synthetic sonic matter of *Contours* is shaped and forged into a tapestry of a rather impressionistic kind. However, it would be a mistake to regard *Contours* solely as a decorative arras. Rather, it exhibits very specific attention to the structural details of sound composition. In the conclusion of this chapter, I maintain that a constructivistic attitude hides behind what at first may sound like a pure interplay of fascinating sound colors. In later years (certainly after *Sud* [for tape, 1985]) Risset explored altogether different compositional approaches, no less interesting but perhaps (to my ears) less representative of his central contribution to the birth and development of computer music. A piece written over a decade later, *Invisible* (soprano and tape, 1995), in some ways marks a return to the compositional style of *Contours*, although the two pieces were realized with very different techniques.

In 1987, I undertook an analysis of *Contours* (Di Scipio 1988) in which I scrutinized many of the Music V code listings that Risset had written for this piece as well as his graphical sketches and written annotations. For me, these materials were recorded traces of the compositional process. I examined them in order to outline the sound design criteria adopted by the composer and to elucidate the connection between these materials and the overall structure of the piece. It was my first thorough analytical attempt of this kind. At the time, I was aware of a similar effort by Denis Lorrain (1980), whose insight into the tape part of *Inharmonique* provided a helpful starting point. In retrospect, the efforts that I undertook in my analysis of *Contours* were particularly significant in that they allowed me to define a suitable methodological approach for the analysis of electroacoustic music repertoires (for both computer and noncomputer technologies). More recently, I have resumed this analytical approach in an attempt to better ground it on a more stable music-theoretical base (Di Scipio 1995a, 1995b, 1997a, 1997b).

In this chapter, I survey the 1987 analysis of *Contours* and discuss a number of issues of which I was relatively aware at that time. I avoid direct reference to the details of Music V computer code. Readers interested in the technical details of the Music V code are referred to the listings supplied in the Appendix. Those not familiar with Music V should be able to read the chapter without difficulty, as it never directly refers to computer code particulars. Nevertheless, I want to stress that Music V code is not at all difficult to read provided one has a basic knowledge of the standard electroacoustic equipment of classic analog studios (i.e., oscillators, filters, function generators). The composer Iannis Xenakis, who has pursued a completely opposite approach to computer music, has enthusiastically described Music V as "a magnificent manipulatory language . . . the realization of the dream of the electronic music composer in the fifties" (Xenakis 1992, 246). Indeed, in the late 1950s Max Mathews initiated a research agenda that eventually led him and others, including Risset, to the creation of Music V (Mathews 1969; Risset 1969). Subsequently, Mathews' work with Music V became a reference for many sound synthesis software developers.[1]

ANALYSIS PATH (THE METHOD)

In the preface to his "Introductory Catalog of Computer Synthesized Sounds," Risset described Music V data as "the computer 'score'" for sound (Risset 1969, 5). Recently, he has used definitions such as "writing for sound" and "a truly exhaustive score for sound."[2] Clearly, these definitions are of the utmost relevance, particularly when the analysis concerns the actual compositional work pursued with Music V. The computer "sound score" allows an observer to analyze compositionally significant traits of a sound structure. Consequently, this provides the possibility to characterize the musical idea captured in the sounds that it generates. In Risset's own words, studying the Music V listings, "one is able to analyze the scores, not only the notes, but also the sounds."[3] This notion is crucial in that it reflects the basic assumption that, for Risset, composing is not only a matter of assembling sounds but also of creating the sounds themselves. Timbre then becomes an outcome of composing, a dimension central to the making of the piece, the very object of the composer's concern. In this sense, timbre can be considered as a kind of "musical form," something that is carefully shaped and made available for aesthetic judgment and appreciation. In computer music a composer's actions pertaining to timbre are partially captured in the computer. As a result, the computer score constitutes a form of notation that, although very different from standard musical notation, provides documentation for observation and study by those other than the composer.

The full score of *Contours* is a collection of all the text files that Risset created for the computer representation of both the sound synthesis algorithms ("instruments" in Music V parlance) and the list of sound events ("note list"). Each text file contains a sequence of computer instructions consistent to a particular method of sound synthesis, as well as note list parameters, usually arranged in temporal order. I refer to this "instrument + note list" as a "programming sequence." During the creation of the piece, Risset submitted each sequence to the Music V compiler and generated a separate sound structure. The finished piece resulted from the mixing of many such structures. The mixing of these structures was achieved with analog, not digital, means. This was done because not only was digital mixing slow and impractical with a computer such as the T1600, but the more interactive approach of a conventional mixing board allowed Risset to better control the balance of several sound layers. Despite some drawbacks (background noise and synchronization problems), in the end this procedure saved computer time and, significantly, allowed for a more detailed digital representation of the separate sound structures (with many overlapping sound layers, very few bits would be left for each separate sound layer).[4]

The total duration of *Contours* is 9:43. At the time of my analysis, I obtained an analog tape recording that Risset had sent for some concerts in Italy. After starting the analytical work, a compact disc release appeared a few months afterward (Neuma Records 450-71, 1988). The CD is identical to the analog copy (however, it does present some digital artifacts not present in the analog tape). In this chapter, I refer to the compact disc release for the indicated timings.

The programming sequences that I examined in detail include those that the composer in his sketches labeled as TRIT12 (PASSAGE EN TRITON PAR DNL), FANF04, FANF10, PHAS08 (PHASING HARMONIQUE), PHAS6, PHAS7, PHAS17, PLF405, LB1010, LB1022, BELLS1. In the following survey, I focus on those sequences that can be considered most representative of the piece. My discussion examines the synthesis techniques adopted, including classic methods such as waveshaping (also called "nonlinear distortion," NLD) frequency modulation (FM), and various additive synthesis methods.[5] Although such techniques operate in different ways, they do share a common objective: they all allow the composer to consider sound in terms of dynamic spectra. This is by no means irrelevant, for these methods require decisions that concern the frequency and amplitude of each frequency component or group of components. For Risset, these technical possibilities are firmly grounded in the frequency-domain representation of sound signals (i.e., the Fourier paradigm), where the minimal controlling units are the oscillations of a given (but possibly changing) frequency and amplitude.

This annotation may seem obvious; however, this is not so, for there are other ways of musically thinking about sound, and different modes of sound signal representation lend themselves to different technical possibilities. For example, consider the computer-synthesized works by Herbert Brün (post-1966) or Iannis Xenakis (post-1977) (Di Scipio 1997a, 1997b). In these works the sound signal representation is of an entirely different kind. The parameters themselves, by which the sound material is made available to musical development, are far from similar. In general, any particular sound signal representation framework reflects a particular compositional and cognitive-aesthetic attitude toward sound and music and reflects practical solutions to problems that arise from specific historical-technological circumstances. Moreover, deciding on a particular representation framework has significant consequences to the process of composing and, in the end, determines the boundaries within which a composer can mold and articulate his or her materials. Conversely, different aesthetic views and styles of musical expression lead composers to adopt different sound representations, thus circumscribing the range of applicable tools, as well as the achievable musical results.

In the analysis of *Contours*, my basic task was one of decomposing, rebuilding, and ultimately interpreting the sound structuring strategies adopted by Risset within the particular sound representation domain. In considering such strategies, we can characterize the "compositional task-environment" (Laske 1991) and possibly understand how electroacoustic composition transforms *sound* into *music*. With this particular work, there lies a chance to grasp in what sense *Contours* is the audible rendition of "a story of emergence and dissolution," as Risset himself has described this work.[6]

COMPOSITIONAL SPACE (THE OVERALL DESIGN STRATEGY)

To clarify the discussion, it is useful to begin with an illustration of some general principles that emerged from the analysis and to describe how they were operated upon during the actual compositional process (I describe six analysis samples). This description is possible only post hoc, as the analytical work by necessity followed a more exploratory and largely bottom-up approach.

All relevant decisions in the composition of *Contours* can be delimited by two design criteria:

1. *spectral shaping*: in determining the frequency and amplitude sets of the spectrum, allowing for a wide range of results extending from perfect harmonicity to various kinds of controlled inharmonicity;
2. *time patterning*: in determining the start time and duration values of individual partials of the spectrum, allowing for a wide range of results extending from perfect synchrony, to the complete scattering of partials.

These two criteria define the *space for possible actions* that Risset had defined for himself in the making of the piece. I should stress that this is a space for possible actions *in sound*. The audible results of the actions pursued within that space can be framed by the following double opposition:

1. *harmonic* versus *inharmonic* spectrum;
2. *fusion* versus *fission* of partials.

(Here *fusion* indicates that different partials are summed and coalesce into a single, perceptually homogeneous sound image, while *fission*, in contrast, signifies that partials yield a more composite sonority.) The two terms of this double opposition are comparable to two orthogonal linear dimensions. Their coupling creates a bidimensional space where all events designed by the composer can be appropriately mapped. Ultimately, this is a *perceptual* space, as, in fact, the design criteria involved are themselves very relevant to the psychoacoustic relationship between sound as a physical phenomenon and sound as a perceptual phenomenon. In short, we have a musical space in two perceptual dimensions, as shown in the simple schema of Example 7.1.

The title of this piece refers to studies in musical psychoacoustics in which the notion of "contour" is meant to abstract the pattern of pitch directions (the "up" and "down" patterns) in a sequence of tones, disregarding their interval size. These studies have shown that pitch sequences can be heard as similar insofar as they present the same contour. Fusion, the term cited earlier to circumscribe the compositional space, is itself a term with a scientific pedigree, for it was part of the consonance theory put forth by Carl Stumpf over a century ago (1883). It is also especially similar to the notion of *spectral fusion* proposed by Stephen McAdams (1982).

In addition to being a prominent composer, Risset is a well-respected author of numerous contributions in the field of psychoacoustics. He is the coordinator

Example 7.1
Schematic View of the Compositional Space for *Contours*

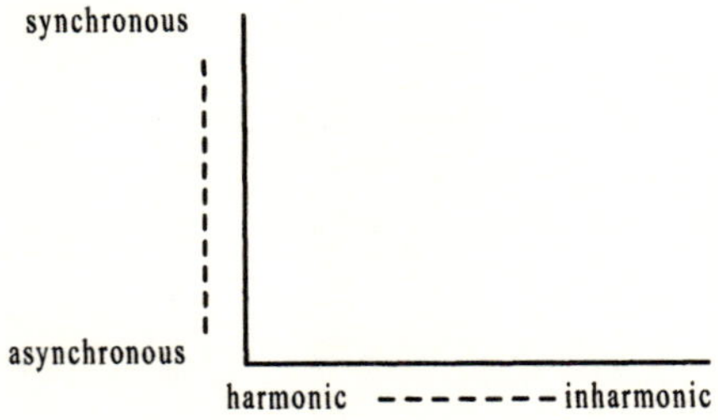

of scientific projects pursued in this field at LMA in Marseilles, France (financed for research, this institute only occasionally hosts composers, apart from Risset). It is important to note that Risset's work often includes a research methodology centered toward the study of perceptual illusions. For example, he has explored pitch paradoxes caused by unusual spectral properties, showing that particular arrangements of partial frequencies can affect and even confuse the pitch perception mechanisms (Risset 1978b, 1986). In a simple and much praised experiment, Risset created spectra that, when doubled in frequency, cause the listener to hear the sound pitch shift a semitone lower rather than an octave higher (Risset 1978a).

Analysis Sample 1

Contours begins with sounds generated from the programming sequence TRIT12 (see the computer score in the Appendix). The synthesis instrument in this sequence is based on the technique of waveshaping—the nonlinear distortion of a signal (usually sinusoidal) by a more complex shaping function (Arfib 1979).[7] This method generates only sounds with a harmonic spectrum (unless the operations are manipulated in ways to produce different results). For TRIT12, Risset uses polynomial functions in order to distort an input sine tone. Frequency values in the note list are extremely low, approximately 32, 46, and 65 Hz, corresponding to C, F♯, and C an octave higher. However, these frequencies are not heard as such but act as purely "nominal" frequencies. Instead, the particular shaping functions adopted cause the output to include, alternatively, the 11th, 16th, or the 22nd harmonics of the input frequency.

As illustrated in Example 7.2, the output sound comprises a narrow band of packed frequencies (ca. 700–740 Hz), roughly corresponding to a much higher F♯. Because the amount of distortion varies with time, as from some control function, this sound is heard as a sustained sound with a very slowly changing spectrum. Given the particular shaping functions, interplay between C and F♯ is present, with the C gradually giving way to the F♯ and vice versa.

Example 7.2
"Nominal" Frequencies and Resultant Sounding Frequencies (shown as pitches) in the Programming Sequence TRIT12

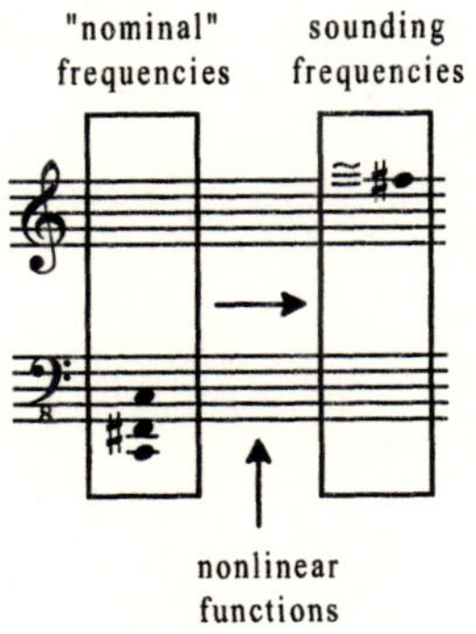

For TRIT12, the following observations apply:

1. The frequency values specified by the composer in the Music V note list do not correspond to the frequencies in the audible result. These values are nominal frequencies and may be thought of as "absent fundamentals." Pitch is unclear, and the output sound is heard as a chord in which the notes of that chord are a complex function of the absent fundamental frequency.
2. The partials of the output sound do not have harmonic frequency relations, yet they were generated as harmonics of absent fundamentals. This results from the mechanism of the waveshaping technique.
3. With respect to the fundamental, the 11th, 16th, and 22nd harmonics generated correspond to intervals of tritone, octave, and tritone.[8] The absent fundamentals themselves (C, F♯, C) are contained within these interval relations.

With TRIT12 Risset obtains a prolonged sound structure of a rather neutral color. The sound color is indirectly achieved through the interplay of specific intervals. If different intervals had been used, the resultant sound color would have produced altogether different results. It is by no accident that this particular sonority is stated at the beginning of the piece. As more material appears, the sound of TRIT12 (and similar sequences) remains in the background as a kind of "pedal," preserving the interplay of C and F♯ to the listener but subliminally transferred to the dimension of timbre.

Analysis Sample 2

The sound synthesis technique of the programming sequence FANF04 (see Appendix) is basic frequency modulation (FM), very similar to the original implementation of this technique developed by Chowning (1973). Although FM lends itself to a large variety of sound results, Risset is here interested in using it for a very specific task: the simulation of trumpet tones. Synthesis parameters are set in order to achieve perfect harmonic spectra (carrier: modulator ratio = 1),[9] yielding sounds that have a clearly recognizable pitch. Because the same envelope function is used for both the amount of modulation (index) and amplitude, Risset keeps the spectrum bandwidth directly proportional to the overall signal amplitude. This allows for the simulation of a particular sound characteristic of brass instruments: the perceived intensity of the sound event is a function not only of the actual amplitude level but also of its "brightness" (spectrum-rich high frequencies) (Risset 1966; Risset and Mathews 1969). The onset time of high-order partials is also important and should be slower than that of the low-order partials. The dynamics of FM systems lends itself particularly well to this effect.

Example 7.3 depicts a transcription of what is produced with FANF04. This musical passage occurs at 0:09. In the programming sequence FANF10, there is a similar passage at 0:50. As shown in Example 7.4, FANF10 is an extension of FANF04. Both are rather straightforward in their overall conception as well as in the actual sound. The simulation of trumpet tones is overt. FANF04 begins with three tritones in sequence at a relative distance of whole-tone and minor-third (C-F#, A#-E, G-C#). The same is observed in the first of five musical phrases generated with FANF10 (D#-A, C#-G, A#-E). In the FANF10, there is a repeat-

Example 7.3
Transcription of Programming Sequence FANF04 (starting at 0:09)

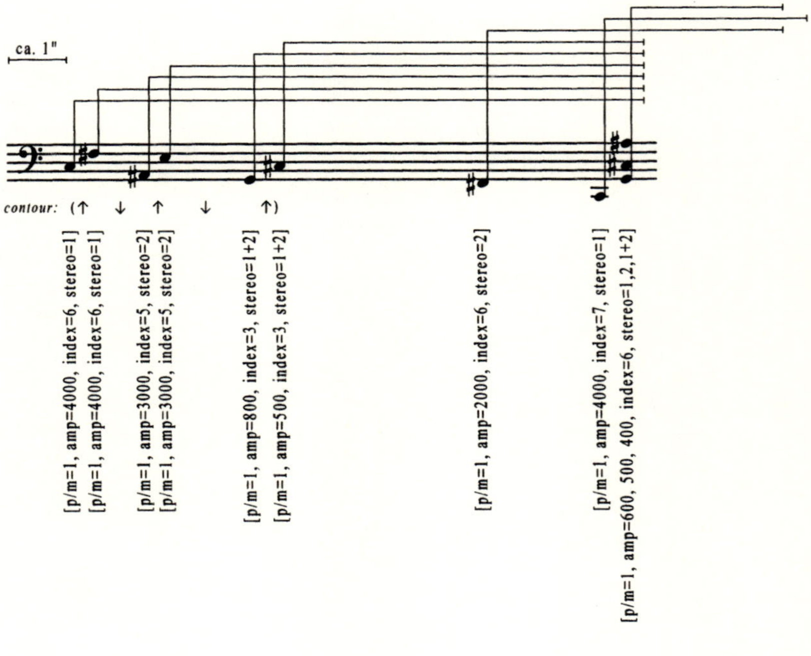

Example 7.4
Transcription of Programming Sequence FANF10 (starting at 0:50)

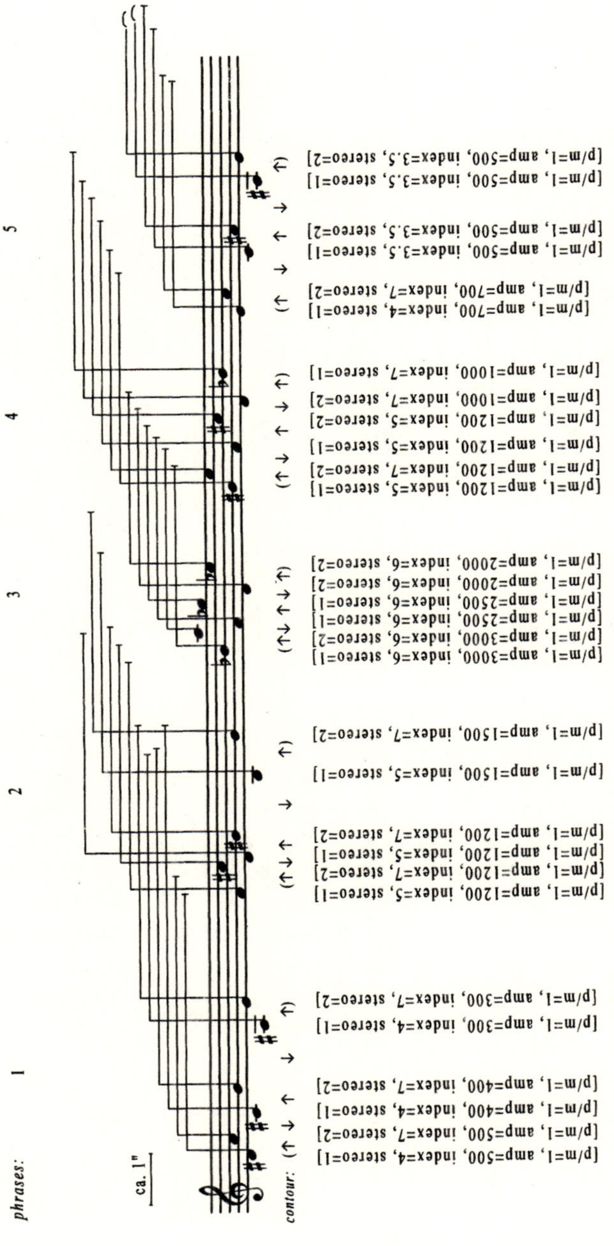

ing pattern of stereo positions: "left / right / left / right" or "left / left / right / right / left / left / right / right" Pitches also yield a repetitive pattern, although the intervals vary considerably. In all five phrases there is an identical contour: "up / down / up / down / up." On a larger scale, the overall pitch organization of FANF10 exhibits an archlike shape in which the climax (third phrase) features the widest intervals of the entire musical passage.

When listening to FANF10, both the local contour (the "up" and "down" patterns in each phrase) and the stereo pattern ("left" and "right") may result in a perceptual rearrangement of the auditory image due to a phenomenon known as *auditory stream segregation* (McAdams and Bregman 1979): the ear tends to group sounds in two distinct, but overlapping, streams (three descending notes), although the sounds are actually presented as a single stream (six notes with a zigzag pitch contour). This phenomenon is usually explained in terms of principles associated with Gestalt psychology, such as "proximity," "similarity," and "common fate" (the notion of "melodic contour" itself implies perceptual mechanisms that reflect gestalt principles).

For FANF04 and FANF10, the following observations apply:

1. All sounds have a harmonic spectrum or at least are perceived as such (slight deviations constitute no exception to the ear; they simply add beats, resulting in slowly moving variations in the amplitude of partials).
2. The frequencies in the note list correspond to the fundamental tones of the perceived sound.
3. Timbre is perfectly homogeneous and is heard as a typical brass-sounding instrument, in particular, the trumpet.

These elements allow the listener to *clearly* recognize a particular melodic contour, although a variety of intervals are actually employed. As shown, the initial phrase features tritones shifted apart by a smaller interval, while the phrases that follow include larger and larger intervals, with the last phrase finally returning to tritones and whole tones. The overall pitch structure resembles a typical archlike shape. At times, auditory stream segregation takes place, and two parallel contours can be heard simultaneously. For example, the third musical phrase of FANF10 can be heard as two overlapping pitch streams, one of descending major-thirds (A#-F#-D) and the other of descending minor-thirds (A-F#-D#).

Analysis Sample 3

Programming sequence PHAS08 consists of five instruments, all of which implement the same sound synthesis technique: the summation of a given number of oscillators. The only difference between these instruments is the total number of oscillators, which ranges from one to eight, and the stereo positioning of the output sound (see Appendix for details).

Audio functions used for each oscillator are calculated as summations of harmonically related sine-wave periods. Risset used three primarily harmonic sets (Example 7.5) that include specific arrangements of partials and extend upward to high-order components (to the 22nd). (Psychoacousticians refer to such spectra, those missing some of the harmonic partials, as "hol(e)y" spectra). Nominal frequency values in the note list are extremely low, very near the lower limit of the audible range, and correspond to the pitches C, F#, and C an octave higher. As neither the nominal fundamentals (the maximum common divisor of the harmonic set) nor the harmonic ratios among partials can be reconstructed by the ear, in some cases, the resulting spectrum may be perceived as inharmonic.

This method, paradoxically, enables the composer to create inharmonic spectra by using table functions (which by necessity can include only harmonically related frequency components). It was introduced in Risset's *Catalog* (1969, 63), where it was used to simulate the sound of struck metallic surfaces. In *Contours*, however, the goal is different. In each instrument, the oscillators are assigned slightly different frequency values, with differences in the order of hundredths of hertz. This causes the components to beat among themselves. In this way, Risset creates prolonged sound textures animated by a kind of internal rhythm (i.e., by the rising and falling amplitude patterns as a result of these beats). Moreover, various note events overlap, and this adds to the complexity of the actual beat pattern. Nominal fundamentals in the note list are the tritone and octave (C, F# and C). The interplay of overlapping events causes the high-order components of independent, but overlapping, (in)harmonic spectra to create a variety of beat combinations, with rhythmic patterns comprising-various tempi (beat rate) and accentuation (phase relationships between partials).

Example 7.5
Harmonic Spectra of Audio Functions Used in Programming Sequence PHAS08

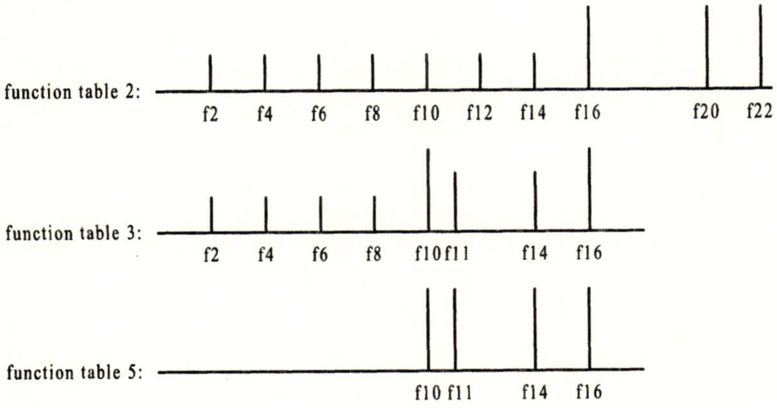

For example, consider the third event in the PHAS08 note list (nominal fundamental: F♯): the lower component (10th harmonic), which has a frequency of 23.1*10 = 231 Hz, beats with one of the components (14th harmonic) in the fourth event (nominal fundamental: C), having a frequency of 16.4*14 = 229.6 Hz. This quasi unison (approximately A♯) will beat at a rate of 231–229.6 = 1.4 Hz. It also overlaps with other beats that have their own distinctive beat rates. After closely examining all the frequency combinations in PHAS08 (the number of overlapping note events multiplied by the amount of components in the audio functions adopted), a common divisor for beat periods was not found. In the output sound, these aperiodic beat patterns are heard as a kind of polyrhythmic texture of (in)harmonic partials.[10]

Example 7.6 illustrates an approximate graphical rendition of PHAS08. As shown, more prominent pitch relationships belong to the whole-tone scale. Pitches C, E, F♯, and A♯ (B♭) are emphasized due to the particular amplitude arrangement of their harmonic components in the audio functions. Stronger harmonics include the 11th and 22nd (tritones to the fundamental), the 16th (octave), the 10th (major-third), and the 14th (second or major-seventh). (For a good example of this strategy, see function table 5 in Example 7.5).

For PHAS08 (and PHAS17, not examined here) the following observations apply:

1. Frequency values in the note list are purely nominal. These values, laced at the lower limit of the audible range, are a means of creating intricate patterns of beats among partials. In the perceived sound texture and dependent upon the relative distance between beating frequencies, the amplitude of components rises and falls at different rates.
2. Spectra are mathematically harmonic; however, due to their extremely low fundamental frequencies, they are perceived as inharmonic by the ear.
3. Pitches emerge more from precisely constructed spectra (harmonic composition of the audio functions) than from the nominal fundamentals of the note list. However, both the emergent pitches and the nominal fundamentals consist of either a tritone or two overlapping tritones shifted by a second.

The fluid timbre of the resulting sound structure of PHAS08 is heard between the second and third minute of the piece. In his annotations, Risset refers to this sonority as a "cascade of harmonics." Example 7.7 presents a sonogram of a short excerpt of the PHAS08 sound output. In this image, the "visual rhythms" replicate the patterns of beats among quasi-identical frequencies. Given the interplay of tritones and octaves, PHAS08 may be considered as a kind of expansion of the sonic image first introduced in TRIT12. Therefore, it assumes a similar musical function, namely, that of a "pedal" (but more intricate than TRIT12) where certain pitches are at the same time hidden and revealed across the time-varying pattern of beats.

Example 7.6
Transcription of PHAS08

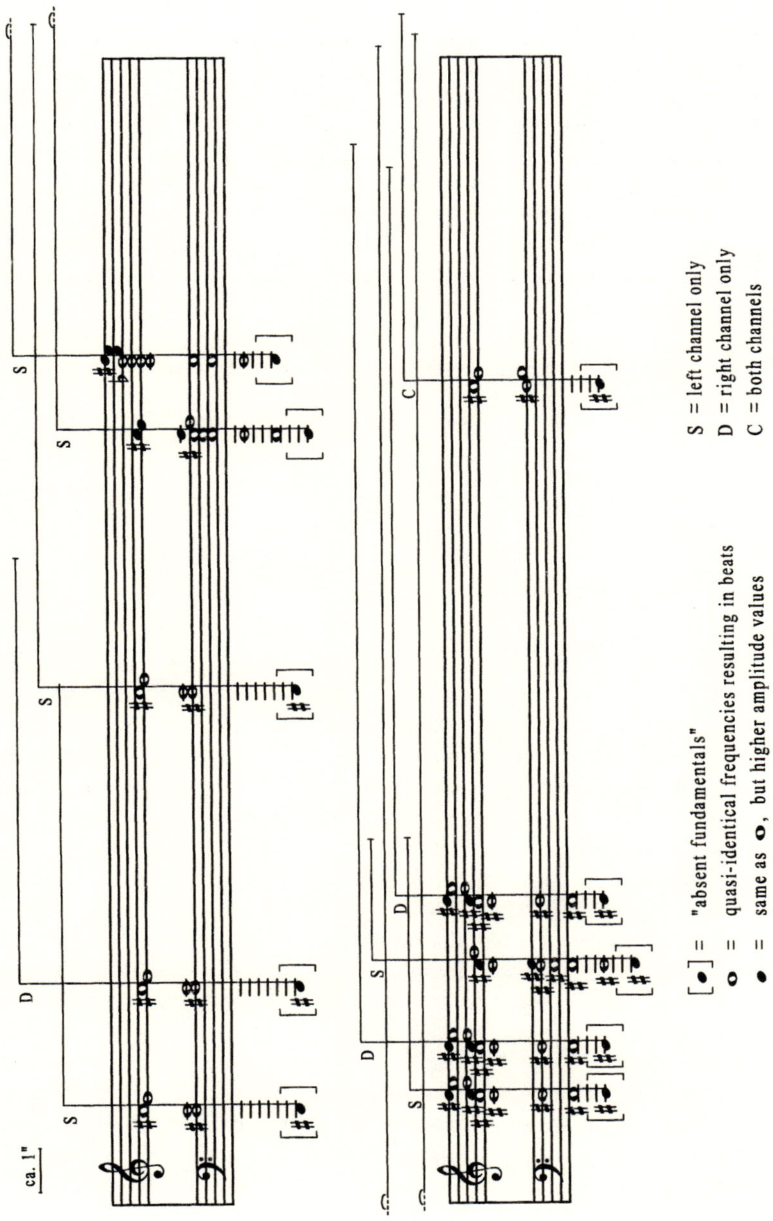

Example 7.7
Sonogram of the Second Structure Generated with Programming Sequence PHAS08 (1:56–2:03)

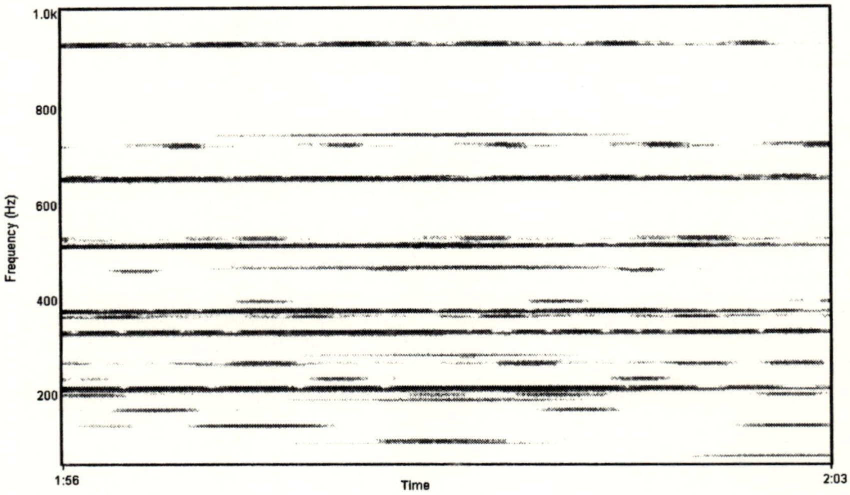

Analysis Sample 4

Music V is considered a "general purpose" sound synthesis program. In principle, it does not "prejudice" the operation of any particular approach of sound synthesis, nor is it biased toward any particular compositional methods for the creation of event lists. Essentially, it is entirely dependent on data supplied by the user. This is generally seen as a much-valued feature of computer music systems, as it makes it possible for the user to freely determine the details of his or her musical construction. However, this "generality" is at the expense of the program's "strength" in terms of interaction (ease of access to information) and of process automation (automation of a specific series of repeated actions or instructions). Therefore, while it is of great value for a large variety of musical tasks, in the pursuit of each task it does demand a fair amount of work from the user. (This "inverse relation of generality and strength" is typical of all problem solving, including computer programs, so it is no surprise that it also applies to computer music applications [Truax 1980].)

Still, it is possible to "steer" Music V toward more specific purposes. I refer to the use of PLF instructions. By means of PLF instructions Music V passes a small set of data to an external program written in Fortran, which then returns a comparatively larger set of data composed according to some well-defined procedure.

Risset's PLF405 programming sequence (see Appendix for details) takes full advantage of this method of creatively "prejudicing" the program. The synthesis algorithm itself represents possibly the most basic of sound synthesis techniques: a sine wave oscillator with an amplitude envelope. However, through the use of PLF instructions Risset links the Music V compiler to external program routines of his own design, transforming a single oscillator into a larger number of oscillators, each with its own parameter values. In other words, a single note event in the Music V note list is transformed into an implicit list comprising many note events. The event parameters (start time, duration, frequency) do not apply as such but simply provide the raw data in order that a larger number of separate events can be calculated.

In short, this is an additive synthesis implementation with automated controls. It should be seen as a very useful tool, not only considering that the amount of input data would otherwise be enormous (particularly if the output sound requires many partials) but also because groups of partials can now be composed according to some built-in compositional rule. This rule, which may be of any kind, is captured in a Fortran program especially created for this purpose. The program, once completed and transferred to the Music V compiler, represents stored knowledge acquired in software, which applies at the level of development internal to the sound.

In the PLF405 sequence, Risset utilizes two PLF instructions, the first invoking a Fortran program subroutine labeled PLF4 and the second invoking subroutine PLF2. An example of the original manuscript for Risset's PLF4 is shown in Example 7.8. (This figure is given not so much to illustrate the code itself but to provide the reader a sample of the documentation used during this analysis.)

In his annotations, Risset notes that PLF4 is used for "harmonic/nonharmonic prolongation, in the desired order and with the desired time lags."[11] The compositional rule that it captures can be explained as follows. Given a base-frequency f_0, calculate a series of partials in which the frequencies are either

$$f_n = f_0 * Pn \qquad \text{or} \qquad f_n = f_0 \,/\, Pn$$

With P integer (as is always the case with the PLF405 sequence) the result will produce a series of either harmonic frequencies (first option)[12] or subharmonic frequencies (second option). The composer freely selects between the two. With the PLF2 program, frequencies are calculated as either

$$f_n = f_0 + Pn \qquad \text{or} \qquad f_n = f_1 * P^{n-1}$$

The first calculation results in a shift of all the harmonics in the series (the final spectrum may not be harmonic), while the second results in frequencies arranged in a geometric series (this is especially utilized in the LB1010 programming sequence, the next analysis sample).

Example 7.8
Risset's Manuscript of His PLF4 Fortran Program

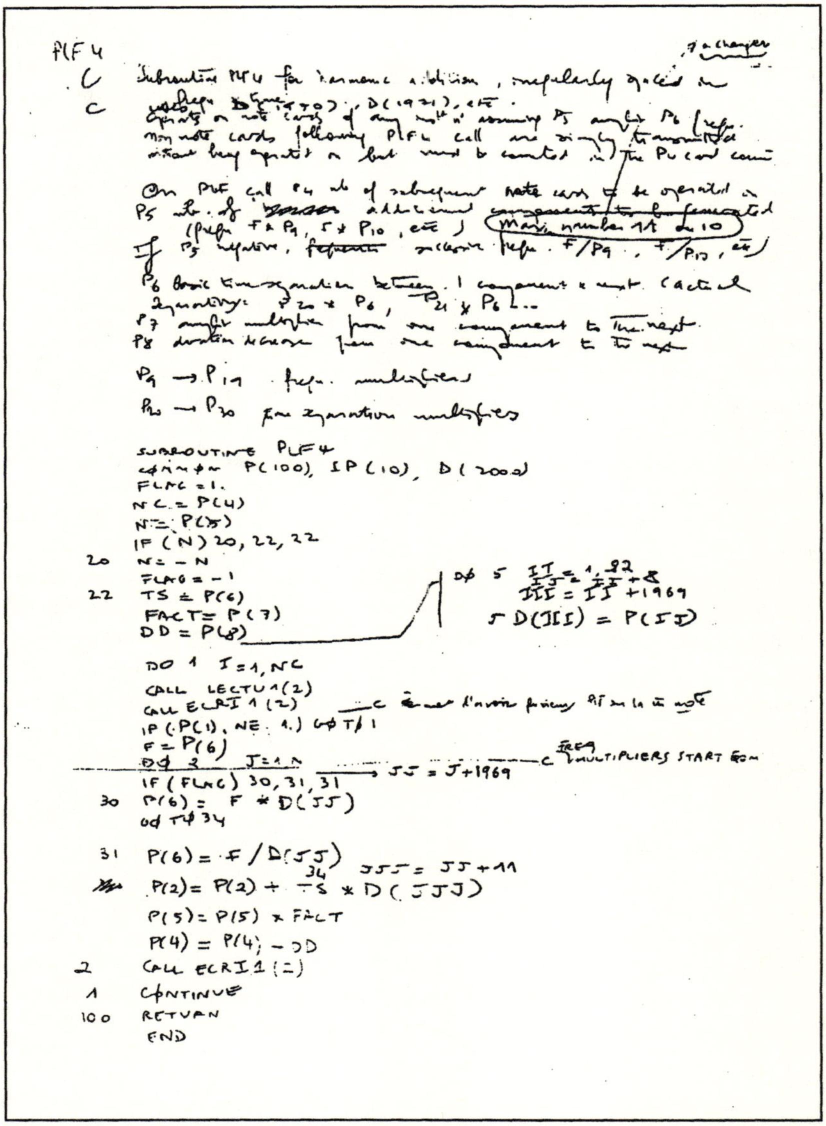

```
      SUBROUTINE PLF4
      COMMON P(100), IP(10), D(2000)
      FLAG = 1.
      NC = P(4)
      N = P(5)
      IF (N) 20, 22, 22
20    N = -N
      FLAG = -1
22    TS = P(6)
      FACT = P(7)
      DD = P(8)
      DO 1 I=1,NC
      CALL LECTU1(2)
      CALL ECRI1(2)
      IF (P(1).NE.1.) GOTO 1
      F = P(6)
      IF (FLAG) 30,31,31
30    P(6) = F * D(JJ)
      GO TO 34
31    P(6) = F / D(JJ)
34    P(2) = P(2) + TS * D(JJJ)
      P(5) = P(5) * FACT
      P(4) = P(4) - DD
2     CALL ECRI1(2)
1     CONTINUE
100   RETURN
      END
```

Note: This routine, called up from within Music V, allows for automated controls of additive synthesis parameters, such as implemented in *Contours* programming sequence PLF405. Several such manuscripts were scrutinized as part of the analysis.

With both programs, Risset supplies himself with yet another crucial possibility: by specifying a base value for the entry-delay time between partials, an entire geometrical series of entry-delays is calculated by the computer. Even negative entry-delay values can be used, which cause the partials to actually resonate prior to the note's start time (the start time can then be considered as a "nominal start time"). Durations can also be controlled by a geometric series. In short, Risset makes it possible to exert extremely subtle controls over the time patterning of the sound components. For example, components can enter at different times before or after the nominal start time, creating an asynchronous effect in which the various components do not coalesce into a fused, homogeneous whole. With little asynchrony, the effect is usually heard as a more complex attack transient of the sound. With larger values, the listener might even distinguish individual partials as if they were separate events. This spectral fission allows the ear to "analytically" listen to the sound (this may also be possible with the patterns of beats in PHAS08, but to a lesser degree). The sound image splits into many individual elements, similar to a chords's splitting into component notes when played "arpeggiato." Risset had already made use of "spectral arpeggi" in one of his earliest computer pieces, *Mutations* (1969).[13]

Example 7.9 illustrates an approximate graphical rendition of the sound structure generated with PLF405. Three events are depicted that have increasing amounts of time scattering of partials. Entry-delay times extend from fractions of a second (first event) to several seconds (third event). As shown, some of the fundamental frequencies are arranged with chords comprising tritones separated by whole tones. This occurs in the first and second event (C-F♯, A♯-E), with the third event consisting of a more extended cluster (in fact, an all-interval chord). Sound structures of this kind are heard at 2:47 (mixed with PHAS08) and are at their most pronounced in the piece at around 4:00.

For PLF405, the following observations apply:

1. Each nominal frequency value of the note list is a base-value used for calculating a larger number of frequency values. It may or may not have any direct effect on the perceived pitches (this depends on the degree of temporal scattering of partials).
2. At times, the auditory image is one of an articulated cluster of smaller sound units, with varying degrees of spectral fission.
3. With occurrences of spectral fission, each component becomes a separate sound event, although its frequency is a harmonic of the nominal fundamental (base-value).

The melodic contour, veiled within the chords of the note list, is projected and multiplied, giving rise to a composite sound object. In his annotations, Risset uses the term "harmonic fog" to refer to sound events of this kind.

Analysis Sample 5

Sequence LB1010 (as well as LB1022 and others not discussed here) focuses on the possibility of creating well-studied series of inharmonic frequencies (see

Example 7.9
Transcription and Graphical Rendition of Programming Sequence PLF405 (starting at 2:47)

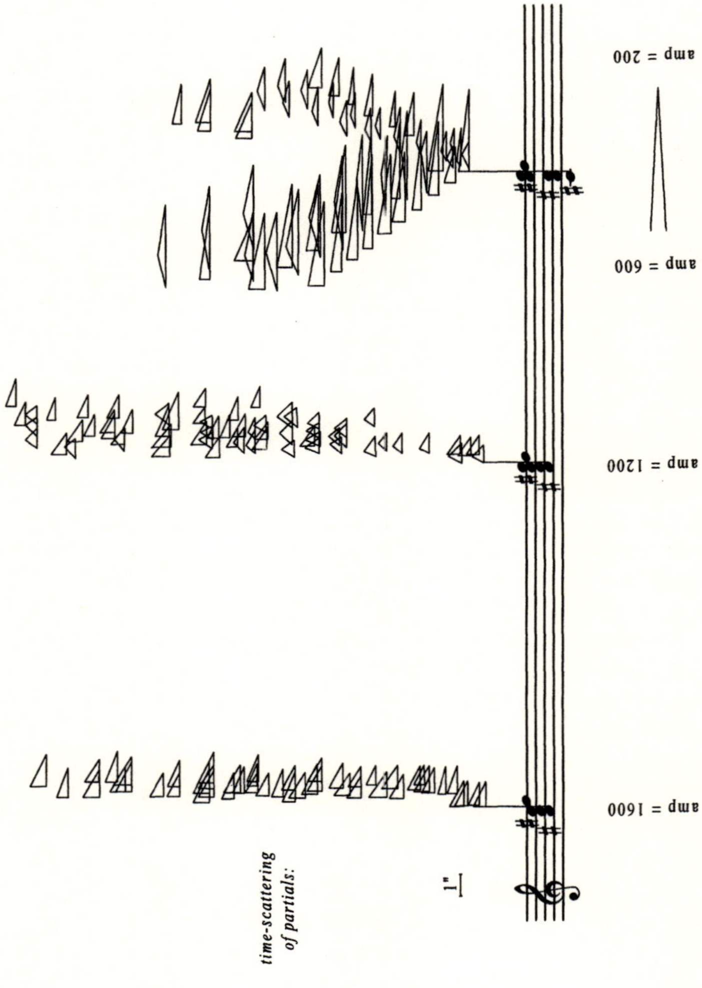

Appendix for details). Again, Risset employs his PLF2 Fortran program, exploiting the rule

$$f_n = f_1 * P^{n-1}$$

with P as a fractional number. As observed, this produces a geometric series of partials that represents a particular distortion of the harmonic setting. Unlike McAdams' "stretched" and "compressed" spectra (McAdams 1982) in a geometric series of partials the distance between low-order partials is "compressed" (smaller than in the full harmonic set), while the distance between high-order partials is "stretched" (larger than the full harmonic set). In particular, LB1010 has either

$P = 1.414$ (i.e., a tritone interval ratio)
or
$P = 1.333$ (i.e., a natural fourth interval ratio)

The resultant group of partials resembles chords of tritones or chords of fourths.

In the LB1010 note list, base-frequencies are arranged in sequences such as A#, E, F#, C or G#, D, F#, C, E, A# (the second covering the complete whole-tone scale). Similar to PLF405, Risset also introduces significant asynchrony among partials. Entry-delay values, whether positive or negative, are in the range of seconds, with the output sound consisting of dispersed partials with inharmonically related frequencies. When listening, it is nearly impossible to recognize what component belongs to what series or what component is derived from what base-frequency. The result is more of a texture with countless microscopic, metallic sounds, which is also due to the fact that partials have the sharpest attack, with onset time as short as one digital sample (this introduces transient artifacts and creates a kind of spectral development within each microscopic event). Here, the notion of timbre grows closer to the properties of a global, compound sound image, with perhaps a dreamlike quality to it. I would say that such a vague, holistic timbral characteristic has much of the usual "feel" or "color" of whole-tone scales. That is, timbre, at this point, is dependent on the intervallic content at least as much as on the spectral composition. Example 7.10 illustrates an approximate and, by necessity, far from complete rendition of the sound structure generated with LB1010 (heard at 6:40). As shown, synthesis parameters were controlled in such a way that an archlike gesture is produced (as was also found in FANF10; see Example 7.4). Two identical chords of nominal frequencies contain the full whole-tone pitch set, with the entry-delay and duration patterns of the second chord being the retrograde (negative geometric ratios) of the first.

Soon after this archlike structure, a similar, but much shorter, gesture occurs at 7:09, constituting an almost perfect copy of the former (see the sonogram in Example 7.11).

Example 7.10
Transcription and Graphical Rendition of Programming Sequence LB1010 (starting at 6:40)

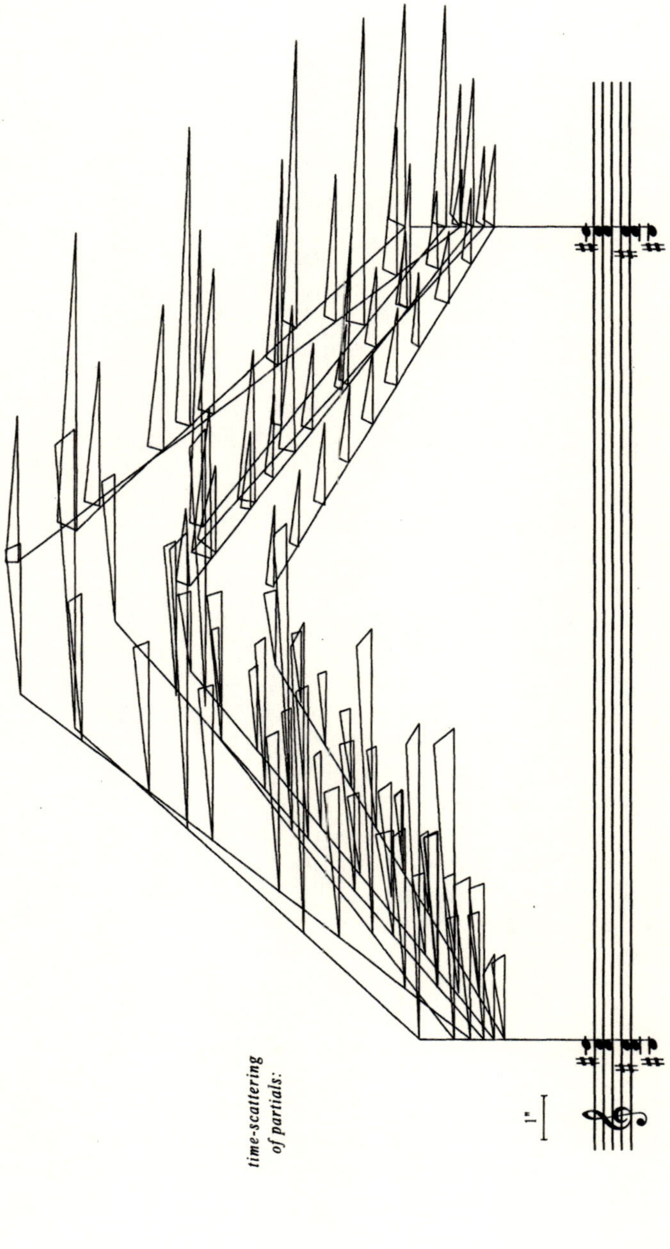

Example 7.11
Sonogram of the Sound Structures heard at 6:40 and 7:09

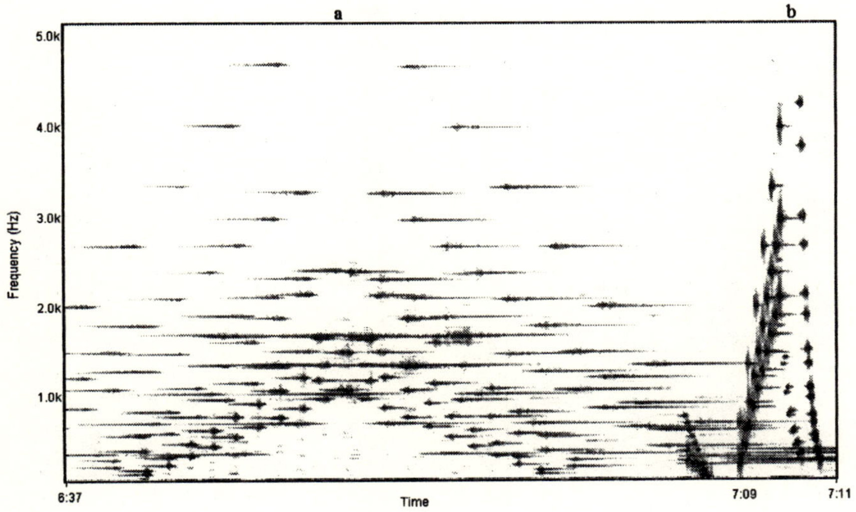

Note: The two events (*a* and *b*) are identical except for the time parameters entry-delay and duration. Due to the different temporal scale, they are perceived as very different gestalten. The first event corresponds to the event graphically depicted in Example 7.10.

For LB1010, the following observations apply:

1. Pitch perception is more statistical and does not match the fundamental frequencies of the note list (similar to PLF405, these are base-values passed to the PLF2 subroutine). Spectra are inharmonic partials arranged in a geometric series.
2. Pitch content is strictly limited to the whole-tone scale. Intervals are projected and dispersed within a rather intricate texture. Nearly unrecognizable, pitches still affect the overall sound color: the particular musical "feel" that we usually experience when listening to whole-tone scales, phrases, or chords here becomes a factor in the formation of timbre.
3. It is difficult (if not impossible) to discern which partial belongs to which inharmonic series (with the exception of when entry-delays are short enough to determine an "arpeggiato chord of partials," a kind of articulated, but not completely dispersed, sonority).

The second observation is emphasized, as it implies that attributes typically belonging to a certain perceptual dimension (pitch) are successfully projected onto a different perceptual dimension (timbre), thus determining an original form of auditory gestalt. This particular pitch collection—one having a role in the history of modern music from the time of Debussy but also having premodern and non-European origins—is transmuted into fluid sound textures, in a dimension

Example 7.12
Sonogram of the Sound Structure from 5:37–5:54

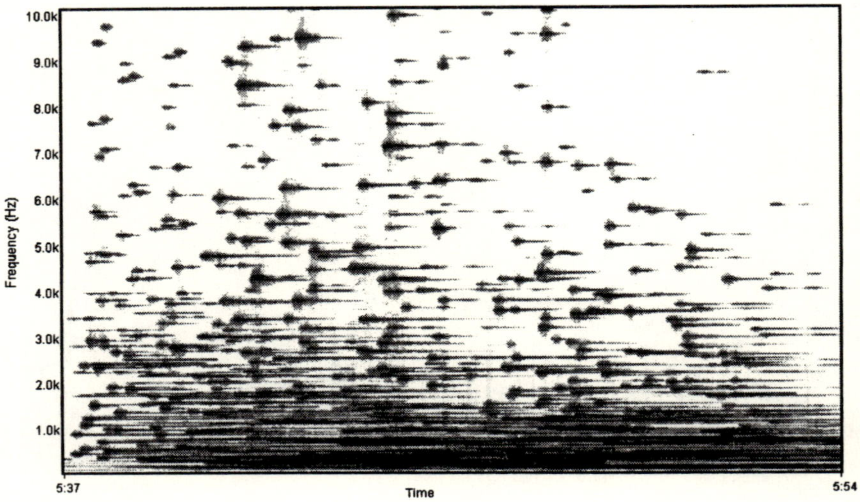

that we usually experience as timbre. Conversely, timbre is clearly (although concealed from the ear) a function of particular intervals and at the same time a function fo the temporal scattering of partials.

In Contours, LB1010 is not the only example of this kind. Another, more dense musical passage is heard from 5:37–5:54 (Example 7.12). However, this example does not bear the archlike shape of LB1010; rather, it more resembles a "cloud of sounds," a statistical distribution of minute, random sonic events. This moment represents the most radical example of spectral fission in the piece, in sharp contrast to the perfect fusion observed in the trumpetlike sounds of FANF04 and FANF10.

Analysis Sample 6

Additive synthesis and external Fortran routines are again utilized in the programming sequence labeled BELLS1 (see Appendix). Compared to the previous two samples, the strategy is this time much simpler. Frequency values are selected from an array of predetermined values (created with the instruction SV1) such that very little or no computation is needed in order to assign each sound partial its own frequency. Through examining these arrays, one observes that Risset worked out two spectral typologies. The first is represented by the values found in array 790 (in Hz): 185, 185.5, 261, 260, 392, 554, and 932. Discarding the repetitions, these values correspond to the pitches F♯, C, G, C♯, A♯. The second typology is represented by the inharmonic frequency ratios found in array 1280: 1, 2.79, 5.44, 8.93, 13.17, 18.13, 23.71, 29.8, and 36.2. These ratios are used for the specific purpose of simulating the sound of chimes (e.g., Pierce 1983, 181). Clearly, the simulation is successful provided the appropriate envelopes and amplitude values are used: partials must have a perfectly synchronous attack, and the high-order partials must decay faster than the low-order partials.

The spectrum of bell-like sounds usually obscures the perception of pitch. In BELLS1 the pseudofundamental frequencies correspond to the critical pitches of C, F♯, A♯, and E, with the bell-like spectrum somehow distorting the perceived interval size between these pitches. Yet in no way does it distort the overall contour shape. It is noteworthy to point out that the pitch contour heard from bell-like sounds at 4:53, created with a programming sequence very similar to BELLS1, is only slightly different (but in essence identical) from the one heard from the trumpetlike sounds at 0:09 (FANF04). Indeed, the nominal fundamentals *are* the same (C-F♯, A♯-E, G-C♯), with the differences resulting from the changed spectral context to pitch perception.

For BELLS1, the following observations apply:

1. Pitch perception is unclear, yet the contour shape is preserved.
2. Within the preserved contour, intervals are recognizable as tritones, whole tones, and minor thirds, although they have actually deviated from their normal size.
3. Each bell-like sound is a whole, consistent unit. There is minimal spectral fission, notwithstanding the inharmonic spectra.[14]

The sounding results of BELLS1 (and similar programming sequences not examined here) are heard as musical phrases of bells, chimes, and other struck metal surfaces. Examples occur at 4:53 and 5:16 in the piece.

MUSICAL PATH (STEPPING THROUGH THE COMPOSITIONAL SPACE)

Throughout the piece spectra made with programming sequences such as LB1010 and BELLS1 are farthest from the harmonic spectrum. However, while LB1010 creates a temporal scattering of partials, BELLS1 provides an example of perfect spectral fusion. A separate, but parallel, contrast is established between sequences FANF04 and PLF405. Here the FANF04 sounds have perfectly fused harmonic spectrum, while the PLF405 sounds, which also have harmonic spectrum, in addition include various degrees of temporal dispersion.

Overall, there exists an orientation within the musical flow that can be explained in terms of the double opposition sketched earlier in this chapter: (1) harmonic versus inharmonic spectrum and (2) synchronous versus asynchronous timing of partials. Example 7.13 illustrates an approximate mapping of the analysis samples within the bidimensional space opened up by these two orthogonal dimensions. (Although the path across the compositional space throughout the piece is not as linear as depicted in Example 7.13, for clarity we can assume it as such.) At the beginning of the piece there is a predominance of harmonicity and

Example 7.13
Programming Sequences Mapped onto the Compositional Space as Illustrated in Example 7.1

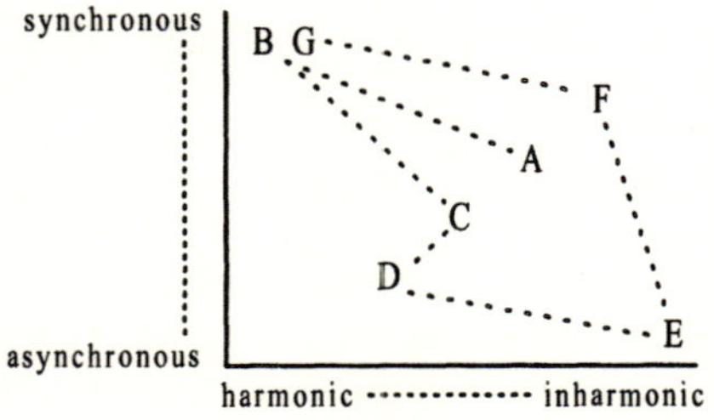

Note: A=TRIT12, B=FANF04 and FANF10, C=PHAS08, D=PLF405, E=LB1010, F=BELLS1, G=simulation of singing voice (not analyzed in this chapter).

synchrony (perfect fusion), as in FANF04 and similar sequences. The piece then proceeds toward a decomposition of the spectrum (spectral fission), first through intricate patterns of beats among pseudo-inharmonic partials (PHAS08), followed by a dispersion of harmonically related partials (PLF405). The most pronounced fission occurs within the temporal scattering of inharmonically related components of LB1010. Later, BELLS1 yields yet another element of spectral fusion, although its sounds contain inharmonic spectrum. The pitch contour first projected in FANF04 is now stated once again; however, it is slightly distorted by the perceptual conflict introduced with the bell-like inharmonic spectrum.

The path concludes with an intriguing coda (composed with programming sequences not examined here). In the midst of a myriad of sounds reminiscent of small chimes and other metallic surfaces (e.g., glockenspiel), there suddenly enters a soprano voice, followed soon after by a baritone. With such sounds, the ear cannot make out the partials, as they are perfectly integrated into a single, compact auditory image. These synthetic voices have an amazingly realistic quality. Risset employed an FM method that had been proposed ad hoc for the computer simulation of the singing voice (Chowning 1980). The late appearance of these "ghost" voices (at 8:19) against a background of fully dispersed partials highlights the contrast between spectral fusion and fission. In a sense, it also emphasizes that the contrast itself is an effect of mere illusion, the phenomenal domain of skilled simulation where things are perceived as real only due to the composer's virtuosic ability in manipulating his material in close contact with the mechanisms of auditory perception.

As mentioned, the many programming sequences that Risset created for *Contours* do not represent separate fragments or sections of the piece. They were mixed together after the computer synthesis, and most were made to overlap in order to produce more dense and articulated musical results. With this said, however, we should notice that the overall musical development of *Contours* is, indeed, in discrete steps. In each instance where the relationship of pitch to timbre is worked out with a different sound design strategy, something similar to a new episode is introduced, possibly cross-faded with the preceding one. This is not to say that the listener can detect a clear-cut segmentation in the musical flow. The musical form preserves a sense of continuity, but perhaps in a way resembling turning over leaves when reading a book or, in a similar way, skimming through the pages of a catalog. We are presented with a number of musical pages that illustrate different ways to work out the subject matter at hand—the changing relationship of pitch to timbre based on a restricted pitch set. This notion suggests that there is a kind of "didactic" infrastructure to this music (remember Risset's 1969 "Introductory Catalog"). Possibly, this is concerned with the scientific concerns that lay at the core of Risset's compositional experience. Indeed, the notion of a catalog-like framework can remind us of an ancient tradition developed at the interface between science and art from the Middle Ages through the Renaissance. In those times, authors of scholarly treatises preferred less to illustrate a theory of their discipline than to collect a list of significant example phenomena. Consider, as an example, Villard de Honnecourt's *Album* (thirteenth century). This album is a collection of notable examples illustrating how one could engineer portraits and buildings. Villard did not propose a verbal description of successful methods to be used in painting or architecture but offered the reader thirty-three separate sheets demonstrating various geometrical proportions and shapes of objects, animals, and human faces (Villard's fundamental concern with the geometry of natural organisms is reminiscent of D'Arcy Thompson *On Growth and Form* [1961]). The *Album* provided visual cues as to practical ways to start and work out designs (Example 7.14). Jean-Claude Risset's writings (as well as his lectures) are often in a similar spirit, as they do not bear on his aesthetics or artistic intentions but simply propose interesting things to do and listen for, together with the basic know-how for making them audible. In this perspective, his music provides empirical evidence for his efforts toward an understanding of auditory perception. This may explain the catalog-like or episodic development of *Contours* (and other pieces as well).

At this point, it is not difficult to establish some loose connection between this particular way of casting musical matter and one of the most ancient forms of knowledge, or at least one of the most ancient means to record and represent knowledge: for the early (pre-Socratic) Greeks, as well as for the Sumerians, Babylonians, and Assyrians, knowledge "was made of many pieces of information obtained in different ways from different sources" and finally gathered together to the benefit of many (Feyerabend 1987, 98). Knowledge was a matter of recording as many observed facts as possible to what is relevant to the senses. Later, someone might eventually propose some explanation or *theory* (i.e., some way for "looking through" observed facts and understanding their truth). As a knowledge-level experience captured in sound and recorded in concrete traces (like computer program listings), a piece such as *Contours* ultimately offers a list of audible facts that the composer considers very relevant and artistically fruitful to illustrate for the benefit of our understanding of human perception.

Example 7.14
One of the Thirty-three Sheets from Villard de Honnecourt's Album (thirteenth century)

CONCLUSION (CONSTRUCTIVISTIC IMPRESSIONISM)

This analysis has shown that in *Contours* Risset establishes a very close relationship between pitch and timbre. Overall, the piece develops through a number of changes in how this relationship is implemented and perceived by the listener. In Risset's words, the goal was to create "a suggestive yet illusory world, free of material constraints, by playing directly, so to speak, upon perceptual mechanisms, thus . . . guiding perception toward one mode or another (e.g., synthetic vs. analytic)" (Risset 1985, 18).

The composer focuses his own as well as the listener's attention on a rather restricted pitch collection. He utilizes a variety of intervals, but central to the musical development of the work are intervals of the whole-tone scale. At times, the auditory image is kept rather simple, as to allow pitches to be clearly recognizable. At these points, the listener can reasonably well follow the organization *between* sounds, the pitch profile emerging clearly to the ear (synthetic mode of perception). At other times however, pitch is not so easily discerned and remains a purely nominal value in the computer score. What is revealed to the ear is the organization *in* the sound, the inner structure of a composite, textural sonority (analytic mode of perception).

As mentioned, Risset projects the gestalt properties of the pitch contour into the realm of timbre. Ultimately, this represents a possible, albeit subjective, answer to the question put forth by Arnold Schoenberg in the final lines of his *Harmonielehre* (1922): "[W]ho can ever pretend to have a theory for the compositional laws of timbre?" Clearly, Risset does not pretend to have any generalizable theory of the kind, and yet his work overtly suggests that a musically meaningful structuration of timbre can profitably lean on perceptual and cognitive criteria involved in the structuring of pitch relationships. This surely defines a music-theoretical position of primary relevance in much electroacoustic and computer music. Yet, as a particular position among many, it may be (and has been) put into question. For our purposes, however, the important point is less to discuss this position than to put it into evidence based on analytically observed facts.

I want to also stress that Risset manages the transformations within the relationship of pitch to timbre by means of various sound synthesis methods. These methods, invariably, are strictly functional to the compositional concept and are never taken as independent or neutral technical options. To investigate them is an attempt to observe how their implementation brings forth the music that we experience as listeners.

Finally, the composer's notion that *Contours* is "a story of emergence and dissolution" becomes less enigmatic. Risset refers to different degrees of clarity in the perception of the particular pitch contour representing the basic kernel of the piece. The opposition of "emerging and dissolving" and the notion that the opposition is itself subjected to development (implemented in various manners) represent a musical idea born by working the tools of the compositional process themselves (i.e., it concerns the very means by which the composer creates the sounds and their organization). In this sense, this idea functions as an *operative metaphor*—a metaphor concerning not only *what* to do (the final musical results) but also *how* to do it (the compositional process). Of course, it also provides an effective guideline for listening.

Viewing *Contours* only as a pure arras of elegant sonorities would be misleading. It is true that there is a significant legacy to an impressionistic style, as represented by both the whole-tone scale and the naturalistic, but dreamlike, sonorities. It is also true that the concept of an "illusory world" and of virtual sound sources compares very well with a musical aesthetic in which reality is perceived as if in a dream. Central to this conception is also the notion of "simulation," which pervades Risset's sound world and reappears repeatedly in the analysis samples. However, this latter notion already marks an interesting departure from an impressionistic style. Hughes Dufourt has observed (in a 1998 paper presentation at Goethe Institut in Rome, unpublished) that "simulation" was a relevant keyword concept for cyberneticians in the 1950s and 1960s (likewise, "information" and "feedback"), having nontrivial implications of epistemological nature. Risset's work is rooted in that particular aspect of the cybernetician mind-set. Simulation tasks make it available to sense the experience of logical-mathematical knowledge and findings pursued in more abstract scientific search. Thus, they are a crucial element in the agenda of an "experimental epistemology" (which Edgar Morin terms the knowledge of knowledge—how can you know that you know?). Indeed, the analysis of *Contours* shows that the great care taken by Risset in shaping the internal structure of sound and its perceivable connection to the overall musical development testifies to a rather constructivistic attitude.

Though hidden behind a curtain of crystalline and evocative sound textures, Risset's focus on the structural element is somehow very present to the listener. The manner in which he molds the changing relationship of pitch to timbre, within and throughout the sonic matter, has little of a mere contemplative attitude. The final artifact of a very particular approach of composing, *Contours* preserves traces of a unique interplay, which may be better described—in more philosophical terms—as an interplay between the primacy of perception (senses, body) and the primacy of reason (intellect, mind).

APPENDIX (examples of some of the Music V listings used in *Contours*)

Analysis Sample 1: TRIT12

P2=start time
P3=instrument number
P4=duration in secs.
P5=amplitude (absolute 16-bit value)
P6=frequency in Hz
P7=envelope function number
P8=index function number
P9=polynomial function number
P10=tremolo frequency (cycles per duration)

Orchestra:

```
SV3 0 1 255 1 .05 0 -12.75 ;

INS 0 1 ;
SET P7 ; IOS P5 P20 B3 F1 P30 ;
SET P8 ; IOS V1 P20 B4 F2 P29 ;
IOS V3 P10 B6 F8 P27 ;
MLT B4 B6 B6 ;
AD2 V6 B5 B6 ; AD2 B4 B6 B4 ;
IOS B4 P6 B4 F3 P23 ;
AD2 V1 B4 B4 ;
SET P9 ; FON B3 B4 B5 F4 V2 ;
STR B5 V4 B1 ; END ;          - channel 1 -

INS 0 2 ;
SET P7 ; IOS P5 P20 B3 F1 P30 ;
SET P8 ; IOS V1 P20 B4 F2 P29 ;
IOS V3 P10 B6 F8 P27 ;
MLT B4 B6 B6 ;
AD2 B6 V5 B6 ; AD2 B4 B6 B4 ;
IOS B4 P6 B4 F3 P23 ;
AD2 V1 B4 B4 ;
SET P9 ; FON B3 B4 B5 F4 V2 ;
STR V4 B5 V1 ; END ;          - channel 2 -
```

Score:

```
GEN 0 1 1 0 1 0 5 1 10 1 340 .7 330 1 430 0 511 ;
GEN 0 1 2 0 0 .95 170 1 340 1 511 ;
GEN 0 2 3 1 1 ;
GEN 0 84 0 0 0 0 0 0 0 0 0 0 01 1 ;
GEN 0 1 5 0 0 0 5 1 80 .7 140 1 430 0 511 ;
GEN 0 1 6 1 0 1 170 .97 340 .9 400 0 511 ;
GEN 0 8 7 0 0 0 0 0 0 0 0 0 0 0 0 0 0 0 0 1 1 ;
GEN 0 2 8 .3 .7 .24 .1 .033 0 .6 .25 .37 .14 .071 6 ;
NOT 0 1 10 2000 65.4 1 2 4 6 ;
NOT 2 2 14.14 4000 65.45 1 2 4 8 ;
NOT 9.5 1 15.5 4000 46.25 5 6 7 9 ;
GEN 15 8 4 0 0 0 0 0 0 0 0 0 0 0 0 0 0 0 0 0 0 0 0 0 0 1 1 ;
NOT 17.3 2 14 3000 32.7 1 6 4 10 ;
SEC 32 ;
```

Analysis Sample 2: FANF04

P2= start time
P3= duration
P4= amplitude
P5= carrier frequency
P6= modulating frequency
P7= modulation index
P8= envelope function number

Orchestra:

```
SV3 0 1 0 1 ;

INS 0 2 ;
SET P9 ; IOS V2 P10 B3 F4 P20 ;
MLT B3 P8 B4 ; OSC B4 P7 B4 F1 P29 ;
AD2 P6 B4 B4 ;
MLT B3 P5 B5 ;
IOS B5 B4 B3 F1 P28 ;
STR B3 V1 B1 ; END ;          - channel 1 -
INS 0 4 ; ............ same as above .........
STR V1 B3 B1 ; END ;          - channel 2 -

INS 0 6 ; ............ same as above .........
STR B3 B3 B1 ; END ;          - channels 1 and 2 -
```

Score:

```
GEN 0 2 1 1 1 ;
GEN 0 1 4 0 0 1 4 .4 7 .6 15 .1 30 .2 250 .03 480 0 511 ;
GEN 0 1 5 0 0 1 6 .6 11 .7 30 .35 250 .5 340 .2 480 0 511 ;
GEN 0 1 6 0 0 1 10 .6 16 .8 35 .3 250 .5 340 .2 480 0 511 ;

NOT 0 2 9.7 4000 130.8 130.8 6 4 ;
NOT .25 2 9.45 4000 185 185 6 4 ;
NOT 1.16 4 8.5 3000 116.5 116.5 5 4 ;
NOT 1.5 4 8.2 3000 164.8 164.8 5 4 ;
NOT 3 6 6.7 800 98 98 3 5 ;
NOT 3.5 6 6.2 500 138.6 138.6 3 5 ;
NOT 7 4 5.5 2000 92.5 92.6 6 6 ;
NOT 9 2 4 4000 65.4 65.5 7 6 ;
NOT 9.5 2 3 600 98 98 3 5 ;
NOT 9.51 4 3 500 138.6 138.5 3 5 ;
NOT 9.495 6 3 400 233 233 3 5 ;
SEC 14 ;
```

Analysis Sample 3: PLF405

for the PLF4 program:

P2= start time for the PLF computation in MUSIC V's PassIII
P3= label number of the program
P4= amount of explicit NOTes to transform with the PLF (NOTes subjected to transformations are those next to the PLF instruction in the note list)
P5= amount of implicit notes to generate for each explicit NOTe in the note list
P6= entry-delay between implicit notes
P7= amplitude ratio between implicit notes
P8= subtrahend from the duration of note f_{n+1}
P9...P19= ratios of each implicit note frequency f_{n+1} to the frequency value in P6 of the explicit NOTe
P20...P30= multiplier of P6 (entry-delay) for each implicit note f_{n+1}
NB - In the PLF4 program, if P5 > 0 then the partials (implicit notes) are calculated as $f_n = f_0 * nP9$, with f_0 = P6 of the explicit NOTe and n <= P5 of the PLF; viceversa, if P5 < 0, then the partials are calculated as $f_n = f_0 / nP9$, where f_0 = P6 of the explicit NOTe and n <= absolute value of the PLF's P5.

for the PLF2 program:
P2= start time for the PLF computation in Music V's PassIII
P3= label number of the program
P4= amount of explicit NOTes to transform with the PLF (NOTes subjected to transformations are those next to the PLF instruction in the note list)
P5= amount of implicit notes to generate for each explicit NOTe in the note list
P6= entry-delay between implicit notes
P7= amplitude ratio between implicit notes
P8= subtrahend from the duration of note f_{n+1}

P9= addend or multiplier of the PLF's P5.
NB - In PLF2, if P5 < 0 partials (implicit notes) are calculated as $f_n = f_0 + nP9$, where f_0 = P6 of the explicit NOTe ed n <= the absolute value of the PLF's P5; if P5 > 0, then partials are calculated as $f_n = f_0 * P9^{n-1}$ where f_0 = P6 of the NOTe and n = PLF's P5. If P9 = 0, partials will follow the harmonic series.

Orchestra:

```
SV3 0 1 0 ;

INS 0 3 ;
IOS P5 P7 B3 F4 P8 ;
IOS B3 P6 B3 F2 P9 ;
STR B3 V1 B1 ; END ;            - channel 1 -

INS 0 4 ;
IOS P5 P7 B3 F4 P8 ;
IOS B3 P6 B3 F2 P9 ;
STR V1 B3 B1 ; END ;            - channel 2 -

INS 0 5 ;
SET P7 ; OSC P5 P8 B3 F5 P10 ;
IOS B3 P6 B3 F1 P11 ;
STR B3 V1 B1 ; END ;            - channel 1 -

INS 0 6 ;
SET P7 ;
OSC P5 P8 B3 F5 P10 ;
IOS B3 P6 B3 F1 P11 ;
STR V1 B3 B1 ; END ;            - channel 2 -
```

Score:

```
GEN 0 2 1 1 1 ;
GEN 0 2 2 0 0 0 0 0 0 1 1 0 1 1 1 12 ;
GEN 0 2 3 0 0 0 0 0 0 0 0 0 1 1 0 0 1 0 1 1 17 ;
GEN 0 4 4 .001 0 1 15 .2 100 .7 180 .1 230 .001 250 .001 255 1 280 .1 320 .6 360 .15 470 .001 511;
GEN 0 4 5 0 0 .01 1 1 2 .001 505 0 511 ;
GEN 0 4 6 0 0 .001 1 .2 60 1 200 .1 400 .001 505 0 511 ;
GEN 0 4 7 0 0 .001 1 1 60 .7 140 .06 400 .001 505 0 511 ;

NOT 0 3 44 2000 32.7 44.5 0 ; NOT 0 4 44 2000 23.126 44.6 233 0 ;
PLF 0 4 3 11 .2 1 .03   2 4 3 6 5 9 7 11 10 13 11 3 2 4 3 5 3 4 5 4 6 3 ;
NOT 6 5 1.2 1600 466.1 5 0 ; NOT 6 5 1.2 1600 659.2 5 0 ;
PLF 0 4 4 11 .22 1 .03 3 5 4 7 6 4 6 6 9 7 11 3 2 4 3 6 3 4 5 4 6 3 ;
NOT 6 6 1.2 1600 523.25 5 0 ; NOT 6 6 1.2 1300 740 5 0 ;
PLF 0 4 2 11 .36 1 0    11 10 13 16 9 15 13 11 8 10 14 3 2 4 3 5 3 4 5 4 6 3 ;
NOT 24 5 1 1600 466.1 6 0 ; NOT 24 6 1 1600 659.26 7 0 ;
PLF 0 4 2 11 .2 1 0    8 5 7 6 4 9 5 6 7 5 11 12 3 2 4 2 6 2 3 5 0 ;
NOT 24.3 6 1 1600 523.25 7 0 ; NOT 24.3 6 .8 1600 784 6 0 ;
PLF 0 2 2 10 -.6 1 0 0 ;
NOT 36 5 4 600 277.1 5 0 ; NOT 36 5 4 600 349.2 6 0 ;
PLF 0 2 2 8 -.75 1 0 0 ;
NOT 36 6 4 400 466.1 5 0 ; NOT 36 6 4 400 740 6 0 ;
PLF 0 2 2 6 -1 1 0 0 ;
NOT 36 5 4 400 659.2 6 0 ; NOT 36 6 4 400 784 5 0 ;
PLF 0 2 2 10 .2 1 0 0 ;
NOT 36 5 2 300 277 5 0 ; NOT 36 5 2 300 350 6 0 ;
PLF 0 2 2 8 .25 1 0 0 ;
NOT 36 6 2 200 466 5 0 ; NOT 36 6 2 200 740 6 0 ;
PLF 0 2 2 6 .332 1 0 0 ;
NOT 36 5 2 200 659 5 0 ; NOT 36.1 6 2 200 783 6 0 ;
SEC 44 ;
```

Analysis Sample 4: LB1010

Orchestra:

```
INS 0 1 ;
IOS P6 P7 B3 F3 P20 ;
IOS B3 P6 B3 F1 P19 ;
STR B3 V1 B1 ; END ;

INS 0 2 ;
IOS P6 P7 B3 F3 P20 ;
IOS B3 P6 B3 F1 P19 ;
STR V1 B3 B1 ; END ;

INS 0 3 ;
IOS P6 P7 B3 F4 P20 ;
IOS B3 P6 B3 F1 P19 ;
STR B3 V1 B1 ; END ;

INS 0 4 ;
IOS P6 P7 B3 F4 P20 ;
IOS B3 P6 B3 F1 P19 ;
STR V1 B3 B1 ; END ;

INS 0 5 ;
IOS P6 P7 B3 F5 P20 ;
IOS B3 P6 B3 F1 P19 ;
STR B3 V1 B1 ; END ;

INS 0 6 ;
IOS P6 P7 B3 F5 P20 ;
IOS B3 P6 B3 F1 P19 ;
STR V1 B3 B1 ; END ;

INS 0 7 ;
IOS P6 P7 B3 F7 P11 ;
IOS B3 P6 B3 F8 P10 ;
STR B3 V1 B1 ; END ;

INS 0 8 ;
IOS P6 P7 B3 F7 P11 ;
IOS B3 P6 B3 F8 P10 ;
STR V1 B3 B1 ; END ;
```

Score:

```
GEN 0 2 1 1 1 ;
GEN 0 4 3 0 1 .001 2 1 90 .001 500 0 512 ;
GEN 0 4 4 0 1 .001 2 1 400 .001 500 0 512 ;
GEN 0 4 5 0 1 0 3 1 6 .02 150 .0003 503 0 512 ;
GEN 0 4 7 .001 0 .2 100 1 300 .1 456 .001 509 0 511 ;
GEN 0 2 8 0 0 0 0 0 0 0 0 0 0 1 1 0 0 1 0 1 16 ;
NOT 0 7 12 2000 23.12 ; NOT 2 8 11 2000 23.5 ;
PLF 0 2 2 8 .1 .9 0 1.414 ;
NOT 7 1 .4 500 233 ; NOT 7.04 1 .4 500 261.6 ;
PLF 0 2 2 7 .1 .9 0 1.414 ;
NOT 7.01 2 .4 500 329.6 ; NOT 7.03 2 .4 500 370 ;
PLF 0 2 2 6 .14 .8 0 1.333 ;
NOT 7.7 3 5 200 233 ; NOT 7.74 3 .5 200 329.6 ;
PLF 0 2 2 6 .14 .8 0 1.333 ;
NOT 7.71 4 .5 500 261.6 ; NOT 7.73 4 .5 500 370 ;
PLF 0 2 2 6 .166 1 0 0 ;
NOT 12 1 .6 400 34.5 ; NOT 12.02 1 .6 400 48.633 ;
PLF 0 2 2 7 .1428 1 0 0 ;
NOT 12.01 2 .6 300 45.857 ; NOT 11.99 2 .6 200 74.714 ;
PLF 0 2 2 8 .125 1 0 0 ;
NOT 12.03 1 .6 200 32.375 ; NOT 11.99 2 .6 200 116.6 ;
PLF 0 2 2 10 1 1 0 ;
NOT 18 3 2 400 207.6 ; NOT 18.01 3 2 400 293.6 ;
```

```
PLF 0 2 2 8 1.25 1 0 ;
NOT 18 4 3.75 400 370 ; NOT 18.01 4 3.76 400 523 ;
PLF 0 2 2 4 2.5 1 0 ;
NOT 18 3 7.5 400 659 ; NOT 18 4 7.51 400 932 ;
PLF 0 2 2 10 -1 1 0 ;
NOT 38 1 3.75 200 ; NOT 38.02 2 2 200 293.6 ;
PLF 0 2 2 8 -1.25 1 0 ;
NOT 38 1 3.75 200 370.7 ; NOT 38.03 1 3.76 200 325.4 ;
PLF 0 2 2 4 -2.5 1 0 ;
NOT 38 1 7.5 200 659.3 ; NOT 38.01 2 7.62 200 932.4 ;
PLF 0 2 2 10 -1.414 .9 0 ;
NOT 43 1 7 200 103.7 ; NOT 43.05 1 7 200 146.9 ;
PLF 0 2 2 8 -1.7676 .8 0 ;
NOT 43.01 2 7 200 185 ; NOT 43.04 2 7 200 262 ;
PLF 0 2 2 6 -2.166 .75 0 ;
NOT 43.02 1 7 200 330 ; NOT 42.99 2 7 200 467 ;
PLF 0 2 2 9 -.16 1 0 0 ;
NOT 46 5 .5 200 103.7 ; NOT 46.04 5 .5 200 146.9 ;
PLF 0 2 2 7 .2 1 0 0 ;
NOT 46.03 6 .4 150 166 ; NOT 46.01 6 .4 160 232 ;
PLF 0 2 2 5 .25 1 0 0 ;
NOT 46.02 5 .3 100 320 ; NOT 45.99 6 .3 100 467 ;
SEC 62 ;
```

Analysis Sample 5: BELLS1

Orchestra:

```
INS 0 1 ; END ;

SV2 0 3 1 ;
INS 0 3 ;
IOS P5 P7 B3 F2 P10 ;
IOS B3 P6 B3 F1 P11 ;
    STR B3 V1 B1 ;
    END ;
```

Score:

```
GEN 0 2 1 1 1 ;
GEN 0 4 2 0 0 .5 1 .3 8 1 11 .05 300 .001 500 0 511 ;
GEN 0 4 3 .001 1 .4 50 .02 200 1 220 .1 280 .4 350 .02 400 .15 450 .001 500 0 511 ;
GEN 0 4 4 0 0 1 1 .05 220 .3 280 .005 460 .001 490 0 511 ;
SV1 0 700 7 723 207.6 3 208.12 12 200 300.625 6 160 326.76 9 200 531.875 5 100 531 5 120 740 3
    100 925 2.3 100 ;
SV1 0 760 7 1019 261.6 3 185 9 150 186.67 160 254.375 12 180 255.2 12 290 393.125 6 200 555
    4.5 200 925 2.6 150 ;
SV1 0 790 7 1019 261.6 3 166 9 150 186.5 8 160 261.6 12 180 260.8 12 190 392 6 200 554.4 4.5
    200 932.3 2.5 150 ;
SV1 0 880 8 603 261 3 261 11 250 392 5 100 659 8 200 740 6.5 75 733.5 6 75 932.3 4.5 100
    1174 3 50 1700.4 2 50 ;
SV1 0 1210 11 1400 226 3 224 20 150 225 18 100 368 13 150 369 11 270 476 6.5 400 680 7 260
    800 5 220 1094 4 200 1200 3 200 1504 2 180 1628 1.5 200 ;
SV1 0 1250 7 450 394 3 240 10 160 277 9.5 120 385 8.8 160 606 5 100 100 7 60 670 6.5 60 312
    450 ;
SV1 0 1280 9 976 349 3 675 24 200 124 16 200 343 22 200 1138 17 200 1634 6 200 2249 3 200
    2911 2 200 3700 1.5 200 4504 .6 200 ;
etc...
```

NOTES

1. There exists a "tradition" of music software systems, within which Music V has long played a paradigmatic role. I think that such a tradition, with its several ramifications, should be a subject for study. The analysis of any kind of musical repertoire cannot abstract from a knowledge of the particular *lutherie*, of that particular music technology. The study of electroacoustic and computer music is no exception. Musicologists interested in these repertoires cannot exempt themselves from an awareness, if not insight, of the particular technologies in play.
2. J. C. Risset, quoted in Veitl (1997, 58). (The author quotes from interviews that she conducted with the composer).
3. Ibid.
4. Risset comments on this in his *Catalog* (Risset 1969, 97).
5. In the present chapter, I cannot describe sound synthesis techniques in detail; comprehensive descriptions are available in numerous computer music textbooks (e.g., Dodge and Jerse 1985, 1998; Roads 1996).
6. Risset quoted in the program notes of the Musica Verticale Concert Series (Rome, 1984) and the booklet of the Neuma compact disc.
7. In 1969, Risset had already implemented a kind of waveshaping to create "clarinet-like sounds by nonlinearity" (Risset 1969, 32).
8. Throughout this chapter, intervals are reduced to their octave-modulus.
9. Slight deviations are also included, causing beats between FM "side-bands." However, to the ear the sound remains that of a full harmonic set of partials, up to the 7th or 8th harmonic.
10. Risset used the same method in *Inharmoniques* (sequences PHASE6 and PHASE7, discussed in Lorrain 1980) and in *Passage* (approximately two minutes after the beginning of the piece). There, however, beating partials were at a fixed relative distance of 0.2 Hz, which caused periodic beat patterns.
11. "prolongation harmonique/sousharmonique dans l'ordre voulu et les intervalles de temps voulu".
12. To get the full harmonic series, one has to set $P = 1$.
13. A historical annotation: *Mutations* was Risset's second entirely computer-generated work. As the first (*Suite for Little Boy*, 1968) had been composed as the sound track for a play by Pierre Halet, *Mutations* is indeed Risset's first independent composition of the kind. The work was commissioned by Pierre Schaeffer's GRM (Paris) in a time when Schaeffer and his colleagues were quite skeptical regarding the musical use of the computer (Schaeffer 1971). In order for the work to be commissioned, a negotiation with Schaeffer was pursued by Henri Chiarucci, a friend of both Schaeffer and Risset. Clearly, *Mutations* was the first digital work ever composed at GRM and did not include any *concrète* sound sources.
14. With some of these bell-like sounds, the higher partials *may* be perceptually segregated. However, this remains a matter of speculation as far as the sounds are heard not in isolation, but in context.

REFERENCES

Arfib, D. (1979). "Digital Synthesis of Complex Spectra by Means of Multiplication of Non-linear Distorted Sine Waves." *Journal of the Audio Engineering Society* 27, no. 10: 87–118.

Chowning, J. (1973). "The Synthesis of Complex Audio Spectra by Means of Frequency Modulation." *Journal of the Audio Engineering Society* 21, no. 7: 526–534.

Chowning, J. (1980). "Computer Synthesis of the Singing Voice." In *Sound Generation in Winds, Strings, and Computers,* edited by J. Sundberg and E. Jansson. Stockholm: Royal Swedish Academy of Music, 4–13.

Di Scipio, A. (1988). "Un'analisi dettagliata di *Contours*, di J. C. Risset." Internal report, CSC Università di Padova.

Di Scipio, A. (1995a). "Da *Concret PH* a *Gendy301*. Modelli compositivi nella musica elettroacustica di Xenakis." *Sonus-Materiali per la Musica Contemporanea* 7 (nos. 1–2–3: 61–92). English translation: "From *Concret PH* to *Gendy301*. Compositional Models in Xenakis' Electroacoustic Music." *Perspectives of New Music* 36, no. 2 (1998): 201–243.

Di Scipio, A. (1995b). "On Different Approaches to Computer Music as Different Models of Compositional Design." *Perspectives of New Music* 33, nos. 1–2: 360–402.

Di Scipio, A. (1997a). "Herbert Brün, la composizione come prassi critica immanente." *Sonus-Materiali per la Musica Contemporanea* 9, nos. 1–2–3: 70–93.

Di Scipio, A. (1997b). "The Question of 2nd Order Sonorities in Xenakis' Electroacoustic Music." *Organised Sound* 2, no. 3: 165–178.

Dodge, C., and Jerse, T. (1985, 1998). *Computer Music: Synthesis, Composition and Performance*. New York: Schirmer Books.

Feyerabend, P. (1987). *Farewell to Reason*. London: Verso.

Laske, O. (1991). "Towards an Epistemology of Composition." *Interface-Journal of New Music Research* 20, nos. 3–4: 235–269.

Lorrain, D. (1980). "Analyse de la bande magnetique de l'oeuvre de J. C. Risset's *Inharmonique*." Rapports IRCAM no. 26.

Mathews, M. (1969). *The Technology of Computer Music*. Cambridge: MIT Press.

McAdams, S. (1982). "Spectral Fusion and the Creation of Auditory Images." In *Music, Mind and Brain: The Neuropsychology of Music*, edited by M. Clynes. New York: Plenum Press, 279–298.

McAdams, S., and Bregman, A. (1979). "Hearing Musical Streams." *Computer Music Journal* 3, no. 4: 26–44.

Pierce, J. (1983). *The Science of Musical Sound.* New York: W. H. Freeman.

Risset, J. C. (1966). "Computer Study of Trumpet Tones." Internal report, Bell Labs.

Risset, J. C. (1969). "An Introductory Catalog of Computer Synthesized Sounds." Internal report, Bell Labs.

Risset, J. C. (1978a). "Hauteur et timbre des sons." Rapports IRCAM n.11.

Risset, J. C. (1978b). "Paradoxes d'hauteur." Rapports IRCAM n.10.

Risset, J. C. (1985). "Computer Music Experiments, 1964–. . ." *Computer Music Journal* 9, no. 1: 11–18.

Risset, J. C. (1986). "Son musical et perception auditive." *Pour la Science* 11.

Risset, J. C., and Mathews, M. (1969). "Analysis of Musical Instrument Tones." *Physics Today* 22, no. 2: 23–40.

Roads, C. (1995). *The Computer Music Tutorial*. Cambridge: MIT Press.

Schoenberg, A. (1922). *Harmonielehre*. Wien: Universal Edition.

Schaeffer, P. (1971). "La musique et les ordinateurs." *La Revue Musicale*, v. 268–269: 57–92.

Stumpf, C. (1883). *Tonpsychologie*. Leipzig: Hirzel.

Thompson, D'A. (1961). *On Growth and Form*. Cambridge: Cambridge University Press.

Truax, B. (1980). "The Inverse Relationship between Generality and Strength." *Interface-Journal of New Music Research* 9, no. 1.

Veitl, A. (1997). *Politiques de la musique contemporaine: le compositeur, la 'recherche musicale' et l'Etat en France de 1958 à 1991*. Paris: L'Harmattan.

Xenakis, I. (1992). *Formalized Music: Thought and Mathematics in Music*. Stuyvesant, New York: Pendragon (rev. and extended version of the 1971 edition).

8

Looking into *Sequence Symbols*

James Dashow

SOME BRIEF FACTS

Sequence Symbols is a work conceived in terms of electronic sounds, in particular, those obtainable from digital synthesis and from the spectacular transformational control that this method provides. The piece was mulled over for about two months, completely worked out in my head one day during my half-hour walk to the Padova University Computer Center, and actually realized on paper, at the terminal, and finally on magnetic tape over a four-month period, February to May 1984. It was premiered at the Ars Electronica Festival in Linz, Austria, in September of that year and since has had and continues to have a variety of performances and broadcasts here and there. It was included on the *Perspectives of New Music* (23, no. 2) cassette tape in a stereo mixdown of the original quadraphonic version, and a slightly revised, remixed version was released on Wergo Compact Disc (WER 2010-50) in 1987. You really have to hear it in a fairly large hall in order to be able to perceive the variable spatial and sense-of-depth effects that are important "orchestrational" aspects of the piece, from a structural standpoint as well as for simply enjoying the sound. At any event, play your compact disc nice and loud, maybe turning up the bass control to counteract at least one of the minor drawbacks of digital synthesis.

AN INTRODUCTION

It should come as no surprise when I say that I cannot account for many of the decisions, ideas, and thought processes that went into the creation of this piece. It is still a cause of wonder to me, during the course of working on a composition, when the ideas start to flow, and I get not only a sense of the whole piece but how to go about doing it, even in its smallest details. How do you talk about something like that? Which leads me to several other questions. What should an analysis of a musical work provide? What is real analysis as opposed to description or opinion, informed or otherwise? Does analysis help you hear a piece, especially if you are talking about abstract procedures that seem to have little or no bearing on the perceived result? *How* can analysis help you hear a piece?

In his book *The Tacit Dimension*, Michael Polanyi observes that "an unbridled lucidity can destroy our understanding of complex matters. Scrutinize closely the particulars of a comprehensive entity and their meaning is effaced, our conception of the entity is destroyed" (Polanyi [1966] 1983, 18). Attention to particulars as revealed by some kinds of musical analysis tells you nothing about what you're actually hearing and, at the worst, can destroy your comprehending the piece as a whole, that something that is far greater than the linear sum of its individual details. But Polanyi then adds that "the detailing of particulars, which by itself would destroy meaning, serves as a guide to their subsequent integration and thus establishes a more secure and more accurate meaning of them" (Polanyi [1966] 1983, 19). Most appropriate for musical analysis, which, in order to completely fulfill its function, is that it must not fail to take into account the second part of Polanyi's recipe, the subsequent integration of particulars.

It is essential that the particulars analyzed here be integrated in subsequent listenings. For this reason, I talk about those particulars that directly support and contribute to important *heard* aspects of the piece. If you know that a particular phrase is intended as an upbeat, for example, you can contribute to the phrase by hearing it as an upbeat, adding your own upbeat emotional response to it, expecting perhaps an arrival point that may be stated directly or ambiguously or even delayed. You are now actively participating in the listening, putting something of yourself into the music, and by being thus more involved in the piece, you can enjoy it and understand it more. For music this application of Polanyi's important idea of reintegrating particulars into the comprehensive entity of which they are its parts seems particularly valid and fruitful.

The comprehensive entity here is a musical structure coming alive; it's being relived as you listen to it, *because* you are listening to it. "Structure" is meant in much the same way as Piaget defines it in his book *Structuralism*: "As a first approximation, we may say that a structure is a system of transformations. Inasmuch as it is a system and not a mere collection of elements and their properties, these transformations involve laws: the structure is preserved or enriched by the interplay of its transformation laws . . . the notion of structure is comprised of three key ideas: the idea of wholeness, the idea of transformation, and the idea of self-regulation" (Piaget 1968, 5). Thus, the interaction and cross-influences of ideas and processes in the piece determine the sense of wholeness of the work, the resulting transformations determine the shape and progression of the work's ideas, and these developments are constrained by a self-referential context derived from a few general background principles, described later. It is the idea of temporal *organic* structure that I want to emphasize here, the whole structural process becoming a living, transforming thing while you listen to it; analysis should help prepare you to hear a work in these terms, to perceive actively the procedures and their results and the wholeness that they construct over time. A tall order, but certainly a worthy goal.

To this end it is often illuminating to know what composers themselves want you to hear, to learn from them about some of those particulars that they labored over that aren't immediately apparent, about the musical framework in which they have chosen to work. This kind of information can increase the degree of active participation on the part of the listener in the sense previously mentioned.

So, that's what this chapter touches on. This piece about a piece contains some statements in order to create the context of musical thinking that serves for my framework, a mention of some of the musical issues that were important during the work's composition, and finally the technical stuff: the characteristics of my computer orchestra, my ideas about functionally structuring timbre, and a look at the piece itself in terms of what I think are the structurally important aspects, as suggested by the Piagetian model. Those of you who prefer only the nuts and bolts can skip the following couple of sections. For the rest of you who are still with me, on we go.

SOME BACKGROUND CONSIDERATIONS

I hear vertically. Listening to even the most linear music, I tend to try to capture areas of vertical definition, no matter how fleeting or how merely implied they might be. Music derives much of its fascination and power from its capacity to develop these two dimensions, the linear and the vertical, simultaneously in time but at different rates and to different degrees. Works that dismiss the importance of one or the other of these dimensions, I think, tend to be disappointing.

So, my approach to electronic music is very much influenced by an awareness of the vertical dimension. Sounds generated by electronic instruments certainly don't lack fascinating linear (or successional) possibilities, but it is often difficult to control with any consistency or coherence the simultaneous aspect of these sounds, especially on a large structural scale. Digital synthesis of electronic sounds, however, provides very powerful means for developing methods that enable the composer to control the vertical dimension in electronic music to any degree.

To this end, I have developed, and continue to develop, synthesis techniques for the computer based on the idea that electronic sounds may be conceived of as *chords*, in the traditional sense of the word. The frequencies in a particular sound that go to make up its characteristic timbre are considered to be members of a chord; those frequencies that are structurally more important with respect to larger-scale aspects of the composition are considered to be *harmonized* by the other frequencies in the sound. That the various frequencies that make up the timbre of electronic sounds can be given different degrees of importance in this way suggests most strongly that hierarchical relationships can be built into these sounds and that the component frequencies of a timbre can have a variety of meaningful functional properties. Timbre is no longer merely orchestrational;

it can become functional with respect to the frequencies that compose it. This further suggests that composers can consciously develop electronic music on many structural levels, endowing their work with the kind of power, subtlety, and conviction found in traditional (discrete pitch) musical systems of the past.

Specific relationships among the frequencies are no longer limited to the familiar scalar ratios or traditional harmonic (integer or near integer) ratios. The *inharmonic* sounds that are the most characteristic and unique features of electronic music display an enormous variety in the ratios between frequency components, ratios that are sometimes called microtonal relationships in other musical contexts. Unlike microtonal systems, inharmonic sounds make use of irregular divisions of the continuous audio frequency spectrum rather than the systematic divisions of various kinds of scales, semitone and not. A certain kind of timbre is the result of specific frequency components, their relative phases and amplitudes. These components can be manipulated in digital synthesis in order to create a functional system or system of systems that permits the evolution of large-scale hierarchies, all based on timbre. As such, an *inharmonic music* could be considered a more global, all-encompassing system. Just as the chromaticism of the late nineteenth century contains and enlarges on the largely diatonic mode of composition of the end of the eighteenth century, and the free, nontonal music of this century has a similar relationship to chromatic tonal music, I suggest that an inharmonic music, where the *composer* decides how the audio spectrum will be divided up, represents another such enlargement of the musical vocabulary. The equal-tempered scale is only *one* of the possible ways of establishing a system of (or structuring) frequency relationships.

It is from this point of view that I develop my music. I compose what one might call a background level based on the equal-tempered scale, networks of note-groups that are related by common tones: which common tones at what time, their articulation by means of octave transfer are important aspects at this level. The note-groups themselves are made up of those intervals that produce the kinds of timbre in which I'm interested. Through a variety of techniques, described elsewhere (Dashow 1978, 1980), a specific dyad or trichord can be made to generate families of electronic sounds, or chord-spectra, all of which have the generating pitches, the dyad or trichord, in common. The other components of the chord-spectrum form what I consider to be the *harmonization* of those generating pitches, and each chord has its own timbre as a result of this harmonization, with greater or lesser differentiation among the chord-spectra of any one family or between families. In other words, systems of chord-spectra can be structured any way the composer likes using relationships of common generating frequencies or common generating intervals as a basis.

I consider that the chord-spectra generated by one dyad are a means for *prolonging*, literally, that dyad in time. The variety of timbres that a single dyad can produce through frequency or amplitude modulation, signal multiplication, exponential modulation, and other related procedures provides the means for the rich textural elaboration of a musical work's surface while maintaining the continuous or prolonged presence of the generating dyad on a background level.

This is comparable to a familiar diatonic practice of placing a fixed chord (e.g., in the winds) as background to fast moving scalar patterns (in the strings). The functional-harmonic significance of the scalar patterns is determined by the chords; different kinds of chords force different functional interpretations on the same scalar patterns. With the electronic chord-spectra, the background pitches, organized into dyads, emerge from the choice of spectra that are chosen from among those that the dyads can be made to generate. The functional significance of the chord-spectra is determined by its generating dyad and by its timbre, which is, again, what I am calling the harmonization of the dyad. (I am fully aware of rhythmic and dynamic factors in contributing to the overall functional sense of a chord; as long as we're talking about digital synthesis, one could add velocity of spatial movement, sense of depth and presence, and a variety of other factors unique to composing for digital electronic instruments as important aspects in determining the "functionality" of a sound or series of sounds. I am here mainly concerned with the frequency content of electronic sounds and how to control their relationships on a variety of levels. The methods that I use permit going beyond merely stringing together arbitrary series of nice sounds: I can attribute a sense of large-scale coherence to these sounds by controlling their frequency content through relationships to a fully structured background level.)

With this approach, the adaptation to the electronic realm of notions derived from previously successful modes of composition can yield fresh results owing to the expanded frequency vocabulary that digital electronic synthesis provides. Mixtures of sounds, generated by different dyads, can be organized into tension-release patterns; interesting approaches to counterpoint, which can be clarified by composing a line's spatial movement, its degree of reverberation, extraordinary rhythm structures (things you wouldn't dream of asking a live performer to do—the computer can perform *any* rhythmic figure that you can imagine) can expand the traditional techniques. One important result encountered here is that the difference between timbre and chord is obscured, and, in fact, the ambiguity that arises—at what point does a frequency become an independent element, and at what point is it merely a timbral phenomenon?—is here exploited and made a fundamental issue.

I should point out that the generating-dyad techniques are designed to be used with those signal-generating processes that are, from the standpoint of computer synthesis, computationally economical. The advantages of using such algorithms, besides their relative speed of execution, include a reduction of score input data—fewer numbers are needed to describe the desired sound—and perhaps most important, a *limitation* of the kinds of sounds available. Whereas in additive synthesis, the selection of component frequencies is completely unlimited, and hence the composer spends an enormous amount of time experimenting, synthesis by algorithm (as mentioned before, frequency modulation, signal multiplication, and so forth) makes certain choices for the composer—the principle by which frequencies are combined and their dynamic evolution—and thereby produces immediately a limited selection of useful sounds with which the composer can get right to work. As in any system, the limitations challenge, rather than stifle, invention, and one has easily obtainable families of sounds within whose framework a functionally coherent inharmonic music can begin to be realized. Most of my own work has been within these algorithmic systems. I have, however, been developing a generating dyad application for additive synthesis situations. A pair of pitches can be made to generate a variety of inharmonic partial series, through a distortion of the equation representing harmonic partials and inharmonic scales and through distortions of the equation representing the equal tempered system (Dashow 1986).

ABOUT *SEQUENCE SYMBOLS* GENERALLY

Sequence Symbols makes use of a mixture of inharmonic sound-generating algorithms and additive synthesis. The former are used exclusively with the generating dyad principle; the latter is used for explicit articulation of the underlying pitch structure at important points, especially where the development of the pitch structure in itself generates an interesting texture as orchestrated by additive synthesis and other subsidiary factors such as complex delay-line and reverberation patterns. At other moments, the pitch structure is played clearly, then followed by an inharmonic harmonization; or the reverse can happen: an inharmonic passage is followed by the specific unfolding of the pitch structure that generated it. The resulting flux of contrasting timbres, textures, and sections contributes in a fundamental way to the piece's overall large-scale rhythm. The sense of form of the piece, its wholeness, is determined by this rhythm. The real work involved in this piece (the four months) was to translate my sense of that form (my half-hour walk) into the chord-spectra that realize it.

These contrasts all participate in the piece's basic *pairs of events* concept and the fundamental notion of *progression by interruption*. Much effort went into building up interlocking networks of *antecedent-consequent* on both the small and large scale. Locally, the notion of upbeat-downbeat is intimately tied to larger-scale antecedent-consequent relations, while the interruptions create over longer time spans an expectation of a consequent or, in some cases, delay the arrival of the *right* consequent. The interruption itself assumes formal dimensions such that an ambiguity is intentionally created between the motion *A-interrupt-A'*, two-part structure, and *A-B-A*, three-part structure. This, I think, creates a large-scale tension over the whole work that is never really resolved; perhaps you could think of it, borrowing an appropriate metaphor from theoretical physics, as a stable, broken symmetry.

Several ideas are intertwined through this procedure of articulation and interruption. Some ideas are first stated in a fully expanded version and gradually reduced over the course of the work to their essence; others are begun as fragments and gradually expanded to their fullest expression. The most important instance of the latter process is the interruption itself becoming an independent contrasting section requiring its own (well-delayed) consequent. Finally, the rhythm of interruption contributes significantly to the flow of the work. Certainly, I was extremely conscious of the rhythm created by local interruptions and delayed consequents, of the rhythm generated by the sense of simultaneous expansion and contraction of different idea-strands, and of the large-scale rhythm that the various sections produced through differing timbres and kinds of interruption, tensions resolved or delayed.

It is hard to talk specifically about many aspects of the piece, especially the rhythmic dimension. The sounds that I use, through their contrasting degrees of tension, timbre, phrase structure, and so on, create the local sense of motion and direction, while their participation in the more global background structure generates the larger-scale movement and direction of the piece. At best I can draw your attention to these aspects in terms of one major dimension, the underlying pitch structure. I want to emphasize that after more than fifteen years of experience with chord-spectra and their associated generating pitches, I now compose in terms of those generating dyads and trichords that give me the kinds of sounds that I want. I prepare for each new composition by generating several hours of a sound catalog consisting of the chord-spectra that various intervals can be made to generate, especially *combinations* of these chord-spectra (always full of surprises!); finally I begin organizing my thinking around the available possibilities and hence around the intervals that produced them. Just as you think about a piece for orchestra in terms of the instruments at your disposal, so the resources of various inharmonic sound-generating algorithms as constrained by the generating-pitch method largely determine the way that I conceive my pieces. I accept these constraints because I have found that successions and combinations of electronic sounds gain an extraordinary coherence when constructed according to the principles of this approach, a coherence that suggests that a genuine language can be forged out of this abundance of basic materials.

I concentrate my discussion on the underlying pitch structure, which determines the possible chord-spectra available at any one time, antecedent-consequent articulation at various levels, and the workings out of some of the more important interrupts. This isn't, by any means, an exhaustive analysis, but I hope that the remarks that follow help you perceive what I consider to be some of the work's more significant aspects and, of course, permit you to participate as a more active listener to *Sequence Symbols* and thereby enjoy it more fully.

THE ORCHESTRA

The overall digital sound-synthesis language used for realizing *Sequence Symbols* was the well-known Music 360, originally written by Barry Vercoe of the Massachusetts Institute of Technology (MIT) and subsequently expanded by the author at the Centro di Sonologia Computazionale (CSC), University of Padova (Italy). Music 360 is written in a combination of IBM Assembler and Fortran. It is a completely programmable language, and the composer who takes the trouble to learn Assembler and Fortran finds that he or she has an extraordinarily flexible and powerful sound synthesis tool at his or her disposal.

The user writes programs in this language. Each program fragment, which in my case I dedicated to a particular algorithm, is conceived of as an individual instrument, and all the instruments together form the orchestra. My 1984 orchestra for *Sequence Symbols* consists of eighteen different instruments, thirteen of which are complex signal generators, the other five being signal processors, each of the latter containing several different kinds of processors, selectable with a software switch (you write 1 or 2 or 3 etc. at the appropriate place in the score data to get the program to become processor 1, processor 2, etc.). Some of the signal generators are also double instruments, insofar as the same setup of unit generators that produce one kind of sound can be slightly altered (again, with a software switch) to produce another kind of sound. The specific instruments and their fundamental algorithms are as follows.

Instrument 1—Frequency Modulation

Generating-dyad technique is used here to find the frequency values for the modulator and carrier frequency. If the dyad is given by an upper frequency (HZU) and a lower frequency (HZL), and their sideband positions in the FM spectrum are given by an upper sideband (SBU) and a lower sideband (SBL), respectively, then the modulator (MOD) and carrier (CAR) frequencies can be found by

$$\begin{aligned} \text{MOD} &= (\text{HZU} - \text{HZL}) / (\text{SBU} - \text{SBL}) \\ \text{CAR} &= \text{HZU} - (\text{SBU} * \text{MOD}) \end{aligned}$$

Instrument 2—Frequency Modulation with Up to Four Modulators Software Switchable to Discrete Linear Summation

In frequency modulation mode, the MOD and CAR frequencies are calculated as for instrument 1; a second, third, and fourth modulator are added in series to the first modulator, and the frequencies for each of these modulators is calculated by multiplying modulator 1 by any desired factor.

In discrete linear summation mode, the sound is generated by the following equations (after Moorer 1976):

$$\frac{(1-A^2)\sin\theta}{1+A^2-2A\cos\beta} \quad \text{or} \quad \frac{\sin\theta - A\sin(\theta-\beta)}{1+A^2-2A\cos\beta}$$

Instrument 3—Frequency Modulation, Single Pitch Version

Carrier is set to specific pitch (PCH), modulator is determined by multiplying PCH by any desired factor: MOD = PCH * factor or, if PCH is declared to be at sideband *N*, carrier is calculated, then modulator as before. In either case, an optional second modulator is calculated as for Instrument 2, MOD2 = MOD1 * any factor.

Instrument 4—PN (Partial Numbers) Instrument, or Switch to Nonlinear Distortion

A chord of usually two, three, or four frequencies or pitches (Pchl, Pch2, Pch3, etc.) is generated by a single oscillator reading a complex-function table that is the sum of two, three, or four partials. Ratios of Pchl:Pch2:Pch3: etc. are adjusted to become whole-number ratios. These numbers then become the partial numbers of a function (used in the table-lookup operation of the oscillator unit generator) driven by the frequency calculated by Pch1/partial number of Pchl.

Example: if pitches are 8.00, 9.03, and 10.01, the ratios between them are:

9.03 : 8.00 = 8ve + m3 = 2.3784
10.01 : 8.00 = 2 8ves + m2 = 4.2378
10.01 : 9.03 = m7 = 1.7818

Readjusting ratios to whole numbers, 157 : 88 : 37 (closest fit . . . 10.01 slightly sharp, but OK) generate a function with partial numbers 37, 88, 157, whose driving frequency is the lowest of the three pitches, 8.00 (= 262 Hz) divided by the partial number that will generate it:

driving Hz = 262/37 = 7.0811

Switch to nonlinear distortion:

- window width and function-center location are variable
- the window width can be modulated at audio rates
- the basic function table uses sum of sines (low partial numbers) that offer a variety of slopes as transfer function, rather than usual Chebychev. Result is a constantly changing distortion function, harmonic content constantly changing.

Instrument 5—Foldover

This instrument takes advantage of one of the defects of digital synthesis: when you call for a frequency, HZ, that is greater than half the sampling rate, SR, your computer will generate not that frequency but rather the frequency given by SR – HZ, which in many circumstances is inharmonic to the context in which it occurs. Since inharmonic sounds are what we're after, this is a welcome result. A frequency so generated is called a foldover frequency. By calling for a pitch PCH to be generated as a foldover frequency by a particular partial number PN in a complex function (that has many other partials in it), the desired pitch sounds within an inharmonic chord whose components are provided by the other partials in the function. The necessary frequency, F0, is calculated by the computer according to the following equation:

$$F0 = \frac{SR * N \pm PCH}{PN}$$

By simply varying N, the integer multiplier of the SR, and keeping all else constant, an interesting variety of inharmonic "harmonizations" of PCH can be obtained. (See Dashow 1978 for specific details.)

Instrument 6—AMRM

An amplitude modulation (AM) circuit is treated as one part of a ring-modulation (RM), or signal multiplication, circuit; the other part is simply a third oscillator. For simple sine-wave tables, there are six components in the resultant spectrum. A generating trichord determines the frequencies for the three oscillators, and there are ninety-six possible chord-spectra, all of which have the three frequencies of the generating trichord in common. (Equations and procedure can be found in Dashow 1978.)

Instrument 7—AMVARY

Amplitude modulation with a complex carrier (sum of two or three partials). Score data preprocessed by a Fortran subroutine generate the appropriate complex sine table functions that yield three (or two) generating pitches as different components of each chord-spectrum. There are three different ways of manipulating the data, resulting in anywhere from six to twenty-four different chord-spectra, each of which has the generating pitches among its components (see Dashow 1980).

Instrument 8—RMCMPLX

A complex ring-modulation signal is generated by multiplying together two sums of sines (two components per oscillator) as shown by the following equation:

$$(\sin m\alpha + \sin n\alpha) * (\sin x\beta + \sin y\beta)$$

Each such multiplication yields the following eight resultant components:

$$m\alpha \pm x\beta$$
$$m\alpha \pm y\beta$$
$$n\alpha \pm x\beta$$
$$n\alpha \pm y\beta$$

A generating dyad can be made to sound as any two of these eight components. One of the frequencies of the dyad can be generated as a negative frequency (phase reversed), thereby doubling the possibilities. A total of thirty-two chord-spectra can be obtained by multiplying together the same two oscillators (each using its own fixed function table with the appropriately calculated frequencies), all of which have the same generating dyad among their components (see Dashow 1980).

Instrument 15—Noise Modulation

A single pitch is slightly frequency modulated with white noise during the attack portion, and/or ring modulated with "fractal" (l/f) noise. 1/f can be used for vibrato as well.

Instrument 16—Super Oscil

Economic additive synthesis: one call to the super oscil routine produces the sum of *N* oscils, where *N* is in the range 2–30. The frequency of each of the *N* oscils may differ by anywhere from a very few Hz, for chorus effects, to specific intervals, to create inharmonic chords. For the latter, the generating dyad method can be used to determine the frequencies of these spectra.

Instrument 17—Wave Shape Modulation

This modulates the zero-crossing location of the carrier wave at audio rates, producing harmonic or inharmonic spectra, depending on the modulation rate's relationship to the carrier, set to a specific pitch value, PCH. Unlike FM (and more like acoustic instruments), as the "modulation index" goes higher, more harmonics become audible, but the lower harmonics *do not* disappear; rather, they continue to grow, but at slower rate as more energy is distributed to higher components. The equations (Mitsuhashi 1980) used by the computer are as follows:

$$f(a,x) = \left[\begin{array}{ll} (1-a)*(x+1)*(x-a) & -1 \le x < a \\ -(1+a)*(x-a)*(x-1) & a \le x < 1 \end{array} \right.$$

a = zero-crossing point
x = current phase (from phase + sampling increment)
All calculations are within the limits of ± 1; sampling increment, phase, zero-crossing point all have to be reset to within these limits.

Instrument 18—XPN, XPN MOD

A positive sine table is subjected to dynamically varying exponentiation; then the output is readjusted to ± 1. As exponent increases, spectrum gets brighter, and upper partials begin to sound. Exponent can vary slowly (according to specific envelope) or can be modulated at audio rates. The modulation factor

= integer * carrier: harmonic spectra
= irrational * carrier: inharmonic spectra

Exact frequency content produced by exponential modulation is still unknown (see Dashow 1986).

New Instrument 5—ISFP

Based on an algorithm by Giuseppe Englert, sound, SIG, is the result of a logical choice between two other sounds, VSIG and WSIG, as follows:

SIG = (VSIG > WSIG ? VSIG : WSIG)

The current value of SIG is set to the current value of VSIG if VSIG is greater than the current value of WSIG; otherwise, SIG is set to WSIG. VSIG and WSIG can be simple or complex, related by harmonic or inharmonic intervals, dynamically variable in time, and so on. Option for linear interpolation between successive values of SIG at arbitrarily chosen rates.

SIGNAL PROCESSORS

Instrument 10—RMOD/XPN/VSR

1. RMOD option: multiplies any incoming sound by an oscillator whose frequency is related in some way to the source sound. Can be a complex multiplier from OSCIL4F, a special-purpose unit generator whose output is an interpolation between four functions. Multiplication depth is dynamically variable.
2. XPN option: any incoming sound is subjected to exponentiation. Exponent is dynamically variable, slowly or modulated at audio rates.
3. VSR option: resamples any incoming sound at any sampling rate less than the audio sampling rate with which the sound was originally synthesized. The new sampling rate is dynamically variable in time or may be *modulated* at audio rates that are related in some way to the incoming source. Slope between newly resampled points is obtained by interpolation from a table containing a ½ pos sine or ¼ $\sin^2$. Slope may be dynamically varied by exponentiation. Exponentiation may be audio-modulated. Often produces foldover, which is a primary source of interesting inharmonic sounds. Mathematical expression for spectral content is exceedingly difficult to determine.

Instrument 11—Filters/Comb Filter

1. One or two filters, in parallel or series, act on incoming source signal. Filters (Beauchamp 1979) may be low-pass, high-pass, band-pass, or band-reject (notch); choice of filter types is set at note initialization time. A pair of filters can be a complementary low-pass and high-pass creating a wide band-pass (presence filter) or a wide-band notch. Center frequency and Q may be varied dynamically.
2. Comb filter sets its loop time (LPT) to l/Hz to cause either resonance or cancellation of frequency Hz and its harmonics. LPT can be altered by reinitializing the comb filter to create a dynamically changing resonance pattern.

Instrument 12—Echo; Matrix Delay

1. Long recirculating echoes may be obtained, up to 6.4 seconds if all four units are chained together. Includes an Alpass filter option to avoid unwanted resonances at smaller loop times.
2. Matrix circuit (Puckette 1983) uses output of sum and difference of two multiple-tap, multiple-feedback delay lines to create a highly blended wall of sound out of original discrete attacks. By varying the feedback factor and the internal feedback filters' cut-off frequency, significant timbre transformations take place.

Instrument 13—Delay Line with Chorus Effect

Continuous shifting of delay time creates a Doppler effect and, when mixed with the original signal, causes significant enrichment of sound (chorus effect).

Special features include:

1. Negative feedback
2. Allpass option
3. Dynamically variable feedback factor
4. Dynamically variable delay time change rates
5. Synchronization between features 3 and 4
6. Random delay times

Instrument 14—Reverberation

Mono reverb is made into stereo by phase shifting and added delay between channels. Used often for special exaggerated reverb effects such as twelve seconds reverberation time, which provides interesting sustain and decay patterns to originally short attacks.

Final postreverberation (Puckette 1983) done by separate quadraphonic unit: eight delay lines, four of which are tapped eight times, the other four tapped only once; complex internal matrix with low-pass filters on feedback.

SOME SPECIFICS

The chromatic group A in Example 8.1 was chosen as the fundamental pitch group. The complement, group B, is the transposition of group A at the interval

Example 8.1
Chromatic Groups A and B

Example 8.2
Different Interval Types

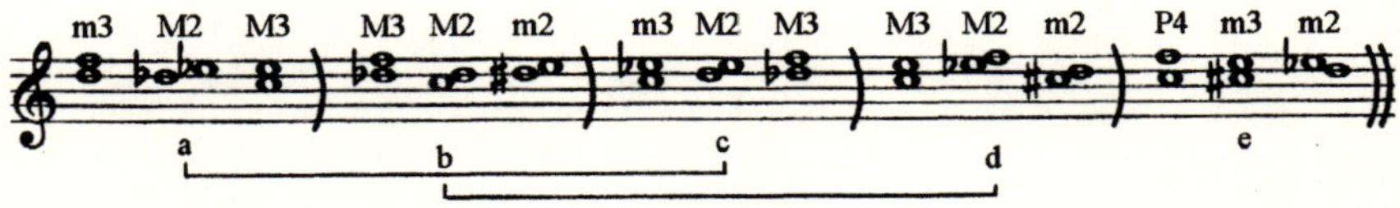

of a tritone; the group is inversionally neutral; that is, the inversion and the original are identical. Different transpositions, other than that at the tritone, have different numbers of common tones with the original: the transposition up a major third or down a major third has the same number of tones in common with the original, but the specific common pitches are different. The important aspect for the generating-dyad technique is that the six-note group may be divided into a variety of intervals. The criterion followed was that each such division must be into three *different* interval types (or dyads), and no interval is to be repeated. The possibilities are shown in Example 8.2.

Divisions *a* and *c* are closely related: the interval pattern is the same (M3, m3, M2), but the specific pitches that make up the intervals are different. The same relationship obtains between divisions *b* and *d* (M3, M2, m2). Division *e* is a clear contrast, having a unique interval, the perfect fourth. Divisions *a* and *b* together and *c* and *d* together very strongly suggested an antecedent-consequent relationship, and *e* suggested a contrasting role, which will be realized through the notion of interruption.

It should be noted that only six kinds of interval are considered: the major and minor second, the major and minor third, the perfect fourth, and the tritone. All intervals greater than these (but less than the octave) are considered inversions of the basic six (M6 is m3, m7 is M2, etc.) and hence of the same interval class, as are distributions of these intervals over more than one octave. However, the generating-dyad technique produces considerably different chord-spectra for each version, as just defined, of an interval, such that the family of sounds produced by a specific interval may now be expanded to include all chord-spectra generated by the same interval-*class*, that is, all those chord-spectra generated by the same two pitch classes regardless of register. Thus, a kind of hierarchy emerges where two pitch-class sets give rise to six fundamental intervals from which can be derived first their inversions (producing the remaining five intervals within the octave), then these same intervals spread over more than one octave. Again, I want to emphasize that *each* of these intervals, fundamental and derived, can generate its own local families of chord-spectra using the previously described techniques. From one point of view we can consider this to be a very elaborate and complex hierarchical system; from another point of view, it is legitimate to question the notion of pitch-class identity at the chord-spectra level, given the rather significant difference between the actual sounds generated by, say, a minor seventh and an octave-and-a-minor-seventh. The ambiguity of this situation, especially with respect to perception of the immediate background-level pitch structure, is exploited rather than resolved.

The piece begins by articulating group A as division *a* dyads, which are transformed into the complement collection group B type *b* in inverted form (Example 8.3a). Group A doesn't suddenly become group B; rather, there is overlapping of elements from one group with elements of the other (small note-heads in Example 8.3a), which is locally only a transition area but sets the all-important precedent of a third *derived* harmonic area that will grow to structural and procedural importance as the piece progresses. A two-part structure is established by means of the motion from A to B, antecedent-consequent is implied within this motion because of the complementary relationship between groups A and B, and the high rhythmic energy of this initial idea creates the expectation of a larger-scale consequent motion to the whole, to be satisfied using the progression type *c* to type *d*.

Instrument 5, the foldover instrument, is used to generate the chord-spectra around the pitches. Each dyad has its own rapid rate of change of the *N* factor (see "Orchestra" earlier), creating an immediate sense of highly charged energy that will seek a lower, more stable level over the time span of the piece, while various interruptions continually delay this discharging (I have found it most convenient to borrow from the vocabulary of contemporary particle physics those terms that, used as metaphors, express vividly and accurately some of the large-scale processes at work in my music, or at least the way I tend to think about them). I like to compare this event to the theoretical description of electrons as being able to exist at different energy levels: when charged to a higher energy level, they then emit light while returning to their proper, stable, energy level within the particular atom of which they are a part. The high energy level at the beginning of *Sequence Symbols* is discharged gradually; the "emitted light" is the piece itself.

Again, with reference to Example 8.3a, the larger-scale antecedent-consequent is unbalanced—twenty-six seconds for the antecedent, only ten seconds for the consequent before the first real interrupt takes place, using instrument 1 (FM) for contrast, especially with respect to timbre. Completion of the consequent is, from the standpoint of duration, suspended, creating a sense of expectation; although the harmonic motion was completed, the second group A to group B parallels the first twenty-six-second event, and the time for the consequent motion is considerably reduced, a concentration of energy and momentum that motivates an interruption to avoid this tendency to build up energy

Example 8.3a
Opening of *Sequence Symbols* (0:00–1:40)

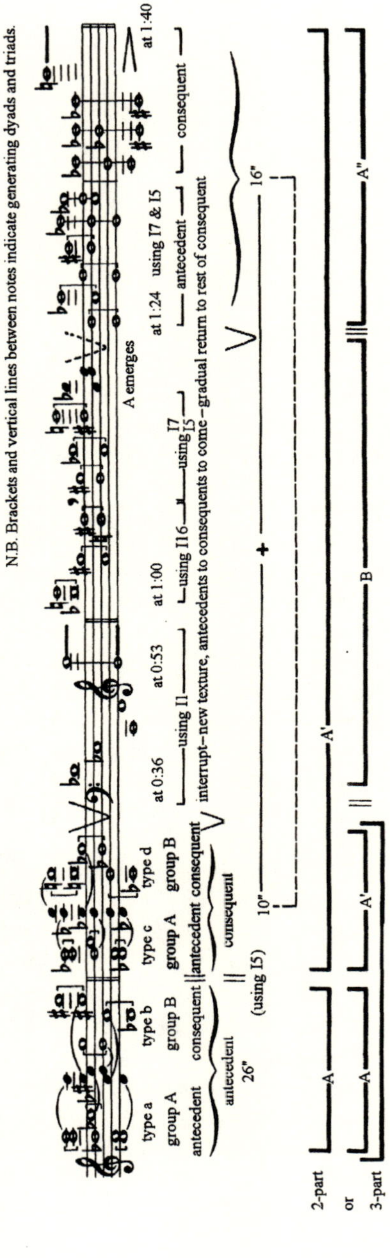

Example 8.3b
Closure Section of Opening (1:40–2:09)

continuously by shorter, ever more concentrated segments that can result only in a sort of self-destruct. The resumption at time 1:24 of instruments 5 and 7 in a group A to group B progression lasts for sixteen seconds, completing the necessary time-span complementation to the initial event pair, but with a noticeably reduced energy sense; and at 1:40 there begins a winding down toward a local closure. But the interrupt, from 0:36 to 1:24, has introduced several new textures that will be seen to be antecedents to long-delayed consequents and has, above all, introduced the fundamental contrast between accumulation of energy and winding down of energy, one of the key procedures that will contribute significantly to the sectional progression of the piece.

Locally, each contrasting idea in this first and extended interrupt, articulated by different instruments (instrument 1, then instrument 16, then instrument 7), flows into the next, and each freely manipulates the possible interval combinations, in dyads and triads, of groups A and B. Each *specific* interval, it will be remembered, produces families of chord-spectra. The combinations here used yield the kind of bright charged sound appropriate for this stage of the piece. As the interrupt extends, the sense is created that the interrupt is an independent structure, not merely a delay in the consequent completion; an ambiguity is intentionally created, suggesting a complex, two-part structure or a less complex, three-part structure. The piece constantly plays on this formal ambiguity, which is a source of tension and evolution throughout.

Even the winding down is interrupted at 1:40 by a reassertion of the earlier interrupt ideas, which here function to delay the completion of the winding-down gesture, as well as a transition to the beginning of the next section at 2:09. The winding down is, in a sense, suspended, and this, too, needs to be completed later (Example 8.3b). The two major features of this second interrupt are the modified repetition of previous interrupt ideas, but here *not* as a consequent but as a part of an ongoing developmental chain: each separate idea is to be treated to developmental procedures—gradual expansion or contraction, realignment of note groups intervallically or with respect to pitch content, and so on—and altered versions of these ideas will occur as ambiguously functioning interrupts. All this allows for the blending of, and cross-influence between, various kinds of procedures that result in the working out of ideas on multiple levels or in multiple dimensions simultaneously.

Example 8.4
(2:09–3:09)

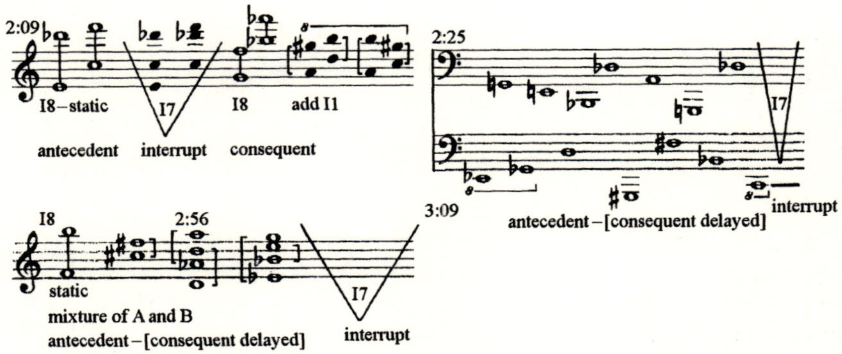

At 2:09 the first version of the static-chord idea occurs, an idea that will be considerably developed during the piece. This idea reflects various dimensions that have already been expressed but represents a major variant, or rather hybrid, of them. Antecedent-consequent is here extended, with respect to time, and blended with the developmental-chain procedure: each consequent can be considered antecedent to the next phrase (using this particular texture) that follows (Example 8.4). Instrument 8 is used exclusively for this texture, employing the simple "ring modulation" algorithm that yields a tremendous variety of chord-spectra for each generating dyad. Instrument 7, which is similar as the interrupt between successive instrument 8 phrases. At 2:25 there is a more elaborate version of the first interrupt idea (instrument 1 at 0:36), fully formed to in sound but which dynamically changes its timbre at faster rates, is used again suggest its being an antecedent to some consequent to follow. Here is the first instance of emergence to full development of an idea earlier expressed in reduced form—an indication of one of the many strands being worked out in this piece. This phrase is again a free intervallic development following the implications of the breakup of groups A and B, barely hinted at in the closure around 2:00.

The instrument 7 interrupt leaves the consequent of this phrase (begun at 2:25) suspended, and the static instrument 8 idea reappears under the chain-development procedure, at around 2:50; each pair of generating dyads is a mix of two notes from group A and two notes from group B, and each four-note group contains a prominent tritone, the one interval not explicitly present in groups A and B. The emergence of the tritone through shuffling around of the note groups will have important consequences later on. This interval makes specific what was implied by the original transposition relation between groups A and B.

The static instrument 8 phrase now becomes antecedent to a delayed consequent—a dramatic instrument 7 interrupt, crescendo up to 3:09, clears the way for yet another antecedent: a new, contrasting, pitch-only (no chord-spectra) idea that attempts to reestablish the original group A and B associations—an

Example 8.5
(3:09–3:40)

indication of the continuing structural influence of the original groupings (Example 8.5). A complete halt occurs at this point, another kind of interrupt, but also because we have by now three delayed consequents to contend with, conflict between the old original note groups and the developmental progress of the new groupings—a highly complex situation (suggesting a sort of functional overload, perhaps) that requires taking a breath before trying to sort things out. The simple device of silence is a subtly effective way of prolonging the accumulated tension without adding new events to it.

What follows at 3:27 are small events that pick up the fallen momentum, as upbeat to 3:40, where one of the delayed consequents occurs, the static instrument 8 developmental chain, here consisting of three harmonic areas, each, again, with pairs of generating dyads consisting of two notes from group A and two from group B (Example 8.6). Once again, the consequent becomes antecedent to what will follow in the chain; the interrupt at 4:10 confirms this idea, but here the interrupt is prolonged with a contrasting idea that continues the work of building up momentum after the halt before 3:40. This prolonged interruption is itself interrupted at 4:33 with instrument 1 (FM) textures that continue the developmental strand begun at 0:53 with similar kinds of chord-spectra. Example 8.7 shows the generating dyads at this point, a continued manipulation of the basic note groups; one of the dynamic functions of the continuing interruptions is to try displacing any particular collection of generating dyads that is not "correct"; that is, the interrupts act to break up any accumulation of dyads that does not represent a stable collection. *The piece itself will eventually define what "stable" means in this context.* There is no note group or concept that is a priori more privileged than any other; rather it is one of the composer's tasks to establish and define constructs that convince the listener of their functional correctness *for each particular composition.* Once the listener begins to gather ideas about the composer's intentions (his definitions and constructions), the piece can be experienced more fully and certainly with more involvement. The composer also recommends that you listen to this piece at least a second time (these comments, an interruption to be sure, form a kind of reduced consequent to the Introduction section of this chapter).

The interrupt at 4:49 then dislodges the collection begun at 4:33 and lets in one of the delayed consequents, a development of the freely derived interval idea

Example 8.6
(3:40–4:33)

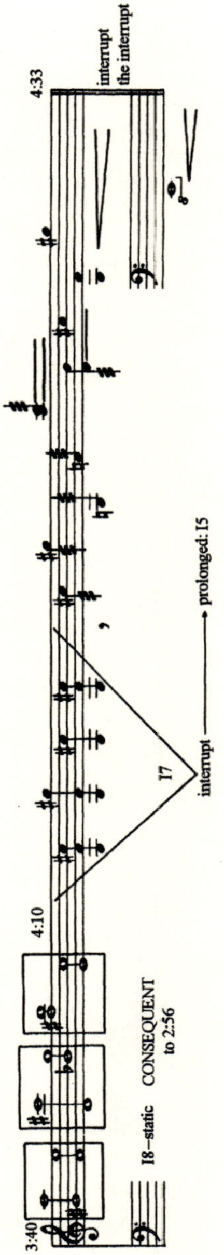

Example 8.7
(4:33–5:20)

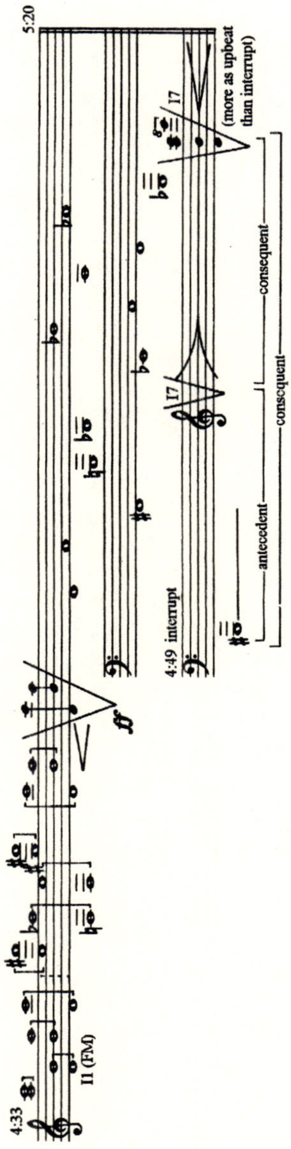

begun at 2:25. Using the same procedure as at the beginning of the piece, that of dividing the consequent up into subunits, this consequent phrase creates its own antecedent-interrupt-consequent construction. There is a small-scale sense of completion of one strand here (the successfully realized delayed consequent), yet the instrument 7 added on to the end of this passage functions as an upbeat to 5:20 rather than as an interrupt. The pitches used in this phrase are not considered a stable group—the added upbeat ensures that tension is maintained between a first real coming to completion in one domain and an unsatisfied stage in the transforming of the note groups from one stable configuration to another.

At 5:20, the instrument 8 static idea resumes its developmental chain, here with an extremely suspended effect, almost no motion, which leads to the contrasting "start-stop" texture at 5:46, the interrupt phrase or section now compressed to a motivic level. Here the interrupt procedure assumes an autonomous existence as a fully formed articulation, and here a significant pair of complementary note groups (Examples 8.8a and 8.8b) occurs, groups that represent an expansion of the original groups—covering a tritone rather than a perfect fourth—while one group is the involution[1] of the other at a transposition of the fourth, rather than one group being identical to the other at the transposition of a tritone. "Stability" for an evolved note group begins to mean that collection of pitches that demonstrates some clearly identifiable, relatively simple, logical relationship to the original group. By relatively simple, I mean the kind of relationship that involves noncomplex terms (as in mathematics, relationships between integers rather than between more complex factors such as irrational or imaginary numbers). The stable group is built around a consistent inner structure as well, rather than being bound by more complex or irregular kinds of relationships; the latter situation can be considered less stable. Although these definitions are arbitrary, I want to emphasize that they are the concepts I have chosen to work with; again, it is one of the tasks of this specific piece to create the context that will succeed in making these concepts convincing.

It is not by accident that this group locally disintegrates to a recalling of the original groups—at 6:54 the consequent to 3:09 finally arrives, ironically as an interrupt to the newly defined stable point (which was, to complete the irony, articulated by a developed version of what has hitherto always been a destabilizing event, the interrupt).

It should be pointed out that this return to rigidly structured groups partakes of another emerging procedure, the oscillation between freely developing groups (the dissolution of stabilized relationships) and fixed forms that demonstrate clear inter- and intranote relationships: this oscillation represents but one of the multiple dimensions that participate in, and resonate to, the changing tensions being prolonged and manipulated at various levels of composition. It should be added that the articulation of local note groups, which are mixtures of pitches from groups A and B, and the progression of different *kinds* of groups that result, are paralleled by the method for constructing actual events, which usually consists in borrowing features of previously stated events and combining them to create transformed ideas whose origins are, nevertheless, still clear.

Example 8.8a
Expanded Fundamental Note Groups

Example 8.8b
Using the Expanded Groups (5:46–6:54); Return to the Original Groups (6:54–7:12)

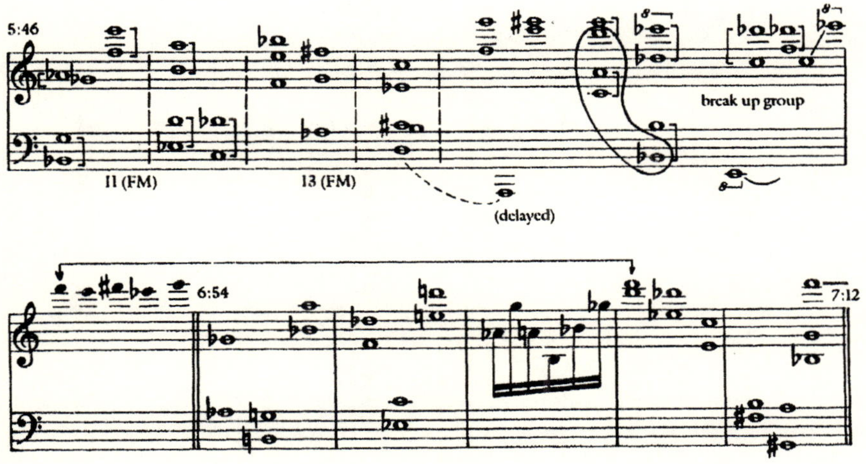

This tendency toward stable note-group configurations signals the coming of the main arrivals of the work, the climactic sections. At 7:12 begins the fully expanded version of the freely articulated pitches-only idea; the succession of notes are not grouped into dyads in order to be harmonized in terms of the inharmonic chord-spectra. Every group of four pitches, circled in Example 8.9, is made up of one of the intervallic combinations derived from the main groups, as shown in Example 8.2. For example, the first four notes describe m2, M2 (as m7), M3 (as m6); the next four notes (D-B-B♭-E♭) outline m3, m2, P4 (as P5), and so on. Tension is maintained by the passage's contrasting a freely (with respect to the pitch content of groups A and B) changing flux of notes with the rigidly fixed intervallic successions (those making up groups A and B) from which the notes are derived.

The sound-synthesis technique is unique here—four different timbres, one per channel (in the original quadraphonic version), articulate the same single line at different rates of speed and with different rhythms; each timbre (voice) is passed through a complex four-channel matrix delay line algorithm (a quadra-

Example 8.9
Main Arrival, First Part (7:12–8:10)

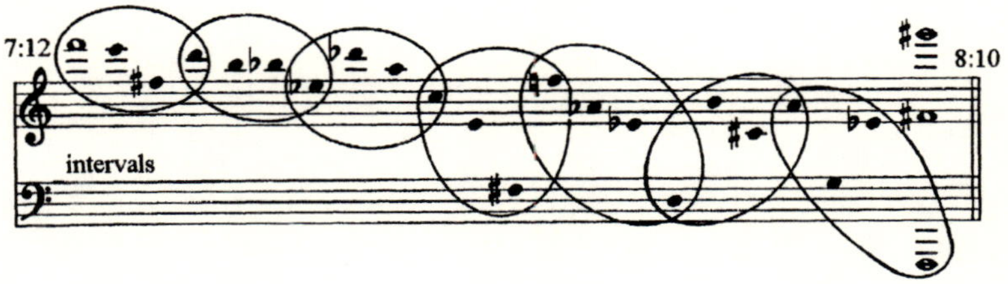

phonic version of instrument 12, described in the "Orchestra" section), and the whole ensemble is passed yet again through another signal-processing algorithm, a quadraphonic matrix reverberator. The effect is to create chords out of the contiguous pitches of the descending line and to orchestrate them with a constantly changing timbral complex. The aim was to provide a clear sense of downbeat and arrival with this rather deluxe timbral and spatial orchestration.

This arrival is prolonged by means of the equally climactic inharmonic section that begins at 8:10. Instruments 7, 8, and 5, which were previously used to achieve light and transparent chord-spectra, are now adjusted to yield dense, rich inharmonic sounds, accompanied by FM instruments 1 and 3. The background note groups at this point are shown in Example 8.10; their local evolution is toward stable groups, especially those that fill the tritone interval. This is the high point of one of the central developmental strands, although not the end of that development, as we shall see. The climax is, then, in two parts, clearly separated by timbral distinctions. Ironically, there is *not* an antecedent-consequent relationship here, rather a single structure divided into two contrasting subsections, the second of which is also divided in two. Then a pause.

The conditions for this pause are exactly the opposite of those motivating the pause just before 3:40, after several unresolved or unsatisfied antecedent events had been insistently crowded together. Here, instead, the prolonged stretch of intense climactic arrival and completion needs more of a stop for "catching our breath." You could almost attribute antecedent-consequent to these two pauses—but I won't insist on it.

But there is a sense that some dimensions are not yet finalized, some processes set in motion that have not spent themselves, some workings out yet to be done. One of these is the development of intervallic progressions with respect to more or less stable note groups. The resumption of the start-stop idea (Example 8.11) after the pause does just this. Once again, this idea has the function of picking up momentum after a pause that has rather let things wind down. A loud and very sudden interrupt reasserts for the last time the original *type* of grouping, but not the same pitches, of groups A and B, and there follows the last version of static instrument 8 idea, now working out a series of groups directed toward the final and most stable note group (Example 8.12a), the goal (the "normal" energy

Example 8.10
Main Arrival, Second Part (8:10–9:44)

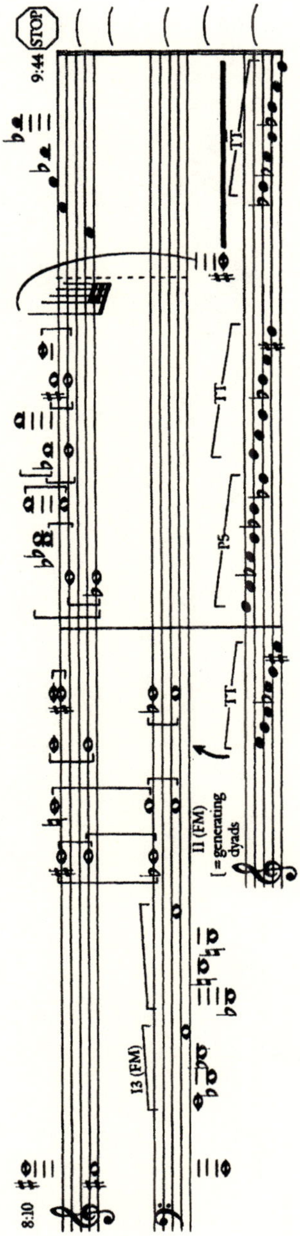

Example 8.11
Transformations of Groups A and B (10:08)

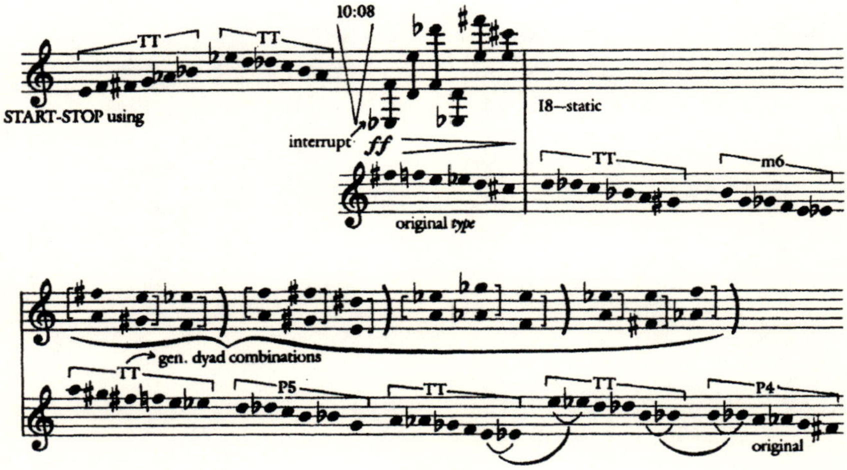

Example 8.12a
Final "Stable" Group Transformation

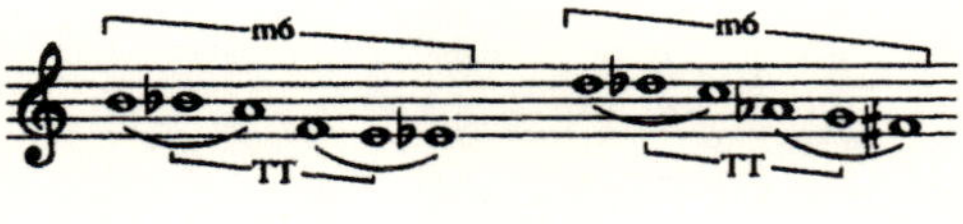

Example 8.12b
(11:04 to the end)

level) of the original groups (that were so highly charged at the outset). The goal groups are made up of three pitches from group A and three pitches from group B; the tritone relationship is now preserved specifically *within* each group, not *between* them. These groups provide the intervallic material (Example 8.12b) for the chord-spectra played by instrument 8; the timbres associated with the static idea are made to prolong the finally arrived goal groups with a moderately fast turnover of chord-spectra types that achieves a relaxed, almost lyrical quality, a resolving effect; again the quadraphonic matrix-delay processing is working together with multiple chorus effects to obtain as rich a sound as possible.

The single tones that flash in and out are simply the generating dyads played by themselves using the timbre at 6:54 (end of Example 8.8b) and with the same kind of quadraphonic spatial manipulation. Just as the first major section finished off with a local closure and an offhand sort of coda (one of whose functions was to add the first touch of emphasis to the breaking up of the original A and B groups, Example 8.3b), so this whole section beginning after the two-part climax is a closure or winding down on a much larger scale, but with a final emphasis on the definitively constructed stable groups, in contrast to the local function of the earlier, first codalike passage.

Then comes the gesture of the final chord transformed by multiple feedback echo circuits, high-pass filtered to almost nothing—a last coda to the whole work. This particular sound event occurs only here; but it is a consequence of earlier, smaller such subsections with a similar function: to end.

POSTSCRIPT

It's been about seventeen years since the composition of *Sequence Symbols*, and a lot, to put it mildly, has transpired since then. The procedures described in this chapter, originally written for *Perspectives of New Music*, have undergone a great deal of expansion and development, the result of which is a full-blown and highly detailed method of musical composition that I call the dyad system.

The dyad system offers a wide range of techniques for composing not only electronic music but also instrumental music without electronics. The fundamental ideas have remained: everything is derived from dyads, or trichords. But now the system offers means for developing the pitch structure as well as for the elaboration of electronic sounds based on that pitch structure, and vice versa. Further, the notion of a linear hierarchy in constructing a work with the system has been replaced by a concept of a circular or spherical hierarchy where the starting point is arbitrary and the way in which the hierarchy is structured becomes part of the composition: it, too, is purely contextual along with all other elements of a given work.

The two basic rules of the dyad system with respect to pitch organization run as follows:

given a collection of unique pitch-classes (6 or 7 or 8 are generally the most useful),

1. *preserving the pitch-class content of the collection, change the dyadic disposition*; in other words you group the pitch collection into different subgroupings of three dyads (for six pitches), two dyads and a trichord (for seven pitches), and for eight pitches either four dyads or two trichords and a dyad. Depending on which sized collection you begin with, you generate a different number of groupings (typically 15 groups for a six pitch-class collection, 105 for seven pitches, and 220 for eight pitches grouped as one dyad and two trichords. Each of these subdivisions of a given pitch collection is called a *group*.
2. *preserving the dyadic content of the collection, change the pitch classes that constitute the dyads*; for dyads, read also "trichord" as well. Here, each group, as generated by rule 1, maintains the internal intervallic identity of each dyad or trichord, but the actual pitches that make up these internal intervals change, such that the relation between (external to) the dyads/trichords changes. Each of these pitch collections so derived is called a *type*. Again, depending on the dimensions of the pitch collection, the number of derived types can range from as many as forty, for six note collections, to lesser numbers for larger pitch collections.

These rules are a generalization of my approach to the generating dyad procedures employed in *Sequence Symbols*, as previously described. The collection of dyads/trichords so derived is first composed into what will be their actual articulations as real intervals in the work (mn2 dyads become mj7's or mn9's or 8ve and mn9, and so on), based on the desired texture (if the work is only instrumental) or on what kinds of electronic sounds those real intervals can be made to generate with the various generating dyad algorithms. In the latter kind of music, as mentioned earlier, it is not uncommon to first design a musical idea in terms of electronic sounds and then elaborate either the rest of the electronic work or eventual instrumental parts in terms of the dyads that were used to generate those sounds.

A detailed account of the dyad system has been published in *Perspectives of New Music* (37, no.1 [Winter 1999], Part 1, and 37, no. 2 [Summer 2000], Parts 2 and 3). Included in the article are descriptions of many more generating dyad algorithms, mainly for the control of additive synthesis, that work very efficiently with such digital sound synthesis programs as Music 30, Csound, and the like. The advent of extremely powerful home computing systems means that the necessary experimentation and accumulation of experience with these sounds can now be done in the composer's personal studio without the pressures of certain institutional customs that all too often accompanied the creation of digitally synthesized music, a phenomenon typical of the times that saw the composition of *Sequence Symbols*. Nowadays, the availability of a great deal of excellent signal processing software for personal computers means that there is a far greater variety of timbral elaboration possible than was the norm back in the 1970s and early 1980s. The sounds produced by the generating dyads when processed by the many different kinds of chorus effects, filters, delay lines, reverbs, and multiband compressors and limiters are truly rich and varied, opening up tremendous resources for electronic music composition without at all obscuring the fundamental dyad structure.

NOTE

1. "The projection *down* from the lowest tone of a given chord, using the same intervals in the order of their occurrence [going *up* from the lowest tone] in the given chord we may call the involution of the given chord" (Hanson 1960, 17). The involution is also more easily derived by simply reversing the intervallic order of any simultaneity, starting on the same bottom or top note. Thus, the involution of a C major triad is the C minor triad, and vice versa.

REFERENCES

Beauchamp, J. (1979). Filter equations, sent as a personal communication to the author.

Dashow, J. (1978). "Three Methods for the Digital Synthesis of Chordal Structures with Non-Harmonic Partials." *Interface* 7: 69–94.

Dashow, J. (1980). "Spectra as Chords." *Computer Music Journal* 4, no. 1 (Spring): 43–52.

Dashow, J. (1986). "New Approaches to Digital Sound Synthesis and Transformation." *Computer Music Journal* 10, no. 4 (Winter): 56–66.

Hanson, H. (1960). *Harmonic Materials of Modern Music.* New York: Appleton-Century-Crofts.

Mitsuhashi, Y. (1980). "Waveshape Parameter Modulation in Producing Complex Audio Spectra." *Journal of the Audio Engineering Society* 28 (December): 879–895.

Moorer, J. A. (1976). "The Synthesis of Complex Audio Spectra by Means of Discrete Summation Formulae." *Journal of the Audio Engineering Society* 24 (November): 717–727.

Piaget, J. (1968). *Structuralism.* English translation by C. Maschler, 1970. New York: Harper and Row. Reprint of Basic Books original English edition New York: Harper Colophon Books.

Polanyi, M. (1966, 1983). *The Tacit Dimension.* New York: Doubleday. Republication of the original edition, Gloucester, MA: Peter Smith.

Puckette, M. (1983). Personal communication and conversations at the MIT Experimental Music Studio.

Selected Discography of the Electroacoustic Music of James Dashow

Archimedes, Act I, scene 2 (first version), electronic music (1988), Wergo CD WER 2018-50.

Disclosures, for cello and electronic sounds (1988–1989), Scarlatti Classica MZQ737707 and Neuma CD 450-90.

First Tangent to the Given Curve, for piano and electronic sounds (1995–1996), Capstone CPS-8645.

Le Tracce di Kronos, i Passi, for clarinet, dancer and computer (1995), Scarlatti Classica MZQ737707 and Centaur CD CRC 2310.

Mappings, for cello and electronic sounds (1974), ProViva ISPV 177 and Neuma CD 450-90.

Media Survival Kit, a lyric satire for radio broadcast, for voices, instruments, and electronic sounds (1995–96), Scarlatti Classica MZQ737707.

Mnemonics, for violin and computer (1981–1982; revised 1984, computer part generated 1985), Wergo CD WER 2018-50.

Morfologie, for trumpet player and computer (1993), Neuma CD 450-90.
Oro, Argento & Legno, for flute and computer (1987), Capstone CPS-8659 and Wergo CD WER 2018-50.
Reconstructions, for harp and electronic sounds (1992), ProViva ISPV 177.

9

Oppositional Dialectics in Joji Yuasa's *The Sea Darkens*

Kristian Twombly

INTRODUCTION

Composer Joji Yuasa (b. Koriyama, Japan, 1929) was one of the first Japanese composers to work with electronic media. During the 1950s, along with fellow composers Toru Takemitsu and Kuniharu Akiyama, he was a member of the *Jikken Kobo* (Experimental Workshop). Yuasa (who was originally trained as a medical doctor and did not begin composing until well into his twenties) has produced notable electronic compositions that utilize a variety of techniques, including *musique concrète*, cross-synthesis, and subtractive synthesis. In addition, he has also produced noteworthy examples of multimedia composition. His music is often concerned with various concepts of synthesis: the synthesis of language, of diverse sonic materials, and of divergent cultural models (he has worked extensively in Japan, Europe, and the United States, and each of these cultures has had a profound influence on his music). Yuasa has noted that his music is rooted in the interplay of two fundamental oppositions: universality and individuality. In his view, music should not only express one's "cosmology" or experiences but on some level it should also be understood as a more universal expression: "[U]niversality—expresses my interest in spatial temporal structure. Such a point of view holds that music is an entity of transition of sonic energy on a time axis."[1] In contrast, Yuasa's notion of individuality is concerned with locality: a composer is naturally affected by the cultural and musical conditions present in the environment in which he or she composes.

PRELIMINARY OBSERVATIONS

The composition *A Study in White* (1987) consists of two text-based, computer-synthesized works.[2] The first, which is the subject of this chapter, is entitled *The Sea Darkens* and constitutes a setting of a haiku written by the Japanese poet Bashõ (1644–1694).

Umi kurete	The sea darkens
kamono koe	voices of sea gulls
honokani shiroshi	sound faintly white.

The text of the second piece, *I've Lost It*, is drawn from the writings of R. D. Laing.

The Sea Darkens exemplifies Yuasa's aforementioned penchant for oppositional dialectics. Foremost among these is the juxtaposition of spoken text with that of pure white noise,[3] as well as the juxtaposition of language, which is presented through numerous and complete readings of the text in both its original Japanese and in English translation. (Isolated words and fragments of the text are also dissected and transformed in various ways throughout the work.) In addition, there is a variety of local oppositions of register, gesture, and tone color. The interaction of these contrasting materials provides the basis for the formal structure of much of the work as well as the dramatic tension of the piece, and the synthesis of these materials near the end of the piece constitutes the work's dénouement.

As is the case with most electroacoustic music, there is no score for *The Sea Darkens*. Traditional approaches to the study of pitch and rhythm seemed inappropriate for the analysis of this piece. Thus, I felt that more specialized tools for analysis were needed to fully explore this work's many sonic nuances, and to this end I found the sonogram to be a very useful tool.

Historical precedent for the use of sonograms in the analysis of electroacoustic works (as well as for the analysis of instrumental compositions) is well documented. Most notable in this regard is the work of Robert Cogan, who has used sonograms to examine works by such diverse composers as Edgard Varèse, Claude Debussy, Elliot Carter, and Billie Holliday, among many others.[4] His analysis of Varèse's *Poème Electronique* represents one of the first milestones in the theoretical examination of music composed for the electroacoustic medium.[5] Sonograms provide the ability to examine the acoustical properties of a variety of sonic materials not readily accessible through traditional methods of analysis. As Cogan states in the introduction of his book *Music Seen, Music Heard*, "[A] spectrograph allows us to *see* what we are hearing and to grasp music's rich material physicality; indeed, it shows us more than we realize that we are hearing."[6] With this tool, the theorist can now observe a large part of what is actually heard. Essentially, he is now able to analyze music not by examining its *input*, or notation, but rather its *output*, or sound spectra.

A sonogram is a graphical representation of sound in which frequency is plotted on the vertical axis and time is plotted on the horizontal axis. More intense (louder) sounds are represented by darker images, less intense sounds, by lighter ones. In this analysis, all observations and calculations are based on a monophonic reduction of a stereo recording.[7] All sonograms were generated using Sound Technology Inc. SpectraPLUS FFT program.[8] An example of just such a graphic representation, a thirteen-inch segment of *The Sea Darkens*, is shown in Example 9.1.

At the center of the image, the dark area represents a single unvoiced articulation of the word "white." The region of greatest intensity, between ca. 500 and 5,000 Hz, changes over time, delineating a general upward motion tracking the diphthong ("ai"), which is characteristic of the word's vowel structure. The darker bands within the image reflect the formants of the spoken sound (frequency bands emphasized naturally by the human voice).

The basic sound materials utilized by Yuasa in *The Sea Darkens* consists of two readings of the text, one in English and the other in Japanese. To this material Yuasa employs various sound transformation techniques throughout the work, each producing different results. For example, with the aid of a phase vocoder (which is used to cross-synthesize the spoken text with bands of white noise), the text is at times articulated as filtered white noise, producing a sound much like a whispered reading of the text. As will be shown, examples of this are found at the end of each of the two main parts of the composition.

Through the sound transformation technique known as time stretching, the variable speed of sound events can, on occasion, destroy the intelligibility of the word(s) being articulated. The very rapid series of the word "shiro/shiroshi" ("white" in Japanese) at the beginning of part II exemplify this technique. These have been reduced to very short vocalizations, which at first are rapidly repeated and then gradually lengthened, creating a general ritardando effect. In contrast, full readings of the text are frequently and significantly lengthened.

Through the use of a high pass filter, the high sounds of extracted word fragments, such as "white" and "shiro(shi)," are emphasized through the filtering out of frequencies below ca. 500 Hz. For the full readings of the text, a low pass filter is used to allow sounds generally lower than 750 Hz to sound. In some

Example 9.1
Articulation of "White" (0:36–0:49)

cases, a band pass filter (allowing frequency bands to pass through unfiltered) appears to be used.

The composer has also added reverberation, which, in general, is at first used sparingly and then, as the piece unfolds, gradually less frequently. By the end of the piece, the sounds are quite dry.

ANALYSIS

The Sea Darkens is 6:27 long as measured from the beginning of its first sound to the end of the final decay of the last sound. This duration is used as the basis of all calculations throughout the analysis. The piece is clearly separated into two distinct parts by an extended period of silence that begins at about 2:31 (the only such silence in the entire piece). Part I extends from 0:00 to 2:40; Part II, from 2:40 to the end, 6:27. Each part begins with unvoiced articulations of word fragments and concludes with complete readings of the poem that have been filtered into pitch bands. Unvoiced articulations of the text are achieved as the result of cross-synthesis of a reading of the spoken text with white noise, and I refer to all sound produced in this manner as unvoiced articulations.

Example 9.2 presents a sonogram of the entire piece that shows the two parts of the composition. Each part is similar in a number of ways. Most strikingly is that each begins with a passage dominated by white noise and then gradually moves toward more pitched material. Pitched passages are, of course, represented in the sonogram by a series of relatively narrow horizontal bands, while those dominated by white noise appear as large, densely filled shapes. Additionally, each part begins with short, rapid articulations of words and word fragments, gradually giving way to full readings of the text. Furthermore, a loud statement of the word "white" precedes the appearance of pitched material in both parts, at 0:42 and 3:22.

Part I begins with word fragments consisting largely of unvoiced articulations of the words "white" and "shiroshi" ("white" in Japanese) as well as the first two syllables of "shiroshi," "shiro" (Example 9.3). From the outset of its initial entrance, the filtered, pitch-banded voiced readings are separated from the unvoiced word fragments by register. Pitched material is generally low, below 1,500 Hz, while the word fragments are high, ca. 500–8,000 Hz (Example 9.4). Part I concludes with an unvoiced reading of the complete text in Japanese.

Part II, separated by a long silence from the end of part I (Example 9.5), begins much like part I, with unvoiced word fragments. This time, however, the fragments comprise mainly articulations of "shiro." At approximately 3:30 into the piece, an extended glissando encompassing a very wide frequency range is heard, which leads to a section of pitch bands that comprise the entire frequency range of the piece, ca. 50–8,000 Hz (Example 9.6). Part II ends much like part I, however, this time with a voiced reading of the complete text not in Japanese but in English.

Example 9.2
Whole Piece (0:00–6:27)

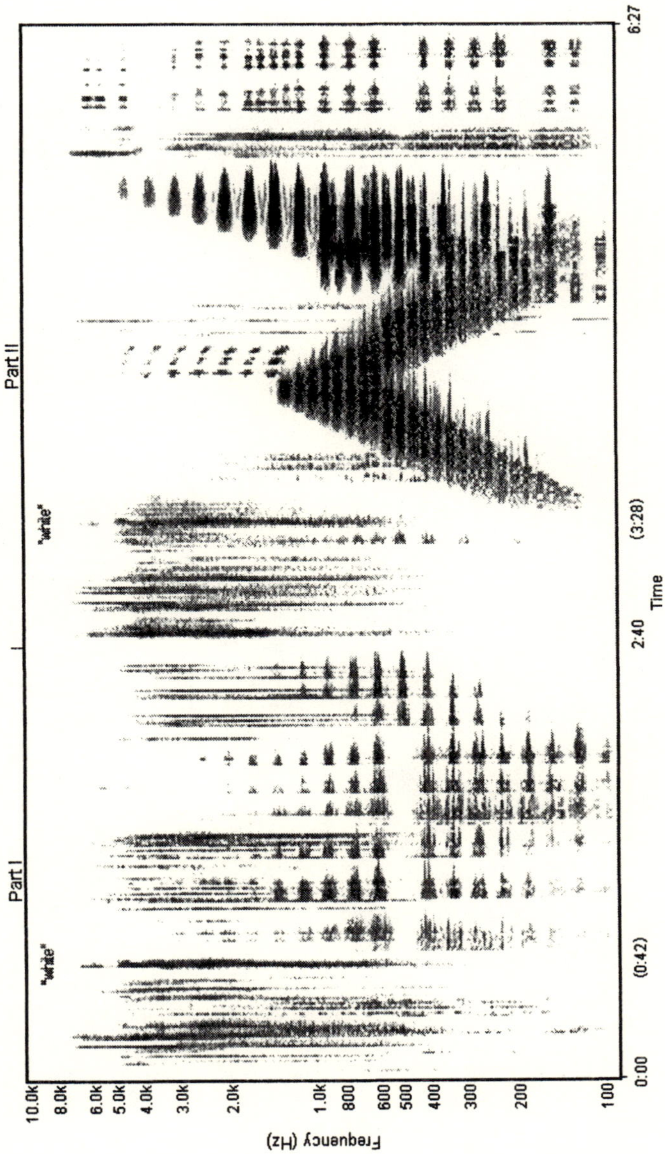

Example 9.3
Beginning of Part I (0:00–0:47)

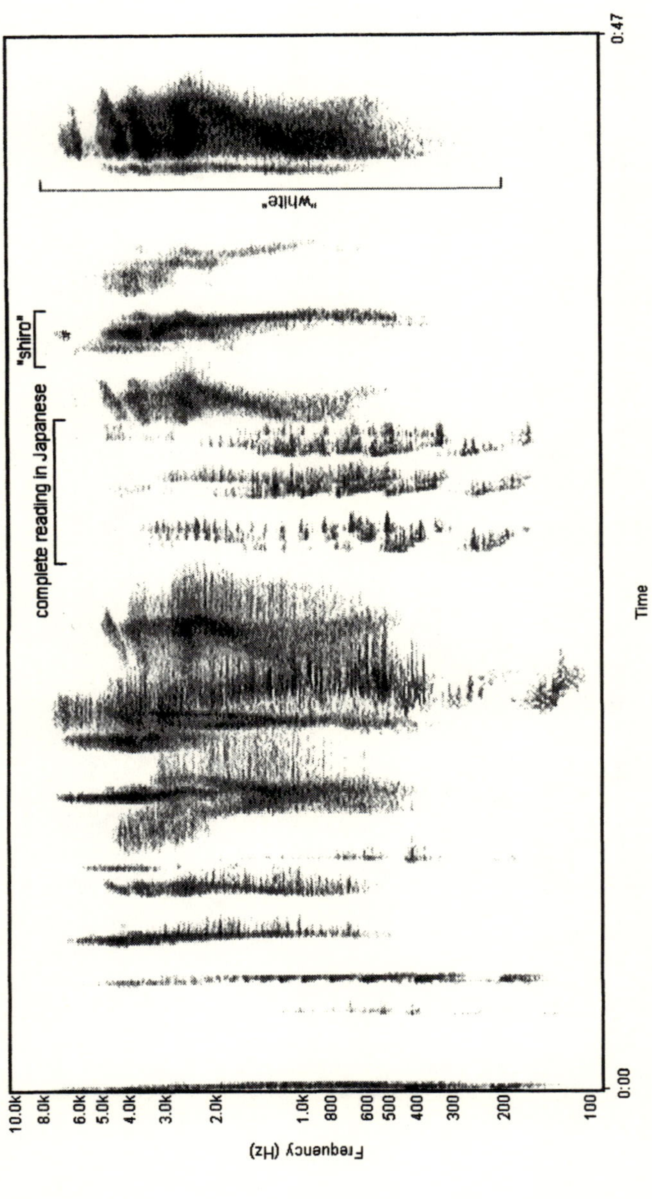

Example 9.4
Frequency Separation of White Noise and Pitched Material in Part I (0:54–1:33)

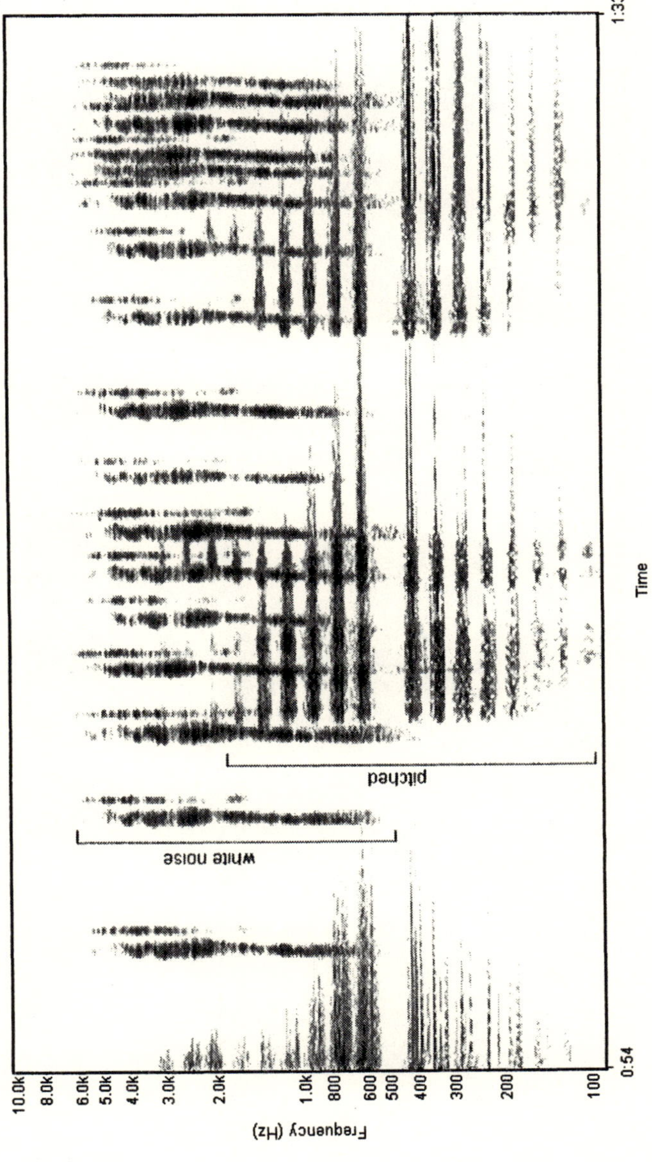

Example 9.5
Detail from the End of Part I to the Beginning of Part II (2:09–3:09)

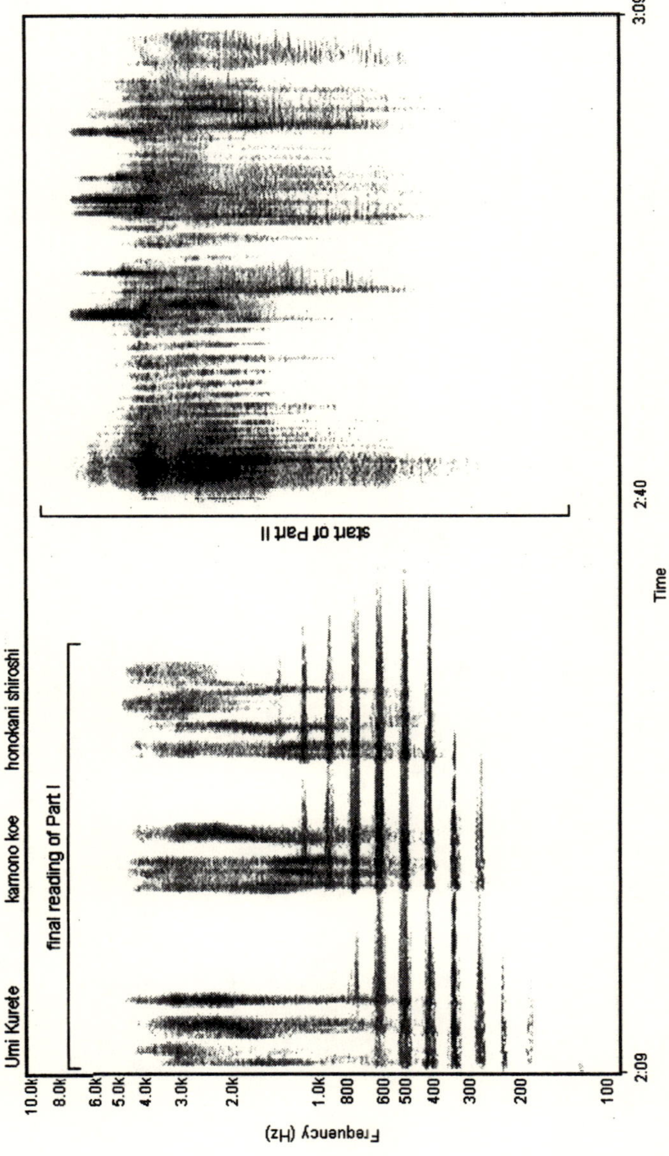

Example 9.6
Glissando and Area of Pitched Bands from Part II (3:19–5:46)

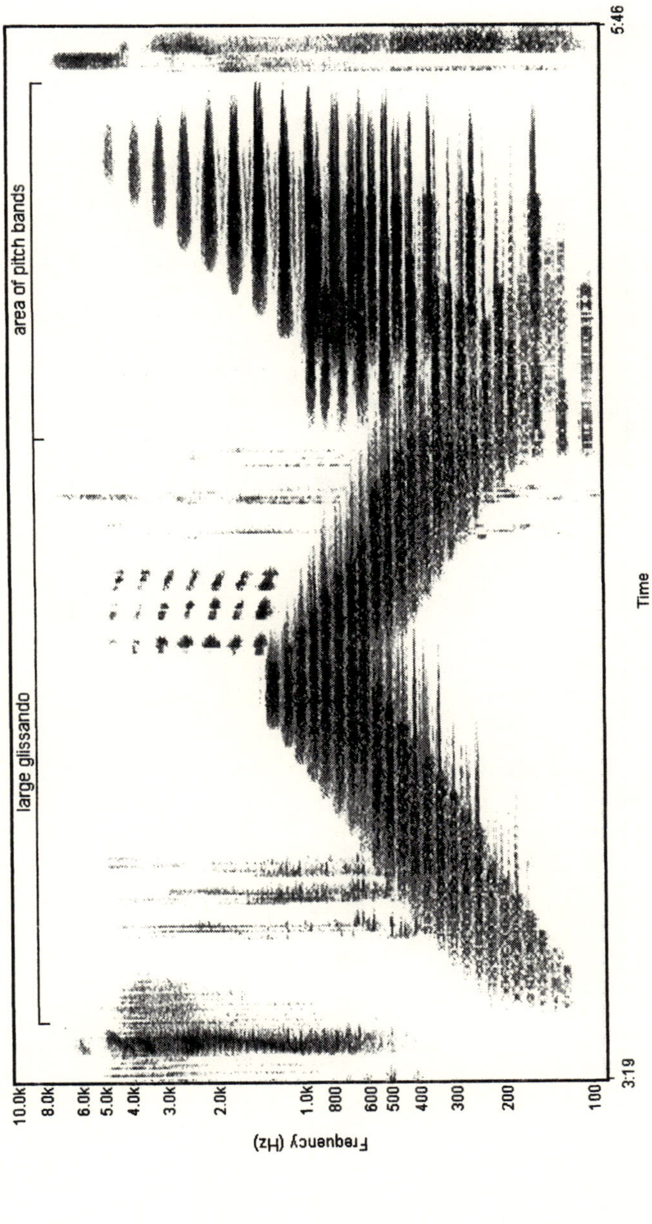

Example 9.7
Part I (0:00–2:40)

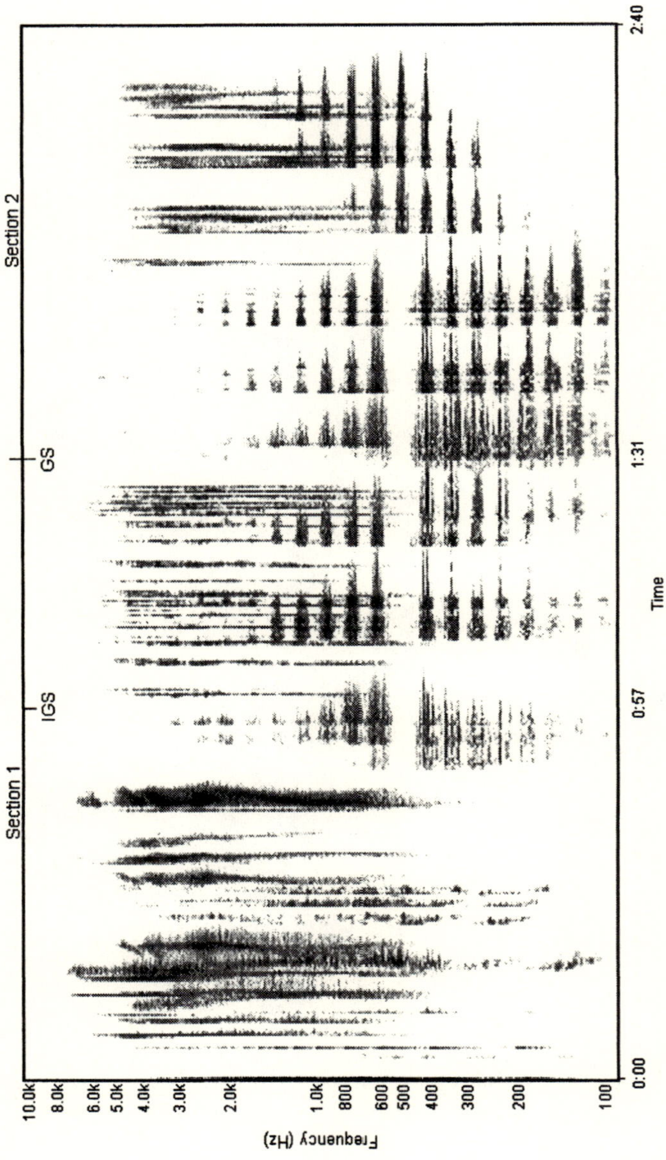

Example 9.8
Part I, Section 1 (0:00–1:33)

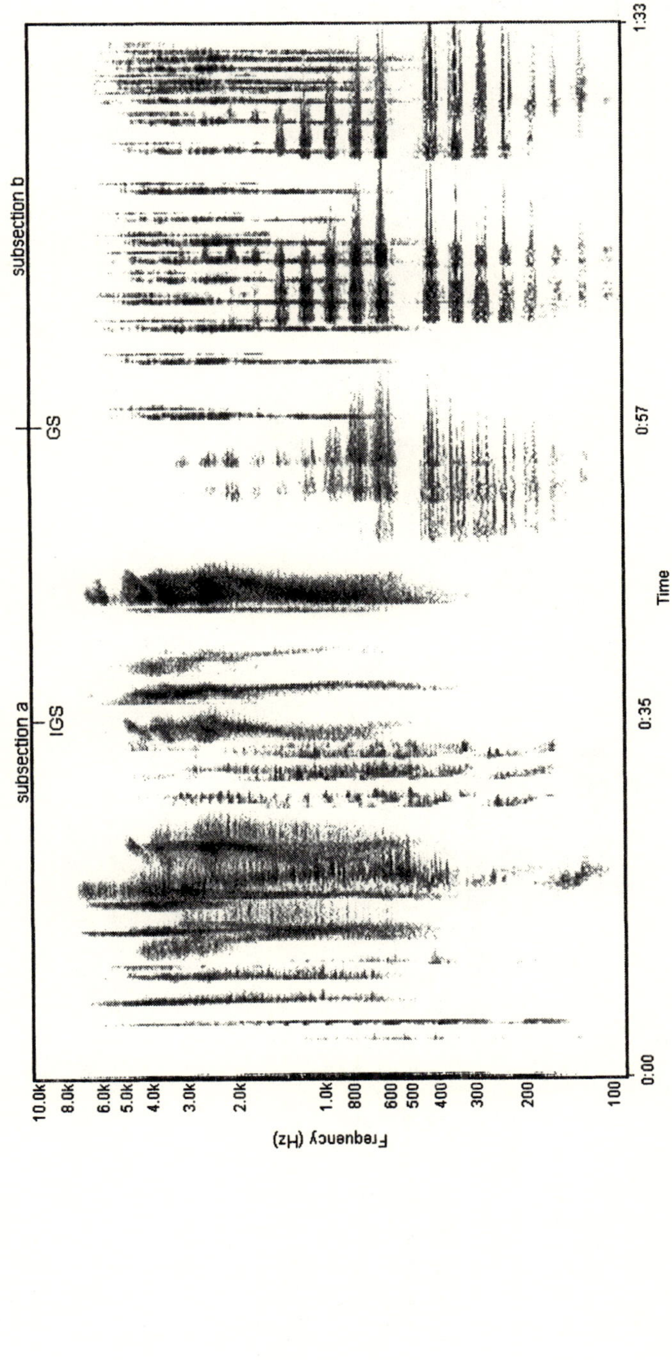

Example 9.9
Part I, Section 1, Subsection a (0:00–0:58)

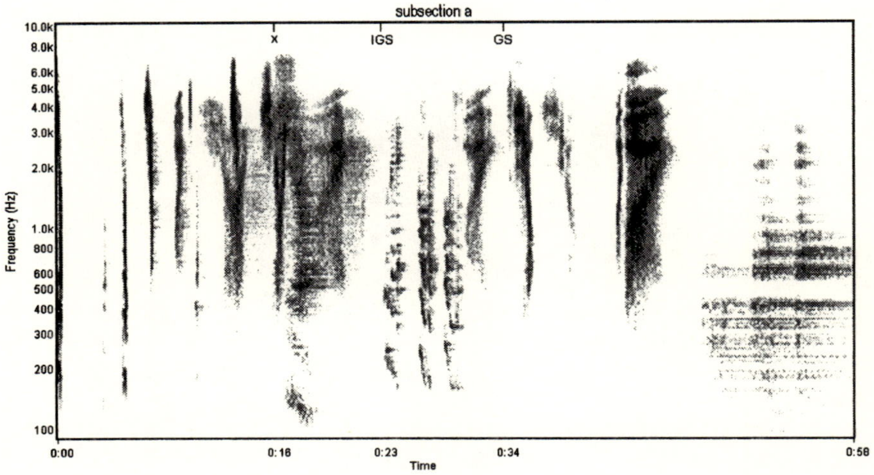

Example 9.10
Part I, Section 1, Subsection b (0:58–1:33)

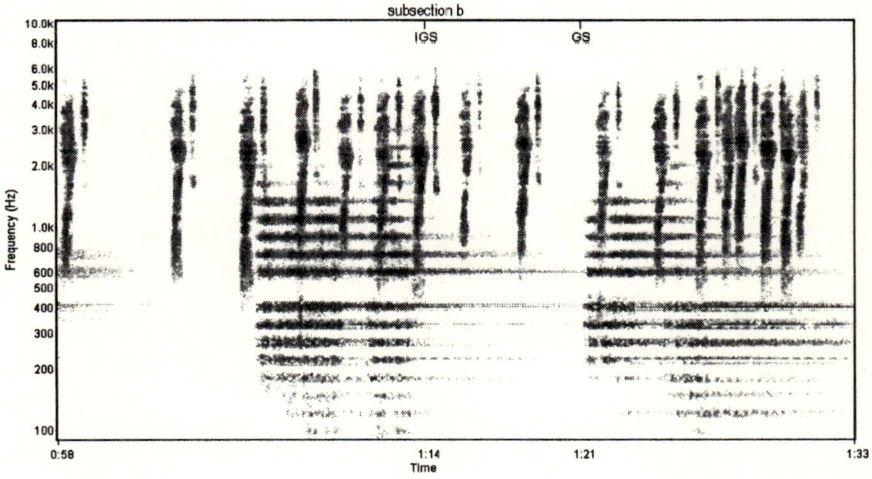

Before proceeding to a discussion of the oppositional structure of the work, I'd like to present a discussion of the temporal framework of the composition. This framework unifies all the diverse elements of the composition as they unfold. Remarkably, the proportions of the Golden Section (GS) and the Inverse Golden Section (IGS) (approximately 0.618 and 0.382, respectively) define all major part, section, and subsection boundaries in the piece. In addition, the related proportions of the Fibonacci series play an important role in shaping the piece. The Golden Section, well known and documented since Greco-Roman times, has been used in an organic attempt to classify subjects as diverse as architecture and zoology according to proportion of design. The proportions of Greek facades and the decreasing size of chambers in a chambered Nautilus are examples of such relationships. In music, one often discovers that composers partition a work into formal units using the GS or IGS. Often climactic moments of a piece occur at these points. The use of these proportions in music has been widely discussed. The work of many important twentieth-century composers, including Edgard Varèse, Karlheinz Stockhausen, Bela Bartok, and Claude Debussy, to name a few, reflects their importance.[9]

Numbers derived from the Fibonacci series (FS), a summation series starting with 0 and 1, are related to the Golden Section in a special way. Each adjacent pair of integers in the series 0, 1, 1, 2, 3, 5, 8, 13, 21, 34, and so on approximates the GS, and this approximation grows closer as one moves further through the series.

2/3 = 0.667   3/5 = 0.6   5/8 = 0.625   8/13 = 0.615   13/21 = 0.619

Ratios between nonadjacent pairs separated by exactly one value of the series result in an approximation of the Inverse Golden Section (0.382), and these approximations also grow closer as one moves further through the series.

2/5 = 0.4   3/8 = 0.375   5/13 = 0.385   8/21 = 0.381   13/34 = 0.382

As theorist Jonathan Kramer has noted,[10] the Fibonacci series appears to have been used more extensively by composers through history than the Golden Section, perhaps because of the greater ease of translating integers into beats, measure numbers, and pitch values, as opposed to the proportion 1:0.618.

As stated, the total duration of *The Sea Darkens* is 6:27. The Inverse Golden Section occurs at 2:28, coinciding with the longest silence of the piece, which, as noted, separates part I from part II (see Example 9.2).[11] Although twelve seconds separate the IGS from the beginning of part II, Yuasa treats this structural point quite musically, challenging the listener's perception of sectional division. Part II begins at the next articulated sound, with the only sound heard after the IGS and before the start of part II being the ringing of the final sound of part I.

Within part I both the GS and IGS are emphasized, and part I is subdivided further into two sections at these points (Example 9.7). In fact, each significant, form-defining event falls on a GS point. Examples 9.8–9.10 show the sectional and subsectional divisions found in part I, along with the indicated GS and IGS points. The first full readings in both Japanese and English fall on these points, as does the very rapid series of articulations of "white."

Within part II, Yuasa moves away from a straightforward use of GS and IGS relationships by extending proportions higher into the Fibonacci series. As mentioned, the FS more closely approximates the GS as one moves further through the series (3/5 = .6, 21/34 = .617, etc.). In addition, if an integer in the series is skipped, the IGS proportion is produced in a similar manner (2/5 = .4, 13/34 = .382). By utilizing the IGS proportion in this manner and applying that value outside the original measurement, Yuasa creates a different, but still proportional, form in part II (Example 9.11).

Part II is divided into 3 sections: sections 3, 4, and 5 of the entire composition (Example 9.12). Each is characterized by distinctive gestures. Sections 3 and 5 are equal in length while the ratio of section 4 to either section 3 or 5 is 5:13, reflecting relationships of the Fibonacci series. Internally, sections 3 and 5 show no further significant FS or GS partitioning. However, section 4 exhibits many instances of such proportions. As stated, the long glissando that constitutes section 4 is subdivided into two subsections: the initial glissando followed by a filtered pitch band region. The beginning of this filtered region falls on the GS (point z, 1:21 into the piece) of section 4. The final Japanese reading begins at the IGS (point y, 0:50) of section 4.

Example 9.11
Visual Representation of "Extraction" of the IGS in Part II

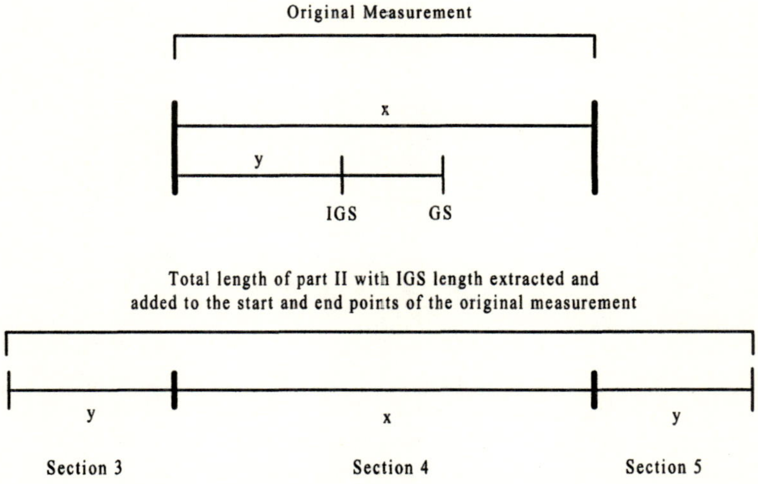

Example 9.12
Part II (2:40–6:27)

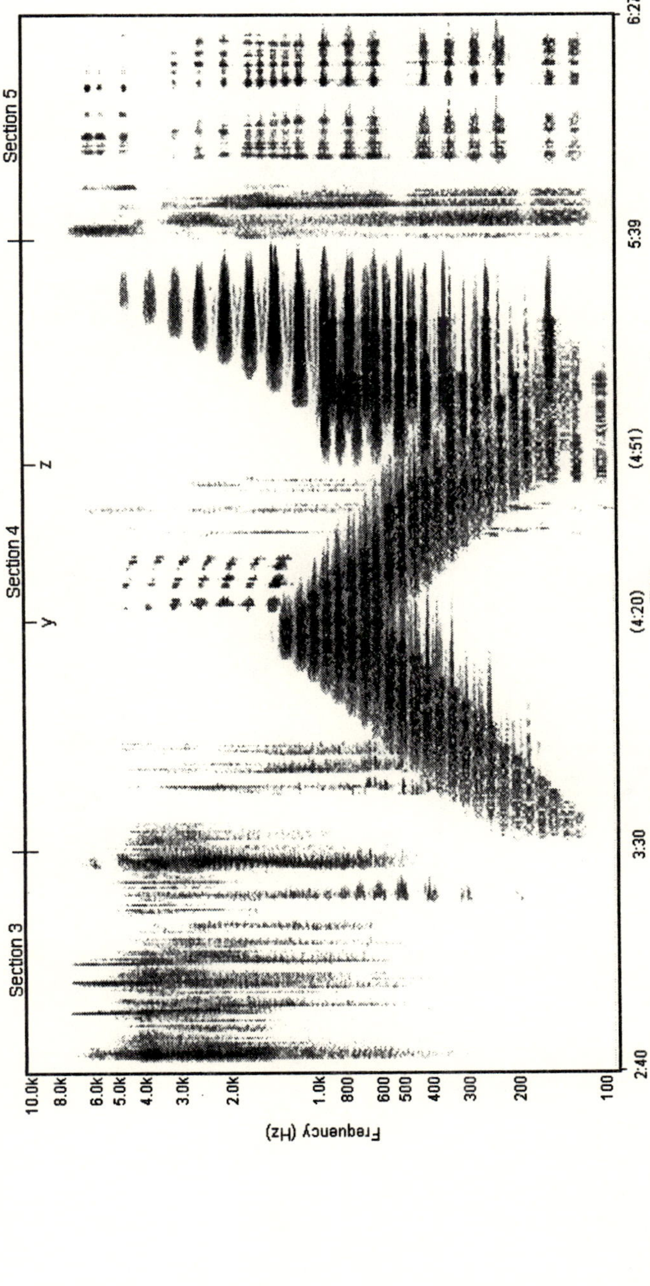

Example 9.13
Detail of "White" (0:36–0:49)

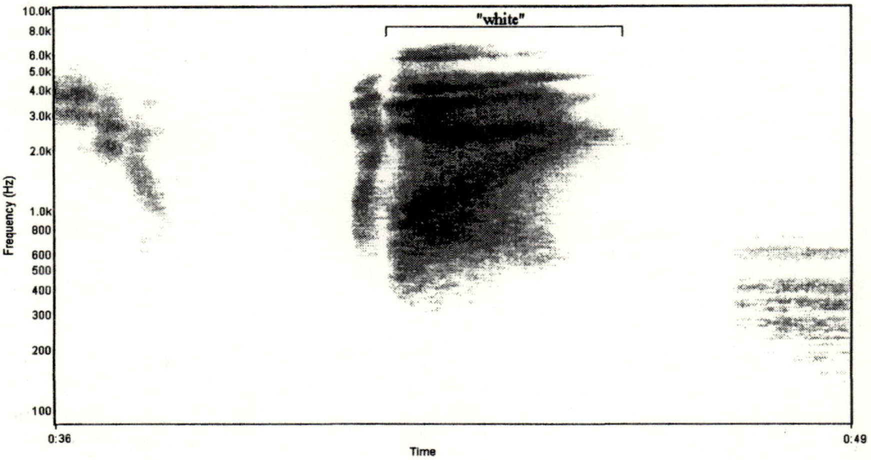

Example 9.14
Detail of Repeated "Shiro(shi)" (2:45–2:52)

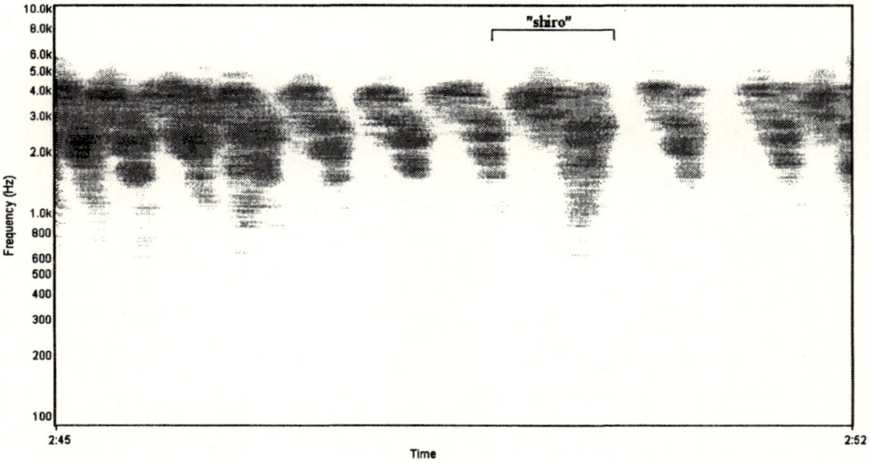

OPPOSITIONS

As mentioned, much of Yuasa's output is concerned with oppositions, whether sonic, linguistic, or cultural. In *The Sea Darkens* his oppositional dialectics are demonstrated quite beautifully. Indeed, the dialogue between the various oppositions within the work constitutes much of the work's dramatic structure, and language determines several of these contrasts. Each reading of the haiku is in either Japanese or English. The original Japanese haiku is read by a female voice, while its English translation is read by a male voice. For white noise passages, word fragments from the text ("white" and "shiro[shi]") provide the source material, while the source material for pitched sounds are derived from full readings of the text. In addition, these two sound types are further defined through their registral separation: white noise is generally high (500–8,000 Hz), while pitched material is low (below 750 Hz).

On a more local level, an intriguing opposition occurs between the words "white" and "shiro(shi)," which are both articulated as white noise. The English word "white" has a natural *upward glissando* because of its diphthong "ai" (Example 9.13). Notice the upward sweep of the phoneme bands, especially starting at ca. 1,000 and 3,200 Hz. The Japanese word fragment "shiro," in contrast, has a natural *downward glissando*, starting with its first vowel "ee" and moving to its second and much lower vowel "oh." Example 9.14 illustrates several, successive articulations of "shiro." Thus, oppositions occur not only between the two languages but also between the acoustical designs of the words themselves—words that Yuasa consistently emphasizes throughout the work.

The material that opens each of the work's two parts is derived from yet another linguistic opposition. "White" is the main source for white noise in part I, while "shiro" is the primary source for white noise in part II. The conclusion of each part displays a similar oppositional relationship. The end of part I features a complete reading of the text in Japanese, while part II ends with a complete reading of the text in English.

Moreover, the reading that concludes part I contains a clear separation of two different types of sound material (see Example 9.5), while the end of the entire piece synthesizes these two types of sonic material. At the end of part I the sonic space is subdivided into two regions, an upper region filled with white noise and a lower region filled with pitched bands of sound. Both are drawn from a transformed reading of the complete text in Japanese. At this moment the two opposing materials, white noise and pitch bands, are clearly separated, despite the fact that they are presented simultaneously within the same reading. At the end of part II, however, the full English reading of the text begins as white noise and concludes as pitched material (Example 9.15).

Significantly, the white noise and pitched material are not separated at this point but are instead merged. This appears to be the result of a gradual narrowing of the filters, which produce pitch bands. In the first line of the text, the bands are wide, and we hear the text articulated as broad bands of white noise. For the second line of text, the bands are reduced in size, and the reading appears more pitched. In the third line, the bands are very narrow (tightly

Example 9.15
The Final Complete Reading of the Text, in English (5:39–6:27)

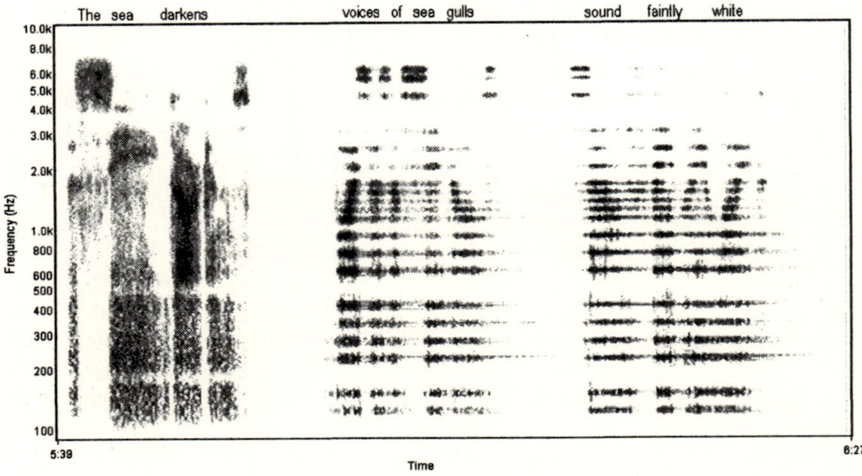

filtered), and we hear a distinct set of pitches resonating through the text, in all frequency regions. Notably, for the final line, both the voiced and unvoiced components of the words (low to high vowels and consonants) are filtered in such a way as to create pitches. In fact, the beginning of the last line is so finely filtered that the "s" consonant is transformed into a whistlelike tone. This leads to yet another synthesis of the two basic sonic oppositions of the piece—white noise and pitched sound, both of which have now merged into a single set of pitched bands.

Ultimately, the final reading of the text serves as the climax of the piece, as it resolves many of the composition's internal oppositions. Prior to the final reading, the composer has made an effort (through register, language, and length of articulations) to separate pitched material from white noise throughout much of the piece. However, Yuasa has foreshadowed the same synthesis of oppositions in the last reading of part I (2:09–2:31). Here, for the first time, he presents a reading of the text that *simultaneously* occurs as both white noise and filtered pitch bands. Although these contrasting sound materials are not merged here (as they are at the end of the piece), a partial synthesis is still achieved through their simple, simultaneous juxtaposition. At this moment, both white noise and pitched sounds are articulated by the same reading, yielding an incomplete synthesis that foreshadows the final, complete synthesis heard at the end of the piece (for Yuasa makes an effort to ensure that the two sonic environments of white noise and pitch continue to maintain their separation a while longer). It is not until the final reading, which begins as white noise and then gradually evolves to highly focused pitched bands at the end of the work, that we become aware that the synthesis of both the linguistic and sonic content of the composition has been completed. This moment serves as the raison d'être of the oppositional dialogue that lies at the heart of this piece.

NOTES

1. From a lecture given by Joji Yuasa at Hamilton University (29 March, 1992).
2. Realized at the Center for Musical Experiment (CME) at the University of California, San Diego.
3. White noise has also played a prominent role in Yuasa's electronic work. In his book *Mind Models: New Forms of Musical Experience* (New York: Praeger, 1975), Roger Reynolds gives a brief discussion of *ICON* (1966–1967), a Yuasa work that uses white noise as the only sound source.
4. Robert Cogan, *New Images of Musical Sound* (Cambridge: Harvard University Press, 1984).
5. Robert Cogan, "Varèse: An Oppositional Sonic Poetics," *Sonus* 11, no. 2 (1991): 26–35.
6. Robert Cogan, *Music Seen, Music Heard: A Picture Book of Musical Design* (Cambridge: Publication Contact International, 1998).
7. *A Study in White* was released on the Wergo label, *Computer Music Currents 7* (WER 2027).
8. SpectraPLUS (version 2.32.02), Sound Technology Inc., Campbell, CA.
9. Robert Cogan and Pozzi Escot, *Sonic Design: The Nature of Sound and Music* (Englewood Cliffs, NJ: Prentice-Hall, 1976); Jonathan Kramer, *Time in Music: New Meanings, New Temporalities, New Listening Strategies* (New York: Schirmer Books, 1988), 308–310; Roy Howat, *Debussy in Proportion: A Musical Analysis* (Cambridge: Cambridge University Press, 1983).
10. Kramer, *Time in Music.*
11. Other than the 12" discrepancy, all other section dimensions fall within 0.5" of the actual GS and IGS calculations.

Index

About the Contributors

KONRAD BOEHMER (Berlin, 1941) studied composition with Gottfried Michael Koenig (1959–1961) and philosophy, sociology, and musicology at the University of Cologne, writing his doctoral thesis on the theory of open form in new music ("Zur Theorie der offenen Form in der neuen Musik," 1966). From 1961 to 1963, he was active at the electronic music studios of the WDR (West German Broadcasting Company) in Cologne. In 1966, he moved to the Netherlands and worked until 1968 at the Institute of Sonology at Utrecht University. He then became music editor of the Dutch weekly newspaper *Vrij Nederland* and in 1972 Professor of music history and new music theory at the Royal Conservatory in The Hague, where since 1994 he has been Director of the Institute of Sonology. In the 1970s and 1980s he was repeatedly guest professor at the "Latin-American Courses for Contemporary Music," as well as extensively in the US and Europe. His composition *Information* was presented with the Dutch AVRO-award (1966), and the electronic work *Aspekt* was awarded the first prize of the Fifth Paris Biennale in 1968. His music drama *Doktor Faustus* was awarded the Rolf-Liebermann prize in 1983. In 1985, the city of Rotterdam awarded him the Pierre-Bayle-Prize for his writings on music and musical life.

JAMES DASHOW has had commissions, awards, and grants from the Bourges International Festival of Experimental Music, the Guggenheim Memorial Foundation, Linz Ars Electronica Festival, the Fromm Foundation, the Biennale di Venezia, the U.S. National Endowment for the Arts, RAI (Italian National Radio), the American Academy and Institute of Arts and Letters, the Rockefeller Foundation, Il Cantiere Internazionale d'Arte (Montepulciano, Italy), the Koussevitzky Foundation, Prague Musica Nova, and the Harvard Musical Association of Boston. In June 2000 he was awarded the prestigious Prix Magistere at the Thirtieth Festival International de Musique et d'Art Sonore Electroacoustiques in Bourges. A pioneer in the field of computer music, Dashow was one of the founders of the Centro di Sonologia Computazionale at the University of Padova, and has taught at the Massachusetts Institute of Technology (MIT), Princeton University and the Centro para la Difusion di Musica Contemporanea in Madrid, and, most recently (March, 2002), Musica Viva in Lisbon; he conducts masterclasses regularly in the U.S. and Europe. He served as the first vice president of the Computer Music Association and was for many years the producer of the radio program *Il Forum Internazionale di Musica Contemporanea* for Italian National Radio. He has written theoretical and analytical articles for *Perspectives of New Music*, the *Computer Music*

Journal, *La Musica*, and *Interface*. He is the author of the Music30 language for digital sound synthesis. His music has been recorded on WERGO (Mainz), Capstone Records (New York), Neuma (Boston), RCA-BMG (Roma), ProViva (Munich), Scarlatti Classica (Roma), CRI (New York), and Pan (Roma). He is currently at work on an opera for Planetarium production, based on the life of Archimedes. Dashow makes his home in the Sabine Hills north of Rome.

PASCAL DECROUPET (1965) studied musicology at the University of Liège from 1982 to 1986 and trombone at the Liège Conservatory up to 1988. Various foreign residencies (Berlin, Paris, Basel, Bonn) followed, in connection with research on a dissertation on serial music and a research project of the DFG on the Darmstadt Summer Courses (Humboldt University, Berlin). Currently, he is Lecturer in music theory and music of the twentieth century at the University of Liège and Director of the Studio for Electronic Music there. He has published on questions of analysis and aesthetics of music in the twentieth century, most notably, the chapters "Konzepte serieller Musik," "Elektronische Musik," "Aleatorik und Indetermination," and "Erweiterungen des Materials" in *Im Zenit der Moderne: Die Internationalaen Ferienkurse für neue Musik Darmstadt 1946-1966*, edited by Gianmario Bario and Hermann Danuser (1997).

THOMAS DELIO is a distinguished composer and theorist. His music is published by Smith Publications/Sonic Art Editions and recorded on such labels as Wergo, Neuma, Capstone, Spectrum, 3D Classics. He has published numerous essays about various aspects of twentieth century music in such journals as *Interface*, *Sonus*, *Journal of Music Theory*, *Musical Quarterly*, *Contemporary Music Review* and *Artforum*. He has also published numerous books, including *The Music of Morton Feldman*, *Circumscribing the Open Universe*, *Contiguous Line: Issues and ideas in the Music of the '60s and '70s*, and *Words and Spaces*.

AGOSTINO DI SCIPIO (Naples, 1962) has composed tape works and works for live instrumentalists and interactive computer systems. Recently he was also involved in the creation of interactive sound installations. His music has been performed in several countries in Europe, Asia, and North and South America. Awards or honorable mentions from the Bourges electroacoustic music competition (*Event*, for flute, clarinet and tape, 1991; *5 piccoli ritmi*, tape 1996; *5 interazioni cicliche alle differenze sensibili*, for string quartet and interactive computer processing, 1998), Ars Electronica, Linz (*7 piccole variazioni sul freddo*, for trumpet and interactive computer processing, 1995), and CIME, São Paulo (*5 interazioni cicliche alle differenze sensibili*, 1998). Works are available on Neuma Records ("Electroacoustic Music VI"), NoteWork ("Roma Soundscape remix"), and ORF ("Ars Electronica 95"). He has been composer in residence at CSC (University of Padova, since 1987), visiting faculty member at the Deparmtment of Communications of Simon Fraser University (Burnaby, B.C., 1993), and visiting composer at Sibelius Academy (Helsinki, 1995), electronic music teacher at Conservatory of Bari, and member of the board of directors of AIMI (Italian Association of Musical Informatics). His writings and research papers in unconventional sound synthesis methods, algorithmic composition, and issues in music analysis and the history and methods of music technology have appeared in many international journals. The author of essays on Iannis Xenakis' electronic and computer music, as well as on H. Brün's and J. C. Risset's computer music, and the editor of the anthology *Teoria e prassi della musica nell'era dell'informatica,* Di Scipio edited the Italian translation of a number of volumes, including G. M. Koenig's *Genesi e forma* and Michael Eldred's *Heidegger, Hölderlin & John Cage.*

JEROME KOHL has taught music theory, the history of music theory, and music analysis at the University of Washington and the University of British Columbia. He is currently editor and chief translator of the English edition of Karlheinz Stockhausen's *Texte* (forthcoming). From 1985 to 2001 he was the managing editor of *Perspectives of New Music,* where he recently also guest-edited a three-part Festschrift in honor of Stockhausen's seventieth birthday. He has published articles and reviews on Stockhausen, Stravinsky, and other twentieth-century subjects in *Perspectives of New Music, In Theory Only, Contemporary Music Review, Journal of Music Theory,* and *Notes.* At the Stockhausen 70 Symposion at the University of Cologne in November 1998, he gave a paper titled "Die Rezeption der Musik und Gedanken Stockhausens in Amerika," published in the proceedings of that meeting, in volume 4 of the series *Signale aus Köln: Beiträge zur Musik der Zeit* (1999). In October 2000, he participated in the Stockhausen 2000 Symposion in Cologne with a paper titled "Der Aspekt der Harmonik in *Licht,*" which is forthcoming in the proceedings of that conference.

OTTO LASKE was born in Silesia, now Poland, and educated in Germany (where he came under the influence of the Frankfurt School of Social Research (Dr. phil., 1966) and the Darmstadt School of New Music). He emigrated to the U.S. in 1966 to study computer music (M. Mus., 1968). Laske has taught music in the Netherlands (Instituut voor sonologie), Canada (McGill University), and the U.S. (U. of Pittsburgh; U. of Illinois), and has been active in theoretical as well as applied A.I. and is a pioneer of cognitive musicology. In the 1980s, he was a Cofounder and Artistic Director of NEWCOMP, Inc., the New England Computer Arts Association. In the 1990s, he undertook studies in developmental psychology at Harvard University, and founded Laske and Associates, LLC, a company specializing in the assessment of human capability in organizations. Laske has written seventy works for instruments, voices, and tape, and is a published poet. For more information on his musicological work, see J. N. Tabor's *Otto Laske: Navigating New Musical Horizons* (Greenwood Press, 1999). For more information on his compositional work, see www.emf.org\subscribers, and www.symsound@symbolic.sound\eighth-userDir.html.

THOMAS LICATA is a composer and theorist. He received his doctorate from the University of Maryland at College Park where he studied with Thomas DeLio. Much of his doctoral research was concentrated on the implementation of various computer applications to the composition and analysis of electroacoustic music. After receiving his doctorate he continued his studies of electroacoustic music at the Institute of Sonology in the Netherlands. He has taught at the University of Maryland and Clark University. Currently, he teaches at Hartwick College in New York.

JEAN-CLAUDE RISSET (1938) worked for three years with Max Mathews at Bell Laboratories to develop the musical resources of computer sound synthesis: imitation of real-timbres (brass synthesis, 1965); pitch paradoxes, synthesis of new timbres and sonic development processes (1967–1969). He has written numerous musical works, most of which resort to computer synthesis in conjunction with instruments or human voice. He has published a catalog of computer synthesized sounds (1969) and set up computer sound systems at Orsay (1970–1971), the University of Marseille-Luminy (1974), and IRCAM, where Pierre Boulez asked him to head the Computer Department (1975–1979). As a composer in residence at the Media Labratory, MIT (1987–1989), he implemented the first real-time interaction between performer and computer with acoustic piano sounds. Presently "Directeur de recherché" (CNRS), he works on computer music in Marseille. Among other distinctions, he has been awarded: Golden NICA, Ars Electronica (1987); Grand Prix National de la Musique (1990); Gold medal, Centre National de la Recherche Scientifique (1999).

KRISTIAN TWOMBLY received degrees in music theory and composition from the University of Maryland where he studied with Thomas DeLio. His main areas of interest include computer applications to music theory and composition, as well as art theory. He has composed numerous experimental works for electroacoustic and instrumental ensembles, including a recent sonic installation celebrating the opening of the new Clarice Smith Performing Arts Center of the University of Maryland. As a theorist, his interests lie mainly in music post-1950, including computer applications and indeterminancy. He teaches music at the University of Maryland at College Park, and electronic music at the University of Maryland at Baltimore County.

ELENA UNGEHEUER studied musicology, ethnology, and psychology at the University of Bonn. Her dissertation there has been published *Wie die elecktronische Musik 'erfunden' wurde..Quellenstudie zu Werner Meyer-Epplers Entwurf zwischen 1949 und 1953* (1992). She is Lecturer at the Robert-Schumann-Hochschule in Düsseldorf. Her main areas of research are in musical acoustics, music psychology, music and media (from storage media to multimedia), organology, music after 1950, and music history as cultural history.